Coral Reef Conservation

Coral reefs are the 'rainforests' of the ocean, containing the highest diversity of marine organisms and facing the greatest threats from humans. As shallow-water coastal habitats, they support a wide range of economically and culturally important activities, from fishing to tourism. Their accessibility makes reefs vulnerable to local threats which include over-fishing, pollution and physical damage. Reefs also face global problems, such as climate change, which may be responsible for recent widespread coral mortality and increased frequency of hurricane damage.

This book summarizes the current state of knowledge about the status of reefs, the problems they face and potential solutions. The topics considered range from concerns about extinction of coral reef species to economic and social issues affecting the well-being of people who depend on reefs. The result is a multidisciplinary perspective on problems and solutions to the coral reef crisis.

ISABELLE M. CÔTÉ is a professor at Simon Fraser University, Vancouver, Canada where she leads the Tropical Marine Ecology Group.

JOHN D. REYNOLDS is a professor at Simon Fraser University, Vancouver, Canada where he holds the Tom Buell Chair in Aquatic Conservation.

Conservation Biology

Conservation biology is a flourishing field, but there is still enormous potential for making further use of the science that underpins it. This new series aims to present internationally significant contributions from leading researchers in particularly active areas of conservation biology. It will focus on topics where basic theory is strong and where there are pressing problems for practical conservation. The series will include both single-authored and edited volumes and will adopt a direct and accessible style targeted at interested undergraduates, postgraduates, researchers and university teachers. Books and chapters will be rounded, authoritative accounts of particular areas with the emphasis on review rather than original data papers. The series is the result of a collaboration between the Zoological Society of London and Cambridge University Press. The series editors are, Professor John Gittleman, Professor of Biology at the University of Virginia, Charlottesville, Dr Rosie Woodroffe of the University of California, Davis and Dr Guy Cowlishaw of the Institute of Zoology, Zoological Society of London and Professor Michael Samways, Stellenbosch University, South Africa. The series ethos is that there are unexploited areas of basic science that can help define conservation biology and bring a radical new agenda to the solution of pressing conservation problems.

Published Titles

1. *Conservation in a Changing World*, edited by Georgina Mace, Andrew Balmford and Joshua Ginsberg 0 521 63270 6 (hardcover), 0 521 63445 8 (paperback)
2. *Behaviour and Conservation*, edited by Morris Gosling and William Sutherland 0 521 66230 3 (hardcover), 0 521 66539 6 (paperback)
3. *Priorities for the Conservation of Mammalian Diversity* edited by Abigail Entwistle and Nigel Dunstone 0 521 77279 6 (hardcover), 0 521 77536 1 (paperback)
4. *Genetics, Demography and Viability of Fragmented Populations* edited by Andrew G. Young and Geoffrey M. Clarke 0 521 78207 4 (hardcover), 0 521 79421 8 (paperback)
5. *Carnivore Conservation* edited by Gittleman *et al.* 0 521 66232 X (hardcover), 0 521 66537 X (paperback)
6. *Conservation of Exploited Species* edited by Reynolds *et al.* 0 521 78216 3 (hardcover), 0 521 78733 5 (paperback)
7. *Conserving Bird Biodiversity* edited by Ken Norris, Deborah J. Pain 0 521 78340 2 (hardcover), 0 521 78949 4 (paperback)
8. *Reproductive Science and Integrated Conservation* edited by Holt *et al.* 0 521 81215 1 (hardcover), 0 521 01110 8 (paperback)
9. *People and Wildlife, Conflict or Co-existence?* edited by Woodroffe *et al.* 0 521 82505 9 (hardcover), 0 521 53203 5 (paperback)
10. *Phylogeny and Conservation* edited by Andrew Purvis, John L. Gittleman, Thomas Brooks 0 521 82502 4 (hardcover), 0 521 53200 0 (paperback)
11. *Large Herbivore Ecology* edited by Danell *et al.* 0 521 83005 2 (hardcover), 0 521 53687 1 (paperback)
12. *Top Predators in Marine Ecosysyems* edited by Ian Boyd, Sarah Wanless and C. J. Camphuysen 0 521 84773 7 (hardcover), 0 521 61256 X (paperback)

Coral Reef Conservation

Edited by
ISABELLE M. CÔTÉ
JOHN D. REYNOLDS
Simon Fraser University

CAMBRIDGE UNIVERSITY PRESS
Cambridge, New York, Melbourne, Madrid, Cape Town, Singapore, São Paulo

Cambridge University Press
The Edinburgh Building, Cambridge CB2 2RU, UK

Published in the United States of America by Cambridge University Press, New York

www.cambridge.org
Information on this title: www.cambridge.org/9780521855365

First published 2006

Printed in the United Kingdom at the University Press, Cambridge

A catalogue record for this publication is available from the British Library

ISBN-13 978-0-521-85536-5 hardback
ISBN-10 0-521-85536-5 hardback

ISBN-13 978-0-521-67145-3 paperback
ISBN-10 0-521-67145-0 paperback

Contents

Contributors

ANGEL C. ALCALA
Silliman University–Angelo King Center for Research and Environmental Management (SUAKCREM)
Silliman University Marine Laboratory
Dumaguete City 6200
Philippines

RICHARD B. ARONSON
Dauphin Island Sea Laboratory
101 Bienville Boulevard
Dauphin Island, AL 36528
USA

RICHARD BOAK
Water Management Consultants Ltd
23 Swan Hill
Shrewsbury SY1 1NN
UK

KATRINA BROWN
School of Development Studies
University of East Anglia
Norwich NR4 7TJ
UK

LISA J. BROWNING
Reefology
39 Brompton Road
Southsea PO4 9AJ
UK

EMILY CORCORAN
Coral Reef Unit
c/o UNEP–World Conservation Monitoring Centre
219 Huntingdon Road
Cambridge CB3 0DL
UK

ISABELLE M. CÔTÉ
Department of Biological Sciences
Simon Fraser University
Burnaby, B.C. V5A 1S6
Canada

DEOLALL DABY
School of Science
University of Mauritius
Reduit
Mauritius

RICHARD E. DODGE
Nova Southeastern University
Oceanographic Center
8000 North Ocean Drive
Dania Beach, FL 33004
USA

R. ANDREW O. FINLAY
Atkins Water
Woodcote Grove
Ashley Road
Epsom KT18 5BW
UK

LORNA R. E. FOX
Reefology
39 Brompton Road
Southsea PO4 9AJ
UK

TOBY A. GARDNER
Centre for Ecology, Evolution and Conservation
School of Environmental Sciences
University of East Anglia
Norwich NR4 7TJ
UK

JENNIFER A. GILL
Centre for Ecology, Evolution and Conservation
School of Biological Sciences
University of East Anglia
Norwich NR4 7TJ
UK

DAVID GILLIAM
Nova Southeastern University
Oceanographic Center
8000 North Ocean Drive
Dania Beach, FL 33004
USA

STEFAN HAIN
Coral Reef Unit
c/o UNEP–World Conservation Monitoring Centre
219 Huntingdon Road
Cambridge CB3 0DL
UK

ALASTAIR R. HARBORNE
Marine Spatial Ecology Laboratory
School of Biosciences
University of Exeter
Exeter EX4 4PS
UK

EMILY HARDMAN
Marine Science Laboratories
University of Wales at Bangor
Menai Bridge LL57 5AB
UK

JULIE P. HAWKINS
Environment Department
University of York
York YO10 5DD
UK

J. HAROLD HUDSON
Florida Keys National Marine Sanctuary
PO Box 1083
Key Largo, FL 33037
USA

DAVID J. HUTCHINSON
School of Biological Sciences
University of Liverpool
Liverpool L69 7ZB
UK

WALTER C. JAAP
Florida Fish and Wildlife Research Institute
100 8th Avenue SE
St Petersburg, FL 3370
USA

GUY JOBBINS
SEAM Programme
Egyptian Environmental Affairs Agency
30 Misr Helwan al Zerae
Maadi
Cairo
Egypt

REBECCA KLAUS
Marine Science Laboratories
University of Wales at Bangor
Menai Bridge LL57 5AB
UK

NANCY KNOWLTON
Center for Marine Biodiversity and Conservation–0202
Scripps Institution of Oceanography
University of California at San Diego
La Jolla, CA 92093
USA

TIM McCLANAHAN
Wildlife Conservation Society
Coral Reef Conservation
Bamburi, Kenyatta Beach
Mombasa
Kenya

PETER J. MUMBY
Marine Spatial Ecology Laboratory
School of Biosciences
University of Exeter
Exeter EX4 4PS
UK

PORTIA NILLOS
Silliman University–Angelo King Center for Research and Environmental Management (SUAKCREM)
Silliman University Marine Laboratory
Dumaguete City 6200 Philippines

WILLIAM F. PRECHT
PBS&J
Ecological Sciences Program
2001 NW 107th Avenue
Miami, FL 33172
USA

JOHN D. REYNOLDS
Department of Biological Sciences
Simon Fraser University
Burnaby, B.C. V5A 1S6
Canada

CALLUM M. ROBERTS
Environment Department
University of York
York YO10 5DD
UK

GARRY R. RUSS
School of Marine Biology and Aquaculture
James Cook University
Townsville 4811
Australia

RICHARD SHAUL
Sea Byte, Inc.
P. O. Box 14069
Bradenton, FL 34280
USA

CHARLES SHEPPARD
Department of Biological Sciences
University of Warwick
Coventry CV4 7AL
UK

JAMES SPURGEON
Jacobs Babtie
London Road
Reading RG6 1BL
UK

JOHN R. TURNER
Marine Science Laboratories
University of Wales at Bangor
Menai Bridge LL57 5AB
UK

AMANDA C. J. VINCENT
Project Seahorse
Fisheries Centre
University of British Columbia
Vancouver, B.C. V6T 1Z4
Canada

ANDREW R. WATKINSON
Centre for Ecology, Evolution and Conservation
Schools of Biological and Environmental Sciences
University of East Anglia
Norwich NR4 7TJ
UK

SUE WELLS
56 Oxford Road
Cambridge CB4 3PW
UK

CLIVE WILKINSON
Global Coral Reef Monitoring Network
c/o Australian Institute of Marine Science
P. O. Box 772
Townsville 4810
Australia

Foreword

The world's coral reefs are vitally important for their biodiversity value, including the large range of goods and services that they provide to people who have few alternative resources available. Coral reefs support 10% of the world's fishing harvest, provide vital coastal protection, and harbour a third of the world's marine species.

Yet, as this volume makes clear, coral reefs and the livelihoods they support are under grave threat from a range of competing pressures. These include coastal development, unsustainable fishing practices, pollution, the growth of tourism and the consequences of climate change. These pressures threaten around half of the world's reefs.

The United Kingdom has a particular responsibility towards helping to solve the problems facing the world's coral reefs. Through our Overseas Territories, we are ranked 12th among the world's nations for tropical reefs under our jurisdiction. Furthermore, recent research has shown that we also have significant areas of cold-water reefs off our shores, which harbour unique species assemblages that are under threat, principally from fishing trawlers. The UK has used the Common Fisheries Policy to protect cold-water corals such as the Darwin Mounds.

Coral reef conservation is also a key part of our wider international agenda, which seeks to promote sustainable development and poverty reduction while safeguarding the biodiversity that is crucial to people around the world. The recent report by the Royal Commission on Environmental Pollution, *Turning the Tide*, underlines ongoing degeneration of the marine environment. The sustainable management of our seas is an enormous environmental challenge.

To meet the challenge of solving the coral reef crisis we need to be strategic and flexible in developing our responses, recognizing that we often need to follow different tracks simultaneously. We need to keep up the pressure on tackling climate change by reducing greenhouse gases. The coral reef community can play a vital role in helping to secure international action by publicizing the findings reported in this volume, of extreme sensitivity of coral to increases in sea temperatures, which has severe implications for coastal communities.

As we tackle climate change, we need to mainstream coral reef conservation management approaches into national sustainable development and investment strategies, as well as those of international agencies and programmes, donors and financial institutions. We need countries and organizations to change their thinking and adopt integrated marine and coastal management strategies.

We also need to apply more specific measures that address sectoral threats directly. We need to focus on tackling excessive and destructive fishing; we need networks of marine protected areas; and we need appropriate regulatory action to control land-based pollution.

To deliver these policies and measures effectively, we also need to improve the way we work together and take forward our policies. This means effective partnerships embracing governments, agencies, intergovernmental bodies, non-governmental organizations (NGOs) and the private sector, which enable decisions and implementation to be undertaken at the local level wherever possible. In short, we need improved governance based on stronger participation by all interested parties.

An excellent example of international coordination is provided by the International Coral Reef Initiative (ICRI). We are delighted to have shared responsibility for ICRI over the last two years with the Government of Seychelles and with the assistance of the UNEP World Conservation Monitoring Centre in Cambridge. This has been a significant undertaking in our Department of Environment, Food and Agriculture, which has contributed some £200 000 to run ICRI during our stewardship, including helping to deliver some tangible outcomes under a small grants programme.

We feel that ICRI has established a sense of an international coral reef community, providing a strong voice in international environment and development decisions. This has strengthened the hand of coral reef conservation when decisions taken by countries are translated into actions on the ground. At the recent Small Island Developing States Conference in Mauritius (January 2005), ICRI joined with governments, NGOs and agencies in a major initiative to help develop marine protected areas throughout the Small Island regions over the coming years.

The last element I would draw attention to in building a strategic approach to coral reef conservation is the need for increased funding of assessment and science. I am delighted that the conference that led to this book included the UK launch of the 2004 Status of Coral Reefs of the World report. I commend this as an excellent piece of work by the Global Coral Reef Monitoring Network.

Some of the messages in the Report and amplified in this book are stark, but it is not all bad news. It is heartening to be able to point to cases where effective management has shown that coral reef degradation can be stopped and reversed. This underlines the importance of our devising effective strategies which centre on conservation of the resources on which communities depend, and which demonstrate long-term commitment by all parties.

Ben Bradshaw, MP
Minister for Nature Conservation and Fisheries, UK

Preface

Coral reefs are found in the waters of more than 100 countries in tropical regions of the world, and provide food, income and cultural benefits to hundreds of millions of people. They cover a mere 0.1% of the ocean surface, yet they host a disproportionate amount of biodiversity, including nearly one-third of the world's marine fish species.

Coral reefs are under threat around the world. Recent estimates suggest that approximately 20% of the world's coral reefs have been destroyed and show no immediate prospect of recovery. Of those remaining, one-quarter are under imminent risk of collapse and another quarter face a long-term threat of collapse. For example, a recent comprehensive survey from the Caribbean found that since 1977, live coral cover across this region has decreased from 50% to 10%. This 80% decline in 25 years exceeds the rates of loss for any biome, including tropical forests. Equivalent measures of coral loss are not yet available for other regions, though 80–95% of coral cover was lost throughout large tracts of the Indian Ocean during the 1998 coral bleaching event, and there has been little recovery from many of these sites.

The main causes of coral reef degradation clearly originate from human activities, driven by growing human populations in coastal areas and lack of effective management of reef resources. They include over-fishing, which can damage reefs directly and also through the removal of herbivores that keep macroalgae in check, pollution and sedimentation due to coastal development and runoff from deforested lands, and warming of oceans due to climate change. There are no easy solutions to any of these problems. Climate change is particularly worrisome, with its links to coral bleaching and mortality. Future projections of rises in sea temperatures are bleak, and the problem can only be combated with concerted global efforts, which are difficult to muster.

The implications of coral reef deterioration for loss of biodiversity are profound. Governments of the world are committed to the target of the

World Summit on Sustainable Development, set in Johannesburg in 2002, for a reduction in the rate of loss of the world's biodiversity by 2010. With the marine habitat that holds the highest diversity of species per unit area under such threat, this target will be very difficult to achieve.

The loss of the world's reefs also has profound implications for the millions of people who depend on them for food and income. Healthy reefs are estimated to provide up to US$375 billion per year in goods and services globally. These benefits include fisheries, tourism, protection of coastal developments against storms, generation of beach sand, sources of pharmaceuticals, and the provision of key biogeochemical services (i.e. nitrogen fixation, waste assimilation, detoxification of hydrocarbons, oxygen production and sequestration of carbon).

This book stems from a conference that we organized in London in December 2004. The meeting was sponsored by the Zoological Society of London and by the Fisheries Conservation Foundation, to whom we are extremely grateful. Prominent speakers from a wide range of disciplines were asked to help place the coral reef crisis in context of the implications for both biodiversity and loss of ecosystem services that are vital to people's livelihoods. The meeting also served as the UK launch point for the biennial *Coral Reefs of the World Report* (2004) by the Global Coral Reef Monitoring Network.

In Part I, 'Setting the stage', Clive Wilkinson begins with a sobering review of the state of the world's coral reefs. Although some of the reefs affected by the 1998 mass bleaching event have recovered, many have not. Recovery has been better in more remote areas unaffected by severe anthropogenic impacts, but coral reefs of the world continue to decline under a mix of predominantly human stresses. How extraordinary these changes are can only be understood when placed in a historical context. William Precht and Richard Aronson offer such a perspective for Caribbean coral reefs and suggest that the unprecedented convergence of coral community compositions across reefs of the region began in the very recent past and was initiated primarily by disease outbreaks and bleaching episodes. The changes occurring on coral reefs can also not be appreciated in an ecological vacuum. Peter Mumby and Alastair Harborne demonstrate elegantly the connectivity and interdependence of coral reefs, mangroves and seagrasses and argue convincingly for a seascape perspective. Finally, Emily Corcoran and Stefan Hain shatter the myth of corals as exclusive denizens of warm, tropical waters and review the distribution and only recently realized plight of cold-water corals. Anyone who needs to be convinced that there is indeed something very special 'down there' need only look at

Plate 4.4! The authors note that a key difference between temperate and tropical reefs is the fact that the former face a single predominant threat: trawling, giving some hope for effective management.

Coral reefs are exploited for the resources they contain. The impacts of this exploitation are reviewed in Part II, *Uses and abuses: ecological and socio-economic issues.* Tim McClanahan considers the challenges to achieving sustainability in coral reef fisheries. These include managing a highly species-rich catch, targeted by varied and overlapping gear owned by a large number of people wholly dependent on this activity for their livelihood. Tim's review of food fisheries is complemented by Amanda Vincent's chapter, which provides the most comprehensive review to date of the trade in live fish and non-food items extracted from coral reefs. She points out the increasingly global reach of the trade in reef products, and the depletions of some species such as groupers and large wrasses that ensue. For other species, her review highlights concerns about the lack of information on population impacts of extractive activities. Guy Jobbins shows that tourism can be a mixed blessing for coral reefs. Tourism brings in much-needed revenues and incentives to protect reefs. However, the infrastructure required by tourists, and the actions of the visitors themselves, can threaten the very ecosystems that drew people to a given area. Guy illustrates these trade-offs using the South Sinai as a case study and suggests non-intuitive links between destination marketing, visitor 'quality' and coral reef degradation.

We have included human alteration of the global climate among the many abuses sustained by coral reefs. Although the direct impacts of climate change on reefs, such as the incidence of coral bleaching caused by elevated sea temperatures, are well documented, the longer-term impacts of bleaching-induced coral mortality are less often considered. Charles Sheppard shows that these effects can be far ranging, from shifts in coral community composition as a result of differential mortality among species, to increases in wave energy reaching the shoreline, and accelerated beach erosion, resulting from the impaired protective function afforded by eroding dead coral.

In Part III, various authors explore *The way forward.* Their chapters cover three general topics: developing or strengthening assessment methods, involving communities in conservation, and rethinking management strategies. Assessing what we have lost and what we have left is not as straightforward as it seems. Isabelle Côté and colleagues propose a new and statistically robust method of estimating the rate of ecological change on coral reefs. This method generates hard-hitting figures of coral loss, which are useful for lobbying for action and for gauging how far we are from meeting the 2010 biodiversity objective. We have spared the reader yet another review of the importance of marine protected areas (MPAs). Instead, Sue Wells tackles a neglected but important aspect of coral reef MPAs: how to assess the effectiveness of their management. She emphasizes how we should adopt business-like criteria to assessing MPA management effectiveness. John Turner and colleagues show how careful environmental impact assessment can reduce or mitigate some of the more damaging effects of coastal development on coral reefs. They offer a new method of impact assessment which calls for continuous monitoring of reefs during construction and responsive feedback action by developers. Another form of assessment is reviewed by James Spurgeon, who points toward the next generation of economic models to improve our estimates of the value of coral reefs. He argues that the omission of the intrinsic value of reefs from previous approaches has led to a gross undervaluation of these ecosystems.

It is widely acknowledged that community support is crucial to the success of all conservation endeavours. The veracity of this statement is tested quantitatively by Angel Alcala and co-authors. They compare the outcomes of coral reef MPAs with and without community-led management and find that, although both types of MPAs have equal success in enhancing fisheries, those involving local communities experience fewer conflicts with stakeholders. Engaging communities in coral reef conservation is clearly desirable, but sometimes difficult to achieve. Education offers an important means to raise awareness of the importance of reefs and instil a sense of pride and ownership. Lisa Browning and colleagues review the positive impacts of education programmes associated with coral MPAs. On the strength of this evidence, they make the case that education should be an integral part of coral conservation effort and not a poorly planned afterthought, as is often currently the case. Bottom–up approaches to community involvement are necessary, but are not enough without a change in top–down influences. Kate Brown highlights the key reasons why stakeholders are seldom involved in coral reef conservation, and shows why a full understanding of the social and political contexts is vital for success in reef management. Anyone who thinks that better studies of conservation biology alone will turn things around should take a close look at her Fig. 15.2, which shows that in Tobago, taxi drivers have the same perceived influence over the local marine park as conservation organizations!

Two chapters on coral reef management address opposite extremes of spatial scale. Walt Jaap and colleagues examine coral reef restoration techniques, which are usually applied to small areas of reef after damage from ship groundings and other physical impacts. There seems to be little that cannot be fixed nowadays, given sufficient time and money. High-tech restoration is a luxury that few countries can currently afford, but we can expect a growing demand for use of the simpler techniques amid increasing human activities around reefs. At the other end of the spectrum, Callum Roberts and co-authors propose a radical shift in the scale at which coral reef conservation efforts should be aimed. Marine reserves are still the best tool we have to protect reefs, but their so-far haphazard establishment must be transformed into a spatially coherent regional network to preserve and enhance key processes of reef recovery, such as recruitment, which occur at large geographic scales.

The concluding chapter could easily have been a sad goodbye to coral reefs, an obituary to a much admired old friend, but it is not. Nancy Knowlton offers us instead a cautiously optimistic credo, highlighting evidence of recovery here and positive human action there as small rays of hope. Indeed it isn't all gloom and doom. We hope that the contributions of the 39 authors in this book will help consolidate the knowledge base from which people can move forward in their efforts to restore the world's coral reefs and the vital resources that they contain.

Isabelle M. Côté
and
John D. Reynolds
Vancoover, January 2006

PART I

Setting the stage

1

Status of coral reefs of the world: summary of threats and remedial action

CLIVE WILKINSON
Australian Institute of Marine Science

INTRODUCTION

While the history of active coral reef research stretches back over 100 years, the concern for the declining status of coral reefs is relatively recent, probably less than 25 years. The first major attempt to alert the global coral reef science community to the threats posed to coral reefs was in 1981 by Edgardo Gomez, who subtitled the 4th International Coral Reef Symposium in Manila, May 1981, as *The Reef and Man* (Gomez, 1982). Similarly Bernard Salvat and David Stoddart raised the alarm in 1982 (Salvat, 1980, 1982; Stoddart, 1982). At this time, most coral reef researchers worked from field stations during vacations; field stations specifically chosen that were adjacent to healthy and flourishing coral reefs seemingly not affected by human impacts. There was a small group of coral reef scientists who were working in developing countries, however, who were aware of an impending crisis for coral reefs.

Since that 1981 Symposium, there has been a steady increase in the involvement of coral reef scientists in the applied aspects of coral reef management (summarized in Knowlton, this volume). A paper published by Don Kinsey in 1988 succinctly summarized the stresses to coral reefs (Kinsey, 1988). Similarly there were other reports of localized damage to coral reefs by coral reef scientists (Brown, 1987; Gomez, 1988; Pauly and Chua, 1988; Grigg and Dollar, 1990), but it was not until 1992 that global attention was alerted to the threats facing coral reefs. That was the year of

Coral Reef Conservation, ed. Isabelle M. Côté and John D. Reynolds.
Published by Cambridge University Press.

the United Nations Conference on Environment and Development in Rio de Janeiro and the 7th International Coral Reef Symposium in Guam. The two plenary addresses in Guam focused on the threats facing coral reefs, with alarming predictions of a bleak future if remedial action was not taken (Buddemeier, 1993; Wilkinson, 1993). Immediately following this symposium, Bob Ginsburg organized a landmark conference in Miami that recognized the apparent crisis facing coral reefs, although there was insufficient information for a full assessment (Ginsburg, 1993). One of the reports of decline was the collapse of the Discovery Bay coral reefs of Jamaica, a 'model' coral reef studied by many coral reef scientists (Goreau, 1959; Hughes, 1989, 1994). These conferences all acted as catalysts to initiate the International Coral Reef Initiative (ICRI) in 1995, the Global Coral Reef Monitoring Network (GCRMN) in 1996, and Reef Check in 1998 (Hodgson, 1999). The decline of coral reefs was confirmed with 14 reports presented at the 8th International Coral Reef Symposium in Panama, 1996, the findings of which were used to produce the first *Status of Coral Reefs of the World: 1998* report by the GCRMN (Wilkinson, 1998).

There is indeed a crisis facing coral reefs with a range of stresses acting sometimes in isolation, but usually in concert, in many parts of the world. This chapter is a summary of the *Status of Coral Reefs of the World: 2004* report that was finalized in early December 2004 based on more than 240 contributors from 96 countries (Wilkinson, 2004). The report was published by the Australian Institute of Marine Science and the Global Coral Reef Monitoring Network and is available online at www.aims.gov.au or www.gcrmn.org.

CORAL REEFS IN A HISTORICAL PERSPECTIVE

It is instructive to review the recent history of coral reefs during the last 10 000 years of human activities. Much of this overview is derived from the research of Jeremy Jackson and colleagues (Jackson, 1997; Jackson *et al.*, 2001; Pandolfi *et al.*, 2003). Additional historical information is presented by Precht and Aronson (this volume).

10 000 years ago

The history of modern coral reefs can be traced readily back about 10 000 years when sea levels were rising as the ice melted to end the Pleistocene. Over a period of about 5000 years, sea levels rose 110 to 120 m (approximately 240 cm per 100 years compared to the current predicted rate of approximately 50 cm per 100 years). The early Holocene was a period of rapid coral reef growth as corals settled on limestone and other hard substrata in tropical and subtropical regions. The Pleistocene also facilitated human migrations during low sea level. These early human populations undoubtedly exploited coral reef resources, seen in archaeological evidence of major harvesting of fishes, molluscs, dugongs, manatees and especially turtles in most areas. That rate of exploitation most probably increased as human populations grew and technology increased (Jackson *et al.*, 2001).

1000 years ago

Human populations had occupied most available land adjacent to coral reefs, including the vast expanses of the Pacific Ocean, with the exception of some Indian Ocean islands and very remote islands and atolls. These peoples continued to exploit coral reef resources for food and building materials. By current standards, most of these reefs would have been regarded as predominantly pristine with healthy corals, and large, well-structured fish and invertebrate communities. The available human technology allowed the exploitation of some of the larger fauna (turtles, dugongs and giant clams) in shallow water, but there was little capacity to harvest organisms in deeper water. These indigenous populations remained relatively small and some small island populations were developing traditional management of coral reef resources to ensure sustainability.

100 years ago

The consensus opinion of authors from the 94 countries included in the 2004 report (Wilkinson, 2004) is that reefs were generally 'healthy' 100 years ago with high coral cover and relatively 'natural' fish populations. Exploitation was increasing, but the harvesting of fishes and many invertebrates was within sustainable limits for the reefs. The exceptions again were the large fauna: dugong, manatee, turtles and giant clams. Pollution was not regarded as a problem and sediment damage was limited, although the land clearing in the tropics for agriculture was increasing. There was no concept of a 'coral reef problem' and little consideration was given to the need for management of the resources, except possibly pearl shell in the Pacific.

Since 1992

The first global assessment of coral reefs produced by Sue Wells and colleagues in 1988 contained many references to degraded reefs (Wells, 1988).

The World Environment Summit at Rio in 1992 set an agenda for global marine conservation with Chapter 17 of Agenda 21; then there were alarming predictions about the future of coral reefs (Wilkinson, 1993). There followed a landmark conference in Miami which concluded that, while there was insufficient information to assess the status of the world's coral reefs, there was an apparent crisis facing coral reefs (Ginsburg, 1993). The ICRI started in 1995 as a means of stimulating diplomatic and international agency focus on coral reefs, especially because of their considerable strategic and economic importance. The GCRMN and Reef Check followed soon after to document this apparent global decline in coral reef status.

2004

The collective opinions of the 240 authors who contributed to the *Status of Coral Reefs of the World: 2004* report (Wilkinson, 2004) are summarized in Table 1.1. The estimates are:

- that 20% of the world's coral reefs have been effectively destroyed and show no immediate prospects of recovery;
- approximately 40% of the 16% of the world's reefs seriously damaged by coral bleaching in 1998 are either recovering well or have recovered;
- approximately 24% of the remaining reefs in the world are under imminent risk of collapse through human pressures; and
- a further 26% of the remaining reefs are under a longer-term threat of collapse.

The losses of the reefs are attributed to direct damage from human activities on coral reefs: poor land management practices that result in the release of sediments, nutrients and other pollutants; over-fishing and particularly fishing with destructive methods; coral predators such as the crown-of-thorns starfish and coral diseases; and increasing water temperatures that result in lethal coral bleaching and exacerbated coral diseases.

A similar assessment of global reef status was obtained by Reef Check, a predominantly volunteer monitoring programme that has obtained data from more than 750 coral reefs in 70 coral reef countries in 2003. They report that the living coral cover lost during the 1998 bleaching event has been largely replaced by new growth, although often very variable in extent and location. Reef Check reports that many key human impact indicators, such as food fish, continue to decline, with the number of sites not reporting medium- to large-sized serranids and a key target species in the Indo-Pacific, the humphead wrasse (*Cheilinus undulatus*), having

Table 1.1. A summary of the current status of coral reefs in 17 regions of the world designated as Nodes within the GCRMN. These estimates were developed by the authors of the chapters in Wilkinson (2004), and from the Reefs at Risk analyses (Bryant *et al.*, 1998; Burke *et al.*, 2002; Burke and Maidens, 2004). These assessments should be regarded as indicative, because there are insufficient coral reef monitoring data for many regions to make definitive statements on losses and authoritative predictions for the future. The proportion of reefs in column 3 has increased from 11% reported in Wilkinson (2000), with the addition of more damaged reefs and those that have not recovered from 1998 (column 4)

Chapter number and region of the world	Reef area ($km^2 \times 1000$)	Destroyed reefs (%)	Reefs recovered / reefs destroyed in 1998 (% / %)	Reefs at critical stage (%)	Reefs at threatened stage (%)
4. Red Sea	17.64	4	2 / 4	2	10
5. The Gulfs	3.80	65	2 / 15	15	15
6. East Africa	6.80	12	22 / 31	23	25
7. SW Indian Ocean	5.27	22	20 / 41	36	31
8. South Asia	19.21	45	13 /65	10	25
9. SE Asia	91.70	38	8 / 18	28	29
10. E and N Asia	5.40	14	3 / 10	23	12
11. Australia, PNG	62.80	2	1 / 3	3	15
12. SW Pacific Islands	27.06	3	8 / 10	18	40
13. Polynesian Islands	6.73	2	1 / 1	2	3
14. Micronesian Islands	12.70	8	1 / 2	3	5
15. Hawaiian Islands	1.18	1	NA	2	5
16. US Caribbean	3.04	16	NA	56	13

(cont.)

Table 1.1. *(cont.)*

Chapter number and region of the world	Reef area ($km^2 \times 1000$)	Destroyed reefs (%)	Reefs recovered / reefs destroyed in 1998 (% / %)	Reefs at critical stage (%)	Reefs at threatened stage (%)
17. North Caribbean	9.80	5	3 / 4	9	30
18. Central America	4.63	10	NA	24	19
19. East Antilles	1.92	12	NA	67	17
20. S Tropical America	5.12	15	NA	38	15
Total	284.30	20	6.4 / 16	24	26

Notes:
Column 1: The countries in each region are listed in Wilkinson (2004).
Column 2: Coral reef area from the *World Atlas of Coral Reefs* (Spalding *et al.*, 2001).
Column 3: Reefs 'destroyed' with 90% of the corals lost and unlikely to recover soon.
Column 4: Proportion of reefs recovered of the losses in 1998 from global coral bleaching (% / %).
Column 5: Reefs at a critical stage with 50% to 90% loss of corals, likely to join those in the Destroyed reefs column in 10 to 20 years.
Column 6: Reefs threatened with moderate signs of damage, 20% to 50% loss of corals and likely to be added to the Destroyed reefs column in 20–40 years.
NA. Not applicable, as there were no climate change related losses in 1998.
Columns 4 and 5 are based on the very high to high risk (combined), and the medium risk categories of the *Reefs at Risk* process (Burke and Maidens, 2004).

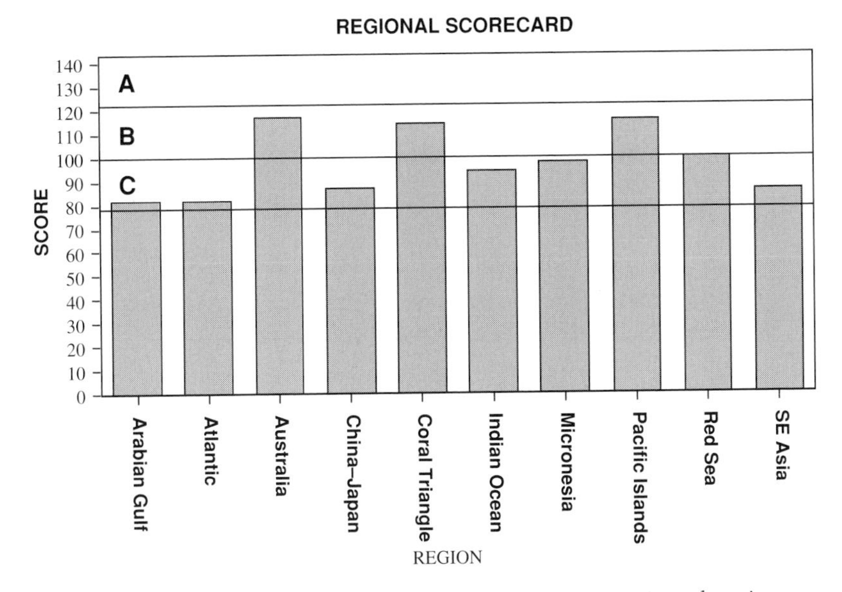

Figure 1.1 Sum of the 18 indicator grades (A = 4, B = 3, etc.) in each region from Reef Check surveys in 2002–2003; a perfect score would be 144. (Source: Gregor Hodgson, Reef Check.)

increased from 90% to 95% from 1997 to 2003 (Hodgson and Liebeler, 2002; www.ReefCheck.org). A regional scorecard based on the 18 categories of data recorded by Reef Check shows variation among regions of the world in the health of coral reefs (Fig. 1.1). This shows that Australia, the Pacific Islands and Coral Triangle (between Indonesia, the Philippines and Papua New Guinea) had the least damaged reefs in 2003, whereas the Arabian Gulf and Atlantic reefs were in the worst condition.

STATUS OF CORAL REEFS OF THE WORLD BY REGIONS

The following sections are summaries of the more detailed chapters in the *Status of Coral Reefs of the World: 2004* report (Wilkinson, 2004). The information on damage from the major tsunami of 26 December 2004 is derived from reports received after these chapters were written.

The Red Sea and Gulf of Aden (Kotb *et al.*, 2004)

The Red Sea reefs continue to be in relatively good health, because there are few direct anthropogenic threats. There is virtually no runoff from the land, fishing is at a relatively low level, although key target species like sharks are being removed, and tourism is largely concentrated in a few areas. Shipping, over-development of tourism without sufficient controls on sewage pollution and sediment runoff, coral bleaching and the crown-of-thorns starfish are the major future problems. The political awareness and will for conservation are not widespread, and monitoring and management capacity remain weak. Damage from coral bleaching in 1998 has been largely reversed in many areas.

Arabian/Persian Gulf region (Regional Organization for the Protection of the Marine Environment Sea Area) (Rezai *et al.*, 2004)

The reefs off the Arabian Peninsula have shown little recovery after they were largely destroyed during severe coral bleaching events in 1996 and 1998. The only recovery is larvae recruiting from reefs in deeper water that were less affected; however, there is an apparent shift in the recruiting coral species to lower-profile, slow-growing and more resistant species (e.g. species of *Porites, Favia* and *Cyphastrea*). Prior oil exploitation, shipping activities, and military conflicts that had resulted in some major oil spills have caused minimal previous damage. Near-shore reefs on the Iranian coast have also been affected by bleaching, but at a low level, whereas some of the offshore reefs in deeper water retain healthy corals. Awareness is increasing in this region; however, there are some major development projects that are destroying coral reefs. A monitoring network was formed in late 2003 with Iran as the host country.

East Africa (Obura *et al.*, 2004)

There has been significant, but very patchy, recovery of reefs devastated in 1998, with better recovery on reefs that are well managed. Coral regrowth is estimated at about 30–50%. The growing coastal population of 22 million people poses the largest threat to the reefs, with land-based activities and over-fishing increasing. There have been significant improvements in the management of coral reef marine protected areas (MPAs) in the last two to four years, due to national and regional initiatives, and greater commitments to increase the area of MPAs and improve fisheries management (see McClanahan, this volume). Regional and international NGOs are assisting communities in developing their own co-management places for MPAs, often based around tourist destinations. Ecological and socio-economic monitoring and research on coral reefs is expanding in the region due to local and international efforts. Damage to the coral reefs from the tsunami was relatively minor (D. Obura, pers. comm.).

South West Indian Ocean islands (Ahamada *et al.*, 2004)

There has been some recovery of the coral reefs damaged in 1998. However, recent bleaching damage to the new coral recruits is slowing recovery (see also Sheppard, this volume). There are some exceptional sites that were highly resilient to the bleaching damage, but human stresses and natural disturbances pose a constant threat to these reefs. Coral reefs on the Southern Islands (Madagascar, Mauritius, Réunion) suffered less damage in 1998, but natural disturbances have caused some coral mortality. There has been a marked increase in awareness of the need for coral reef management and conservation, and all countries have active monitoring programmes to assist in environmental decision-making. There are more monitoring sites, including remote reefs like Tromelin, Juan da Nova, Europa (France) and Cosmoledo, Assumption and Aldabra (Seychelles). The Global Environment Facility has just announced a continuation of funding for monitoring activities, which are expanding and providing information for governments. Damage to the coral reefs from the tsunami was relatively minor (D. Obura, pers. comm.).

South Asia (Rajasuriya *et al.*, 2004)

While there has been encouraging coral reef recovery in the Maldives, Chagos, Sri Lanka and Lakshadweep (India) after the massive coral bleaching mortalities in 1998, there has not been a parallel rise in awareness about the importance of coral reefs and the need for effective conservation. The possible exception is India, where there have been great advances in coral reef science with the publication of several major coral guidebooks and the formation of senior government committees and some stakeholder groups. Monitoring in the Maldives has assumed a lower priority, although there is high economic dependence on coral reef resources; insufficient national funds are allocated for monitoring or management, with the tourism sector filling the gaps. Management capacity continues to be weak in most countries with the drive for development taking priority over environmental conservation. There are, however, some excellent examples of effective management and successes in reef protection through community control. Many of the MPAs in the Maldives are managed by tourist resorts to protect their resources. Poverty continues to drive over-exploitation of fishes, invertebrates and coral rock. There was massive damage in India, the Maldives and Sri Lanka from the tsunami, but damage to the reefs was less important than damage to shorelines and coral islands. Some reefs were virtually destroyed; however, the majority escaped major damage and should recover rapidly once debris is removed (A. Rajasuriya, pers. comm.). Some reefs of the Andaman Islands have been uplifted and exposed to the air (K. Venkataraman, pers. comm.).

Southeast Asia (Tun *et al.*, 2004)

There has been a continual decline in reef condition across the region, with some signs of coral recovery in Indonesia and possibly Burma. Continued reef decline in the Philippines, Vietnam, Thailand and Singapore is occurring within the area of highest coral reef diversity. Direct human pressures remain high, dominated by over-fishing and damaging fishing, pollution from the land, excess sediment flow onto the reefs from coastal development, dredging and deforestation; and reclamation of coral reef areas continues for industries, airports and marinas. However, there are more active management initiatives throughout the region, and monitoring programmes have improved and expanded, after a decade of little progress. Some countries lack the expertise and resources for monitoring and there is a critical lack of effective coordination. Several major projects are starting to address the issues with assistance from United Nations and non-governmental organization (NGO) agencies, but there is a major need for regional coordination and cooperation, and a sharing of resources for coral reef monitoring and management. Damage from the tsunami along the Andaman Sea and Indian Ocean coastlines of Burma, Indonesia, Malaysia and Thailand was severe in some places, but generally far less than damage on land. Some shallow reefs were destroyed in Northern Sumatra as they were uplifted 2 to 3 m out of the water (G. Hodgson, pers. comm.).

East Asia (Kimura *et al.*, 2004)

Pressures from human activities remain the major threats to coral reefs in East and North Asia. These have been exacerbated by coral bleaching and some severe, recent typhoons. Sediment runoff is a major problem in many areas and rapid development is threatening reefs. Fishing pressures remain at extreme levels in most areas. Coral reefs continue to decline in areas of high human activity, whereas remote reefs are recovering from the bleaching losses of 1998. All countries are developing coral conservation and management programmes, and it is anticipated that these programmes could be effective in conserving coral reefs in the future, provided that there are no repeat bleaching episodes and that growing human populations do not increase pressures on coral reefs. Mariculture is supplementing stocks of coral reef fishes and invertebrates, but also resulting in local pollution. Coral bleaching has occurred since 2002, but most corals recovered.

Australia and Papua New Guinea (Miller and Sweatman, 2004)

Coral reefs in this region remain in relatively good condition, despite some recent setbacks. However, the level of resource monitoring and management is markedly different in both countries. Papua New Guinea has few trained people, minimal resources and low political will for coral reef conservation in a country where human pressures on the reefs are relatively low, but increasing rapidly. The only potentially effective model for conservation in Papua New Guinea is a decentralized, community-based system for reef resource management driven largely by NGOs. Australia has set an example for the world in coral reef conservation by declaring 33% of the whole Great Barrier Reef area as a highly protected zone; similarly 34% of the Ningaloo Reef tract of Western Australia has also been given protection. Good central planning, legislation, enforcement, research and monitoring support these activities. The reefs of the Great Barrier Reef show highly dynamic patterns of short periods of decline from disturbances, followed by longer periods of recovery. There is an apparent, longer-term trend of gradual decline, especially on inshore reefs affected by coastal pollution. The other major threats are coral bleaching and crown-of-thorns starfish outbreaks. There was a major bleaching event in 2002 and an outbreak of coral disease, but the mortality caused localized declines in coral cover, and many of the areas are recovering.

Southwest Pacific (Lovell *et al.*, 2004)

Coral reefs in the Southwest Pacific are generally in good condition, although there was extensive coral bleaching during 2000–2002. Some coral reefs have shown full recovery of live coral cover, whereas others have not recovered. The greatest threats to reefs continue to be human activities and cyclones, with reefs of New Caledonia, Samoa, Solomon Islands and Vanuatu having been damaged by cyclones since 2002. Other threats are crown-of-thorns starfish plagues and disease. The human pressures of overexploitation and pollution are concentrated around the cities and towns, and in lagoons. There is increased participation of governments, NGOs, scientists, volunteers and local communities in coral reef protection and conservation, with more plans for sustainable management of resources. Monitoring training and field surveys have increased; however, there is a lack of sustainable funding and support, and political will for the necessary conservation measures is weak.

Southeast Pacific (Vieux *et al.*, 2004)

The coral reefs of Polynesia Mana are predominantly healthy and under a low risk of damage in the immediate future. The reefs are probably the least degraded in the world as they are remote from large land masses and human influences; however, predicted global climate change, threats of more cyclones and coral bleaching are the major concern. Monitoring is developing, with some countries having ongoing programmes, whereas others are starting. Local populations are reviving cultures and traditions for sustainable reef management. Political awareness and will for coral reef conservation are increasing, but more effort is needed to combat the threats of increased sedimentation, over-fishing, dredging and nutrient pollution. If governments fail to implement coral reef resource management and do not remedy the causes of human stresses to the reefs around the heavily populated islands, these reefs will continue to decline, especially with lower fish stocks.

Micronesia (Kelty and Kuartei, 2004)

Micronesia contains some of the most diverse and pristine reefs in the world, but the cumulative impacts of sedimentation, increasing population demands, commercial fisheries, coastal pollution, ship groundings and recreational activities are apparent on many reefs. Human population growth is the main factor behind increasing disturbance. Isolated reefs are in good condition, but many reefs near population centres, and around the high islands, are declining with decreases in coral cover, reduced fish abundance, increased sediment damage and poor resilience to disease and bleaching. Coral reef monitoring and management continue to improve, with significant regulations banning scuba fishing, 'live rock' collection, and hunting of turtles and marine mammals. Monitoring activities have been boosted by increased support for the Palau International Coral Reef Center and more awareness in Micronesian countries. Governments and NGOs are developing more MPAs, and combining these into networks to conserve biodiversity.

Northeast (American) Pacific (Friedlander *et al.*, 2004)

The Hawaiian archipelago is one of the most isolated in the world, with many endemic species. The northwestern Hawaiian Islands are mostly uninhabited atolls and banks and generally in excellent condition with the only potential threats being coral bleaching and marine debris. The main Hawaiian Islands have 1.2 million residents and receive 7 million tourists each year who use the heavily developed tourism infrastructure; coral reefs are estimated to be worth US$10 billion per year to the economy. The major pressures are from land-based sources of pollution, over-fishing, recreational overuse and alien species. Fishing pressures vary considerably between the islands, with the remote reefs having large populations of apex predators, whereas there are very few remaining on the main volcanic islands. US government funding and expanded partnerships amongst organizations have resulted in more monitoring, mapping and research efforts to guide management decisions.

The American Caribbean (Kelty *et al.*, 2004)

There were massive losses in coral cover in the 1980s and 1990s from coral diseases, bleaching and human damage. However, the losses appear to have stabilized at much lower levels of coral cover, with evidence of coral recovery. Fishing pressures continue in both the economically depressed regions of Puerto Rico, and also along the coastlines of Florida and US Virgin Islands. The major recent change has been multinational fishing on the isolated and uninhabited Navassa reef, where the once healthy populations of major target fishes have been severely depleted in the last two years. Monitoring is demonstrating negative trends in reef community health, especially in existing MPAs. This is providing a stimulus for better management to protect coastal resources by reducing anthropogenic stresses. An essential need is to strengthen cross-boundary and cross-jurisdictional agreements to facilitate ecosystem-based management and information and technology transfer. Mapping, monitoring and management of coral reefs of Florida, Flower Garden Banks, Puerto Rico, US Virgin Islands and Navassa have all improved, with increased government awareness and funding.

Northern Caribbean and western Atlantic (Jones *et al.*, 2004)

Coral cover in the northern Caribbean remains low, averaging 20% cover, compared to what existed in the 1960s. There are a few sites in most countries with 30–50% coral cover; however, most sites have 3–10% cover. There has been little recovery of the formerly abundant *Acropora* spp. coral cover, and diseases, bleaching and pollution are still resulting in coral loss. Patchy recovery of the *Diadema* sea urchin is occurring, but algae still dominate on many reefs. Fishing is still intense, and many grouper populations are virtually extinct, such that it is rare to see large fishes on the reefs. All countries report significant threats to coral reefs, including over-fishing, land-based sources of pollution, and regional or global factors such as coral bleaching and disease. Over-fishing of algal grazing fishes is the major cause of macroalgal overgrowth of corals. National capacity to implement and enforce fisheries regulations is inversely proportional to fishing intensity. Most countries have adequate legislation, but enforcement is inadequate or lacking, and many MPAs lack effective management. Although progress in coastal management is being made in most countries, poor financial resources often impede the implementation of laws and policies.

Central or Mesoamerica (Arrivillaga and Garcia, 2004)

Natural disturbances, such as hurricanes, coral diseases, *Diadema* mortality and coral bleaching, combined with anthropogenic stresses, such as nutrient enrichment, sedimentation, over-fishing and direct damage of the corals, all threaten the coral reefs of this region. A new regional initiative between Belize, Guatemala, Honduras and Mexico has gathered considerable support for public and private conservation efforts, and resulted in coordinated environmental monitoring of coral reefs, which is producing substantial trend data. NGOs are active in the region and assisting communities with co-management of their resources to reverse major declines in fisheries stocks. Tourism is expanding very rapidly and will have positive effects in providing alternative uses for coral reefs and employment for communities, but the rapid and often uncontrolled pace of development is damaging coastal lands and increasing demand for quality seafood, e.g. lobsters and groupers.

The eastern Antilles (Bouchon *et al.*, 2004)

The coral reefs of the French West Indies and nearby islands have steadily declined since the early 1980s. This has stimulated long-term monitoring on the French islands and increased Reef Check activities in the other island states with the support of the United Nations Environment Programme (UNEP) Regional Coordinating Unit in Jamaica. Reef Check rapid assessments are filling gaps where there were no current data, and training local fisheries and dive operator staff. All reefs face a common set of threats: high rates of sedimentation, due to deforestation and bad land management, which affect mainly the reefs in the enclosed bays; algal proliferation due to an overload of nutrients in the coastal waters from excessive use of fertilizers and poor wastewater treatment; and chronic over-fishing and harvesting of reef resources. More MPAs have been declared, but many remain without adequate management. Many of these islands were damaged by a series of major hurricanes in mid-2004. There are no available data on the fate of the reefs; however, it is anticipated that many sustained wave and sediment damage.

Southern tropical America (Garzón-Ferreira *et al.*, 2004)

Most coral reefs in this region have undergone major changes in the last 30 years, but particularly during the 1980s. There have been considerable losses of live coral cover in many reef areas, while algae have become dominant. However, some areas of high coral cover occur on both the Caribbean (means between 20% and 40%) and Pacific (means above 40%) coasts. The coral reefs are strongly influenced by continental runoff containing large amounts of sediments and high concentrations of nutrients from large rivers on the South American mainland. The other major threats are coral bleaching, disease outbreaks and phytoplankton blooms, and direct human pressures from deforestation, increased sedimentation, coastal development, sewage pollution and over-fishing. An additional threat is the demands of a strongly developing tourism industry for seafood. There are major gaps in financial support for coral reef monitoring and management, and governments are not fully aware of or concerned about the fate of their coral reefs.

THREATS AND STRESSES TO CORAL REEFS

The authors of the *Status of Coral Reefs of the World: 2004* report (Wilkinson, 2004) identified the major threats and stresses to coral reefs around the world (Table 1.2). These frequently occur simultaneously, and will result in varying degrees of damage to specific coral reefs. For example, on reefs close to human populations, pollution is a greater threat in some areas, whereas over-fishing is more destructive in others. By contrast, on remote reefs global climate change poses the major threat. However, poor awareness of the problem and insufficient political will are usually causal agents behind damage to coral reefs and threats to their future survival (Table 1.2).

Table 1.2. Summary of threats and stresses affecting coral reefs

General category	Specific threat	Description
Global change	Coral bleaching	Loss of photosynthetic zooxanthellae from coral tissues caused by elevated sea surface temperatures due to global climate change
	Rising levels of CO_2	Increased concentrations of CO_2 in sea water due to increasing water temperatures, resulting in decreased calcification rates in coral reef organisms
	Diseases, plagues and invasives	Increases in frequency of diseases and plagues of coral predators; increasingly linked to human disturbances in the environment
Direct human pressures	Over-fishing (and global market pressures)	The harvesting of fishes and invertebrates beyond sustainable yields, including the use of damaging practices (bomb and cyanide fishing)
	Sedimentation	Increased rate of sediments and mud deposited on coral reefs, stemming from poor land use, deforestation, and dredging
	Nutrients and chemical pollution	Both organic and inorganic chemicals carried with sediments, in untreated sewage, wastes from agriculture, animal husbandry and industry; includes complex organics and heavy metals
	Development of coastal areas	Modification of coral reefs for urban, industrial, transport and tourism developments, including reclamation and the mining of coral reef rock and sand beyond sustainable limits
Governance, awareness and political will	Rising poverty, increasing populations, alienation from the land	Increasing numbers of poor and dispossessed people relying on coral reef resources for subsistence and exploiting them beyond sustainable limits
	Poor capacity for management and lack of resources	Lack of trained personnel for coral reef management, raising awareness, enforcement and monitoring; lack of adequate funding and logistic resources to implement effective conservation
	Poor political will, and oceans governance	Political ignorance, indifference or inertia; corruption in governance of resources at global and regional levels

True natural threats are not considered in this chapter, as coral reefs generally have strong potential to recover from tropical cyclonic storms, freshwater inundation, geological events such as earthquakes, volcanoes or tsunamis, and low levels of plagues and diseases. The caveat about recovery is that additional anthropogenic stresses are not imposed on the reefs, and the level of these natural disturbances does not increase in future. Such an increase, however, is one of the predicted scenarios of global climate change (Kleypas *et al.*, 1999; Bellwood *et al.*, 2004; Hoegh-Guldberg, 2004). It is predicted that tropical storms could increase in frequency and severity, and the major global ocean currents may change (Intergovernmental Panel on Climate Change Working Group I, 2001; Intergovernmental Panel on Climate Change Working Group II, 2001; Timmermann, 1999).

Pressures on reefs are increasing as human populations and economies increase (Wilkinson, 1993; Birkeland, 2004), resulting in direct damage to coral reefs, either inadvertently via pollution or directly through the extraction of resources, e.g. fishes, rock, sand. There is another category for which the direct cause is not obvious. These are stresses that are natural in origin, but are probably exacerbated by human activities. This category includes: stresses arising from global climate change, with increased coral bleaching (Hoegh-Guldberg, 1999; Wilkinson, 1999, 2002); diseases of corals and other reef organisms (Harvell *et al.*, 2002); plagues of coral predators and other damaging animals; and invasive species that threaten to disturb the ecological balance on coral reefs by out-competing local species (Table 1.2). All these stresses have increased markedly in the past 30 years.

Global change threats

Coral bleaching

The major emerging threat to coral reefs in the last decade has been coral bleaching and mortality associated with global climate change, especially major El Niño–La Niña events. The 1998 global coral bleaching event effectively destroyed 16% of the world's coral reefs, with most damage throughout the Indian Ocean and the western Pacific (Wilkinson *et al.*, 1999; Wilkinson, 2000). The damage appeared to be a 1-in-1000-year event in many regions based on the past history of coral reefs (Fig. 1.1). Very old corals (around 1000 years old) died from bleaching during 1998 and there is no record or memory of similar bleaching mortality in official government records or in the memories of traditional cultures. What is uncertain is whether the major climate shifts of 1998 will prove to be a 1-in-1000-year event in the future. The evidence is strongly against that assumption, with predictions that coral bleaching like that seen in 1998 will become a regular event in approximately 50 years time (Hoegh-Guldberg, 1999, 2004; see also Sheppard, this volume), although by then most of the susceptible corals may have been lost from many coral reefs. There is a strong probability that some rare and restricted corals may become totally extinct. There has been no recurrence of the major coral bleaching episodes of 1998, although there have been some more localized bleaching events in 2000 and 2003 causing damage to reefs.

The other major predicted threats from global climate change are: an increase in the frequency and intensity of tropical storms; more frequent and severe switches in global climate, such as El Niño – La Niña changes; a rise in sea level; a potential shift in ocean currents; and an increase in the dissolved concentration of the greenhouse gas carbon dioxide in sea water (Wilkinson and Buddemeier, 1994). There are suggestions that the first effect of more frequent and severe storms has already happened, but clusters of severe storms such as that which happened in the Caribbean in 2004 are known from historical records and no definitive trend has emerged so far. It is apparent that the interval between El Niño events has shortened from about 12 years to less than seven years, but the record is too short for confirmation. It is also too early to assess whether the large ocean currents will change (Timmerman, 1999). Sea level rise will not threaten coral reefs, but will have potentially disastrous consequences for low-lying coral islands, especially atoll countries like the Maldives, Tuvalu, Marshall Islands and Kiribati (Wilkinson and Buddemeier, 1994). Sheppard (this volume) covers many of these longer-term impacts of global climate change.

Rising levels of carbon dioxide

The threat of increasing concentrations of atmospheric CO_2 dissolving in sea water and altering the carbonate–bicarbonate balance (lower pH, lower carbonate ion concentration) is becoming more likely as greenhouse gas concentrations continue to increase. The oceans are sequestering about one-third of all human-induced CO_2 emissions (Feely *et al.*, 2004). Increased dissolved CO_2 has the potential to decrease rates of calcification in tropical and cold-water corals, molluscs, calcifying algae and foraminifera. All of these organisms make major contributions of calcium carbonate in many marine ecosystems. The potential was reported by Smith and Buddemeier (1992), and has since been confirmed in experiments on reef-building organisms in the laboratory and in large coral mesocosms with calcification rates declining significantly under higher CO_2 concentrations (Kleypas *et al.*, 1999). There was a 10–40% reduction in coral calcification under doubled CO_2 concentrations, the scenario that is predicted to occur within 50 years (Kleypas *et al.*, 1999; Feely *et al.*, 2004). The increasing atmospheric CO_2 concentrations may result in synergistic pressures, possibly increasing already acute coral reef stresses like bleaching and diseases by reducing coral resilience.

Diseases, plagues and invasives

The other major global threat to coral reefs is through an apparent proliferation of coral reef diseases and plagues of destructive organisms. These threats are increasing in incidence and severity, with strong correlations with damaging human activities, whether through pollution from poorly managed watersheds, heat stress to corals, or through over-fishing of the organisms that control plagues (Jackson *et al.*, 2001).

Coral diseases are reported to affect more than 150 species of Caribbean and Indo-Pacific corals, and new examples continue to be added to the 29 described diseases (Harvell *et al.*, 2002; Rosenberg and Ben-Haim, 2002; Willis *et al.*, 2004). Diseases have caused more damage to the coral reefs in the wider Caribbean than in the Indo-Pacific region; however, the recent increases in marine diseases worldwide emphasizes the need for more research and also points to potential linkages to other stresses on corals as possible instigators of disease (Harvell *et al.*, 2002; Rosenberg and Ben-Haim, 2002).

It is apparent that plagues of predators, such as crown-of-thorns starfish (*Acanthaster planci*), are increasingly reported around areas of human activities, with the possibility that either the plagues are initiated or exacerbated by over-fishing and/or that increases in nutrients from the land favour the planktonic stages of the starfish (Birkeland, 1982; Jackson *et al.*, 2001). Unfortunately, definitive explanations for the outbreaks do not exist after decades of intensive research, although the best explanation for current outbreaks is through a removal of fishes that consume juvenile starfish (Jackson *et al.*, 2001). There have been widespread, large-scale losses of coral cover and biodiversity on many reefs and these plagues can be added as another large-scale threat to the integrity of coral reefs. The highest densities of crown-of-thorns starfish in recent years have been in Tanzania, Kenya and on the Great Barrier Reef.

The potential threats from invasive species have largely been ignored until recently. While there is the likelihood that such invasives could disrupt the ecological balance of coral reefs, there is little evidence of significant deleterious effects on ecosystem processes or biodiversity. The most serious incidence was the suspected introduction through the Panama Canal of a disease that killed the sea urchin *Diadema antillarum* in the Caribbean in the early 1980s (Lessios, 1995). There is now evidence of invasive species causing damage in Hawaii and parts of the Caribbean. The most likely causes of invasive introductions are through ballast-water or the hulls of cargo ships, or through the release of aquarium specimens in the wrong habitat (Davis, 2005).

Direct human pressures

Direct human pressures continue to rise in almost all coral reef areas of the world, as human populations grow and increase their demand for more resources, e.g. human activities on land result in more pollution of reefs, and over-fishing disrupts the ecological balance. These are the stresses that are most amenable to intervention by resource managers and governments, acting in concert with local user communities. Coral reefs remote from land influences or managed to reduce human pressures have the greatest recovery potential and resilience to other pressures, like global climate change bleaching and disease.

Over-fishing

As human populations increase and regional economies grow, there is a parallel increase in the demand for seafood. Most coral reefs within range of small fishing boats, including motor-powered aluminium boats, are now over-fished with the key target species being those that are closely associated with coral reefs, i.e. the groupers, snappers and large wrasses (Pauly and Chua, 1988; Pauly *et al.*, 1998). As catches decrease, fishers target all fish species, using more efficient methods of traps, fine-mesh nets and spears; the final resort is to use bombs and cyanide to catch the few remaining fish. This fishing down the food chain from the predators, to omnivores, to herbivores, and eventually to planktivores has multiple effects on a coral reef (Hughes, 1994; Pauly *et al.*, 1998). Coral reefs with reduced fish populations are more susceptible to overgrowth by macroalgae, plagues of coral predators, and probable increases in disease (McClanahan *et al.*, 2000; McClanahan, this volume). In addition, fishing results in direct physical damage to the reef framework, thereby further exacerbating the effects of over-fishing. Damage results from anchors, nets and traps and especially the use of explosives to stun fish hiding in the corals (Burke *et al.*, 2002).

One of the most effective measures to protect biodiversity, including fishes, is the establishment and enforcement of no-take MPAs (Roberts *et al.*, this volume). However, many national and international fisheries management authorities contend that improvement in fish abundance in areas near MPAs has to be demonstrated before more MPAs are implemented. This suggests that no-take MPAs are experiments in managing fish stocks and must be scientifically validated. The inverse is the reality. No-take MPAs on coral reefs do conserve biodiversity and retain natural ecosystems, and constitute the 'control' in the 'experiment', which is to determine whether fishing or selectively removing one component (fish) from an ecosystem causes an ecological imbalance. Thus, the hypothesis should be: 'Does fishing remove fish from an ecosystem and does over-fishing affect the biodiversity and ecological balances on a coral reef?' The no-take zone then becomes the control for this experiment as an un-fished ecosystem.

Unless fishing pressures can be reduced through the provision of alternative livelihoods and employment for fishers, through sustainable aquaculture and through establishing more no-take MPAs, it is predicted that there will be more collapses in fisheries stocks. Daniel Pauly and colleagues have a pessimistic view on the possibility of managing coral reef fisheries in developing countries and suggest that current approaches towards establishing sustainable coral reef fisheries are unlikely to yield success (Pauly *et al.*, 2002), whereas the International Society for Reef Studies (2004) and others recommend the essential measures needed to achieve sustainability in coral reef fisheries, although with some pessimism (see also McClanahan, this volume).

Destructive fishing

Over-fishing is often accompanied by damaging practices to compensate for the depletion of fish stocks and to feed the demand for high-priced species for Asian restaurants and the aquarium trade. Bomb fishing is largely restricted to Southeast and East Asia, although it has occurred in eastern Africa and parts of the Pacific. Bombs are used when fish stocks drop, making hook-and-line, net and trap fishing unprofitable. Cyanide was first used to catch small aquarium fish, but its use has expanded to capture live fish for the restaurant trade (Vincent, this volume). The fish can be resuscitated after being stunned, although there is usually permanent liver damage. The use of cyanide, however, usually results in death of corals and other reef organisms, producing a wasteland (Johannes and Riepen, 1995; Barber and Pratt, 1997; Sadovy and Vincent, 2002).

Sediment pollution

Most developments within reef catchment areas increase sediment flow onto coral reefs. This results in reduced photosynthesis in corals, increased rates of disease and bioerosion, and eventual burial of corals. The rate of sediment release into the oceans is increasing, as more coastal lands are developed to accommodate rising urban populations and increases in agriculture (Fabricius, 2005). One of the major increases is through tropical deforestation, often by clear-felling for tropical timbers and agriculture, such as oil palm plantations in Southeast Asia and the western Pacific. These impacts are clearly being felt in Indonesia, Papua New Guinea, the Solomon Islands and throughout the wider Caribbean. In parts of Micronesia, steep upland forest areas are being cleared to grow the root crop 'sakau', a type of mildly intoxicating 'kava'.

Nutrient pollution

Nutrient pollution has been studied extensively on many coral reefs, e.g. the Kaneohe Bay story (Hunter and Evans, 1995). Excess nutrients favour the growth of macroalgae when the populations of grazing fishes and sea urchins are reduced. They increase phytoplankton growth in sea water, thereby reducing light energy penetration to the light-dependent corals. They also favour the growth of other competitors of corals, especially those that bore into coral skeletons, such as sponges, molluscs, worms and burrowing algae, and probably make corals more susceptible to disease. All reefs near human populations or adjacent to large land masses suffer some degradation from nutrient pollution. The control of catchment pollution through an extensive water-quality programme is seen as one of the major issues for the management of the Great Barrier Reef (Haynes and Schaffelke, 2004).

Development on coral reefs

As populations increase on the coast, so do the pressures to alienate land from the sea as 'development'. There are currently large plans to 'reclaim' coral reef areas in the Persian/Arabian Gulf, especially in United Arab Emirates, in the Red Sea along the coast of Saudi Arabia, in Singapore and recently in peninsular Malaysia and southern Japan to build airports on coral reefs to attract tourists. Virtually all coastal developments result in sediment damage to fragile corals; however, some activities have long-lasting effects. The building of marinas, groynes and causeways around coral reefs disrupts currents and often causes major displacements of sediment. Causeways on some Pacific islands have resulted in considerable coral death and reduced fisheries in coral lagoons.

Many countries have prohibited the mining of coral rock and sand from sensitive areas on and around coral reefs. This ban was in recognition of the damage that excessive mining caused to reefs and their potential to provide other goods and services, such as fish productivity, shoreline protection and attracting tourists. Mining is still practised in some countries where there are limited sources of sand and limestone on land, or where governments do not enforce the regulations, such as in South Asia.

Governance, awareness and political will

The human component of poor governance and low political will in many coral reef countries, combined with occasional unintended consequences of actions by international agencies, is resulting in collateral damage to coral reefs (see Brown, this volume). Many countries reported that there was inadequate governance capacity and a lack of awareness of the problems facing coral reefs

Rising poverty, increasing populations, alienation from the land

Many tropical countries have rapidly increasing coastal populations and consequent rising levels of poverty, which put increasing pressures on coral reefs to provide food and other resources, usually beyond sustainable limits (Wilkinson, 1993; Birkeland, 2004). There is a global trend towards a migration of populations to coastal areas in search of work, as agricultural lands lose fertility or are divided into smaller parcels for family members. These increased pressures have caused, and will cause, collapses of coral reefs and phase shifts towards algal-dominated reefs at the expense of corals. Moreover, the increases in populations and the associated increases in pollution and resource exploitation will undermine attempts at conserving coastal resources. These three problems have to be faced in order to implement sustainable management of coral reef resources.

Poor capacity for management and lack of resources

Of the 100 coral reef countries and states reported in Wilkinson (2004), 21 have populations under 100 000, and a further 23 have populations under 1 million. These countries must establish the full range of government and be represented on United Nations (UN) bodies and multilateral environmental agreements. In addition, they are responsible for the management of a large component of global biodiversity. These governments have often declared MPAs and passed well-drafted legislation to protect coral reefs, but there is little follow-up action to manage the MPAs and enforce the regulations, principally because they lack the capacity and financial and logistic resources for the task. There is also often insufficient awareness of the threats facing coral reefs and the potential solutions. For example, the many small to large states in the Wider Caribbean have declared 285 MPAs, but only 16 are regarded as effectively managed (Burke and Maidens, 2004). Similarly in Southeast Asia, only 10% to 20% of more than 630 MPAs are effectively managed, with well-prepared management plans that are enforced (Tun *et al.*, 2004).

Low political will and oceans governance

Many developing country governments focus on solving the immediate needs of providing health, housing, education and nutrition for their populations, and postpone action on the longer-term, and potentially more difficult problems of ensuring that environmental goods and services are conserved for the future. The resources needed to build management capacity by training young graduates in environmental management, and providing the funding and logistic resources to implement effective conservation, are low on the priority list; authors report that some governments consider that the environmental problems can be solved after the immediate problems. Conservation efforts are often taken on by the multilateral environmental agreements and NGOs, working at the local government level.

Inter-sectoral disputes and poor coordination are contributing factors towards poor environmental management. The 'traditional' management approach was consensus-based or 'integrated coastal management', often with the whole or large sections of the community involved in discussions before decisions were made about resource use. The resources were considered as the 'common property' of the community. Most developing countries have now adopted 'Western' or 'modern' methods of governance, with a cash economy, the concept of free access to all marine areas, and a sectoral government approach, e.g. a fisheries department seeking to maximize fish harvests, a forestry department aiming to maximize returns from trees, and an environment department tasked with conserving resources and ecosystems. Moreover, many of these governments must simultaneously consider the potential impacts of global climate change throughout the economy and on particular ecosystems.

The critical issues to improve coral reef (and oceans) governance are: a firm basis of local, national and international environmental policies and regulations to ensure the sustainable use of coral reef resources; effective mechanisms to implement and enforce those policies and regulations, including reviews of the effectiveness of the mechanisms in conserving resources; and improved capacity for coral reef management in these countries and the provision of resources for actions to avert the potential collapse in coral reef resources.

International agencies assisting coral reef countries
Many international agencies, including organizations of the UN, national donors and NGOs, assist countries with activities to conserve coral reef biodiversity, reduce threats, introduce integrated coastal management, and assist communities to develop alternative and sustainable livelihoods. These efforts are achieving considerable successes. However, many international agencies are inadvertently exacerbating the problem of poor capacity in many developing countries.

For example, the major multilateral environmental agreements concerned with coral reefs – the Convention on Biological Diversity, the Framework Convention on Climate Change, the World Heritage Convention, as well as the CITES, Ramsar and Migratory Species conventions which focus on protecting biodiversity – all seek to assist countries with natural resource conservation and environmental management. However, this assistance often depends on the production of regular reports to convention secretariats and the need to attend annual or biannual meetings in distant lands. Unfortunately, these reporting and meeting requirements and some training programmes divert the few trained environmental staff from direct activities aimed at conserving coral reef resources. Thus, there would be considerable benefits if the meeting and reporting requirements of the multilateral environmental agreements and other UN agencies could be rationalized to ensure that more time and resources are spent on activities directly related to resource conservation.

The Kyoto protocol to reduce the flow of greenhouse gases into the atmosphere and slow the accelerating rate of global climate change was drafted in Japan in 1997 (www.unfccc.int/essential_background/convention/items/2627.php). This protocol, which is minimalist in its ambitions to slow climate change, has only come into force as a UN-ratified convention in late 2004, with 84 parties signing and 124 either ratifying or acceding to the convention; some major greenhouse gas emitting countries, such as the USA, are not included. Thus, seven years have potentially been lost in reducing the threats to the world's ecosystems, including coral reefs. These delays result in cynicism amongst the smaller coral reef countries that are likely to be adversely affected by climate change but are not major emitters of greenhouse gases.

TWO EXAMPLES OF DAMAGE AND CONSERVATION

Two regions of the world illustrate variations in both the damage to coral reefs and activities aimed at conserving them. The Great Barrier Reef (GBR) of Australia is an example of particularly active conservation, supported by a strong scientific base and supportive local community. In mid-2004, 33% of the whole province of the GBR (the GBR World Heritage Area) was given highly protected status (or no-take zones) by the Parliament of Australia (www.gbrmpa.gov.au). This is an increase from 5% of the GBR with the focus on the coral reefs that were zoned for protection in 1981. The heightened protection was considered necessary by the single management agency, the Great Barrier Reef Marine Park Authority, following increasing evidence that existing multiple-use zoning was inadequate to conserve biodiversity. For example, dugong populations have declined by 97% since the 1960s; nesting loggerhead turtles declined by 50–80% over four decades; commercial and recreational fishing have doubled since 1990; populations of major target species of fishes have been reduced and are now composed of smaller individuals; the annual flow of sediments and nutrients into the GBR has increased fourfold; and the reefs have suffered from severe coral bleaching, a series of cyclones and outbreaks of crown-of-thorns starfish. Many marine organisms rely on several adjacent ecosystems, thus the planning process focused on conserving a representative sample of all ecosystems ('ecoregions' or 'bioregions'), including seagrass beds, sandy and muddy bottoms and deep continental shelf slopes.

The process for reviewing the zoning of the Great Barrier Reef Marine Park started with the collation of all available scientific information, followed by community involvement, which together led to the identification of 70 bioregions within the Marine Park. There were a number of guiding principles to achieve the overall goal, including extending no-take protection to at least 20% of each bioregion. There was strong community involvement throughout the review process, with more than 31 000 public submissions received. The resulting new zoning includes the world's largest network of no-take areas (114 530 km^2).

Support for the rezoning was helped by the government offering assistance to affected parties such as commercial fishers, who might have reduced earning potential from the reduction in line-fishing and trawling areas.

In contrast, there has been a significant and catastrophic degradation of coral reef status in the Wider Caribbean (including the nearby Atlantic coral reefs), accompanied by largely ineffective attempts at removing the human stresses and implementing effective resource conservation. Coral cover has declined by approximately 80% over 25 years, from about 50% cover on many reefs to approximately 10% now (Gardner *et al.*, 2003; Côté *et al.*, this volume). These declines are attributed to coral bleaching and disease, hurricanes, and chronic problems of over-fishing, nutrient and sediment pollution and coastal modification (Burke and Maidens, 2004). The decline is particularly evident with the formerly dominant and major reef-building corals, *Acropora cervicornis* and related species and hybrids, and *A. palmata* (Precht and Aronson, this volume). These were severely affected by coral diseases and bleaching in the 1980s and 1990s, such that they have now been listed under the Endangered Species Act (ESA) of the USA (B. Plater, pers. comm.).

There has been some recent recovery in the major reef-building coral species in parts of the Wider Caribbean (Precht and Aronson, this volume), with fewer reported incidences of disease and major bleaching events. However, this should be treated with caution as the long-term trend is for an increase in the severity and extent of coral bleaching (McWilliams *et al.*, 2005). The long-term prognosis for Caribbean reefs is also discouraging as human pressures continue to mount with increasing populations. There are currently 116 million people living within 100 km of a Caribbean coast, which is a 20% increase in the past 10 years (Burke and Maidens, 2004).

The *Reefs at Risk* analysis for the Caribbean in 2004 (Burke and Maidens, 2004) and the report on impacts of climate change on Caribbean coral reefs from the Pew Center for Global Climate Change (Buddemeier *et al.*, 2004) found that:

- In the Caribbean, 64% of coral reefs are threatened by high levels of human activities, especially the eastern and southern Caribbean, Greater Antilles, Florida Keys, Yucatan and the Mesoamerican Barrier Reef.
- Coastal development threatens 33% of the region's reefs. The threat is greatest in the Lesser and Greater Antilles, Bay Islands of Honduras, Florida Keys, Yucatan and southern Caribbean.
- Land-based sources of pollution and sediments threaten 35% of Caribbean coral reefs, most notably in Jamaica, Hispaniola, Puerto Rico, the high islands of the Lesser Antilles, Belize, Costa Rica and Panama. Pollution and damage from ships threaten 15% of coral reefs, especially around large ports and cruise tourism centres.
- Over-fishing threatens more than 60% of Caribbean coral reefs, particularly on narrow coastal shelves near human population centres.
- Diseases and rising sea surface temperatures threaten reefs across the Caribbean.
- Ineffective MPA management threatens Caribbean coral reefs, with only 6% of 285 MPAs rated as effectively managed.

- There will be large economic losses if coral reef degradation continues, with a predicted loss of US$350–870 million per year by 2015 of the US$3100–4600 million of current annual benefits from fisheries, dive tourism and shoreline protection services.

These pressures and the threats of global climate change pose major threats for future recovery of Caribbean reefs. Many of these reefs are within the territorial waters of small developing states, with little capacity and few resources to implement effective management. Most reefs continue to be damaged by over-fishing such that surveys, especially by Reef Check (www.ReefCheck.org) and AGRRA (www.agrra.org), show that some fish stocks are close to collapse throughout, with very few reefs having populations of breeding fish. Moreover, there are very few areas with highly protected MPAs and most of those that do exist are not enforced.

RECOMMENDATIONS FOR THE FUTURE OF CORAL REEFS

The authors of the chapters in Wilkinson (2004) made a series of recommendations to reduce the stresses on coral reefs so as to reverse their declining status in their regions. These recommendations have many features in common with the 'Okinawa Declaration' and the Action Statement from the 2nd International Tropical Marine Ecosystems Management Symposium, as well as the statements from *Reefs at Risk* (Burke and Maidens, 2004), the Pew Center for Global Climate Change (Buddemeier *et al.*, 2004) and elsewhere (Birkeland, 2004).

Action to conserve coral reefs

These recommendations focus on:

- reducing and, where possible, removing the direct pressures on coral reefs through integrated catchment and coastal management to minimize the inflow of polluting sediments and nutrients into reef waters;
- managing coral reef fisheries in an attempt to make them sustainable and prohibit damaging fishing practices;
- improving fisheries yields by protecting breeding stocks in no-take MPAs, protecting spawning sites, and also in selective breeding programmes to satisfy the Asian restaurant market for live reef fish;

- involving local communities in the design and management of MPAs and enforcement of regulations;
- developing networks of MPAs that are larger, contain the most resistant and resilient coral and other organism populations, and are connected to ensure a free transfer of new larvae to restock the reefs and repair damage; and
- acting locally and globally to reduce the emissions of greenhouse gases that are driving global climate change inexorably towards massive destruction of coral reefs and the possible extinction of many coral reef species.

Action to improve oceans governance

Many countries reported there was insufficient capacity to implement actions to conserve natural resources. The main issues are for countries to have: environmental policies and regulations for effective conservation; implementation mechanisms for policies and regulations to improve coral reef management and conservation; and the capacity for coral reef management and resources for direct action with communities.

Environmental policies and regulations

There are many international policies and regulations, with the Law of the Sea Convention, the Climate Change Convention and the multilateral environmental agreements (e.g. World Heritage, CITES, Ramsar and Migratory Species). Most governments have developed strong national legislation, thus the urgent issue is not to develop more of these, but ensure that they are implemented. There is a need is to:

- ensure that local user communities and the private sector are aware of these environmental policies and regulations and have access to their provisions to manage environments on the ground;
- ensure that the international community provides incentives for communities and governments to manage their resources sustainably. Market-based incentives are an effective mechanism to assist communities;
- increase recognition in national and international policy development that sustainable development and poverty reduction in many countries are not achievable without integrated watershed and marine ecosystem management;

- recognize the role that effective management of coral reef resources can play in sustainable development and poverty alleviation.

Implementation mechanisms for policies and regulations

Implementation is where most effort is required. There is an urgent need to develop effective mechanisms to convert the legal instruments into effective implementation in the natural environment, and to:

- develop integrated oceans, integrated natural resource and integrated catchment management groups that include all stakeholders, especially local communities and the private sector, supported by governments, that can make decisions across all sectors of government;
- devolve sufficient authority to communities to develop and run their own no-take MPAs and implement enforcement (all well supported by state and national governments);
- develop joint enforcement mechanisms with government and communities acting in concert to enforce environmental laws aimed at conserving resources;
- strengthen jurisdiction and the imposition of penalties under existing laws to demonstrate to communities that their actions are supported and that infringements are treated seriously in the courts;
- reduce the reporting and meeting requirements of UN agencies and multilateral environmental agreements and make them more relevant to small countries, possibly through developing regional meetings that combine several international marine environmental instruments with more attention to practical issues;
- facilitate the access of small countries to international conventions and instruments as collaborating blocks and reduce their meeting and reporting requirements by forming groups of states with similar cultures, problems and resources;
- review the effectiveness of implementation of international conventions and instruments to ensure that they are assisting in conserving the marine resources;
- undertake an objective appraisal of the performance of current international and regional environmental agencies to ensure that their current activities meet the stated objective of conserving environmental resources.

Capacity for coral reef management

Most coral reef countries lack trained personnel for coral reef management, awareness raising, enforcement and monitoring. Moreover, they lack the necessary resources to implement effective management. Thus there is a need to:

- assist in the training of environmental resource managers and ensuring that they are provided with in-country employment;
- assist countries in the development of alternative livelihoods to combat poverty and reduce the need to over-exploit coral reef resources;
- assist developing countries in the design, implementation and management of networks of MPAs to conserve their resources;
- consolidate the training provided by UN agencies and multilateral environmental agreements to ensure that they are targeted on resources, issues and problems relevant to conserving national resources;
- provide adequate and long-term financial and logistic resources for developing countries to undertake environmental planning for the longer term, rather than the three- to five-year funding cycle of projects;
- assist in the recognition of appropriate traditional knowledge and methods of environmental management and help governments harmonize these with state and national laws;
- develop the 'capacity to build capacity' and use 'train-the-trainers' and peer-to-peer exchanges as low-cost mechanisms to ensure that capacity building is a self-sustaining mechanism.

CONCLUSIONS

Coral reefs of the world continue to decline under a mix of predominantly human stresses arising from increasing exploitation of resources and developments on the land, fuelled by increasing populations. Coral reefs in the Indian Ocean and western Pacific are recovering after the 1998 El Niño–La Niña global coral bleaching event, with stronger recovery in well-managed and remote reefs; however, there is not uniform recovery and many reefs damaged in 1998 show few signs of recovery, because there are inadequate supplies of new coral larvae.

Action will be required at local, national and international scales to implement better management practices, to make fisheries more sustainable and improve yields by protecting breeding stocks, to protect reefs from direct damage and to integrate conflicting approaches to management in the watersheds and adjacent waters around coral reefs. It is widely recognized that one of the better methods of protecting coral reefs is through

MPAs and affording them the highest level of protection possible. The declaration of 33% of the Great Barrier Reef World Heritage Area with highly protected status is an example for other governments. Many MPAs have been declared recently by governments around the world; however, few MPAs have effective management and most are ignored by local populations. There is strong recognition amongst international agencies that developing countries need scientific, logistic and financial support to designate and manage coral reef MPAs to safeguard biodiversity of global importance.

Fundamental to supporting these actions is a wider involvement of the public and stakeholders in management processes, as well as an improved understanding of the importance of coral reefs, especially the economic value of coastal ecosystems. Understanding the linkages between human activities and changes in coral reef condition is critical for implementing the necessary changes in management, and strengthening political will and community support for these changes. Stronger partnerships will need to be developed between all sectors involved in coral reef exploitation and conservation. The World Summit on Sustainable Development in 2002 called for the establishment of networks of larger MPAs and a major international effort to reduce losses in biodiversity, including the biodiversity on coral reefs. This call lies at the heart of efforts to conserve coral reefs for future generations.

ACKNOWLEDGEMENTS

I thank the contributors to the *Status of Coral Reefs of the World: 2004* report and the support of the Zoological Society of London and the Fisheries Conservation Foundation for opportunity to present this material on 16 December 2004 in London.

REFERENCES

Ahamada, S., Bijoux, J., Bigot, L. *et al.* (2004). Status of the coral reefs of the South West Indian Ocean island states. In *Status of Coral Reefs of the World: 2004*, vol. 1, ed. C. Wilkinson, pp. 189–211. Townsville, QLD: Australian Institute of Marine Science.

Arrivillaga, A. and Garcia, M. A. (2004). Status of coral reefs of the Mesoamerican Barrier Reef Systems Project Region, and reefs of El Salvador, Nicaragua and the Pacific Coasts of Mesoamerica. In *Status of Coral Reefs of the World: 2004*, vol. 2, ed. C. Wilkinson, pp. 473–91. Townsville, QLD: Australian Institute of Marine Science.

Barber, C. V. and Pratt, V. R. (1997). *Sullied Seas: Strategies for Combating Cyanide Fishing in Southeast Asia and Beyond*. Washington, DC: World Resources Institute and International Marinelife Alliance.

Bellwood, D. R., Hughes, T. P., Folke, C. and Nystrom, M. (2004). Confronting the coral reef crisis. *Nature*, **429**, 827–33.

Birkeland, C. (1982). Terrestrial runoff as a cause of outbreaks of *Acanthaster planci* (Echinodermata: Asteroidea). *Marine Biology*, **69**, 175–85.
(2004). Ratcheting down the coral reefs. *BioScience*, **54**, 1021–7.
Bouchon, C., Miller, A., Bouchon-Navaro, Y., Portillo, P. and Louis, M. (2004). Status of coral reefs in the French Caribbean Islands and other islands of the Eastern Antilles. In *Status of Coral Reefs of the World: 2004*, vol. 2, ed. C. Wilkinson, pp. 493–507. Townsville, QLD: Australian Institute of Marine Science.
Brown, B. B. (1987). Worldwide death of corals: natural cyclic events or man-made pollution? *Marine Pollution Bulletin*, **18**, 9–13.
Bryant, D., Burke, L., McManus, J. and Spalding, M. (1998). *Reefs at Risk: A Map-Based Indicator of Potential Threats to the World's Coral Reefs*. Washington, DC: World Resources Institute.
Buddemeier, R. W. (1993). Corals, climate and conservation. *Proceedings 7th International Coral Reef Symposium*, **1**, 3–10.
Buddemeier R. W., Kleypas, J. A. and Aronson, R. (2004). *Coral Reefs and Global Climate Change: Potential Contributions of Climate Change to Stresses on Coral Reef Ecosystems*. Pew Center for Global Climate Change. Available online at http://www.pewclimate.org/docuplods/Coral_Reefs.pdf
Burke, L. and Maidens, J. (2004). *Reefs at Risk in the Caribbean*. Washington, DC: World Resources Institute.
Burke, L., Selig, E. and Spalding, M. (2002). *Reefs at Risk in Southeast Asia*. Washington, DC: World Resources Institute.
Davis, J. B. (ed.) (2005). Invasive species: their threat to MPAs, and how practitioners are responding. *MPA News: International News and Analysis on Marine Protected Areas*, **6**(6). Avilable online at http://depts.washington.edu/mpanews/MPAS9.htm
Fabricius, K. E. (2005). Effects of terrestrial runoff on the ecology of corals and coral reefs: review and synthesis. *Marine Pollution Bulletin*, **50**, 125–46.
Feely, R. A., Sabine, C. L., Lee, K. *et al.* (2004). Impact of anthropogenic CO_2 on the $CaCO_3$ system in the oceans. *Science*, **305**, 362–6.
Friedlander, A., Aeby, G. and Brainard, R. (2004). Status of coral reefs in the Hawaiian Archipelago. In *Status of Coral Reefs of the World: 2004*, vol. 2, ed. C. Wilkinson, pp. 411–30. Townsville, QLD: Australian Institute of Marine Science.
Gardner, T. A., Côté, I. M., Gill, J. A., Grant, A. and Watkinson, A. R. (2003). Long-term region-wide declines in Caribbean corals. *Science*, **301**, 958–60.
Garzón-Ferreira, J., Cortés, J., Croquer, A. (2004). Southern tropical America: coral reef status and consolidation as GCRMN Regional Node. In *Status of Coral Reefs of the World: 2004*, vol. 2, ed. C. Wilkinson, pp. 509–22. Townsville, QLD: Australian Institute of Marine Science.
Ginsburg, R. N. (ed.) (1993). *Global Aspects of Coral Reefs: Health Hazards and History*, 7–11 June 1993, University of Miami, Miami, FL.
Gomez, E. D. (1982). Opening remarks. *Proceedings 4th International Coral Reef Symposium*, **1**, 1.
(1988) Overview of environmental problems in the East Asian Seas region. *Ambio*, **17**, 166–9.
Goreau, T. F. (1959). The ecology of Jamaican coral reefs. I. Species composition and zonation. *Ecology*, **40**, 67–90.

Grigg, R. W. and Dollar, S. J. (1990). Natural and anthropogenic disturbances on coral reefs. In *Ecosystems of the World*, vol. 25, *Coral Reefs*, ed. Z. Dubinsky, pp. 439–52. New York: Academic Press.
Harvell, C. D., Mitchell, C. E. and Ward, J. R. (2002). Climate warming and disease risks for terrestrial and marine biota. *Science*, **296**, 2158–62.
Haynes, D. and Schaffelke, B. (eds.) (2004). *Catchment to Reef: Water Quality Issues in the Great Barrier Reef Region*, CRC Reef Research Centre Technical Report No. 53. Townsville, QLD: CRC Reef Research Centre.
Hodgson, G. (1999). A global assessment of human effects on coral reefs. *Marine Pollution Bulletin*, **38**, 345–55.
Hodgson, G. and Liebeler, J. (2002). *The Global Coral Reef Crisis: Trends and Solutions: 5-Year Reef Check Report*. Los Angeles, CA: Reef Check Foundation. Institute of the Environment, University of California at Los Angeles.
Hoegh-Guldberg, O. (1999). Climate change, coral bleaching and the future of the world's coral reefs. *Marine and Freshwater Research*, **50**, 839–66.
(2004). Coral reefs in a century of rapid environmental change. *Symbiosis*, **37**, 1–31.
Hughes, T. P. (1989). Community structure and diversity of coral reefs: the role of history. *Ecology*, **70**, 275–9.
(1994). Catastrophes, phase shifts, and large-scale degradation of a Caribbean coral reef. *Science*, **265**, 1547–51.
Hunter, C. L. and Evans, C. W. (1995). Coral reefs in Kaneohe Bay, Hawaii: two centuries of western influence and two decades of data. *Bulletin of Marine Science*, **57**, 501–15.
Intergovernmental Panel on Climate Change Working Group I (2001). *Climate Change 2001: the Scientific Basis*, contribution of Working Group I to the 3rd Assessment Report of the Intergovernmental Panel on Climate Change, eds. J. T. Houghton, Y. Ding, D. J. Griggs *et al.* Cambridge: Cambridge University Press. Available online at http://www.grida.no/climate/ipcc_tar/wg1/index.htm.
Intergovernmental Panel on Climate Change Working Group II (2001). *Climate Change 2001: Impacts, Adaptation and Vulnerability*, contribution of Working Group II to the 3rd Assessment Report of the Intergovernmental Panel on Climate Change, eds. J. J. McCarthy, O. F. Canziani, N. A. Leary, D. Dokken and K. S. White. Cambridge: Cambridge University Press. Available online at http://www.grida.no/climate/ipcc_tar/wg2/index.htm.
International Society for Reef Studies (2004). *Briefing Paper No. 4*. Available online at http://www.fit.edu/isrs/
Jackson, J. B. C. (1997). Reefs since Columbus. *Coral Reefs*, **16** (Suppl.), S23–S32.
Jackson, J. B. C., Kirby, M. X., Berger, W. H. *et al.* (2001). Historical overfishing and the recent collapse of coastal ecosystems. *Science*, **293**, 629–38.
Johannes, R. E. and Riepen, M. (1995). *Environmental, Economic and Social Implications of the Live Reef Fish Trade in Asia and the Western Pacific*. Jakarta: The Nature Conservancy.
Jones, L., Warner, G., Linton, D. *et al.* (2004). Status of coral reefs in the Northern Caribbean and Western Atlantic Node of the GCRMN. In *Status of Coral Reefs of the World: 2004*, vol. 2, ed. C. Wilkinson, pp. 451–72. Townsville, QLD: Australian Institute of Marine Science.

Kelty, R. and Kuartei, J. (eds.) (2004). Status of the coral reefs in Micronesia and American Samoa. In *Status of Coral Reefs of the World: 2004*, vol. 2, ed. C. Wilkinson, pp. 381–409. Townsville, QLD: Australian Institute of Marine Science.

Kelty, R., Andnrews, K., Wheaton, J., *et al.* (2004). Status of coral reefs in the US Caribbean and Gulf of Mexico: Florida, Flower Garden Banks, Puerto Rico, US Virgin Islands, Navassa. In *Status of Coral Reefs of the World: 2004*, vol. 2, ed. C. Wilkinson, pp. 431–50. Townsville, QLD: Australian Institute of Marine Science.

Kimura, T., Dai, C. F. and Pae, S. (2004). Status of coral reefs in East and North Asia: China, Hong Kong, Taiwan, Korea and Japan. In *Status of Coral Reefs of the World: 2004*, vol. 1, ed. C. Wilkinson, pp. 277–301. Townsville, QLD: Australian Institute of Marine Science.

Kinsey, D. W. (1988). Coral reef response to some natural and anthropogenic stresses. *Galaxea*, **7**, 113–28.

Kleypas, J. A., Buddemeier, R. W. and Archer, D. (1999). Geochemical consequences of increased atmospheric carbon dioxide on coral reefs. *Science*, **284**, 118–20.

Kotb, M., Abdulaziz, M. and Al-Agwan, Z. (2004). Status of coral reefs in the Red Sea and Gulf of Aden in 2004. In *Status of Coral Reefs of the World: 2004*, vol. 1, ed. C. Wilkinson, pp. 137–54. Townsville, QLD: Australian Institute of Marine Science.

Lessios, H. A. (1995). *Diadema antillarum* 10 years after mass mortality: still rare, despite help from a competitor. *Proceedings of the Royal Society of London B*, **259**, 331–7.

Lovell, E., Sykes, H., Deiye, M. *et al.* (2004). Status of coral reefs in the South West Pacific: Fiji, Nauru, New Caledonia, Samoa, Solomon Islands, Tuvalu and Vanuatu. In *Status of Coral Reefs of the World: 2004*, vol. 2, ed. C. Wilkinson, pp. 337–61. Townsville, QLD: Australian Institute of Marine Science.

McClanahan, T. R., Sheppard, C. R. and Obura, D. O. (eds.) (2000). *Coral Reefs of the Indian Ocean: Their Ecology and Conservation*. New York: Oxford University Press.

McWilliams, J. P., Côté, I. M., Gill, J. A., Sutherland, W. J. and Watkinson, A. R. (2005). Accelerating impacts of temperature-induced coral bleaching in the Caribbean. *Ecology*, **86**, 2055–66.

Miller, I. and Sweatman, H. (2004). Status of coral reefs in Australia and Papua New Guinea in 2004. In *Status of Coral Reefs of the World: 2004*, vol. 2, ed. C. Wilkinson, pp. 303–35. Townsville, QLD: Australian Institute of Marine Science.

Obura, D., Church, J., Daniels, C. *et al.* (2004). Status of coral reefs in East Africa 2004: Kenya, Tanzania, Mozambique and South Africa. In *Status of Coral Reefs of the World: 2004*, vol. 1, ed. C. Wilkinson, pp. 171–88. Townsville, QLD: Australian Institute of Marine Science.

Pandolfi, J. M., Bradbury, R. H., Sala, E. (2003). Global trajectories of the long-term decline of coral reef ecosystems. *Science*, **301**, 955–8.

Pauly, D. and Chua, T.-E. (1988). The overfishing of marine resources: socioeconomic background in southeast Asia. *Ambio*, **17**, 200–6.

Pauly, D., Christensen, V., Dalsgaard, J., Froese, R. and Torres Jr, F. (1998). Fishing down marine food webs. *Science*, **279**, 860–3.

Pauly, D., Christensen, V., Guénette, S. *et al.* (2002). Towards sustainability in world fisheries. *Nature*, **418**, 689–95.

Rajasuriya, A., Zahir, H., Venkataraman, K., Islam, Z. and Tamelander, J. (2004). Status of coral reefs in South Asia: Bangladesh, Chagos, India, Maldives and Sri Lanka. In *Status of Coral Reefs of the World: 2004*, vol. 1, ed. C. Wilkinson, pp. 213–33. Townsville, QLD: Australian Institute of Marine Science.

Rezai, H., Wilson, S., Claereboudt, M. and Riegl, B. (2004). Coral reef status in the ROPME Sea Area: Arabian/Persian Gulf, Gulf of Oman and Arabian Sea. In *Status of Coral Reefs of the World: 2004*, vol. 1, ed. C. Wilkinson, pp. 155–70. Townsville, QLD: Australian Institute of Marine Science.

Rosenberg, E. and Ben-Haim, Y. (2002) Mini-review: microbial diseases of corals and global warming. *Environmental Microbiology*, **4**, 318–26.

Sadovy, Y. J. and Vincent, A. C. J. (2002). Ecological issues and the trades in live reef fishes. In *Coral Reef Fishes: Dynamics and Diversity in a Complex Ecosystem*, ed. P. F. Sale, pp. 391–420. San Diego, CA: Academic Press.

Salvat, B. (1980). Death for the coral reefs. *Oryx*, **15**, 341–4.

(1982). Preservation of coral reefs: scientific whim or economic necessity? Past, present and future. *Proceedings 4th International Coral Reef Symposium*, **1**, 225–9.

Skirving, W., Strong, A., Heron, S., Liu, G. and Arzayus, F. (2004). Coral bleaching: was 1998 a portent of the future or a 1-in-a-1000 year event? Satellite-derived data. In *Status of Coral Reefs of the World 2004*, vol. 1, ed. C. Wilkinson, pp. 22–3. Townsville, QLD: Australian Institute of Marine Science.

Smith, S. V. and Buddemeier, R. W. (1992). Global change and coral reef ecosystems. *Annual Review of Ecology and Systematics*, **23**, 89–118.

Spalding, M., Ravilious, C. and Green, E. (2001). *World Atlas of Coral Reefs*. Berkeley, CA: UNEP World Conservation Monitoring Centre and University of California Press.

Stoddart, D. R. (1982). Coral reefs: the coming crisis. *Proceedings 4th International Coral Reef Symposium*, **1**, 33–6.

Timmermann, A., Oberhuber, J., Bacher, A. *et al.* (1999). Increased El Niño frequency in a climate model forced by future greenhouse warming. *Nature*, **398**, 694–6.

Tun, K., Chou, L. M. and Cabanban, A. (2004). Status of coral reefs, coral reef monitoring and management in Southeast Asia, 2004. In *Status of Coral Reefs of the World: 2004*, vol. 1, ed. C. Wilkinson, pp. 235–75. Townsville, QLD: Australian Institute of Marine Science.

Vieux, C., Aubanel, A. and Axford, J. (2004). A century of change in coral reef status in Southeast and Central Pacific: Polynesia Mana Node, Cook Islands, French Polynesia, Kiribati, Niue, Tokelau, Tonga, Wallis and Futuna. In *Status of Coral Reefs of the World: 2004*, vol. 2, ed. C. Wilkinson, pp. 363–80. Townsville, QLD: Australian Institute of Marine Science.

Wells, S. M. (ed.) (1988). *Coral Reefs of the World:* vol. 1, *Atlantic and Eastern Pacific;* vol. 2, *Indian Ocean, Red Sea and Gulf;* vol. 3, *Central and Western Pacific*. Nairobi: UNEP/Gland, Switzerland: International Union for Conservation of Nature and Natural Resources.

Wilkinson, C. R. (1993). Coral reefs of the world are facing widespread devastation: can we prevent this through sustainable management practices? *Proceedings 7th International Coral Reef Symposium*, **1**, 11–21.
(ed.) (1998). *Status of Coral Reefs of the World: 1998*. Townsville, QLD: Australian Institute of Marine Science.
(1999). Global and local threats to coral reef functioning and existence: review and predictions. *Marine Freshwater Research*, **50**, 867–78.
(ed.) (2000). *Status of Coral Reefs of the World: 2000*. Townsville, QLD: Australian Institute of Marine Science.
(ed.) (2002). *Status of Coral Reefs of the World: 2002*. Townsville, QLD: Australian Institute of Marine Science.
(ed.) (2004). *Status of Coral Reefs of the World: 2004*. Townsville, QLD: Australian Institute of Marine Science.
Wilkinson, C. R. and Buddemeier, R. W. (1994). *Global Climate Change and Coral Reefs: Implications for People and Reefs*, Report of the UNEP–IOC–ASPEI–IUCN Global Task Team on Coral Reefs. Gland, Switzerland: International Union for Conservation of Nature.
Wilkinson, C. R., Linden, O., Cesar, H. *et al.* (1999). Ecological and socioeconomic impacts of 1998 coral mortality in the Indian Ocean: An ENSO impact and a warning of future change? *Ambio*, **28**, 188–96.
Willis, B. L., Page, C. and Dinsdale, E. (2004). Coral diseases on the Great Barrier Reef. In *Coral Health and Disease*, eds. E. Rosenberg and Y. Loya, pp. 69–104. Berlin: Springer-Verlag.

2

Death and resurrection of Caribbean coral reefs: a palaeoecological perspective

WILLIAM F. PRECHT
PBS&J, Miami

RICHARD B. ARONSON
University of South Alabama

INTRODUCTION

In the last three decades reef corals have suffered catastrophic levels of mortality throughout the tropics, a trend which has been especially pronounced in the Caribbean and western Atlantic region (Ginsburg, 1994; Gardner *et al.*, 2003; Ginsburg and Lang, 2003). Since the late 1970s and early 1980s, the structure of most Caribbean reefs has changed dramatically, with a fundamental shift in dominance from corals to macroalgae (Knowlton, 1992). This phase shift from coral- to macroalgae-dominated benthic reef communities has been driven largely by a drastic reduction in the abundance of branching elkhorn (*Acropora palmata*) and staghorn (*Acropora cervicornis*) corals (Aronson and Precht, 2001a, 2001b), coupled with reduced herbivory (Glynn, 1990; Carpenter, 1997).

Although the temporal and spatial signals of recent change in the Caribbean are relatively straightforward (Aronson and Precht, 2001b; Gardner *et al.*, 2003; Ginsburg and Lang, 2003; Kramer, 2003), the causes remain controversial. A number of hypotheses have been developed, with top–down (over-fishing), bottom–up (eutrophication and pollution) and side–in (habitat destruction and global change) models dominating the literature. Reliance on weak inference in many of these studies, however, has hindered the progress of reef science and confounded the direction

Coral Reef Conservation, ed. Isabelle M. Côté and John D. Reynolds.
Published by Cambridge University Press.

and emphasis of ecosystem management. In this chapter, we examine the principal models and evaluate their utility as explanations of the ecological changes that have been observed on Caribbean reefs. We discuss recent evidence pointing to regional- and global-scale disturbances as the dominant drivers in the system and emphasize the need to develop regional solutions to the ongoing crisis.

OUR APPROACH

A question of critical significance to scientists, managers and policy-makers is whether recent changes on Caribbean reefs are something new or part of a long-term pattern of repeated community shifts (Aronson and Precht, 2001c). Without an appropriately scaled baseline against which to measure change, we could end up trying to manage noise rather than responding to signals (Aronson, 2001; Jackson, 2001). Because coral reefs are both geological and biological entities, the logical sequence must be to observe the effects of disturbance in ecological time, detect any historical changes in the palaeoecological record, discern whether recent patterns are unprecedented on a relevant temporal scale, and deduce the multiscale processes behind those patterns. Focusing on the Quaternary history of reef development along the north coast of Jamaica, we asked the question: 'How do past ecological responses of coral reef systems, recorded in the fossil and sub-fossil record, aid in understanding the current crisis on coral reefs?' Although others have taken this approach, our reading of the ecological and palaeoecological record departs significantly from previous interpretations.

THE MODELS

The reef system along the north coast of Jamaica in the vicinity of Discovery Bay is the sad-eyed poster child for reef degradation in the Caribbean (Done, 1992; Knowlton, 1992, 2001; Liddell and Ohlhorst, 1993; Hughes, 1994; Sebens, 1994; Steneck, 1994; Paine *et al.*, 1998; Nyström *et al.*, 2000; Jackson *et al.*, 2001; Scheffer *et al.*, 2001; Palumbi, 2002; Elmqvist *et al.*, 2003; Pandolfi *et al.*, 2003; Scheffer and Carpenter, 2003; Bellwood *et al.*, 2004; Sobel and Dahlgren, 2004). In fact, Pandolfi *et al.* (2005) considered Jamaican reefs to be among the most degraded in the world, being composed of 'little more than rubble, seaweed, and slime'. The Jamaican reefs that were initially used to define typical Caribbean reef structure and zonation (Goreau, 1959; Goreau and Goreau, 1973) also contributed substantially to our perception that most or all Caribbean reefs are now in a severe state of degradation (discussed in Aronson and Precht, 2001a). The model of reef decline, derived from observations in Jamaica, is that the shift from a more desirable, coral-dominated state to a less desirable, macroalgae-dominated state was primarily a consequence of over-fishing and coastal eutrophication (e.g. Bellwood *et al.*, 2004; Pandolfi *et al.*, 2005).

According to Bellwood *et al.* (2004) and references therein, Jamaican reefs as originally described had been over-fished for decades or possibly centuries, with no apparent negative effects on the coral assemblages. Increased nutrient loading, a result of altered land use following European colonization, did not promote overgrowth by macroalgae as long as herbivorous fish suppressed the algae. Once predatory and herbivorous fish were extracted, the herbivorous echinoid *Diadema antillarum* became superabundant and maintained the coral-dominated state. In 1980, Hurricane Allen initiated the phase shift by causing substantial coral mortality (Woodley *et al.*, 1981). The shift away from coral dominance was exacerbated in 1983–84 when *D. antillarum* populations suffered a regional mass mortality from a water-borne pathogen (Lessios *et al.*, 1984; Lessios, 1988). Along the entire north coast of Jamaica, the resident *D. antillarum* population suffered >98% mortality in less than one week (Hughes *et al.*, 1985). The loss of *Diadema*, combined with decades of intense fishing pressure, resulted in a dramatic increase in macroalgal cover on many Jamaican reefs (Liddell and Ohlhorst, 1986, 1993; Hughes *et al.*, 1987; Hughes, 1989, 1994; Aronson, 1990; Precht, 1990; Knowlton, 1992; Aronson and Precht, 2001a). Jackson (2001) argued that the ecological redundancy of the *D. antillarum* obscured the effects of the loss of herbivorous fishes for well over a century until they too were lost (but see Jackson (1997) for the reverse argument, that *Diadema* were historically abundant). In addition, Jackson and colleagues (Jackson, 2001; Jackson *et al.*, 2001) asserted that overgrowth by macroalgae following the mass mortality of *D. antillarum* was responsible for the sudden and catastrophic mortality of corals, not only in Jamaica (Hughes, 1994) but throughout the wider Caribbean, during the 1980s.

This scenario based on Discovery Bay and nearby sites is widely accepted as a model for the recent dynamics of Caribbean reefs. But is this model correct? What roles, if any, do over-fishing and nutrification play in the story? Although some mortality of massive corals (i.e. coral heads) in Jamaica can be attributed to overgrowth by macroalgae (Hughes, 1994; River and Edmunds, 2001; but see de Ruyter van Steveninck *et al.*, 1988; McCook *et al.*, 2001a), it is our contention that coral mortality itself was the crucial precondition for macroalgal dominance (Aronson and Precht,

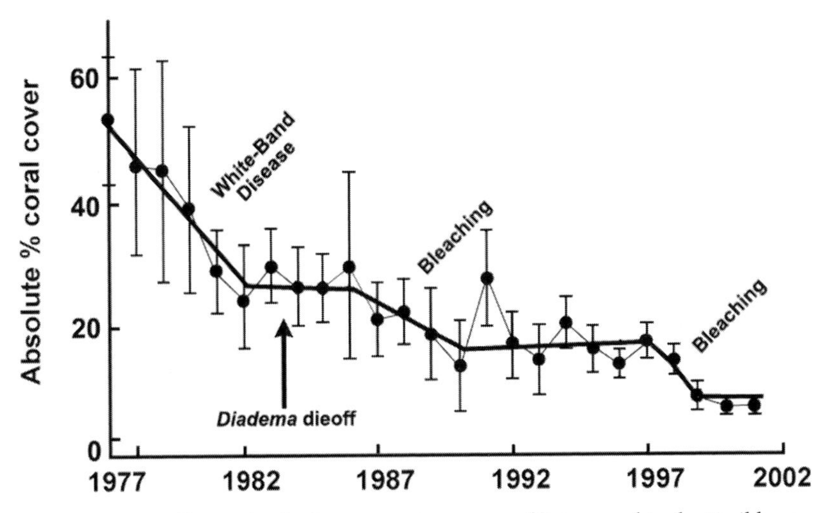

Figure 2.1 Change in absolute percentage cover of living coral in the Caribbean from 1977 to 2001, based on the meta-analysis of Gardner *et al.* (2003). Means weighted by sample size (•) are shown with 95% bootstrapped confidence intervals. The decline is not monotonic, but rather it is stepwise in response to proximate causes of coral mortality. The most significant decline, from 1977 to 1982, is related to the loss of Caribbean acroporids from white-band disease. Two additional declines, from 1987 to 1990 and from 1997 to 1999, are associated with major Caribbean-wide bleaching events. Note that there was essentially no response to the mass mortality of *Diadema antillarum* in 1983–84. (Figure modified with permission from Gardner *et al.* (2003).)

2001a, 2001b; Aronson *et al.*, 2002a; see also Ostrander *et al.*, 2000; McCook *et al.*, 2001b; Williams *et al.*, 2001; Szmant, 2002; McManus and Polsenberg, 2004). This is especially so for rapidly growing taxa like the *Acropora* species, which can out-compete algae for space and light (Rylaarsdam, 1983). The rapid decline of *Acropora* in the late 1970s and early 1980s predated the mass mortality of *D. antillarum* (Fig. 2.1). The loss of *D. antillarum* clearly triggered the dramatic increase in macroalgal abundance in Jamaica, but that effect was predicated on coral mortality. The scaling up of the Discovery Bay model of Knowlton (1992) and Hughes (1994) to the rest of the Caribbean has been perpetuated in the literature by a series of essays, self-citations of previous reviews, and *ad hoc* revisions (Nyström *et al.*, 2000; Jackson, 2001; Jackson *et al.*, 2001; Jackson and Sala, 2001; Scheffer *et al.*, 2001; Palumbi, 2002, 2005; Elmqvist *et al.*, 2003; Pandolfi *et al.*, 2003; Scheffer and Carpenter, 2003; Bellwood *et al.*, 2004) and by an explicit attempt to suppress legitimate scientific debate (Pandolfi *et al.*,

2005), all of which have retarded ecological discovery (see Elner and Vadas (1990) for a similar critique in a different context).

Hypothesis I: Top–down impacts – over-fishing

Over-fishing is considered to be among the most significant threats to reef ecosystems (Roberts, 1995; Jackson, 2001; Jackson *et al.*, 2001). High-intensity fishing reduces species diversity and can lead to extirpations of target species, but other species suffer as well through collateral effects. Several studies have demonstrated negative effects of fishing on tropical resources (Roberts, 1995; Rogers and Beets, 2001). Results from marine protected areas also suggest that connections between fish faunas and the reef benthos can be important (McClanahan and Muthiga, 1988). In addition to fishing pressure, destruction of mangrove and seagrass habitats has led to dramatic declines of some reef fishes, including the largest herbivorous fish in the Caribbean, the rainbow parrotfish *Scarus guacamaia* (Mumby *et al.*, 2004; see also Mumby and Harbourne, this volume).

It has been proposed that historical declines in predators and herbivores have gone unrecognized as potential agents of change on coral reefs (Jackson, 2001; Jackson *et al.*, 2001; Bascompte *et al.*, 2005). Bellwood *et al.* (2004) asserted that, due to the resultant shift from fish-dominated to urchin-dominated herbivory, reefs are on a predictable trajectory toward complete collapse. Pandolfi *et al.* (2003) argued that benthic communities on coral reefs have actually been in decline for centuries and that by default the only reasonable explanation is over-fishing. They based much of their argument on archaeological evidence, which indicates that stocks of reef fish were over-exploited, at least locally, before European colonization of the Caribbean (e.g. Wing and Wing, 2001). The depletion of large predators, the subsequent switch to over-fishing of herbivores and the associated cascading effects (Aronson, 1990; Pauly *et al.*, 1998; Steneck, 1998; Jackson *et al.*, 2001) have (putatively) led to collapse of reef ecosystems at the global scale (Pandolfi *et al.*, 2003).

When did over-fishing begin? Based on Jackson's (2001) reading of the historical literature, Jamaican and other Caribbean reefs were already so severely over-fished in the nineteenth century that salted cod (called 'salt fish' in Jamaica) had to be imported from northern latitudes to stave off human starvation. This interpretation, however, is contrary to the economic history of salt fish. Cod was supplied from New England and the Maritime Provinces of Canada beginning in the seventeenth century as the main source of cheap protein for the enslaved African population in the Caribbean in exchange for molasses and rum (Kurlansky, 2003). Jamaican reefs are certainly over-fished today and have been for decades at least (Munro, 1983), but it is uncertain whether over-fishing dates to colonial times. The recent increase in the Jamaican population and an increasing demand for fresh fish have led to unremitting pressure on local fish stocks and recent expansion of the fishery to offshore banks, which were seldom or never exploited before the 1970s (Koslow *et al.*, 1988).

In the view of Pandolfi *et al.* (2003), historical over-fishing weakened the trophic linkage between herbivores and benthic algae, reducing the resilience of coral assemblages and releasing the algae to overgrow corals following other perturbations such as the loss of *Diadema*. Jackson and Johnson (2000) suggested that a prominent feature of the effects of humans on coral reefs has been the time lag between the initial removal of large consumers and the subsequent (recent) collapse of coral assemblages. They linked this time lag to compounded episodes of disturbance that were required, in their conceptual model, for the sudden development of alternative communities (Knowlton, 1992; Hughes, 1994). Jackson and Johnson (2000; Jackson, 2001; Jackson *et al.*, 2001) interpreted the time lag between the declines of vertebrates and corals as evidence for a causal relationship, in apparent contradiction to the idea of Pandolfi *et al.* (2003) that coral assemblages had already been in decline for a long time.

There is no doubt that fish and corals interact on Caribbean reefs. This interaction, however, does not prove that reef communities or metacommunities are tightly integrated or ecologically locked, as Jackson (1994) argued. It is equally clear that over-fishing has removed entire functional groups of fish on some reefs, leading to trophic cascades (Pennings, 1997; Pauly *et al.*, 1998; Sala *et al.*, 1998), but there is no evidence that the reef-coral assemblages have been compromised by these actions. Rather, the recent transition to macroalgal dominance is the consequence of coral species' individual responses to a number of simultaneous perturbations including, but not limited to, over-fishing. Contrary to claims by Jackson (1997), there is also no credible evidence that the prehistoric megafauna of tropical seas – green sea turtles and manatees – were keystone herbivores on reefs (see, e.g., Bjorndal, 1997; Domning, 2001), or that hunting these herbivores nearly to extinction in historical times was the beginning of the end of reef communities.

Using ratios of jaw size : test size in museum specimens collected over the century before 1983, Levitan (1992) uncovered a small but positive relationship between population density of *D. antillarum* and increasing levels of human exploitation pressure through time. Levitan noted that the human impact may have been small relative to natural geographic variation; nevertheless, his study supported Hay's (1984) contention that *Diadema* density was positively related to fishing pressure. Bellwood *et al.* (2004), following a number of previous authors, speculated that 'crowded conditions' of the *Diadema* populations contributed to their collapse by increasing their susceptibility to disease. The mass mortality of remote and relatively sparse populations, however, appeared to be density independent (Gittings *et al.*, 1994). It is certainly plausible that *Diadema* populations were inflated on heavily fished reefs.

An important issue with regard to the over-fishing argument, however, is whether or not all reefs of the Caribbean have had the same history of resource exploitation. With the exception of some islands like Jamaica and Haiti, and possibly St Croix (Hay, 1984), there is little evidence to support the claim that herbivorous fish have been removed throughout the entire region by sustained fishing pressure, leaving *Diadema* as the only grazer of any consequence (see Lessios *et al.*, 2001). In fact, on most Caribbean reefs over-fishing has led to preferential removal of larger-bodied piscivores (sharks, groupers, snappers and jacks) and invertivores (triggerfish and larger wrasses such as the hogfish *Lachnolaimus maximus*), and not primary consumers (parrotfishes, surgeonfishes and damselfishes). The resulting compensatory response, therefore, should have been an increase and not a decrease in the sizes and numbers of herbivorous prey species. Recently, Bascompte *et al.* (2005) suggested on theoretical grounds that historical over-fishing of sharks in the Caribbean may have led to the loss of herbivorous fishes through a trophic cascade that involved the release of groupers from predation; however, there is no empirical evidence that sharks historically were hunted or exploited in preference to groupers or other large piscivores in the Caribbean (see Baum *et al.*, 2003), raising questions about the historical importance of this trophic linkage.

Diadema clearly had a negative impact on herbivorous fishes prior to 1983–84. Short-term increases in grazing and long-term increases in population sizes of herbivorous fishes were reported subsequent to the regional demise of the sea urchins (Carpenter, 1986, 1988, 1990a; Morrison, 1988; Robertson, 1991). Significantly, the increase in grazing pressure by herbivorous fishes was not sufficient to compensate for the loss of *Diadema*. The main problem with generalizing the over-fishing scenario beyond Discovery Bay is that macroalgal cover has increased on protected and moderately fished reefs, as well as on heavily fished ones, although to a lesser degree (e.g. de Ruyter van Steveninck and Bak (1986) for Curaçao, Netherlands Antilles; Levitan (1988) for St John, US Virgin Islands; Carpenter (1990a,

1990b) for St Croix, US Virgin Islands; McClanahan and Muthiga (1998) and McClanahan *et al.* (1999) for Belize). These results imply that *Diadema* was the most important shallow-water herbivore even on lightly fished reefs, contrary to the prevailing model (e.g. Bellwood *et al.*, 2004) but in substantial agreement with surmises of the historical importance of the species (Jackson, 1997; Lessios *et al.*, 2001).

Hypothesis II: Bottom–up impacts – nutrient enrichment

Declining water quality is the factor most often blamed in the popular press for the demise of coral reefs. The reasoning here is tautological (Szmant, 2002): the increased abundance of algae observed on reefs supports the a priori assumption that nutrient loading must be the cause. Many who advocate nutrient pollution as the primary factor behind coral reef decline have further proposed connections to development, agricultural runoff and human waste, especially in Florida (discussed in Precht and Miller, 2006). On a regional scale, it has been suggested that the entire Caribbean basin may be enriched due to its semi-enclosed geography and increased runoff from poor land-use practices, coastal development and deforestation (Muller-Karger *et al.*, 1989).

A number of reviews published in the last several years have assessed the role of nutrient enrichment in the decline of corals, and the relationships among nutrients, algae and competition between algae and corals (Hughes *et al.*, 1999; Aronson and Precht, 2001a; McCook *et al.*, 2001a; Szmant, 2002; McClanahan *et al.*, 2003; McManus and Polsenberg, 2004). These papers have all concluded that the increased abundance of algae on reefs is not due to nutrients but rather to the increased availability of substratum for algal colonization as a result of coral mortality (see Williams *et al.* (2001) for an experimental demonstration). The loss of herbivores may not explain coral mortality, but it was clearly a factor in the increased algal abundance on Caribbean reefs, based on evidence ranging from the obvious effects of the demise of *D. antillarum* (Lessios, 1988), to the observed inverse relationship between algal cover and herbivorous fish biomass on 19 reefs throughout the region (Williams and Polunin, 2001). Although few data exist to suggest that changes in reef communities were caused by localized pollution in Jamaica (see Cho and Woodley, 2002), and few historical data exist regarding correlated changes in nutrient pollution, algal abundance and coral cover (Szmant, 2002), strenuous debate continues about the importance of increased nutrient concentrations to the demise of coral populations (Lapointe, 1997, 1999; Lapointe *et al.*, 1997; Hughes *et al.*, 1999; Miller *et al.*, 1999; Aronson and Precht, 2000).

Szmant (1997, 2002) suggested that the level of topographic complexity on a reef indirectly influences the effects of nutrient input and uptake. In the absence of overfishing or mass mortalities of herbivores, topographic complexity determines the availability of shelter for herbivores. The recent mass mortality of the acroporids greatly reduced the topographic complexity of these reefs, indirectly reducing herbivory and thereby lowering rates of consumption of algae in the face of pulsed or chronic nutrification. Although the necessary modelling has not been done to quantify the relationships among the various nutrient sources and sinks, it is clear that identifying sewage from leaking cesspits and stormwater or agricultural runoff from poor farming practices as the primary causes of reef degradation is an oversimplification (Precht and Miller, 2006).

The point is that corals have died and macroalgae have risen to dominance on reefs throughout the Caribbean regardless of whether they were near or far from centres of human population, and regardless of whether or not they were exposed to nutrient loading or intense fishing pressure (Aronson and Precht, 2001a, 2001b; Gardner *et al.*, 2003; Ginsburg and Lang, 2003; Kramer, 2003). For instance, Lapointe *et al.* (1997; Lapointe, 1997) used the offshore barrier reef tract of Belize as an example of an oligotrophic reef system and as an alleged contrast in community change to the (supposedly eutrophic) north coast of Jamaica (Lapointe, 1997). Like Jamaica, however, the Belizean reefs have lost coral over the past several decades, with concomitant increases in macroalgae but in the absence of nutrient enrichment, primarily in habitats previously dominated by acroporids (Rützler and Macintyre, 1982; Littler *et al.*, 1987; Aronson *et al.*, 1994; McClanahan and Muthiga, 1998; McClanahan *et al.*, 1999; Aronson and Precht, 2001b; McClanahan *et al.*, 2002, 2003, 2004; Precht and Aronson, 2002) – exactly the opposite of Lapointe's contention.

High-temperature anomalies, coral and urchin diseases, and hurricanes are stressors that have well-known effects on coral assemblages at multiple spatial and temporal scales (Aronson and Precht, 2001a; Szmant, 2002; Gardner *et al.*, 2005; Precht and Miller, 2006; see next section). These extreme events have strongly influenced the trajectory of reef communities, yet authors advocating diminished water quality as the primary cause of reef decline have largely ignored them. There are a few clear examples of reef decline resulting from nutrient enrichment (e.g. Kaneohe Bay, Hawaii: reviewed in Grigg, 1995), but an association in time between near-shore nutrient enrichment and coral mortality, followed by a shift toward macroalgal dominance, does not by itself prove a causal connection. In fact, the evidence linking anthropogenic nutrients to reef degradation in Jamaica remains purely correlative. It is well documented that local point sources of nitrate-rich water enter Discovery Bay (D'Elia *et al.*, 1981); however, the water on the fore reef at Discovery Bay is oligotrophic (Cho and Woodley, 2002). The most important consequences of increased nutrification may lie in an increase in the incidence and severity of coral diseases (Bruno *et al.*, 2004; Sutherland *et al.*, 2004) and in the reduced ability of coral reefs to recover from natural and (increasingly frequent) anthropogenic disturbance events (McCook *et al.*, 2001b). There are significant public-health and economic reasons to reduce pollution, and obviously coral reefs will benefit as well. Improving water quality is imperative, but without ameliorating the main causes of coral mortality or increasing the abundance of keystone herbivores it is unrealistic to think that Caribbean reefs will recover to their former state.

Hypothesis III: Side–in impacts – disease, bleaching and hurricanes

Pandolfi *et al.* (2003) postulated that the 'recent widespread and catastrophic episodes of coral bleaching and disease have distracted attention from the chronic and severe historical decline of reef ecosystems'. It is clear from both historical and recent data, however, that the proximal causes of the decline in coral cover on Caribbean reefs were recent disease outbreaks, coral bleaching events and hurricanes (Aronson and Precht, 2001a, 2001b; Harvell *et al.*, 1999; Bythell *et al.*, 2000; Lugo *et al.*, 2000; Gardner *et al.*, 2003, 2005; Hughes *et al.*, 2003; Precht and Miller, 2006). Major disease events have changed the way reefs look over relatively short timescales, and even though scientists were present to observe the changes we still do not fully understand the causes (Harvell *et al.*, 2004). For example, we know that in the early 1980s a disease killed almost all the *Diadema* in the Caribbean (Lessios *et al.*, 1984), but the pathogen remains unidentified (however, see Bauer and Agerter, 1987).

The mass mortality of *D. antillarum* is one of two major disease outbreaks that have swept through the Caribbean in the last 25 years, reshaping how coral reefs look and function. The second epizootic, white-band disease (WBD), sharply reduced populations of acroporid corals from the late 1970s to the early 1990s, and it still affects acroporids throughout the region (Green and Bruckner, 2000; Aronson and Precht, 2001b; Precht *et al.*, 2002). The loss of the acroporids due to WBD significantly reduced the three-dimensional structure of the reefs and effectively eliminated two of the major framework-building corals from the region (Bythell and Sheppard, 1993; Aronson and Precht, 2001b; Precht *et al.*, 2002, 2004). Thus, two lethal, essentially concurrent epizootics constituted a perturbation with regional consequences unprecedented in at least the preceding half century.

It is now apparent that for more than two decades WBD epizootics have been the primary cause of mortality of *Acropora* over wide areas of the Caribbean and western Atlantic (Shinn, 1989; Bythell and Sheppard, 1993; Aronson and Precht, 2001a, 2001b), with losses in excess of 95% regionally (Precht *et al.*, 2002). Robinson (1973), reporting on the reef condition of Buck Island National Monument in the US Virgin Islands, was the first to discuss mortality related to WBD. Subsequently, Gladfelter (1982) recognized the devastating effects of WBD on acroporids in St Croix. Unfortunately, by the time the Gladfelter manuscript was published in 1982 most of the acroporids throughout the region, including Jamaica, had been extirpated. As Hubbard *et al.* (2005) recently commented, 'Bill [Gladfelter] was the first to note and describe White Band Disease. It was not until years later that the rest of us caught up and realized the significance of this event.'

At Discovery Bay, WBD had been observed on *A. cervicornis* thickets prior to the passage of Hurricane Allen in 1980 and was probably responsible for substantial post-hurricane mortality (Knowlton *et al.*, 1990). Had Hurricane Allen not destroyed the acroporid populations along the north coast of Jamaica, they would have succumbed to WBD as they did elsewhere in the Caribbean (Precht and Aronson, 2002). In reality, the focus on hurricane impacts to Jamaican reefs proved to be an intellectual distraction from the Caribbean-wide WBD story (Aronson and Precht, 2001a). The misdiagnosis of regional causality was aggravated by the loss of *Diadema* in 1983–84 (Sheppard, 1993) and the destructive effects of Hurricane Gilbert in Jamaica in 1988 (Woodley, 1992). Contrary to the assertions of Jackson (1997), Pandolfi *et al.* (2003) and others, conditions in the 1960s and early 1970s do in fact represent the legitimate baseline for the status of healthy coral populations in the Caribbean (Kramer, 2002).

Even after 20 years, the aetiology of WBD remains largely unknown, and recent reports suggest that there are several varieties of the disease with differing characteristics and pathologies (Antonius, 1981; Gladfelter, 1982; Peters *et al.*, 1983; Peters, 1997; Richardson, 1998; Ritchie and Smith, 1998; Richardson and Aronson, 2002; Bythell *et al.*, 2004; Sutherland *et al.*, 2004). Significantly, there is no association of WBD outbreaks with proximity to human influences such as fishing pressure or coastal eutrophication; reefs both near and far from human population centres have been affected (Aronson and Precht, 2001b; Ginsburg and Lang, 2003; Kramer, 2003).

As mentioned earlier, it could be argued that the Caribbean is so small that the entire region lies in close proximity to sources of anthropogenic stress (Connell, 1997; Roberts, 1997; Jackson, 2001; Andréfouët *et al.*, 2002).

Kramer (2003) pointed out that deeper reef sites throughout the Caribbean (>20 m depth), below which *Acropora* and *Diadema* were never numerically important, still have relatively high coral cover (~26%) and low macroalgal cover. The health of deep reefs emphasizes the dramatic effects of the two diseases on shallow-reef community structure and the transition from coral to macroalgal dominance. One reef system in particular, the Flower Garden Banks in the northern Gulf of Mexico off the coast of Texas, highlights the requirement of coral mortality to initiate the coral–algal transition. The Flower Garden Banks are deep, cool-water reefs that support high coral cover and abundant fish populations, and the cold-sensitive acroporids have been historically absent. Because there were no acroporids, the Flower Garden Banks were blind to the major disturbances that ravaged acroporid populations elsewhere in the late 1970s and 1980s. In 1985, within one year of the loss of *Diadema* from these banks, macroalgae increased from ~5% to 14%, mostly on open space, and have fluctuated ever since. Coral cover, however, did not decline (Gittings *et al.*, 1994), and it has remained steady at approximately 50% from the late 1970s to the present (Aronson *et al.*, 2005b).

Beginning in the 1970s and continuing to today, diseases and disease-like syndromes have appeared in corals other than the acroporids, including the *Montastraea annularis* species complex (Antonius, 1977; Edmunds, 1991; Bruckner and Bruckner, 1997; Santavy and Peters, 1997; Goreau *et al.*, 1998; Garzón-Ferreira *et al.*, 2001). Diseases that attack slow-growing, massive corals, especially the *M. annularis* species complex, may be the most threatening to the geologic structure of Caribbean reefs (Knowlton, 2001; Ginsburg and Lang, 2003). Other environmental stressors such as pollution, nutrient loading, increased iron supply and African dust could be associated with disease outbreaks, yet few firm connections have been established (Epstein *et al.*, 1998; Harvell *et al.*, 1999; Shinn *et al.*, 2000; Hayes *et al.*, 2001; Jackson *et al.*, 2001; Richardson and Aronson, 2002; Bruno *et al.*, 2004).

Based on palaeoecological reconstructions from cores of Holocene reefs in Belize, Aronson and Precht (1997; Aronson *et al.*, 2002a) concluded that the mass mortality of acroporids due to WBD was a novel event in at least the last 3000 years. The recent mortality of centuries-old *Montastraea* colonies throughout the region also emphasizes the emergent nature of the coral diseases. These observations in turn support the hypothesis of a human link to reef diseases (Ward and Lafferty, 2004), and hence to recent reef degradation.

In addition to disease, bleaching has become a major cause of coral mortality in the last few decades. Bleaching, the loss of algal symbionts and/or their pigments, can be a response to a number of stresses (Williams and Bunkley-Williams, 1990). These stresses vary regionally and seasonally, and they may act singly or synergistically to cause corals to bleach (Fitt *et al.*, 2001). The most obvious is temperature-induced stress (Jokiel, 1997). Corals are typically exposed during local summertime to temperatures near the upper limits of their thermal tolerances (Glynn, 1993; Hoegh-Guldberg, 1999), which is why coral reefs are often considered to be the ecosystems most threatened by global warming (Glynn, 1991, 1996; Hoegh-Guldberg, 1999, 2004; Walther *et al.*, 2002; Hughes *et al.*, 2003). Field and laboratory studies have shown unequivocally that sustained, anomalously high summertime water temperatures are associated with coral reef bleaching (Glynn and D'Croz, 1990; Podestá and Glynn, 1997). If temperatures are elevated above the average maximum for a prolonged period, colonies of many coral species will die (Glynn, 1983; Aronson *et al.*, 2002b).

Substantial impacts on reef community structure have been observed during periods of warmer-than-normal sea temperatures. At least six major periods of mass coral bleaching have occurred since 1979 and the incidence of mass bleaching is increasing in both frequency and intensity (Hoegh-Guldberg, 1999; Walther *et al.*, 2002; Hughes *et al.*, 2003). The most severe episode occurred in 1998, in which an estimated 16% of the world's reef-building corals died (Walther *et al.*, 2002). The increased and widespread nature of coral bleaching events over the past two decades is convincingly correlated with increases in maximum sea-surface temperature (Kleypas *et al.*, 2001). Global warming will likely exacerbate the situation (Hoegh-Guldberg, 1999, 2004; Walther *et al.*, 2002; Hughes *et al.*, 2003). Although long-term data are generally not available on how coral species richness and community structure have changed after bleaching events, we suspect these changes will be large (Wellington *et al.*, 2001; Szmant, 2002; Hughes *et al.*, 2003). In Jamaica, substantial mortality of remaining non-acroporid coral populations can be attributed in part to bleaching events in the late 1980s (Sebens, 1994; W. F. Precht, unpublished data).

Exactly how do coral mortality and the loss of herbivores interact in the transition to macroalgal dominance? Aronson *et al.* (2002b) noted that coral mortality throughout the region has generally been followed by the proliferation of fleshy and filamentous (non-coralline) macroalgae, because populations of herbivores have not been able to keep pace behaviourally or numerically with algal growth in the large areas of space opened by the death of corals. San Salvador Island, Bahamas, serves as an unreplicated illustration.

San Salvador is a small, low-lying carbonate island with low fishing pressure and excellent water quality. The economy of the island is driven almost entirely by underwater ecotourism. In the early 1980s the reefs of San Salvador suffered catastrophic losses of acroporid corals, especially *A. cervicornis*, related to the WBD pandemic (Shinn, 1989; Aronson and Precht, 2001a), followed by the loss of *Diadema* in 1983. Other corals, however, including especially the *M. annularis* species complex, remained unaffected by these two disturbances (W. F. Precht, personal observation; see Curran *et al.* (1994) for a discussion of increases in *Porites porites* on dead *A. cervicornis* rubble). While some increases in macroalgae were observed in the following decade, a bleaching event in 1995 followed by Hurricane Lili in 1996 resulted in a significant decline of the remaining coral species including the *Montastraea* spp. (from 14% cover in 1994 to 5% in 1997): with dramatic increases in macroalgae (from 17% cover in 1994 to 44% in 1997: Ostrander *et al.*, 2000). In the absence of *Diadema*, the shift to macroalgal dominance occurred without changes in the high abundance of herbivorous fish or nutrient concentrations, highlighting the combined importance of coral mortality and the absence of *Diadema*.

LESSONS LEARNED

The Pleistocene record

Most of us agree that understanding the primary causes of coral mortality in a historical context is important if we are to confront the coral reef crisis (Aronson *et al.*, 2003; Gardner *et al.*, 2003; Pandolfi *et al.*, 2003). The fossil record is the best place to observe the natural variability of coral reefs long before human impacts. Jackson (1991, 1992), Pandolfi (1999, 2002), Pandolfi and Jackson (1997) and Aronson and Precht (2001a) have shown that, almost without exception, Pleistocene fossil-reef sections in the Caribbean exhibit patterns of species composition and zonation similar to modern reefs at the same location (at least as they were prior to the 1980s). Thus, Pleistocene reef-coral assemblages within the same general type of environment (e.g. lagoon, fore reef) are more distinct between reefs of the same age from different locations than between reefs formed at different times in the same location. Pandolfi (2001, 2002) suggested that the Pleistocene data point to a high degree of order and predictability in coral assemblages over broad spatial and temporal scales. Present trends are not predicted from history, implicating *Homo sapiens* as the vector of this change (Stokstad, 2001).

In Jamaica, limestone outcrops spanning 0–6 m above present sea level represent coral reefs deposited ~125 Ka during the last major interglacial high sea stand (Marine Isotope Stage 5e: Boss and Liddell, 1987). The 125-Ka Pleistocene bank/barrier reef exposed along the eastern margin of Rio Bueno Harbor, on the north coast of the island, is dominated by assemblages of *Acropora palmata, A. cervicornis, Montastraea annularis* species complex and *Porites porites* in the fore-reef facies (Liddell *et al.*, 1984) and follows the classic coral zonation scheme of Goreau (1959). The same suite of species characterized the living fore-reef community in the waters just below at Rio Bueno and at nearby Discovery Bay prior to the 1980s (Precht and Hoyt, 1991). This suggests that well-preserved, zoned, acroporid-dominated communities were the norm, at least during high sea stands, and that dominance by macroalgae was not a common attribute of the Pleistocene fossil record (see Jackson (1992) for a similar description for Barbados).

Using the fossil record of Caribbean reefs as a baseline representing the pristine condition, it is possible to test the impact of over-fishing on reef community structure. We cannot estimate the abundance of most fish on Pleistocene reefs, but there is one exception: the threespot damselfish *Stegastes planifrons*. Prior to the recent decline of *Acropora*, threespot damselfish were common residents of intermediate to shallow depths (<25 m) on fore-reef terraces throughout the Caribbean (Kaufman, 1977, 1983). Their preferred microhabitat was thickets of *A. cervicornis* (Kaufman, 1981). Threespots are highly territorial and actively kill the corals by biting living tissue. By aggressively defending their territories against other herbivores, threespots allow the growth of dense algal gardens on the coral skeletons. Although many reef fish tend algal gardens, threespots produce gardens within stands of living coral. On the fore-reef terrace at Discovery Bay, threespot territories infested up to 40% of the living coral surfaces prior to 1980 (Kaufman, 1977, 1981). A common feature of threespot territories was *A. cervicornis* branches covered by clusters of gall-like structures called chimneys. Chimneys were formed at the margins of the territories by the healing of coral skeleton over algae-infested lesions from damselfish bites (Fig. 2.2). The frequency of bites was lower at the margins than in the centres of the territories, providing scope for limited recovery in the marginal portions.

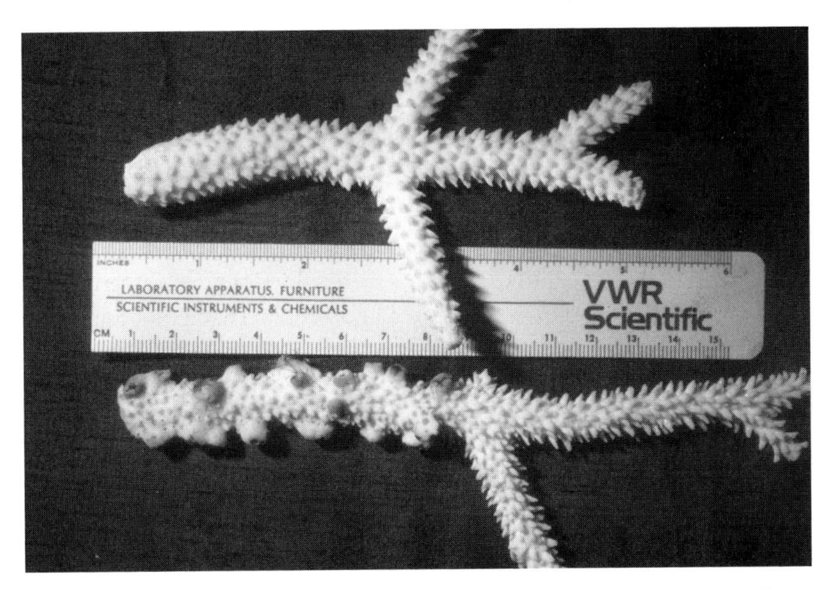

Figure 2.2 Photograph of *Acropora cervicornis* branches collected from the fore reef at Discovery Bay, Jamaica. Bottom colony shows numerous gall-like structures that represent coral growth around lesions caused by spot-biting of the threespot damselfish, *Stegastes planifrons*. The lesions are colonized by filamentous algae, and coral growth can eventually heal over them entirely.

One of the questions posed by Kaufman's (1977) initial work at Discovery Bay was: 'Were the recent numbers of threespots inflated due to decades of over-fishing, which released the damselfish from predation and increased their impact on the reef?' (see also Ogden, 1995). To test this hypothesis, Kaufman (1981) sampled fossil *A. cervicornis* branches from the Pleistocene Falmouth Formation at nearby Rio Bueno. His result – an abundance of chimneys on taphonomically unaltered *A. cervicornis* branches – suggests that threespot territories are a persistent attribute of Caribbean reef ecology. Thus, the type and intensity of at least one form of biological disturbance were not related in any obvious manner to the recent over-exploitation of predatory reef fish.

In addition, we evaluated Jackson's (1997) assertion (*contra* Hay, 1984) that *Diadema* were historically abundant on at least some Caribbean reefs. Using sediment core samples from the shallow fore reef at the Long-Term Study (LTS) reef at Discovery Bay (5 m depth) in 1978, we compared the abundance of diadematid test and spine fragments to bulk samples taken from the same lithofacies in the Falmouth Formation at Rio Bueno (Fig. 2.3). The results, 3.8% *Diadema* fragments in 1978 versus 3.7%

Figure 2.3 Outcrop photograph of exposed fore-reef facies in Pleistocene Falmouth Formation, Rio Bueno, Jamaica. Depth estimate of this *Acropora cervicornis* zone is ~5 m based on comparison with reef crest datum. Analysis of biotic constituents of sediment from this lithofacies is presented in Table 2.1.

Table 2.1. Percentage constituent composition for sediments on the West Fore Reef (WFR), Discovery Bay, Jamaica, at 5 m depth compared with sediments from the equivalent facies in the Pleistocene (125 000 years ago) Falmouth Formation at nearby Rio Bueno (RB); standard errors are in parentheses

Category	WFR, 1978 ($n = 6$)	RB, 125 Ka (East Shore) ($n = 6$)
Hard corals (Scleractinia and Milleporina)	48.2 (6.6)	45.3 (5.9)
Halimeda	34.6 (7.5)	41.5 (4.5)
Coralline red algae	5.1 (2.4)	2.3 (1.8)
Foraminifera	2.4 (1.2)	2.0 (0.8)
Mollusks	3.6 (0.6)	3.2 (0.7)
Diadematid echinoids	3.8 (1.2)	3.7 (1.1)
Others (echinoderms, sponge spicules, bryozoans, etc.)	1.9 (0.7)	1.8 (0.5)
Unidentified	0.4 (0.2)	0.2 (0.1)

~125 Ka, reveal a remarkable fidelity through time and space. Other categories of sediment grains (coral fragments, *Halimeda* segments, etc.) are also remarkably similar in these samples (Table 2.1). If we take these comparative data at face value, it appears that *Diadema* was always an important herbivore on Jamaican reefs (see also Gordon and Donovan, 1992; Donovan and Gordon, 1993). The implication could be profound: it may well be that herbivorous fish are ecologically redundant to the keystone herbivore, *D. antillarum* (see Carpenter, 1986), and not the other way around on shallow Caribbean reefs.

The Holocene record

On reefs in protected, lagoonal environments, the Holocene sub-fossil record renders an accurate picture of stasis and change in the composition of coral assemblages on a centennial to millennial scale, with minimal information loss (Aronson *et al.*, 2002a, 2004, 2005a). Coring studies in Belize (Aronson and Precht, 1997; Aronson *et al.*, 2002a) and Panama (Aronson *et al.*, 2004) suggest that corals grew actively and continuously for millennia until the last few decades. To discover whether the recent phase shift in Jamaica was unprecedented in the late Holocene, we extracted eight push-cores from the reef at Columbus Park in Discovery Bay (Wapnick *et al.*, 2004). This lagoonal reef, which is in a protected setting relative to the fore reef, was dominated by *A. cervicornis* until about 1980. The *A. cervicornis* population in Columbus Park was killed by WBD at approximately the same time that Hurricane Allen decimated acroporid populations on the fore reef.

The cores consisted almost entirely of *A. cervicornis* rubble. Samples of *A. cervicornis* from the bases of the cores were radiocarbon-dated to 440–1260 calendar years before 1950. The *A. cervicornis* in the cores showed significantly less internal bioerosion than 20-year-old *A. cervicornis* rubble from the modern death assemblages in Columbus Park and on the fore reef of Discovery Bay, indicating generally shorter *post mortem* exposure at the sediment–water interface in the past. In the centuries to millennia preceding the 1980s, *A. cervicornis* grew continuously and was buried rapidly, and multi-decadal interruptions in population growth were rare or did not occur at all (Wapnick *et al.*, 2004).

Our results agree with quantitative ecological observations over the last 50 years, supporting the premise that the circumstances leading to the recent demise of *A. cervicornis* were unique to our times. The cores show millennial-scale stasis of the coral assemblage, punctuated by change in the last few decades. This study and palaeoecological analyses throughout the region do not support the hypothesis that corals were already in decline prior to modern times. On the contrary, regional coral mortality and species turnover began in the very recent past, they were driven in the first instance by disease outbreaks and bleaching episodes (and to a lesser extent by hurricanes), and they occurred whether herbivorous fish were abundant (as in Belize) or not (as in Panama and Jamaica).

PREDICTING THE FUTURE: RESILIENCE AND RECOVERY

Recent changes on Caribbean reefs could persist for decades or longer and it is unclear how future global climate change will interact with disease and other stressors (Brown, 1997; Harvell *et al.*, 2001; Kleypas *et al.*, 2001). The virulence of some coral diseases increases with increasing temperature, suggesting that coral mortality will accelerate in the face of global warming (Rosenberg and Ben-Haim, 2002). Human activities are continuing to present novel challenges that compound the difficulty of predicting ecosystem-scale responses to global climate change. The combined effects of multiple anthropogenic stressors could alter ecosystem resilience and prevent the recovery of affected reefs (Knowlton, 1992, 2001; Peters *et al.*, 1997; Nyström *et al.*, 2000; McCook *et al.*, 2001b). On the other hand, where environmental stress has been reduced, corals have increased

Figure 2.4 Underwater photograph taken at the Long-Term Study (LTS) reef at 6 m depth on the West Fore Reef at Discovery Bay, Jamaica, in March 2004. Recovery of the herbivorous sea urchin *Diadema antillarum* has reduced macroalgal cover from >60% to <5%, while increasing the cover of crustose coralline algae and the abundance of coral recruits on a substratum of *Acropora* rubble. In the last few years there has been a conspicuous increase in recruits of *A. palmata*, one of which appears in the centre of the photograph. (See also Plate 2.4 in the colour plate section.)

in abundance. For example, in Jamaica the return of *Diadema* to some areas has been associated with a reduction in macroalgal cover, an increase in the abundance of juvenile corals and ultimately an increase in coral cover (Fig. 2.4), providing evidence that the coral–macroalgal phase shift is reversible (Aronson and Precht, 2000; Edmunds and Carpenter, 2001; Cho and Woodley, 2002; Idjadi *et al.*, 2006).

What factors could forestall recovery? Disease pathogens are still present, bleaching events are increasing in frequency and intensity, hurricanes continue to set back reef succession, predators continue to take their toll on remnant coral populations, and a variety of other stressors continue to affect corals (Hughes, 1989, 1994; Knowlton *et al.*, 1990; Knowlton, 1992; Bruckner *et al.*, 1997; Hughes and Connell, 1999; Aronson and Precht, 2001c; Baums *et al.*, 2003; Sutherland *et al.*, 2004). Suitable substratum may limit larval recruitment where populations of fleshy macroalgae remain high (Hughes and Tanner, 2000). The loss of topographic complexity may also control the numbers of herbivores. If herbivory remains low, fleshy macroalgae will continue to be the most abundant benthic components of Caribbean reefs. If herbivory increases, however, we anticipate a return to coral dominance. Prolific growth rates of the acroporids in Jamaica before 1980 (see Rylaarsdam, 1983; Tunnicliffe, 1983), combined with their low to intermediate potential for sexual recruitment and their high rate of fragmentation once established (Tunnicliffe, 1981), suggest that recovery on a decadal time scale is possible in all of the habitat types occupied prior to recent events (Woodley, 1992; Precht *et al.*, 2004). If one or both of the *Acropora* species do not recover, however, then weedy, brooding corals such as *Porites* and *Agaricia* will become increasingly abundant (Hughes, 1994; Kojis and Quinn, 1994; Knowlton, 2001), at least in the near term.

While most Caribbean reefs have been declining for the past two decades (Gardner *et al.*, 2003), coral cover has been increasing on a reef at Dairy Bull, 2 km east of Discovery Bay. In 2004, Dairy Bull had almost 100% more living coral cover and 90% less macroalgal cover at 6 m depth than it did in 1995 (Edmunds and Bruno, 1996; Idjadi *et al.*, 2006). The most conspicuous increase in coral cover was new growth of *A. cervicornis*. This species was rare throughout the 1990s, but by 2004 it had increased to more than 10% absolute cover (Fig. 2.5). The 2004 value is similar to the 14–16% cover reported for *A. cervicornis* at the same depth in the late 1970s on the West Fore Reef at Discovery Bay (Rylaarsdam, 1983).

The cover of several other species of reef-building corals also increased significantly at Dairy Bull (Idjadi *et al.*, 2006). In fact, the benthic community at Dairy Bull in 2004 was similar to Jamaican reefs of the 1970s, when average coral cover was ~55% (Huston, 1985; Liddell and Ohlhorst, 1987; Hughes, 1994). The dramatic reduction of macroalgae at Dairy Bull to only ~6% cover by 2004 put macroalgae back to pre-1983 values (Liddell and Ohlhorst, 1987; Carpenter, 1990b; Côté *et al.*, this volume). The persistence of substantial coral populations at Dairy Bull in the 1990s, especially long-lived colonies of *Montastraea annularis* species complex, probably preempted space and prevented macroalgal dominance (Edmunds and Bruno, 1996; Aronson and Precht, 2001a). The *M. annularis* complex also maintained a high degree of structural heterogeneity (topographic complexity), which apparently promoted the recovery of *D. antillarum*. The increase in *Diadema* almost certainly reduced macroalgal biomass and facilitated coral recruitment.

At intermediate depths (6–20 m) on the fore reef at Discovery Bay, in contrast, topographic relief was reduced to a far greater extent by storm damage and bioerosion after 1980 than at Dairy Bull, and to date there has not been any appreciable regeneration of topography through coral growth.

Figure 2.5 Underwater photograph of *Acropora cervicornis* thickets filling in the voids between large, century-old colonies of *Montastraea annularis* at ~6 m depth at Dairy Bull Reef, Jamaica, in July 2003. The view in this photograph is reminiscent of the coral assemblage of the north coast of Jamaica in the 1960s and 1970s. This reef has shown dramatic increases in coral cover and reductions in macroalgae in the past few years, coincident with the recovery of *Diadema antillarum* and in the near-absence of herbivorous fish. (See also Plate 2.5 in the colour plate section.)

Coral cover at Discovery Bay is ~5% in this depth range, and macroalgae cover >60% of the substratum (Morrison, 1988; Liddell and Ohlhorst, 1993; Aronson *et al.*, 1994; Andres and Witman, 1995). Structural complexity is an important difference between Dairy Bull and nearby reefs (Bechtel *et al.*, 2006), and it may be that reefs without it are less resilient. If this scenario is accurate, *M. annularis* species complex is a foundation taxon (Bruno and Bertness, 2001) that facilitated the recovery of the keystone herbivore *D. antillarum*, leading to the dramatic decline of the formerly dominant macroalgae. Considering that there is now anecdotal evidence for similar dynamics at other locations throughout the Caribbean (Fig. 2.6), we could well be witnessing the incipient recovery of *Acropora* populations and a return to the coral-dominated state.

Jamaican reefs have been characterized as so polluted and over-fished that they cannot recover under current levels of protection (Pandolfi *et al.*, 2003, 2005). In reality there is no compelling evidence that coral decline or recovery were caused or hindered by pollution and over-fishing. In fact, fishing pressure continues to be severe on reefs along the north coast of

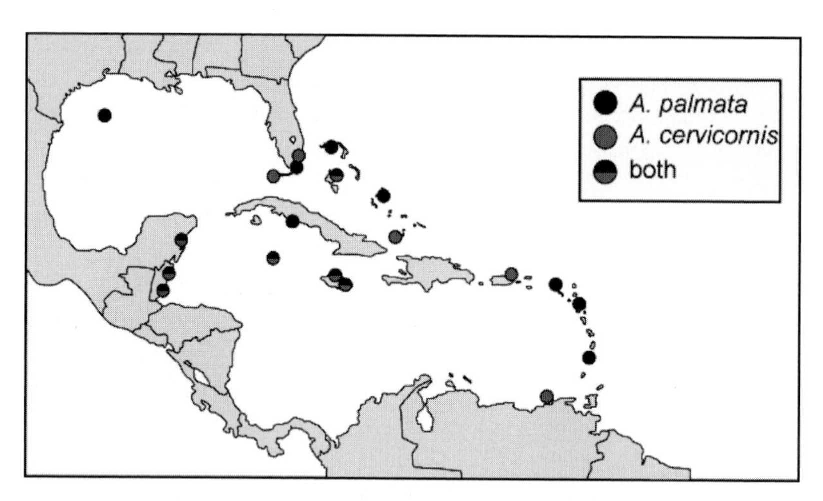

Figure 2.6 Map of the Caribbean basin showing the locations of known recent increases in populations of acroporid corals. Stands of *Acropora cervicornis* and *A. palmata* have recently been observed on some reefs in the Bahamas (J. Feingold, personal communication; W. F. Precht, personal observation), Belize (M. Robbart, I. Macintyre, P. Mumby, personal communications), Bonaire (B. Zimmer, personal communication), British Virgin Islands (Rogers, 2000), Cuba (P. Alcalado, personal communication), Florida (Precht and Aronson, 2004; S. Miller, personal communication), the Flower Garden Banks (Precht and Aronson, 2004), Jamaica (Idjadi *et al.*, 2006; G. Warner, personal communication), Grand Cayman Island (T. Austin, personal communication prior to passage of Hurricane Ivan in the summer of 2004), Mexico (J. Bruno, personal communication), Puerto Rico (W. F. Precht, personal observation), Turks and Caicos Islands (P. Mumby, personal communication), the US Virgin Islands (Rogers *et al.*, 2002), and other locations (see Bruckner, 2002; Kramer, 2003).

Jamaica (Woodley and Sary, 2002). Fish and other vertebrate consumers remain essentially absent, and it is unlikely that water quality (sediment loads, dissolved nutrient concentrations, etc.) has improved over the last ten years (Aronson and Precht, 2000; Cho and Woodley, 2002). Herbivorous vertebrates have been scarce at Dairy Bull for decades (Munro, 1983), and they have not been principally responsible for removing algae from the reef. The rapid reversal of the coral–macroalgal phase shift clearly proves that algal dominance is not the inevitable and irreversible consequence of overfishing.

The practical implications of this most recent recovery are profound. First, devising restoration and management programmes that enhance critical components of the ecosystem (i.e. the keystone species, *Diadema antillarum*: see Miller and Szmant, 2006; Jaap *et al.*, this volume) could be far more effective at promoting the success of corals and far less costly than undertaking large, landscape-scale approaches (Simberloff, 1998) such as instituting and enforcing draconian no-take regulations over vast areas (e.g. Bellwood *et al.*, 2004; Pandolfi *et al.*, 2005), especially in developing nations. Second and perhaps more important, understanding the recovery process is crucial in defining the ecological and environmental parameters that govern the system. Whether the coral- and algal-dominated states are stable alternatives, each of which resists conversion to the other, or whether instead the coral–macroalgal transition is an easily reversible phase shift, is critical in determining the resilience of reef communities in the Caribbean (Scheffer *et al.*, 2001; Scheffer and Carpenter, 2003; Bellwood *et al.*, 2004). We agree with Petraitis and Dudgeon (2004) that no experimental evidence exists to support the idea of alternative stable states on coral reefs and that the switch between coral- and macroalgae-dominated communities was merely a phase-shift response to changes in environmental conditions (see Sammarco *et al.* (1974) and Sammarco (1982) for whole-reef manipulations). The rapid reversion to coral dominance at Dairy Bull (Idjadi *et al.*, 2006) and the ongoing recovery of shallow reef communities around Jamaica (Aronson and Precht, 2000; Edmunds and Carpenter, 2001; Cho and Woodley, 2002; Bechtel *et al.*, 2006) appear to be predicated almost exclusively on the recovery of *Diadema* populations.

It seems ironically appropriate that the same Jamaican reefs that framed the story of reef decline for the region are now the bell-wether for resilience and recovery. The results from Jamaica provide evidence that even without their full complement of taxa, trophic components and/or functional groups, coral reefs are still astoundingly resilient systems. On the other hand, if we do not reduce the major causes of coral mortality, especially bleaching and disease, we will be faced with coral mortality continuing to exceed rates of growth and recovery at the scale of the region.

SUMMARY AND OUTLOOK

Most Caribbean reefs have experienced a recent phase shift in benthic community structure, the principal features of which have been a decline in coral cover and an increase in macroalgal cover and biomass. The main events of this change have been sudden die-offs of *Acropora cervicornis, A. palmata, Diadema antillarum* and, more recently, long-lived massive corals. Locally, the phase shift has been exacerbated by long-term depletion of herbivorous fishes. The phase shift is especially well documented in Jamaica, but the same general pattern of coral mortality followed by increased macroalgal abundance has been observed throughout the region, both near and far from sources of anthropogenic stress and fishing pressure.

The transition from coral to macroalgal dominance was a novel event in at least the last centuries to millennia. In particular, acroporid corals dominated continuously for millennia until the last three decades, when outbreaks of disease coupled with other sources of mortality caused regional turnover. Interestingly, acroporids and other corals are now recovering on some Caribbean reefs, even though fishing pressure has not declined and water quality has not improved.

Palaeoecological and ecological data indicate that coral mortality is largely decoupled from changing levels of herbivory and water quality, and that reef dynamics on a regional scale are at best weakly linked to present and past fishing pressure. Nevertheless, herbivory, especially herbivory by *Diadema*, may be the critical component in the ability of a reef to recover from disturbance events. For almost 20 years after the loss of *Diadema* from the region, other herbivores were unable to control the macroalgae that colonized and dominated the open space left by coral mortality. Now, the removal of macroalgae and the resultant rapid phase-shift reversal in some shallow reef communities appears to be linked to the recovery of *Diadema* populations. The recovery of *Diadema* itself may be the key to facilitating coral recovery.

Improving water quality and conserving stocks of reef fish should be and clearly are high priorities of management, but the positive, localized impact on corals will be minimal in the face of regional- to global-scale stressors such as disease and increasing sea-surface temperature. Establishing marine protected areas may have a positive impact on fishery resources, especially targeted species, but the impact that such protections will have on the corals remains unclear (Jones *et al.*, 2004). In the face of multiple disturbances, then, the restoration of keystone/foundation species may be more important in reversing reef degradation than large-scale ecosystem-based approaches (Power *et al.*, 1996).

Some authors have claimed that reef scientists have failed in protecting the world's reefs (Risk, 1999; Bellwood *et al.*, 2004; Pandolfi *et al.*, 2005). We argue that no form of locally based stewardship, scientific management or scientific policy could have changed the overall trajectory of coral loss or ameliorated the major disturbances responsible for reef decline at the regional scale, especially outbreaks of disease in corals and urchins, hurricanes and storms, and coral bleaching events. The recent decline of corals is a global environmental catastrophe that requires global solutions. Although local management efforts are surely necessary to protect reef ecosystems from a variety of smaller-scale human disturbances, only by addressing the coral reef crisis at the highest levels of government will we be able to find the appropriate long-term solutions. It is imperative that managers and policy-makers directly address the range of factors that have decimated coral populations and hinder their recovery; therefore, understanding the causal links between human-induced global change and reef health must be our most pressing challenge for the future (Buddemeier *et al.*, 2004). Unfortunately, vigorous management strategies to alleviate these stressors are not yet politically expedient.

CONCLUSIONS

Coral populations have declined drastically on reefs throughout the Caribbean since the 1980s. In particular, the elkhorn coral *Acropora palmata* and the staghorn coral *A. cervicornis* have experienced catastrophic mortality throughout the region. Because these two species were dominant space occupants in shallow and intermediate depths, respectively, their loss precipitated biotic turnover on a regional scale. The phase shift to macroalgal dominance was exacerbated by the regional mass mortality of the herbivorous sea urchin *Diadema antillarum* in 1983–84. Recently, there have been reports of top–down coral recovery related to an increase in grazing by *D. antillarum*. This reversal of fortune on some Caribbean reefs is occurring without changes in reef-fish assemblages or pressure from fishers, calling into question the hypothesis that over-fishing is the primary cause of collapse of reef ecosystems. Macroalgal dominance of Caribbean reefs may not be the inevitable consequence of over-fishing. Coral mortality is decoupled from fish abundance, and reef dynamics on a regional level are at best weakly linked to present and past levels of fishing pressure. On the other hand, recovery of the sea urchin *D. antillarum* is probably the key to facilitating coral recovery throughout the region.

ACKNOWLEDGEMENTS

We are indebted to John Bruno, Pete Edmunds, Bill Fitt, Bob Ginsburg, Peter Glynn, Denny Hubbard, Jeremy Jackson, Les Kaufman, Joanie Kleypas, Judy Lang, Jim Leichter, Don Levitan, Steven Miller, Thad Murdoch, Martha Robbart, Caroline Rogers, Gene Shinn, Steve Vollmer, Cheryl Wapnick and Jeremy Woodley for many discussions over many years, which helped us focus our thoughts. Special thanks are due to Isabelle Côté and John Reynolds for inviting us to participate in the Zoological Society of London – Coral Reef Conservation Symposium and Workshop. Financial support was provided by the US National Science Foundation (grant EAR-9902192 to R.B.A.) and the National Geographic Society (grant

7041-01 to R.B.A.). We thank Northeastern University's Three Seas (East/West) Marine Biology Program and the staff of the Discovery Bay Marine Laboratory (DBML) for making our research in Jamaica possible. This is DBML Contribution Number 571 and Contribution Number 361 from the Dauphin Island Sea Lab.

REFERENCES

Andréfouët, S., Mumby, P. J., McField, M., Hu, C. and Muller-Karger, F. E. (2002). Revisiting coral reef connectivity. *Coral Reefs*, **21**, 43–8.

Andres, N. G. and Witman, J. D. (1995). Trends in community structure on a Jamaican reef. *Marine Ecology Progress Series*, **118**, 305–10.

Antonius, A. (1977). Coral mortality in reefs: a problem for science and management. *Proceedings 3rd International Coral Reef Symposium*, **2**, 617–23.

(1981). The 'band' diseases in coral reefs. *Proceedings 4th International Coral Reef Symposium*, **2**, 6–14.

Aronson, R. B. (1990). Onshore–offshore patterns of human fishing activity. *Palaios*, **5**, 88–93.

(2001). The limits of detectability: short-term events and short-distance variation in the community structure of coral reefs. *Bulletin of Marine Science*, **69**, 331–2.

Aronson, R. B. and Precht, W. F. (1997). Stasis, biological disturbance, and community structure of a Holocene coral reef. *Paleobiology*, **23**, 326–46.

(2000). Herbivory and algal dynamics on the coral reef at Discovery Bay, Jamaica. *Limnology and Oceanography*, **45**, 251–5.

(2001a). Evolutionary paleoecology of Caribbean coral reefs. In *Evolutionary Paleoecology: The Ecological Context of Macroevolutionary Change*, eds. W. D. Allmon and D. J. Bottjer, pp. 171–233. New York: Columbia University Press.

(2001b). White-band disease and the changing face of Caribbean coral reefs. *Hydrobiologia*, **460**, 25–38.

(2001c). Applied paleoecology and the crisis on Caribbean coral reefs. *Palaios*, **16**, 195–6.

Aronson, R. B., Edmunds, P. J., Precht, W. F., Swanson, D. W. and Levitan, D. R. (1994). Large-scale, long-term monitoring of Caribbean coral reefs: simple, quick, inexpensive techniques. *Atoll Research Bulletin*, **421**, 1–19.

Aronson, R. B., Macintyre, I. G., Precht, W. F., Wapnick, C. M. and Murdoch, T. J. T. (2002a). The expanding scale of species turnover events on coral reefs in Belize. *Ecological Monographs*, **72**, 233–49.

Aronson, R. B., Precht, W. F., Toscano, M. A. and Koltes, K. H. (2002b). The 1998 bleaching event and its aftermath on a coral reef in Belize. *Marine Biology*, **141**, 435–47.

Aronson, R. B., Bruno, J. F., Precht, W. F. *et al.* (2003). Causes of reef degradation. *Science*, **302**, 1502.

Aronson, R. B., Macintyre, I. G., Wapnick, C. M. and O'Neill, M. W. (2004). Phase shifts, alternative states, and the unprecedented convergence of two reef systems. *Ecology*, **85**, 1876–91.

Aronson, R. B., Macintyre, I. G. and Precht, W. F. (2005a). Event preservation in lagoonal reef systems. *Geology*, **33**, 717–20.

Aronson, R. B., Precht, W. F., Murdoch, T. J. T. and Robbart, M. L. (2005b). Long-term persistence of coral assemblages on the Flower Garden Banks, northwestern Gulf of Mexico: implications for science and management. *Gulf of Mexico Science*, **23**, 84–94.

Bascompte, J., Melián, C. J. and Sala, E. (2005). Interaction strength combinations and the overfishing of a marine food web. *Proceedings of the National Academy of Sciences, USA*, **102**, 5443–7.

Bauer, J. C. and Agerter, C. J. (1987). Isolation of bacteria pathogenic for the sea urchin *Diadema antillarum* (Echinodermata: Echinoidea). *Bulletin of Marine Science*, **40**, 161–5.

Baum, J. K., Myers, R. A., Kehler, D. G. *et al.* (2003). Collapse and conservation of shark populations in the northwest Atlantic. *Science*, **299**, 389–92.

Baums, I. B., Miller, M. W. and Szmant, A. M. (2003). Ecology of a corallivorous gastropod, *Coralliophila abbreviata*, on two scleractinian hosts. I. Population structure of snails and corals. *Marine Biology*, **142**, 1083–91.

Bechtel, J. D., Gayle, P. and Kaufman, L. (2006). The return of *Diadema antillarum* to Discovery Bay: patterns of distribution and abundance. *Proceedings 10th International Coral Reef Symposium* (in Press).

Bellwood, D. R., Hughes, T. P., Folke, C. and Nyström, M. (2004). Confronting the coral reef crisis. *Nature*, **429**, 827–33.

Bjorndal, K. A. and Jackson, J. B. C. (1997). Foraging ecology and nutrition of sea turtles. In *The Biology of Sea Turtles*, eds. P. L. Lutz and J. A. Musick, pp. 259–74. Boca Raton, FL: CRC Press.

Boss S. K. and Liddell, W. D. (1987). Back-reef and fore-reef analogs in the Pleistocene of north Jamaica: implications for facies recognition and sediment flux in fossil reefs. *Palaios*, **2**, 219–28.

Brown, B. E. (1997). Disturbances to reefs in recent times. In *Life and Death of Coral Reefs*, ed. C. Birkeland, pp. 354–79. New York: Chapman and Hall.

Bruckner, A. W. (2002). *Proceedings of the Caribbean* Acropora *Workshop: Potential Application of the US Endangered Species Act as a Conservation Strategy*, Technical Memorandum NOAA-OPR-24. Silver Spring, MD: National Oceanic and Atmospheric Administration.

Bruckner, A. W. and Bruckner, R. J. (1997) The persistence of black-band disease in Jamaica: impact on community structure. *Proceedings 8th International Coral Reef Symposium*, **1**, 601–6.

Bruckner, R. J., Bruckner, A. W. and Williams Jr, E. H. (1997). Life history strategies of *Coralliophila abbreviata* Lamarck (Gastropoda: Coralliophilidae) on the southwest coast of Puerto Rico. *Proceedings 8th International Coral Reef Symposium*, **1**, 627–32.

Bruno, J. F. and Bertness, M. D. (2001). Habitat modification and facilitation in benthic marine communities. In *Marine Community Ecology*, eds. M. D. Bertness, M. E. Hay and S. D. Gaines, pp. 201–18. Sunderland, MA: Sinauer.

Bruno, J. F., Petes, L. E., Harvell, C. D. and Hettinger, A. (2004). Nutrient enrichment can increase the severity of coral diseases. *Ecology Letters*, **6**, 1056–61.

Buddemeier, R. W., Kleypas, J. A. and Aronson, R. B. (2004). *Coral Reefs and Global Climate Change: Potential Contributions of Climate Change to Stresses on Coral Reef Ecosystems*. Arlington, VA: Pew Center on Global Climate Change.

Bythell, J. C. and Sheppard, C. (1993). Mass mortality of Caribbean shallow corals. *Marine Pollution Bulletin*, **26**, 296–7.

Bythell, J. C., Hillis-Starr, Z. M. and Rogers, C. S. (2000). Local variability but landscape stability in coral reef communities following repeated hurricane impacts. *Marine Ecology Progress Series*, **204**, 93–100.

Bythell, J. C., Pantos, O. and Richardson, L. (2004). White plague, white band, and other 'white' diseases. In *Coral Health and Disease*, eds. E. Rosenberg and Y. Loya, pp. 351–65. Berlin: Springer-Verlag.

Carpenter, R. C. (1986). Partitioning herbivory and its effects on coral-reef algal communities. *Ecological Monographs*, **56**, 345–63.

(1988). Mass mortality of Caribbean sea urchin: immediate effects on community metabolism and other herbivores. *Proceedings of the National Academy of Sciences, USA*, **85**, 511–14.

(1990a). Mass mortality of *Diadema antillarum*. I. Long-term effects on sea urchin population dynamics and coral reef algal communities. *Marine Biology*, **104**, 67–77.

(1990b). Mass mortality of *Diadema antillarum*. II. Effects on population densities and grazing intensity of parrotfishes and surgeonfishes. *Marine Biology*, **104**, 79–86.

(1997). Invertebrate predators and grazers. In *Life and Death of Coral Reefs*, ed. C. Birkeland, pp. 198–229. New York: Chapman and Hall.

Cho, L. L. and Woodley, J. D. (2002). Recovery of reefs at Discovery Bay, Jamaica and the role of *D. antillarum*. *Proceedings 9th International Coral Reef Symposium*, **1**, 331–8.

Connell, J. H. (1997). Disturbance and recovery of coral assemblages. *Coral Reefs*, **16**, S101–S113.

Curran, H. A., Smith, D. P., Meigs, L. C., Pufall, A. E. and Greer, M. L. (1994). The health and short-term change of two coral patch reefs, Fernandez Bay, San Salvador Island, Bahamas. In *Proceedings of the Colloquium on Global Aspects of Coral Reefs: Health, Hazards and History*, compiled R. N. Ginsburg, pp. 147–53. Miami, FL: Rosenstiel School of Marine and Atmospheric Science, University of Miami.

D'Elia, C. F., Webb, K. L. and Porter, J. W. (1981). Nitrate-rich groundwater inputs to Discovery Bay, Jamaica: a significant source of N to local reefs? *Bulletin of Marine Science*, **31**, 903–10.

de Ruyter van Steveninck, E. D. and Bak, R. P. M. (1986). Changes in abundance of coral-reef bottom components related to mass mortality of the sea urchin *Diadema antillarium*. *Marine Ecology Progress Series*, **34**, 87–94.

de Ruyter van Steveninck, E. D., Van Mulekon, L. L. and Breenan, A. M. (1988). Growth inhibition of *Lobophora variegata* (Lamouroux) Womersley by scleractinian corals. *Journal of Experimental Marine Biology and Ecology*, **115**, 169–78.

Domning, D. P. (2001). Sirenians, seagrasses, and the Cenozoic ecological change in the Caribbean. *Palaeogeography, Palaeoclimatology, Palaeoecology*, **166**, 27–50.

Done, T. J. (1992). Phase shifts in coral reef communities and their ecological significance. *Hydrobiologia*, **247**, 121–32.

Donovan, S. K. and Gordon, C. M. (1993). Echinoid taphonomy and the fossil record: supporting evidence from the Plio-Pleistocene of the Caribbean. *Palaios*, **8**, 304–6.
Edmunds, P. J. (1991). Extent and effect of black-band disease on a Caribbean reef. *Coral Reefs*, **10**, 161–5.
Edmunds, P. J. and Bruno, J. F. (1996). The importance of sampling scale in ecology: kilometer-wide variation in coral reef communities. *Marine Ecology Progress Series*, **143**, 165–71.
Edmunds, P. J. and Carpenter, R. C. (2001). Recovery of *Diadema antillarum* reduces macroalgal cover and increases abundances of juvenile corals on a Caribbean reef. *Proceedings of the National Academy of Sciences, USA*, **98**, 5067–71.
Elmqvist, T., Folke, C., Nyström, M. *et al.* (2003). Response diversity, ecosystem change, and resilience. *Frontiers in Ecology and the Environment*, **1**, 488–94.
Elner, R. W. and Vadas, R. L. (1990). Inference in ecology: the sea urchin phenomenon in the northwestern Atlantic. *American Naturalist*, **136**, 108–25.
Epstein, P. R., Sherman, B., Spanger-Siegfried, E. *et al.* (1998). *Marine Ecosystems: Emerging Diseases as Indicators of Change*, Health, Ecological and Economic Dimensions of Global Change Program. Cambridge, MA: Harvard Medical School.
Fitt, W. K., Brown, B. E., Warner, M. E. and Dunne, R. P. (2001). Coral bleaching: interpretation of thermal tolerance limits and thermal thresholds in tropical corals. *Coral Reefs*, **20**, 51–65.
Gardner, T. A., Côté, I. M., Gill, J. A., Grant, A. and Watkinson, A. R. (2003). Long-term region-wide declines in Caribbean corals. *Science*, **301**, 958–60.
(2005). Hurricanes and Caribbean coral reefs: impacts, recovery patterns, and role in long-term decline. *Ecology*, **86**, 174–84.
Garzón-Ferreira, J., Gil-Agudelo, D. L., Barrios, L. M. and Zea, S. (2001). Stony coral diseases observed in southwestern Caribbean reefs. *Hydrobiologia*, **460**, 65–9.
Ginsburg, R. N. (compiler) (1994). *Proceedings of the Colloquium on Global Aspects of Coral Reefs: Health, Hazards and History*. Miami, FL: Rosenstiel School of Marine and Atmospheric Science, University of Miami.
Ginsburg, R. N. and Lang, J. C. (2003). Foreword: Status of coral reefs in the western Atlantic – results of initial surveys, Atlantic and Gulf Rapid Reef Assessment (AGRRA) Program. *Atoll Research Bulletin*, **496**, vii–xiii.
Gittings, S. R., Bright, T. J. and Hagman, D. K. (1994). Protection and monitoring of reefs on the Flower Garden Banks, 1972–1992. In *Proceedings of the Colloquium on Global Aspects of Coral Reefs: Health, Hazards and History*, compiled R. N. Ginsburg, pp. 181–7. Miami, FL: Rosenstiel School of Marine and Atmospheric Science, University of Miami.
Gladfelter, W. B. (1982). White band disease in *Acropora palmata*: implications for the structure and growth of shallow reefs. *Bulletin of Marine Science*, **32**, 639–43.
Glynn, P. W. (1983). Extensive bleaching and death of reef corals on the Pacific coast of Panama. *Environmental Conservation*, **10**, 149–54.

(1990). Feeding ecology of selected coral-reef macroconsumers: patterns and effects on coral community structure. In *Ecosystems of the World*, vol. 25, *Coral Reefs*, ed. Z. Dubinsky, pp. 365–400. Amsterdam: Elsevier.
(1991). Coral reef bleaching in the 1980s and possible connections with global warming. *Trends in Ecology and Evolution*, **6**, 175–9.
(1993). Coral reef bleaching: ecological perspectives. *Coral Reefs*, **12**, 1–17.
(1996). Coral reef bleaching: facts, hypotheses and implications. *Global Change Biology*, **2**, 495–509.
Glynn, P. W. and D'Croz, L. (1990). Experimental evidence for high temperature stress as the cause of El Niño-coincident coral mortality. *Coral Reefs*, **8**, 181–91.
Gordon, C. M. and Donovan, S. K. (1992). Disarticulated echinoid ossicles in paleoecology and taphonomy: the last interglacial Falmouth Formation of Jamaica. *Palaios*, **7**, 157–66.
Goreau, T. F. (1959). The ecology of Jamaican coral reefs. I. Species composition and zonation. *Ecology*, **40**, 67–90.
Goreau, T. F. and Goreau, N. I. (1973). The ecology of Jamaican coral reefs. II. Geomorphology, zonation and sedimentary phases. *Bulletin of Marine Science*, **23**: 399–464.
Goreau, T. J., Cervino, J., Goreau, N. *et al.* (1998). Rapid spread of diseases in Caribbean coral reefs. *Revista de Biologia Tropical*, **46**(Suppl. 5), 157–71.
Green, E. and Bruckner, A. W. (2000). The significance of coral disease epizootiology for coral reef conservation. *Biological Conservation*, **96**, 347–61.
Grigg, R. W. (1995). Coral reefs in an urban embayment in Hawaii: a complex case history controlled by natural and anthropogenic stress. *Coral Reefs*, **14**, 253–66.
Harvell, D., Aronson, R., Baron, N. *et al.* (2004). The rising tide of ocean diseases: unsolved problems and research priorities. *Frontiers in Ecology and the Environment*, **2**, 375–382.
Harvell, C. D., Kim, K., Burkholder, J. M. *et al.* (1999). Emerging marine diseases: climate links and anthropogenic factors. *Science*, **285**, 1505–10.
Hay, M. E. (1984). Patterns of fish and urchin grazing on Caribbean coral reefs: are previous results typical? *Ecology*, **65**, 446–54.
Hayes, M. L., Bonaventura, J., Mitchell, T. P. *et al.* (2001). How are climate and marine biological outbreaks functionally linked? *Hydrobiologia*, **460**, 213–20.
Hoegh-Guldberg, O. (1999). Climate change, coral bleaching and the future of the world's coral reefs. *Marine and Freshwater Research*, **50**, 839–66.
(2004). Coral reefs and projections of future change. In *Coral Health and Disease*, eds. E. Rosenberg and Y. Loya, pp. 463–84. Berlin: Springer-Verlag.
Hubbard, D. K., Zankl, H., Van Heerden, I. and Gill, I. P. (2005). Holocene reef development along the northeastern St Croix shelf, Buck Island, US Virgin Islands. *Journal of Sedimentary Research*, **75**, 97–113.
Hughes, T. P. (1989). Community structure and diversity of coral reefs: the role of history. *Ecology*, **70**, 275–9.
(1994). Catastrophes, phase shifts and large-scale degradation of a Caribbean coral reef. *Science*, **265**, 1547–51.
Hughes, T. P. and Connell, J. H. (1999). Multiple stressors on coral reefs: a long-term perspective. *Limnology and Oceanography*, **44**, 932–40.
Hughes, T. P. and Tanner, J. E. (2000). Recruitment failure, life histories, and long-term decline of Caribbean corals. *Ecology*, **81**, 2250–63.

Hughes, T. P., Keller, B. D., Jackson, J. B. C. and Boyle, M. J. (1985). Mass mortality of the echinoid *Diadema antillarum* in Jamaica. *Bulletin of Marine Science*, **36**, 377–84.
Hughes, T. P., Reed, D. C. and Boyle, M.-J. (1987). Herbivory on coral reefs: community structure following mass mortalities of sea urchins. *Journal of Experimental Marine Biology and Ecology*, **113**, 39–59.
Hughes, T. P., Szmant, A. M., Steneck, R., Carpenter, R. and Miller, S. (1999). Algal blooms on coral reefs: what are the causes? *Limnology and Oceanography*, **44**, 1583–6.
Hughes, T. P., Baird, A. H., Bellwood, D. R. (2003). Climate change, human impacts, and the resilience of coral reefs. *Science*, **301**, 929–33.
Huston, M. A. (1985). Patterns of species diversity in relation to depth at Discovery Bay, Jamaica. *Bulletin of Marine Science*, **37**, 928–35.
Idjadi, J. A., Lee, S. C., Bruno, J. F. *et al.* (2006). Rapid phase-shift reversal on a Jamaican coral reef. *Coral Reefs* (in press).
Jackson, J. B. C. (1991). Adaptation and diversity of reef corals. *BioScience*, **41**, 475–82.
(1992). Pleistocene perspectives of coral reef community structure. *American Zoologist*, **32**, 719–31.
(1994). Community unity? *Science*, **264**, 1412–13.
(1997). Reefs since Columbus. *Coral Reefs*, **16**, S23–S32.
(2001). What was natural in the coastal oceans? *Proceedings of the National Academy of Sciences, USA*, **98**, 5411–18.
Jackson, J. B. C. and Johnson, K. G. (2000). Life in the last few million years. *Paleobiology*, **26**, 221–35.
Jackson, J. B. C. and Sala, E. (2001). Unnatural oceans. *Scientia Marina*, **65**(suppl. 2), 273–81.
Jackson, J. B. C., Kirby, M. X., Berger, W. H. *et al.* (2001). Historical overfishing and the recent collapse of coastal ecosystems. *Science*, **293**, 629–38.
Jokiel, P. L. (1997). Temperature stress and coral bleaching. In *Coral Health and Disease*, eds. E. Rosenberg and Y. Loya, pp. 401–25. Berlin: Springer-Verlag.
Jones, G. P., McCormick, M. I., Srinivasan, M. and Eagle, J. V. (2004). Coral decline threatens fish biodiversity in marine reserves. *Proceedings of the National Academy of Sciences, USA*, **101**, 8251–3.
Kaufman, L. (1977). The three spot damselfish: effects on benthic biota of Caribbean coral reefs. *Proceedings 3rd International Coral Reef Symposium*, **1**, 559–64.
(1981). There was biological disturbance on Pleistocene coral reefs. *Paleobiology*, **7**, 527–32.
(1983). Effects of Hurricane Allen on reef fish assemblages near Discovery Bay, Jamaica. *Coral Reefs*, **2**, 43–7.
Kleypas, J. A., Buddemeier, R. W. and Gattuso, J.-P. (2001). The future of coral reefs in an age of global change. *International Journal of Earth Sciences (Geologische Rundschau)*, **90**, 426–37.
Knowlton, N. (1992). Thresholds and multiple stable states in coral reef community dynamics. *American Zoologist*, **32**, 674–82.
(2001). The future of coral reefs. *Proceedings of the National Academy of Sciences, USA*, **98**, 5419–25.

Knowlton, N., Lang, J. C. and Keller, B. D. (1990). Case study of natural population collapse: post-hurricane predation on Jamaican staghorn corals. *Smithsonian Contributions to the Marine Sciences*, **31**, 1–25.

Kojis, B. L. and Quinn, N. J. (1994). Biological limits to Caribbean reef recovery: a comparison with western South Pacific reefs. In *Proceedings of the Colloquium on Global Aspects of Coral Reefs: Health, Hazards and History*, compiled R. N. Ginsburg, pp. 353–9. Miami, FL: Rosenstiel School of Marine and Atmospheric Science, University of Miami.

Koslow, J. A., Hanley, F. and Wicklund, R. (1988). Effects of fishing on reef fish communities at Pedro Bank and Port Royal Cays, Jamaica. *Marine Ecology Progress Series*, **43**, 201–12.

Kramer, P. A. (2003). Synthesis of coral reef health indicators for the western Atlantic: results of the AGRRA Program (1997–2000). *Atoll Research Bulletin*, **496**, 1–57.

Kramer, P. R. (compiler) (2002). Report from the status and trends working group. In *Proceedings of the Caribbean* Acropora *Workshop: Potential Application of the US Endangered Species Act as a Conservation Strategy*. Technical Memorandum NOAA–OPR-24, ed. A. Bruckner, pp. 28–37. Silver Spring, MD: National Oceanic and Atmospheric Administration.

Kurlansky, M. (2003). *Cod: Biography of the Fish that Changed the World*. London: Penguin Books.

Lapointe, B. E. (1997). Nutrient thresholds for bottom–up control of macroalgal blooms on coral reefs in Jamaica and southeast Florida. *Limnology and Oceanography*, **42**, 1119–31.

(1999). Simultaneous top–down and bottom–up forces control macroalgal blooms on coral reefs. *Limnology and Oceanography*, **44**, 1586–92.

Lapointe, B. E., Littler, M. M. and Littler, D. S. (1997). Macroalgal overgrowth of fringing coral reefs at Discovery Bay, Jamaica: bottom–up versus top–down control. *Proceedings 8th International Coral Reef Symposium*, **1**, 927–32.

Lessios, H. A. (1988). Mass mortality of *Diadema antillarum* in the Caribbean: what have we learned? *Annual Review of Ecology and Systematics*, **19**, 371–93.

Lessios, H. A., Robertson, D. R. and Cubit, J. D. (1984). Spread of *Diadema* mass mortality through the Caribbean. *Science*, **226**, 335–7.

Lessios, H. A., Garrido, M. J. and Kessing, B. D. (2001). Demographic history of *Diadema antillarum*, a keystone herbivore on Caribbean reefs. *Proceedings of the Royal Society of London B*, **268**, 2347–53.

Levitan, D. R. (1988). Algal–urchin biomass responses following mass mortality of *Diadema antillarum* Philippi at Saint John, US Virgin Islands. *Journal of Experimental Marine Biology and Ecology*, **119**, 167–78.

(1992). Community structure in times past: influence of human fishing pressure on algal–urchin interactions. *Ecology*, **73**, 1597–605.

Liddell, W. D. and Ohlhorst, S. L. (1986). Changes in benthic community composition following the mass mortality of *Diadema antillarum*. *Journal of Experimental Marine Biology and Ecology*, **95**, 271–8.

(1987). Patterns of reef community structure, north Jamaica. *Bulletin of Marine Science*, **40**, 311–29.

(1993). Ten years of disturbance and change on a Jamaican fringing reef. *Proceedings 7th International Coral Reef Symposium*, **1**, 144–50.

Liddell, W. D., Ohlhorst, S. L. and Coates, A. G. (1984). *Modern and Ancient Carbonate Environments of Jamaica. X. Sedimenta*. Miami, FL: Rosenstiel School of Marine and Atmospheric Science, University of Miami.
Littler, M. M., Taylor, P. R., Littler, D. S., Sims, R. H. and Norris, J. N. (1987). Dominant macrophyte standing stocks, productivity and community structure on a Belizean barrier reef. *Atoll Research Bulletin*, **302**, 1–24.
Lugo, A. E., Rogers, C. and Nixon, S. (2000). Hurricanes, coral reefs and rainforests: resistance, ruin and recovery in the Caribbean. *Ambio*, **29**, 106–14.
McClanahan, T. R. and Muthiga, N. A. (1988). Changes in Kenyan coral reef community structure and function due to exploitation. *Hydrobiologia*, **166**, 269–76.
(1998). An ecological shift among patch reefs of Glovers Reef Atoll, Belize over 25 years. *Environmental Conservation*, **25**, 122–30.
McClanahan, T. R., Aronson, R. B., Precht, W. F. and Muthiga, N. A. (1999). Fleshy algae dominate remote coral reefs of Belize. *Coral Reefs*, **18**, 61–2.
McClanahan, T. R., Cokos, B. A. and Sala, E. (2002). Algal growth and species composition under experimental control of herbivory, phosphorus and coral abundance in Glovers Reef, Belize. *Marine Pollution Bulletin*, **44**, 441–51.
McClanahan, T. R., Sala, E., Stickels, P. A. *et al.* (2003). Interaction between nutrients and herbivory in controlling algal communities and coral condition on Glover's Reef, Belize. *Marine Ecology Progress Series*, **261**, 135–47.
McClanahan, T. R., Sala, E., Mumby, P. J. and Jones, S. (2004). Phosphorous and nitrogen enrichment do not enhance brown frondose 'macroalgae'. *Marine Pollution Bulletin*, **48**, 196–9.
McCook, L. J., Jompa, J. and Diaz-Pulido, G. (2001a). Competition between corals and algae on coral reefs: a review of evidence and mechanisms. *Coral Reefs*, **19**, 400–17.
McCook, L. J. Wolanski, E. and Spagnol, S. (2001b). Modeling and visualizing interactions between natural disturbances and eutrophication as causes of coral reef degradation. In *Oceanographic Processes of Coral Reefs: Physical and Biological Links in the Great Barrier Reef*, ed. E. Wolanski, pp. 113–25. Boca Raton, FL: CRC Press.
McManus, J. W. and Polsenberg, J. F. (2004). Coral–algal phase shifts on coral reefs: ecological and environmental aspects. *Progress in Oceanography*, **60**, 263–79.
Miller, M. W., Hay, M. E., Miller, S. L. *et al.* (1999). Effects of nutrients versus herbivores on reef algae: a new method for manipulating nutrients on coral reefs. *Limnology and Oceanography*, **44**, 1847–61.
Miller, M. W. and Szmant, A. M. (2006). Lessons learned from experimental key-species restoration. In *Reef Restoration Handbook: The Rehabilitation of an Ecosystem Under Siege*, ed. W. F. Precht. Boca Raton, FL: CRC Press.
Morrison, D. (1988). Comparing fish and urchin grazing in shallow and deeper coral reef algal communities. *Ecology*, **69**, 1367–82.
Muller-Karger, F. E., McClain, C. R., Fisher, T. R., Esaias, W. E. and Varela, R. (1989). Pigment distribution in the Caribbean Sea: observations from space. *Progress in Oceanography*, **23**, 23–64.

Mumby, P. J., Edwards, A. J., Arias-Gonzalez, J. E. *et al.* (2004). Mangroves enhance the biomass of coral reef fish communities in the Caribbean. *Nature*, **427**, 533–6.

Munro, J. L. (ed.) (1983). *Caribbean Coral Reef Fishery Resources.* Manila: International Center for Living Aquatic Resources Management.

Nyström, M., Folke, C. and Moberg, F. (2000). Coral reef disturbance and resilience in a human-dominated environment. *Trends in Ecology and Evolution*, **15**, 413–17.

Ogden, J. C. (1995). Coral reef decline in the Caribbean region. *Proceedings of the 2nd European Regional Meeting of the International Society for Reef Studies, Publications de la Service Geologique du Luxembourg*, **29**, 224.

Ostrander, G. K., Armstrong, K. M., Knobbe, E. T., Gerace, D. and Scully, E. P. (2000). Rapid transition in the structure of a coral reef community: the effects of coral bleaching and physical disturbance. *Proceedings of the National Academy of Sciences, USA*, **97**, 5297–302.

Paine, R. T., Tegner, M. J. and Johnson, E. A. (1998). Compounded perturbations yield ecological surprises. *Ecosystems*, **1**, 535–45.

Palumbi, S. R. (2002). *Marines Reserves: A Tool for Ecosystem Management and Conservation.* Arlington, VA: Pew Oceans Commission.

(2005). Germ theory for ailing corals. *Nature*, **434**, 713–14.

Pandolfi, J. M. (1999). Response of Pleistocene coral reefs to environmental change over long temporal scales. *American Zoologist*, **39**, 113–30.

(2001). Pleistocene persistence and the recent decline in Caribbean coral communities. *Paleobios*, **21** (suppl. 2), 100.

(2002). Coral community dynamics at multiple scales. *Coral Reefs*, **21**, 13–23.

Pandolfi, J. M. and Jackson, J. B. C. (1997). The maintenance of diversity on coral reefs: examples from the fossil record. *Proceedings 8th International Coral Reef Symposium*, **1**, 397–404.

Pandolfi, J. M., Bradbury, R. H., Sala, E. *et al.* (2003). Global trajectories of the long-term decline of coral reef ecosystems. *Science*, **301**, 955–8.

Pandolfi, J. M., Jackson, J. B. C., Baron, N. *et al.* (2005). Are US coral reefs on the slippery slope to slime? *Science*, **307**, 1725–6.

Pauly, D. W., Christiansen, J., Dahsgaard, J., Froese, R. and Torres Jr, F. C. (1998). Fishing down marine food webs. *Science*, **279**, 860–3.

Pennings, S. C. (1997). Indirect interactions on coral reefs. In *Life and Death of Coral Reefs*, ed. C. Birkeland, pp. 249–72. New York: Chapman and Hall.

Peters, E. C. (1997). Diseases of coral reef organisms. In *Life and Death of Coral Reefs*, ed. C. Birkeland, pp. 114–39. New York: Chapman and Hall.

Peters, E. C., Yevich, P. P. and Oprandy, J. J. (1983). Possible causal agent of 'white band disease' in Caribbean acroporid corals. *Journal of Invertebrate Pathology*, **41**, 394–6.

Peters, E. C., Gassman, N. J., Firman, J. C., Richmond, R. H. and Power, E. A. (1997). Ecotoxicology of tropical marine ecosystems. *Environmental Toxicology and Chemistry*, **16**, 12–40.

Petraitis, P. S. and Dudgeon, S. R. (2004). Detection of alternate stable states in marine communities. *Journal of Experimental Marine Biology and Ecology*, **300**, 343–71.

Podestá, G. P. and Glynn, P. W. (1997). Sea surface temperature variability in Panamá and Galápagos: extreme temperatures causing coral bleaching. *Journal of Geophysical Research*, **102**, 15749–59.
Power, M. E., Tilman, D., Estes, J. A. *et al.* (1996). Challenges in the quest for keystones. *BioScience*, **46**, 609–20.
Precht, W. F. (1990). Geologic and ecologic perspectives of catastrophic storms and disturbance on coral reefs: lessons from Discovery Bay, Jamaica. *Geological Society of America Annual Meeting Program with Abstracts*, **22**, A331.
Precht, W. F. and Aronson, R. B. (2002). The demise of *Acropora* in the Caribbean: a tale of two reef systems. In *Proceedings of the Caribbean* Acropora *Workshop: Potential Application of the US Endangered Species Act as a Conservation Strategy*, Technical Memorandum NOAA–OPR-24, ed. A. Bruckner, p. 147. Silver Spring, MD: National Oceanic and Atmospheric Administration.
(2004). Climate flickers and range shifts of reef corals. *Frontiers in Ecology and the Environment*, **2**, 307–14.
Precht, W. F. and Hoyt, W. H. (1991). Reef facies distribution patterns, Pleistocene (125 Ka) Falmouth Formation, Rio Bueno, Jamaica, W. I. *American Association of Petroleum Geologists Bulletin*, **75**, 656–7.
Precht, W. F. and Miller, S. (2006). Ecological shifts along the Florida reef tract: the past as a key to the future. In *Geological Approaches to Coral Reef Ecology*, ed. R. B. Aronson. New York: Springer-Verlag.
Precht, W. F., Bruckner, A. W., Aronson, R. B. and Bruckner, R. J. (2002). Endangered acroporid corals of the Caribbean. *Coral Reefs*, **21**, 41–2.
Precht, W. F., Robbart, M. L. and Aronson, R. B. (2004). The potential listing of *Acropora* species under the US Endangered Species Act. *Marine Pollution Bulletin*, **49**, 534–6.
Richardson, L. L. (1998). Coral diseases: what is really known? *Trends in Ecology and Evolution*, **13**, 438–43.
Richardson, L. L. and Aronson, R. B. (2002). Infectious diseases of reef corals. *Proceedings 9th International Coral Reef Symposium*, **2**, 1225–30.
Risk, M. J. (1999). Paradise lost: how marine science failed the world's coral reefs. *Marine and Freshwater Research*, **50**, 831–7.
Ritchie, K. B. and Smith, G. W. (1998). Type II white-band disease. *Revista de Biologia Tropical*, **46**(Suppl. 5), 199–203.
River, G. F. and Edmunds, P. J. (2001). Mechanisms of interaction between macroalgae and scleractinians on a coral reef in Jamaica. *Journal of Experimental Marine Biology and Ecology*, **261**, 159–72.
Roberts, C. M. (1995). Effects of fishing on the ecosystem structure of coral reefs. *Conservation Biology*, **9**, 988–95.
(1997). Connectivity and management of Caribbean coral reefs. *Science*, **278**, 1454–7.
Robertson, D. R. (1991). Increases in surgeonfish populations after mass mortality of the sea urchin *Diadema antillarum* in Panama indicate food limitation. *Marine Biology*, **111**, 437–44.
Robinson, A. (1973). Natural vs. visitor-related damage to shallow water corals: recommendations for visitor management and the design of underwater nature trails in the Virgin Islands. National Park Service, Unpublished internal report, US Department of the Interior, St Thomas, US Virgin Islands.

Rogers, C. S. (2000). Is *Acropora palmata* (elkhorn coral) making a comeback in the Virgin Islands? *Reef Encounter*, **27**, 15–17.
Rogers, C. S. and Beets, J. (2001). Degradation of marine ecosystems and decline of fishery resources in marine protected areas in the US Virgin Islands. *Environmental Conservation*, **28**, 312–22.
Rogers, C., Gladfelter, W., Hubbard, D. *et al.* (2002). *Acropora* in the US Virgin Islands: a wake or an awakening? In *Proceedings of the Caribbean* Acropora *Workshop: Potential Application of the US Endangered Species Act as a Conservation Strategy*, Technical Memorandum NOAA–OPR-24, ed. A. Bruckner, pp. 95–118. Silver Spring, MD: National Oceanic and Atmospheric Administration.
Rosenberg, E. and Ben-Haim, Y. (2002). Microbial diseases of corals and global warming. *Environmental Microbiology*, **4**, 318–26.
Rützler, K. and Macintyre, I. G. (1982). The habitat distribution and community structure of the barrier reef complex at Carrie Bow Cay, Belize. In *The Atlantic Barrier Reef Ecosystem at Carrie Bow Cay, Belize*, vol. 1, *Structure and Communities*, eds. K. Rützler and I. G. Macintyre, pp. 9–45. Washington, DC: Smithsonian Institution Press.
Rylaarsdam, K. W. (1983). Life histories and abundance patterns of colonial corals on Jamaican reefs. *Marine Ecology Progress Series*, **13**, 249–60.
Sala, E., Boudouresque, C. F. and Harmelin-Vivien, M. (1998). Fishing, trophic cascades, and the structure of algal assemblages: evaluation of an old but untested paradigm. *Oikos*, **83**, 425–39.
Sammarco, P. W. (1982). Echinoid grazing as a structuring force in coral communities: whole reef manipulations. *Journal of Experimental Marine Biology and Ecology*, **61**, 31–55.
Sammarco, P. W., Levinton, J. S. and Ogden, J. C. (1974). Grazing and control of coral reef community structure by *Diadema antillarum* Philippi (Echinodermata: Echinoidea): a preliminary study. *Journal of Marine Research*, **32**, 47–53.
Santavy, D. L. and Peters, E. C. (1997). Microbial pests: coral diseases in the western Atlantic. *Proceedings 8th International Coral Reef Symposium*, **1**, 607–12.
Scheffer, M. and Carpenter, S. R. (2003). Catastrophic regime shifts in ecosystems: linking theory to observation. *Trends in Ecology and Evolution*, **18**, 648–56.
Scheffer, M., Carpenter, S., Foley, J. A., Folke, C. and Walker, B. (2001). Catastrophic shifts in ecosystems. *Nature*, **413**, 591–6.
Sebens, K. P. (1994). Biodiversity of coral reefs: what are we losing and why? *American Zoologist*, **34**, 115–33.
Sheppard, C. (1993). Coral reef environmental science: dichotomies, not the Cassandras, are false. *Reef Encounter*, **14**, 12–13.
Shinn, E. A. (1989). What is really killing the corals? *Sea Frontiers*, **35**, 72–81.
Shinn, E. A., Smith, G. W., Prospero, J. M. *et al.* (2000). African dust and the demise of Caribbean coral reefs. *Geophysical Research Letters*, **27**, 3029–32.
Simberloff, D. (1998). Flagships, umbrellas, and keystones: is single-species management passé in the landscape era? *Biological Conservation*, **83**, 247–57.
Sobel, J. and Dahlgren, C. (2004). The cautionary tale of Caribbean reef decline. In *Marine Reserves: A Guide to Science, Design, and Use*, eds. J. Sobel and C. Dahlgren, pp. 43–50. Washington, DC: Island Press.

Steneck, R. S. (1994). Is herbivore loss more damaging to reefs than hurricanes? Case studies from two Caribbean reef systems. In *Proceedings of the Colloquium on Global Aspects of Coral Reefs: Health, Hazards and History*, compiled R. N. Ginsburg, pp. 220–6. Miami, FL: Rosenstiel School of Marine and Atmospheric Science, University of Miami.
(1998). Human influences on coastal ecosystems: does overfishing create trophic cascades? *Trends in Ecology and Evolution*, **13**, 429–30.
Stokstad, E. (2001). Humans to blame for coral loss. *Science*, **293**, 593.
Sutherland, K. P., Porter, J. W. and Torres, C. (2004). Disease and immunity in Caribbean and Indo-Pacific zooxanthellate corals. *Marine Ecology Progress Series*, **266**, 273–302.
Szmant, A. M. (1997). Nutrient effects on coral reefs: a hypothesis on the importance of topographic and trophic complexity to reef nutrient dynamics. *Proceedings 8th International Coral Reef Symposium*, **2**, 1527–32.
(2002). Nutrient enrichment on coral reefs: is it a major cause of coral reef decline? *Estuaries*, **25**, 743–66.
Tunnicliffe, V. (1981). Breakage and propagation of the stony coral *Acropora cervicornis*. *Proceedings of the National Academy of Sciences, USA*, **78**, 2427–31.
(1983). Caribbean staghorn coral populations: pre-Hurricane Allen conditions in Discovery Bay, Jamaica. *Bulletin of Marine Science*, **33**, 132–51.
Walther, G.-R., Post, E., Convey, P. *et al.* (2002). Ecological responses to recent climate change. *Nature*, **416**, 389–95.
Wapnick, C. M., Precht, W. F. and Aronson, R. B. (2004). Millennial-scale dynamics of staghorn coral in Discovery Bay, Jamaica. *Ecology Letters*, **7**, 354–61.
Ward, J. R. and Lafferty, K. D. (2004). The elusive baseline of marine diseases: are diseases in ocean ecosystems increasing? *Public Library of Science: Biology*, **2**, 542–7.
Wellington, G. M., Glynn, P. W., Strong, A. E. *et al.* (2001). Crisis on coral reefs linked to climate change. *Eos*, **82**, 1, 5.
Williams Jr, E. H. and Bunkley-Williams, L. (1990). The world-wide coral reef bleaching cycle and related sources of coral mortality. *Atoll Research Bulletin*, **335**, 1–71.
Williams, I. D. and Polunin, N. V. C. (2001). Large-scale associations between macroalgal cover and grazer biomass on mid-depth reefs in the Caribbean. *Coral Reefs*, **19**, 358–66.
Williams, I. D., Polunin, N. V. C. and Hendrick, V. J. (2001). Limits to grazing by herbivorous fishes and the impact of low coral cover on macroalgal abundance on a coral reef in Belize. *Marine Ecology Progress Series*, **222**, 187–96.
Wing, S. R. and Wing, E. S. (2001). Prehistoric fisheries in the Caribbean. *Coral Reefs*, **20**, 1–8.
Woodley, J. D. (1992). The incidence of hurricanes on the north coast of Jamaica since 1870: are the classic reef descriptions atypical? *Hydrobiologia*, **247**, 133–8.
Woodley, J. D. and Sary, Z. (2002). Development of a locally managed fisheries reserve at Discovery Bay, Jamaica. *Proceedings 9th International Coral Reef Symposium*, **2**, 627–33.
Woodley, J. D., Chornesky, E. A., Clifford, P. A. *et al.* (1981). Hurricane Allen's impact on Jamaican coral reefs. *Science*, **214**, 749–55.

3

A seascape-level perspective of coral reef ecosystems

PETER J. MUMBY AND ALASTAIR R. HARBORNE
University of Exeter

INTRODUCTION

Tropical coastal areas are often categorized into three major systems: coral reefs, seagrass beds and mangroves. All three systems often occur in close proximity (Fig. 3.1) and a number of habitats are represented within each (e.g. patterns of habitat zonation in coral reefs: Sheppard, 1982). Many physical and ecological processes transcend individual habitats with some particularly striking examples among the three principal systems. A well-known example is the trapping of riverine sediments in estuarine mangroves that might otherwise discharge onto reefs and cause coral mortality through sedimentation (Pannier, 1979; Torres *et al.*, 2001). Other examples of abiotic linkages include the runoff of cool, low-salinity water from precipitation (Andréfouët *et al.*, 2002) and the discharge of hot water from relatively calm lagoons, both of which can cause coral bleaching (reviewed in Glynn, 1993).

Ecological linkages among habitats include the migration of organisms on either an ontogenetic or diurnal basis. Many snappers (Family Lutjanidae), grunts (Haemulidae) and parrotfish (Scaridae) species, for example, undertake ontogenetic shifts in habitat use from seagrass beds or mangroves to their adult coral reef habitat (McFarland *et al.*, 1985; Lindeman *et al.*, 1998; de la Morinière *et al.*, 2002; Mumby *et al.*, 2004a). Grunts also undertake diurnal migrations from their night-time foraging habitat of seagrass beds to their daytime resting habitat on coral reefs (Ogden and Ehrlich, 1977; Burke, 1995). Interestingly, the daytime defecation of fish

Coral Reef Conservation, ed. Isabelle M. Côté and John D. Reynolds.
Published by Cambridge University Press.

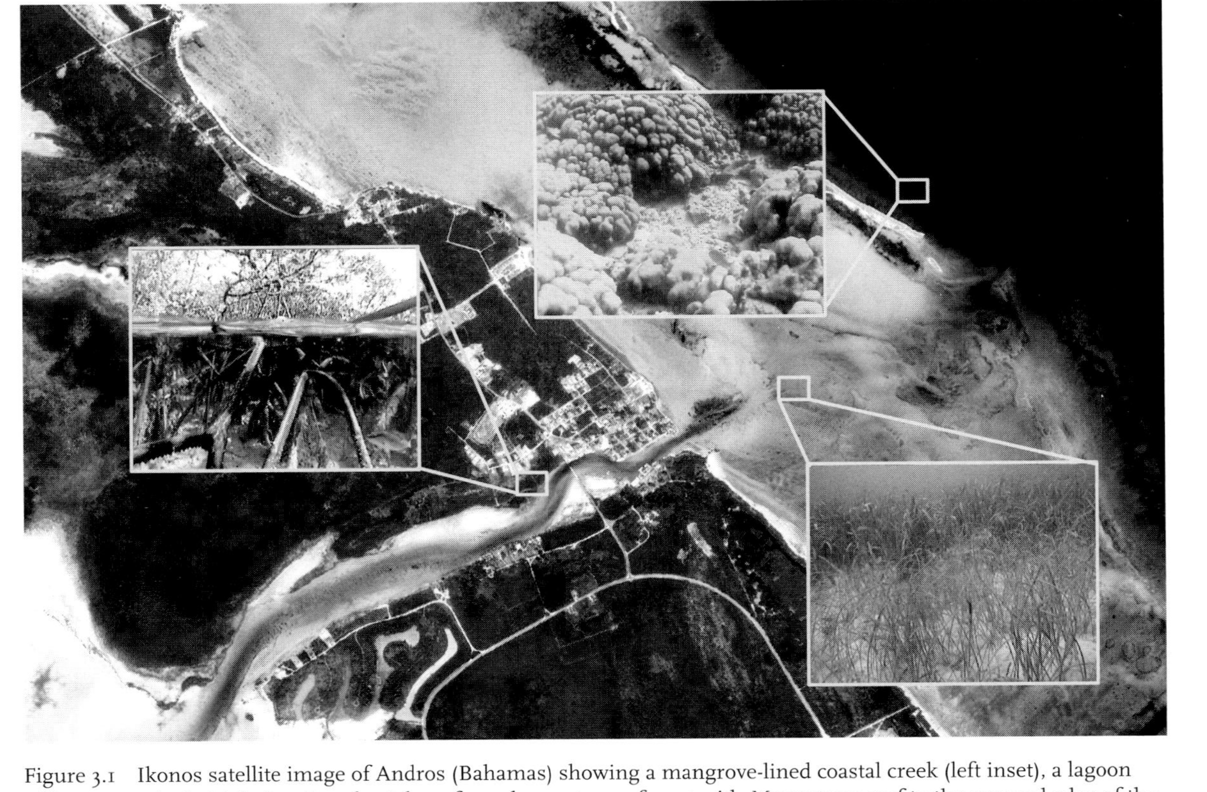

Figure 3.1 Ikonos satellite image of Andros (Bahamas) showing a mangrove-lined coastal creek (left inset), a lagoon with seagrass beds (right inset) and patch reefs, and an outer reef crest with *Montastraea* reef to the seaward edge of the image (middle inset). (See also Plate 3.1 in the colour plate section.)

facilitates a transfer of nutrients from the seagrass beds that is large enough to cause local increases in the growth rate of corals (Meyer *et al.*, 1983; Meyer and Schultz, 1985).

Whilst the importance of seascape-level processes has been clearly stated (Ogden and Gladfelter, 1983; Hatcher, 1997a; Ogden, 1997), the vast majority of coral reef studies have a much narrower focus. Taking a random sample of 100 papers from the journal *Coral Reefs* between 1981 and 2000, we found that only 4% considered processes within a wider seascape of multiple habitats and only 2% considered non-reef systems such as shallow seagrass beds. This skew towards studies of individual reef habitats is understandable given the difficulties in replicating experiments at multiple scales. However, the vast majority of reef management decisions have to consider threats and activities occurring across entire catchments. Coastal development, for example, is often followed by increases in fishing intensity, sediment runoff, dredging, nutrification and so on. From a management perspective, the interrelatedness and functioning of coral reefs need to be understood at the seascape level.

Here, we attempt to review the present state of coral reef 'seascape ecology' and suggest further avenues for research. We begin by describing the remote-sensing methods used to describe a seascape, most of which result in a habitat map. We then describe the functioning and characteristics of each habitat by reviewing ecosystem processes across the seascape. Using ontogenetic shifts in fish habitat use as a case study, we then describe processes that link multiple habitats. Finally, we discuss the uptake of seascape-level processes within ecosystem models and reserve selection algorithms. Our ultimate objective is to encourage the development of ecosystem models that integrate processes occurring across the seascape. Such models will underpin decision-support tools for management and provide a mechanism for linking the outcomes of ecological studies to policy.

MAPPING THE SEASCAPE

Virtually every ecosystem on the planet has been studied using remote sensing. Tropical coastal resources such as mangroves, seagrass beds and coral reefs have probably received as much attention as any other system. Their popularity among the remote-sensing community stems in part from the characteristic shallow clear water associated with many tropical coastal areas (Fig. 3.1). Clear water transmits relatively high levels of photosynthetically active radiation (PAR) which is a biological necessity for photosynthetic organisms inhabiting the benthos (e.g. the algal symbionts of hermatypic corals). Clear water also allows remote-sensing instruments to measure the light reflected from the benthos and has stimulated intensive coastal research since the launch of the multispectral scanner (MSS) sensor on the Landsat satellite in 1972.

A detailed review of remote-sensing methods for tropical coastal environments is beyond the scope of this chapter but the following review articles may prove useful. For the application of remote sensing to tropical coastal management, see Green *et al.* (1996, 2000) and for a recent overview of sensors and applications see Mumby *et al.* (2004c).

Remote sensing of coral reefs

Remote sensing provides information on several parameters that are important to reef science and management. The easiest of these to map are coral reef boundaries. The next level of sophistication is to distinguish principal geomorphological zones of the reef (see Table 3.1). For management purposes, such information may be used to provide a background for planning but these maps may also have more sophisticated ecological uses which include the stratification of field sampling regimes. Maps of reef geomorphology have been made with considerable success (e.g. Ahmad and Neil, 1994).

Mapping the ecological components of coral reefs is considerably more difficult than patterns of geomorphology (Bainbridge and Reichelt, 1989). Ecological components may be defined in various ways including assemblages of coral species (e.g. Done, 1983), assemblages of coral and non-coral species, or assemblages of species and substrata (Sheppard *et al.*, 1995; Mumby and Harborne, 1999). The choice depends on the ecological objective and physiognomy of the area. For example, coral species assemblages would be appropriate in places where coral cover was high, but perhaps less so where coral cover rarely exceeded 20%. Irrespective of their foundation, maps with an ecological basis will be referred to as 'habitat maps' (see Table 3.2). Maps of reef habitat are a useful planning tool which, among other uses, allow management boundaries to be located and representative reef habitats to be identified (McNeill, 1994). Generally, discrimination of more than five reef habitats requires high spatial resolution (pixel width <10 m) and, more importantly, high spectral resolution in which the blue and green ranges of the electromagnetic spectrum are divided into at least six, narrow (~ 20 nm) bands (Mumby *et al.*, 1998).

Few studies have attempted to map the health or status of reefs directly. A study in French Polynesia used a high-resolution airborne multispectral

Table 3.1. Hierarchical classification scheme and quantitative characteristics, for the geomorphological zones typically found on Caribbean coral reefs

First tier		Second tier	
Label	Characteristics	Label	Characteristics
Back reef	Usually shallow, <2 m		
Reef crest	Often emergent at low tide		
Spur and groove		Low-relief spurs and grooves	Spurs <5m in height
		High-relief spurs and grooves	Spurs >5m in height
Fore reef	Reef with $<45^{\circ}$ slope		
Escarpment	Either reef or lagoon with $>45^{\circ}$ slope		
Patch reef		Dense patch reef	Aggregated coral colonies (living or dead) where colonies cover $>70\%$ of the benthos
		Diffuse patch reef	Dispersed coral colonies (living or dead) where colonies cover $<30\%$ of the benthos
Lagoon floor	Lagoon floor with $<45^{\circ}$ slope	Shallow lagoon floor	Depth <12 m
		Deep lagoon floor	Depth >12 m

Source: Redrawn from classification scheme developed by Mumby and Harborne (1999).

Table 3.2. Hierarchical classification scheme, and quantitative characteristics, for the benthic communities typically found on Caribbean coral reefs

First tier		Second tier	
Label	Characteristics	Label	Characteristics
Coral classes	>1% hard coral cover; relatively high rugosity	Branching corals	*Acropora* spp. visually dominant
		Sheet corals	*Agaricia* spp. visually dominant
		Ribbon and fire corals with green calcified algae	*Agaricia tenuifolia* visually dominant
		Montastraea reef	*Montastraea annularis* visually dominant
Algal dominated	>50% algal cover; 1% hard coral cover	Green algae	~3 gorgonians m^{-2}
		Fleshy brown algae and sparse gorgonians	Monospecific *Lobophora* beds
		Lobophora	Rare assemblage dominated by red algae with encrusting sponges
		Euchema and *Amphiroa*	
Bare substratum dominated	Dominated by bare substratum; <1% hard coral; low rugosity	Bedrock/rubble and dense gorgonians	>3 gorgonians m^{-2} (usually >8 m^{-2}) and ~30% algal cover
		Bedrock/rubble and sparse gorgonians	~3 gorgonians m^{-2} and little algal cover
		Rubble and sparse algae	No gorgonians
		Sand with sparse algae	>90% sand
		Mud	No gorgonians
		Bedrock	
Seagrass dominated	>10% seagrass cover; low rugosity	Sparse seagrass	Standing crop 1–10 g m^{-2}; cover <30%
		Medium density seagrass	Standing crop 11–80 g m^{-2}; cover 30 ± 70%
		Dense seagrass	Standing crop >80 g m^{-2}; cover >70%
		Seagrass with distinct coral patches	Seagrass visually dominant, coral cover may reach 3%, gorgonians may be present

Source: Modified from classification scheme developed by Mumby and Harborne (1999).

sensor (1-m pixels, ten spectral bands) to classify individual pixels as either live *Porites*, recently dead *Porites* (within last 6 months after a bleaching event), old-dead *Porites*, dead *Pocillopora, Halimeda* and *Hydrolithon onkodes* (Mumby *et al.*, 2001, 2004b). Although reef-scale estimates of coral cover were of a similar accuracy and precision to field survey, attempts to map coral cover must be repeated under a variety of physical and biological conditions to gauge the applicability of this result to other reefs.

Remote sensing of seagrass beds

Ecologists and managers of seagrass systems require a suite of data on the status of seagrass habitats (for an overview see Phillips and McRoy, 1990). Seagrass boundaries have been mapped extensively with aerial photography (Ferguson *et al.*, 1993; Sheppard *et al.*, 1995; Kirkman, 1996) and by showing the location and extent of seagrass habitat, they may indicate the health of coastal systems (Dennison *et al.*, 1993). Similarly, SPOT multispectral (20-m pixels, three bands) imagery has been used to highlight the seagrass die-off in Florida Bay (Robblee *et al.*, 1991). A more detailed study in the Bahamas obtained a quantitative empirical relationship between Landsat TM (30-m pixels, three bands) and seagrass biomass (Armstrong, 1993). Mumby *et al.* (1997) obtained similar quantitative relationships between seagrass standing crop and data from Landsat TM, SPOT XS and Compact Airborne Spectrographic Imager (CASI) (1-m pixels, six bands).

Remote sensing of mangroves

Mangroves often grow in dense stands and have complex aerial root systems which make extensive field sampling logistically difficult. Remote sensing offers a rapid and non-intrusive means of making large-scale measurements on a variety of mangrove parameters. Maps of mangrove have been used to plan aquaculture (Biña, 1982), assess deforestation rates (Ibrahim and Yosuh, 1992), examine mangrove zonation (Vibulsresth *et al.*, 1990) and predict the sensitivity of mangal to oil spills (Jensen *et al.*, 1991).

The simplest and most easily attainable mapping objective is locating mangrove versus non-mangrove systems. Both satellite and airborne methods appear to achieve this objective with reasonable accuracy. Segregating mangrove into its constituent assemblages is more problematic. In general, satellite sensors can discriminate mangrove zonation on the basis of tree height but not species composition (Gray *et al.*, 1990; Green *et al.*, 1998a). To discriminate and map more detailed zonation, aerial photography or multispectral airborne remote sensing is required. Green *et al.* (1998b) found that the airborne multispectral instrument CASI could distinguish the peripheral *Rhizophora* habitats that are functionally important as nurseries for many organisms (see 'Case study', p. 94).

To summarize, detailed habitat maps of the seascape can be created from airborne imagery. High-resolution satellite data such as Ikonos (4-m pixels, three spectral bands) can also be used for detailed habitat mapping but there is a greater requirement for extensive field survey in order to distinguish features on the image.

HABITAT-LEVEL SEGREGATION OF ECOSYSTEM PROCESSES

As the list of deleterious impacts to coral reefs grows ever larger, it is increasingly important to understand how reefs function at a range of spatial scales and how anthropogenic impacts affect ecosystem processes. Better understanding of processes will illuminate the consequences of disturbance both at the ecological scale and in changes to reef goods and services, such as coastal protection and fisheries productivity (Moberg and Folke, 1999).

In this section we briefly review six ecosystem processes and assess the 'functional value' of individual coastal habitats across the seascape. Functional value, as used here, indicates the relative importance of a given habitat to a particular process. For example, we document that a seagrass bed has a higher (more important) functional contribution to primary production than, say, a sand flat. Space limitations preclude a full review of processes (but see Harborne *et al.*, 2006) so our aim here is to highlight how diverse empirical studies can be integrated to the spatial pattern of processes across the seascape. We focus on the functional values of shallow (euphotic) habitats in Caribbean seascapes with additional information from the Indo-Pacific where necessary.

Wave energy dissipation

Waves and currents do not travel passively across a reef and are significantly modified by benthic habitats creating wave height and energy gradients (e.g. Sheppard, 1982, this volume; Sebens, 1997). Perhaps the most obvious example of energy dissipation across a reef is the creation of lagoons to the leeside of coral reefs that provide suitably calm conditions for seagrass beds and mangroves (e.g. Moberg and Rönnbäck, 2003). Lugo-Fernández *et al.* (1994) showed in Puerto Rico that the height of waves generated by both trade and local winds decreased as they travelled across the fore reef. The reduction of wave heights was 19.5% from a depth of 20 m to 10 m and 26% from 20 m to 5 m. There was a concomitant reduction in wave energy of 35% from 20 m to 10 m and 45% from 20 m to 5 m. Although wave energies are dissipated across the fore reef, there are limited data on the role of different habitats in wave energy dissipation. However, it is clear that spur and groove zones affect water movement significantly because strong on-shelf flow can be entrapped and advected up deep grooves at the shelf margin, and subsequently over the reef crest, and these areas typically have high levels of turbulence (Roberts *et al.*, 1977).

Water movement is altered significantly as it flows across the fore reef but the reef crest also has a vital role in the hydrodynamics of a reef ecosystem. For example, Suhayda and Roberts (1977) studied water movement across the reef crest and showed that wave height and period were typically reduced by approximately 50% and that this varied with water depth. Lugo-Fernández *et al.* (1994) have shown that wave heights decrease an average of 82% across the reef crest, with a simultaneous 97% energy loss. Lugo-Fernández *et al.* (1994) calculated that the transmission coefficients, which quantify the wave energy that crosses the reef crest, were 18% for trade-wind-generated waves and 39% for locally generated waves and, therefore, shorter waves transmit more energy. Suhayda and Roberts (1977) also highlighted that wave-driven currents flowed onshore continuously over the reef crest and had the greatest velocity at low tide when wave breaking was most intense.

Community primary productivity

Patterns of primary productivity vary significantly across habitats and depend on their community composition. Furthermore, there are overarching spatial controls on primary productivity, the most obvious of which is light availability (reviewed by Larkum, 1983; Hatcher, 1990). Gross primary productivity decreases with increasing depth on a fore reef as light and photosynthetic area decrease. However, the relationship between productivity and changing depth is complicated by photoadaption, grazing, self-shading, topographic complexity, stability of the reef surface and disturbance regimes (Barnes and Devereux, 1984; Hatcher, 1997b). Much of the research on primary productivity has focused on the coral–algal symbiosis to the detriment of work on algae, seagrass and phytoplankton. Filamentous (turf) algae are a particularly important component of the epilithic algal community because they exploit the high surface area that the complex topography of a reef provides (Littler and Littler, 1984; Hatcher, 1997b). Macroalgae are also important primary producers (e.g. Hillis-Colinvaux, 1980; Rogers and Salesky, 1981; Hatcher, 1988) and are particularly abundant when grazing pressure is reduced, such as in deeper water or following outbreaks of disease in herbivores (Lessios, 1988; Precht and Aronson, this volume).

Although algae are major primary producers on reefs, their contribution within lagoons can be significantly lower than rates reported for seagrasses, mangroves and benthic microalgae (e.g. Lewis, 1977; Bach, 1979). Indeed, mangrove forests and seagrass beds are among the world's most productive ecosystems (e.g. Odum, 1956; Lugo and Snedaker, 1974). Seagrass beds frequently contribute large portions of the primary production of coastal ecosystems (e.g. Thayer *et al.*, 1984; Fourqurean *et al.*, 1992). Mangrove primary production dominates mangal systems with leaf litter, reproductive propagules, twigs and dead trees being the major component of energy flow pathways (rather than direct herbivory). Algae and seagrass on and under the prop roots also contribute to the total primary production of mangal systems (Hogarth, 1999).

Differences in benthic community composition and their interactions with light, topography, grazers and water movement lead to areal primary productivity and community respiration varying predictably between habitats, sometimes by an order of magnitude (Hatcher, 1997b). The large number of studies dedicated to primary productivity on coral reefs has allowed a succession of authors to propose standard empirical values for coral reef zones. For example, Kinsey (1983) suggested that shallow unperturbed Pacific reef systems have four or five 'modes' of metabolic performance, particularly 'coral / algal', 'algal pavement' and 'sand / rubble'. The concept of modes of metabolic performance has been extended by Hatcher (1988, 1990) who presented a figure summarizing, from the available literature, primary productivity for entire reefs plus six reef zones and seven major benthic taxa contributing to reef productivity. Hatcher's work clearly shows variation between reef habitats and also demonstrates that the majority of productivity measurements have been made on reef flats.

Density of herbivores

Herbivory is a vital process in trophic energy flow on a coral reef (e.g. Lubchenco and Gaines, 1981). Differences in herbivore density among habitats are largely influenced by topography, proximity to nearby shelter, predator abundance, density of territorial competitors and local availability of food resources (Lewis and Wainwright, 1985). For fish, grazing is mainly inversely related to tidal exposure and wave action and positively correlated with the availability of shelter from predators (Hixon, 1997). Therefore, the density of herbivorous fish is highest on shallow, rugose sections of the reef and lowest in areas that are deep or topographically simple, or where water movement interferes with feeding (Hay, 1981). The fish taxa generally regarded as the most important of the Caribbean macroherbivore community are the parrotfish, surgeonfish (Acanthuridae) and damselfish (Pomacentridae) (e.g. Ogden, 1976). Parrotfish commonly predominate in slightly deeper areas (>5 m) than surgeonfish (e.g. Lewis and Wainwright, 1985) but most adult parrotfish decrease in density in the deeper reef habitats (Van Rooij *et al.*, 1996). Juveniles of many parrotfish and surgeonfish species commonly use specific nursery areas, particularly seagrass beds but also shallow reefal zones such as the back reef, patch reefs, reef crest and *Acropora cervicornis* zones (e.g. Nagelkerken *et al.*, 2000). Non-planktivorous damselfish defend small contiguous territories against intruding fish and the distinct biotic patches within damselfish territories are functionally different from benthic communities outside territories (e.g. Hay, 1985). Many damselfish habitat preferences are highly specific and general substratum complexity is a poor predictor of recruitment within a habitat (Booth and Beretta, 1994). For example, threespot damselfish *Stegastes planifrons* are most often associated with live and dead *A. cervicornis* (Itzkowitz, 1977).

Diadema antillarum is a key herbivore on reefs but populations were dramatically reduced in the early 1980s by a mass mortality caused by a water-borne pathogen (Lessios, 1988; Precht and Aronson, this volume) and much of the work on the ecology of *Diadema* pre-dates this event. Naturally, *Diadema* has intermediate abundances in very shallow water, because excessive wave action affects grazing rates (Foster, 1987). Densities are highest at 5–10 m and then decrease with increasing depth, and *Diadema* is effectively absent from below 20–25 m (e.g. Ogden and Lobel, 1978). Even at reduced densities, *Diadema* generally accentuates patterns of fish grazing. For example, Lewis and Wainwright (1985) and Littler *et al.* (1987) showed that the order of herbivory intensity, from lowest to highest rates, was seagrass bed (too shallow for fish, limited shelter), lower fore reef, outer ridge (both too deep for many herbivores), upper fore reef and then the rubble and carbonate pavement of the back reef (shallow with plenty of shelter and fast algal growth rates).

Herbivores have an important role in seagrass beds, despite their limited abundances. Thayer *et al.* (1984) state that although only a few species feed directly on living blades, larger herbivores can have a profound effect on the biogeochemical processes occurring within a seagrass meadow. For example, green turtles can affect nitrogen cycling in their grazing plots by reducing their capacity to trap and retain organic matter (reviewed by Thayer *et al.*, 1984).

Density of piscivores

Tertiary producers in a coral reef ecosystem encompass a wide range of taxa but here the discussion will be limited to piscivorous fishes. Piscivores are a diverse group that can comprise up to 53% of the species in an area (Hixon, 1991). Patterns of total piscivore density across a reef profile are difficult to find. Similarly, there has been little systematic work demonstrating absolute or relative predation rates across mangrove, lagoon and reef habitats. Even across the reef itself, such empirical data are scarce compared to the information available on herbivory and its consequent effects on algal zonation. However, the habitat preferences of individual species (e.g. Nassau grouper, *Epinephelus striatus*) are relatively well established, often because of their commercial importance.

Work by Eggleston (1995) showed that recently settled Nassau groupers have a disproportionately high association with coral clumps (especially *Porites* spp.) which are covered by macroalgae (especially *Laurencia*) in off-reef tidal creek systems and lagoons. Larger juveniles tend to reside outside or adjacent to algal-covered coral clumps and, like smaller juveniles, are mostly solitary (Eggleston, 1995). When juvenile *E. striatus* are large enough (typically 120–150 mm) they tend to exhibit an ontogenetic habitat shift from patches of macroalgal and *Porites* spp. to patch reef habitats (Eggleston, 1995). On patch reefs, *E. striatus* (like all serranids) exhibit high site fidelity to territories (e.g. Eggleston *et al.*, 1997). It has long been recognized that groupers move into deeper water as they mature and adult *E. striatus* are widely dispersed on coral-rich fore reefs (e.g. Bardach, 1958). Adults are highly sedentary living among the benthic community in holes, caves and crevices (Eggleston, 1995; Chiappone *et al.*, 2000) and densities are commonly linked to high or moderate topographical relief (e.g. Sluka and Sullivan, 1996). Reproductively active *E. striatus* have further specific habitat requirements for transient mass spawning events but these are poorly understood. Mass spawning sites have commonly been seen near continental shelf breaks or the edges of insular shelves (Domeier and Colin, 1997).

Adult snappers generally have a weaker habitat dependence than serranids because they lead less sedentary lives and are less reliant on an ambush strategy (Parrish, 1987). Ontogenetic shifts in snapper habitat use are often similar to those of grunts, which are described in the case study below (see pp. 94–101).

Community calcification rates

Biological calcium carbonate production, calcification, is dominated by contributions from corals, coralline red algae and calcareous green algae (Smith, 1983). Depth, light, turbidity and sedimentation rate are major controls of coral growth and calcification rates (Hubbard and Scaturo, 1985). Depth (light) is particularly important because coral calcification and primary productivity are positively correlated (Gattuso *et al.*, 1999) and coral growth rates (and primary productivity) generally decline with increasing depth. However, the relationship between depth and growth rate is rarely linear and generally within the upper 10–15 m of a reef, growth depends on the species present and other local environmental factors rather than absolute depth. Below 10–15 m, growth rate generally declines dramatically and monotonically with increasing depth (Buddemeier and Kinzie, 1976). Similarly to corals, there is significant inter- and intraspecific variation in calcification rates of algae but rates are generally higher for the aragonite-depositing green and brown algae than those for calcite-depositing coralline reds (Borowitzka, 1983). There seems little systematic research focusing on spatial changes in algal calcification rates but Steneck (1997) has shown that red coralline algal biomass is highest in the turbulent shallows and lowest at 40 m. In contrast, calcifying green and brown algae are most common in habitats with light grazing pressure, a pattern that has been significantly altered by over-fishing, the mass mortality of *Diadema* and anthropogenic nutrient inputs. The increase of macroalgal biomass on Caribbean reefs has affected the distribution of calcareous plants, which are now found in almost every habitat type (Hughes, 1994).

Community calcification rates are highest in shallow (<10 m) areas (Smith and Buddemeier, 1992). Within shallow zones, calcification is highest for areas of continuous coral, lower for algal pavement and lowest for sand and rubble (Done *et al.*, 1996; Gattuso *et al.*, 1998). From a literature review, Smith and Kinsey (1976) proposed two common calcification rates for shallow reef communities: 4 kg $CaCO_3$ m^{-2} yr^{-1} for seaward areas and 0.8 kg $CaCO_3$ m^{-2} yr^{-1} for protected areas because of variations in water motion. They suggested that the 'standard' rates are insensitive to coral versus coralline algal dominance. Smith (1983) suggested that 90–95% of coral reef areas calcifies at the lower rate and 5–10% calcifies at the higher rate and extended the concept by introducing a higher rate of 10 kg $CaCO_3$ m^{-2} yr^{-1}. Most of the data summarized by Smith and Kinsey (1976) were from Pacific reefs but data have been published for a range of Caribbean habitats by, for example, Chave *et al.* (1972) in Barbados. Chave *et al.* (1972) generated theoretical data for shallow sand flats (0.4 kg $CaCO_3$ m^{-2} yr^{-1}), coral mounds on sand (10 kg), algal ridges (9 kg) and complete coral coverage on outer slopes (60 kg). In a regional assessment of fore reef carbonate production since Caribbean benthic community phase shifts, Vecsei (2001) gave a value for very shallow fore reefs with dense ramose coral framework of approximately 10 kg $CaCO_3$ m^{-2} yr^{-1}. Furthermore, Vecsei (2001) showed that production rates decrease exponentially with depth. For framework reefs values were 10.1–17.3 kg $CaCO_3$ m^{-2} yr^{-1} at 0–10 m, 4.5–8.1 kg at 10–20 m and 0.8–3.0 kg at 30–40 m. The new 'Submersible Habitat for Analysing Reef Quality' (SHARQ), developed by Yates and Halley (2003), is an excellent tool for assessing community calcification (and dissolution) rates in a range of habitats. Existing data using SHARQ have studied daily community calcification rates in Florida and compared patch reefs, dense and sparse seagrass beds and a sand area (Yates and Halley, 2003). Net calcification, averaged across a series of samples, was highest on patch reefs (1.14 g $CaCO_3$ m^{-2}) and lowest in dense seagrass beds (0.25 g $CaCO_3$ m^{-2}). Calcification rates in sparse seagrass beds and on a single sandy area were approximately equivalent (0.44 and 0.41 g $CaCO_3$ m^{-2} respectively).

Density of bioeroders

The process of bioerosion creates a proportion of the carbonate sediments that fill interstitial framework spaces during reef accretion. Although the effect of bioerosion varies significantly in space, Fagerstrom (1987) suggests that the contribution of bioerosion to sediment production equals that of physical abrasion. The taxonomic composition of bioeroders is reviewed by Risk and MacGeachy (1978) and Glynn (1997). Perry (1998b) provides a comprehensive assessment of invertebrate macroboring communities across a Caribbean reef, revealing the magnitude of framework removal. Working in Jamaica, Perry (1998b) showed that sponges were the dominant macroborers on fore reef sites while sipunculans and polychaetes were only important at back reef, lagoon and shallow fore reef sites. Bivalves were important within back reef and lagoon patch reef habitats. Overall, macroboring was highest in the back reef and deep (>20 m) fore reef habitats. In addition to boring species, a major component of bioerosion in most habitats is grazing by herbivorous fish and urchins (Bruggemann *et al.*, 1996). For example, the rate of bioerosion by herbivorous fish is highest in the shallows and decreases with depth (Bruggemann *et al.*, 1996). Even after its mass mortality, *Diadema* remains a significant source of bioerosion on shallow Jamaican fore reefs (Perry, 1999). Herbivorous fish, particularly parrotfish and surgeonfish, may be less significant bioeroders than *Diadema*, although post-mortality data are scarce, but they are wider ranging and a geologically significant agent in the transformation of reefs into sediment (Gygi, 1975; Ogden, 1977).

Microborers (e.g. cyanobacteria, chlorophytes, rhodophytes and fungi) are an important component of the bioeroding community and, being largely photosynthetic, their distribution across the reef is linked to light levels. In Belize, May *et al.* (1982) documented endolithic microorganisms in mounted carbonate fragments along a reef transect. Analysis showed two assemblages; the upper photic zone (less than 12 m) was dominated by cyanophytes and chlorophytes and the lower photic zone was characterized by rhodophytes. There was some evidence that the unidentified subsurface microborers in the shallow lagoon were fungi and bacteria. Perry (1998a) also showed that in Jamaican sediments there were two distinct microboring communities associated with the transition from upper to lower photic zone. In water shallower than 18 m the sediments were dominated by cyanobacteria and chlorophytes; in contrast below a depth of 18 m rhodophytes and fungi were most abundant. In more turbid water with greater rates of light attenuation, the community shift may occur at 5–10 m (Perry and Macdonald, 2002). The highest infestation of carbonate grains by microborers was in low-energy back reef habitats (Perry, 1998a).

Functional values of habitats within coral reef seascapes

Many studies of coral reefs are confined to benign environments and our understanding of many processes is therefore incomplete at a seascape scale. However, the previous sections have attempted to summarise the disparate and extensive literature of functional values for typical Caribbean habitat types. To clarify these patterns, we categorize each of the six processes into four broad categories ('none', 'low', 'medium' or 'high') for different habitat types and plot these across a schematic reef profile (Fig. 3.2).

Inevitably, a series of caveats are required when assessing Fig. 3.2. For example, there are few empirical data on how functional values change when environmental parameters are altered by natural or anthropogenic influences (e.g. increased turbidity). Furthermore, many studies pre-date significant changes to Caribbean coral reefs such as the reductions of *Diadema antillarum* and acroporids throughout much of the region (e.g. Aronson and Precht, 2001; Precht and Aronson, this volume). Such changes will have profound effects on processes such as biological

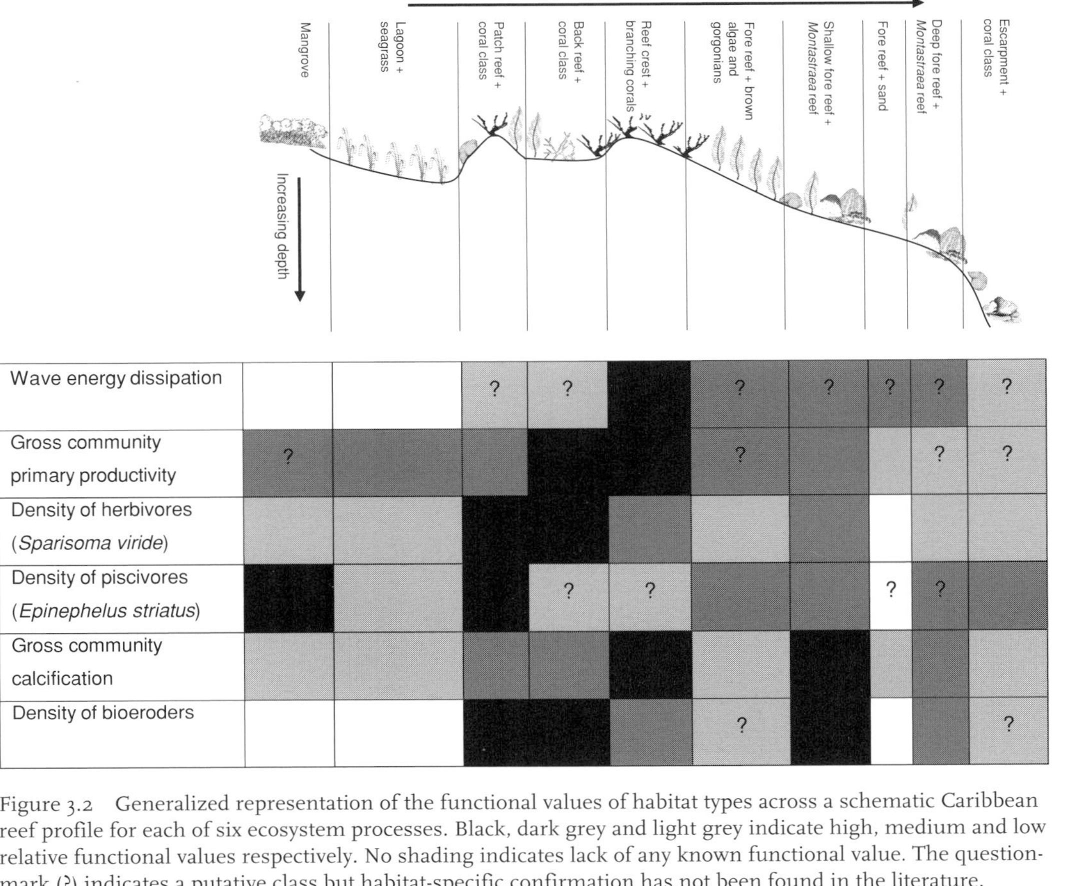

Figure 3.2 Generalized representation of the functional values of habitat types across a schematic Caribbean reef profile for each of six ecosystem processes. Black, dark grey and light grey indicate high, medium and low relative functional values respectively. No shading indicates lack of any known functional value. The question-mark (?) indicates a putative class but habitat-specific confirmation has not been found in the literature.

production, biogeochemical cycling and accretion, and further empirical work may be required on these 'modified' habitats to assess their current functional values.

Combining functional values (Fig. 3.2) with remotely sensed imagery will allow the translation of habitat maps into maps of ecosystem processes. Although these static 'process maps' have disadvantages compared to more dynamic modelling approaches (discussed below) they are relatively simple to generate and may facilitate insight into ecological and management questions. For example, layers representing calcification, bioerosion and sediment production, and settlement could be linked with bathymetry to model reef growth under different scenarios of sea-level change.

It is also possible to gain some insight into overall functional roles of habitats by converting functional values to ordinal values and generating an ordination using non-metric multidimensional scaling (Fig. 3.3) (see Clarke, 1993 for more details on methods). Perhaps the most conspicuous feature of this ordination is the spread of habitats, despite the limited number of processes considered, indicating that each habitat has a relatively unique set of functional values. Incorporating other processes into the analysis will provide further insights into the functioning of tropical marine habitats and facilitate the identification of suites of key habitats for conserving particular ecosystem goods and services.

CONNECTIVITY AMONG HABITATS: CASE STUDY OF MANGROVES, SEAGRASS BEDS, PATCH REEFS AND FORE REEFS

Mangrove forests are one of the world's most threatened tropical ecosystems with global loss exceeding 35% within the last two decades (Valiela *et al.*, 2001). Juvenile coral reef fishes often inhabit mangroves (Rooker and Dennis, 1991; Claro and Garcia-Arteaga, 1993; Ley *et al.*, 1999; Nagelkerken *et al.*, 2001) but the importance of these nurseries to reef fish has only recently been investigated and may differ between the Indo-Pacific and Atlantic.

A recent study from the western Caribbean found surprising impacts of mangroves on adult reef fish (Mumby *et al.*, 2004a). Using a comparative approach involving four atolls and the Belize Barrier Reef, the study used Landsat TM satellite imagery to categorize the availability of mangroves into two levels: scarce (<5 km of mangrove perimeter per 200 km^2 area) and rich (>70 km mangrove perimeter per 200 km^2). The mangrove nursery habitat

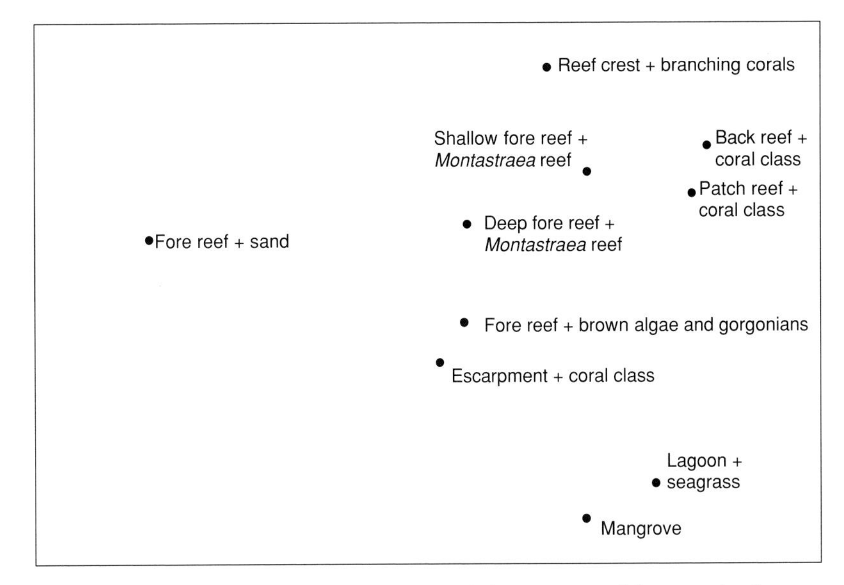

Figure 3.3 Ordination of the standard ten habitats assigned functional values within each section of this chapter. Variables used were those represented in Fig. 3.2. Each variable was converted to an ordinal value (no function value = 0; low functional value = 1; medium = 2; high = 3). In mutidimensional scaling ordination, the distance between the data points is related to how similar the suites of characteristics describing each point are; thus, patch reef and back reef share very similar functional values for the six ecosystem processes considered, and both are more similar (i.e. closer) to *Montastraea* (deep) than to either seagrass or sand. The relatively low stress indicates that the two-dimensional distances depicted here are a good representation of the multidimensional similarity in functional values between habitats.

was dominated by red mangrove *Rhizophora mangle*, which has prop roots permanently inundated even at low tide. Mangroves were found within 10 km of the reef habitat and connected by shallow seagrass beds and patch reefs. The study had three principal conclusions.

First, only one reef fish species appears to have a strong functional dependency on mangroves as a nursery habitat: the rainbow parrotfish (*Scarus guacamaia*). This is the largest herbivorous marine fish in the Atlantic (Randall, 1967), reaching 1.2 m in length, and is listed as vulnerable on the IUCN *Red List of Threatened Species* (IUCN, 2002). Juveniles of the species were only ever observed in mangroves and adults were only found on reefs with fairly extensive mangrove nurseries. Such functional dependency means that *S. guacamaia* is vulnerable to local extinction from habitat

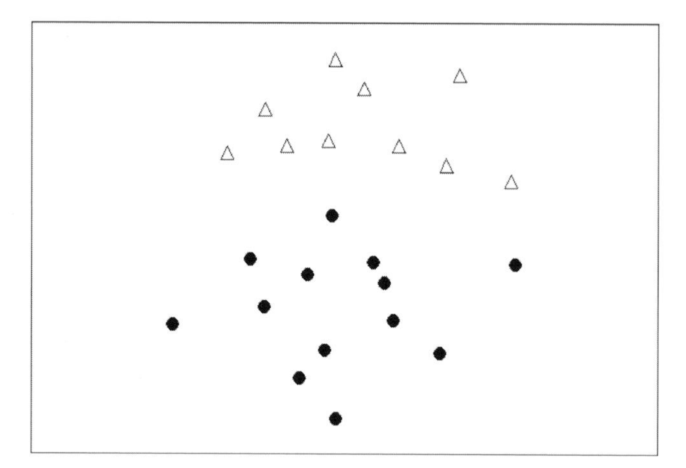

Figure 3.4 Ordination of reef fish community structure across six atoll and barrier reef systems of Belize and Mexico. Open triangles denote sites with rich mangroves whereas full circles denote sites with scarce mangrove resources. See Fig. 3.3 for a note on the interpretation of ordination figures.

loss as well as over-fishing. Indeed, anecdotal information from Glover's Reef (D. Wesby, pers. comm.) suggests that *S. guacamaia* has undergone local extinction in the last 30 years. Schools of this parrotfish were commonly observed in the 1960s when several of the islands had well-developed mangrove habitats. All functional mangrove was cleared at this site in the late 1960s and early 1970s, and in the mid to late 1970s *S. guacamaia* was heavily fished. The parrotfish is no longer fished and has either recovered or survived at low densities at mangrove-rich sites. Its extinction at Glover's Reef seems most likely due to the removal of its nursery habitat. Loss of a single adult *S. guacamaia* would constitute a 10% reduction in total parrotfish biomass within its territory. Therefore, a combination of mangrove deforestation and fishing can significantly reduce the total level of grazing in shallow reef environments.

Second, whilst the presence of most fish species does not depend on the extent of mangroves near coral reefs, mangroves can strongly influence the community structure of fish assemblages (Fig. 3.4). Even those species which never use mangrove nurseries can be influenced indirectly because many interact with species that benefit directly from mangroves. Using a multivariate version of analysis of variance (ANOVA) (namely ANOSIM: see Clarke, 1993), the study found that patterns of community structure of reef-obligate fish species were more strongly related to mangrove extent ($R = 0.59$, $p < 0.05$) than they were to differences among atolls in general

($R = 0.49$, $p < 0.01$). An implication of this observation is that studies of the ecology and population dynamics of reef-obligate species should bear in mind the wider seascape configuration of the study site. For example, the presence of extensive mangrove nurseries could be added as a binary covariate in studies of fish density across reef habitats.

The third, and possibly most striking, conclusion of the study was that the standing crop of fishes that use mangrove nurseries was often considerably greater when a reef habitat was connected to mangroves. For example, the biomass of bluestriped grunt (*Haemulon sciurus*) was over 2000% greater on patch reefs, 650% greater on shallow fore reefs and 55% greater on outer *Montastraea* reefs (depth ~10 m) in mangrove-rich systems (Table 3.3). Other species of snappers, grunts and parrotfish also benefited positively from mangrove extent (Table 3.3). A number of these species (e.g. yellowtail snapper *Ocyurus chrysurus* and schoolmaster *Lutjanus apodus*) are commercially important, which means that mangrove nurseries may enhance the production of a fishery.

Mangroves may enhance adult fish biomass in two ways. First, efflux of detritus and nutrients may enrich primary production in neighbouring ecosystems but this hypothesis is not well supported (Ogden, 1997). Second, mangrove nurseries may provide a refuge from predators and/or plentiful food which increases the survivorship of juveniles (Laegdsgaard and Johnson, 2001). The study in Belize provided data that were consistent with the latter hypothesis. For example, the size–frequency distribution of bluestriped grunt *H. sciurus* suggests an ontogenetic shift in habitat use from seagrass to mangroves to patch reefs and finally fore reefs, their main adult habitat (Fig. 3.5). The resulting 'intermediate nursery habitat' hypothesis is outlined below and in Fig. 3.6.

Figure 3.6 stylizes the bluestriped grunt and rainbow parrotfish at various stages of development (A–G). Various workers have hypothesized that ontogenetic migrations may reflect either (1) a need for different food sources (Parrish and Zimmerman, 1977) as fish grow, (2) that larger fish outgrow the shelter offered by nursery habitats (Shulman, 1985; Rooker and Dennis, 1991) or (3) that greater access to ocean currents helps to disperse larvae after reproduction (de la Morinière, 2002). Many species, including bluestriped grunt, inhabit seagrasses (A) before moving to mangroves once they reach a larger size of around 6 cm in total length (see also McFarland, 1979; McFarland *et al.*, 1985). Once in mangroves (B), studies of diet suggest that many fishes continue to feed nocturnally in the seagrass. Workers in Curaçao found that 63.5% of the stomach contents of juvenile bluestriped grunt comprised crustaceans (Order Tanaidacea) which were mainly found

Table 3.3. Impact of mangrove extent on the biomass of fish in patch reef, shallow fore reef, and *Montastraea* reef habitats in Belize; mean biomass (kg km^{-2}) with standard error in parentheses

	Patch reef				Shallow fore reef				*Montastraea* reef			
Species	Scarce mangrove	Rich mangrove	Significant factor	Biomass increase	Scarce mangrove	Rich mangrove	Significant factor	Biomass increase	Scarce mangrove	Rich mangrove	Significant factor	Biomass increase
Striped parrotfish *Scarus iserti*	–	–	–		–	–	–		1 530 (118)	2 170 (111)	M/	42%
Bluestriped grunt *Haemulon sciurus*	1 205 (329)	33 349 (9 274)	M	2 667%	56 (38)	425 (120)	M	659%	288 (53)	447 (55)	M, R	55%
French grunt *H. flavolineatum*	5 256 (1460)	15 307 (4114)	M, R	191%	516 (101)	1 600 (249)	M	210%	1 398 (149)	1 643 (139)	ns	
White grunt *H. plumieri*	5 174 (1614)	16 280 (3591)	M	214%	317 (72)	843 (304)	M	165%	523 (62)	863 (69)	M	65%
Grunts (all)	11 636 (2089)	67 370 (12971)	M, R	478%	889 (152)	3 031 (497)	M	240%	2 288 (188)	3 210 (192)	M, R, S/	40%
Yellowtail snapper *Ocyurus chrysurus*	769 (441)	410 (95)	R*		659 (150)	892 (187)	ns		3 098 (486)	6 715 (1 323)	M, S/	116%
Schoolmaster *Lutjanus apodus*	739 (354)	6 192 (1566)	M	737%	622 (336)	2 392 (722)	M	284%	1 767 (226)	1 898 (259)	S/	
Snappers (all)	2 890 (1228)	16 707 (4805)	M	478%	1882 (745)	4428 (1055)	M	135%	5 883 (796)	12 223 (1503)	M, S	107%

Notes: The importance of mangroves and reef system in explaining patterns of biomass was tested using nested General Linear Model ANOVA. Data were transformed using the Box–Cox method but on one occasion (*), the fit was poor ($p > 0.02$) and the significance of mangroves could not be tested. Significant ($p < 0.05$) factors are M (mangrove), R (reef system) and S (site). Site was only entered into a few tests (denoted /) because site-level data (individual transects) often had to be pooled to increase sample size. Where mangroves exerted significant influence, the increase in mean biomass is expressed as a percentage of the level in mangrove-scarce systems. Patch reef area was entered as a covariate for patch reefs but the slopes did not differ from zero (the test was not significant, ns). *Scarus iserti* was not surveyed on patch reefs or shallow fore reefs. (all) denotes all species in family, not just those in table. Neither the biomass nor density of species in seagrass beds differed significantly between mangrove-rich and mangrove-scaree sites.

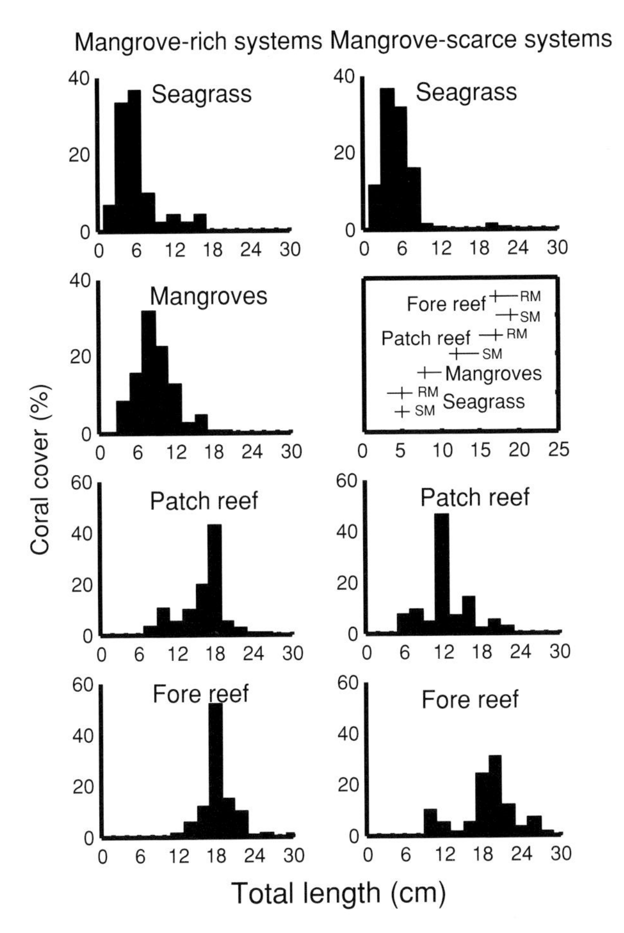

Figure 3.5 Ontogenetic patterns of habitat use in bluestriped grunt *Haemulon sciurus*. Shifts in median length between seagrass, mangrove, patch reef and fore reef are all significant within each system (Kruskal–Wallis test with Mann–Whitney comparisons among medians, $p < 0.0002$). Inter-system comparisons reveal that median lengths and densities between seagrass systems do not differ significantly (Mann–Whitney tests, $p > 0.05$) whereas lengths on patch reefs are significantly greater in mangrove-rich systems ($p < 0.05$). Data are pooled from all systems within each mangrove category. Inset figure shows median and inter-quartile size range of *H. sciurus* and demonstrates that the gap in median fish length between seagrass and patch reefs is greater in systems with rich mangrove (RM) than scarce mangrove (SM).

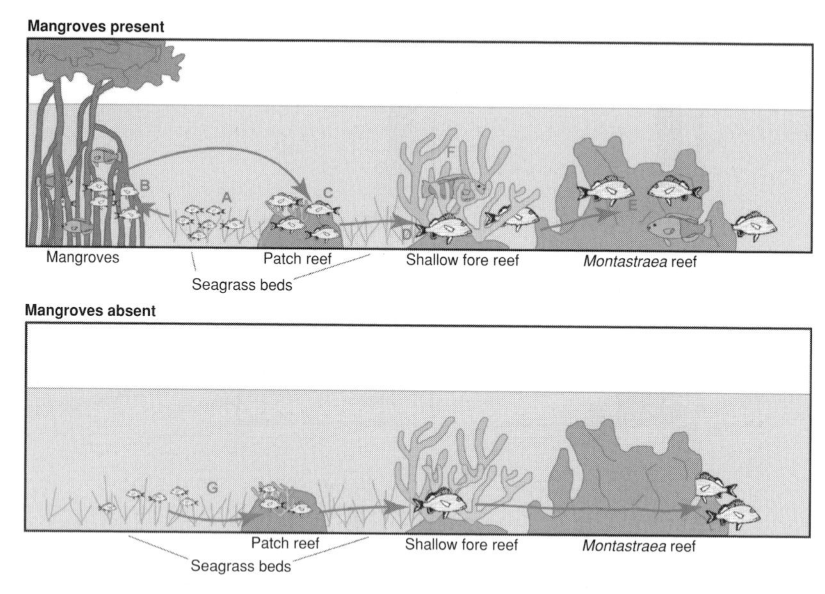

Figure 3.6 Schematic diagram showing ontogenetic shifts in habitat for reef fish.

in the zooplankton and sediment of seagrass beds rather than mangroves (de la Morinère *et al.*, 2003). Mangroves serve as an intermediate nursery habitat before the fish migrate to patch reefs (C). The benefits accrued from mangroves probably involve a refuge from predators and/or plentiful food which increases the survivorship of juveniles (Laegdsgaard and Johnson, 2001). If mangrove is not present, bluestriped grunt move directly from seagrass to patch reefs, appearing on patch reefs (G) at a smaller size and at lower density (260 ha^{-1} compared to 3925 ha^{-1} in mangrove-rich systems). Since the biomass of predators is often greater on reefs than in mangroves (30 t km^{-2} versus 18 t km^{-2}), the chances of grunt survival may be lower if migrating directly to reefs. In the presence of mangroves, the biomass of bluestriped grunt is significantly enhanced on patch reefs, shallow fore reefs and *Montastraea* reefs (C, D, E). Rainbow parrotfish (F) has a functional dependency on mangroves and is rarely seen where mangroves are absent.

Studies in the Indo-Pacific (Birkeland and Amesbury, 1988) found positive impacts of nurseries on the number of juvenile fishes but not on adult fish. This may not be surprising given that adult fish populations are regulated by other factors including larval supply, predation and fishing (Caley *et al.*, 1996). Moreover, fluctuations of tidal height are generally greater in the Indo-Pacific than in the Atlantic, and therefore the mangrove prop-root environment will tend to be ephemeral and possibly of lower overall value than it is in the Caribbean. Nonetheless, the main implication of this study is that corridors of connected habitats should be protected explicitly (see also Roberts *et al.*, this volume).

A RESEARCH AGENDA FOR CONSERVATION SCIENCE AT THE SEASCAPE SCALE

Developments in remote sensing have largely removed the difficulty in describing the structure of coral reef seascapes. Whilst habitat maps of coral reefs are now widely available, their use for coastal management continues to be limited. This is not a criticism of the managers, but a reflection of the scarcity of process-level information necessary to interpret such maps. Interpretation is intrinsically linked to having models that make use of spatial information and allow managers to predict the impact of various management options on the system (e.g. Borsuk *et al.*, 2004; Wooldridge and Done, 2004). We close the chapter by considering the integration of information on pattern and process and the inevitable need for further research.

New research into seascape-level phenomena

Most studies of inter-habitat processes have addressed nutrient transport (Weibe, 1987), diurnal migrations (Ogden and Buckman, 1973; Burke, 1995) or ontogenetic shifts in habitat use (Appeldoorn *et al.*, 1997; Lindeman *et al.*, 1998; Nagelkerken and van der Velde, 2002). These studies have documented important phenomena and we believe that the availability of accurate habitat maps, advanced chemical tracers (Swearer *et al.*, 1999) and tagging methods (Walsh and Winkelman, 2004) will pave the way for better quantitative information in future. Quantitative process-level understanding is critical if we are to translate empirical studies into dynamic models and algorithms that can be applied to real seascapes. For example, the case study described earlier on mangrove nurseries (Mumby *et al.*, 2004a) does not identify (1) the distance over which fishes will migrate from mangroves to coral reefs, (2) whether particular habitats or physical environments (e.g. deep channels) serve as barriers to migration, or (3) quantitative mortality and colonization rates of fishes per habitat. All three types of information would be required to provide a powerful and flexible model of the system.

The sheer scale of seascape-level studies presents a formidable challenge to empiricists. Experimental manipulations are almost impossible at these scales and studies often have to take a comparative and inductive approach (Petraitis and Latham, 1999). It is clearly important, therefore, to use an appropriate study design that attempts to distinguish *all plausible hypotheses*, not just the ecologist's favourite! Moreover, novel statistical approaches, such as the use of epidemiological causal criteria (Fabricius and De'Ath, 2004), are likely to be required to distinguish competing hypotheses.

Seascape-level models

The modelling of coral reef ecosystems is gaining momentum (Atkinson and Grigg, 1984; Preece and Johnson, 1993; McClanahan, 1995; Opitz, 1996; Kleypas *et al.*, 1999; Langmead and Sheppard, 2004; Wolanski *et al.*, 2004; Wooldridge and Done, 2004; Mumby and Dytham, 2006). With the exception of Wolanski *et al.* (2004), none of these can be considered seascape models; most focus on a specific habitat within an ecosystem. Given the patchiness in our habitat-level understanding of process (see pp. 85–94), it remains a considerable challenge to create meaningful models of individual reef habitats. However, habitat-level models still provide useful insight into the management of marine resources, particularly when the habitat being modelled is widely used for extractive activities. For example, McClanahan (1995) used an energy-based model to examine fishing strategies in Kenya and was able to compare the expected ecological and catch outcomes when targeting piscivores, herbivores or invertivores. A key recommendation was to protect keystone invertivores (the triggerfish *Balistaphus* and *Balistes*) as their exploitation would lead to increases in sea urchin densities and competitive exclusion of herbivorous fish (see McClanahan, this volume). Similarly, Mumby (2006) used a spatial simulation model to explore the sensitivity of *Montastraea* reefs to the exploitation of parrotfishes. In the absence of the sea urchin *Diadema antillarum* (Lessios *et al.*, 1984), Caribbean fore reefs are largely dependent on parrotfishes to control the cover of macroalgae. Even relatively minor depletions of grazers can reduce the resilience of these reefs, leading to a reduction in coral cover (Fig. 3.7), which if left unresolved, will cause a decline in the structural complexity and quality of the habitat (Glynn, 1997). The main conclusion was that parrotfish exploitation should be regulated throughout the reef system, not just within no-take marine reserves.

Extending individual-habitat models to seascape scales will reveal potentially surprising, but important phenomena. More importantly, seascape-level models are more likely to become decision-support tools because

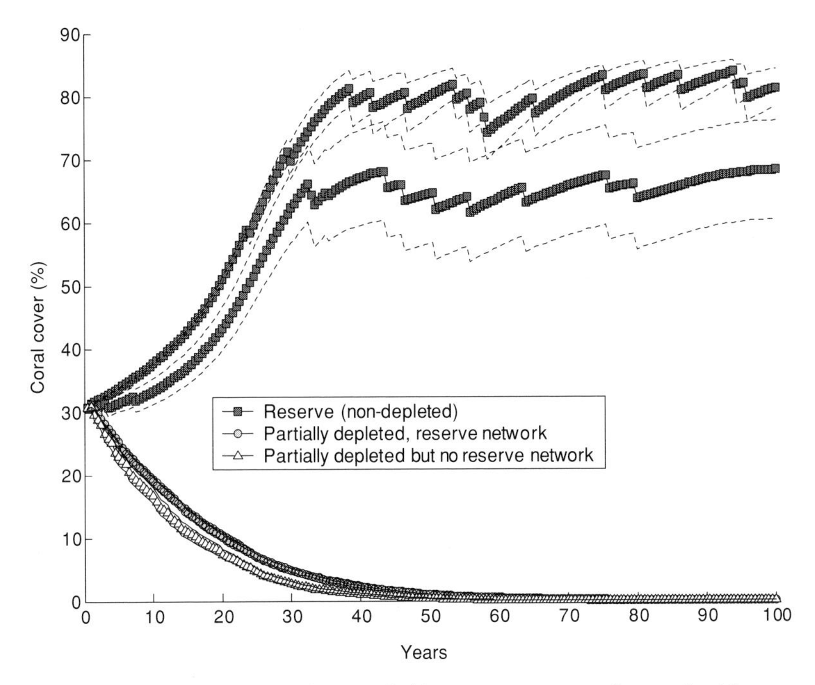

Figure 3.7 Effects on coral cover of adding a reserve network to reefs with partially depleted parrotfishes. Grazers are not depleted in reserves (two connected reefs shown in black). Hurricanes occur at an average interval of 40 years. Reefs are connected using a stock-recruitment relationship. Dashed lines represent standard error from 10 simulations. From Mumby (2006).

they must, by definition, embody suitably large spatial scales, such as entire catchments. Reconciling the competing needs of multiple users at these scales is the very essence of coastal management (Brown, this volume). Some fisheries stock-production models consider ontogenetic shifts in habitat use (e.g. Ault *et al.*, 1999). It would be useful to extend this perspective to other ecosystem processes. For example, a model of coral–algal–grazer disturbances in *Montastraea* reefs (Mumby, 2006) could be coupled to the management of mangroves because of the shared link of grazing parrotfishes that use mangroves as nurseries (see 'Case study', p. 94). In this case, the process of grazing on coral reefs could be modelled at seascape scales, revealing indirect links between mangrove deforestation and, say, the resilience of coral reefs.

Algorithms for conservation planning

Whilst decision-support tools can be driven directly from ecosystem models, many advances in ecological understanding are implemented through algorithms. For example, there are dozens of algorithms to quantify measures of patchiness, connectivity and fragmentation among habitats in a landscape (Farina, 1998). Similarly, several sophisticated algorithms exist to optimize the inclusion of sites within reserve networks based on management targets and given opportunity costs (Possingham *et al.*, 2000). The problem occurs in making such algorithms relevant to the ecosystem.

Few coral reef studies have quantified the degree to which habitats serve as a proxy of diversity or community structure across a range of spatial or temporal scales (but see Ward *et al.*, 1999; Friedlander *et al.*, 2003). Not surprisingly, then, it is difficult to predict how changes in habitat area, patch size or spatial context within the seascape will impact populations or communities of organisms. Recently, however, a few studies have begun using landscape patch metrics to assess the composition of communities within seagrass beds (e.g. Pittman *et al.*, 2004). These sorts of studies will be pivotal in linking monitoring data from remote sensing to either biodiversity or process-level impacts on the ground. For example, at what point does fragmentation of a seagrass bed influence the composition and persistence of organisms within it? What are the implications of changes in community structure for ecosystem functioning? How does this relationship change in other physical environments? Can we infer the present level of stress on the ecosystem from its spatial composition?

A widely used premise for conservation planning is the inclusion of representative habitats (McNeill, 1994). Managers can then use optimization tools to identify a set of reserves that minimize the cost of assigning a certain level of protection to each habitat (Possingham *et al.*, 2000). However, what criteria should be used? Are all habitats equally important? Should some habitats be considered more important, or requiring a larger degree of protection, than others? To what extent should particular habitats be selected in groups or corridors? Answers to these questions require all the steps outlined in this chapter, namely, (1) an appreciation for the degree to which habitats serve as proxies of biodiversity, (2) models that identify the resilience of individual habitats to anticipated sources of stress (e.g. coral bleaching), both with and without management, and (3) seascape models that modify the predictions of (2) given a particular seascape configuration.

In summary, we have set out a challenging research agenda for an improved 'seascape ecology' of coral reefs. Although the benefits of such research are clear in improving spatial decision-making, we also believe a top–down approach to the science is warranted. That is, we should begin by consolidating our present understanding in simple models that may require many assumptions and improve the models as fresh insight into the mechanisms and scales of seascape processes become available. Finally, it is vital that the certainty we have in such models is made explicit so that users are fully aware of the models' capability.

CONCLUSIONS

Seascape-level studies of coral reefs are gaining momentum, partly because of unprecedented access to remotely sensed data and new tools for tracking the dispersal and migration of organisms. In general, understanding of ecosystem processes is biased towards benign habitats and greater research effort is needed in fore reef environments. Where appropriate, ecosystem models should incorporate processes at seascape scales. To achieve this, ecological studies should focus on rates rather than static variables, and attempt to quantify the area, quality and connectivity among habitats. Seascape-level models will underpin future decision-support tools and help guide the development of meaningful algorithms for selecting sites for management activities.

ACKNOWLEDGEMENTS

We thank the National Science Foundation (OCE-0119976) Biocomplexity Grant and the Royal Society for funding.

REFERENCES

Ahmad, W. and Neil, D. T. (1994). An evaluation of Landsat Thematic Mapper (TM) digital data for discriminating coral reef zonation: Heron Reef (GBR). *International Journal of Remote Sensing*, **15**, 2583–97.

Andréfouët, S., Mumby, P. J., McField, M., Hu, C. and Muller-Karger, F. E. (2002). Revisiting coral reef connectivity. *Coral Reefs*, **21**, 43–8.

Appeldoorn, R. S., Recksiek, C. W., Hill, R. L., Pagan, F. E. and Dennis, G. D. (1997). Marine protected areas and reef fish movements: the role of habitat in controlling ontogenetic migration. *Proceedings 8th International Coral Reef Symposium*, **2**, 1917–22.

Armstrong, R. A. (1993). Remote sensing of submerged vegetation canopies for biomass estimation. *International Journal of Remote Sensing*, **14**, 621–7.

Aronson, R. B. and Precht, W. F. (2001). White-band disease and the changing face of Caribbean coral reefs. *Hydrobiologia*, **460**, 25–38.

Atkinson, M. J. and Grigg, R. W. (1984). Model of a coral reef ecosystem. II. Gross and net benthic primary production at French frigate shoals, Hawaii. *Coral Reefs*, **3**, 13–22.

Ault, J. S., Luo, J. G., Smith, S. G. *et al.* (1999). A spatial dynamic multistock production model. *Canadian Journal of Fisheries and Aquatic Sciences*, **56**, 4–25.

Bach, S. D. (1979). Standing crop, growth and production of calcareous siphonales (Chlorophyta) in a south Florida lagoon. *Bulletin of Marine Science*, **29**, 191–201.

Bainbridge, S. J. and Reichelt, R. E. (1989). An assessment of ground truth methods for coral reef remote sensing data. *Proceedings 6th International Coral Reef Symposium*, **2**, 439–44.

Bardach, J. E. (1958). On the movements of certain Bermuda reef fishes. *Ecology*, **39**, 139–46.

Barnes, D. J. and Devereux, M. J. (1984). Productivity and calcification on a coral reef: a survey using ph and oxygen electrode techniques. *Journal of Experimental Marine Biology and Ecology*, **79**, 213–31.

Biña, R. T. (1982). Application of Landsat data to coral reef management in the Philippines, In *Great Barrier Reef Remote Sensing Workshop*, vol. 1, ed. D. Hopley, pp. 1–39. Townsville, QLD: James Cook University.

Birkeland, C. and Amesbury, S. S. (1988). Fish-transect surveys to determine the influences of neighboring habitats on fish community structure in the tropical pacific. In *Regional Co-operation on Environmental Protection of the Marine and Coastal Areas of the Pacific*, UNEP Regional Seas Reports and Studies No. 97, ed. A. L. Dahl, pp. 195–202. Paris: UNEP.

Booth, D. J. and Beretta, G. A. (1994). Seasonal recruitment, habitat associations and survival of pomacentrid reef fish in the United States Virgin Islands. *Coral Reefs*, **13**, 81–9.

Borowitzka, M. A. (1983). Calcium carbonate deposition by reef algae: morphological and physiological aspects. In *Perspectives on Coral Reefs*, ed. D. J. Barnes, pp. 16–28. Manuka, ACT: Brian Clouston for Australian Institute of Marine Science.

Borsuk, M. E., Stow, C. A. and Reckhow, K. H. (2004). A Bayesian network of eutrophication models for synthesis, prediction and uncertainty analysis. *Ecological Modelling*, **173**, 219–39.

Bruggemann, J. H., Van Kessel, A. M., Van Rooij, J. M. and Breeman, A. M. (1996). Bioerosion and sediment ingestion by the Caribbean parrotfish *Scarus vetula* and *Sparisoma viride*: implications of fish size, feeding mode and habitat use. *Marine Ecology Progress Series*, **134**, 59–71.

Buddemeier, R. W. and Kinzie, R. A. (1976). Coral growth. *Oceanography and Marine Biology Annual Review*, **14**, 183–225.

Burke, N. C. (1995). Nocturnal foraging habitats of french and bluestriped grunts, *Haemulon flavolineatum* and *H. sciurus*, at Tobacco Caye, Belize. *Environmental Biology of Fishes*, **42**, 365–74.

Caley, M. J., Carr, M. H., Hixon, M. A. *et al.* (1996). Recruitment and the local dynamics of open marine populations. *Annual Review of Ecology and Systematics*, **27**, 477–500.

Chave, K. E., Smith, S. V. and Roy, K. J. (1972). Carbonate production by coral reefs. *Marine Geology*, **12**, 123–40.

Chiappone, M., Sluka, R. and Sullivan Sealey, K. (2000). Groupers (Pisces: Serranidae) in fished and protected areas of the Florida Keys, Bahamas and northern Caribbean. *Marine Ecology Progress Series*, **198**, 261–72.

Clarke, K. R. (1993). Non-parametric multivariate analyses of changes in community structure. *Australian Journal of Ecology*, **18**, 117–43.

Claro, R. and Garcia-Arteaga, J. P. (1993). Estructura de las communidades de peces asociados a los manglares del groupo insular sabana-camaguey, Cuba. *Avicennia*, **10**, 60–83.

de la Morinère, E. C. (2002). Post-settlement life cycle migrations of reef fish in the mangrove-seagrass-coral reef continuum. Ph.D. thesis, Katholieke Universiteit Nijmegen, Amsterdam.

de la Morinère, E. C., Pollux, B. J. A., Nagelkerken, I. and van der Velde, G. (2003). Diet shifts of Caribbean grunts (Haemulidae) and snappers (Lutjanidae) and the relation with nursery-to-coral reef migrations. *Estuarine Coastal and Shelf Science*, **57**, 1079–89.

de La Morinière, E. C., Pollux, B. J. A., Nagelkerken, I. and Van der Velde, G. (2002). Post-settlement life cycle migration patterns and habitat preference of coral reef fish that use seagrass and mangrove habitats as nurseries. *Estuarine and Coastal Shelf Science*, **55**, 309–21.

Dennison, W. C., Orth, R. J., Moore, K. A. (1993). Assessing water quality with submersed aquatic vegetation: habitat requirements as barometers of Chesapeake Bay health. *BioScience*, **43**, 86–94.

Domeier, M. L. and Colin, P. L. (1997). Tropical reef fish spawning aggregations: defined and reviewed. *Bulletin of Marine Science*, **60**, 698–726.

Done, T. J. (1983). Coral zonation: its nature and significance. In *Perspective on Coral Reefs*, ed. D. J. Barnes, pp. 107–47. Manuka, ACT: Brian Clouston for Australian Institute of Marine Science.

Done, T. J., Ogden, J. C., Wiebe, W. J. and Rosen, B. R. (1996). Biodiversity and ecosystem function of coral reefs. In *Functional Roles of Biodiversity: A Global Perspective*, eds. H. A. Mooney, J. H. Cushman, E. Medina, O. E. Sala and E.-D. Schulze, pp. 393–429. New York: John Wiley.

Eggleston, D. B. (1995). Recruitment in Nassau grouper *Epinephelus striatus*: post-settlement abundance, microhabitat features and ontogenic habitat shifts. *Marine Ecology Progress Series*, **124**, 9–22.

Eggleston, D. B., Lipcius, R. N. and Grover, J. J. (1997). Predator and shelter-size effects on coral reef fish and spiny lobster prey. *Marine Ecology Progress Series*, **149**, 43–59.

Fabricius, K. E. and De'Ath, G. (2004). Identifying ecological change and its causes: a case study on coral reefs. *Ecological Applications*, **14**, 1448–65.

Fagerstrom, J. A. (1987). *The Evolution of Reef Communities*. New York: John Wiley.

Farina, A. (1998). *Principles and Methods in Landscape Ecology*. London: Chapman and Hall.

Ferguson, R. L., Wood, L. L. and Graham, D. B. (1993). Monitoring spatial change in seagrass habitat with aerial photography. *Photogrammetric Engineering and Remote Sensing*, **59**, 1033–8.

Foster, S. A. (1987). The relative impacts of grazing by Caribbean coral reef fishes and *Diadema*: effects of habitat and surge. *Journal of Experimental Marine Biology and Ecology*, **105**, 1–20.

Fourqurean, J. W., Zieman, J. C. and Powell, G. V. N. (1992). Phosphorus limitation of primary production in Florida bay: evidence from C : N : P ratios of the dominant seagrass *Thalassia testudinum*. *Limnology and Oceanography*, **37**, 162–71.

Friedlander, A. M., Brown, E. K., Jokiel, P. L., Smith, W. R. and Rodgers, K. S. (2003). Effects of habitat, wave exposure and marine protected area status on coral reef fish assemblages in the Hawaiian archipelago. *Coral Reefs*, **22**, 291–305.

Gattuso, J.-P., Frankignoulle, M. and Wollast, R. (1998). Carbon and carbonate metabolism in coastal aquatic ecosystems. *Annual Review of Ecology and Systematics*, **29**, 405–34.

Gattuso, J. P., Allemand, D. and Frankignoulle, M. (1999). Photosynthesis and calcification at cellular, organismal and community levels in coral reefs: a review on interactions and control by carbonate chemistry. *American Zoologist*, **39**, 160–83.

Glynn, P. W. (1993). Coral reef bleaching: ecological perspectives. *Coral Reefs*, **12**, 1–17.

(1997a). Bioerosion and coral-reef growth. In *Life and Death of Coral Reefs*, ed. C. Birkeland, pp. 68–95. New York: Chapman and Hall.

Gray, D. A., Zisman, S. A. and Corves, C. (1990). *Mapping the Mangroves of Belize*. Edinburgh: Department of Geography, University of Edinburgh.

Green, E. P., Mumby, P. J., Edwards, A. J. and Clark, C. D. (1996). A review of remote sensing for the assessment and management of tropical coastal resources. *Coastal Management*, **24**, 1–40.

Green, E. P., Clark, C. D., Mumby, P. J., Edwards, A. J. and Ellis, A. C. (1998a). Remote sensing techniques for mangrove mapping. *International Journal of Remote Sensing*, **19**, 935–56.

Green, E. P., Mumby, P. J., Edwards, A. J., Clark, C. D. and Ellis, A. C. (1998b). The assessment of mangrove areas using high resolution multispectral airborne imagery. *Journal of Coastal Research*, **14**, 433–43.

Green, E. P., Mumby, P. J., Edwards, A. J. and Clark, C. D. (2000). *Remote Sensing Handbook for Tropical Coastal Management*, Coastal Management Sourcebooks No. 3. Paris: UNESCO.

Gygi, R. H. (1975). *Sparisoma viride* (Bonnaterre), the stoplight parrotfish, a major sediment producer on coral reefs of Bermuda. *Ecologiae Geologicae Helvetiae*, **68**, 327–59.

Harborne, A. R., Mumby, P. J., Micheli, F. *et al.* (2006). The functional value of Caribbean coral reef, seagrass and mangrove habitats to ecosystem processes. *Advances in Marine Biology* (in press).

Hatcher, B. G. (1988). Coral reef primary productivity: a beggar's banquet. *Trends in Ecology and Evolution*, **3**, 106–11.

(1990). Coral reef primary productivity: a hierarchy of pattern and process. *Trends in Ecology and Evolution*, **5**, 149–55.

(1997a). Coral reef ecosystems: how much greater is the whole than the sum of the parts? *Proceedings 8th International Coral Reef Symposium*, **1**, 43–56.

(1997b). Organic production and decomposition. In *Life and Death of Coral Reefs*, ed. C. Birkeland, pp. 140–74. New York: Chapman and Hall.

Hay, M. E. (1981). Spatial patterns of grazing intensity on a Caribbean barrier reef: herbivory and algal distribution. *Aquatic Botany*, **11**, 97–109.

(1985). Spatial patterns of herbivore impact and their importance in maintaining algal species richness. *Proceedings 5th International Coral Reef Congress*, **4**, 29–34.

Hillis-Colinvaux, L. (1980). Ecology and taxonomy of *Halimeda*: primary producer of coral reefs. *Advances in Marine Biology*, **17**, 1–327.

Hixon, M. A. (1991). Predation as a process structuring coral reef fish communities. In *The Ecology of Fishes on Coral Reefs*, ed. P. F. Sale, pp. 475–508. San Diego, CA: Academic Press.

(1997). Effects of reef fishes on corals and algae. In *Life and Death of Coral Reefs*, ed. C. Birkeland, pp. 230–48. New York: Chapman and Hall.
Hogarth, P. J. (1999). *The Biology of Mangroves.* Oxford: Oxford University Press.
Hubbard, D. K. and Scaturo, D. (1985). Growth rates of seven species of scleractinean corals from Cane Bay and Salt River, St. Croix, USVI. *Bulletin of Marine Science,* **36**, 325–38.
Hughes, T. P. (1994). Catastrophes, phase shifts and large-scale degradation of a Caribbean coral reef. *Science,* **265**, 1547–51.
Ibrahim, M. and Yosuh, M. (1992). Monitoring the development impacts on the coastal resources of Pulau Redang marine park by remote sensing. In *3rd ASEAN Science and Technology Week Conference,* vol. 6, eds. L. M. Chou and C. Wilkinson, pp. 407–13. Singapore: University of Singapore.
Itzkowitz, M. (1977). Spatial organization of the Jamaican damselfish community. *Journal of Experimental Marine Biology and Ecology,* **28**, 217–41.
IUCN (2002). *Red List of Threatened Species.* Gland, Switzerland: IUCN.
Jensen, J. R., Lin, H., Yang, X. *et al.* (1991). The measurement of mangrove characteristics in southwest Florida using spot multispectral data. *Geocarto International,* **2**, 13–21.
Kinsey, D. W. (1983). Standards of performance in coral reef primary production and carbon turnover. In *Perspectives on Coral Reefs,* ed. D. J. Barnes, pp. 209–20. Manuka, ACT: Brian Clouston for Australian Institute of Marine Science.
Kirkman, H. (1996). Baseline and monitoring methods for seagrass meadows. *Journal of Environmental Management,* **47**, 191–201.
Kleypas, J. A., Mcmanus, J. W. and Menez, L. A. B. (1999). Environmental limits to coral reef development: where do we draw the line? *American Zoologist,* **39**, 146–59.
Laegdsgaard, P. and Johnson, C. (2001). Why do juvenile fish utilize mangrove habitats? *Journal of Experimental Marine Biology and Ecology,* **257**, 229–53.
Langmead, O. and Sheppard, C. (2004). Coral reef community dynamics and disturbance: a simulation model. *Ecological Modelling,* **175**, 271–90.
Larkum, A. W. D. (1983). The primary productivity of plant communities on coral reefs. In *Perspectives on Coral Reefs,* ed. D. J. Barnes, pp. 221–230. Manuka, ACT: Brian Clouston for Australian Institute of Marine Science.
Lessios, H. A. (1988). Mass mortality of *Diadema antillarum* in the Caribbean: what have we learned? *Annual Review of Ecology and Systematics,* **19**, 371–93.
Lessios, H. A., Robertson, D. R. and Cubit, J. D. (1984). Spread of *Diadema* mass mortality through the Caribbean. *Science,* **226**, 335–7.
Lewis, J. B. (1977). Processes of organic production on coral reefs. *Biological Reviews,* **52**, 305–47.
Lewis, S. M. and Wainwright, P. C. (1985). Herbivore abundance and grazing intensity on a Caribbean coral reef. *Journal of Experimental Marine Biology and Ecology,* **87**, 215–28.
Ley, J. A., McIvor, C. C. and Montague, C. L. (1999). Fishes in mangrove prop-root habitats of northeastern Florida bay: distinct assemblages across an estuarine gradient. *Estuarine, Coastal and Shelf Science,* **48**, 701–23.
Lindeman, K. C., Diaz, G. A., Serafy, J. E. and Ault, J. S. (1998). A spatial framework for assessing cross-shelf habitat use among newly settled grunts and snappers. *Proceedings Gulf and Caribbean Fisheries Institute,* **50**, 385–416.

Littler, M. M. and Littler, D. S. (1984). Models of tropical reef biogenesis: the contribution of algae. *Progress in Phycological Research*, **3**, 323–64.

Littler, M. M., Taylor, P. R., Littler, D. S., Sims, R. H. and Norris, J. N. (1987). Dominant macrophyte standing stocks, productivity and community structure on a Belizean barrier reef. *Atoll Research Bulletin*, **302**, 1–18.

Lubchenco, J. and Gaines, S. D. (1981). A unified approach to marine plant-herbivore interactions. I. Populations and communities. *Annual Review of Ecology and Systematics*, **12**, 405–37.

Lugo, A. E. and Snedaker, S. C. (1974). The ecology of mangroves. *Annual Review of Ecology and Systematics*, **5**, 39–64.

Lugo-Fernández, A., Hernández-Ávila, M. L. and Roberts, H. H. (1994). Wave-energy distribution and hurricane effects on margarita reef, southwestern Puerto Rico. *Coral Reefs*, **13**, 21–32.

May, J. A., Macintyre, I. G. and Perkins, R. D. (1982). Distribution of microborers within planted substrates along a barrier reef transect, Carrie Bow Cay, Belize. In *The Atlantic Barrier Reef Ecosystem at Carrie Bow Cay, Belize*, vol. 1, *Structure and Communities*, ed. I. G. Macintyre, pp. 93–107. Washington, DC: Smithsonian Institution Press.

McClanahan, T. R. (1995). A coral reef ecosystem-fisheries model: impacts of fishing intensity and catch selection on reef structure and processes. *Ecological Modelling*, **80**, 1–19.

McFarland, W. N. (1979). Observations on recruitment in haemulid fishes. *Proceedings Gulf and Caribbean Fisheries Institute*, **32**, 132–8.

McFarland, W. N., Brothers, E. B., Ogden, J. C. *et al.* (1985). Recruitment patterns in young french grunts, *Haemulon flavolineatum* (family Haemulidae), at St. Croix, Virgin Islands. *Fisheries Bulletin*, **83**, 413–26.

McNeill, S. E. (1994). The selection and design of marine protected areas: Australia as a case study. *Biodiversity and Conservation*, **3**, 586–605.

Meyer, J. L. and Schultz, E. T. (1985). Migrating haemulid fishes as a source of nutrients and organic matter on coral reefs. *Limnology and Oceanography*, **30**, 146–56.

Meyer, J. L., Schultz, E. T. and Helfman, G. S. (1983). Fish schools: an asset to corals. *Science*, **220**, 1047–9.

Moberg, F. and Folke, C. (1999). Ecological goods and services of coral reef ecosystems. *Ecological Economics*, **29**, 215–33.

Moberg, F. and Rönnbäck, P. (2003). Ecosystem services of the tropical seascape: interactions, substitutions and restoration. *Ocean and Coastal Management*, **46**, 27–46.

Mumby, P. J. (2006). The impact of exploiting grazers (Scaridae) on the dynamics of Caribbean coral reefs. *Ecological Applications* (in press).

Mumby, P. J. and Dytham, C. (2006). Metapopulation dynamics of hard corals. In *Marine Metapopulations*, eds. J. P. Kritzer and P. F. Sale. San Diego, CA: Academic Press (in press).

Mumby, P. J. and Harborne, A. R. (1999). Development of a systematic classification scheme of marine habitats to facilitate regional management and mapping of Caribbean coral reefs. *Biological Conservation*, **88**, 155–63.

Mumby, P. J., Green, E. P., Edwards, A. J. and Clark, C. D. (1997). Measurement of seagrass standing crop using satellite and digital airborne remote sensing. *Marine Ecology Progress Series*, **159**, 51–60.

Mumby, P. J., Green, E. P., Clark, C. D. and Edwards, A. J. (1998). Digital analysis of multispectral airborne imagery of coral reefs. *Coral Reefs*, **17**, 59–69.
Mumby, P. J., Chisholm, J. R. M., Clark, C. D., Hedley, J. D. and Jaubert, J. (2001). Spectrographic imaging: a bird's-eye view of the health of coral reefs. *Nature*, **413**, 36.
Mumby, P. J., Edwards, A. J., Arias-Gonzalez, J. E. *et al.* (2004a). Mangroves enhance the biomass of coral reef fish communities in the Caribbean. *Nature*, **427**, 533–6.
Mumby, P. J., Hedley, J. D., Chisholm, J. R. M., Clark, C. D. and Jaubert, J. (2004b). The cover of living and dead corals using airborne remote sensing. *Coral Reefs*, **23**, 171–83.
Mumby, P. J., Skirving, W., Strong, A. E. *et al.* (2004c). Remote sensing of coral reefs and their physical environment. *Marine Pollution Bulletin*, **48**, 219–228.
Nagelkerken, I. and van der Velde, G. (2002). Do non-estuarine mangroves harbour higher densities of juvenile fish than adjacent shallow-water and coral reef habitats in Curaçao (Netherlands Antilles)? *Marine Ecology Progress Series*, **245**, 191–204.
Nagelkerken, I., van der Velde, G., Gorissen, M. W. *et al.* (2000). Importance of mangroves, seagrass beds and the shallow coral reef as a nursery for important coral reef fishes, using a visual census technique. *Estuarine, Coastal and Shelf Science*, **51**, 31–44.
Nagelkerken, I., Kleijnen, S., Klop, T. *et al.* (2001). Dependence of Caribbean reef fishes on mangroves and seagrass beds as nursery habitats: a comparison of fish faunas between bays with and without mangroves/seagrass beds. *Marine Ecology Progress Series*, **214**, 225–35.
Odum, H. T. (1956). Primary production in flowing waters. *Limnology and Oceanography*, **1**, 102–17.
Ogden, J. C. (1976). Some aspects of herbivore–plant relationships on Caribbean reefs and seagrass beds. *Aquatic Botany*, **2**, 103–16.
(1977). Carbonate-sediment production by parrot fish and sea urchins on Caribbean reefs. In *Reefs and Related Carbonates: Ecology and Sedimentology*, eds. G. H. Frost, M. P. Weis and J. B. Saunders, pp. 281–8. Tulsa, OK: American Association of Petroleum Geologists.
(1997). Ecosystem interactions in the tropical coastal seascape. In *Life and Death of Coral Reefs*, ed. C. Birkeland, pp. 288–97. New York: Chapman and Hall.
Ogden, J. C. and Buckman, N. S. (1973). Movements, foraging groups and diurnal migrations of the striped parrotfish *Scarus croicensis* Bloch (Scaridae). *Ecology*, **54**, 589–96.
Ogden, J. C. and Ehrlich, P. R. (1977). The behavior of heterotypic resting schools of juvenile grunts (pomadasyidae). *Marine Biology*, **42**, 273–80.
Ogden, J. C. and Gladfelter, E. H. (1983). *Coral Reefs, Seagrass Beds and Mangroves: Their Interaction in the Coastal Zones of the Caribbean*. Paris: UNESCO.
Ogden, J. C. and Lobel, P. S. (1978). The role of herbivorous fishes and urchins in coral reef communities. *Environmental Biology of Fishes*, **3**, 49–63.
Opitz, S. (1996). *Trophic Interactions in Caribbean Coral Reefs*,. Technical Report No. 43. Manila: International Center for Living Aquatic Resources Management.
Pannier, F. (1979). Mangroves impacted by human-induced disturbances: a case study of the Orinoco Delta mangrove ecosystem. *Environmental Management*, **3**, 205–16.

Parrish, J. D. (1987). The trophic biology of snappers and groupers. In *Tropical Snappers and Groupers: Biology and Fisheries Management*, ed. S. Ralston, pp. 405–63. Boulder, CO: Westview Press.

Parrish, J. D. and Zimmerman, R. J. (1977). Utilization of fishes of space and food resources on an offshore Puerto Rican coral reef and its surroundings. *Proceedings 3rd International Coral Reef Symposium*, **1**, 297–303.

Perry, C. T. (1998a). Grain susceptibility to the effects of microboring: implications for the preservation of skeletal carbonates. *Sedimentology*, **45**, 39–51.

(1998b). Macroborers within coral framework at Discovery Bay, north Jamaica: species distribution and abundance and effects on coral preservation. *Coral Reefs*, **17**, 277–87.

(1999). Reef framework preservation in four contrasting modern reef environments, Discovery Bay, Jamaica. *Journal of Coastal Research*, **15**, 796–812.

Perry, C. T. and MacDonald, I. A. (2002). Impacts of light penetration on the bathymetry of reef microboring communities: implications for the development of microendolithic trace assemblages. *Palaeogeography, Palaeoclimatology, Palaeoecology*, **186**, 101–13.

Petraitis, P. S. and Latham, R. E. (1999). The importance of scale in testing the origins of alternative community states. *Ecology*, **80**, 429–42.

Phillips, R. C. and McRoy, C. P. (1990). *Seagrass Research Methods*, Monographs on Oceanographic Methodology No. 9. Paris: UNESCO.

Pittman, S. J., McAlpine, C. A. and Pittman, K. M. (2004). Linking fish and prawns to their environment: a hierarchical landscape approach. *Marine Ecology Progress Series*, **283**, 233–54.

Possingham, H., Ball, I. and Andelman, S. (2000). Mathematical models for identifying representative reserve networks. In *Quantitative Methods for Conservation Biology*, eds. S. Ferson and M. Burgman, pp. 291–306. New York: Springer-Verlag.

Preece, A. L. and Johnson, C. R. (1993). Recovery of model coral communities: complex behaviours from interaction of parameters operating at different spatial scales. In *Complex Systems: From Biology to Computation*, eds. D. G. Green and T. Bossomaier, pp. 69–81. Amsterdam: IOS Press.

Randall, J. E. (1967). Food habitats of reef fishes of the West Indies. *Studies in Tropical Oceanography*, **5**, 665–847.

Risk, M. J. and MacGeachy, J. K. (1978). Aspects of bioerosion of modern Caribbean reefs. *Revista de Biologia Tropical*, **26** (Suppl. 1), 85–105.

Robblee, M. B., Barber, T. R., Carlson, P. R. *et al.* (1991). Mass mortality of the tropical seagrass *Thalassia testudinum* in Florida bay (USA). *Marine Ecology Progress Series*, **71**, 297–99.

Roberts, H. H., Murray, S. P. and Suhayda, J. N. (1977). Physical processes in a fore-reef shelf environment. *Proceedings 3rd International Coral Reef Symposium*, **2**, 507–15.

Rogers, C. S. and Salesky, N. H. (1981). Productivity of *Acropora palmata* (Lamarck), macroscopic algae and algal turf from Tague Bay reef, St. Croix, U.S. Virgin Islands. *Journal of Experimental Marine Biology and Ecology*, **49**, 179–87.

Rooker, J. R. and Dennis, G. D. (1991). Diel, lunar and seasonal changes in a mangrove fish assemblage off southwestern Puerto Rico. *Bulletin of Marine Science*, **49**, 684–98.

Sebens, K. P. (1997). Adaptive responses to water flow: morphology, energetics and distribution of reef corals. *Proceedings 8th International Coral Reef Symposium*, **2**, 1053–8.
Sheppard, C. R. C. (1982). Coral populations on reef slopes and their major controls. *Marine Ecology Progress Series*, **7**, 83–115.
Sheppard, C. R. C., Matheson, K., Bythell, J. C. *et al.* (1995). Habitat mapping in the Caribbean for management and conservation: use and assessment of aerial photography. *Aquatic Conservation Marine and Freshwater Ecosystems*, **5**, 277–98.
Shulman, M. J. (1985). Recruitment of coral reef fishes: effects of distribution of predators and shelter. *Ecology*, **66**, 1056–66.
Sluka, R. and Sullivan, K. M. (1996). The influence of habitat on the size distribution of groupers in the upper Florida keys. *Environmental Biology of Fishes*, **47**, 177–89.
Smith, S. V. (1983). Coral reef calcification. In *Perspectives on Coral Reefs*, ed. D. J. Barnes, pp. 240–7. Manuka, ACT: Brian Clouston for Australian Institute of Marine Science.
Smith, S. V. and Buddemeier, R. W. (1992). Global change and coral reef ecosystems. *Annual Review of Ecology and Systematics*, **23**, 89–118.
Smith, S. V. and Kinsey, D. W. (1976). Calcium carbonate production, coral reef growth and sea level change. *Science*, **194**, 937–9.
Steneck, R. S. (1997). Crustose corallines, other algal functional groups, herbivores and sediments: complex interactions along reef productivity gradients. *Proceedings 8th International Coral Reef Symposium*, **1**, 695–700.
Suhayda, J. N. and Roberts, H. H. (1977). Wave action and sediment transport on fringing reefs. *Proceedings 3rd International Coral Reef Symposium*, **2**, 65–70.
Swearer, S. E., Caselle, J. E., Lea, D. W. and Warner, R. R. (1999). Larval retention and recruitment in an island population of a coral-reef fish. *Nature*, **402**, 799–802.
Thayer, G. W., Bjorndal, K. A., Ogden, J. C., Williams, S. L. and Zieman, J. C. (1984). Role of larger herbivores in seagrass communities. *Estuaries*, **7**, 351–76.
Torres, R., Chiappone, M., Geraldes, F., Rodriguez, Y. and Vega, M. (2001). Sedimentation as an important environmental influence on Dominican Republic reefs. *Bulletin of Marine Science*, **69**, 805–18.
Valiela, I., Bowen, J. L. and York, J. K. (2001). Mangrove forests: one of the world's threatened major tropical environments. *BioScience*, **51**, 807–15.
Van Rooij, J. M., De Jong, E., Vaandrager, F. and Videler, J. J. (1996). Resource and habitat sharing by the stoplight parrotfish, *Sparisoma viride*, a Caribbean reef herbivore. *Environmental Biology of Fishes*, **47**, 81–91.
Vecsei, A. (2001). Fore-reef carbonate production: development of a regional census-based method and first estimates. *Palaeogeography, Palaeoclimatology, Palaeoecology*, **175**, 185–200.
Vibulsresth, S., Downreang, D., Ratanasermpong, S. and Silapathong, C. (1990). Mangrove forest zonation by using high resolution satellite data. *Proceedings 11th Asian Conference on Remote Sensing*, **1**, D1-1–D1-6.
Walsh, M. G. and Winkelman, D. L. (2004). Anchor and visible implant elastomer tag retention by hatchery rainbow trout stocked into an Ozark stream. *North American Journal of Fish Management*, **24**, 1435–9.

Ward, T. J., Vanderklift, M. A., Nicholls, A. O. and Kenchington, R. A. (1999). Selecting marine reserves using habitat and species assemblages as surrogates for biological diversity. *Ecological Applications*, **9**, 691–8.

Weibe, W. J. (1987). Nutrient pool dynamics in tropical, marine, coastal environments with special reference to the Caribbean and Indo-West Pacific regions. In *Comparison between Atlantic and Pacific Tropical Marine Coastal Ecosystems: Community Structure, Ecological Processes and Productivity*, ed. C. Birkeland, pp. 19–42. Paris: UNESCO.

Wolanski, E., Richmond, R. H. and McCook, L. (2004). A model of the effects of land-based, human activities on the health of coral reefs in the Great Barrier Reef and in Fouha bay, Guam, Micronesia. *Journal of Marine Systems*, **46**, 133–44.

Wooldridge, S. and Done, T. J. (2004). Learning to predict large-scale coral bleaching from past events: a Bayesian approach using remotely sensed data, in-situ data and environmental proxies. *Coral Reefs*, **23**, 96–108.

Yates, K. K. and Halley, R. B. (2003). Measuring coral reef community metabolism using new benthic chamber technology. *Coral Reefs*, **22**, 247–55.

4

Cold-water coral reefs: status and conservation

EMILY CORCORAN AND STEFAN HAIN
UNEP – World Conservation Monitoring Centre, Cambridge, UK

INTRODUCTION

Although their existence has been known for centuries, the observation and study of cold-water coral habitats in their natural surroundings began only in the last decade. Scientists around the globe gained access to increasingly sophisticated instrumentation, such as manned and remote operated submersibles, to explore deep-water environments. Their findings challenged conventional wisdom; coral reefs are not only confined to shallow and warm tropical and subtropical regions, but there are a variety of coral ecosystems thriving in deep, dark and cold waters around the globe. Some of these cold-water corals construct banks or reefs as complex as those in tropical areas. Analyses have confirmed that some of these living banks and reefs are up to 8600 years old (Mikkelsen *et al.*, 1982; Hovland *et al.*, 2002), and geological records show that cold-water coral reefs have existed for millions of years.

Cold-water corals grow in dark deep waters. They have no light-dependent symbiotic algae in their tissue and must depend on currents to supply particulate and dissolved organic matter and zooplankton. Many of these cold-water corals produce calcium carbonate skeletons that resemble bushes or trees to support colonies of polyps, maximizing their ability to capture their food efficiently. The result is a complex three-dimensional habitat which provides a multitude of microniches for the associated fauna.

It is only recently that an understanding has developed of the complexity of these cold-water coral ecosystems that are largely hidden and ignored

Coral Reef Conservation, ed. Isabelle M. Côté and John D. Reynolds.
Published by Cambridge University Press.

because they can only be observed with complex and expensive equipment. Like their tropical counterparts, cold-water corals are home to thousands of other species, in particular sponges, polychaete worms (or bristle worms), crustaceans (crabs, lobsters), molluscs (clams, snails, octopuses), echinoderms (starfish, sea urchins, brittle stars, feather stars), bryozoans (sea moss) and fish. Most of the studies have been carried out at higher latitudes, but there are now observations of cold-water coral reefs off the coasts of Africa, South America and in the Pacific, indicating their wide distribution through all seas and oceans (Zibrowius, 1973, 1980; Cairns, 1982, 1984, 1995). Many of these wait to be explored and studied in more detail to fill the knowledge gaps of marine deep-water ecosystems and reef-forming processes.

Researchers are also beginning to realize that coral reefs represent a continuum. At one end, the evolution of light-dependent symbioses has allowed corals to survive under low nutritional regimes in the shallow waters of the tropics. Cold-water corals are at the other end of the spectrum, thriving as carnivorous animals, adapted to capture food in deeper and colder waters. Unfortunately, as the understanding of the distribution, biological dynamics and rich biodiversity of cold-water ecosystems expands, there is clear evidence that many of these vulnerable ecosystems are being damaged by human activities (Hall-Spencer *et al.*, 2002; Masson *et al.*, 2003; Grehan *et al.*, 2004). Undoubtedly, the greatest and most irreversible damage is due to the increasing intensity of deep-water trawling which relies on the deployment of heavy gear, which 'steamrollers' over the sea floor destroying virtually all in its path. There is also concern about the potential effects of oil and gas exploration, in particular the potential smothering effects of drill cuttings. Cold-water coral reefs have recently become an important topic on the political agenda of various national and international bodies due to the realization that many of the most spectacular examples discovered so far could be gone in one or two decades, if corrective action is not taken quickly.

In this chapter, we summarize and update the information contained in the report *Cold-Water Coral Reefs: Out of Sight – No Longer Out of Mind* (Freiwald *et al.*, 2004) about the current knowledge of cold-water coral reefs, their similarities to and differences from tropical, warm-water reefs, the key species and their distribution, and the threats that cold-water coral reefs face from various human activities. We also provide an overview of the emerging national and international efforts to protect and manage cold-water coral reefs sustainably.

DESCRIPTION AND SIMILARITIES WITH TROPICAL WARM-WATER CORAL REEFS

Cold-water coral reefs, like their tropical warm and shallow-water counterparts, are built predominately by stony corals (Scleractinia). A comparison between warm- and cold-water coral reefs shows some striking differences and similarities (Table 4.1). Cold-water coral reefs flourish along the edges and trenches of continental shelves with a suitable hard bottom substratum for the larvae to settle and where cold water currents provide a regular food supply of suspended organic matter and zooplankton. In higher latitudes, such conditions can be found in relatively shallow waters, whereas in the tropics cold-water coral reefs grow beneath the warm and light-flooded surface layers that are home to their shallow-water cousins, which rely on photosynthetic symbionts for additional food supply. In contrast to the large number and variety of coral species found in warm-water reefs, cold-water coral reefs are mostly composed by one or two species. There are only around six reef-building cold-water coral species, all of which show a number of adaptations to their colder, deeper and more stable environment: their calcareous skeletons grow more slowly and are more delicate than warm-water corals. The complex three-dimensional structures they form are very fragile and prone to physical damage. The main similarity between cold-water and warm-water coral reefs is their ecological function and importance. Both provide habitat, feeding grounds and nursery for many associated species. If warm-water reefs are 'the tropical rainforest of the sea', cold-water coral reefs are their temperate counterpart. Unfortunately, both types of reef are threatened by a number of human activities. Although visualizing the problems in cold, dark deep waters is considerably more difficult than for tropical coral reefs, recent underwater footage shows that a large number of coral reefs have been impacted or destroyed by the use of active fishing gear (especially bottom trawls).

KEY COLD-WATER CORAL SPECIES

Colonies formed by stony corals (Scleractinia) in cold and usually deep waters can vary in size from small, scattered colonies no more than a few metres in diameter to vast reef complexes measuring several tens of metres in height and kilometres in length (Fig. 4.1).

In the North Atlantic, the Mediterranean Sea and the Gulf of Mexico, *Lophelia pertusa* and *Madrepora oculata* are the most abundant reef-builders.

Table 4.1. Some similarities and differences between cold-water and warm-water coral reefs

	Cold-water coral reefs	Warm-water coral reefs
Distribution	Potentially in all seas, and at all latitudes	In subtropical and tropical seas between 30° N and 30° S
Number of states, countries and territories with corals	41 so far	109
Area covered	Unknown: studies indicate global coverage that could equal, or exceed warm-water reefs	284 300 km^2
Country with largest coral reef area	Unknown: at least 2000 km^2 estimated in Norwegian waters	Indonesia (51 020 km^2)
Largest reef complex	Unknown: Røst Reef (100 km^2) (discovered 2002) in northern Norway probably the largest	Great Barrier Reef (more than 30 000 km^2), Australia
Temperature range	4°–13 °C	18–32 °C (some outside this range)
Salinity range	32–38.8 (%)	33–36 (%)
Depth range	39–3383 m	0–100 m
Nutrition	Uncertain: probably suspended organic matter and zooplankton	Suspended organic matter and photosynthesis
Symbiotic algae	No	Yes
Growth rate	Up to 25 mm yr^{-1}	Up to 150 mm yr^{-1}
Number of reef-building coral species	Around 6	Around 800
Reef composition	Mostly composed of one or a few species	Mostly composed of numerous species
Age of living reefs	Up to 8500 years	Up to 9000 years
Status	Unknown: most reefs studied show physical damage; some reefs in NE Atlantic completely lost to bottom trawling	30% irreversibly damaged; another 30% at severe risk of being lost in the next 30 years
Rate of regeneration/ recovery	Unknown: slow growth rate indicates that if regeneration /recovery is possible, it might take decades to centuries for damaged reef to regain ecological function	Slow (years to decades): regeneration /recovery may lead to reduced coral diversity, species composition shifts or phase shifts to algal-dominated ecosystem, especially when human pressures are evident

Table 4.1. (*cont.*)

	Cold-water coral reefs	Warm-water coral reefs
Main threats: natural and induced by climate change	Unknown: climate change may cause large changes in current systems affecting the living conditions	Increased episodes of higher sea surface temperatures will lead to more widespread and lethal coral bleaching
Main threats from human activities	• Bottom fisheries • Oil and gas exploration and production • Placement of pipelines and cables • Others, e.g. pollution, research activities, dumping	• Over-fishing and destructive fishing (especially with bombs and cyanide) • Pollution and sedimentation from land-based sources and coastal development • Tourism and anchoring
Ecological importance	Reefs provide habitat and feeding grounds for many deep-water organisms; probably have recruitment and nursery functions including commercial fish species. The species richness on these reefs and full ecological importance unknown	Estimated 1 million plant and animal species are associated with warm-water coral reefs. There are approximately 4000 coral reef fish species (a quarter of all marine fish species)
Socio-economic importance	Unknown: initial observations suggest important for local fisheries, including coastal line/net fisheries and deep-water fisheries (especially around seamounts)	Provide coastal protection and livelihoods for more than 1 billion people; net potential benefits provided by reefs estimated at US$30 billion yr^{-1}
International awareness and attention	Increased over last 2–3 years	Increasing over last 1–2 decades, especially after bleaching events in the 1990s; more than 100 non-governmental and intergovernmental organizations involved

Figure 4.1 Model of a cold-water reef, composed of various underwater photos taken on Norwegian *Lophelia* reefs. (Courtesy of Fosså *et al.*, 2000.) (See also Plate 4.1 in the colour plate section.)

The former forms cauliflower-like colonies measuring up to around 4 m across and consisting of thousands of translucent white to yellow, orange or red-coloured coral polyps. As the colony develops, adjacent branches tend to fuse, thereby considerably strengthening the entire framework. The species has a global distribution and is best known from the East Atlantic, stretching from the south-western Barents Sea along the continental margin down to West Africa. The largest cold-water coral reef known so far, the Røst Reef, was discovered in 2002 in northern Norway and is the size of Manhattan. It has been built primarily by *L. pertusa* (Fig. 4.2).

Like *Lophelia*, corals of the *Madrepora* group are cosmopolitan; two of this group, *Madrepora oculata* and *M. carolina*, form branched colonies which are generally much more fragile than *Lophelia* and tend to break easily. This limits their capacity to build large frameworks or reefs. However, they are often associated with other reef-building corals such as *L. pertusa* and *Goniocorella dumosa*.

The continental slope off Atlantic Florida and North Carolina is the home of reefs constructed by *Oculina varicosa*. This species can occur in both deep and shallow waters, where the species often possesses symbiotic algae similar to tropical shallow reef corals. The shape of *Oculina* colonies

Figure 4.2 Living *Lophelia pertusa* colonies on top of a Norwegian reef. (Courtesy of André Freiwald, IPAL-Erlangen.) (See also Plate 4.2 in the colour plate section.)

varies from short, stout branches in the surf zone to taller and more fragile spherical, bushy or finger-like structures in deeper areas, which can measure up to 150 cm in diameter.

Solenosmilia variabilis is widely distributed in the South Pacific and Atlantic Ocean, whereas *Goniocorella dumosa* is restricted to waters around New Zealand, South Africa, Indonesia and Korea. Both species are the most prominent reef-building species in the southern hemisphere, especially around seamounts and oceanic banks off Tasmania and New Zealand. *Gomiocorella dumosa* is frequently found in water depths of 300 to 400 m, whereas *S. variabilis* aggregations often occur on the summits of seamounts at 1000 to 1400 m. The biology and ecology of both species are poorly known.

Enallopsammia profunda is endemic to the western Atlantic from the Antilles in the Caribbean, to Massachusetts, north-eastern USA. The species can form massive finger-like colonies up to 1 m thick at 150 to 1750 m deep. *Enallopsammia profunda* is often associated with *L. pertusa*, *M. oculata* and *S. variabilis*.

Cold-water coral ecosystems are not exclusively the domain of stony corals. Other groups of corals with solid or calcified skeletons, such as black corals (Antipatharia) or lace corals (Stylasteridae), form branched or tree-like structures in cold water. In addition, there are numerous groups of soft corals such as precious corals, sea fans and bamboo corals, which form rich, strikingly colourful communities in colder and deeper waters, such as

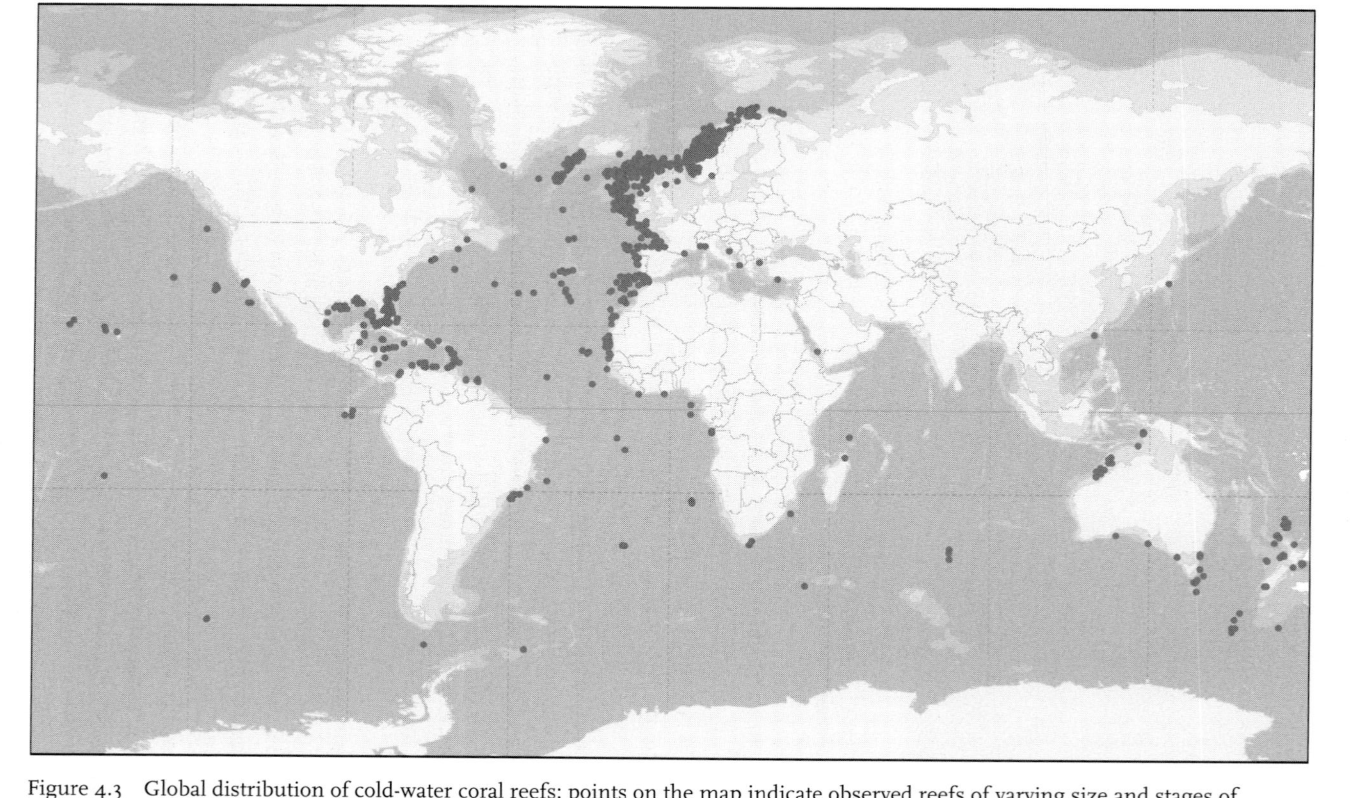

Figure 4.3 Global distribution of cold-water coral reefs: points on the map indicate observed reefs of varying size and stages of development but not the actual area covered. The high density of reefs shown in the North Atlantic reflects the intensity of research in this region. Further discoveries are expected worldwide, particularly in the deeper waters of subtropical and tropical regions. (Courtesy of UNEP-WCMC, sourced from A. Freiwald, from various sources.)

Table 4.2. List of countries known to have cold-water corals; further discoveries are expected, particularly in the deeper waters off the coasts of tropical and subtropical countries

Angola	Guyana	Nicaragua
Australia	Haiti	Norway
Brazil	Honduras	Portugal
Canada	Iceland	Russia
Cape Verde	Indonesia	Seychelles
Chile	Ireland	South Africa
China	Italy	Spain
Colombia	Jamaica	Surinam
Cuba	Japan	Sweden
Denmark (Greenland Faroes)	Madagascar	United Kingdom
Dominican Republic	Mauritania	United States of America
Ecuador	Mexico	Venezuela
France	Morocco	Western Sahara
Ghana	New Zealand	

the 'octocoral gardens' off Nova Scotia, Canada, along the Aleutians and the North Pacific coasts as well as on seamounts off Canada, the USA, Japan and in New Zealand waters.

These cold-water corals create hard substrata on otherwise sandy or muddy bottoms that favour the settlement and growth of a wide range of other attached invertebrates such as sponges, bryozoans and molluscs. The combination of all these make up the cold-water coral reefs and ideal habitats for a wide range of other species, including many of high commercial importance.

DISTRIBUTION OF COLD-WATER CORALS

Cold-water coral reefs occur in fjords, along the edge of the continental shelf and around offshore sub-marine banks and seamounts in almost all of the world's seas and oceans (Fig. 4.3). They are known from the territorial waters of 41 countries (Table 4.2), but this will be an underestimate as there have been no systematic searches. Most studies have been carried out in high latitudes, where these corals are observed from 40 m to depths of hundreds of metres. In tropical areas, warm-water masses overlie the cold, nutrient-rich waters, which explains why cold-water coral reefs are usually found at greater depths.

Cold-water coral ecosystems are defined as large areas of corals at a given locality. Almost all known coral ecosystems share a number of environmental attributes or factors. Their preferred locations are found in areas with suitable conditions. These are:

- Strong topographically guided bottom currents prevent deposition of sediments, thereby creating current-swept hard substrata that facilitate colonization by habitat-forming corals. Generally, these grounds are pre-existing topographic highs of various scales that form obstacles in the current path: they can be boulder fields, moraine ridges, drumlins, the flanks of oceanic banks, seamounts, sedimentary mounds and occasionally artificial substrata such as wrecks and oil rigs.
- The flow of water is funnelled through narrow passages such as straits (e.g. Florida Strait, Strait of Gibraltar, Cook Strait, New Zealand) or channels, fjord troughs (e.g. in Scandinavia, New Zealand and Chile) and submerged canyons and gullies.
- Nearby nutrient-rich waters stimulate the development of high phytoplankton and zooplankton levels, providing a major food source for the coral communities.

THREATS TO COLD-WATER CORAL REEFS

Cold-water corals are long-lived, slow-growing and fragile, which makes them especially vulnerable to physical damage. Since the mid-1980s, the deeper parts of the world's oceans have come under increasing pressure from human activities to exploit their biological and mineral resources, raising concern among academia as demonstrated by the call for action from more than 1000 scientists and 69 countries at the annual meeting of the American Association for the Advancement of Science in Seattle, USA, in February 2004. Recent surveys of cold-water coral reefs have shown reef damage or destruction in many locations around the world e.g. off eastern Florida (Reed *et al.*, 2005), on the summits of some south Tasmanian seamounts (Koslow *et al.*, 2001); on oceanic banks in New Zealand waters (Probert *et al.*, 1997); the octocoral gardens in Alaskan waters (Shester and Ayers, 2005) and coral grounds off Nova Scotia (Gass and Willison, 2005); and *Lophelia* reefs in Scandinavian waters (Fosså *et al.*, 2002), off western Ireland (Hall-Spencer *et al.*, 2002) and in the northern Rockall Trough (ICES, 2002, 2003). The main documented and potential sources of threats to cold-water corals are listed below.

Bottom-trawling and other bottom fishing

Fishing gear dragged along the sea floor, such as bottom-trawls or dredges, is considered the greatest threat to cold-water coral reefs. Bottom-trawling on deep shelves and along the continental margins to 1500 m depth and beyond has increased dramatically since the late 1980s. Large and heavy gear is used in these operations, with nets as large as 55 m across and 12 m high. The bottom of the net opening is weighted by chains or cables with heavy discs or rollers, and the mouth of the net is held open by beams or vanes (known as 'doors'), which can weigh as much as 6 tonnes. On a typical 15-day fishing trip in the north-east Atlantic, a trawler sweeps approximately 33 km^2 of seabed (Hall-Spencer *et al.*, 2002).

Although fishermen try to avoid trawling over large coral reefs and coral-topped carbonate mounds, there is a great deal of direct and collateral damage to coral grounds, both in waters within and beyond the limits of national jurisdiction (Gianni, 2004). Visual observations provide clear evidence that trawl doors plough through the seabed and smash or disrupt corals. Groundline rollers flatten corals and coral-covered boulders, while the strengthened base of the trawl net can tear or break coral further (Fig. 4.4). It is estimated that a single 15-minute trawl can completely destroy a cold-water coral reef which has taken thousands of years to grow. Even if not impacted directly, further damage might be caused by the sediments disturbed by trawling which can smother nearby corals.

In addition to bottom trawls and dredges, there are a number of fishing techniques, such as bottom-set gillnets and bottom-set long-lines, as well as pots and traps, which come into contact with the sea floor and thereby pose threats to cold-water coral reefs. In most cases, anchors and weights are used to fix this gear at or close to the seabed, causing physical damage to the fragile reefs. Lost fishing nets and lines are frequently observed entangled in the corals, but recovery of such lost gear might cause further disruption.

Hydrocarbon exploration and production

Exploration and production of oil and gas can have severe effects on coral habitats, including physical impact from the placement of structures (oil platforms, anchors, pipelines), damage from discharges of rock cuttings, drilling fluids and chemicals, or from discharges from the wells. In areas such as European waters, oil companies are required to conduct environmental impact assessments before carrying out most activities. This has

Figure 4.4 (a) Intact reef. (Courtesy of the JAGO-Team.) (b) Reef after a trawl has passed. (Courtesy of Fosså *et al.*, 2002.) (c) Coral caught in trawl gear. (Courtesy of Jim Reid, DFO-Canada.) (d) Lost net on reef. (Courtesy of IFREMER, ARK-19/3a, 2003.) (See also Plate 4.4 in the colour plate section.)

Figure 4.4 (*cont.*)

led to the discovery of several cold-water coral reefs, and avoided or reduced the risk of damage to them. However, the challenge is to ensure that such regulation occurs everywhere and that the industry works to the highest possible environmental standards.

Cable and pipeline placement

Telecommunication and electricity cables, and oil and gas pipelines criss-cross all seas and oceans. In waters shallower than 1500 m, these cables and pipelines are usually buried within the seabed, especially to prevent accidental damage by trawling. The potential threats to cold-water coral reefs originate from the physical impact of cables and pipelines as they are laid in coral reef areas, and from the resuspended sediments from the burying methods, which can smother nearby corals.

Bioprospecting and destructive scientific sampling

There has been considerable recent research by scientists, and biotechnology and pharmaceutical companies in deep-water ecosystems. This occurred after they shifted from shallow water to sample cold-water corals and sponges. Most of this research is carried out with manned and remotely operated submersibles, such that the potential damage to deep reefs is minimized; however, damage occurs when sampling gear is dragged over the bottom.

Waste disposal, dumping and pollution

The oceans have long been regarded as a place to dump wastes. Ropes and fishing equipment are frequently found on cold-water coral reefs, mostly through accidental loss. The deliberate dumping or disposal of material (such as dredged sediments) on coral reef ecosystems will physically damage corals or bury them.

The damage to cold-water corals from marine pollution, including environmental toxicants, radioactive wastes and sewage, is unknown; however, there is sufficient concern in the scientific community that chronic pollution of the ocean will result in damage to many marine ecosystems and losses of biodiversity.

Coral exploitation and trade

A number of cold-water corals are exploited for trade, such as precious coral species (*Corallium*) and black corals (*Antipatharia*) (see Vincent, this volume, for a discussion of trade in tropical corals). The threats originate where specimens are harvested unsustainably or with unselective gear such as coral draggers, i.e. an iron bar with chains to trap pieces of coral, which also causes considerable habitat damage.

Future threats

There are future threats that could damage cold-water coral reefs. There has been considerable discussion of deep-sea mining for minerals, especially manganese-rich nodules and mineral concentrates on 'black smokers' in tectonically active areas. While this has not started, there is strong potential for adverse effects on corals through direct impacts and resuspension of sediments.

The capture of CO_2 from the atmosphere and sequestration into deep waters has been proposed as a mechanism to reduce greenhouse gas global warming (Herzog *et al.*, 1997). It is uncertain whether this disposal would significantly reduce atmospheric CO_2 and there are concerns that the dissolution of CO_2 will lower the alkalinity (pH) of sea water, thereby impairing the ability of corals to lay down calcium carbonate structures (Kleypas *et al.*, 1999; Haugan, 2004). The rise of CO_2 levels in the atmosphere is already lowering the pH in sea water, which could affect the calcification of tropical corals, and potentially also affect cold-water corals. Climate change may also affect water currents and thus change living conditions for cold-water corals.

STATUS OF COLD-WATER CORALS: REGULATIONS AND MEASURES

Regulations and measures have been enacted recently by some countries to protect a few cold-water coral ecosystems. However, most of the world's cold-water coral reefs are not under protection and are under serious threat of destruction, especially from bottom-trawlers. It is very expensive to examine and survey cold-water coral reefs in their natural deep-water surroundings. Therefore information on the status of these coral reefs remains incomplete and geographically biased, with very little information on the cold-water coral reefs occurring in deeper tropical waters. Concerted studies have only been conducted on these ecosystems during the last ten years and these have been predominantly spot investigations to determine the presence of the reefs and associated animals.

Various countries and regional bodies have adopted, or are establishing, regulations and measures to protect and manage vulnerable marine habitats, including cold-water coral reefs. The regulations and measures vary considerably depending on the specific threat, status and location of the reefs. The measures range from a requirement for environmental impact assessments prior to activities, the prohibition or expansion of operations and bottom-trawling on cold-water coral reef areas, to specific management plans and regulations, such as a ban on all or certain types of fishing gear (especially those which are dragged along the sea floor) where cold-water coral reefs are known to exist.

Some cold-water coral reef locations have been designated by national or international agreements as 'habitats of particular concern', 'special areas of conservation' or 'marine protected areas' (MPAs). The MPAs have been used by countries in their territorial and exclusive economic zone waters to protect sensitive or valuable marine species and habitats against harmful human activities. MPAs can vary in size and the degree of protection, from reserves totally closed to all activities, to multiple-use areas that allow human uses compatible with specific conservation objectives (see Roberts *et al.*, this volume).

The World Summit on Sustainable Development (WSSD) agreed in 2002 on the establishment of MPAs consistent with international law and based on scientific information, including representative networks, by 2012. The specific goals and targets were to ensure practical and timely implementation of this commitment, and this included the need to designate cold-water coral reef locations as MPAs. Cold-water coral reefs also occur in the international waters of the high seas, beyond national jurisdiction. The protection of these reefs is now the focus of international efforts to protect vulnerable high-seas habitats and to create a legal basis for protection consistent with the UN Convention on the Law of the Sea (UNCLOS). This is currently being discussed at the international level, mainly under UNCLOS and the Convention on Biological Diversity. Some of the actions taken by national governments in the Atlantic, Indian and Pacific Oceans are discussed below.

In 2003, the OSPAR Commission for the Protection of the Marine Environment of the North-East Atlantic identified *Lophelia* reefs as a threatened and/or declining habitat. In the light of the commitments made at the Ministerial Meeting of the OSPAR Commission in 2003, OSPAR has started to compile information on these reefs (and other marine habitats of a similar status as a basis for further measures to be taken to protect the cold-water coral reefs in the region (OSPAR, 2003).

In November 2004, the Convention on Future Multilateral Cooperation in North-East Atlantic Fisheries (NEAFC Convention) agreed to close five seamounts and a section of the Reykjanes Ridge on the high seas off

Iceland in the NEAFC Regulatory Area for three years to bottom-trawling and static gear, in order to protect vulnerable deep-water habitats (including cold-water coral reefs).

At its General Meeting in Okinawa (3–4 July 2004), the International Coral Reef Initiative (ICRI) adopted a Decision on Cold-Water Coral Reefs. In April 2005 ICRI was asked to agree that cold-water coral reefs should become a standard agenda item for ICRI General Meetings and set out terms of reference and a programme of work for an *ad hoc* committee to implement. The cold-water coral reef activities under ICRI will focus on the ecology and conservation of these ecosystems with the aim to identify opportunities to raise awareness and recognition of cold-water coral reefs and the threats that they face. They encourage the additional study and monitoring of cold-water coral reefs and recommend that the *ad hoc* committee work with the ICRI Secretariat to identify and invite countries that are known to have cold-water coral reefs but are not currently members of ICRI to participate. ICRI will identify opportunities for capacity-building and review what implementation modalities, if any, might be needed, including a review of the potential implications for ICRI's current work and the potential role of ICRI operational networks.

Atlantic Ocean

Most continental shelves of the northeastern and northwestern Atlantic Ocean have suitable environmental conditions for cold-water corals. Some of the reefs found in these regions, especially on the eastern seaboard stretching from Norway to West Africa, are among the best studied and constitute the basis for most of our knowledge on cold-water coral reefs. However, new reefs are being discovered continually even among these relatively well-known parts of the Atlantic Ocean. The largest *Lophelia* reef so far (about 100 km^2) was found in 2002.

In April 2005, a major four-year international research project 'Hotspot Ecosystem Research on the Margins of European Seas' (HERMES) was launched with funding from the European Union to study cold-water coral reefs and other deep-water marine environments in more detail. The cold-water coral reef work under HERMES will focus on various sites in the East Atlantic (from northern Norway to Mauritania, including some sites in the Mediterranean).

Norwegian Shelf, northeast Atlantic

There are many cold-water coral reefs along the shelf break and the edges of the deep troughs of the Norwegian Shelf, including the largest and the shallowest *Lophelia* reefs, which is the Røst Reef, approximately 35 km × 2.8 km, southwest of the Lofoten Islands. There are also several reefs in Norwegian fjords, including the Selligrunnen Reef at 39 m in the Trondheimsfjord. Scientific cruises and fishing reports indicate that the mid-Norwegian shelf sector between 62° 30′ N and 65° 30′ N and the shelf break between 62° 30′ N and 63° 50′ N contain the densest occurrence of corals, at 200 to 400 m depth.

There has been trawling along the continental shelf break and on the shelf banks since the mid-1980s, including robust rock-hopper trawls, which have allowed larger vessels to fish in rougher and previously inaccessible areas. These have caused the complete destruction of coral reefs in some places.

Norway was the first country to implement protection of cold-water corals in European waters. The need for urgent action to protect these reefs emerged after the Norwegian Institute of Marine Research estimated that probably between 30% and 50% of the cold-water coral reefs in Norwegian waters had been partially or totally damaged by bottom-trawling. In 1999, Norwegian fisheries authorities established a regulation for the protection of cold-water coral reefs against fisheries damage with the Sea-Water Fisheries Act within Norway's exclusive economic zone (EEZ). This regulation prohibits intentional destruction of coral reefs and requires precaution when fishing in the vicinity of known reefs. Furthermore, the regulation gives special protection to particularly valuable coral reefs by totally banning the use of fishing gear that is dragged along the bottom, and may come in contact with the reefs. So far five reefs have received this special protection: the Sula Reef, Iverryggen Reef, Røst Reef, Tisler Reef and Fjellknausene Reef. The Selligrunnen *Lophelia* reef has also been temporarily conserved by the environmental authorities through the Norwegian Nature Conservation Act.

The Norwegian government has outlined further measures to protect cold-water coral reefs, including a proposal to protect a selection of reefs against all threats as part of a national representative network of MPAs. The process of establishing this network started in 2001 and is due to end in 2006–2007.

Rockall Trough, Darwin Mounds and Porcupine Seabight, northeast Atlantic

Knowledge of the occurrence of corals on the Rockall Trough, Darwin Mounds and Porcupine Seabight area to the west of Ireland and the UK has increased considerably as a result of targeted studies funded by the Atlantic Frontier Environmental Network, the Natural Environment Research Council (NERC) and industrial consortia of the UK (Managing Impacts on the Marine Environment), and the European Commission (Atlantic Coral Ecosystem Study) and Environmental Controls on Mound Formation along the European Margin projects.

Lophelia pertusa occurs along the relatively shallow flanks of the Rockall Bank and to a lesser degree on Porcupine Bank at 180 to 300 m depth. The slopes of the Rockall Trough and the northern and eastern parts of the Porcupine Seabight are covered in coral carbonate mounds at 500 to 1200 m depth. These *Lophelia* reefs are associated with clusters of giant carbonate mounds which rise 10 to 300 m above the sea floor, with the densest living corals on the summits of mounds where current flow is generally strongest.

There has been deep-sea fishing over this entire area since 1989. Although no quantitative analyses have been made in the wider Rockall–Porcupine area, the damage from the trawlers has been frequently documented with visual inspections. Some of the carbonate mounds are probably too steep for existing trawling gear, but low-relief mounds are much more vulnerable to trawling.

A special area of concern is the Darwin Mounds, approximately 100 km^2 in the northern Rockall Trough and 185 km off northwest Scotland. These series of mounds 1000 m deep were discovered in 1998 during an environmental survey by a consortium of oil companies and the UK government. The mounds are probably 'sand volcanoes' formed by fluid release, and are colonized by *L. pertusa* and a rich associated community. Just two years after their discovery, there was direct evidence that the mounds had been trawled (Masson *et al.*, 2003). The UK government requested urgent action through the European Commission in August 2003 and an emergency measure was imposed to prohibit bottom-trawling and similar activities within the Darwin Mounds. This action for the conservation and sustainable exploitation of the fisheries resources was taken under the common fisheries policy. In March 2004, the European Council permanently prohibited such fishing in an area of approximately 1300 km^2.

The UK intends to designate the Darwin Mounds as a special area of conservation under the EC Habitats Directive. However, there is no national legislation to specifically protect cold-water coral species in UK waters. *Lophelia pertusa* reefs now feature in the non-statutory UK Biodiversity Action Plan, which recommends conservation and research on their distribution and designation within MPAs, and *L. pertusa* reefs are being considered as nationally important features within a review conducted by the UK Department for Environment, Food and Rural Affairs (Defra).

Ireland has formed a working group of all sectors to determine policy to conserve cold-water corals after evidence was presented of fishing damage in 2001 (Grehan *et al.*, 2004). In June 2003, the Irish government also decided to protect some cold-water coral under the EC Habitats Directive. The Department of the Environment, Heritage and Local Government is now identifying suitable sites, in consultation with major stakeholders.

Azores, Madeira and Canary Islands

Lophelia reefs occur off the Canary Islands and often at depths greater than 1000 m around the Atlantic islands of Madeira and the Azores. These reefs are part of the belt of reefs in the northeast Atlantic stretching from northern Norway to West Africa. After evidence of damage from trawlers was obtained, the EC proposed in 2004 mechanisms to protect these vulnerable deep-water coral reefs from trawling around the Azores, Madeira and Canary Islands. This extends the temporary protection from trawling by a special access regime. The new regulations will guarantee continuity of protection for these areas as part of EC legislation.

Atlantic Canada

Corals have long been known in Atlantic Canada, because they frequently appear as by-catch in fishing trawls, long-lines and gillnets. The Department of Fisheries and Oceans at the Bedford Institute of Oceanography began studies in 1997 by interviewing fishers and fishing observers on commercial vessels. They extended this with video and photographic observation of cold-water corals collected during research cruises. Cold-water corals are widespread off Nova Scotia, Newfoundland and Labrador, and extend northwards to the Davis Strait.

The Scotian Shelf off Nova Scotia has coral reefs occurring predominantly between 190 and 500 m, with corals frequently caught in fishing gear. The distribution and status of these corals were reviewed in 1997 by the Ecology Action Centre, which identified three major areas where closures were implemented on the outer continental shelf and slopes: the Gully, a large submarine canyon on the Scotian Shelf with the highest diversity of coral species in Atlantic Canada; the Northeast Channel, with a high density of gorgonian corals; and the Stone Fence, with the first *L. pertusa* reef to be discovered in Canada.

The Department of Fisheries and Oceans is designating the Gully as the first MPA in Atlantic Canada under the Oceans Act (1997), after draft regulations were released for public comment in 2003. The MPA prohibits damaging activities to protect species in this ecosystem, including deep-sea corals. All activities, including research, will be excluded from one of the three zones. There is little evidence of fisheries damage, and the halibut long-line fishery will be permitted to continue in part of the MPA. Remotely operated vehicle (ROV) surveys in 2000 and 2001 in the Northeast Channel confirmed that octocorals grew in areas with cobbles and boulders, but 29% of all surveys showed that colonies had been damaged by long-line and trawl fishing for redfish (*Sebastes* spp.).

The Canadian government declared 424 km² around Romey's Peak as a multiple-use conservation area in 2002, because of a high density of gorgonian corals in the Northeast Channel. About 90% of the area is now a 'restricted bottom fisheries zone' and closed to all bottom fishing, with the remaining open only to authorized long-line fishing. There is an ongoing observation program to survey the level of fishing activity and any damage.

The first *L. pertusa* reef in Atlantic Canada was found off the Stone Fence at the mouth of the Laurentian Channel in 2003. This is a small reef, 1 km long and several hundred metres wide, but has been heavily damaged by fishing. A 15-km² area around the reef has been closed to all bottom fishing under the Fisheries Act to allow the corals to recover.

US Atlantic and Pacific waters

Cold-water coral ecosystems and habitats occur along the continental shelf and slope of both the Atlantic and the Pacific coasts of the USA, in Alaskan waters of the Bering Sea, and on island slopes and seamounts in the US Caribbean and Pacific.

Currently, there is no US legislation that specifically conserves cold-water corals, although recent bills regarding protection of these resources from trawl fishing damage have been proposed in the US House of Representatives and Senate. The Magnuson–Stevens Fishery Conservation and Management Act governs the conservation and management of fishery resources in the US EEZ from 3 to 200 nautical miles offshore. It requires the Secretary of Commerce, via the National Oceanic and Atmospheric Administration (NOAA) and eight Regional Fishery Management Councils, to develop and maintain fishery management plans for resources under their jurisdiction. Although primarily established to ensure sustainable fisheries, fishery management plans provide some protection from fishing damage for a number of cold-water coral resources. National Marine Sanctuaries and environmental compliance in the management of outer continental shelf natural gas and oil leases by the Minerals Management Service of the US Department of the Interior may provide additional protection for some cold-water corals.

Northeast United States

The US waters north of Cape Hatteras contain numerous cold-water hard corals, soft corals and hydrocorals. The major structure-forming corals are primarily octocorals (*Paragorgia, Acanthogorgia* and *Primnoa*). Species that depend on a hard base are most abundant in the canyons along the continental slope and on the New England seamount chain (which extends beyond the US EEZ). The distribution and abundance of cold-water corals in this region remain poorly known, and only a few surveys have been conducted. In 2004, the New England and Mid-Atlantic Fishery Management Councils recommended the protection of two submarine canyons with known cold-water coral resources from monkfish bottom-trawling.

Southeast United States and Gulf of Mexico

These waters contain the best-developed deep coral reefs in US waters formed from the stony *Oculina, Lophelia* and *Enallopsammia* corals. The status of the *Oculina* reefs, which are only found at a depth of 60–100 m off eastern Florida, have deteriorated since they were documented in the 1960s. The narrow reef area stretches some 167 km along the shelf break about 32 to 68 km offshore. Submersible dives sponsored by NOAA in the 1970s showed large coral reefs rich in shrimp and fish such as groupers, which became a target for commercial and recreational fishery in the following years. This geographically restricted reef area is one of the first known examples of cold-water coral reefs living in close proximity to warm-water corals, although they are in deeper waters and further offshore.

In 1984, a substantial portion (315 km^2) of this *Oculina* reef ecosystem became the first cold-water coral MPA in US waters; a decision prompted by the recommendation of the South Atlantic Fishery Management Council. Trawling, dredging and other disruptive activities, such as anchoring, were banned within the Oculina Bank Habitat Area of Particular Concern (OHAPC). In 1994, the OHAPC was closed to fishing for snapper and grouper species for ten years as a precautionary measure. This area, now known as the Oculina Experimental Closed Area, was closed to test the effectiveness of a fishery reserve for the restoration of fish stocks. In 2003, the area was extended in order to update the research plan and better evaluate the current results. The OHAPC was enlarged in 2000 to 1029 km^2 with the prohibition of fishing for snapper and grouper species only applying within the Oculina Experimental Closed Area.

Despite considerable efforts to protect the *Oculina* reefs off eastern Florida, recent ROV and submersible surveys show that illegal trawling and fishing activities have reduced much of the reef habitat to coral rubble. Consequently, NOAA recently increased surveillance and enforcement of the OHAPC. However, recently discovered *Oculina* reefs outside the OHAPC are vulnerable to damage caused by legal fishing.

In addition to *Oculina* reefs, deep-water banks of *Lophelia pertusa* and *Enallopsammia profunda* corals occur at depths of 700–850 m along the base of the Florida–Hatteras slope, off the coasts of North and South Carolina, Georgia and Florida. These cold-water reefs are only beginning to be explored, but appear to be the most extensive cold-water reefs in the northwest Atlantic. The South Atlantic Fishery Management Council is considering new MPAs to protect these coral habitats from fishing damage.

Lophelia pertusa and *Madrepora oculata* coral aggregations also occur in the US EEZ along the continental slope of the Gulf of Mexico. Impacts from fishing gear and oil and gas exploration or development are potential threats in these areas.

United States and Canadian west coast, Alaska and Aleutian Islands

Cold-water corals, especially octocorals, are widely distributed along the Pacific continental shelf, continental slope, and seamounts of North America. Much of the available information on the distribution of cold-water corals in this region comes from records of coral by-catch in fisheries. Recent submersible explorations in Alaska have revealed exceptionally rich coral and sponge habitats. Validated information on fishing impacts on coral grounds is available from the Aleutian Islands. US federal fishery observer data indicate extensive sponge and coral by-catch occurred in the Aleutian Islands fisheries. The North Pacific Fishery Management Council prepares fishery management plans for US EEZ around Alaska, and has protected more than 180 000 km^2 in the Gulf of Alaska from trawling. The Council is currently considering options for additional protection measures for cold-water coral habitats on the continental shelf, Aleutian Islands and Alaskan seamounts.

United States insular Pacific

Cold-water corals, especially octocorals, occur in the waters around Hawaii, other US islands and seamounts of the central and western Pacific. Trawling has not been permitted in the US EEZ of the central and western Pacific since 1983. There are black coral and precious coral beds in Hawaii, where there is a limited, but well-managed, fishery for several species used to make jewellery. Recently, the black coral fishery has been threatened by an invasive soft coral species, *Carijoa riise*, from the Caribbean. The soft coral has been found overgrowing and killing up to 90% of black coral colonies in surveyed areas below 75 m (NOAA, 2004).

Pacific and Indian Oceans

Little is known about the status of cold-water corals in the Pacific and Indian Oceans. The corals are presumed to be widely dispersed on the many thousands of seamounts, as well as on the continental slopes of islands and continents. However, only a small number of these sites have been visually surveyed, showing that coral density declines below 1000 to 1500 m. The density of precious corals in the North Pacific is greatest at 100 to 400 m and 1000 to 1500 m, and coral abundance seems to depend directly on the productivity of the overlying waters.

Many seamounts shallower than 1500 m have been commercially exploited for mineral resources and fish, with more than 70 commercial fish species taken off seamounts as well as 20 species of precious corals (Grigg, 1984; Rogers, 1994). Since the mid-1960s, successive waves of fisheries have targeted the extensive coral and fish resources off seamounts in the North and South Pacific, and Atlantic and Indian Oceans. Fishing effort has often been massive: between 1969 to 1975 there were 18 000 trawler days of effort by the former Soviet Union fleet trawling on a few seamounts in the southeast Emperor–northern Hawaiian Ridge system, and more than 100 Japanese and Taiwanese vessels started a second wave of coral fishing on central North Pacific seamounts in 1981 (Grigg, 1993).

Seamount fisheries are particularly vulnerable to overexploitation due to their isolation, and most species taken are often particularly long lived and show infrequent recruitment. These fisheries are characterized by a 'boom and bust' cycle. At the end of the 1970s, when the pelagic armorhead (*Pseudopentaceros* spp.) fishery collapsed, seamount fisheries shifted first to the southwest Pacific for orange roughy (*Hoplostethus* spp.) around New Zealand and Tasmania and then to the Indian Ocean, North Atlantic Ridge and the southeast Atlantic off Namibia. Tropical and subtropical seamounts have been exploited for alfonsino (*Beryx* spp.) (Koslow *et al.*, 2000), but precise locations of these fisheries are often not recorded, particularly when they occur in international waters (e.g. the central Indian Ocean) or when they involve poaching within the EEZ of another country.

There are few observations of the damage of this fishing on benthic communities; however, coral by-catch from orange roughy fisheries around New Zealand and Tasmania has been substantial, particularly in the early years when 1–15 tonnes of coral by-catch were taken per trawl (Probert *et al.*, 1997; Anderson and Clarke, 2003). Based on photographic evidence, Koslow *et al.* (2001) found virtually no coral cover, living or dead, on heavily fished seamounts off Tasmania, in marked contrast to unfished or lightly fished seamounts.

There is usually little overlap in coral species composition between groups of seamounts; no species have been found in common between seamounts south of Tasmania and those on the Norfolk Ridge or Lord Howe Rise in the northern Tasman Sea and southern Coral Sea. This high degree of endemism greatly increases the risk of extinction of biodiversity by the large-scale removal of bottom fauna from seamounts. Very few of the seamounts in the Pacific and Indian Oceans have been protected, and only a few countries have adopted measures to conserve seamount habitats and ecosystems in their territorial waters.

Seamounts in the Australian EEZ

The summits of seamounts south of Tasmania and within the Australian EEZ are rich in the reef-building cold-water coral *Solenosmilia variabilis* which provides a good habitat for a diverse range of other animals, including many fish species. In 1999, the Australian government declared the Tasmanian Seamounts Marine Reserve under the National Parks and Wildlife Conservation Act 1975. The key objectives of the management plan are (1) to add a representative sample of this unique seamount region to the National Representative System of Marine Protected Areas; and (2) to protect the high biodiversity values of the seamount benthic communities from human-induced disturbance.

The reserve has two management zones with different objectives and permissible activities. There is a highly protected zone near the bottom which is managed to protect the coral reef ecosystems, and where no fishing or petroleum or mineral exploration is permitted. Above this there is a managed resource zone from the ocean surface to 500 m depth, which allows tuna long-line fishing in the surface waters.

Seamounts in the New Zealand EEZ

The key goals of the New Zealand government are to maintain the biodiversity and productive ecosystems on seamounts within their EEZ. The Ministry of Fisheries protected 19 representative seamounts under a Seamounts Management Strategy from bottom trawling and dredging in 2001 (Anonymous, 2001), and a national strategy has addressed protection of deepwater biodiversity from bottom trawling since September 2004. These seamounts are distributed around the EEZ, including the Chatham Rise, sub-Antarctic waters, and the east and west coasts of the North Island. The protected seamounts vary from the very large Bollons Seamount in the sub-Antarctic to tiny seamounts on the Chatham Rise. Although little is known about their fauna, it is hoped this precautionary approach will protect representative components of the animals and habitats. None of these seamounts has been fished, except for Morgue, which was included to study recolonization and regeneration after the fishing stopped.

INFORMATION, MANAGEMENT AND RESEARCH

The distribution of cold-water corals and reefs is still poorly known. Information is especially lacking for the tropical and subtropical deep-water areas near developing countries and small island developing states. Most location records are held by individual experts and scientific institutions, or by companies exploring the deep waters for commercial purposes. There is a need to combine this information from the various sources, maintain the data in secure places, and present summary information to all stakeholders to improve conservation and management. However, it is particularly time-consuming and expensive to gather these data using the latest deep-sea technology and instruments. Modelling the potential distribution of cold-water coral reefs will focus further research and habitat mapping, especially in the tropical and subtropical areas where direct observations of the reefs are very limited. The results of modelling activities should be verified with existing records and observations and should be widely distributed.

Knowledge about the biology of cold-water corals is also poor; there is little information on the structure and function of cold-water coral ecosystems. There is also little understanding of the effects of different human activities on these corals and reefs and their capability to regenerate. Furthermore, cold-water coral field research is expensive, and can potentially cause damage to the systems being studied. Therefore there is a need for good international coordination of marine research programmes so that research efforts can be focused to achieve cost efficiency and minimise damage to the coral habitats.

Monitoring and assessment

Most regulations and measures to protect cold-water coral reefs have only been established recently, and little information exists about their efficacy in achieving conservation objectives. Since many of these areas occur far offshore or in international waters, monitoring, surveillance and enforcement of measures will be expensive and pose special challenges. More regulations and measures are going to be established soon, therefore it is becoming increasingly important to compile and share information about the range of management strategies adopted by various countries and organizations, and to develop monitoring and assessment tools to evaluate and redefine the approaches taken to protect the reefs. This will help to guide countries in their efforts to manage cold-water coral reefs, especially those countries with fewer resources for basic research.

As emphasized in a number of chapters in this book, appropriate monitoring is vital for the conservation, protection and sustainable management of ecosystems. The monitoring of remote and deep-water habitats is still challenging and requires the development of methods and equipment that are robust, practicable, flexible and cost-efficient, so that they can be customized to local conditions and applied in waters of both developed and developing countries. Monitoring efforts should be able to describe the status of undisturbed reefs, and the state and recovery of damaged reefs, as well as the environmental and socio-economic effects of conservation and management regulations and measures.

In light of the increasing amount of data and information becoming available from various sources, there is a need to consider establishing and maintaining database facilities and regular publications on the health and status of cold-water coral reefs, similar to those in place for warm-water tropical reefs, which are able to assist resource managers in coral reef conservation. The activities carried out by countries and international organizations (including UNEP) *inter alia* under the umbrella of ICRI, are a first step in this direction.

CONCLUSIONS

Cold-water coral reefs are long-lived, fragile and unique ecosystems in the colder parts of our oceans. They represent vulnerable biodiversity hotspots with important ecological functions in the deeper waters of the marine realm, comparable to the better-known warm-water reefs in shallow tropical waters. However, there are still large gaps in our knowledge about the distribution and biology of cold-water coral reefs, and their importance for associated faunas (including commercial fish species). Almost every survey shows impacts of human activities and the signs of deliberate or accidental damage to cold-water coral reefs (especially from bottom-trawling), regardless of where and at what depth these corals occur. This means that further scientific research on cold-water coral reefs has to go hand in hand with urgent, concerted action for their conservation, protection and sustainable management, to ensure that these ancient reefs, together with the goods and services they supply, are not lost forever. The recommendations given in Freiwald *et al.* (2004) provide a framework for activities and actions to be taken at national, regional and global level, including the need to raise the awareness of cold-water coral reefs; to stimulate further research and monitoring; to share resources, information, knowledge and lessons learned; and to adopt precautionary regulations and measures designed to conserve and manage these reefs sustainably. With more and more information on the state and threats to cold-water coral reefs emerging (Freiwald and Roberts, 2005), countries are taking or considering action to protect cold-water coral reefs in their national waters as part of their commitment to internationally agreed targets and goals such as the reduction in the rate of biodiversity loss by 2010 and the establishment of ecologically representative networks of marine protected areas by 2012. Following concerns raised at the UN General Assemblies in 2003 and 2004 (United Nations, 2004), international processes have been set up under the Convention on Biological Diversity and the UN Convention on the Law of the Sea concerning the protection of marine biodiversity (including cold-water coral reefs) in sea areas beyond the limits of national jurisdiction. Multi-stakeholders consultations involving governments, international organizations, industry and business are being held to explore and formulate innovative and balanced agreements, which take into account the various interests and concerns, and which can be implemented effectively and successfully. Cold-water coral reefs are certainly no longer 'out of mind', and it is hoped that we will be able to protect these magnificent ecosystems before it is too late.

ACKNOWLEDGEMENTS

This text is largely based on an updated and revised summary of the UNEP–WCMC Biodiversity Series Report No. 22, *Cold-Water Coral Reefs: Out of Sight – No Longer Out of Mind* (Freiwald *et al.*, 2004).

REFERENCES

Anderson, O. F. and Clark, M. R. (2003). Analysis of bycatch in the fishery for orange roughy, *Hoplostethus atlanticus*, on the South Tasman Rise. *Marine and Freshwater Research*, **54**, 643–52.

Anonymous (2001). Seamount closures. *Seafood New Zealand* (June) 1–21.

Cairns, S. D. (1982). *Antarctic and Subantarctic Scleractinia*, Antarctic Research Series No. 34. Washington, DC: American Geophysical Union.

(1984). New records of ahermatypic corals (Scleractinia) from the Hawaiian and Line Islands. *Bishop Museum Occasional Papers*, **25**, 1–30.

(1995). *The Marine Fauna of New Zealand: Scleractinia (Cnidaria: Anthozoa)*. Auckland, New Zealand: New Zealand Oceanographic Institute.

Freiwald, A. and Roberts, J. M. (eds) (2005). *Cold-Water Corals and Ecosystems*. Berlin: Springer-Verlag.

Freiwald, A., Fosså, J. H., Grehan, A., Koslow, T. and Roberts, J. M. (2004). Cold-Water Coral Reefs: *Out of Sight–No Longer Out of Mind*, Biodiversity Series No. 22, Cambridge: UNEP-WCMC. Available online at. http://www.unep-wcmc.org/resources/publications/UNEP_WCMC_bio_series/22.htm

Fosså, J. H., Mortensen, P. B. and Furevik, D. M. (2002). The deep-water coral *Lophelia pertusa* in Norwegian waters: distribution and fishery impacts. *Hydrobiologia*, **471**, 1–12.

Gass, S. E. and Willison, J. H. M. (2005). An assessment of the distribution of deep-sea corals in Atlantic Canada by using both scientific and local forms of knowledge. In *Cold-Water Corals and Ecosystems*, eds. A. Freiwald and J. M. Roberts, pp. 223–45. Berlin: Springer-Verlag.

Gianni, M. (2004). *High Seas Bottom Trawl Fisheries and their Impacts on the Biodiversity of Vulnerable Deep-Sea Ecosystems: Options for International Action*. Gland, Switzerland: IUCN.

Grehan, A. J., Unnithan, V., Olu, K. and Opderbecke, J. (2004). Fishing impacts on Irish deep-water coral reefs: making the case for coral conservation. In *Proceedings of the Symposium on the Effects of Fishing Activities on Benthic Habitats: Linking Geology, Biology, Socioeconomics and Management*, 12–14 November 2002. Bethesda, MD: American Fisheries Society.

Grigg, R. W. (1984). Resource management of precious corals: a review and application to shallow water reef building corals. *Marine Ecology*, **5**, 57–74.

(1993). Precious coral fisheries of Hawaii and the US Pacific Islands. *Marine Fisheries Review*, **55**, 50–60.

Hall-Spencer, J., Allain, V. and Fosså, J. H. (2002). Trawling damage to Northeast Atlantic ancient coral reefs. *Proceedings of the Royal Society of London B*, **269**, 507–11.

Haugan, P. M. (2004). *Possible Effects of Ocean Acidification*. Bergen, Norway: University of Bergen.

Herzog, H., Drake, E. and Adams, E. (1997). *CO_2 Capture, Reuse, and Storage Technologies for Mitigating Global Climate Change*. Final Report, DOE Order No. DE-AF22–96PC0125. Cambridge, MA: Massachusetts Institute of Technology.

Hovland, M. T., Vasshus, S., Indreeide, A., Austdal, L. and Nilsen, Ø. (2002). Mapping and imaging deep-sea coral reefs off Norway, 1982–2000. *Hydrobiologia*, **471**, 13–17.

ICES (2002). *Report of the Study Group on Mapping the Occurrence of Cold-Water Corals*, CM 2002/ACE:05. Copenhagen: International Council for the Exploration of the Sea.

(2003). *Report of the Study Group on Cold-Water Corals (SGCOR) for the Advisory Committee on Ecosystems (ACE)*, Copenhagen: International Council for the Exploration of the Sea.

Kleypas, J. A., McManus, J. W. and Menez, L. A. B. (1999). Environmental limits to coral reef development: where do we draw the line? *American Zoologist*, **39**, 146–59.

Koslow, J. A., Boehlert, G. W., Gordon, J. D. M. *et al.* (2000). Continental slope and deep-sea fisheries: implications for a fragile ecosystem. *ICES Journal of Marine Science*, **57**, 548–57.

Koslow, J. A., Gowlett-Holmes, K., Lowry, J. K. *et al.* (2001). Seamount benthic macrofauna off southern Tasmania: community structure and impacts of trawling. *Marine Ecology Progress Series*, **213**, 111–25.

Masson, D. G., Bett, B. J., Billett, D. S. M. *et al.* (2003). The origin of deep-water, coral-topped mounds in the Northern Rockall Trough, Northeast Atlantic. *Marine Geology*, **194**, 159–80.

Mikkelsen, N., Erlenkeuser, H., Killingley, J. S. and Berger, W. H. (1982). Norwegian corals: radiocarbon and stable isotopes in *Lophelia pertusa*. *Boreas*, **11**, 163–71.

NOAA (2004). National Oceanic and Atmospheric Administration, Coral Reef News, Coral Reef Conservation Program. Volume 1 No. 3, p. 4

OSPAR (2003). Available onlin at http://212.219.37.107/hosted/ospar/ospar.html.

Probert, P. K., McKnight, D. G. and Grove, S. L. (1997). Benthic invertebrate bycatch from a deep-water trawl fishery, Chatham Rise, New Zealand. *Aquatic Conservation: Marine and Freshwater Ecosystems*, **7**, 27–40.

Reed, J. K., Shepard, A. N., Koenig, C. C. and Scanlon, K. M. (2005). Mapping, habitat characterization, and fish surveys of the deep-water *Oculina* Coral Reef Marine Protected Area: a review of historical and current research. In *Cold-Water Corals and Ecosystems*, eds. A. Freiwald and J. M. Roberts, pp. 443–65. Berlin: Springer-Verlag.

Rogers, A. D. (1994). The biology of seamounts. *Advances in Marine Biology*, **30**, 305–50.

Shester, G. and Ayers, J. (2005). A cost-effective approach to protecting deep-sea coral and sponge ecosystems with an application to Alaska's Aleutian Islands region. In *Cold-Water Corals and Ecosystems*, eds. A. Freiwald and J. M. Roberts. Berlin: Springer-Verlag.

United Nations (2004). Cold-water coral reefs. In *Addendum to the Report of the Secretary-General to the 59th Session of the United Nations General Assembly on Oceans and the Law of the Sea (Document A/59/62/Add.1)*, Part 2, *Vulnerable Marine Ecosystems and Biodiversity in Areas beyond National Jurisdiction*, p. 48. Available on line at http://www.un.org/Depts/los/index.htm.

Zibrowius, H. (1973). Scléractiniaires des Iles Saint Paul et Amsterdam (Sud de l'Océan Indien). *Tethys*, **5**, 747–78.

(1980). Les Scléractiniaires de la Méditerranée et de l'Atlantique nord-oriental. *Mémoires de l'Institut Océanographique, Monaco*, **11**, 1–284.

PART II

Uses and abuses: ecological and socio-economic issues

5

Challenges and accomplishments towards sustainable reef fisheries

TIM McCLANAHAN
Wildlife Conservation Society, Mombasa, Kenya

INTRODUCTION

Sustainable use is the concept that resources should be used in a way that achieves a balance between resource production and human consumption, such that harvesting will not reduce future production and options for resource use. Sustainable management therefore requires a shift in focus from short- to long-term use and profits, and places importance on sustaining species with potential future uses. It is also closely aligned with ecosystem management concepts where resource use is expected to maintain the many ecological processes and diversity while managing for multiple present and future needs of people. These concepts are generally acceptable and desirable to most members of society but the problem with implementing them is that they can frequently conflict with the daily practices and desires of the individuals that collect resources, which are frequently focused on minimizing effort and maximizing short-term harvests and profits (Aswani, 1998) and therefore lead to 'collective action problems' when the resources are being collected by many with the same profit motives (Ostrom, 1990). Further, the continual improvements of technology and increases in human populations have produced harvesting and marketing potential beyond the production potential of most ecosystems. Coral reefs are no exception but because they are often viewed as a 'common-pool resource' with exceptionally high biological diversity and potential uses they pose special problems for management.

Coral Reef Conservation, ed. Isabelle M. Côté and John D. Reynolds.
Published by Cambridge University Press.

The discussion that follows will outline some of the characteristics of the coral reef ecosystem and resource use, and the effects of fishing on coral reefs, and will suggest ways that these characteristics can be managed for sustainability of the harvest and the ecosystem. The challenge to describe and present useful recommendations is large – given that over 100 mostly tropical, poor and culturally diverse countries have coral reef fisheries that range from subsistence gathering of intertidal snails to industrial trawl fishing and the export of luxury items. Consequently, there will ultimately be a need to gather information and develop management systems sufficiently useful for specific people, technologies and coral reef ecosystems but this does not preclude the value of developing global policies and guidelines for programmes of study and management that can assist site-specific management objectives. This, therefore, is the primary purpose of this short overview of fisheries sustainability.

THE CORAL REEF FISHERIES ENVIRONMENT

Coral reefs are limited to tropical environments that experience high light levels, warm water temperatures, high water motion, low nutrients and strong land-based influences, including pollution. The coral reef environment houses many species because coral skeletons, both live and dead, provide refuge from predators for fishes and invertebrates. Reefs are productive both from algal productivity and plankton-derived input but in many places the production is less than the demand by consumers that inhabit the reef and therefore many fish travel away from the coral reef to find additional food. This high concentration of fish makes them excellent fishing grounds and are, therefore, a target habitat for fishermen.

Production and its limits

One of the curiosities of the coral reef ecosystem is the high productivity of the plants and algae but the low net production of fish (Nixon, 1982). The benthic algae production rivals agriculturally intensive and productive systems such as sugar cane but humans can use less than 1% of this production in the form of fisheries (Hatcher, 1997). This occurs because of the high internal demand for this production by the coral reef species themselves, such that most coral reefs maintain a balance between production and consumption, with little if any excess that can be exported or used by humans. Other ecosystems, such as oceanic upwelling systems can produce nearly 50 times more fish than coral reefs for each unit of algal production.

Consequently, coral reefs should not be seen as a source for fisheries production for global trade, but rather as a repository of biological diversity. Nonetheless, coral reefs do support important fisheries for tropical people with reported yields ranging widely from 0.1 to 50 tonnes km^{-2} yr^{-1} (Table 5.1). The annual average reported yields from over 35 fishery studies worldwide is around 6.6 tonnes km^{-2} and may be near the maximum sustained yield but the variation around this mean is larger than the mean itself, suggesting high variation among study sites, which makes reliable estimates and recommendations difficult. There is also considerable variation in the means within ocean basins, with low estimates for the Caribbean, moderate for the Indian Ocean, and the highest yields reported from the Pacific.

Estimated yields vary greatly depending on the ecological productivity, fishing gear, species selection, effort and history of fishing in the coral reef. For example, in lightly fished reef areas, such as the remote Chagos Islands of the Indian Ocean, the catch per person is around 60 kg day^{-1} (Mees *et al.*, 1999) whereas heavily fished reefs in Kenya produce around 3 kg day^{-1} per person (McClanahan and Mangi, 2001). Ironically, the sustainable yields from the Chagos and Seychelles have been estimated at the low end of production between 0.10 and 0.22 tonnes km^{-2} whereas the Kenyan reefs produce around 3–12 tonnes km^{-2} and some reefs have potential for higher production if the high fishing effort could be reduced (Table 5.1). The differences between these two areas are primarily due to the fact that most of the Indian Ocean island fishery is in deep water (up to 150 m), uses non-renewable resources and refrigeration, and is selective, while in Kenya the fishery is less than 10 m deep, uses renewable resources, and is unselective. The Chagos fishery employs about 600 fishermen in 9000 km^2 fishing area and therefore the fishermen density is less than 0.1 fishermen km^{-2}, as compared to around 7000 fishermen in around 500 km^2 fishing areas of Kenya or around 14 fishermen km^{-2} (Mees *et al.*, 1999; McClanahan and Mangi, 2001). Consequently, differences in effort, water depth, aerial extent, technology of the fishery and different histories and selectivity of fishing create difficulties for estimating resource productivity and making precise recommendations on maximum sustained yields. The monetary value of the fishery, which generally ranges from US$1 to 5 kg^{-1} of finfish, will also influence the profitability, incentive, and therefore the effort and associated yields. The catch per person is the most frequently collected statistic for coral reef fisheries, ranging from 1 to 60 kg day^{-1} per person (Dalzell, 1996), but, by itself, is not very helpful in determining the maximum sustainable catch, as it always declines

Table 5.1. Summary of fish yields from coral reefs, site descriptions, and source from the literature; for each region the mean and standard deviation in brackets are provided

Location	Habitat type	Area fished (km^2)	Maximum depth fished (m)	Yield ($t\ km^{-2}\ yr^{-1}$)	Source
Caribbean					
Puerto Rico	Coralline shelf	5 300	100	0.1–1.4	Weiler and Suarez-Caabro (1980)
Jamaica	Coralline shelf	3 422	200	1.2–4.3	Munro (1977)
Jamaica	Coral, seagrass and sand	1 807	50	0.34	Koslow *et al.* (1994)
Belize	Coral, seagrass and sand	709	n.a.	0.55	Koslow *et al.* (1994)
Mean for Caribbean				1.32 (1.54)	
Pacific Ocean					
Ontong Java (Solomon Islands)	Atoll reef and lagoon	122	n.a.	0.6	T. Bayliss-Smith (unpubl. data)
Tarawa (Kiribati)	Atoll reef and lagoon	459	30	7.2	Mees *et al.* (1988)
Ifaluk Atoll	Atoll reef and lagoon	5	n.a.	5.1	Stevenson and Marshall (1974), based on observations by Alkire (1965)
American Samoa	Fringing reef	3	40	8.6–44.0	Wass (1982)
Palau	Fringing and others	450	20	1.7–3.0	Kitalong and Dalzell (1994)
Western Samoa	Fringing reef	300	40	11.4	Zann *et al.* (1991)
Philippines, Apo	Fringing reef	1.5	2–60	11.4–31.8	Alcala (1981), Alcala and Luchavez (1981), Maypa *et al.* (2002)
Hulao-hulao	Barrier reef	0.5	15	5.2	Alcala and Russ (1990)
Sumilon	Fringing reef	0.5	40	14.0–36.9	Alcala and Gomez (1985), Lopez (1986),
Niue	Fringing reef and reef slope	6.2	60	9.3	Dalzell *et al.* (1993)
Nauru	Fringing reef and reef slope	7.5	100	4.5	Dalzell and Debao (1994)

Panilacan	Fringing reef	1.8	29	10.7	Savina and White (1986), Bellwood (1988),
Fiji, Koro and Lakeba	Fringing reefs	8.4	n.a.	5	T. Bayliss-Smith (unpubl data)
Yanuca, Dravuni, Moala, Totoya, Navatu	Fringing reefs	n.a.	n.a.	0.3–10.2	Jennings and Polunin (1995)
Papua New Guinea					
Kavieng	Fringing reefs and patch	207.7	30	0.42	Wright and Richards (1985)
Port Moresby	Reef and lagoon	116	40	5	Lock (1986)
Indonesia	Coraline shelf	2800	60	3.2	Pet-Soede *et al.* (2001)
Mean for Pacific Ocean				10.2 (11.4)	
Indian Ocean					
Tanzania	Coralline shelf	12160	n.a	0.8–5.7	Wijkstrom (1974)
Tanzania	Mixed reefs	4500	n.a.	7–13	McClanahan *et al.* (1999)
Red Sea coast of Saudi Arabia	Coralline shelf and reefs	n.a.	3–60	0.4	Kedidi (1984)
Gulf of Suez (Red Sea)	Coralline shelf and reefs	n.a.	3–60	0.31	Sanders and Kedidi (1984)
Kenya,					
Diani	Fringing reefs	23	5	12	McClanahan *et al.* (1997)
Southern Kenya	Fringing reefs	23	5	3.3–6.6	McClanahan and Mangi (2001)
Mombasa	Fringing reef	3	5	7	Rodwell *et al.* (2003)
Maldives, North Male	Fringing reefs	552	45	0.95	Van der Knaap *et al.* (1991)
Mauritius	Fringing reefs	243	n.a.	3.96–7.5	Munbodh *et al.* (1988)
Chagos	Reef slopes	8926	<70	0.10–0.22	Mees *et al.* (1999)
Chagos	Deep reef slopes	339	7–150	0.72–1.38	Mees *et al.* (1999)
Seychelles	Reef slopes	n.a.	<70	0.17–1.38	Mees (1992)
Mean for Indian Ocean				3.8 (4.1)	
World average, mean (SD)				6.6 (9.0)	

with increased effort and it is seldom measured at the time that a fishery is opened.

To practically estimate the maximum sustained yield for specific coral reefs without relying on the assumptions of the equations and models used by fisheries scientists it is necessary to monitor the catch on a per-unit-area basis over time. When catch-per-area rises there is the potential for further catch but when declining the maximum sustained yield has been exceeded. Consequently, one of the simplest ways to manage a fishery is to reduce effort whenever the total catch for a specific area declines. Catch per area has a few pitfalls that must be acknowledged in order to avoid the common problems that lead to fishing beyond sustainable levels. The two most common problems are that both the effort and area that the catch is measured from are often not constant over time unless carefully checked. It is possible for the total catch at a landing site to be constant or to increase far beyond the maximum sustained yield of the local fishery because the fished area increases and fishers are expending more daily effort. In a declining fishery, fishers will travel further and fish longer and this makes it necessary to change the effort and area parts of this calculation to get unbiased catch-per-area estimates. If these factors are considered and the conditions of the environment that influence production do not change greatly between years, then monitoring the catch per area can give good estimates of fish yields.

Ecological influences on production

Light, water movement, nutrients and aspects of the reef ecology, such as the cover of coral and algae and the abundance of herbivores, influence production by algae and subsequently coral reef fisheries. Consequently, where light penetration is reduced by depth or dirty water, coral fishery yields are also expected to decline, which is one of the incentives for maintaining clean sea water. The full consequences of dirty water are not well understood but they do include reduced growth rates of corals and increased decay rates of dead skeletons (Ferrier-Pages *et al.*, 2000; Carriero-Silva *et al.*, 2005), which will reduce the number of refuges available for fish and invertebrates. There may be other unexpected influences of dirty or nutrient-enriched water such as increases in coral and fish diseases (Diamant *et al.*, 1999; Bruno *et al.*, 2003).

Important aspects of the coral reef community that influence production are the types of primary producers, their rates of production, and the cropping and fertilization influences of herbivores. Coral and calcifying algae have lower consumable production than some of the common and highly productive turf and foliose algae that frequently dominate the reef benthos. Similarly, large leathery frondose algae that are common on reefs without high grazing also have lower production than turf algae (Steneck and Detheir, 1994). Consequently, a very high dominance of coral or calcifying algae associated with high levels of herbivory or leathery frondose algae associated with low levels of herbivores can reduce fish biomass (McClanahan and Graham, 2005) and production, and influence fisheries' yields. Coral provides refuge for coral reef fish and there needs to be a balance between cover by productive algae and corals to achieve both the production and refuge required by fish. Although poorly studied and understood, it is expected that reefs with intermediate levels of coral cover of between ~25% and 50% of the bottom are likely to be optimal for sustaining high fisheries yields.

EFFECTS OF FISHING ON CORAL REEFS

Fishing has direct effects on coral reefs by removing usable biomass in the form of fish and other species, which are fishery targets or are caught incidentally (by-catch). Since coral reefs are complex systems, fishing also has indirect effects, which result from the exploitation itself (e.g. habitat destruction) or its consequences (e.g. 'cascades' resulting from depletion of target species). While side effects on habitat are relatively well known, the indirect effects through food webs and other species interactions are potentially as far reaching but are less understood (Polunin and Pinnegar, 2002).

Direct effects

Fishing increases the total mortality of target and by-catch species and over time this will tend to reduce numbers of individuals and biomass in the stocks involved. This population decline will occur if recruitment remains the same or declines, but not if it increases greatly. Knowledge of recruitment patterns in space and time could help predict stock sustainability. Larval settlement of a few small species onto reefs has been extensively studied (Doherty, 2002), but little is still known about the spatial and temporal patterns of replenishment to fisheries stocks and the effects of this on their exploitation. For only a few reef fishery stocks has age structure been determined (Choat *et al.*, 2003), but the evidence is that reef fishery recruitment varies over time and, as occurs in temperate waters, the catch may often be dominated by particularly strong year-classes (Russ *et al.*, 1996). Consequently, uncertainty of recruitment is one reason for maintaining areas closed to fishing, because the high biomass of large fecund reef fish in an effectively protected area helps to insure against recruitment failure. Some of the most useful data on direct effects of fishing have come from large-scale comparisons of abundances along fishing pressure gradients. These studies show that at low levels of fishing intensity, biomass declines rapidly as fishing effort increases (Jennings and Polunin, 1996) and species with large maximum size are most vulnerable to depletion (Jennings *et al.*, 1999). While long thought to be mostly resilient to exploitation, some large target species on reefs, such as the bumphead parrotfish (*Bolbometopon muricatum*), are now recognized to be vulnerable to local exploitation (Dulvy and Polunin, 2004).

Fishing has the effect of reducing survivorship, and thus with intense exploitation, older age-classes are lost altogether and mean age in a stock declines. Fish are very variable in their growth rate, but because of this lower survivorship and the direct size-selectiveness of fishing, the mean and maximum sizes of fish caught decline with increasing fishing pressure. Other characteristics directly related to body size include fecundity; thus another direct effect of fishing is likely to be reduced egg production. This does not necessarily translate into reduced recruitment, however, because egg output by the spawning stock is not the sole determinant of recruitment. Although poorly known in reef fishes, many other factors including food availability and predation are likely to affect the egg, larval and juvenile stages (Leis and McCormick, 2002).

Indirect effects

In some cases heavy fishing results in the proliferation of some species. Examples include coral-eating starfish and snails and some herbivorous sea urchins that become abundant when predators such as triggerfish, wrasses and emperors are depleted by exploitation (McClanahan, 2000; Dulvy *et al.*, 2004a). High nutrient and plankton levels are expected to increase the recruitment rates of these pest species and contribute to their rapid colonization (Birkeland, 1982) when predation is low (Muthiga, 1996). It appears that the above invertebrates are particularly prone to population outbreaks, but it is unclear why this is so or why others are not.

The loss of coral cover wrought by pest species is expected ultimately to reduce the abundances of fish that require cover for refuge from predators; thus fisheries' yields may also be reduced. In the case of sea urchins, very high numbers can eat virtually all of the algal production and prevent it from being utilized by other species. Where three or more species are controlled in series by predation, they are said to constitute a trophic cascade; such linkages among species in food webs thus have profound implications for the condition of reefs and their biological diversity (Pinnegar *et al.*, 2000). Specifically, such connections are points through which the integrity of whole reef ecosystems is likely to be compromised by fishery exploitation. Furthermore, high densities of sea urchins also lead to erosion of the reef substratum and this may reduce the role that reefs play as wave-energy protectors of soft shores (see Sheppard, this volume), including beaches valuable to the tourism industry. A net effect of the proliferation of some scraping herbivores may be that more money has to be invested in shoreline protection.

Simulation model of effects of fishing on fish species

The changes described above were incorporated into a simple simulation model that was calibrated based on various ecological rate processes reported in the coral reef literature (McClanahan, 1995). Fish and sea urchin species were pooled into larger functional groups and their responses to fishing were estimated based on the choices and intensity of fishing. The model included only benthic production and the main routes of this production through the food web to fishermen (Fig. 5.1). The model produces estimates for the rates of inorganic carbon or calcium carbonate deposition by corals and algae and erosion of the reef framework by herbivorous fish and sea urchin grazers into sand. Fishermen catch rates were estimated for artisanal fisheries, where the maximum catch per man was estimated at 25 kg day^{-1} in reefs with no prior fishing. During model simulations the number of fishermen and their prey selection were varied to determine the outcome of the harvesting rate of each functional group on the rest of the ecosystem and organic and inorganic carbon. For example, fishermen could select piscivores, invertivores, herbivores or any of the possible combinations of these prey. The model was run until no change or a steady state was achieved and then the variables in the model were plotted against the density of fishermen.

The results of this simple model indicate the complexity of interactions and the ecological effects of fishing (Fig. 5.2). Fishing all functional fish groups (Fig. 5.2a) leads to the elimination of piscivores and invertivores at 0.03 and 0.09 fishermen ha^{-1} (= 3 to 9 fishermen km^{-2}) respectively. A large change occurs, however, at 0.07 fishermen ha^{-1} where the maximum catch of around 300 kg ha^{-1} yr^{-1} (= 30 tonnes km^{-2}) is reached. At this fishing intensity, sea urchin wet weight increases to 4500 kg ha^{-1}, which

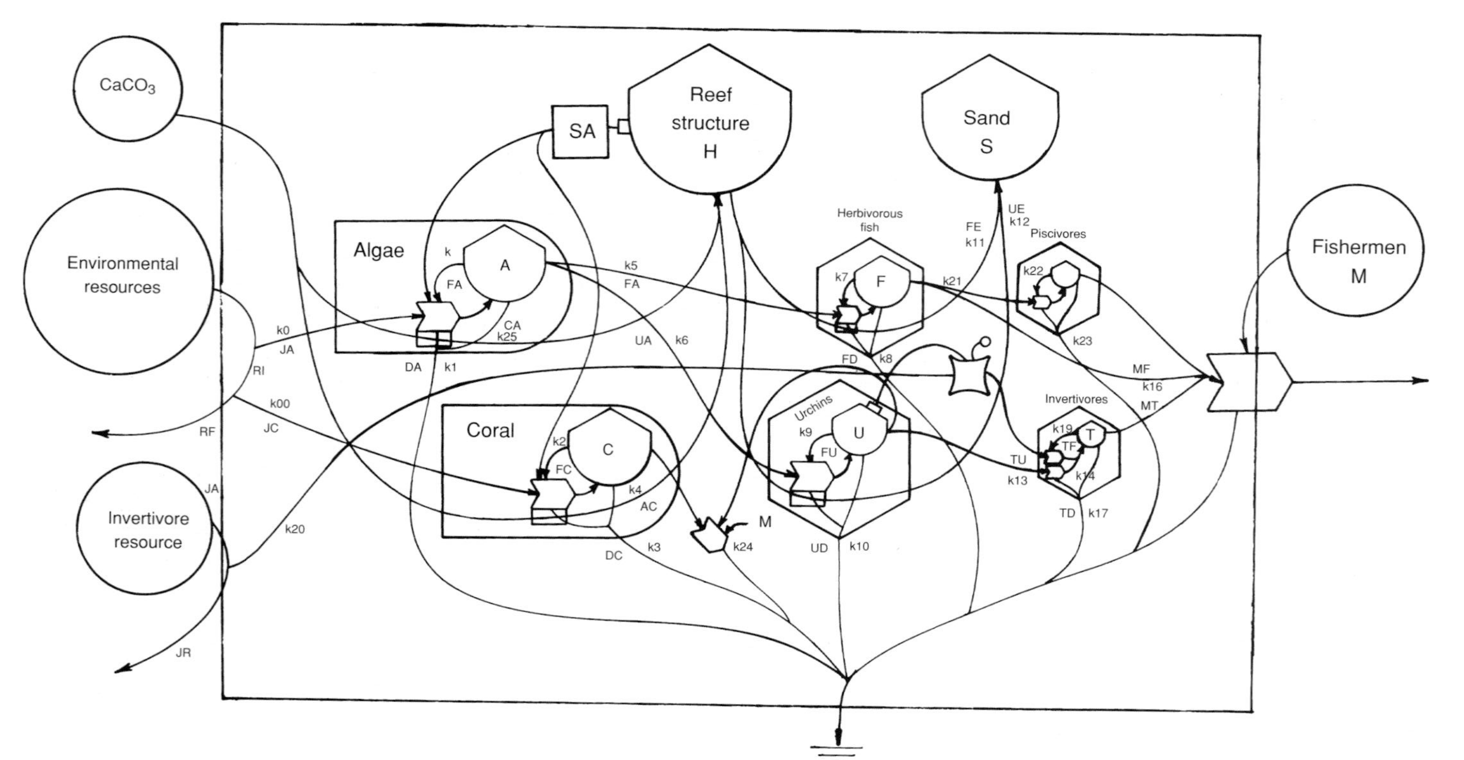

Figure 5.1 Simplified coral reef ecosystem fisheries using an energy-flow diagram. The system is contained within a box and circles are energy or material flows from outside the system. Lines are flows of energy or materials, arrows are interactions, tanks are storages, bullets are primary producers and hexagons are consumers. The full details of the model, abbreviations and calculations are given in McClanahan (1995).

reduces algal wet weight, and gross and net organic carbon productivity. Inorganic carbon (i.e. reef growth) is also reduced at this fishing intensity from 50 to 8 kg ha^{-1} day^{-1}.

The rapid change and loss of fisheries catches and reef process when all fish groups are exploited suggest the need for alternatives and possibly the need to focus fishing on piscivores and herbivores in order to maintain invertivores at a level that will not allow sea urchins to dominate. Fishing only piscivores (Fig. 5.2b) has the effect of keeping sea urchins at low levels and also results in an increase in herbivorous fish, a reduction in algae, and an increase in coral and reef growth to 57 kg ha^{-1} day^{-1}. This fishing strategy would appear to be a benign form of exploitation for the ecosystem, but the maximum yield of fish is less that 3 kg ha^{-1} yr^{-1} and achieved at only 0.02 fishermen ha^{-1}. This is not likely to be a realistic alternative in areas near large human populations that depend on natural resources.

Fishing piscivores and herbivorous fish, but not invertivores, also keeps sea urchins from dominating and the yields are high, at 400 kg ha^{-1} yr^{-1} and are obtained at 10 times the fishing effort (i.e. 0.2 fishermen ha^{-1}), which is optimal when fishing only piscivores. The ecological effect of this fishing regime is, however, less benign as algal wet weight doubles and net productivity is reduced where the maximum yield is achieved. This fishing strategy also has the effect of reducing coral and reef growth to 37 kg ha^{-1} day^{-1} at maximum catch rate. Somewhat unexpectedly the model predicts an eventual increase in reef growth above this maximum yield. This increase is due to calcification by algae alone with little contribution from corals. This result will, of course, depend on the accuracy of the model's estimate of calcification rates by algae, which will depend greatly on the abundance and success of calcifying algal species in these algal-dominated communities. Further, the yields and fishermen densities that the model produces will depend greatly on the algal productivity input of the model and how much is consumed by fisheries resources.

To test the model's relevance and predictive ability we can compare its results with field studies of Kenyan reefs. In Kenya, fishermen densities are estimated to be above 0.07 ha^{-1} and therefore fishing intensity is above the threshold at which a switch to sea urchin dominance is predicted (McClanahan and Mangi, 2001). Plots of the recovery of sites from fishing, following the establishment of marine protected areas, show that reefs often start with sea urchin wet weights of around 4000 kg ha^{-1} and this biomass decreases over time in conjunction with increased predation rates (Fig. 5.3a). After a slow start, there is also an increase in the ratio of calcifying to non-calcifying algae after protection (Fig. 5.3b).

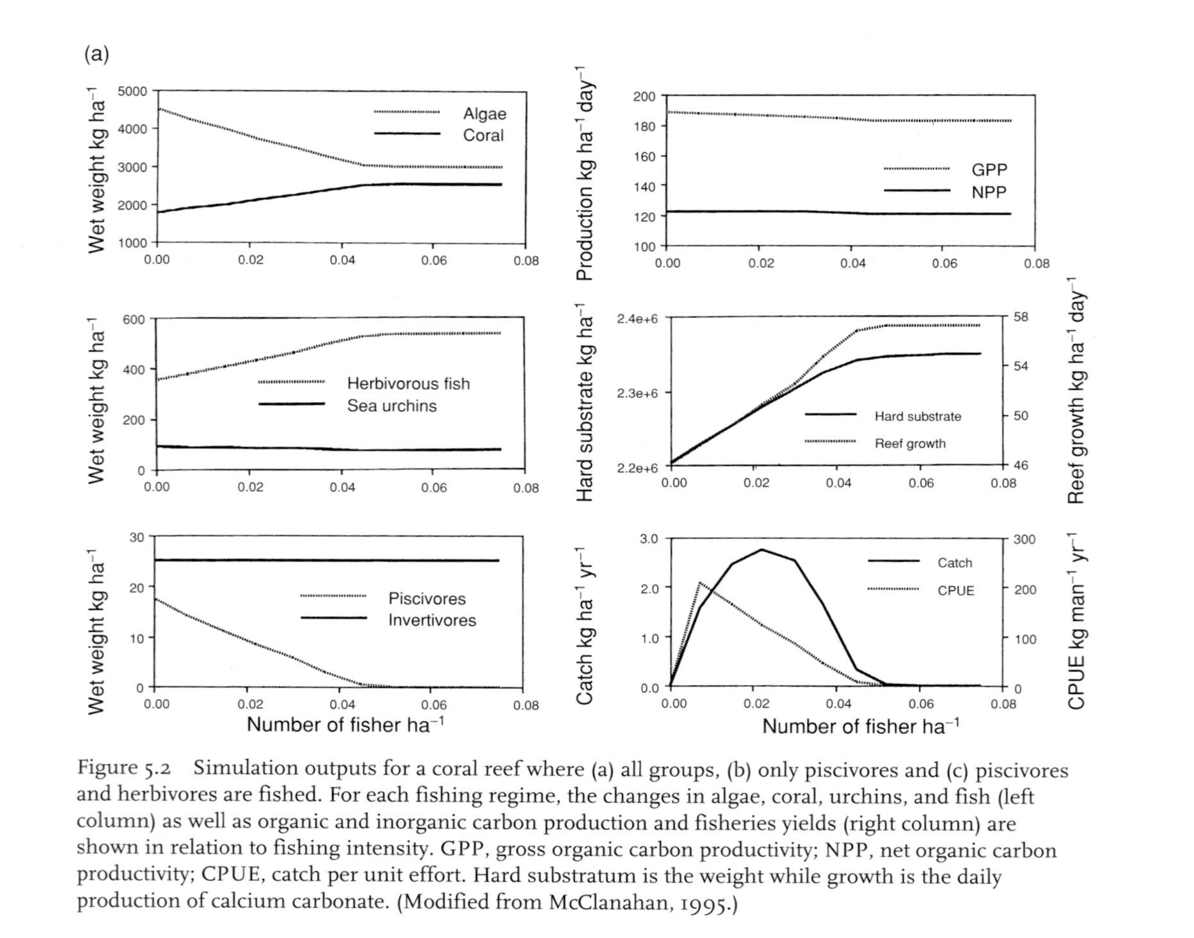

Figure 5.2 Simulation outputs for a coral reef where (a) all groups, (b) only piscivores and (c) piscivores and herbivores are fished. For each fishing regime, the changes in algae, coral, urchins, and fish (left column) as well as organic and inorganic carbon production and fisheries yields (right column) are shown in relation to fishing intensity. GPP, gross organic carbon productivity; NPP, net organic carbon productivity; CPUE, catch per unit effort. Hard substratum is the weight while growth is the daily production of calcium carbonate. (Modified from McClanahan, 1995.)

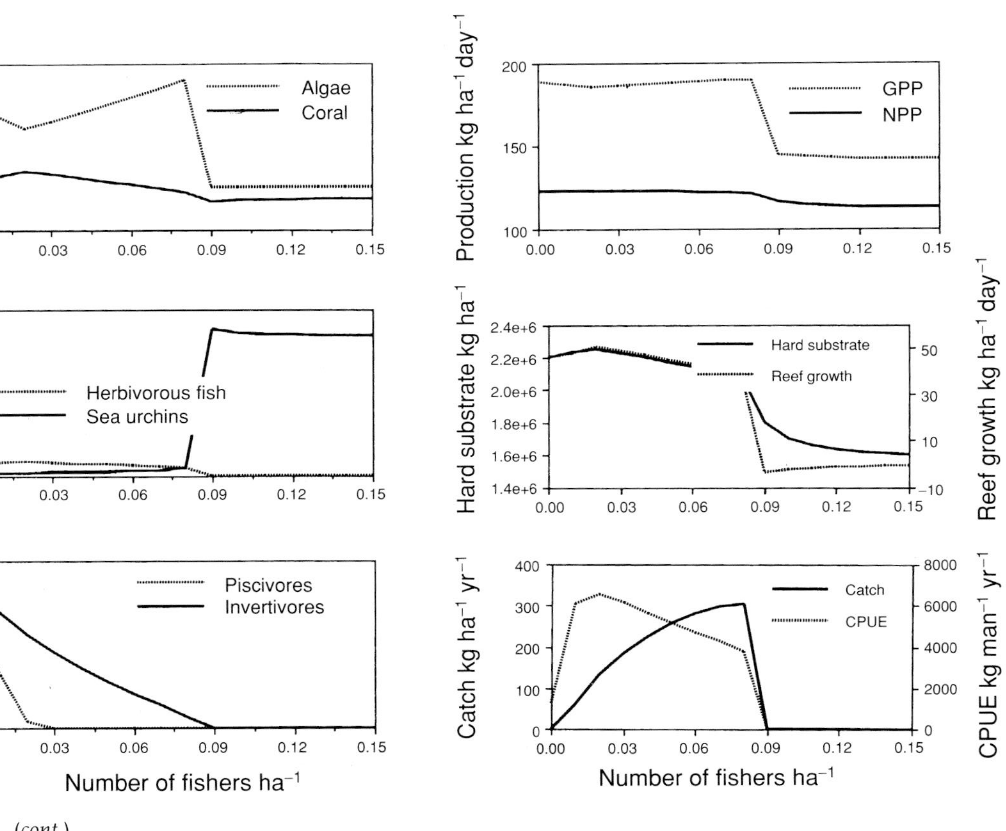

Figure 5.2 *(cont.)*

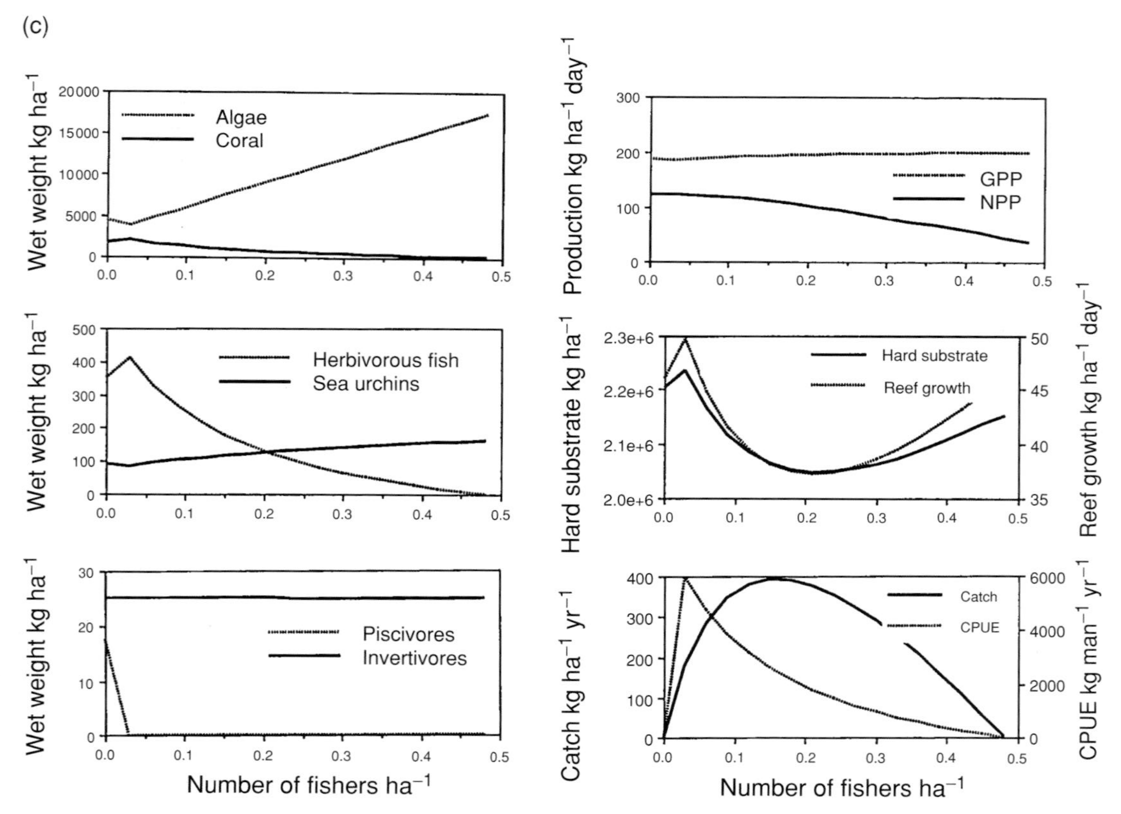

Figure 5.2 *(cont.)*

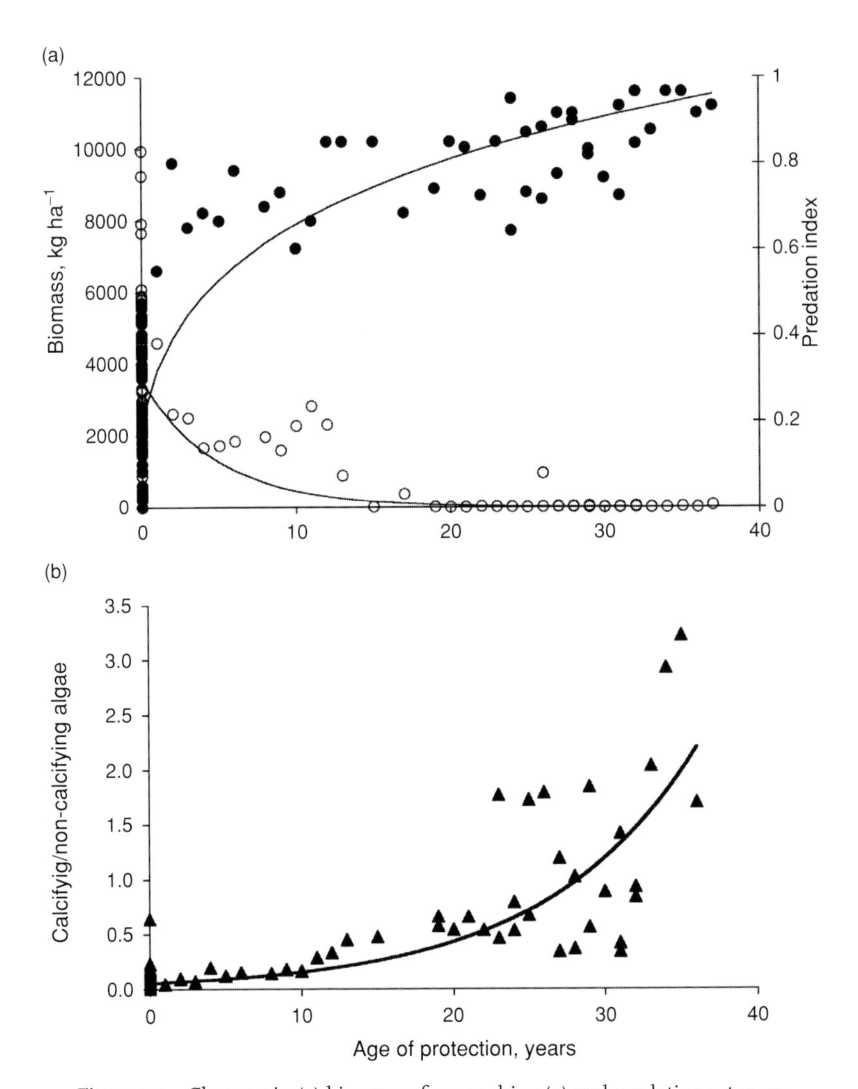

Figure 5.3 Changes in (a) biomass of sea urchins (○) and predation rates on tethered sea urchins (•) and (b) the ratio of calcifying to non-calcifying algae in Kenyan marine protected areas as a function of the time since the closure of the park to fishing.

Fish biomass in fished reefs is around150 kg ha^{-1} and recovers to around 1200 kg ha^{-1} after 20 years (McClanahan and Graham, 2005) (Fig. 5.4). Heavily fished Kenyan reefs still produce fish, but the dominant fisheries species are rabbitfish (*Siganus*) and the seagrass parrotfish (*Leptoscarus*), which feed on seagrass, and other sand and seagrass-associated generalist

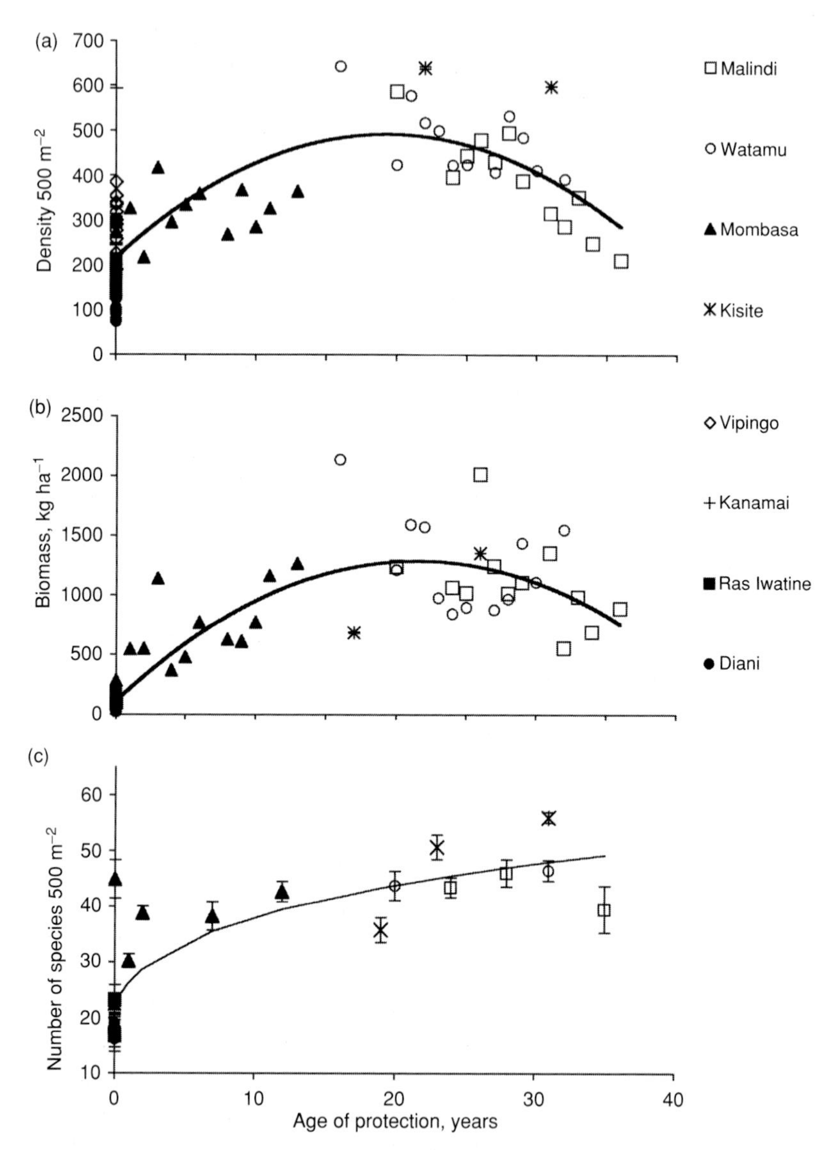

Figure 5.4 Plots of the recovery of (a) fish density, (b) fish biomass and (c) fish diversity in nine families in Kenyan marine protected areas. Eight sites are presented of which four are unprotected and fished reefs with time since closure of zero (Vipingo, Kanamai, Ras Iwatine and Diani); the four areas closed to fishing are Malindi, Watamu, Mombasa and Kisite, and differ in their time since closure. A space-for-time substitution was used such that the four parks are presented along the time axis according to the time since they were closed to fishing.

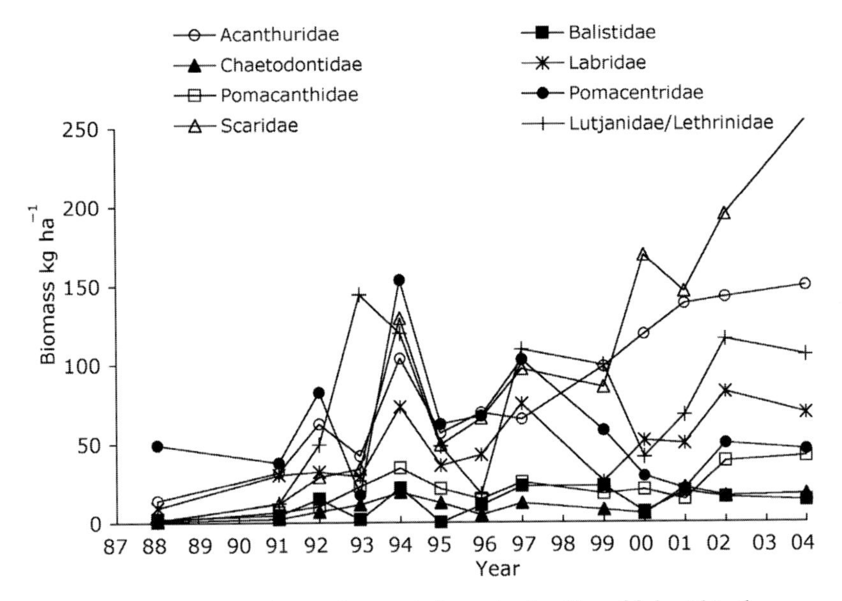

Figure 5.5 Biomass time-series trends for major families of fish within the newly protected Mombasa Marine National Park, which was legally gazetted in 1988 but did not exclude fishers until 1991 (see Fig. 5.7).

and planktonic species that do not depend on the hard bottom coral reef environment.

There are differences among the major fish families in their recovery rates, which are somewhat different from simulation model results (Fig. 5.5). For example, herbivorous parrotfish (Scaridae) have recovered well, but recovery has been slower for herbivorous surgeonfish (Acanthuridae), and triggerfish (Balistidae) appear to have very slow recovery rates. These observations suggest that the model's predictions based on energy production and flow may be more optimistic than actual values perhaps due to important life-history characteristics of species that are not well accounted for when pooling various families into generic functional groups. Nevertheless, the model does have some predictive power and will form the basis for more sophisticated models, which can be developed as more information on important parameters and species' life history accumulates.

Metamodel

Simulation models will change and approximate more realistic conditions as more details are added and better estimates of parameters are produced, and after more tests with field measurements. Nonetheless, despite the slow

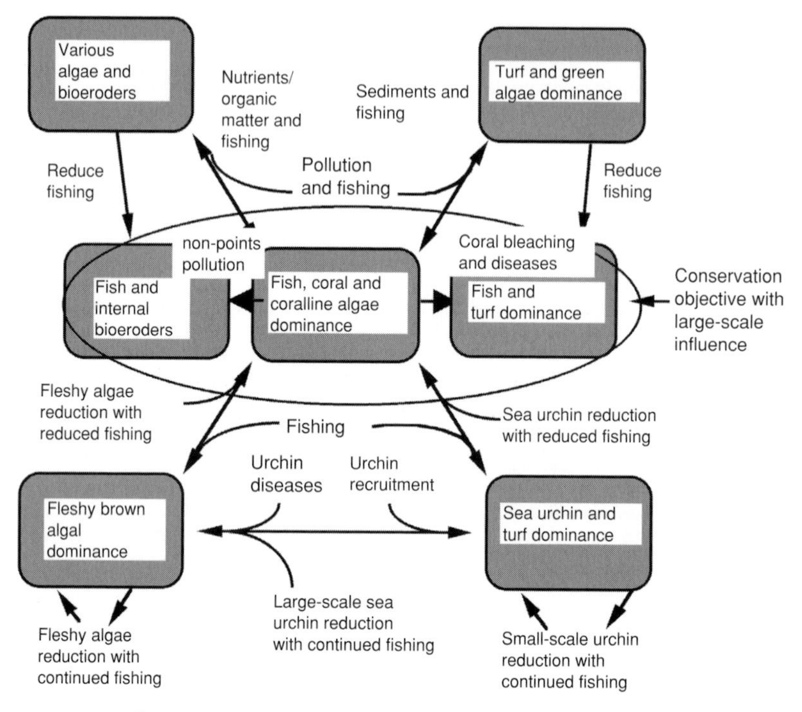

Figure 5.6 Conceptual model of the dominant states (shaded boxes) and hypothesized causative factors that move a coral reef ecosystem between states.

pace of accurate model development, there is a need for a conceptual basis to assist management through simple cause-and-effect relationships. This creates a need for conceptual or metamodels of the ecosystems and how ecosystems will change under various management systems (Fig. 5.6).

Coral reef ecologists have reported a variety of community or ecosystem states that are often described by the dominant organisms or functional groups occurring on reefs. Forces including pollution, fishing, sediments, diseases, warm water and other natural disturbances such as cyclones and various forms of human management are hypothesized to influence the various ecological states. For example, some reef ecologists believe that increases in nutrient concentrations in waters will switch dominance from hard corals to various forms of algae and heterotrophic filter feeders (Bellwood *et al.*, 2004), although others believe that coral mortality must precede the colonization by algae (see Precht and Aronson this volume). Recent studies indicate that nutrients enhance the abundance of small turf-forming and microscopic algae but not the larger frondose brown algae (McClanahan *et al.*, 2003; Carreiro-Silva *et al.*, 2005). Interactions can also be important, with combinations of coral mortality, fishing, nutrient enrichment and sediments likely to interact and produce states different from those produced by the single factor alone (McClanahan *et al.*, 1996; McClanahan and Obura, 1997).

As described above, fishing may increase the abundance of unutilized prey of fished species, resulting in increases of echinoderms such as starfish and sea urchins. In some cases these invertebrates do not recruit or are lost due to disease (Lessios, 1988) and the loss of all herbivores can lead to reefs dominated by frondose algae. In order to achieve the conservation objective of increasing the abundance and diversity of corals and fishes, managers have the option of trying to reduce fishing and pollution as well as reducing pest species or groups such as sea urchins and unpalatable frondose algae. In many cases it is important to attempt a combination of management options, as outcomes will often depend on an interaction of two or more factors (McClanahan *et al.*, 1996, 2001).

MANAGEMENT OPTIONS

Management activities are often focused on reducing catch and effort in the face of increasing numbers of people entering the fishery with more effective technology. There are six basic management options. These include restricting (1) the numbers of people or boats fishing, (2) the time allowed for fishing, (3) the fishing area, (4) gear or technology, (5) the sizes that can be harvested, and (6) the species being selected. Each or a combination of these alternatives will help to limit short-term harvesting in favour of sustaining long-term yields. In many cases more than one, if not all, of these options are needed to sustain the fishery, but what is critical to their success is the acceptability, adoption and enforcement success of the options (see Alcala *et al.*, this volume; Brown, this volume).

Effort

Constraining effort by restricting the number of people or boats is one of the most common management systems employed by government fisheries departments. Requiring fishing and boat licences and adjusting the number of licences or the fee for a licence are common restrictions. Where fisheries departments and associates are able to patrol and check for licences, these restriction can have moderate success but in most fisheries the chances of being caught are minimal, and if fishermen do not feel compelled to comply with government restriction, which is common in many poor tropical countries, there is poor compliance and enforcement and widespread disregard for the licensing system (Sutinen and Kuperan, 1999). This has led to some well-earned cynicism toward this method of restriction and greater hope for catch limits, closed areas, gear restrictions, and community or local social control.

In nations with sports and industrial fishing, failure to sustain fisheries with the above system has often resulted in a switch towards a licence for the maximum quotas or wet weight of fish where the sustainable net offtake of the target species is calculated each year. If the catch is landed at a monitored landing site, then it is possible to control catch by this method, but in tropical artisanal fisheries where catch is landed at many small sites along an undeveloped coastline, it is impractical to monitor catch of individual fishers who may typically catch less than 10 kg day^{-1} per person. This has led to recognition that local social or community control may be one of the better options for managing coral reefs fisheries (Bunce *et al.*, 2000), with stakeholders firmly embedded into the process (Brown, this volume).

Area

Closing areas to fishing is also seen as an option for fisheries management (Russ, 2002) and this has been used by people with traditional management systems where closure ranges from areas inhabited by spirits, as believed by some traditional African people (McClanahan *et al.*, 1997), to areas restricted for harvesting only during feasts when large quantities of meat are needed, as managed by many Melanesian people (Cinner *et al.*, 2005). These traditional area-management systems are considerably different from the modern image of marine parks where tourists are charged park fees by government or private business authorities to enter. The two are not often socially compatible, despite the fact that both prevent access to fishers and have potentially similar ecological consequences (McClanahan *et al.*, 1997).

Closed areas have the added benefit of protecting fish and other components in coral reef ecosystems and have, therefore, received a good deal of attention and excitement as tools for achieving both fisheries sustainability and ecosystem management (Allison *et al.*, 1998; Alcala *et al.*, this volume). They do appear to increase the density, weight and diversity of fish that are the target of fishing when they do work (Mosqueira *et al.*, 2000; Halpern, 2003), but despite the creation of many closed areas only a moderate number have achieved their full management potential (Kelleher *et al.*, 1995). Going from government gazettement to full compliance is complicated by many hurdles that seem to be overcome most frequently in areas with high levels of nature tourism (McClanahan, 1999). Nonetheless, because some coral reef species are slow-growing and slow to recover from fishing (McClanahan, 2000; Russ and Alcala, 2004; McClanahan and Graham, 2005) (Figs. 5.3–5.5), closed areas may be the only way to ensure the persistence of these vulnerable populations and the full range of closed areas needs to be encouraged (McClanahan *et al.*, 2006; Roberts *et al.*, this volume). The types of closed areas will depend greatly on the socio-economic conditions of the sites and should be flexible and utilize systems that are financially sustainable and socially acceptable (Brown, this volume). Large closed areas may be preferable but may only succeed where nature tourism and the economy can afford them, while small-scale and low-cost alternatives will succeed where there is local support but poor external funding (Alcala *et al.*, this volume).

Because the effects of closed areas on fisheries are large scale in space and time and seldom replicated, they are most commonly predicted using simulation models (Rodwell *et al.*, 2002, 2003). Models suggest that fisheries will not benefit unless catch is beyond the maximum sustained yield and also not until the biomass of fish inside the closed area has increased to levels near to its pristine biomass. For example, a recent model with assumptions about adult and larval dispersal and retention sought to predict the optimal closed area size for different levels of fisheries exploitation and found that for a reasonable annual exploitation rate of 40% of the biomass, the optimal reserve size is 10% of the fishing ground (Rodwell *et al.*, 2002). This model was further modified to examine the effects of habitat quality in the reserve, where good habitat quality could increase fish biomass in the park but might also reduce the movement of fish out of the park (Rodwell *et al.*, 2003). If increased biomass was the main effect, then fish yields increased by as much as 40%, but if retention of fish in the closed area was the main effect, then catches declined by around 20%.

The model above was calibrated for conditions near the Mombasa Marine National Park, Kenya, and the actual data indicate that there was a period of significant loss in fish catch and lost fishing area after the establishment of the park, but with time and an increase in the park's fish biomass (Fig. 5.5), there is evidence of increased catch and compensation (Fig. 5.7). Other factors such as changes in the boundary and changes in fishing gear (see below) appear to have had significant effects on fish catches and it may require more than 13 years to determine the equilibrium fisheries yield (McClanahan and Graham, 2005). These results do, however, suggest that there is a considerable time in the early stages of closure in

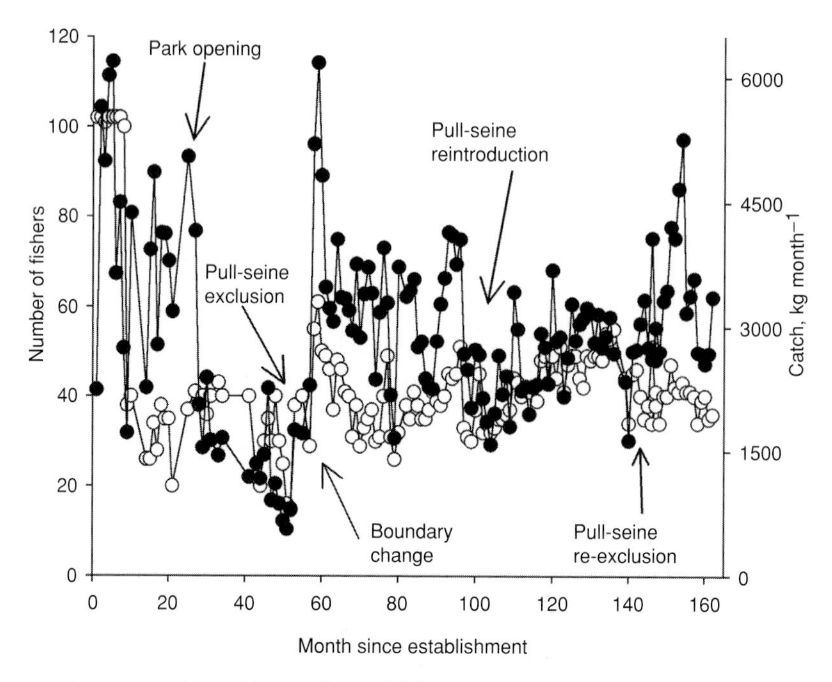

Figure 5.7 Changes in numbers of fishers (○) and monthly catch (•) adjacent to the Mombasa Marine National Park from its establishment in 1991 to 2004. The timings of important change in management, including reducing the size of the park, the elimination of seine nets, reintroduction of modified seine net and its eventual re-exclusion, are shown with arrows.

which total fisheries catches can be low and this is likely to result in conflict between fishers and closed-area managers. Nonetheless, there is subsequently a slow rise in total catch, which may be associated with the increasing fish biomass in the park. Consequently, fish catches in this site are a complex interaction between the sizes of the closed areas, the time since closure, and the types of gear or size of fish caught in the fishery. Managers will need to learn to manipulate these variables over the development of closed area management to optimize fish catch. Despite the weak support for large closed areas by fishers (McClanahan *et al.*, 2005), such areas can ultimately maintain catch by providing a refuge for fish biomass and they also maintain intact coral reef ecosystems and fishing-sensitive species, which become uncommon at even very low levels of fishing effort and require long periods to fully recover (McClanahan, 2000; Russ and Alcala, 2004; McClanahan and Graham, 2005; McClanahan *et al.*, 2006) (Figs. 5.3–5.5).

Gear and size

Increased technological advances in fishing gear are leading to unsustainable harvesting of fish in many areas, but, even among less technologically advanced fisheries, the types of gear used can also result in destruction of habitat and unsustainable fisheries. In coral reefs, a number of gear types destroy reef habitat and should be discouraged. These include nets that are dragged, have heavy weights on the drag-line, heavy traps made with slow- or non-degrading materials, explosives, poisons, and any method that breaks coral to scare or extract fish.

Less obvious is the fact that seemingly different gears can compete for similar resources. As catches decline, the gear that extracts the smallest size and most diverse fish resources may be the 'better competitor' and may reduce the catch of other gear types that select larger and more species-specific targets. Well-managed fisheries should have a mix of gear which ensures that all target species are utilized but without accelerating competition between gears for smaller fish. This requires that mesh size of gears, including the various nets and traps, be similar and lean towards catching the larger size classes of most species, i.e. after fish have reached their asymptotic size and sexual maturity.

An example of analysis of gear overlap and consequences of gear removal is provided for southern Kenya, where an evaluation of 11 402 fish caught over a two-year period found differences in the selectivity of the fish by gear (McClanahan and Mangi, 2004). Hand lines caught mostly emperors (*Lethrinus* spp.), but there was selectivity overlap between spearguns and small traps, both of which caught mostly the speckled parrotfish (*Leptoscarus*), and the largest overlap was found in the catch of seine nets, big traps, and gillnets (Fig. 5.8). Small traps caught smaller fish than spearguns, and seine nets caught the largest number of species and the smallest individuals. Consequently, this evaluation suggests that seine nets and small traps were the two gears that were least likely to maintain maximum sustainable yields because they overlapped in species selectivity and caught smaller individuals than the other gear types. Evidence also exists for lower catch per unit area and per effort in fishing grounds dominated by beach seine use (McClanahan *et al.*, 1997; McClanahan and Mangi, 2001).

To test the hypothesis that the use of seine nets was unsustainable it was necessary to remove them from some of the fish landing sites and evaluate the effects of this removal on the fish catch. A law against beach seine use existed (Fisheries Act Cap 378), but the fisheries department had not enforced this law because it was unlikely to persist unless the government

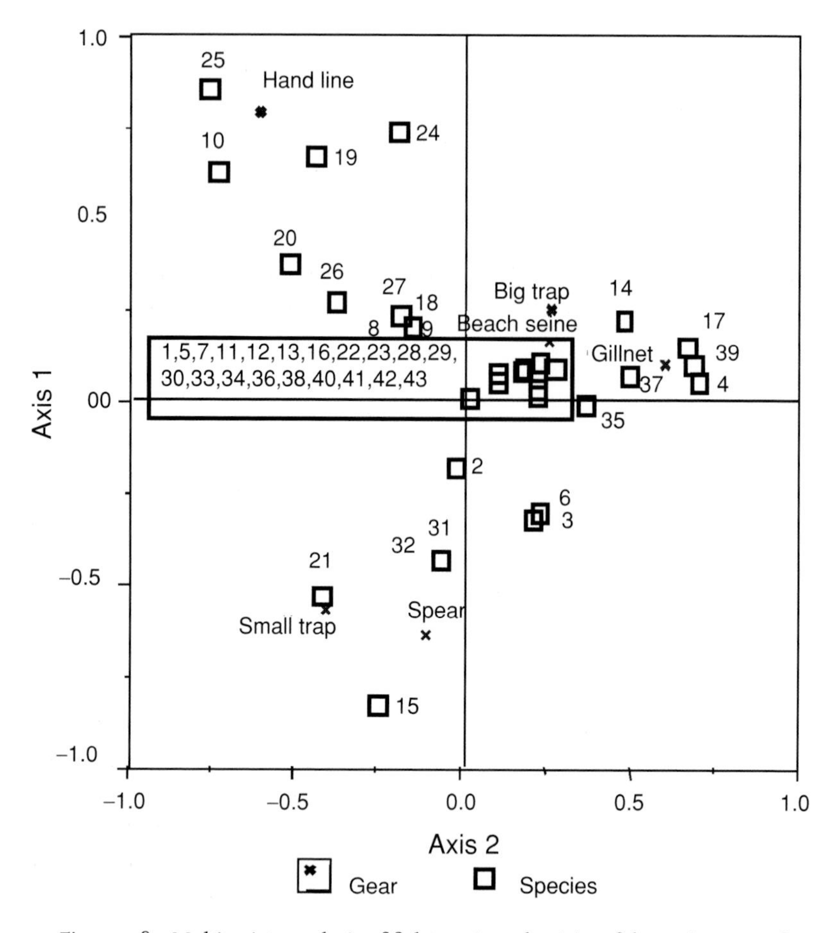

Figure 5.8 Multivariate analysis of fish species selectivity of the main types of fishing gear used in southern Kenya. Gear near the centre of the graph overlap the most in species selectivity with other gear. Position of the species of fish shown with numbers: 1, *Abudefduf sexfasciatus*; 2, *Abudefduf vaigiensis*; 3, *Acanthurus nigrofuscus*; 4, *Acanthurus triostegus*; 5, *Anampses caeruleopunctatus*; 6, *Calotomus carolinus*; 7, *Calotomus spinidens*; 8, *Cheilinus chlorurus*; 9, *Cheilinus trilobatus*; 10, *Cheilio inermis*; 11, *Geres oyena*; 12, *Halichoeres scapularis*; 13, *Hyporhamphus fur*; 14, *Leiognathus equula*; 15, *Leptoscarus vaigiensis*; 16, *Lethrinus elongatus*; 17, *Lethrinus harak*; 18, *Lethrinus lentjan*; 19, *Lethrinus mahsena*; 20, *Lethrinus mahsenoides*; 21, *Lethrinus nebulosus*; 22, *Lethrinus ramak*; 23, *Lethrinus rubrioperculatus*; 24, *Lethrinus sanguineus*; 25, *Lethrinus xanthochilus*; 26, *Lutjanus fulviflamma*; 27, *Lutjanus gibbus*; 28, *Mulloides flavolineatus*; 29, *Parupeneus barberinus*; 30, *Parupeneus macronema*; 31, *Pempheris vanicolensis*; 32, *Plectorhinchus flavomaculatus*; 33, *Pomadasys* sp; 34, *Scarus ghobban*; 35, *Scarus psittacus*; 36, *Scarus sordidus*; 37, *Scolopsis ghanam*; 38, *Secutor insidiator*; 39, *Siganus sutor*; 40, *Sphyraena flavicauda*; 41, *Sprattoloides robustus*; 42, *Carangoides* sp; 43, *Sardinella* sp.

and community leaders came to a joint agreement (McClanahan *et al.*, 2005). A questionnaire on the perceptions of fishermen and government personnel towards gear was developed and this, along with the above field data, was presented to groups of fishers and fisheries personnel. After many discussions, seine nets were identified as the top priority for elimination. This decision led to a joint effort between the fisheries community leaders and fisheries department personnel, which resulted in the partially successful removal of seine nets in Diani and a reversal in the decline in catch that had been measured since 1995 (Fig. 5.9). After two active attempts to eliminate the gear completely, by the fisheries department personnel and local leaders, it remained at some sites but at the end of the study it was reduced considerably.

This study does suggest that seine nets are not maximizing sustainable yields but those fishers using this gear are unlikely to stop using it by choice as it catches smaller fish and is therefore more competitive than the other gear. The owners of this gear are often diversified investors who only deal with the marketing of the catch and many seine fishers are either not full-time fishers or foreigners (McClanahan *et al.*, 1997). These fishers have little interest in long-term sustainability and their selfish but rational choice is to continue to use this gear even in the face of evidence and agreement that it is not the best long-term option for the fishery as a whole. Where there is disagreement between local communities and individual decision-makers who benefit from unsustainable gear, the chances for gear removal are slim without persistent control at some level of leadership. Consequently, gear that catches smaller fish than the alternatives should be eliminated from the fishery or modified to ensure they do not have a competitive size-based advantage. These types of management initiatives generally require constant vigilance by fisheries leaders and managers because the rational selfish interests of fishers will often result in reintroductions of these gears. Fortunately, gear can easily be seen and evaluated and, if needed, confiscated. Gear use is also often grounded in traditions that can be enforced by culture and laws, and this makes them one of the easier restrictions to reach consensus on and enforce.

Species and life-history characteristics

Restrictions on species are not commonly used in the tropics because of the large number of species and the lack of knowledge about which species require restrictions. Nonetheless, modelling studies of functional groups, as described above, suggest that choices that fishermen make

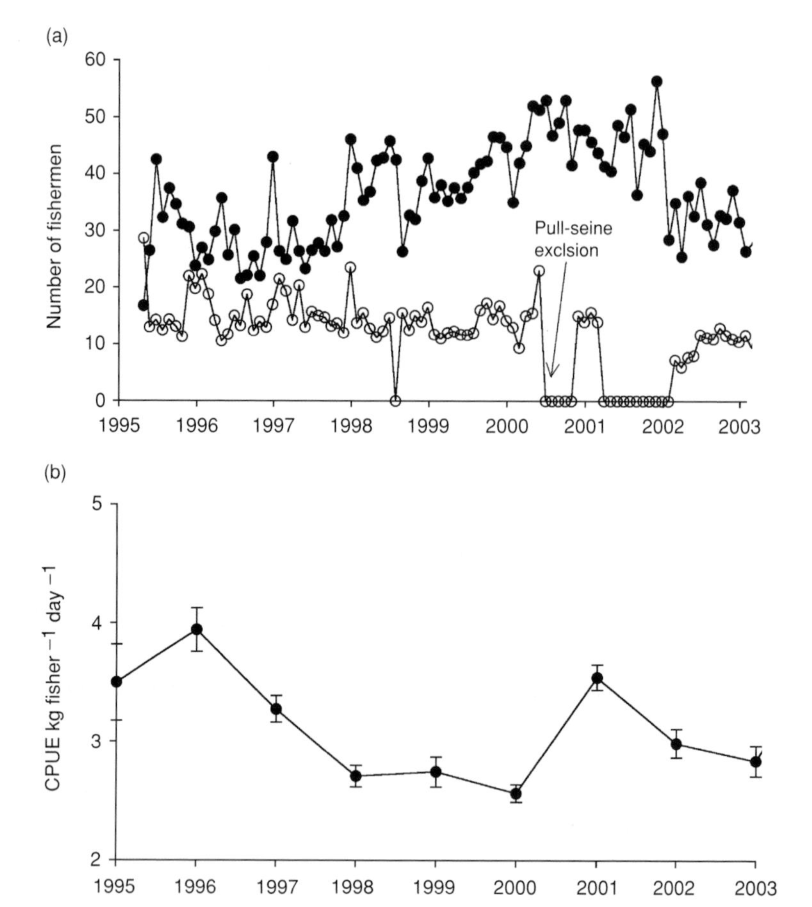

Figure 5.9 Changes in (a) the number of fishers using beach seines (○) and other fishing gear (•), and (b) fish catch per unit effort in the Diani–Chale area of southern Kenya from 1995 to 2003. Beach seines were banned in June 2000 (indicated by arrow), with support from fishers and fisheries personnel, in an effort to reduce the amount of selectivity overlap between different gears.

concerning their catch can greatly influence total yields and ecological processes (McClanahan, 1995). In some cases, not fishing a functional group, such as sea urchin predators, can increase the total yields by ensuring that algal production is channelled into herbivorous fish and not into unutilized sea urchins. The evolution of fisheries is, however, to be selective, often focusing on the high-level predators but eventually fishing species further and further down the food chain (Pauly *et al.*, 1998). This shift maintains the total catch over time, even as effort increases beyond what may be sustainable for some top-level predators and slow-growing species. The species most vulnerable to over-fishing and least able to rebound from fishery depletion are those with slow growth and late maturation. In contrast, species with 'fast' life histories generate a higher yield per unit biomass, and their early maturation makes it more likely that they will spawn before being caught. In the absence of detailed information on growth, reproduction and other biological processes in each species, susceptible species can be identified through the use of life-history proxies and these are easily available, in particular maximum size (Jennings *et al.*, 1999). The distribution of body sizes in an ecosystem is useful for the detection of fishery disturbance, and also helps in predicting fundamental ecosystem processes such as productivity and effects of predation on prey species (Dulvy *et al.*, 2004b).

Restrictions need to be placed on vulnerable species. Restrictions on fishing of spawning aggregations, where many of the carnivorous groupers and snappers congregate for short periods of time to breed, is one clear example. Unrestricted fishing of these aggregations can quickly reduce their populations and interfere with their reproduction (Sala *et al.*, 2001). Furthermore, as mentioned above, restrictions on some specialist predators of sea urchins and starfish, such as triggerfish in the genera *Balistes, Balistoides* and *Balistapus*, or wrasses in the genus *Cheilinus* and many of the parrotfish in the genera *Scarus, Sparisoma, Bolbometopon* and *Chlororus*, are prime candidates for special status and species-level restrictions due to their important role in coral reef ecology.

THE SOCIO-ECONOMIC DIMENSION

Social, cultural and economic forces will often determine the success of restriction options and the challenge for management is to find the right mix of limits for the particular human environment (see Brown, this volume). Many management systems in the past have focused on only a few of these options and if these options are not acceptable to fishers or difficult to enforce there will be poor compliance and success. Consequently, it is recommended that the perceptions towards and feasibility of various options be explored early and repeatedly at intervals during the management process through interviews and public meetings. Once the most acceptable options have been identified, the chances of adoption, compliance and success will improve, although they are not ensured without active management (McClanahan *et al.*, 2005). Once restrictions are established and their failures and successes have been documented, managers can begin the process of adding and modifying restrictions. This process of including users and their percetions in the decisions and adaptive management process is likely to build the social capital required for sustainability (Pretty, 2003; Brown, this volume).

INFORMATION AND MONITORING

Information appropriate to the scale of the resource, the users and its management is a primary ingredient for successful management (Dietz *et al.*, 2003). Conflict resolution, compliance, and building support and adaptation all require that the information is appropriate for decision-making. The level of this information will vary from the most basic concepts of fisheries and ecosystem management to more sophisticated and holistic databases on fishers, the resource and its use, and models of interaction and probabilities of associated outcomes under various scenarios.

In some cases, fishers are not aware of modern fisheries and ecosystem management and the information they need to change unsustainable practices can be as simple as the recognition that fishing effort and fish abundance are related or that a particular gear is destructive to fish habitat. Once fishers are aware of these relationships, there is increased chance that they will adjust their behaviour, management and gear towards more sustainable use. In more sophisticated management environments the outcomes and risks of each management scenario may be calculated and fine-tuned estimates of probabilities are required. In many cases, however, resource-users make decisions based on opportunities for short-term profits and it is the role of managers and society to instil an ethic of compliance that can buffer this behaviour and the consequent fisheries collective action problems or tragedies of the common.

Because decisions are based on multiple conflicts and desires it is best to collect information on a number of aspects of the fishery, not just the fish or the ecosystem, but also the socio-economic environment. This reduces the chances that unexpected consequences, surprises or externalities will disrupt management activities. For example, unemployment or prices of fuel, gear and fish could be as important as fish stock estimates in the decisions made by individuals, politicians or managers. If information about the resource is lacking, the decisions may be made on existing economic information, which can be dangerous when resources are depleted. In many cases the resource-user has informal but invaluable information about resources that needs to be part of the decision-making environment

(Johannes, 2002), but often needs to be distinguished from personal political positions.

Monitoring, or the collection of information over time, is particularly useful when testing for the long-term effects of specific management systems and to generate information that can evaluate the effectiveness of management. In an optimal management environment, monitoring data would be continuously collected and could therefore soon result in changes in management. In practice, there is often missing information and lags in time between recommended changes and compliance with management regulations. The challenge to managers is to find the right mix of information, stakeholder involvement and management action that will facilitate adaptive responses. Additionally, in many of the poor fisheries that are managed at a very local level, there is a need for simple information collection and management decisions. For example, if a particular size or catch per day of a key target species is below a certain level, then this target species would be protected from fishing for a period before testing for this threshold at some later date. Simple management heuristics or thresholds that have been established from prior scientific studies or the experiences of resource-users may be one of the better hopes for managing small-scale coral reef fisheries.

SUSTAINING ECOSYSTEM FUNCTION AND DIVERSITY

Given that it is possible to have a sustainable fishery within a degraded ecosystem and environment it behoves the public and managers to look beyond the mechanics of biomass extraction to the larger issues of the ecology and diversity of the fishing environment. Continuous and long-term fishing of an ecosystem is likely to change the ecosystem significantly in favour of fast-colonizing and fast-growing species that are tolerant of frequent disturbances. These species may be able to maintain high yields into the foreseeable future but there may be a loss of many important components of the coral reef ecosystem. For example, many degraded reefs may be replaced by rubble or seagrass ecosystems that can have productive fisheries but support only a fraction of the species diversity. Coral reef ecosystems are composed of a high diversity of species with life histories considerably different from those that will be selected by the harvesting systems. The challenge is, therefore, to not be complacent with simply achieving fisheries sustainability but to also aim for sustaining the ecosystem and all of its components. Maintaining all components of the ecosystem preserves future options and unforeseeable consequences of the changing environment. This has been one of the arguments in favour of closed or reserve areas but there may also be ways in which fishing itself can be encouraged to maintain this diversity. As mentioned above, fishing methods that destroy coral habitat or eliminate species through destruction of their breeding aggregations will not encourage the broader goal of ecosystem sustainability and should be discouraged.

GLOBAL INFLUENCES

Coral reef products such as shells, shark fin, sea cucumber, live rock, food fish, valuable invertebrates such as conch and lobster, and ornaments are part of the global trade environment. The globalization of these products has created a demand beyond what is locally sustainable (see Vincent, this volume). The trade in coral is presently included under CITES Appendix II and requires permits. Many of the other coral reef products that are equally vulnerable are, however, not well regulated, and the extent of their influence on coral reefs is poorly understood. Trade in these products should be undertaken with caution, only after some estimates of natural populations have been obtained and with assurances that the methods used to collect these species are not destructive to their habitat. Greater restrictions on trade will improve chances that the species are monitored and protected.

CONCLUSIONS

The global value of coral reefs lies in their high biological diversity. They should be managed for this diversity rather than primarily as a source of food or luxury products for the global trade. Nonetheless, many tropical people rely on coral reef fisheries, and management should seek to maintain a local balance between resource production and consumption. Restricting trade in coral reef resources to those species that have been estimated and determined to be above certain ecologically viable thresholds can achieve this balance with populations. Furthermore, temporary local restrictions should be placed on the exploitation of individuals that have not yet reproduced. Some species such as some triggerfish and parrotfish play an important role in coral reef ecology and should not be harvested. Local management can also benefit from thresholds that stop fishing when total catch per area declines or when pest species exceed thresholds. Local, national and international leaders should discourage and ban gear that destroys habitat. Restrictions should be encouraged on gear that catch small individuals and management should promote a mix of gear that do not compete for similar resources or smaller fish. Management systems need to adapt to local conditions and attitudes to be embraced by fishing cultures and self-enforced. Simple adaptive learning heuristics and thresholds for restrictions are needed and should be encouraged such that management can be simple, cost-effective and carried out by local authorities.

ACKNOWLEDGEMENTS

Some of this material is based on the International Society for Reef Studies' *Statement on Sustainable Fisheries*. I thank the following people for their help: J. Maina, A. MacNeil and N. Polunin.

REFERENCES

Alcala, A. C. (1981). Fish yields of coral reefs of Sumilon Island, central Philippines. *Bulletin of the Natural Resource Council of the Philippines*, **36**, 1–7.

Alcala, A. C. and Gomez, E. D. (1985). Fish yields of coral reefs in the central Philippines. *Proceedings 5th International Coral Reef Symposium*, **5**, 521–4.

Alcala, A. C. and Luchavez, J. (1981). Fish yields of the coral reef surrounding Apo Island, Central Visayas, Philippines. *Proceedings 4th International Coral Reef Symposium*, **1**, 69–73.

Alcala, A. C. and Russ, G. R. (1990). A direct test of the effects of protective management on abundance and yield of tropical marine resources. *Journal Consieul Internationale du la Exploration de Mer*, **46**, 40–7.

Alkire, W. (1965). *Lamotrek Atoll and Inter-Island Socio-Economic Ties*. Urbana, IL: University of Illinois Press.

Allison, G. W., Lubchenco, J. and Carr, M. H. (1998). Marine reserves are necessary but not sufficient for marine conservation. *Ecological Applications*, **8**, S79–S92.

Aswani, S. (1998). Patterns of marine harvest efforts in south-western New Georgia, Solomon Islands: resource management or optimal foraging? *Ocean and Coastal Management*, **40**, 207–35.

Bellwood, D. R. (1988). Seasonal changes in the size and composition of the fish yield from reefs around Apo Island, central Philippines, with notes on methods of yield estimation. *Journal of Fish Biology*, **32**, 881–93.

Bellwood, D. R., Hughes, T. P., Folke, C. and Nystrom, M. (2004). Confronting the coral reef crisis. *Nature*, **429**, 827–32.

Birkeland, C. (1982). Terrestrial runoff as a cause of outbreaks of *Acanthaster planci* (Echinodermata: Asteroidea). *Marine Biology*, **69**, 175–85.

Bruno, J. F., Petes, L. E., Harvell, C. D. and Hettinger, A. (2003). Nutrient enrichment can increase the severity of coral diseases. *Ecology Letters*, **6**, 1056–61.

Bunce, L., Townsley, P., Pomeroy, R. and Pollnac, R. (2000). *Socioeconomic Manual for Coral Reef Management*. Townsville, QLD: IUCN.

Choat, J. H., Robertson, D. R., Ackerman, J. L. and Posada, J. M. (2003). An age-based demographic analysis of the Caribbean stoplight parrotfish *Sparisoma viride*. *Marine Ecology Progress Series*, **246**, 265–77.

Carreiro-Silva, M., McClanahan, T. R. and Kiene, W. (2005). The role of inorganic nutrients and herbivory in controlling microbioerosion of carbonate substrate. *Coral Reefs*, **24**, 214–21.

Cinner, J. E., Marnane, M. J., McClanahan, T. R. and Clark, T. H. (2005). Conservation and community benefits from traditional coral reef management at Ahus Island, Papua New Guinea. *Conservation Biology*, **19**, 1714–23.

Dalzell, P. (1996). Catch rates, selectivity and yields of reef fishing. In *Reef Fisheries*, eds. N. V. C. Polunin and C. M. Roberts, pp. 161–92. London: Chapman and Hall.

Dalzell, P. and Debao, A. (1994). *Coastal Fisheries Production on Nauru*, Inshore Fisheries Research, Project Country Assignment Report. Noumea, New Caledonia: South Pacific Commission.

Dalzell, P., Lindsay, S. R. and Patiale, H. (1993). *Fisheries Resource Survey of the Island of Niue*, Inshore Fisheries Research Project Technical Document No. 3. Noumea, New Caledonia: South Pacific Commission.

Diamant, A., Banet, A., Paperna, I. *et al.* (1999). The use of fish metabolic, pathological and parasitological indices in pollution monitoring. II. The Red Sea and Mediterranean. *Helgol Marine Research*, **53**, 195–208.

Dietz, T., Ostrom, E. and Stern, P. C. (2003). The struggle to govern the commons. *Science*, **302**, 1907–12.

Doherty, P. J. (2002). Variable replenishment and the dynamics of reef fish populations. In *Coral Reef Fishes*, ed. P. F. Sale, pp. 327–55. Amsterdam: Academic Press.

Dulvy, N. K. and Polunin, N. V. C. (2004). Using informal knowledge to infer human-induced rarity of a conspicuous reef fish. *Animal Conservation*, **7**, 365–74.

Dulvy, N. K., Freckleton, R. P. and Polunin, N. V. C. (2004a). Coral reef cascades and the indirect effects of predator removal by exploitation. *Ecology Letters*, **7**, 410–16.

Dulvy, N. K., Polunin, N. V. C., Mill, A. C. and Graham, N. A. J. (2004b). Size structural change in lightly exploited coral reef fish communities: evidence for weak indirect effects. *Canadian Journal of Fisheries and Aquatic Sciences*, **61**, 466–75.

Ferrier-Pages, C., Gattuso, J.-P., Dallot, S. and Jaubert, J. (2000). Effect of nutrient enrichment on growth and photosynthesis of the zooxanthellate coral *Stylophora pistillata*. *Coral Reefs*, **19**, 103–13.

Halpern, B. (2003). The impact of marine reserves: do reserves work and does reserve size matter? *Ecological Applications*, **13**, S117–S137.

Hatcher, B. G. (ed.) (1997). *Organic Production and Decomposition*. New York: Chapman and Hall.

Jennings, S. and Polunin, N. V. C. (1995). Brief communications: biased underwater visual census biomass estimates for target-species in tropical reef fisheries. *Journal of Fish Biology*, **47**, 733–6.

(1996). Effects of fishing on the biomass and structure of target reef fish communities. *Journal of Applied Ecology*, **33**, 400–12.

Jennings, S., Reynolds, J. D. and Polunin, N. V. C. (1999). Predicting the vulnerability of tropical reef fishes to exploitation: an approach based on phylogenies and life histories. *Conservation Biology*, **13**, 1466–75.

Johannes, R. E. (2002). The renaissance of community-based resource management in Oceania. *Annual Review of Ecology and Systematics*, **33**, 317–40.

Kedidi, S. M. (1984). *Description of the artisanal fishery at Tuwwal, Saudi Arabia: Catches, Efforts and Catch per Unit Effort – Survey Conducted during 1981–1982*, Report No. FAO/UNDP RAB/81/002/16. Cairo: UNDP/FAO.

Kelleher, G., Bleakley, C. and Wells, S. (eds.) (1995). *A Global Representative System of Marine Protected Areas*. Washington, DC: World Bank.

Kitalong, A. H. and Dalzell, P. (1994). *A Preliminary Assessment of the Status of Inshore Coral Reefs Fish Stocks in Pala*, Inshore Fisheries Research Project Technical Document No. 6. Noumea, New Caledonia: South Pacific Commission.

Koslow, J. A., Aiken, K., Auil, S. and Clementson, A. (1994). Catch and effort analysis of the reef fisheries of Jamaica and Belize. *Fisheries Bulletin*, **92**, 737–47.

Leis, J. M. and McCormick, M. I. (2002). The biology, behavior, and ecology of the pelagic, larval stage of coral reef fishes. In *Coral Reef Fishes*, ed. P. F. Sale, pp. 171–99. Amsterdam: Academic Press.

Lessios, H. A. (1988). Population dynamics of *Diadema antillarum* (Echinodermata: Echinoidea) following mass mortality in Panama. *Marine Biology*, **99**, 515–26.

Lock, J. M. (1986). *Fish Yields of Port Moresby Barrier and Fringing Reefs*, Technical Report of the Fisheries Division of Papua New Guinea No. 86. Part Moresby, Papua New Guinea: Department of Primary Industries.

Lopez, M. D. G. (1986). An invertebrate resource survey of Lingayen Gulf, Philipines. *Canadian Special Publication in Fisheries and Aquatic Science*, **92**, 402–9.

Maypa, A. P., Russ, G. R., Alcala, A. C. and Calumpong, H. P. (2002). Long-term trends in yield and catch rates of the coral reef fishery at Apo Island, central Philippines. *Marine and Freshwater Research*, **53**, 207–13.

McClanahan, T. R. (1995). A coral reef ecosystem-fisheries model: impacts of fishing intensity and catch selection on reef structure and processes. *Ecological Modelling*, **80**, 1–19.

(1999). Is there a future for coral reef parks in poor tropical countries? *Coral Reefs*, **18**, 321–5.

(2000). Recovery of a coral reef keystone predator, *Balistapus undulatus*, in East African marine parks. *Biological Conservation*, **94**, 191–8.

McClanahan, T. R. and Graham, N. A. J. (2005). Recovery trajectories of coral reef fish assemblages within Kenyan marine protected areas. *Marine Ecology Progress Series*, **294**, 241–8.

McClanahan, T. R. and Mangi, S. (2001). The effect of closed area and beach seine exclusion on coral reef fish catches. *Fisheries Management and Ecology*, **8**, 107–21.

(2004). Gear-based management of a tropical artisanal fishery based on species selectivity and capture size. *Fisheries Management and Ecology*, **11**, 51–60.

McClanahan, T. R. and Obura, D. (1997). Sedimentation effects on shallow coral communities in Kenya. *Journal of Experimental Marine Biology and Ecology*, **209**, 103–22.

McClanahan, T. R., Kamukuru, A. T., Muthiga, N. A., Gilagabher Yebio, M. and Obura, D. (1996). Effect of sea urchin reductions on algae, coral and fish populations. *Conservation Biology*, **10**, 136–54.

McClanahan, T. R., Glaesel, H., Rubens, J. and Kiambo, R. (1997). The effects of traditional fisheries management on fisheries yields and the coral-reef ecosystems of southern Kenya. *Environmental Conservation*, **24**, 105–20.

McClanahan, T. R., Muthiga, N. A., Kamukuru, A. T., Machano, H. and Kiambo, R. (1999). The effects of marine parks and fishing on the coral reefs of northern Tanzania. *Biological Conservation*, **89**, 161–82.

McClanahan, T. R., McField, M., Huitric, M. *et al.* (2001). Responses of algae, corals and fish to the reduction of macroalgae in fished and unfished patch reefs of Glover's Reef Atoll, Belize. *Coral Reefs*, **19**, 367–79.

McClanahan, T. R., Sala, E., Stickels, P. *et al.* (2003). Interaction between nutrients and herbivory in controlling algal communities and coral condition on Glover's Reef, Belize. *Marine Ecology Progress Series*, **261**, 135–47.

McClanahan, T. R., Maina, J. and Davies, J. (2005). Perceptions of resource users and managers towards fisheries management options in Kenyan coral reefs. *Fisheries Management and Ecology*, **12**, 105–12.

McClanahan, T. R., Verheij, E. and Maina, J. (2006). Comparing management effectiveness of a marine park and a multiple-use collaborative management area in East Africa. *Aquatic Conservation: Marine and Freshwater Ecosystems* (in press).

Mees, C. C. (1992). *Seychelles Demersal Fishery: An Analysis of Data Relating to Four Key Demersal Species* – Prisipomoides filamentosus, Lutjanus sebae, Aprion uirescens, Epinephelus chlorostigma, Research and Development Report No. 19. Victoria, Seychelles: Seychelles Fisheries Authority.

Mees, C. C., Yeeting, B. M. and Taniera, T. (1988). Small-scale fisheries in the Gilbert group of the Republic of Kiribati, Unpublished Report. Tarawa, Kiribati: Ministry of Natural Resources Development.

Mees, C. C., Pilling, G. M. and Barry, C. J. (1999). Commercial inshore fishing activity in the British Indian Ocean Territory. In *Ecology of the Chagos Archipelago*, eds. C. R. C. Sheppard and M. R. D. Seaward, pp. 327–45. London: Linnean Society.

Mosqueira, I., Côté, I. M., Jennings, S. and Reynolds, J. D. (2000). Conservation benefits of marine reserves for fish populations. *Animal Conservation*, **3**, 321–32.

Munbodh, M., Raymead, T. S. and Kallee, P. (1988). L'importance économique de récifs coralliens et tentatives de l'aquaculture à Maurice. *Journal de la Nature*, **1**, 56–8.

Munro, J. L. (1977). Actual and potential production from the coralline shelves of the Caribbean Sea. *FAO Fisheries Report*, **200**, 301–21.

Muthiga, N. A. (1996). The role of early life history strategies on the population dynamics of the sea urchin *Echinometra mathaei* (de Blainville) on reefs in Kenya. Ph.D. dissertation, University of Nairobi, Kenya.

Nixon, S. W. (1982). Nutrient dynamics, primary production and fisheries yields of lagoons. *Oceanologica Acta*, **Suppl. 4**, 357–71.

Ostrom, E. (1990). *Governing the Commons: The Evolution of Institutions for Collective Action*. Cambridge: Cambridge University Press.

Pauly, D., Christensen, V., Dalsgaard, J., Froese, R., Torres, Jr, F. (1998). Fishing down marine food webs. *Science*, **279**, 861–3.

Pet-Soede, L., Van Densen, W. L. T., Hiddink, J. G., Kuyl, S. and Machiels, M. A. M. (2001). Can fishermen allocate their fishing effort in space and time on the basis of their catch rates? An example from Spermonde Archipelago, S W Sulawesi, Indonesia. *Fisheries Management and Ecology*, **8**, 15–36.
Pinnegar, J. K., Polunin, N. V. C., Francour, P. *et al.* (2000). Trophic cascades in fisheries and protected-area management of benthic marine ecosystems. *Environmental Conservation*, **27**, 179–200.
Polunin, N. V. C. and Pinnegar, J. K. (2002). Trophic ecology and the structure of marine food webs. In *Handbook of Fish and Fisheries*, vol. I, eds. P. J. B. Hart and J. D. Reynolds, pp. 310–20. Oxford: Blackwell Science.
Pretty, J. (2003). Social capital and the collective management of resources. *Science*, **302**, 1912–14.
Rodwell, L., Barbier, E. B., Robert, C. M. and McClanahan, T. R. (2002). A model of tropical marine reserve-fishery linkages. *Natural Resource Modeling*, **15**, 453–86.
(2003). The importance of habitat quality for marine reserve–fishery linkages. *Canadian Journal of Fisheries and Aquatic Sciences*, **60**, 171–81.
Russ, G. R. (2002). Marine reserves as reef fisheries management tools: yet another review. In *Coral Reef Fishes*, ed. P. F. Sale, pp. 421–43. Amsterdam: Academic Press.
Russ, G. R., Alcala, A. C. (2004). Marine reserves: long-term protection is required for full recovery of predatory fish populations. *Oecologia*, **138**, 622–7.
Russ, G. R., Lou, D. C. and Ferreira, B. P. (1996). Temporal tracking of a strong cohort in the population of a coral reef fish, the coral trout, *Plectropomus leopardus* (Serranidae: Epinephelinae), in the central Great Barrier Reef, Australia. *Canadian Journal of Fisheries and Aquatic Sciences*, **53**, 2745–51.
Sala, E., Ballesteros, E. and Starr, R. M. (2001). Rapid decline of Nassau grouper spawning aggregations in Belize: fishery management and conservation needs. *Fisheries*, **26**, 23–30.
Sanders, M. J. and Kedidi, S. M. (1984). *Catches, Fishing Effort, Catches per Fishing Effort, and Fishing Locations for the Gulf of Suez and Egyptian Red Sea Fishery for Reef Associated Fish during 1979 to 1982*, Report No. FAO/UNDP RAB/83/023/02. Cairo: UNDP/FAO.
Savina, G. C. and White, A. T. (1986). A tale of two islands: some lessons for marine resource management. *Environmental Conservation*, **13**, 107–13.
Steneck, R. S., and Dethier, M. N. (1994). A functional group approach to the structure of algal-dominated communities. *Oikos*, **69**, 476–98.
Stevenson, D. K. and Marshall, N. (1974). Generalizations on the fisheries potential of coral reefs and adjacent shallow water environments. *Proceedings 2nd International Coral Reef Symposium*, **1**, 147–56.
Sutinen, J. G. and Kuperan, K. (1999). A socio-economic theory of regulatory compliance. *International Journal of Social Economics*, **26**, 174–93.
Van Der Knaap, M., Waheed, Z., Shareef, H. and Rasheed, M. (1991). Reef fish resource survey in Maldives. *Bay of Bengal Programme Working Paper*, **64**, 58.
Wass, R. C. (1982). The shoreline fishery of American Samoa: past and present. In *Marine and Coastal Processes in the Pacific: Ecological Aspects of Coastal Zone Management*, ed. J. L. Munro, pp. 51–83. Jakarta.

Weiler, D. and Suarez-Caabro, J. A. (1980). Overview of Puerto Rico's small-scale fisheries statistics, 1972–1978. Munro, *CODEMAR*, **1**, 1–27.
Wijkstrom, V. N. (1974). Processing and marketing marine fish: possible guidelines for the 1975–1979 periods. In *International Conference on Marine Resource Development in Eastern Africa*, eds. A. S. Msangi and J. J. Griffin, pp. 55–67. Kingston: University of Rhode Island.
Wright, A. and Richards, A. H. (1985). A multispecies fishery associated with coral reefs in the Tigak Islands, Papua New Guinea. *Asian Marine Biology*, **2**, 69–84.
Zann, L. P., Bell, L. and Sua, T. (1991). *The Inshore Fisheries Resource of Upolu, Western Samoa: Coastal Inventory and Database*, FAO/UNDP Field Report No. 5. Rome: FAO.

6

Live food and non-food fisheries on coral reefs, and their potential management

AMANDA C. J. VINCENT
University of British Columbia

INTRODUCTION

Biology and exploitation of coral reef organisms remain very under-studied, particularly with respect to live food and non-food fisheries. Coral reefs are found in over 100 countries, supporting more than 4000 species of fish and 1000 species of reef-building corals (Paulay, 1997). The resources in these ecosystems are exploited by tens of millions of fishers and supply about 10% of the world's seafood (Moberg and Folke, 1999). Such fisheries can be expected to put a myriad of pressures on reef environments: (1) they remove the organisms directly, thus depleting populations; (2) they harm or disturb other individuals, thus disrupting populations; and (3) they place pressures on the larger reef ecosystem, through community change or habitat damage. Despite their ecological and economic importance, however, coral reef fisheries are largely overlooked in national management plans and in international record-keeping. Such data and analyses as do exist generally refer to fisheries intended for food.

This chapter synthesizes current knowledge about fisheries and trades in five forms of reef product that are primarily or entirely sought for reasons other than nutrition: ostentatious meals, aquarium display, curiosities, traditional medicines and bioprospecting for pharmaceuticals. This chapter thereby complements the previous chapter by McClanahan, which focuses on fisheries based on nutrition. I will here refer to 'live food and non-food' products to embrace these and other forms of exploitation not directed at

Coral Reef Conservation, ed. Isabelle M. Côté and John D. Reynolds.
Published by Cambridge University Press.

supplying nutrition, while the term 'food' alone alludes to dead fish. My intention in writing this chapter is to provoke more interest in assessing the ecological and economic importance of live food and non-food fisheries, and in addressing their management where warranted.

This review is selective and illustrative rather than exhaustive. Among forms of ostentatious eating, I consider only reef fishes traded live for food and not invertebrates or other luxury food products, such as shark fin. I also omit other non-nutritive uses of marine species (e.g. for research and teaching, mariculture seed and feed, bait, leather, and many biotechnology uses). On the other hand, the chapter strays into species living in seagrasses, mangroves, estuaries and other coastal habitats, either to illustrate points or because data are too scarce or indiscriminate to allow distinctions. Most data refer to international trades, both because they represent a large portion of the whole and because data on domestic consumption are even scarcer. Such information is necessarily incomplete, both because the trades are global and complex and because so little documentation exists for most such uses. Deducing trade volumes, for example, is very complicated because (1) data are often combined with those for other goods and products, (2) species are not distinguished, and/or (3) domestic trade is largely undocumented. The chapter should, nonetheless, capture key material and raise issues that need further investigation.

I begin by examining the live reef fish trades, for luxury foods and for aquaria, because these are better documented than the other fisheries in this chapter. I next turn to the trades in dead reef life for curiosities, traditional medicine and bioprospecting for pharmaceuticals. For each use, I briefly review what is known about targeted species, extraction, trade routes, volumes, values and conservation impacts. In the latter part of the paper, I compare and contrast the five forms of exploitation, seeking generalities. The live fish trades for food and aquaria were revealed to have many similarities (Sadovy and Vincent, 2002) but the extent to which these patterns persist across other non-food fisheries needs to be considered. Finally, I comment on management options for these live food and non-food fisheries.

Three reference databases are frequently cited in this chapter:

(1) The Convention on International Trade in Endangered Species of Wild Fauna and Flora (CITES, 2005) places species on Appendices in order to regulate their trade at export (and sometimes import) level. An Appendix I listing effectively precludes trade except for scientific purposes. Appendix II listing, by far more commonly used, permits international trade if accompanied by a certificate asserting that the export does not detrimentally affect the wild population and that the

specimen was obtained legally. CITES collects global trade data for Appendix II listed taxa, and thus provides the basis of some analyses (e.g. Green and Shirley, 1999; Bruckner, 2001).

(2) The Global Marine Aquarium Database (GMAD, 2005) was created in 2000 to collect industry data, and now provides a resource from which to understand the trade (e.g. used in E. Green, 2003; Wabnitz *et al.*, 2003). Its reliability depends on the accuracy and comprehensiveness of reporting by exporters and importers.

(3) The IUCN *Red List of Threatened Species* (IUCN, 2004) provides warnings of changes in population abundances or distributions beyond threshold levels.

LUXURY LIVE FOOD

Targets

Live fishes are in high demand in Asian restaurants, where consumers can select their dinner from among the fish in a display tank. Relatively few species are consumed in high volume, with particular attention to groupers (Serranidae), wrasses (Labridae) and snappers (Lutjanidae) (Sadovy and Vincent, 2002; Sadovy *et al.*, 2003a) (Fig. 6.1). Other taxa of interest include emperors (Lethrinidae), sweetlips (Haemulidae), and seabream (Sparidae). While the humphead (Napoleon or Maori) wrasse (*Cheilinus undulatus*), the high-finned grouper (*Cromileptes altivelis*) and giant grouper (*Epinephelus lanceolatus*) are traded only in small volumes, they are among the most valuable species (Johannes and Riepen, 1995; Lau and Parry-Jones, 1999; Chan, 2001).

The live food trade values reef fish according to their rarity, size, colour and perceived medicinal value. The preferred size is often that which will fit on a plate or serve a group at a banquet, such that fish of 0.6–1.5 kg are most in demand, and those of 0.8–1.2 kg are most valuable (Johannes and Riepen, 1995); most individual fishes in trade measure 30–50 cm total length. Chinese consumers prefer species with red coloration (e.g. coral trout) because the colour is auspicious (Lau and Parry-Jones, 1999), and they also select fish with rare colours (e.g. albino coral trout) and particularly high health value (e.g. giant grouper) (Sadovy, 2001a).

Extraction

In Southeast Asia, about 50–70% of the fish destined for live food are wild caught, primarily by small-scale local fishers (Sadovy *et al.*, 2003a). They are

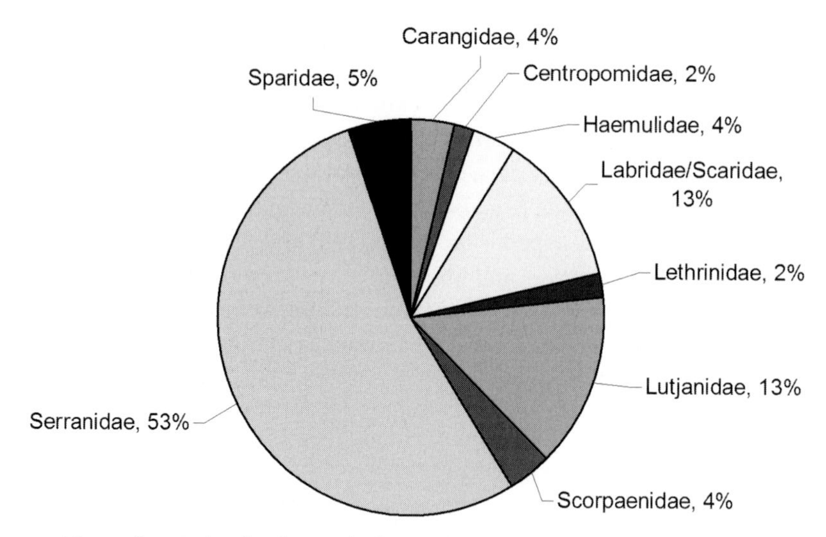

Figure 6.1 Major families in the live reef fish food trade (by number of species). (Source: Sadovy and Vincent, 2002.)

then transferred to buyers who hold them in floating cages (or move them to grow-out operations; see below), before selling them to exporters (Sadovy *et al.*, 2003a). Buyers exert great power in this trade, often fostering the use of destructive fishing methods (Sadovy *et al.*, 2003a).

Most fish for the live food trade come directly from reefs. Reef fish are taken with hook and line, traps, nets and chemicals, sometimes with the aid of artificial reefs or other devices to attract fish. The use of chemicals, particularly cyanide, is very prevalent and contributes to serious concerns about the sustainability of these fisheries; for some species, such as humphead wrasse, poisons are the primary means of capture (Sadovy *et al.*, 2003a). Cyanide is reported to contribute to high mortality rates during capture, holding and transport (Johannes and Riepen, 1995; Bentley, 1999; Johannes and Lam, 1999).

Perhaps 15–40% of the live food fish trade comes from grow-out operations (particularly in mainland China), in which juveniles are caught in the wild, then reared in floating net cages or shallow ponds while being fed wild fish (Sadovy *et al.*, 2003a). Such backyard facilities now provide important economic benefits to local communities (Siar *et al.*, 2002). About 10–15% of live reef fish in global trade come from hatcheries that have closed the life cycles, with a significant proportion produced in Taiwan (Sadovy *et al.*, 2003a).

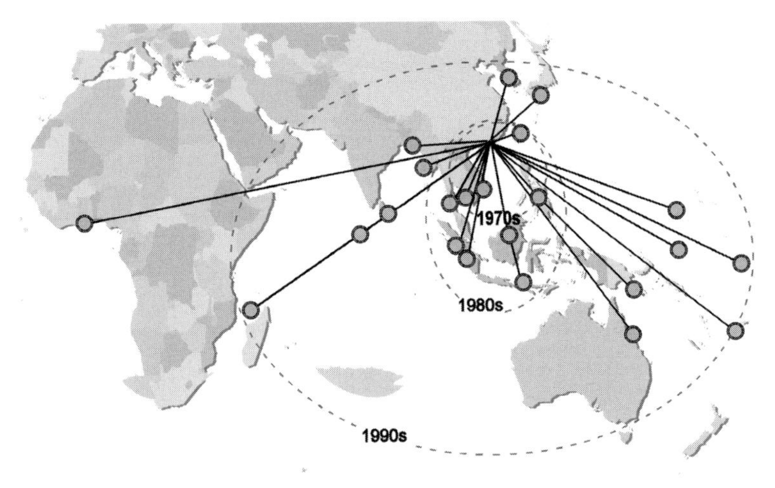

Figure 6.2 Changing sources of live food fish supply to one key destination, Hong Kong. The geographic extents of sources in different decades are marked. (Source: Sadovy and Vincent, 2002.)

Sources and destinations

The trade in live reef fish for food is spreading geographically (Fig. 6.2). Live food fish originated primarily in the northern sector of the South China Sea until the 1980s. Depletions and subsequent geographic shifts mean that live food fish now come from most countries in the Indo-Pacific (Johannes and Riepen, 1995; Chan, 2001). They are caught from Australia to Vietnam – particularly in Indonesia, Malaysia and the Philippines – and in many insular nations far into the Pacific (Johannes and Riepen, 1995; Bentley and Aumeeruddy, 1999; Sadovy and Vincent, 2002). New sources are sought as demand grows, and experimental trades have emerged in California and Fiji (Sadovy *et al.*, 2003a).

Most live food fish are exported by sea or air, depending on the fishery's location and available air links (Sadovy *et al.*, 2003a). The largest single destination and entrepôt is Hong Kong but exports also go to Australia, the USA and many countries with large ethnic Chinese populations in southeast and eastern Asia (Johannes and Riepen, 1995; Indrawan, 1999; Chan, 2001). Perhaps 50% of the live food fishes brought into Hong Kong are re-exported to mainland China, an area with a growing market (Chan, 2001).

Volumes

Data for the live food trade are generally poor or unreliable, partly because of flawed record-keeping and inadequate inspections. However, the best

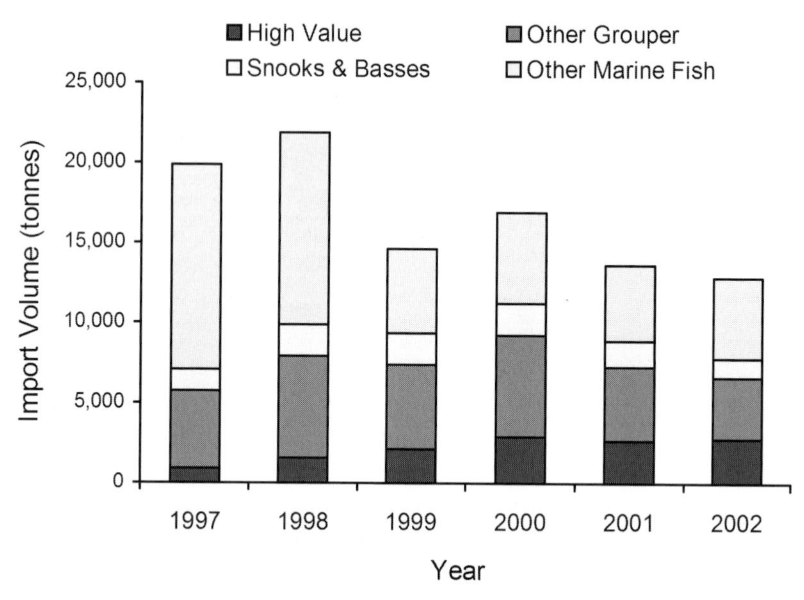

Figure 6.3 Total reported imports of live reef food fish into Hong Kong, China, over the period 1997–2002. High-value species include humpback grouper, humphead wrasse, giant grouper, leopard coral grouper and spotted coral grouper. Underreporting is thought to explain why these figures are lower than other estimates in the text. (Source: Sadovy *et al.*, 2003a.)

available estimates suggest that Hong Kong imported about 1000–2000 tonnes yr^{-1} during the late 1980s and early 1990s (Johannes and Riepen, 1995; Lau and Parry-Jones, 1999; Chan, 2001) and perhaps up to 30 000–35 000 tonnes yr^{-1} in the mid-1990s (Lau and Parry-Jones, 1999; Chan, 2000) (Fig. 6.3).

The global trade in live reef fishes for food is very large. If Hong Kong imports accounted for about 60% of live food trade (as was the case in the mid-1990s: Johannes and Riepen, 1995) then worldwide trade probably totalled about 50 000 tonnes in 1997 (Lau and Parry-Jones, 1999). More recently, however, global trade has been estimated at 30 000 tonnes yr^{-1} or about 30 million fish (at 1 kg each) of just a few species (Sadovy *et al.*, 2003a). Total extraction was perhaps double that, given the probable 50% mortality during handling and transportation (Johannes and Lam, 1999). In the mid-1990s, total take for the live fish trade might have approximately equalled dead grouper landings for all Asian economies combined (Food and Agriculture Organization, 1996).

Values

The trade in live fish for food is very valuable, particular for humpback grouper, humphead wrasse and leopard coral grouper (Sadovy *et al.*, 2003a). The Hong Kong retail trade was estimated to average at least US$350 million annually during 1999–2002, with a probable total of US$500 million in 2002. Given the inferred role of Hong Kong, we can estimate a global trade value of about US$810 million for that year (Sadovy *et al.*, 2003a).

Prices paid to fishers for live coral trouts and humphead wrasses almost doubled between 1995 and 1997, probably because of declining supply (Sadovy and Vincent, 2002), then stabilized (Sadovy *et al.*, 2003a). The advent of the live reef fish trade enhanced income for some fishers, allowing them to earn 75–350% more for live fish than for comparable dead fish for some species in 1999–2002 (Sadovy *et al.*, 2003a). Then, too, the monthly income of cyanide fishers was estimated to be US$150–500 per month during the early 1990s, or 3–10 times that of other fishers in Indonesia (Erdmann and Pet-Soede, 1996). Plate-size fish were the most valuable per unit weight (Johannes and Riepen, 1995). Around the turn of the century, live reef fish retailed at US$5–180 kg^{-1}, with prices varying by species, size, taste, texture, availability and time of year (Sadovy *et al.*, 2003a).

Direct impact

Species in the live food fish trade are particularly vulnerable because they are long-lived and late maturing, with sequential hermaphroditism (Sadovy *et al.*, 2003a). Their brief and easily located spawning aggregations are heavily fished in Micronesia and the Solomon Islands, for example, as well as eastern Indonesia (Johannes and Lam, 1999). The capture and export of hundreds of millions of grouper juveniles per year for grow-out also adds to pressures on wild populations (Bentley, 1999; Sadovy, 2000).

Current levels of live fish production for Southeast Asia and the Maldives well exceed estimates of sustainable extraction (Shakeel and Ahmed, 1997; Sadovy *et al.*, 2003a; Warren-Rhodes *et al.*, 2003). The trade appears to be causing depletions in key target species and in preferred larger sizes of fish in these species (reviewed in Sadovy and Vincent, 2002). For the humphead wrasse, in particular, export fisheries have invariably led to reductions in catch rates and mean sizes, forcing fishers to search further afield (reviewed in Sadovy *et al.*, 2003b). The geographic spread of live reef fish extraction through the Indo-Pacific, away from the consumption hub in Hong Kong, provides further evidence of population declines (see Sadovy

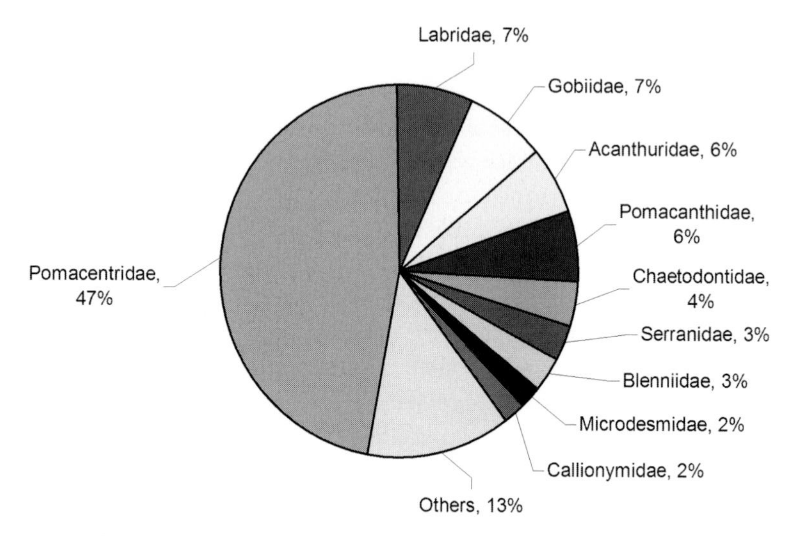

Figure 6.4 Global aquarium trade in marine fish by family. (Source: Wabnitz *et al.*, 2003.)

and Vincent, 2002). Depletion is also evident in the loss of some spawning aggregations, which in turn reduces populations still farther (e.g. Palau: Sadovy *et al.*, 2003a). Fisheries for dead food diminished or eliminated group aggregations in the western Atlantic within a few years (Bohnsack *et al.*, 1989; Sadovy and Eklund, 1999).

Exploitation for the live food trade has contributed directly to the inclusion of many targeted species on the 2004 IUCN *Red List of Threatened Species* (IUCN, 2004), including the Vulnerable and poorly known humphead wrasse *Cheilinus undulatus* (Sadovy *et al.*, 2003b). CITES decided in October 2004 to add this species to Appendix II, requiring that all exports be regulated for sustainability (CITES, 2005). As well, Indonesia, the Maldives, and the Philippines have taken domestic remedial action for humphead wrasse (Donaldson and Sadovy, 2001).

AQUARIUM AND ORNAMENTAL DISPLAY

Targets

A great many marine fishes – including a few also traded live for food – are displayed live for ornaments and/or education. Private and public aquaria around the world purchase 1000–1500 marine fish species for exhibit (Wood, 2001a; Wabnitz *et al.*, 2003). Pomacentrids comprise 47% of global trade and the ten most popular fish species make up about one-third

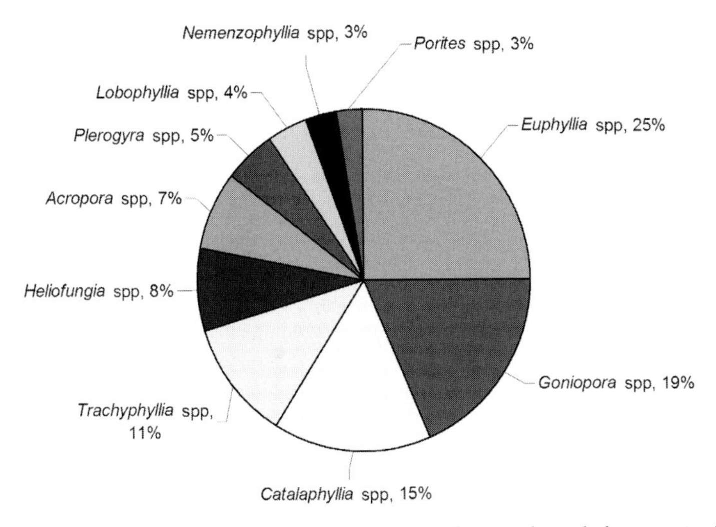

Figure 6.5 Relative amounts of the ten most frequently traded genera in the live coral trade as recorded under CITES 1985–1997. (Source: Green and Shirley, 1999.)

of all trade globally (Wabnitz *et al.*, 2003) (Fig. 6.4). Rarities also find a market, at high cost, for their prestige value (Wood, 2001a). Juveniles – and sometimes males – are highly valued for their attractive colour patterns (e.g. Chan and Sadovy, 1998; Vincent and Sadovy, 1998). Some aquarium fish are juveniles of species that are valued for food (Wabnitz *et al.*, 2003).

Some 140 scleratinian (stony) coral species and 61 soft coral species are thought to be traded for aquaria (Fig. 6.5), although coral taxonomy remains difficult (Wabnitz *et al.*, 2003). Again, the trade is concentrated in relatively few genera (Wabnitz *et al.*, 2003). Nine of the ten species most commonly traded live are massive corals or corals with very large, colourful polyps and prominent tentacles (Bruckner, 2001). Some grow slowly, have low rates of sexual recruitment and/or may be rare; most were much less common in trade prior to 1990 (Bruckner, 2001). According to CITES data, hundreds of tonnes of 'live rock' – reef substratum and its associated invertebrates, microorganisms and coralline algae – are traded each year for aquarium use (Wabnitz *et al.*, 2003). In general, however, CITES data for corals are difficult to interpret because (1) they do not always differentiate between live and dead specimens and (2) dead coral may go to the aquarium (live rock) or curio trades. Thus some of the coral trade cited in this aquarium section may apply to curio uses, and vice versa. GMAD data cover live corals and live rock, but not dead coral used in curios.

Invertebrates other than corals comprise a large part of the aquarium trade, with estimates ranging from 100 to about 500 species of molluscs, shrimps, anemones and other invertebrates (Wood, 2001a; E. Green, 2003; Wabnitz *et al.*, 2003). The giant clams and topshells that are heavily favoured for aquarium display are also valued in shell trades and, in the case of giant clams, as food and ornaments (Wabnitz *et al.*, 2003).

Extraction

The vast majority of organisms sold for marine aquaria come directly from coral reefs (Andrews, 1990; Sadovy and Vincent, 2002; Corbin *et al.*, 2003; Olivier, 2003). The aquarium trade involves a large number of small-scale fishers – e.g. about 2500 in the Philippines alone (Pajaro, 1993) – and many buyers, exporters, wholesalers and retailers (Wabnitz *et al.*, 2003). Most species are caught by hand or using small nets of various designs, sometimes depending on hookah surface air supply (reviewed in Wood, 2001a). Fishers in some of the major supplying countries often use sodium cyanide or other poisons, commonly with the connivance of the buyer. Cyanide played a role in catching perhaps 80% of all aquarium fish in Philippines in the 1980s (Rubec, 1988), and continues to be a problem in many regions despite campaigns and laws to eliminate its use (Wood, 2001b). Poor collection, husbandry, storage and transport practices can mean considerable mortality in trade, in a costly loss that also provokes greater extraction (Wood, 2001a).

Less than 1% of live coral reef fish or live corals in trade is cultured (Green and Shirley, 1999; Moe, 1999). Soft coral farming is feasible but supplies very few specimens (Ellis, 1999). Hobbyists and scientists are actively engaged in aquaculture trials but commercial breeders only produce about 35 fish and 55 coral species (Moe, 2003), whereas 90% of freshwater aquarium fish species come from aquaculture (Olivier, 2003).

Sources and destinations

The aquarium trade is global. Ornamental marine species are exported from 30–45 nations and imported by about the same number (Wood, 2001b; E. Green, 2003) (Fig. 6.6). Exporters' data show that 98% of all fish destined for aquaria originate in the Western Pacific, primarily from developing countries (E. Green, 2003; Wabnitz *et al.*, 2003). Probably about one-third of the marine fishes and invertebrates come from the Philippines, one-third from Indonesia, and the remainder from Brazil, Maldives, Sri Lanka, USA (Hawaii), Vietnam, Australia and others (Wood, 2001a; Wabnitz *et al.*,

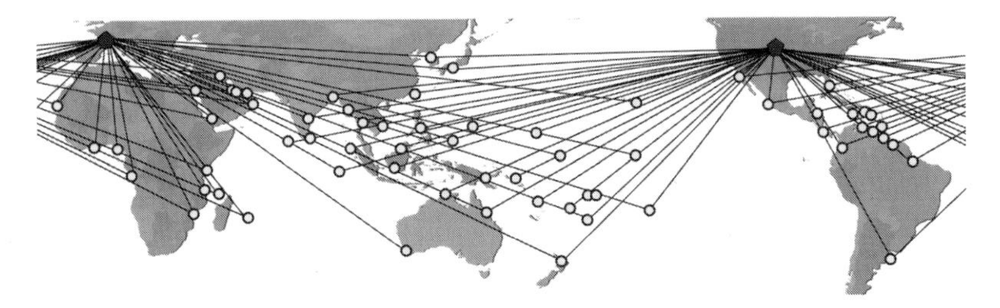

Figure 6.6 Major source countries for the live reef fish aquarium trade, focused on North America and Europe. (Source: Sadovy and Vincent, 2002.)

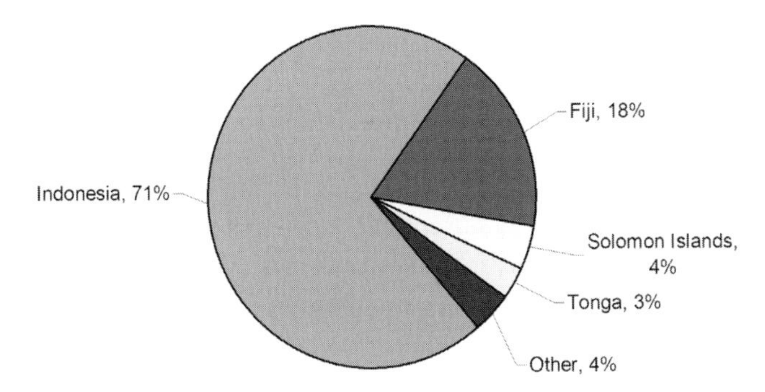

Figure 6.7 Major exporters of live and wild-sourced coral (pieces) in the period 1997–2001. (Source: Wabnitz *et al.*, 2003.)

2003). International air links to markets are a prerequisite for a successful aquarium trade.

Few countries export significant amounts of coral. Indonesia, Fiji, the Solomon Islands and Tonga supplied virtually all live coral exports from 1997 to 2001 (Fig. 6.7), although more countries exported live rock (Wabnitz *et al.*, 2003). This represented a change from the 1970s and 1980s, when the Philippines supplied a high proportion of the corals (Mulliken and Nash, 1993), until a national ban on coral export was enforced in the late 1980s (Bruckner, 2001). Indonesia then emerged as the world's largest coral exporter in 1990, despite its own domestic ban (Bentley, 1998).

The USA is the single largest consumer of marine organisms for the aquarium trade, apparently importing 41–69% of the fish, 73% of the stony corals, 67% of the soft corals, 99% of gorgonian sea fans and 35–80% of other invertebrates (Wabnitz *et al.*, 2003). Some of the high numbers may represent strong participation by US companies in GMAD record-keeping but CITES data (which should be global) are compatible for corals: the USA reportedly imported 70–80% of the live coral, with smaller amounts going

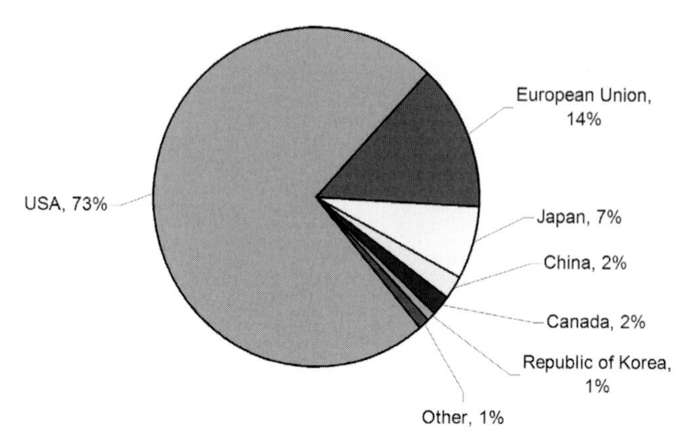

Figure 6.8 Major importers of live and wild-sourced coral (pieces) in the period 1997–2001. (Source: Wabnitz *et al.*, 2003.)

to Germany, Japan and other countries (Bruckner, 2001) (Fig. 6.8). Most other marine organisms went to Europe and Japan, with some to Australia and South Africa (Bruckner, 2001; Wood, 2001b; Wabnitz *et al.*, 2003). The USA bans collection of stony corals and live rock from most of its own reefs, and tightly regulates fish collection domestically (Bruckner, 2001; Wabnitz *et al.*, 2003).

Volumes

Ornamental marine species now supply the hobby interests of 1.5–2 million people (E. Green, 2003) and many public aquaria globally. Much of the industry's growth came in the 1980s, as technology improved sufficiently to permit marine aquaria in the home (Andrews, 1990). The trade in fishes stabilized some time ago, but live coral trade grew steadily in the 1990s (Fig. 6.9).

Crude estimates, adjusted for levels of reporting, suggest that a total of about 20–30 million marine fish were traded each year from 1998 to 2003 for aquarium display, with two-thirds of these coming from coral reefs, representing about one-quarter of all known reef fish species (E. Green, 2003; Wabnitz *et al.*, 2003). Perhaps 9–10 million individual molluscs, shrimps, anemones and other invertebrates and 11–12 million stony and soft corals were in the global live trade every year over the same period (Wabnitz *et al.*, 2003). The trade live corals grew by 30–50% yr^{-1} from negligible levels (about 5% of all corals) in the late 1980s to 1997 (Green and Shirley, 1999; Bruckner, 2001).

A high proportion of the aquarium trade was directed to the USA. The USA imported perhaps 8 million marine ornamental fish in 1992,

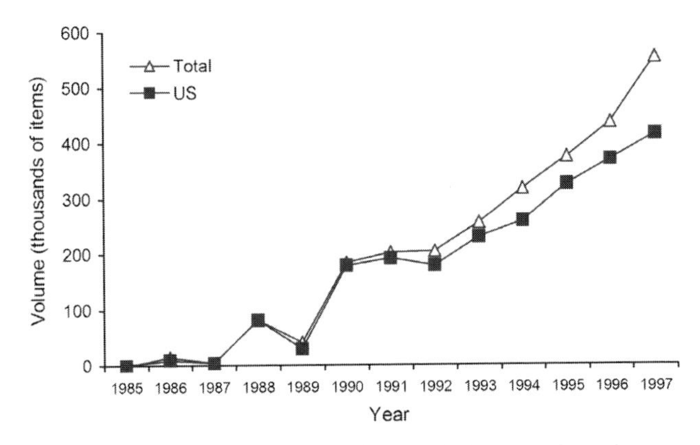

Figure 6.9 Volume of live coral in trade between 1985 and 1997 (CITES data). (Source: Green and Shirley, 1999; Bruckner, 2001.)

although the proportion from coral reefs is unknown (Wood, 2001b). Global trade in all corals generally tracked the USA's imports during the 1990s (Green and Shirley, 1999). If we extrapolate from available GMAD data to all trade (Wabnitz *et al.*, 2003), we deduce that the USA imported approximately 8–8.8 million pieces of live coral and 3.15–8 million marine invertebrates yr^{-1} in the late 1990s. Other importers were much smaller.

Values

Some aquarium species increase greatly in value during trade (Wabnitz *et al.*, 2003). At export, prices can range from US$0.10 to US$500 per fish, depending on the size, species, country of origin and destination (Wood, 2001a). This is often about double what the collector receives, but half what the importer pays. The final retail cost per fish may be 11–14 times what the collector receives, even if there is no buyer as intermediary between fisher and exporter (Wood, 2001a).

The dominant sources of aquarium organisms obtained important earnings from the trade. Exports of marine species from the Philippines and Indonesia were worth about US$12.3 million for 1993 (Wood, 2001a). In 1998, Sri Lanka earned about US$5.6 million by exporting marine species to about 52 countries (Wijesekara and Yakupitiyage, 2001). In 1997, live coral sales were reported to earn about US$5 million for exporting nations (Green and Shirley, 1999). Another estimate, however, claimed that Fiji received about US$12 million yr^{-1} for live coral exports, presumably including live rock; some of these were re-exports from other islands (Smith, 1999).

The trade in live organisms for marine aquaria into the USA, as recorded by the US Fish and Wildlife Service, may have been worth US$200–330 million in 1998 (Wabnitz *et al.* 2003). The total import value of ornamental marine fish specimens around the world was estimated to be at least US$28–30 million yr^{-1} during the 1990s with about one-third from each of the USA and EU, but could have reached US$44 million (Wood, 2001a). Retail value of the marine ornamental fish trade would have been about US$90–300 million (cited in Wood, 2001a) while live corals alone were argued to generate about US$50 million (in 1999 US$) in retail sales in 1997 (Green and Shirley, 1999).

Direct impact

No species collected for the aquarium trade is yet known to be at risk from global extinction (Wood, 2001a). Some areas, such as Australia and the Cook Islands, have sustained their aquarium fisheries without declines in catch per unit effort (CPUE) (Bertram, 1996; Queensland Fisheries Management Authority, 1999). Elsewhere, however, collection of fish for ornamental display may have been excessive, particularly given the destructive fishing techniques that are often employed (e.g. Lunn and Moreau, 2004). A male-biased catch, as in mandarin fish, may contribute to reduced reproductive output of populations (Vincent and Sadovy, 1998). As well, the capture of juvenile fish would probably still put pressure on populations, as those taken are probably much larger than the stage at which high natural mortality occurs.

Localized depletions, with unknown conservation consequences, have certainly been reported in some countries with high extraction and poor fisheries regulations (reviewed in Bruckner, 2001; Wood, 2001a; Wabnitz *et al.*, 2003). Traders in the Philippines, for example, reported lower catches of the most valuable fish species and a potential loss of variety (Vallejo, 1997). In some cases, too, excessive coral collection in the Philippines altered community structure, before take was banned domestically (Ross, 1984). Too little is usually known, however, to determine whether such changes in abundance pose an extinction risk, partly because catch per unit effort and other population parameters are seldom assessed (Wood, 2001a – see below). Reflecting global concerns about overexploitation for all uses, however, all international trade in three aquarium taxa (seahorses, scleratinian corals and giant clams) is controlled under CITES Appendix II (CITES, 2005).

CURIOSITIES

Targets

Large numbers of individuals from a wide array of marine species – some of them also valued in the aquarium trade and/or as food – are sold worldwide as trinkets, jewellery, art, crafts, trophies, lampshades and ornaments. Curios have included raw and processed forms of approximately 5000 species of molluscs, primarily gastropods but also giant clams, capiz shells and other bivalves (Abbott, 1980). In addition, curios have involved 40 species of corals (Wood and Wells, 1988) plus unknown numbers of sponges, sea fans, echinoderms (e.g. sea dollars, sea urchins and sea stars: K. E. Lunn, M. J. Villanueva Noriega and A. C. J. Vincent, unpublished data), crustaceans (e.g. coconut crabs, mangrove crabs: Wells and Wood, 1991), at least 25 fish species (e.g. shark teeth, sawfish rostra, seahorses, pufferfishes: Wells and Wood, 1991; Grey *et al.*, 2005), and marine turtles. The USA documented curio imports of at least 15 species of sharks (including six that may be reef-associated), triggerfish, porcupinefish, pufferfish and five species of seahorses (Grey *et al.*, 2005).

Most of the scarce research on marine curio trades has focused on molluscs, which have long been taken for non-food purposes (Wells, 1988). I focus here on the 'ornamental (or precious) shell', which is used in shell-craft or sold whole for decoration, rather than the 'commercial shell', which is taken for mother-of-pearl and primarily sold worked as buttons (Wells, 1988). Most shells in the curio trade are large, colourful and plentiful, with rarer specimens only sought by specialized collectors (Wood and Wells, 1988).

Almost all corals were traded dead into the 1980s, but live trade then began to grow, surpassing the dead trade by 1997 (Green and Shirley, 1999). Most corals traded dead are shallow-water branching specimens; these are among the most abundant on reefs in the Indo-Pacific and have high rates of growth and sexual recruitment (Bruckner, 2001).

Extraction

Marine curios may be sourced in targeted fisheries, in by-catch from trawlers or other non-selective fishing gear, as by-products of the food fisheries, from strandings ashore or, occasionally, from deaths in the live aquarium trade. As with live food trade, curio traders move from country to country; for example, closure of a coral lease in New Caledonia led a company to move to Fiji (Lovell, 2001a). The vast majority of curio species, including shells, are taken from the ocean alive to obtain a product with good condition and/or good colour (Wells, 1988; Bruckner, 2001). Many species traded as curios – including giant clams, queen conch, echinoderms, sharks and seahorses – were obtained as by-products of the food fishery, or by-catch (Sloan, 1984; Wells, 1988; Munro, 1993; Vincent, 1996). Indeed, for some mollusc species where the shells are used as curios, the edible flesh may be the more valuable commodity, as in queen conch.

Sources and destinations

Marine curios usually originate from coral reefs in developing countries, especially in the Indo-West Pacific (Wells, 1988; Wood and Wells, 1995; Grey *et al.*, 2005). Collecting techniques allow extraction of large numbers of some species (Wells, 1982). The Philippines is inferred to be the major exporter of ornamental shells, with quite possibly their only commercial fishery (Wood and Wells, 1995). Other major sources of ornamental shells in 1985 (in descending order) were thought to comprise Singapore (including re-exports), Taiwan (including re-exports), Indonesia, Thailand, Mexico, Haiti and India (Wood and Wells, 1988; Wood and Wells, 1995).

Corals were exported for curios and aquarium use from at least 66 countries – principally Indonesia but all over the Indo-West Pacific – from 1992 to 1997 (Bruckner, 2001). Taiwan is cited as a source of worked black coral, although it probably originated in another country (Wells and Wood, 1991). It also seems likely that Taiwan sourced sharks from many waters in order to supply 92% of the shark imports to the USA (Grey *et al.*, 2005). The Philippines reputedly supplied 61% of the seahorses and 95% of the porcupinefish entering the USA between 1997 and 2001 (Grey *et al.*, 2005).

Curios are sold domestically, especially where tourism flourishes, but are also traded all over the world. The USA is by far the largest importer of curios and jewellery from marine fauna (Wood and Wells, 1995; US Coral Reef Task Force, 2000 Lovell, 2001a). In 1997, for example, coral imports to the USA constituted 56% of the global trade, while the European Union (EU) consumed 15%, although the proportion used for curios was unclear (Green and Shirley, 1999). Japan is probably another dominant importer (Wells, 1988).

Volumes

Trade in shells and shellcraft was reported to have increased rapidly prior to the 1980s, probably partly because of greater travel and tourism (Wells, 1988; Wood and Wells, 1995), but a dearth of information means that the later trajectory of the trade is unclear. In the 1960s, India was exporting 3–42 t yr^{-1} of cowries and the Maldives was exporting 20–60 t yr^{-1} of cowries (Wells, 1988). It appears that thousands of tonnes of mollusc shells and corals were still sold globally each year in the mid-1980s (Wood and

Wells, 1988). Ornamental shell exports from the Philippines – apparently primarily to the USA – rose from less than 1000 t yr^{-1} in the 1960s to 3400 t in 1979, before subsiding to 2300 t in 1981 and 1000 t in 1985 (Wells, 1988).

Data on the curio trade in species other than molluscs are very scarce. In the 1980s, CITES records show that about 565 t yr^{-1} of coral were traded, primarily dead, but this total had increased to 1221 t by 1997 (Green and Shirley, 1999); the proportion sold for curios remains uncertain (see above). Simply as a rough indication of the scale of trade (although not from coral reefs), Mexican fishers hand-collected an estimated 730 000 sea stars and 48 000 sea urchins each year, destined for domestic retail shops and foreign importers in the USA and overseas (K. E. Lunn, M. J. Villanueva Noriega and A. C. J. Vincent, unpublished data).

It appears that the total volume and value of the USA's curio imports of marine fishes were substantially smaller than similar curio imports for marine invertebrates (see above). From 1997 to 2001, the USA alone annually imported, for curio use, perhaps 29 t of shark parts, more than 200 000 shark teeth, 65 000 seahorses (one-third for curios and two-thirds for traditional medicine) and 20 000 porcupinefish (Grey *et al.*, 2005); many of these were from reef-associated species.

Values

The curio trade could be economically important for some taxa. In 1986, the most recent year with an accessible estimate, the USA's imports of shell-craft (ornamental shells processed prior to export) were worth more than US$10 million, with 75% sourced from the Philippines (Wood and Wells, 1995) (Fig. 6.10). Global exploitation of black corals for jewellery alone was already valued at US$500 million yr^{-1} by 1981 (Green and Hendry, 1999). In comparison, the total value of all fish curio imports to the USA a decade later (from 1997 to 2001) averaged about US$1.7 million yr^{-1} (Grey *et al.*, 2005), with individual seahorses and porcupinefish for curios worth only US$0.16 and US$0.48 respectively at import (Grey *et al.*, 2005).

The curio trade often differs from other non-food fisheries in engaging local people in source communities to add value to the marine resource by processing raw products and thus enhancing employment opportunities (e.g. Salamanca and Pajaro, 1996). Such employment might arguably help to reduce fishing pressure, if sourcing of raw materials were carefully considered and workers were adequately compensated and protected from toxic substances (e.g. chemicals used to etch designs on shells).

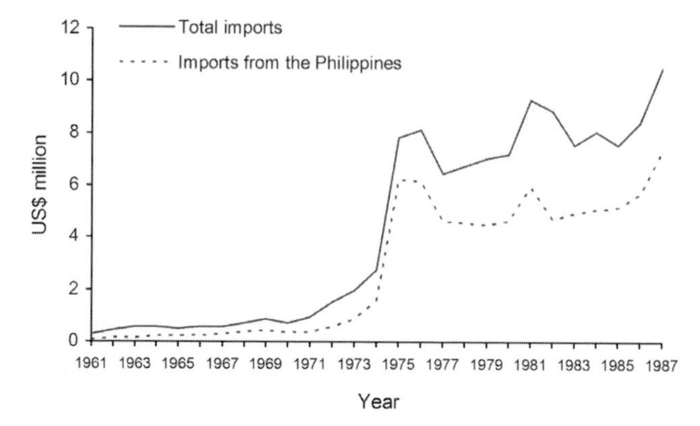

Figure 6.10 Value of US imports of 'articles of shells' 1961 to 1987. (Source: Wood and Wells, 1995.)

Direct impact

The sparse data available indicate that no species has yet been judged as threatened with global extinction by over-collection for curios, but certain species of shells have become extremely scarce in exploited areas (reviewed in Wells, 1988; Wood and Wells, 1995; Ponder and Grayson, 1998). Waste can exacerbate the problem: in some species, shells of all sizes may be taken indiscriminately, without regard for marketability (Magsuci *et al.*, 1980). The shells most vulnerable to overexploitation would include those with narrow geographic ranges, that produce few, bottom-living young, that are large and visible, that are easily harvested on reef flats, or that come from juvenile animals (Wells and Wood, 1991). Anecdotal evidence suggests that over-collection for curios was a concern in Eritrean reef systems (Daw *et al.*, 2001), in the Middle Eastern seas (Fouda, 1995) and in Fiji, where apprehensions about the curio trade in corals led to proposals for an export quota and detailed monitoring (Lovell, 2001a).

Population depletions are not necessarily the direct result of the curio trade. Half of the 32 marine species imported to the USA for curios are considered to be 'Threatened' on the IUCN *Red List of Threatened Species* (and another quarter are 'Data Deficient': Grey *et al.*, 2005), but most are used for purposes other than curios. Construction of buildings, roads and piers from corals, rather than the curio trade, may explain local exhaustion of coral resources in Fiji (Lovell, 2001a). Although the marine curio trade has contributed to the decline in populations of sea turtles (on CITES Appendix I), great white sharks and seahorses (on CITES

Appendix II) and smalltooth sawfish ('Endangered' on the IUCN *Red List*), all of these animals are also under other anthropogenic pressures.

TRADITIONAL MEDICINES

Targets

In many developing countries, people often rely primarily on traditional medicine (TM), or complementary and alternative medicine, in what are acknowledged to be valid means of health care (World Health Organization, 2002). At least 125 forms of TM are recognized, including the codified systems of traditional Chinese medicine (TCM), *Ayurveda*, and *Unani* and the unwritten 'folk' medicines of the Americas, sub-Saharan Africa and the Asia–Pacific region (World Health Organization, 2002). My comments will emphasize consumption for TCM because its trade and conservation issues have been slightly better considered.

An exact tally of marine or coral species in TM – some of which are also used in the aquarium and curio trades – is impossible to deduce. First, most forms of TM rely heavily on oral traditions to disseminate knowledge. Second, many of the species listed in TM pharmacopoeia are not in active use. Third, taxonomy in *materia medica* can be coarse, as when the single listing of seaweed in Ayurvedic medicine in southern India represented up to 14 species of algae (Lipton, 2000). Fourth, the distinction among medicines, tonics and foods is difficult to ascertain in TM (May, 1997). Species primarily consumed as tonic foods – loosely defined as those eaten for general health, rather than under medical guidance – will not be considered in this chapter, although some (e.g. sea cucumber, shark fin or fish maws) are traded in very large volumes.

One preliminary study, mostly of Asian forms of TM, estimated that medicinal value was attributed to nearly 400 marine species, belonging to many phyla (Perry, 2000) (Fig. 6.11). The TCM materia medica list at least 628 marine species (Zeng, 1995). Fewer than 10% of these are currently in regular use in Hong Kong, although new marine species are being added (S.-P. Kwan, unpublished data), including some new to TCM (e.g. Vincent, 1997). Other research has reported use of nine marine medicinals in the Levant (Lev, 2003) and about 20 marine species in Brazil (Costa-Neto, 1999).

Reef-associated species used in TM include sea snakes, sea turtles, seahorses, pufferfish, soft corals, cowries and many more (Tang, 1987; Vincent, 1996; Costa-Neto, 1999; Perry, 2000; Lev and Amar, 2002; S.-P. Kwan,

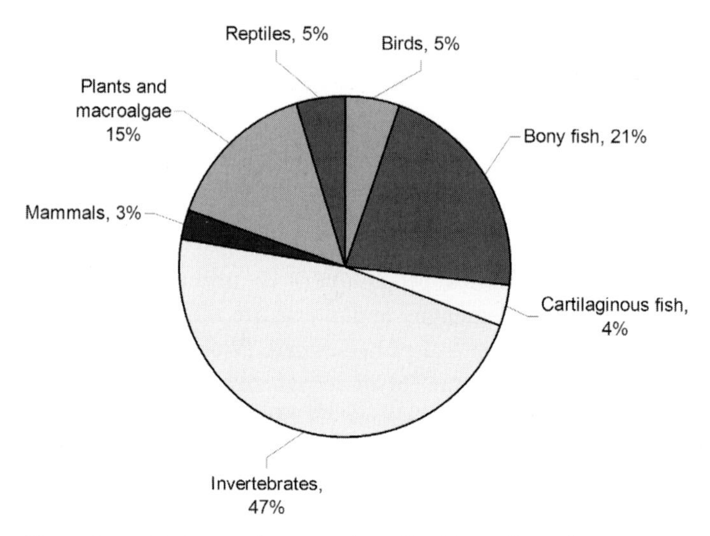

Figure 6.11 Marine taxa known to be utilized in traditional medicine, particularly in Asia (by number of species). (Source: Perry, 2000.)

unpublished data). Much of this section will focus on trade in seahorses for TCM, *hanyak* (Korean TM), *kanpo* (Japanese TM), *jamu* (Indonesian TM) and folk medicines; more is known for these species than for other marine medicinals, although the data do not yet provide enough resolution to distinguish coral reef seahorse species from others. Seahorses are also among the TM species that are heavily traded internationally.

Extraction

Marine medicinals are obtained from the wild in target fisheries, as secondary catch, or as incidental by-catch in non-selective fishing gear. The small-scale fishers that target TM species take them with hook and line, spear, nets, gleaning and hookah gear. Virtually all seahorses used in TM are wild-caught using small nets, by hand or, in seagrass areas, as by-catch in shrimp trawls (Vincent, 1996; McPherson and Vincent, 2004; Giles *et al.*, 2005; Baum and Vincent, 2006). Other reef-associated species in TM, such as some pegasids, are also caught in trawl nets (Pajaro *et al.*, 2004).

Seahorses appear to be the only marine species in which large-scale aquaculture is intended primarily for TM and tonic food uses (author's personal observation). However, no ventures are yet known to have succeeded in sustaining an economically viable business based on sale of seahorses for TM, although many have tried. The largest seahorse farm in mainland China, for example, faces financial and supply challenges

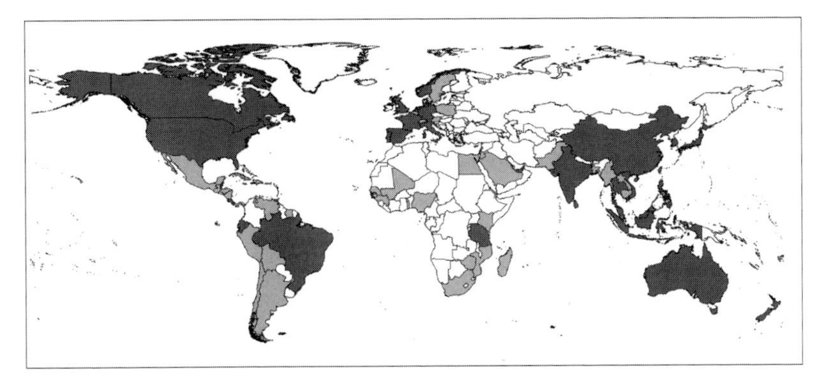

Figure 6.12 Countries known to trade seahorses and/or pipefishes (many data sources do not distinguish them) by 1995 (dark grey) and by 2000 (light grey). (Source: Vincent *et al.*, in press.)

(H. Koldewey and S. Lee, unpublished data). Many seahorse farms intending to supply the TM trade have been forced by economic pressures to redirect their efforts to the aquarium trade (author's personal observation).

Sources and destinations

The trade in marine medicinals can involve large domestic trade and/or substantial international trade, according to the form of medicine and its consumers. We can infer that much of the undocumented extraction of marine species is used domestically, to meet local medicinal needs among dependent people (Marshall, 1998). The international trade is more likely to be visible, although very little has yet been documented.

For seahorses, the largest domestic trade may be in Indonesia, where many tonnes are consumed each year for *jamu* TM (A. Perry, unpublished data). The main exporting nations are India, Philippines, Thailand, Vietnam, and perhaps Mexico (Vincent, 1996; Giles *et al.*, 2005; Baum and Vincent, 2006). Particularly large trade volumes (associated with TCM) travel into and through mainland China, Hong Kong, Singapore and Taiwan (Fig. 6.12).

Volumes

Little is known about the volumes of marine medicinals used in TM. In general, the few official fisheries and trade data that do exist (e.g. national Customs databases, or FAO Yearbook Fisheries Statistics) tend to be for species used primarily in tonic foods, such as sea cucumbers and shark fin.

Crude estimates of trade volumes for seahorses and inferences about their consequence have been produced from field surveys, supplemented by limited official data (Vincent, 1996; McPherson and Vincent, 2004; Giles *et al.*, 2005; Baum and Vincent, 2006; Martin-Smith and Vincent, 2006). Initial surveys (1993–95) found international trade of more than 20 million seahorses in TCM in 1995, involving at least 32 countries; perhaps 90% of that trade went through mainland China, Hong Kong, Singapore, or Taiwan (Vincent, 1996; McPherson and Vincent, 2004). Later surveys (1998–2000) suggested that the trade might have grown somewhat in volume by 2000, then involving nearly 80 countries (A. Vincent, unpublished data).

The use of TM will probably continue to grow (Vincent *et al.*, in press). At the supply end, new trade routes have emerged and new fishing technologies have allowed greater access to, and removal of, marine species. At the demand end, populations in key consumer countries are increasing, China's economy is expanding, Westerners are becoming more interested in TM, and Chinese and Hong Kong governments are institutionalizing TCM in health-care systems (Preparatory Committee on Chinese Medicine, 1997). As well, the increasing advent of patent forms of TM may well enhance market interest.

Values

Many of the marine species used locally for TM may be of low commercial value, even if important medicinally. Organisms that are exported could, however, bring potentially important cash income to the collectors. Some subsistence fishers in the central Philippines depend on seahorses for up to 100% of their seasonal cash income, partly because of the collapse of other resources (M. Pajaro and A. Vincent, unpublished data). At retail level in Hong Kong, some seahorses can sell for up to US$1200 kg^{-1}, although these are not usually coral reef species (Vincent, 1996).

Direct impact

Many marine species used in TM are considered threatened, although not necessarily directly by TM. By 1996, at least 27 species used partly for marine medicinals were included in the IUCN *Red List of Threatened Species* (3 'Critically Endangered', 5 'Endangered', 14 'Vulnerable', 6 'Lower Risk', 4 'Data Deficient') and 23 species were listed on CITES Appendix I or II (Baillie and Groombridge, 1996).

It is difficult to ascertain the role that TM consumption played in creating conservation concern. Many seahorses are included in the IUCN *Red List* (IUCN, 2004) and all are now listed in CITES Appendix II (CITES, 2005). Some population declines of seahorses, as for *Hippocampus comes* in the central Philippines, do appear to have been driven largely by targeted overfishing, primarily for TCM (Vincent, 1996). In other exploited populations with substantial declines (e.g. 15–50% over five years), however, the animals were traded both for TM and for aquarium display (Vincent, 1996). Moreover, many of the seahorses traded for TM – including some species associated with coral reefs – were sourced from bottom-trawls and other non-selective fishing gear (Vincent, 1996; Giles *et al.*, 2005; Baum and Vincent, 2006). One indication that demand may exceed supply comes from the geographic expansion of the sources for seahorses in trade (Fig. 6.12), while total volumes have changed less (A. Vincent, unpublished data).

Many of the marine ingredients in TM for which conservation concern is high – e.g. sea snakes, sea turtles, conch, hard corals – were seldom used by TCM practitioners in Hong Kong and were not considered central to treatment (S.-P. Kwan, unpublished data). Such practitioners further suggested that some of the other marine products they used frequently (e.g. seashells and seaweed) were sufficiently abundant to withstand exploitation while yet more – e.g. abalone shells and cuttlebones – would be obtained as by-products of food collection (S.-P. Kwan, unpublished data). Nonetheless, TM demand will probably also remain high for some core species that could be threatened, such as seahorses.

BIOPROSPECTING

Targets

In contrast to the TM trade, bioprospecting (i.e. seeking commercially exploitable biologically active compounds) on coral reefs is primarily for pharmaceutical products of use in allopathic or Western medicine (Bongiorni and Pietra, 1996). Coral reefs are targeted because of their high levels of biodiversity, warm water, shallow depths (accessible to divers) and wealth of soft-bodied sessile invertebrates (D. Newman, US National Cancer Institute, pers. comm.). These organisms are favoured in bioprospecting because of their bioactive secondary metabolites, used in ecological interactions such as competition for space and protection from fouling and predation (Harper *et al.*, 2001). Porifera is the largest

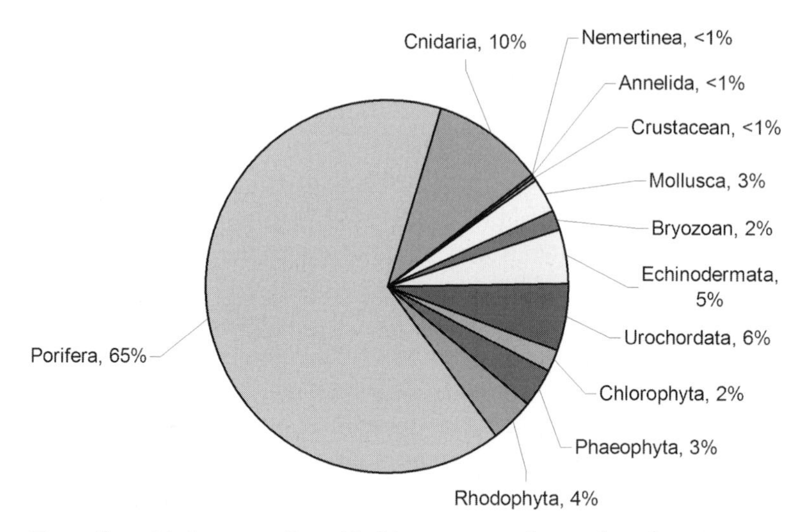

Figure 6.13 Marine taxa collected by bioprospectors (by number of species). (Source: Hunt and Vincent, in press.)

source of marine compounds, followed by Cnidaria, Urochordata, Echinodermata, Rhodophyta and Mollusca (Hunt and Vincent, in press) (Fig. 6.13). Few metabolites are extracted from fish, sea snakes or aquatic mammals (Jha and Xu, 2004).

Commercial confidentiality makes it very difficult to assess the nature, scale and impacts of bioprospecting for marine pharmaceuticals but it clearly taps into a broad array of species. One Spanish pharmaceutical company, PharmaMar, has a library of about 39 000 samples of marine macroorganisms (Rouhi, 2003a), which may or may not each represent a species. As well, the US National Cancer Institute (NCI) processed 18 000 marine extracts between 1975 and 1982 (National Cancer Institute, 2000) and has collected 10 000 samples of marine invertebrates and algae since 1986 (National Cancer Institute, 2005). Such NCI collections include thousands of macroinvertebrates obtained in Palau during the 1990s and 4000–6000 samples obtained from the Great Barrier Reef from 1986 to 1992, in partnership with the Australian Institute of Marine Science. Other such collections of reef organisms include 3500 species (predominantly sponges, cnidarians and ascidians) from tropical Australia, collected by AstraZeneca and Griffith University (Quinn *et al.*, 2002).

Promising biomedical compounds derived from coral reef organisms include a chronic pain treatment synthesized from a coral reef cone (Olivera, 2000), as well as two possible cancer treatments and one anti-asthma drug isolated from sponges in Papua New Guinea (Burgoyne and Andersen, 1992; Williams *et al.*, 1998; Chevallier *et al.*, 2003).

Extraction

Marine species are collected by contractors or research groups, which then supply public bodies and/or pharmaceutical companies. For example, the Coral Reef Research Foundation in Palau collects marine macroorganism samples for the US NCI. The NCI will screen, fractionate and identify possible drugs leads then licence a pharmaceutical company to manage clinical trials of the compound.

Bioprospecting is undergoing some changes. After a period in which natural products research grew rapidly, some pharmaceutical companies reduced their involvement in bioprospecting from the wild, because of concerns about intellectual property rights and the slow rate of compound production when compared with combinatorial chemistry (Rouhi, 2003b). Now, however, natural compounds are again sought, partly as the basis for drug development with combinatorial techniques (Ganesan, 2001; Rouhi, 2003b). Many believe the marine biotechnology industry has yet to achieve its full potential (Zilinskas and Lundin, 1993; Ministry of Economic Development, 2002).

Most bulk compounds used in drug development come from wild supply, synthesis or microbial culture (Munro *et al.*, 1999). By the stage of clinical development, only two or three out of 21 marine drugs were supplied by wild extraction (Hunt and Vincent, in press) (Fig. 6.14). Some compounds can be completely synthesized although others are too complex. Mariculture or aquaculture can also supply some needs, although most marine invertebrates are sufficiently difficult to culture to preclude reliable bulk supply (Mendola, 2003).

Sources and destinations

Bioprospecting largely involves exporting genetic material from coral reefs, primarily in biodiverse tropical developing countries (Fig. 6.15), to the USA, EU and Japan, where compounds can be scanned and pharmaceuticals can be developed (Bongiorni and Pietra, 1996). Little more is understood.

Volumes

Issues of intellectual property mean that data on volumes used in bioprospecting remain elusive. However, companies apparently do want to

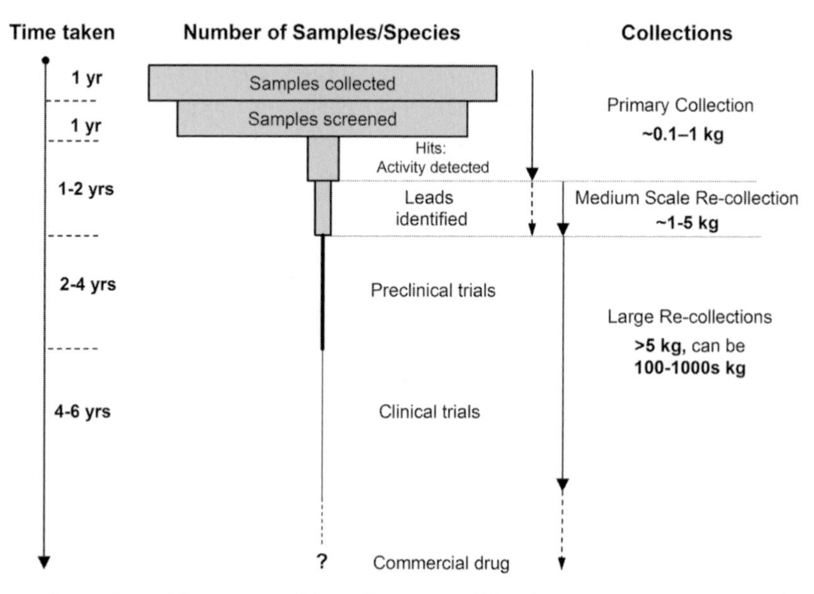

Figure 6.14 The process of drug discovery and development. (Source: Hunt and Vincent, in press.)

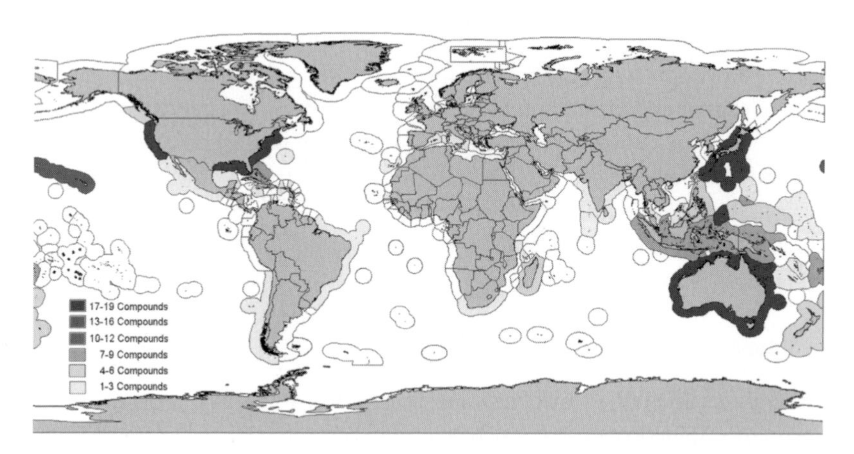

Figure 6.15 Distribution and number of novel marine compounds. The origin (recorded as national exclusive economic zones (EEZs)), and number of novel marine compounds sampled from the literature (American Chemical Society Database) are used as surrogates for location and relative intensity of bioprospecting activity. The data suggest that collection is focused on countries with coral reefs and the national waters of countries that conduct research into marine natural products. (Source: Hunt and Vincent, in press.) (See also Plate 6.15 in the colour plate section.)

know that they can obtain enough material for preclinical and clinical studies before launching into expensive and lengthy research (Cragg, 1998). Miniaturization, better computing and automated techniques mean that screening is generally undertaken on less than 1 kg of material (Hooper *et al.*, 1998; Quinn *et al.*, 2002). Secondary collections to follow up on promising leads, however, tend to be large. For example, secondary collections of coral-reef-associated sponges in the Maldives extracted 400 kg of *Spongia* sp., 500 kg of *Hyrtios erecta* and 350 kg of *Cribrochalina* sp. (Pettit *et al.*, 1993, 1994, 2000). As well, 480 kg of the Palaun sponge *Axinella* sp. and 1 t of the sea hare, *Dolabella auricularia*, were collected in the 1980s (Pettit *et al.*, 1994; Garson, 1997). In 1988, a pharmaceutical company collected 13 t of *Bugula neritina*, a non-reef bryozoan, off the coast of southern California in order to produce just 18 g of bryostatin 1 for use in preclinical and clinical trials (Cragg, 1998). Such large secondary collections may become less necessary in the future because of technological change (Hooper *et al.*, 1998).

Values

Commercial confidentiality makes it difficult to evaluate the economics of this trade. It seems, however, that little of the enormous amount of money involved in drug development – which can take more than a decade and cost up to US$600 million (Kuhlmann, 1997) – is spent on bioprospecting or reaches the source country or its people. Some countries are managing to negotiate support for conservation programmes in exchange for use of their biological resources. In particular, Costa Rica allowed the pharmaceutical company Merck to explore its biodiversity in exchange for $1 million, plus a large share of any royalties (Roberts, 1992), although not necessarily of any patents. Other biodiverse nations have also agreed general financial benefits with pharmaceutical companies. In fact, however, the chances of a profitable discovery are very low (Farrier and Tucker, 2001) and such rewards as do accrue may not offer financial incentives for conservation, going instead to general funds (Barrett and Lybbert, 2000). Future benefits for countries (although often not for local people) may lie in joint ventures, where collection samples are processed and tested in the source country, with technical support from overseas.

Direct impact

A recent workshop found no evidence to suggest that bioprospecting was any more damaging to the marine environment than other scientific collections (J. J. Green, 2003). Conservation concerns are unlikely to arise from primary collections, because of the small amounts that are used at this stage (Cragg, 1998; Munro *et al.*, 1999; Cordell, 2000). If, however, preclinical work justifies (usually much larger) re-collections, then the animal's distribution and abundance become important, because scarcity might preclude progress in drug development (Cragg, 1998). In the case of *B. neritina*, the collection of 13 t sounds substantial, but was easily extracted from docks and pilings and supplied enough for all preclinical and clinical trials (Schaufelberger *et al.*, 1991). Large re-collections of other species, however, may pose problems on at least a local scale (Benkendorff, 2002).

Given the secrecy surrounding sampling, it is difficult to know which specimens of interest to bioprospectors might be on the IUCN *Red List* (IUCN, 2004), although many corals, at least, will be on CITES Appendix II (CITES, 2005). The most common conservation concern is that large collection may significantly reduce local populations, decrease genetic diversity and cause genetic drift (Benkendorff, 2002). In terrestrial systems, for example, bioprospecting is reputed to have caused the decline of plant species, such as the Brazilian *Pilocarpus* spp., used to produce pilocarpine (Pinheiro, 1997). Impacts of bioprospecting are, of course, expected to be more pronounced if the organism is rare or has a restricted distribution relative to the area of collection (Chivian *et al.*, 2003).

COMPARING AND CONTRASTING THE LIVE FOOD AND NON-FOOD FISHERIES

The five live food and non-food trades assessed here cumulatively involve a great many different reef-associated taxa, caught by many different gears, in many different countries, for many different purposes. For example, shells can be sold for food, aquarium display (sometimes associated with live rock), clothing accessories, and manufacture of pottery glazes and floor tiles (Wood and Wells, 1995). As well, seahorses can be traded for aquarium display, curios, traditional medicines or tonic foods (Vincent, 1996). We must carefully consider possible conservation threats, pragmatic approaches to management, realistic evaluations of choices, and efforts to adjust consumption.

All five trades appear to have some commonalities that might set them apart from other reef fisheries (Table 6.1) in that they (1) are exported globally, (2) may focus on rare species, (3) emerged in the last 50–60 years, (4) experienced rapid overall growth over that period, and (5) are already worth a lot of money. The extent of exports in these trades – and their consequent vulnerability to both international pressures and regulations – is an attribute that particularly sets them apart from reef fisheries for dead food. The other common characteristics of wild sourcing, inadequate knowledge, lack of management, possible supplementation from aquaculture and increasing exploitation arguably apply to most reef fisheries and trades.

In some cases, bioprospecting for pharmaceuticals diverges from the other four trades (Table 6.1). In the latter cases, (1) individuals are often selected individually by consumers, (2) fisheries are primarily subsistence and can be combined with food fishing, (3) export volumes may be large relative to populations, and (4) organisms primarily originate in Southeast Asia or insular Pacific nations. In contrast, bioprospecting provides little local employment, although it could offer substantial long-term financial benefits under profit-sharing agreements. As another contrast, participants in bioprospecting reach into more geographically-diverse source areas and actively seek to keep all data confidential for commercial reasons, while the other four trades lack data because of their complexities and dearth of resources. Finally, bioprospecting is likely to be least dependent on wild resources; it is characterised by very small primary collections and infrequent larger collections of soft-bottom sessile invertebrates, with few perceived conservation consequences.

Sometimes, three trades differ from the other two (Table 6.1), as in the following examples. First, aquarium, curio and bioprospecting trades rely on a great diversity of species and have North America and Europe as their main destination. In contrast, the live food and TM trades appear to depend on relatively few species of marine organisms and are primarily directed at ethnic Chinese areas in Asia. Second, species in the aquarium, TM and bioprospecting trades are seldom valued as dead food, while those in the live food and curio trades are more often consumed. Third, the live food, aquarium display, and curio trades essentially involve optional luxury goods, such that consumers could perhaps be influenced to purchase sustainably. In contrast, the TM and bioprospecting trades may be considered more essential because of their importance to health. Even the apparently optional luxury trades may, however, be important to fishers and merchants with few other income-earning opportunities, particularly when value can be added by processing curio species (Lovell, 2001a). The tendency for some species in the luxury trades to become increasingly costly with rarity means that small populations or depletion may not necessarily result in lower exploitation pressure (Sadovy and Vincent, 2002).

Table 6.1. Comparison of attributes across live food and non-food trades. The symbols are as follows: •, yes; (•), somewhat; N, no; ?, uncertain

	Live food	Aquarium	Curios	Traditional medicine	Bioprospecting
Targets					
Dependent on wild populations	•	•	•	•	(•)
Great diversity of species used	N	•	•	N	•
Invertebrates are an important part of the trade	N	•	•	?	•
Few species comprise most of the international trade*	•	•	N	•	N
Most species unstudied	•	•	•	•	•
Consumers select individually, based on appearance*	•	•	•	(•)	N
Smaller individuals can be more valuable than larger individuals of same species*	•	•	N	N	N
Immature individuals often targeted*	•	•	N	N	N
Specimens traded whole	•	•	(•)	•	•
Primarily exploits predators	•	N	N	N	N
Some rare species targeted	•	•	•	•	•
Many species potentially vulnerable to over-fishing	•	(•)	(•)	(•)	?
Target species commonly valued as food in source country	•	N	(•)	N	N
Extraction					
Relatively new fisheries (mostly since WWII)*	•	•	•	(•)	•
Can be combined with food fishing	•	(•)	•	•	N
Mainly supporting subsistence fisheries, with low opportunity costs	•	•	•	•	N
Fisheries rarely managed	•	•	•	•	•
Standard fishery models generally do not apply	•	•	•	•	•

Table 6.1. (*cont.*)

	Live food	Aquarium	Curios	Traditional medicine	Bioprospecting
Some fishing techniques destructive	•	•	N	N	N
Mariculture may help to reduce fishing pressure	•	•	•	•	•
Sources and destinations					
Exported long distances*	•	•	•	•	•
Mainly originating in Southeast Asia and the Pacific Islands, although resource base is shifting*	•	•	•	(•)	N
Export trade supplies wealthy markets*	•	•	•	(•)	•
Exports primarily to North America and Europe*	N	•	•	N	•
Exports primarily to ethnic Chinese areas in Asia*	•	N	N	•	N
Trades poorly monitored	•	•	•	•	•
Trades not included in FAO world production figures	•	•	•	•	•
Animal welfare issues in shipping live organisms*	•	•	N	N	N
High hidden mortalities mean trade numbers are underestimates*	•	•	N	N	N
Volumes and values					
Rapid net growth in the last 50–60 years	•	•	•	(•)	•
Demand expected to grow	•	•	•	•	?
Worth millions of dollars yr^{-1}	•	•	•	•	?
High value per item*	•	•	N	?	N
Rarity confers value*	•	•	(•)	?	N
Luxury/optional items*	•	•	•	N	N
Has linkages to human health issues	•	(•)	N	•	•

Note: * Denotes difference from dead food fisheries on coral reefs.
Source: Partly derived from Sadovy and Vincent (2002).

Table 6.2. Differences between live food trade and aquarium trade fisheries

- Live food trade takes fewer species than aquarium trade
- Live food trade extracts particularly high numbers of juveniles for mariculture
- Live food trade takes larger species/individuals, aquarium trade takes smaller species/individuals
- Value of hardware negligible for live food trade but may be substantial for aquarium trade
- Live food trade culture mainly based on wild capture of juveniles; negligible aquarium trade culture based on hatcheries
- Live food trade has high mortalities and demand for feed in mariculture
- Aquarium trade requires better catch survivorship compared to live food trade catch
- Live food trade is only in Indo-Pacific; aquarium trade is global in tropics/subtropics
- Live food trade has associated human health issues
- Demand for live food trade is in the East; major demand for aquarium trade is in the West
- Aquarium trade is better monitored in international trade
- Live food trade typically has little stability whereas aquarium trade may have long-term stability in specific areas
- Aquarium trade prices generally more stable in the long term
- Public aquaria can promote education and conservation; live trade industry does not

Source: Derived from Sadovy and Vincent (2002).

The two live trades share many commonalities (Table 6.1) but also exhibit some differences (Table 6.2). Management can be particularly challenging because these trades often target (1) males, (2) juveniles, (3) small individuals, and/or (4) colourful individuals; the latter may also be important for some shell collectors in the curio trade. Moreover, the two live trades involve considerable waste of collected specimens through mortality – perhaps also true of breakage in the curio trade – and are the focus of culturing initiatives to help meet demand and provide livelihood opportunities (see below).

CONSERVATION CONSEQUENCES

An overall statement as to conservation concern posed by these five trades would be premature. Too little is known about the life histories, populations, fisheries or consumption patterns for most species exploited for live food and non-food purposes, with many considered 'Data Deficient' on the IUCN *Red List* (IUCN, 2004). The few better-known species are also important in food fisheries and/or have the greatest value in live food and non-food fisheries. At present, we can only try to deduce possible patterns in threats and pressures.

Vulnerability of target species

As with many reef organisms in general, many (but certainly not all) species exploited for live food and non-food purposes have life histories that might make them susceptible to over-fishing (Dulvy *et al.*, 2003), with some combination of small ranges, complex life histories, specialized needs, long lifespans, slow growth and low natural mortality, poor recruitment to the adult population, late maturity, large adult size, highly structured social behaviour, spawning aggregations, hermaphroditism, low reproductive rates, limited larval dispersal, sessile behaviour, site fidelity, and migration (Wells, 1988; Wood and Wells, 1995; Harriot, 1999, 2003; Jennings *et al.*, 1999; Hawkins *et al.*, 2000; Sadovy and Cheung, 2003; Wabnitz *et al.*, 2003). On the other hand, many species traded for aquarium display, curiosities and pharmaceuticals (at least) should be able to withstand substantial exploitation.

Even where commonalities occur, life history is not entirely a predictor of population declines, which occur in live food and non-food targets as diverse as (1) groupers, which are sequential hermaphrodites and form spawning aggregations, (2) seahorses, which provide essential parental care and form site-faithful pairs, and (3) gastropods, which have planktotrophic free-swimming larvae and great dispersal potential; all may encounter depensatory population responses (Allee effects) (Stoner and Ray-Culp, 2000; Sadovy, 2001b; Foster and Vincent, 2004). Moreover, concern is arising both for species with restricted distributions and those that are geographically widespread but heavily exploited (Wood, 2001a); many of the species in the live or non-food trades are at low densities and/or lack refuges inaccessible to fishers and collectors (Wells, 1988; Sadovy *et al.*, 2003b).

Where interest can be generated and resources can be found to undertake biological research, it should focus on the key life-history variables and population dynamics essential for management decision-making (e.g. abundance, age-specific rates of natural mortality, population structure, reproductive timing and location, and intrinsic rates of population increase). Realistically, the sheer number of species that may be exploited in live food and non-food fisheries, and their low profile, is likely to limit such research to the most valuable and/or charismatic. Moreover, many of the species are sufficiently rare – and often cryptic and/or nocturnal – to make life-history research difficult.

Direct impacts on target species

The overall threat posed by live food and non-food fisheries remains unclear. Given that depletions are expected in fished populations, analyses showing fewer individuals or lower biomass in fished areas (e.g. Tissot and Hallacher, 2003) are not, per se, convincing evidence of collapses. Possible indicators of conservation problems (some from Sadovy *et al.*, 2003a) would include (a) declines in population or CPUE continue after initial depletion, (b) the species does not rebound when fishing pressure is reduced, (c) geographic ranges start to contract, and/or (d) larger community or ecosystem changes. All of these metrics, however, require monitoring that may be prohibitively difficult. More feasibly measured indicators of potential conservation concern (some from Sadovy *et al.*, 2003a) would include (e) behaviour that makes a species vulnerable, (f) a relative dearth of adults, (g) juveniles in mariculture or trade, (h) destructive fishing methods, (i) uncontrolled and effectively unmonitored fisheries and/or (j) largely unenforceable protective measures. Even assessing these indicators, however, will require openness to diverse sources of qualitative and quantitative information.

The sustainability of any fishery will have to be assessed at different scales as fishing pressures change. Local depletion is ecologically important but recovery may be possible if exploitation poses no threat on a wider scale. The tendency of some live food and non-food fisheries (especially for live food) to shift among exploitation areas in a form of strip-mining and/or to expand globally can mask declines and remove accountability for population depletion, habitat damage and ecosystem disruption (as with seahorses: Vincent *et al.*, in press). Change in target species, whether by choice or in response to changing availability or market, may also mask depletions and may impose new pressures on additional species. For example, the steady increase in the trade in live corals created pressures on new coral species preferred for aquaria, with their somewhat greater rarity and relatively lower rates of growth and sexual recruitment (Bruckner, 2001).

Impacts on the larger ecosystem

Just as targeted organisms are affected by broader pressures on their ecosystem, so their removal can have consequences for their coral reef ecosystems (Wells and Wood, 1991). Declines could affect many non-target organisms as well as imposing amplified feedback effects on targeted populations. For example, extracting hard corals for aquarium and curio trades may damage and weaken the reef, with consequences for fish and other reef-dependent species. Overexploitation of sea urchins for the curio trade could lead to increased algal cover, which may inhibit the growth of corals (Hughes *et al.*, 1987; Precht and Aronson, this volume). Removal of pufferfish and triggerfish – sought for aquarium display and especially vulnerable to by-catch – may lead to bioerosion of corals, as these fish help to stabilize reef communities by feeding on sea urchins (McClanahan and Shafir, 1990). Impacts should not be assumed, however; depletions of three herbivorous aquarium fish species in Hawaii, for example, had no obvious impacts on macroalgal abundance (Tissot and Hallacher, 2003).

A considerable amount of live food and non-food fishing is targeted, but some fishing methods physically disrupt habitats or remove non-target organisms. Live food and non-food fisheries do not use dynamite or blast fishing but they may involve breakage, overturning, rock removal, dredging and poisoning. Prising corals with iron bars and breaking them to pursue live fish exposed to cyanide would probably reduce fish abundance locally (Dulvy *et al.*, 1995). The use of cyanide in the live fish trades appears to lead to coral bleaching and associated reduced growth and reproduction (Erdmann and Pet-Soede, 1996) although experimental evidence on appropriate temporal and spatial scales is still scarce. Meanwhile, the non-target fish caught with cyanide are sometimes sold as bait or to feed groupers during grow-out mariculture (Johannes and Riepen, 1995; Bentley, 1999). In turn, fyke (bag) nets, used to capture juvenile groupers and wrasses for mariculture, also obtain large volumes of by-catch (Sadovy, 2000).

A further ecosystem impact from live fisheries lies in the introduction of exotic species (Wabnitz *et al.*, 2003); hundreds of thousands of grouper juveniles from all over Southeast Asia are released into Taiwan waters for restocking and public relations exercises (T. Yang, Fish Breeding Association, Taiwan, 31 August 2001, cited in Sadovy *et al.*, 2003a). Other haphazard releases have occurred when people tire of their aquarium displays and release exotic species into local waters (Wood, 2001a; Semmens *et al.*, 2004).

Socio-economic impacts

New live food and non-food fisheries (or any other new fishery) can seem attractive to impoverished fishing communities but their socio-economic benefits and costs are unknown, and are unlikely to be assessed very soon. Fishers are attracted to new opportunities, including those for live food and non-food commodities, by depletion of other marine resources, lack of land or capital, absence of other livelihood options, and/or logistic constraints. The advent of some fisheries for live food, aquaria, curios, and TM – but not bioprospecting, with its relative lack of community involvement – should enable coastal communities to earn income and build essential facilities, at least in the short term. At the same time, live food and non-food trades bring socio-economic costs. First, locals could often otherwise eat quite a number of these species for food. Second, live food and non-food fisheries may not bring enough employment and income to offset their ecological or social damage. Third, the advent of live food and non-food fisheries may create social unrest, with arguments among fishers or between fishers and agents from elsewhere (reviewed for the live food trade in Sadovy *et al.*, 2003a). Fourth, live food and non-food fisheries may lead to more damaging extraction activities, with consequent feedback costs for the marine community. Where live food and non-food trades are ecologically unsustainable, the conservation and human costs accrue to the country where the product originated, not to the destination of the export (Warren-Rhodes *et al.*, 2003).

MANAGEMENT OF WILD CAPTURE

Few countries, particularly developing nations, have established sound management plans for their principal coral reef food fisheries, let alone live food and non-food fisheries. Detailed records are seldom kept, partly because so many fisheries are artisanal or very small scale. Even existing records are commonly incomplete and unreliable, suffering from one or more of the following conditions: effort was not assessed; non-food and food species were (as often) combined; intended consumption was not specified; exports and re-exports became confounded, thus amplifying trade; mortality in the live fish trades was unknown; domestic trade was not represented; the size of any mariculture sector was unclear; and/or much trade proceeded through informal or illegal channels (Wood and Wells, 1995; Vincent, 1996; Green and Shirley, 1999; Bruckner, 2001; Sadovy *et al.*, 2003a).

Given the complexities of the fisheries and the low yields of many species, monitoring and development of management plans for live food and non-food trades may be prohibitively expensive (Sadovy *et al.*, 2003a). Instead, sustainable extraction may best be achieved by utilizing management strategies more suited to the data-poor and dispersed nature of these fisheries (Johannes, 1998; Parma *et al.*, 2003); imperfect or crudely general advice is probably rather better than none at all.

Input controls

One way to manage fishing is to limit effort. Some countries have simply banned exploitation in at least some species traded for live food and non-food purposes (e.g. reviewed in Wood, 2001b). Such bans can be problematic if the species is then fished illicitly, especially if it drops off the conservation agenda (as it is ostensibly 'protected'), or if pressure is deflected to other vulnerable species. As a precautionary means of limiting exploitation, Australia, the Cook Islands, Palau and Tonga (among others) have approached quotas indirectly by limiting the number of active aquarium collectors, while also restricting gear that might result in unsustainable catches (reviewed in Petelo, 2001; Wood, 2001a, 2001b).

Restricting exploitation of particular areas by access, species, time or gear can provide management and conservation benefits: the Solomon Islands use customary ownership while Fiji uses marine tenure to help manage their aquarium trades, putting communities in partnership with industry (Lovell, 2001b; Ramohia, 2001); the Seychelles banned extraction of shells in certain reserves as early as 1981 but found enforcement difficult (Wells, 1988); and many Pacific Islands place temporal restrictions on shell collection (Wells, 1988). In this context, collection zones may need to be sited some distance from areas important to other users, including tourists.

Gear restrictions can improve the sustainability of trades in coral reef organisms for live food and non-food purposes. First, hookah rigs, scuba and outboard engines increase accessibility of deeper or more remote populations, allowing more exploitation and eliminating refugia. Second, use of non-selective fishing gear such as cyanide to target live food and non-food products leads to indiscriminate waste of other organisms of no immediate commercial value. Third, use of non-selective gear in food fisheries can produce by-catch of species with value as non-food commodities, damaging wild populations in the process and potentially fostering demand that must be met by new target fisheries. Moreover, technological advances that allow precision trawling near obstacles now means that even this very non-selective gear can intrude on coral reef ecosystems (R. Kenchington, pers. comm.). For all the concern about gear restrictions, however, even use of apparently appropriate fishing gear can still pose ecological problems if badly deployed (Wood, 2001b).

No-take marine protected areas (MPAs) provide a broad management tool for data-poor fisheries, which can address ecosystem concerns, including those arising from habitat loss (Halpern, 2003). They are proving acceptable or even popular in countries with coral reefs (Wantiez *et al.*, 1997;

White and Courtney, 2002; Martin-Smith *et al.*, 2004; Alcala *et al.*, this volume; Fig. 6.16). Few were specifically designed for the species exploited in live food and non-food fisheries but they may offer benefits nonetheless. No-take MPAs could be valuable for species with vulnerable life-history stages, such as the spawning aggregations targeted by the live reef fish trade. For example, no-take MPAs on the Great Barrier Reef in Australia led to increased abundance and biomass of coral trout, *Plectropomus* spp. (Williamson *et al.*, 2004). At the same time, the tourism often associated with MPAs commonly generates potentially problematic demand for curios and other reef products (Christie *et al.*, 2002), and for seafood.

Output controls

The limited data on populations, fisheries and trades, their impacts, and their change over time, make it difficult to set quotas: (1) there is a substantial risk of setting *ad hoc* limits based on existing practice, without reference to ecological limits; (2) in the absence of species-specific quotas, the fishers may high grade to collect the most valuable (and arguably rarest) species; (3) in the absence of site-specific data, it is difficult to map quotas onto patchy population distributions, in which many live food and non-food species are found.

Selective fishing may be a useful management measure. Minimum size limits can protect populations, especially given the use of juveniles or small fish in many live food and non-food fisheries. Florida has formal restrictions to this end (Wood, 2001b). The difficulty with any size limit lies in finding data to choose a threshold. With respect to the aquarium, curio and TM trade, the CITES technical committee for animals recently endorsed a single minimum size limit for many species as one potential means of ensuring seahorse exports are sustainable under new international trade controls (Foster and Vincent, 2005); although crude, this limit should reduce take until more refined management measures can be contrived. A maximum size limit would help retain larger and more productive individuals on the reef, whether they are corals or fish (Wood, 2001b). An upper limit is, however, less attractive to fishers in trades where larger animals fetch higher prices, such as the TM trade for seahorses (Vincent, 1996; Martin-Smith *et al.*, 2004) (Fig. 6.16). Other options might be to control the removal of organisms by sex or reproductive status, although both have their own risks.

Implementation

Enforcement is a challenge for any restriction or guideline, as proven by the persistence of cyanide fishing despite its illegality in all countries with live

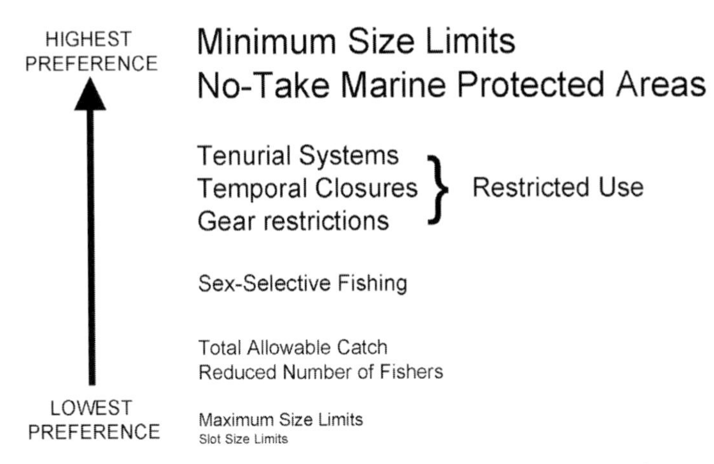

Figure 6.16 Stakeholder preferences for management options in data-poor seahorse fisheries. Font size for each option is proportional to its level of support with maximum size indicating high preference from all six stakeholder groups consulted for that option: Filipino subsistence fishers; Hong Kong TCM merchants; North American public aquarium professionals; Western fisheries scientists; Philippines national policy group; CITES international technical workshop. (Source: Martin-Smith *et al.*, 2004.)

fish exports (Wood, 2001b). Centralized management is expensive, requires considerable administration, and demands outreach, training and monitoring. In Pacific islands, local or traditional ecological knowledge and management techniques, married to pragmatic conservation measures based on ecological principles, probably achieve the greatest probability of population persistence (Johannes, 1981). Some form of community engagement often will be necessary (see Brown, this volume), and will probably be most effective within a national legislative and legal framework, and accompanied by support from regional politicians and police.

ALTERNATIVES TO WILD CAPTURE

Aquaculture

Mariculture is often touted as providing an alternative to management of wild capture fisheries. Approaches to culturing include centralized broodstock facilities, grow-out, and ranching (Wells, 1988; Wells and Wood, 1991; Sadovy *et al.*, 2003a). Among the live food and non-food fisheries, the prospects for aquaculture have been most extensively explored in the trades for food and ornamental display and in pharmaceutical development (Wood, 2001a; Mendola, 2003; Sadovy *et al.*, 2003a), but also for some curio and TM uses, such as queen conch (primarily for food) and seahorses. At present, the collection of post-larvae reef fish for subsequent *ex situ* rearing for live food and aquarium use (Dufour, 1997) is generating considerable discussion. Microbial aquaculture may well be a key element in pharmaceutical development, reducing extraction from the wild (Proksch *et al.*, 2002).

Most culturing ventures pose conservation (and socio-economic) concerns (Sadovy *et al.*, 2003a), ranging from overdependency on wild broodstock (or juveniles in the case of grow-out operations) and/or food (especially for carnivores), escapes of diseased or exotic organisms, local pollution, and/or damage to local habitats (Naylor *et al.*, 2001). As well, not all species can be cultured and not all products from cultured organisms are acceptable to consumers (OmniTrak, 1997; S.-P. Kwan, unpublished data). Moreover, some facilities promote new markets rather than trying to reduce demand for a wild resource, as with a seahorse farm in southern China (H. Koldewey and S. K. H. Lee, unpublished data). Most culturing enterprises will only succeed in reducing pressures on wild populations if fishers find alternative means to earn income and reduce overall extraction. If care is not taken, aquaculture initiatives may undermine opportunities for low-volume and high-value fishing that could sustain fishing communities, thus further threatening the resource. Release of captive-reared species (e.g. a muricid mollusc in Guadeloupe and Martinique: Pointier and Lamy, 1985; or a leopard coral grouper in Japan: Sadovy *et al.*, 2003a), ostensibly for restocking, remains problematic (IUCN, 1998). Just as restocking masks the true state of wild populations, so undocumented trade in cultured products can delay conservation action for wild populations, by inflating their apparent size.

Synthesis and substitution

Synthesis and substitution may help reduce wild capture of marine species for use in TM and pharmaceuticals, although caveats remain. At present, synthesis is largely a viable alternative to bioprospecting. A study of all new small-molecule entities produced between 1981 and 2001 found that 61% were related to or derived from terrestrial or marine natural products, and that the majority are now synthesized (Newman *et al.*, 2003). Some chemical compounds, however, are too complex to be synthesized. And many TM consumers will reject synthesized or substituted products. For example, TM traders in Hong Kong – while certainly willing to adjust consumption to essential minima – argued that each marine medicinal is uniquely important and removing any from the medicinal arsenal would help destroy the integrity of TM. They regarded possible substitutes for seahorses as either unacceptable or impractical (S.-P. Kwan, unpublished data). It is, moreover, not clear that a shift to alternatives for one commodity necessarily reduces pressure on the marine environment as a whole; much depends on how fishers react to the loss of another resource.

CONTROLLING DEMAND

Given the relative wealth of consumers purchasing many live food and non-food products, their role in conservation needs to be considered. If and when marine populations are found to be deleteriously affected by exploitation, three responses are often proposed: find new sources, engage in culturing, and divert species from local consumption to sustain such export trades (some from Sadovy *et al.*, 2003a), with consequent socio-economic concerns. A fourth response, adjusting or reducing demand (as considered here), is insufficiently explored but may be feasible.

Ethical practice and codes of conduct

Industry is obliged to recognize national sovereignty over biological resources, and the need for equitable sharing of benefits from utilizing these resources, as outlined in the 1992 Convention on Biological Diversity. Even where such responsibilities are met (see Values section for bioprospecting), they may not greatly assist source countries, but at least appropriate steps are being taken. In keeping with this and other concerns, industry representatives are becoming involved in self-regulation of many non-food trades, as follows: (1) associations in the aquarium trade range from in-country organizations like AKKII (Indonesia) to PIJAC, the world's largest pet trade association; (2) a shell collectors' organization, the Hawaiian Malacological Society, has an ecological code of conduct; (3) TCM traders in Hong Kong (and particularly the Hong Kong Chinese Medicine Merchants Association) have become engaged in addressing conservation concerns for some marine medicinals (S.-P. Kwan, unpublished data); (4) the International Union of Pure and Applied Chemistry has urged caution when collecting specimens (Andrews *et al.*, 1996). Such codes can include guidelines or restrictions on collection methods, areas, taxa, maximum sample weights/numbers, the qualifications of collectors, as well as the species, size or sex in trade. Associations further worry about waste, which leads to economic loss and repeated exploitation to meet the same need; concerns include deaths in the live fish trades, breakage in the curio trade, and insect damage in the TM trade (Wabnitz *et al.*, 2003).

Ecocertification

Ecological certification schemes provide a formal framework in which consumers may foster sustainable use of coral reef resources, but most still lack measurable impacts. The Marine Stewardship Council (MSC: www.msc.org), set up to evaluate food fisheries globally, has yet to assess any coral reef fisheries. The Marine Aquarium Council (MAC: www.aquariumcouncil.org) has six certified collection areas, all on coral reef habitat. Perhaps because of this engagement with another live trade, for aquarium display, MAC (rather than MSC) is now co-operating with The Nature Conservancy to develop sustainability standards for live food exploitation (fishery, aquaculture, and trade) from reefs (Sadovy *et al.*, 2003a). If such work is to be effective, it will be vital to help developing nations overcome ensuing costs, complexity or technical demands (Chaffee *et al.*, 2003). A further difficulty can be low demand for certified products until consumers understand the problem (e.g. the use of cyanide in the live reef trade: Sadovy *et al.*, 2003a). Once they appreciated the conservation concern, young consumers in Hong Kong indicated a willingness to change eating habits with respect to live food fish (Chan, 2000).

The international treaty, CITES, serves as a form of ecocertification. The vast majority of marine species listed on CITES Appendix II (CITES, 2005) are traded for live food or non-food purposes: humphead wrasse, great white sharks, all seahorses (at least 34 species), giant clams (nine species), queen conch, all hard corals, black coral and some other corals. As well, the marine turtles (of importance in the curio trade) are listed on Appendix I and sea cucumbers (sold in the aquarium trade as well as for food) have also been mooted as potential Appendix II species. In theory, any purchase of these species outside the country of origin should be ecologically sound. In practice, certification schemes, including CITES, are only as good as the assessment and controls allowed by the chain of custody. At least, however, an Appendix II listing enables data to be gathered, challenged and improved.

Legislation and agreements

Many countries have domestic legislation that protects at least some coral reef organisms and/or the reefs themselves (Wells and Wood, 1991). For example, Australia, the USA (Florida and Hawaii) and some Pacific island nations thoroughly control extraction from coral reefs. Bermuda, Kenya, Mauritius, Papua New Guinea and Sri Lanka are among the nations that protect or regulate extraction and/or trade of ornamental species (reviewed in Wood and Wells, 1995; Wijesekara and Yakupitiyage, 2001). In general, however, coral reef resources in developing countries seldom receive the management attention they need.

Given the difficulties in managing multi-species diffuse fisheries, much can be gained by agreeing to global or regional initiatives that work towards sustainability of marine resources. The Asia–Pacific Economic Cooperation group (APEC) and the FAO's Asia–Pacific Fishery Commission (APFIC) are providing important support for the management of live food fisheries. Such regional bodies have the capacity to distil experiences and recommendations and to support appropriate management (Sadovy *et al.*, 2003a). Adopting and using internationally harmonized codes for key commodities – as instituted by Hong Kong for live food fish in 1997 and for seahorses and pipefishes in 1998 – would further increase clarity in international trade.

OUTLOOK

Growth in live food and non-food fisheries has added to diverse pressures on marine environments. Ideally, many of the live food and non-food fisheries could be managed so as to offer high value for low volume of extraction (Sadovy and Vincent, 2002). Principles and criteria for sustainable fisheries include maintaining populations of targeted species and ecosystem integrity, creation of effective fishery management, and compliance with laws and agreements (May *et al.*, 2003). Success in managing these data-poor fisheries will depend on creative engagement from fishers, traders, scientists, managers, consumers, government and other stakeholders. For some species at low abundances, however, even limited additional fishing mortality may have grave consequences, particularly as increasing value with rarity will provoke continued fishing (Sadovy and Vincent, 2002). Moreover, extraction of live food and non-food commodities could damage other food fisheries and marine-based livelihoods.

Anticipating the future of live food and non-food fisheries is difficult. Extraction can change quickly and unpredictably according to consumer preference and variables such as technological advances, transport costs, civil unrest, currency fluctuations and health concerns (Vincent *et al.* in press). Technical advances in aquaculture, aquarium husbandry and drug synthesis will affect demand for wild-sourced animals. National policy will further affect demand, as with government promotion of growth in TM in Hong Kong (Preparatory Committee on Chinese Medicine, 1997).

Further evaluation of the impacts of live food and non-food trades on wild populations must consider their relative pressures on species and their ecosystems when compared with subsistence and industrial fishing pressures, non-selective fishing gear, habitat degradation, eutrophication, invasive species, and climate change. In that context, the aquarium trade removes many fewer fish than the extensive food fisheries (Wood, 2001b) and certainly removes less coral than used for production of lime rock in Indonesia (Cesar, 1996). Moreover, all bioprospecting expeditions over the past 30 years in Australia cumulatively removed fewer soft-bodied benthic organisms than just one trawling experiment in a Great Barrier Reef inter-reefal lagoon (Hunt and Vincent, in press). Arguably, too, loss of coral reef habitat may be a more important threat than any of these five trades.

Calculations of total fisheries' extraction – and overexploitation – from coral reefs would presumably be affected by the inclusion of data for live food and non-food fisheries. Current consumption of reef resources in many countries already exceeds estimated sustainable per capita production levels, on local, regional and global scales (Warren-Rhodes *et al.*, 2003; McClanahan, this volume). Indeed, seafood demand of all countries in the Indo-Pacific may require 2.5 times the region's available coral reef area, imposing a large marine ecological footprint (Warren-Rhodes *et al.*, 2003). To date, however, only extraction for food (including the live reef fish trade for luxury consumption) has been included in such calculations. Given the apparent excessive removal of at least some non-food products, the imbalance between supply and demand of reef resources might be greater than hitherto realized.

CONCLUSIONS

Live food and non-food fisheries add to pressures on already damaged and depleted marine systems. A great many species are traded in large volumes, but usually with unknown conservation consequences. Extraction is both targeted – with rarity sometimes increasing value – and executed with indiscriminate gear. In contrast to most food fisheries on reefs, products from live food and non-food fisheries are traded globally, subject to international pressures and regulations. In common with food fisheries on reefs, however, live food and non-food trades considered in this chapter are taxonomically diverse, dependent on wild populations, mainly unrecorded, growing rapidly, and potentially problematic, at least on a local scale. They also depend on some of the same species. The luxury nature of the live food, aquarium display and curio trades should allow for flexible management, keeping fishers' needs in mind. The potential for some species to be used for both food and non-food purposes, however, complicates assessment and management. Record-keeping for the two live trades is rapidly improving, for all its deficiencies. The three dead trades continue largely undocumented, because of complexity and limited value for most fisheries in the case of the curio and TM trades, and because of commercial confidentiality in the case of bioprospecting. Yet, these fisheries and trades have consequences for reef ecosystems, and the dependent people who largely determine the future of these ecosystems. Questions and concerns about such extraction – real, inferred and anticipated – highlight the need for creative data-poor management, including no-take reserves and areas restricted by access, gear, time or species. The full conservation potential of improved mariculture practices, synthesis, substitution and consumer practices must also be explored. While the overall pressures of live food and non-food fisheries on reef systems may be lower than many other human activities, their impacts on particular species and places may be profound and should be considered in plans for coral reef assessment, management and conservation.

ACKNOWLEDGEMENTS

This is a contribution from Project Seahorse. I am particularly grateful to Bob Hunt for his wonderful support on this work. I also thank Natalie Kim and James Hrynyshyn for their kind input. Isabelle Côté, John Reynolds, Yvonne Sadovy and Elizabeth Wood provided most helpful comments on the manuscript. This work was generously supported by a Pew Marine Fellowship from the Pew Charitable Trusts (USA), by Guylian Chocolates Belgium, and by the John G. Shedd Aquarium (Chicago, USA), through its partnership for marine conservation with Project Seahorse.

REFERENCES

Abbott, R. T. (1980). *The Shell and Coral Trade in Florida*, Special Report No. 3. Washington, DC: TRAFFIC USA.

Andrews, C. (1990). The ornamental fish trade and fish conservation. *Journal of Fish Biology*, **37**(Suppl. A), 53–9.

Andrews, P. R., Borris, R., Dagne, E. *et al.* (1996). Preservation and utilization of natural biodiversity in the context of search for economically valuable medicinal biota. Recommendations. *Pure and Applied Chemistry*, **68**, 2325–32.

Baillie, J. and Groombridge, B. (eds.) (1996). *1996 IUCN Red List of Threatened Animals*. Gland, Switzerland: IUCN.

Barrett, C. B. and Lybbert, T. J. (2000). Is bioprospecting a viable strategy for conserving tropical ecosystems? *Ecological Economics*, **34**, 293–300.

Baum, J. K. and Vincent, A. C. J. (2006). Magnitude and inferred impacts of the seahorse trade in Latin America. *Environmental Conservation* (in press).

Benkendorff, K. (2002). Potential conservation benefits and problems associated with bioprospecting in the marine environment. In *A Zoological Revolution: Using Native Fauna to Assist in Its Own Survival*, eds. D. Lumley and C. Dickman, pp. 90–100. Sydney: Royal Zoological Socitey of New South Wales and Australian Museum.

Bentley, N. (1998). An overview of the exploitation, trade and management of corals in Indonesia. *TRAFFIC Bulletin*, **17**, 67–78.

(ed.) (1999). *Fishing for Solutions: Can the Live Trade in Wild Groupers and Wrasses from Southeast Asia Be Managed?* Petaling Jaya, Selangor: TRAFFIC Southeast Asia.

Bentley, N. and Aumeeruddy, R. (1999). The live reef fishery in the Seychelles. *SPC Live Reef Fish Information Bulletin*, **6**, 5–7.

Bertram, I. (1996). The aquarium fishery in the Cook Islands: is there a need for management? *SPC Live Reef Fish Information Bulletin*, **1**, 10–12.

Bohnsack, J. A., Kumpf, H., Hobson, E. *et al.* (1989). Report on the concept of marine wilderness. *Fisheries*, **14**, 22–4.

Bongiorni, L. and Pietra, F. (1996). Marine natural products for industrial applications. *Chemistry & Industry*, **2**, 54–8.

Bruckner, A. W. (2001). Tracking the trade in ornamental coral reef organisms: the importance of CITES and its limitations. *Aquarium Sciences and Conservation*, **3**, 79–94.

Burgoyne, D. L. and Andersen, R. J. (1992). Contignasterol, a highly oxygenated steroid with the 'unnatural' 14β configuration from the marine sponge *Petrusia contignata* Thiele, 1899. *Journal of Organic Chemistry*, **57**, 525–8.

Cesar, H. (1996). *Economic Analysis of Indonesian Coral Reefs*. Washington, DC: Environment Department, World Bank.

Chaffee, C., Leadbitter, D. and Alders, E. (2003). Seafood evaluation, certification and consumer information. In *Eco-Labelling in Fisheries: What Is It All About?*, eds. B. Phillips, T. Ward and C. Chaffee, pp. 4–13. Oxford: Blackwell Science.

Chan, P. S. W. (2000). The industry perspective: wholesale and retail marketing aspects of the Hong Kong live reef food fish trade. *SPC Live Reef Fish Information Bulletin*, **7**, 3–7.

(2001) Wholesale and retail marketing aspects of Hong Kong's live seafood business. In *Marketing and Shipping Live Aquatic Products, Proceedings of the 2nd International Conference and Exhibition*, November 1999, eds. B. C. Paust and A. A. Rice, pp. 201–6. Seattle, WA: University of Alaska Sea Grant.

Chan, T. T. C. and Sadovy, Y. (1998). Profile of the marine aquarium fish trade in Hong Kong. *Aquarium Sciences and Conservation*, **2**, 197–213.

Chevallier, C., Richardson, A. D., Edler, M. C. *et al.* (2003). A new cytotoxic and tubulin-interactive milnamide derivative from a marine sponge *Cymbastela* sp. *Organic Letters*, **5**, 3737–9.

Chivian, E., Roberts, C. M. and Bernstein, A. S. (2003). The threat to cone snails. *Science*, **302**, 391.

Christie, P., White, A. and Deguit, E. (2002). Starting point or solution? Community-based marine protected areas in the Philippines. *Journal of Environmental Management*, **66**, 441–54.

CITES (2005). Appendix I and Appendix II. Available online at http://www.cites.org/eng/app/appendices.shtml

Cordell, G. A. (2000). Biodiversity and drug discovery – a symbiotic relationship. *Phytochemistry*, **55**, 463–80.
Costa-Neto, E. M. (1999). Healing with animals in Feira de Santana City, Bahia, Brazil. *Journal of Ethnopharmacology*, **65**, 225–30.
Cragg, G. M. (1998). Paclitaxel (Taxol®): a success story with valuable lessons for natural product drug discovery and development. *Medicinal Research Reviews*, **18**, 315–31.
Daw, T. M., Rogers, G. C. C., Mapson, P. and Kynoch, J. E. (2001). Structure and management issues of the emerging ornamental fish trade in Eritrea. *Aquarium Sciences and Conservation*, **3**, 53–64.
Donaldson, T. J. and Sadovy, Y. (2001). Threatened fishes of the world: *Cheilinus undulatus* Ruppell, 1835 (Labridae). *Environmental Biology of Fishes*, **62**, 428.
Dufour, V. (1997). Pacific Island countries and the aquarium fish market. *SPC Live Reef Fish Information Bulletin*, **2**, 6–11.
Dulvy, N., Sadovy, Y. and Reynolds, J. D. (2003). Extinction vulnerability in marine populations. *Fish and Fisheries*, **4**, 25–64.
Dulvy, N. K., Stanwell-Smith, D., Darwall, W. R. T. and Horrill, C. J. (1995). Coral mining at Mafia Island, Tanzania: a management dilemma. *Ambio*, **24**, 358–65.
Ellis, S. (1999). *Farming Soft Corals for the Marine Aquarium Trade*, Report No. 140. Waimanalo, HI: Center for Tropical and Subtropical Aquaculture.
Erdmann, M. V. and Pet-Soede, L. (1996). How fresh is too fresh? The live reef food fish trade in Eastern Indonesia. *NAGA, International Center for Living Aquatic Resource Management Quarterly*, **19**, 4–8.
Farrier, D. and Tucker, L. (2001). Access to marine bioresources: hitching the conservation cart to the bioprospecting horse. *Ocean Development & International Law*, **32**, 213–39.
Food and Agriculture Organization (1996). *Fisheries Statistics and Catch Landings*, vol. 78. Rome: Fisheries Department, FAO.
Foster, S. J. and Vincent, A. C. J. (2004). Life history and ecology of seahorses: implications for conservation and management. *Journal of Fish Biology*, **65**, 1–61.
(2005). Enhancing sustainability of the international trade in seahorses with a single minimum size limit. *Conservation Biology*, **19**, 1044–50.
Fouda, M. M. (1995). *Regional Report, Middle East Seas: Issues and Activities Associated with Coral Reefs and Related Ecosystems*. Dumuguete City, Philippines: *International Coral Reef Initiative Workshop*.
Ganesan, A. (2001). Integrating natural product synthesis and combinatorial chemistry. *Pure and Applied Chemistry*, **73**, 1033–9.
Garson, M. (1997). Biodiversity and bioprospecting. *Australasian Journal of Natural Resources Law and Policy*, **4**, 227–239.
Giles, B. G., Ky, T. S., Hoang, D. H. and Vincent, A. C. J. (2005). The catch and trade of seahorses in Vietnam. *Biodiversity and Conservation*. DOI: 10.1007/s10531-005-2432-6.
GMAD (2005). Global Marine Aquarium Database, Available online at http://www.unep-wcmc.org/marine/GMAD
Green, E. (2003). International trade in marine aquarium species: using the Global Marine Aquarium Database. In *Marine Ornamental Species: Collection, Culture &*

Conservation, eds. C. J. Cato and L. B. Brown, pp. 31–48. Ames, IA: Iowa State University Press.

Green, E. and Shirley, F. (1999). *The Global Trade in Coral*. Cambridge: UNEP–World Conservation Monitoring Centre.

Green, E. P. and Hendry, H. (1999). Is CITES an effective tool for monitoring trade in corals? *Coral Reefs*, **18**, 403–407.

Green, J. J. (2003). Report on the workshop in bioprospecting in the High Seas: Interim summary. In *Proceedings of the Deep Sea 2003 Conference*, 1–5 December 2003, pp. 29–36. Queenstown, New Zealand: Conference Steering Committee.

Grey, M., Blais, A.-M. and Vincent, A. C. J. (2005). The curio trade of marine fish in the United States. *Oryx*, **39**, 413–20.

Halpern, B. S. (2003). The impact of marine reserves: do reserves work and does reserve size matter? *Ecological Applications*, **13**, 117–37.

Harper, M. K., Bugni, T. S., Cropp, B. R. *et al.* (2001). Introduction to the chemical ecology of marine natural products. In *Marine Chemical Ecology*, eds. J. B. McClintock and B. J. Baker, pp. 3–29. Boca Raton, FL: CRC Press.

Harriot, V. J. (1999). Coral recruitment at a high latitude Pacific site: a comparison with Atlantic reefs. *Bulletin of Marine Science*, **65**, 881–91.

(2003). Can corals be harvested sustainably? *Ambio*, **32**, 130–3.

Hawkins, J., Roberts, C. M. and Clark, V. (2000). The threatened status of restricted range coral reef species. *Animal Conservation*, **3**, 81–8.

Hooper, J. N. A., Quinn, R. J. and Murphy, P. T. (1998) Bioprospecting for marine invertebrates. In *Biodiversity, Biotechnology & Biobusiness, Proceedings of the 2nd Asia–Pacific Conference on Biotechnology*, eds. M. Van Keulen and M. A. Borowizka, pp. 109–12. Perth, WA: Murdoch University.

Hughes, T. P., Reed, D. C. and Boyle, M.-J. (1987). Herbivory on coral reefs: community structure following mass mortalities of sea urchins. *Journal of Experimental Marine Biology and Ecology*, **113**, 39–59.

Hunt, B. and Vincent, A. C. J. (in press). Management and sustainability of marine bioprospecting for pharmaceuticals. *Ambio.*

Indrawan, M. (1999). Live reef food fish trade in the Banggai Islands (Suluwesi Indonesia): a case study. *SPC Live Reef Fish Information Bulletin*, **6**, 7–14.

IUCN (1998). *Guidelines for Reintroductions*. Gland, Switzerland: IUCN.

(2004). *Red List of Threatened Species*. Available online at http://www.redlist.org.

Jennings, S., Reynolds, J. D. and Polunin, N. V. C. (1999). Predicting the vulnerability of tropical fishes to exploitation with phylogenies and life histories. *Conservation Biology*, **13**, 466–75.

Jha, R. K. and Xu, Z.-R. (2004). Biomedical compounds from marine organisms. *Marine Drugs*, **2**, 123–46.

Johannes, R. E. (1981). *Words of the Lagoon: Fishing and Marine Lore in the Palau District of Micronesia*. Berkeley, CA: University of California Press.

(1998). The case for data-less marine resource management: examples from tropical nearshore finfisheries. *Trends in Ecology and Evolution*, **13**, 243–6.

Johannes, R. E. and Lam, M. (1999). The live reef food fish trade in the Solomon Islands. *SPC Live Reef Fish Information Bulletin*, **5**, 8–15.

Johannes, R. E. and Riepen, M. (1995). *Environmental, Economic, and Social Implications of the Live Reef Fish Trade in Asia and the Western Pacific*. New York: The Nature Conservancy and Forum Fisheries Agency.

Kuhlmann, J. (1997). Drug research: from the idea to the product. *International Journal of Clinical Pharmacology & Therapeutics*, **35**, 541–52.
Lau, P. P. F. and Parry-Jones, R. (1999). *The Hong Kong Trade in Live Reef Fish for Food*. Hong Kong: TRAFFIC East Asia and World Wide Fund for Nature.
Lev, E. (2003). Traditional healing with animals (zootherapy): medieval to present-day Levantine practice. *Journal of Ethnopharmacology*, **85**, 107–18.
Lev, E. and Amar, Z. (2002). Ethnopharmacological survey of traditional drugs sold in the Kingdom of Jordan. *Journal of Ethnopharmacology*, **82**, 131–45.
Lipton, D. A. (2000). Fishery for marine medicinal species in India: problems and responses. In *Proceedings of the 1st International Workshop on the Management and Culture of Marine Species Used in Traditional Medicines*, 4–9 July 1998, Cebu City, Philippines, eds. M. A. Moreau, H. J. Hall and A. C. J. Vincent, pp. 75–7. Montreal: Project Seahorse.
Lovell, E. R. (2001a). *Status Report: Collection of Coral and Other Benthic Reef Organisms for the Marine Aquarium and Curio Trade in Fiji*. Suva, Fiji: World Wide Fund for Nature.
(2001b). Country report: status of the trade in stony corals, Republic of Fiji. In *Proceedings of the International Workshop on the Trade in Stony Corals: Development of Sustainable Management Guidelines*, ed. A. W. Bruckner, pp. 75–82. Jarkarta, Indonesia: National Oceanic and Atmospheric Administration.
Lunn, K. and Moreau, M.-A. (2004). Unmonitored trade in marine ornamental fishes: the case of Indonesia's Banggai cardinalfish (*Pterapogon kauderni*). *Coral Reefs*, **23**, 344–51.
Magsuci, H., Conlu, A. and Moyano-Aypa, S. (1980). The window pane oyster (*Kapis*) fishery of Western Visayas. *Fisheries Research Journal of the Philippines*, **5**, 74–80.
Marshall, N. (1998). *Searching for a Cure: Conservation of Medicinal Wildlife Resources in East and Southern Africa*. Cambridge: TRAFFIC International.
Martin-Smith, K. M. and Vincent, A. C. J. (2006). Exploitation and trade of Australian seahorses and their relatives (syngnathids). *Oryx* (in press).
Martin-Smith, K. M., Samoilys, M. A., Meeuwig, J. J. and Vincent, A. C. J. (2004). Collaborative development of management options for an artisanal fishery for seahorses in the central Philippines. *Ocean & Coastal Management*, **47**, 165–93.
May, B. (1997). The risks associated with TCM: a review and discussion of the literature. *Pacific Journal of Oriental Medicine*, **10**, 30–44.
May, B., Leadbitter, D., Sutton, M. and Weber, M. (2003). The Marine Stewardship Council (MSC) background, rationale and challenges. In *Eco-Labelling in Fisheries: What Is It All About?*, eds. B. Phillips, T. Ward and C. Chaffee, pp. 14–33. Oxford: Blackwell Science.
McClanahan, T. R. and Shafir, S. H. (1990). Causes and consequences of sea urchin abundance and diversity in Kenyan coral reef lagoons. *Oecologia*, **83**, 362–70.
McPherson, J. M. and Vincent, A. C. J. (2004). Assessing East African trade in seahorse species as a basis for conservation under international controls. *Aquatic Conservation: Marine and Freshwater Ecosystems*, **14**, 521–38.
Mendola, D. (2003). Aquaculture of three phyla of marine invertebrates to yield bioactive metabolites: process developments and economics. *Biomolecular Engineering*, **20**, 441–58.

Ministry of Economic Development (2002). *Bioprospecting in New Zealand: Discussing the Options*. Wellington: Resources and Networks Branch, New Zealand Ministry of Economic Development.

Moberg, F. and Folke, C. (1999). Ecological goods and services of coral reef ecosystems. *Ecological Economics*, **29**, 215–33.

Moe, M. A. (1999) Marine ornamental aquaculture: past, present and future. *1st International Conference of Marine Ornamentals, Abstracts*, 63.

(2003). Culture of marine ornamentals: for love, for money and for science. In *Marine Ornamental Species: Collection, Culture, & Conservation*, eds. C. J. Cato and C. L. Brown, pp. 11–28. Ames, IA: Iowa State University Press.

Mulliken, T. A. and Nash, S. V. (1993). The recent trade in Philippine corals. *TRAFFIC Bulletin*, **13**, 97–105.

Munro, J. L. (1993). Giant clams. In *Nearshore Marine Resources of the South Pacific*, eds. A. Wright and L. Hill, pp. 431–49. Honiara, Solomon Islands: Forum Fisheries Agency.

Munro, M. H. G., Blunt, J. W., Dumdei, E. J. *et al.* (1999). The discovery and development of marine compounds with pharmaceutical potential. *Journal of Biotechnology*, **70**, 15–25.

National Cancer Institute (2000). *Questions and Answers about NCI's Natural Products Branch*. Available online at http://cis.nci.nih.gov/fact/7_33.htm

(2005). *Natural Products Branch: Natural Products Repository*. Available online at http://dtp.nci.nih.gov/branches/npb/repository.html

Naylor, R. L., Williams, S. L. and Strong, D. R. (2001). Aquaculture: a gateway for exotic species. *Science*, **294**, 1655–6.

Newman, D. J., Cragg, G. M. and Snader, K. M. (2003). Natural products as sources of new drugs over the period 1981–2002. *Journal of Natural Products*, **66**, 1022–37.

Olivera, B. M. (2000). ω?-Conotoxin MVIIA: from marine snail venom to analgesic drug. In *Drugs from the Sea*, ed. N. Fusetani, pp. 74–85. Basel, Switzerland: Karger.

Olivier, K. (2003). World trade in ornamental species. In *Marine Ornamental Species: Collection, Culture, & Conservation*, eds. C. J. Cato and C. L. Brown, pp. 49–64. Ames, IA: Iowa State University Press.

OmniTrak. (1997). *Summary of the Taste Test between the Mariculture and Wild-Caught Malabar Grouper*. Honolulu, HI: The Nature Conservancy.

Pajaro, M. (1993). Alternatives to sodium cyanide use in aquarium fish collection: a community based approach. *Sea Wind*, **6**, 3–17.

Pajaro, M. G., Meeuwig, J. J., Giles, B. G. and Vincent, A. C. J. (2004). Biology, fishery and trade of sea moths (Pisces: Pegasidae) in the central Philippines. *Oryx*, **38**, 432–8.

Parma, A. M., Orensanz, J. M., Elías, I. and Jerez, G. (2003). Diving for shellfish and data: incentives for the participation of fishers in the monitoring and management of artisanal fisheries around southern South America. In *Towards Sustainability of Data-Limited Multi-Sector Fisheries, Australian Society for Fish Biology Workshop Proceedings*, eds. S. J. Newman, D. J. Gaughan, G. Jackson *et al.* pp. 8–29. Bunbury, WA: Department of Fisheries.

Paulay, G. (1997). Diversity and distribution of reef organisms. In *Life and Death of Coral Reefs*, ed. C. Birkeland, pp. 298–353. New York: Chapman and Hall.

Perry, A. (2000). Global survey of marine medicinals. In *Proceedings of the 1st International Workshop on the Management and Culture of Marine Species Used in Traditional Medicines*, 4–9 July 1998, Cebu City, Philippines, eds. M. A. Moreau, H. J. Hall and A. C. J. Vincent, pp. 35–43. Montreal: Project Seahorse.

Petelo, A. (2001). The Kingdom of Tonga: status of trade in stony corals. In *Proceedings of the International Workshop on the Trade in Stony Corals: Development of Sustainable Management Guidelines*, ed. A. W. Bruckner, pp. 87–96. Jarkarta, Indonesia: National Oceanic and Atmospheric Administration.

Pettit, G. R., Chicacz, Z. A., Gao, F. *et al.* (1993). Antineoplastic agents. 257. Isolation and structure of spongistatin. *Journal of Organic Chemistry*, **58**, 1302–4.

Pettit, G. R., Gao, F., Cerny, R. L. *et al.* (1994). Antineoplastic agents. 278. Isolation and structure of axinastatins 2 and 3 from a Western Caroline Island marine sponge. *Journal of Medicinal Chemistry*, **37**, 1165–8.

Pettit, G. R., Knight, J. C., Collins, J. C. *et al.* (2000). Antineoplastic agents. 430. Isolation and structure of cribrostatins 3, 4, and 5 from the Republic of Maldives *Cribrochalina* species. *Journal of Natural Products*, **63**, 793–8.

Pinheiro, C. U. (1997). Jaborandi (*Pilocarpus* sp., Rutaceae): a wild species and its rapid transformation into a crop. *Economic Botany*, **51**, 49–58.

Pointier, J. P. and Lamy, D. (1985). Rearing of *Pterynotus phyllopterus*, Mollusca, Muricidae, from Guadeloupe (French West Indies). *Proceedings 5th International Coral Reef Congress*, **5**, 171–6.

Ponder, W. F. and Grayson, J. E. (1998). *The Australian Marine Molluscs Considered to be Potentially Vulnerable to the Shell Trade*. Sydney, NSW: Department of Environment and Heritage.

Preparatory Committee on Chinese Medicine (1997). *Consultation on the Development of Traditional Chinese Medicine*. Hong Kong: PCCM.

Proksch, P., Edrada, R. A. and Ebel, R. (2002). Drugs from the sea: current status and microbiological implications. *Applied Microbiology and Biotechnology*, **59**, 125–34.

Queensland Fisheries Management Authority (1999). Prepared by the Aquarium Fish and Coral Fisheries Working Group. *Queensland Marine Fish and Coral Collecting Fisheries*, Discussion Paper No. 10, Brisbane: Queensland Fisheries Management Authority and Harvest MAC.

Quinn, R. J., de Almeida Leone, P., Guymer, G. and Hooper, J. N. A. (2002). Australian biodiversity via its plants and marine organisms: a high throughput screening approach to drug discovery. *Pure and Applied Chemistry*, **74**, 519–26.

Ramohia, P. (2001) A brief country report: status of trade in stony coral in the Soloman Islands. In *Proceedings of the International Workshop on the Trade in Stony Corals: Development of Sustainable Management Guidelines*, ed. A. W. Bruckner, pp. 83–6. Jarkarta, Indonesia: National Oceanic and Atmospheric Administration.

Roberts, L. (1992). Chemical prospecting: hope for vanishing ecosystems? *Science*, **256**, 1142–3.

Ross, M. A. (1984). A quantitative study of the stony coral fishery in Cebu, Philippines. *Pubblicazioni della Stazione Zoologica di Napoli I: Marine Ecology*, **5**, 75–91.

Rouhi, A. M. (2003a). Rediscovering natural products. *Chemical and Engineering News*, October 13, 77–91.

(2003b). Betting on natural products for cures. *Chemical and Engineering News*, October 13, 93–103.

Rubec, P. J. (1988). Cyanide fishing and the International Marinelife Alliance Net-Training Program. *Tropical Coastal Area Management*, **23**, 11–13.

Sadovy, Y. (2000). *Regional Survey of Fry/Fingerling Supply and Current Practices for Grouper Mariculture: Evaluating Current Status and Long-Term Prospects for Grouper Mariculture in Southeast Asia.* Hong Kong: University of Hong Kong.

(2001a). The live reef fish trade in Hong Kong: problems and prospects. In *Marketing and Shipping Live Aquatic Products, Proceedings of the 2nd International Conference and Exhibition*, November 1999, eds. B. C. Paust and A. A. Rice, pp. 183–92. Seattle, WA: University of Alaska Sea Grant.

(2001b). The threat of fishing to highly fecund fishes. *Journal of Fish Biology*, **59**(Suppl. A), 90–108.

Sadovy, Y. and Cheung, W. L. (2003). Near extinction of a highly fecund fish: the one that nearly got away. *Fish and Fisheries*, **4**, 86–99.

Sadovy, Y. and Eklund, A.-M. (1999). *Synopsis of Biological Data on the Nassau Grouper,* Epinephelus striatus *(Bloch, 1792), and the Jewfish,* E. itajara, Technical Report NMFS-146. Seattle, WA: National Oceanic and Atmospheric Administration.

Sadovy, Y. and Vincent, A. C. J. (2002). Ecological issues and the trades in live reef fishes. In *Coral Reef Fishes: Dynamics and Diversity in Complex Reef Ecosystems*, ed. P. Sale, pp. 391–420. San Diego, CA: Academic Press.

Sadovy, Y., Donaldson, T. J., Graham, T. R. *et al.* (2003a). *While Stocks Last: The Live Reef Fish Food Trade.* Manila: Asian Development Bank.

Sadovy, Y., Kulbicki, M., Labrosse, P. *et al.* (2003b). The humphead wrasse, *Cheilinus undulatus*: synopsis of a threatened and poorly known giant coral reef fish. *Reviews in Fish Biology and Fisheries*, **13**, 327–64.

Salamanca, A. M. and Pajaro, M. G. (1996). The utilization of seashells in the Philippines. *TRAFFIC Bulletin*, **16**, 61–72.

Schaufelberger, D. E., Koleck, M. P., Beutler, J. A. *et al.* (1991). The large-scale isolation of bryostatin 1 from *Bugula neritina* following good manufacturing practices. *Journal of Natural Products*, **54**, 1265–70.

Semmens, B. X., Buhle, E. R., Salomon, A. K. and Pattengill-Semmens, C. V. (2004). A hotspot of non-native marine fishes: evidence for the aquarium trade as an invasion pathway. *Marine Ecology Progress Series*, **266**, 239–44.

Shakeel, H. and Ahmed, H. (1997). Exploitation of reef resources, grouper and other food fishes in the Maldives. *SPC Live Reef Fish Information Bulletin*, **2**, 14–20.

Siar, S. V., Johnston, W. L. and Sim, S. Y. (2002). *Study on Economics and Socio-Economics of Small-Scale Marine Fish Hatcheries and Nurseries, with Special Reference to Grouper Systems in Bali, Indonesia*, Report prepared under APEC Project FWG 01/2001 – Collaborative APEC Grouper Research and Development Network Publication 2/2002. Bangkok: Network of Aquaculture Centers in the Asia–Pacific.

Sloan, N. A. (1984). Echinoderm fisheries of the world: a review. In *Proceedings of the 5th International Echinoderm Conference*, eds. B. F. Keegan and B. D. S. O'Connor, pp. 109–24. Galway, Ireland: A. A. Balkema.
Smith, W. (1999). *Education and Awareness of Marine Environments Project (EAMEP): Concerns and Solutions for the Protection of the Coral Reef in Fiji*. Lautoka, Fiji: Walt Smith.
Stoner, A. W. and Ray-Culp, M. (2000). Evidence for allee effects in an over-harvested marine gastropod: density-dependent mating and egg production. *Marine Ecology Progress Series*, **202**, 297–302.
Tang, W.-C. (1987). Chinese medicinal materials from the sea. *Abstracts of Chinese Medicine*, **1**, 571–600.
Tissot, B. N. and Hallacher, L. E. (2003). Effects of aquarium collectors on coral reef fishes in Kona, Hawaii. *Conservation Biology*, **17**, 1759–68.
US Coral Reef Task Force (2000). *International Trade in Coral and Coral Reef Species: The Role of the United States*, Report to the Trade Subgroup of the International Working Group to the US Coral Reef Task Force, Washington, DC: National Oceanic and Atmospheric Administration Fisheries.
Vallejo, B. (1997). Survey and review of the Philippine marine aquarium fishery industry. *Sea Wind*, **11**, 2–16.
Vincent, A. C. J. (1996). *The International Trade in Seahorses*. Cambridge: TRAFFIC International.
(1997). Trade in pegasid fishes (sea moths), primarily for traditional Chinese medicine. *Oryx*, **31**, 199–208.
Vincent, A. and Sadovy, Y. (1998). Reproductive ecology in the conservation and management of fishes. In *Behavioral Ecology and Conservation Biology*, ed. T. Caro, pp. 209–45. New York: Oxford University Press.
Vincent, A. C. J., Marsden, A. D. and Sumaila, U. R. (in press). The role of globalization in creating and addressing seahorse conservation problems. In *Globalization: Effects on Fisheries Resources*, eds. W. W. Taylor, M. G. Schetcher and L. G. Wolfson. Cambridge: Cambridge University Press.
Wabnitz, C., Taylor, M., Green, E. and Razak, T. (2003). *From Ocean to Aquarium*. Cambridge: UNEP–World Conservation Monitoring Centre.
Wantiez, L., Thollot, P. and Kulbicki, M. (1997). Effects of marine reserves on coral reef fish communities from five islands in New Caledonia. *Coral Reefs*, **16**, 215–24.
Warren-Rhodes, K., Sadovy, Y. and Cesar, H. (2003). Marine ecosystem appropriation in the Indo-Pacific: case study of the live reef food fish trade. *Ambio*, **32**, 481–8.
Wells, S. M. (1982). *Marine Conservation in the Philippines and Papua New Guinea with Special Emphasis on the Ornamental Coral and Shell Trade*, unpublished report. London: Winston Churchill Memorial Trust.
(1988). Impacts of the precious shell harvest and trade: conservation of rare or fragile resources. In *Marine Invertebrate Fisheries: Their Assessment and Management*, ed. J. F. Caddy, pp. 443–54. Rome: FAO.
Wells, S. M. and Wood, E. (1991). *The Marine Curio Trade: Conservation Guidelines and Legislation*. Ross-on-Wye, UK: Marine Conservation Society.

White, A. T., Courtney, C. A. and Salamanca, A. (2002). Experience with marine protected area planning and management in the Philippines. *Coastal Management*, **30**, 1–26.

Wijesekara, R. G. S. and Yakupitiyage, A. (2001). Ornamental fish industry in Sri Lanka: present status and future trends. *Aquarium Sciences and Conservation*, **3**, 241–52.

Williams, D. E., Lassota, P. and Andersen, R. J. (1998). Motuporamines A-C, cytotoxic alkaloids isolated from the marine sponge *Xestospongia exigua* (Kirkpatrick). *Journal of Organic Chemistry*, **63**, 4838–41.

Williamson, D. H., Russ, G. R. and Ayling, A. M. (2004). No-take marine reserves increase abundance and biomass of reef fish on inshore fringing reefs of the Great Barrier Reef. *Environmental Conservation*, **31**, 149–59.

Wood, E. (2001a). *Collection of Coral Reef Fish for Aquaria: Global Trade, Conservation Issues and Management Strategies*. Ross-on-Wye, UK: Marine Conservation Society.

Wood, E. (2001b). Global advances in conservation and management of marine ornamental resources. *Aquarium Sciences and Conservation*, **3**, 65–77.

Wood, E. M. and Wells, S. M. (1988). *The Marine Curio Trade: Conservation Issues*. Ross-on-Wye, UK: Marine Conservation Society.

(1995). *The Shell Trade: A Case for Sustainable Utilization*. Cambridge: IUCN.

World Health Organization (2002). *WHO Traditional Medicine Strategy 2002–2005*. Geneva: WHO.

Zeng, M. (1995). *Zhong-guo Zhong-yao Qu-hua* (Translated as: *Chinese Medicinal Districts in China)*. Beijing: Ke-xue Chu-ban-she.

Zilinskas, R. A. and Lundin, C. G. (1993). *Marine Biotechnology and Developing Countries*. Washington, DC: International Bank for Reconstruction and Development.

7

Tourism and coral-reef-based conservation: can they coexist?

GUY JOBBINS
SEAM Programme, Cairo, Egypt

INTRODUCTION

Tourism is the world's largest industry, with 694 million international tourist arrivals generating revenues of US$514 billion in 2003 (World Tourism Organization, 2004). Estimates of global coastal tourism range between 40% and 70% of the total tourism market, and beach leisure tourism constitutes a major part of the industry. Due to increased disposable incomes, increased leisure time, and falling prices, the industry is still growing rapidly and is expected to reach 1.6 billion arrivals by 2020 (World Tourism Organization, 2001).

Coral reefs contribute to tourism to a tune of US$9.6 billion yr^{-1} globally (Cesar, 2003). National values have been calculated as US$23.2 million yr^{-1} for Bonaire, US$2 million yr^{-1} in Saba, US$23.5 million yr^{-1} in West Lombok and US$682 million yr^{-1} for the Great Barrier Reef (Dixon *et al.*, 1993; Fernandes, 1995; Riopelle, 1995, cited in Cesar, 1996; Driml, 1994). Cesar (2003b) gave a value of US$112 million for Egypt in 2000, including US$23 million in consumer surplus. Reefs not only support niche sub-markets in scuba diving and snorkelling excursions, they also add value to the tourism product through associated images of exoticism and natural beauty.

It is no surprise that in many developing nations with reef resources, tourism is an attractive industry to develop. With long-haul travel becoming cheaper and more available, previously remote areas are becoming part

Coral Reef Conservation, ed. Isabelle M. Côté and John D. Reynolds.

Table 7.1. Predicted average annual growth rates in some destinations, 1995–2020

Region / nation	Average annual growth (%)
Egypt	7.4
Indian Ocean	6.3
Comoros	6.6
Indonesia	7.7
Maldives	6.2
Mauritius	5.3
Philippines	7.7
Reunion	7.1
Thailand	6.9
Caribbean	4.3
Cuba	9.2
Dominican Republic	5.0
Jamaica	3.1
Melanesia / Micronesia / Polynesia	6.5

Source: World Tourism Organization (2001).

of the tourism mainstream. As part of this development, coastal destinations that previously catered to niche markets in independent and adventure travel are becoming oriented to all-inclusive beach resort holidays. Average rates of growth in tourism arrivals for the years 1995–2020 are predicted to be above 6% for many areas supporting coral reefs (World Tourism Organization, 2001) (Table 7.1).

Tourism development poses distinct but potentially manageable threats to coral reefs. In addition to the physical impacts from recreational use by snorkellers and divers, serious problems can be caused by rapid coastal construction and increased environmental loads from what is effectively an increase in the coastal population. Butler's (1980) model of tourism destination life cycles describes a process whereby increasing development and numbers of tourists lead to degradation of the tourism product, a loss of tourism quality and stagnation in the local industry. In a worst-case scenario this could lead to cost-cutting and undervaluation of reef resources, and further environmental degradation.

In reef areas the challenge is not just to manage tourism development to minimize tourism impacts on coral reefs, but also to manage tourism so that the industry itself is sustainable, placing a high value on reef resources. This chapter evaluates these issues using the South Sinai, Egypt, as a case study, and attempts to draw conclusions of relevance for other rapidly growing coastal destinations with significant reef resources.

TOURISM IMPACTS ON REEFS

Impacts from recreational users

Considerable evidence documents the impacts of recreational snorkellers and scuba divers on coral reefs. A variety of studies have shown that physical impacts by fins, loose equipment and gauges, poor buoyancy control (causing resuspension of sediment), as well as trampling on the reef flat, can break corals and reduce hard coral cover (e.g. Woodland and Hooper, 1977; Kay and Liddle, 1989; Neil, 1990; Hawkins and Roberts, 1992, 1993; Talge, 1992; Davis and Tisdell, 1995; Harriot *et al.*, 1997; Muthiga and McClanahan, 1997; Rouphael and Inglis, 1997, 2001; Hawkins *et al.*, 1999; Reboton and Calumpong, 2000; Barker and Roberts, 2004). There is also some evidence that heavy trampling can cause lower fish abundances (Rodgers and Cox, 2003).

Attempts to identify the recreational carrying capacity of reefs have returned values with a substantial range. For example, a study from Sharm el Sheikh, Egypt, suggested that sites might be able to sustain 10 000–15 000 dives yr^{-1} without serious degradation, whilst studies from Bonaire concluded that exceeding 4000–6000 dives yr^{-1} might result in sustained damage (Hawkins and Roberts, 1992; Dixon *et al.*, 1993; Hawkins *et al.*, 1999).

Certain characteristics of divers and dive sites have been associated with increased reef damage. Inexperienced divers, male divers, camera-users, and the initial ten minutes of a dive have all been linked with higher than average rates of contact with the reef (Roberts and Harriott, 1994; Rouphael and Inglis, 2001). Distance from mooring buoys or entry points and the growth forms of coral present also appear to influence the amount of damage sustained (Rouphael and Inglis, 1997; Tratalos and Austin, 2001). Several studies have indicated that a minority of divers are generally responsible for the majority of damage (e.g. Harriott *et al.*, 1997; Talge, 1992).

Medio *et al.* (1997) demonstrated that a detailed 45-minute briefing by researchers prior to diving reduced rates of contact. However, no implementation of such programmes on a large scale within destinations has subsequently been reported, and Barker and Roberts (2004) found that shorter briefings by dive guides had negligible effects on contact rates. Instead, they found intervention by dive leaders during dives to be more effective at reducing contact rates. The larger and usually less controlled snorkelling sector makes management of snorkelling impacts through education and dive leader intervention less likely as a successful strategy. However, the installation of floating jetties and walkways for access across reef flats in intensively used areas has been shown to result in damage being localized to sacrificial areas, with overall benefits in reducing damage (Ormond *et al.*, 1997). Similarly the use of mooring buoys has been demonstrated to reduce incidents of dive and snorkel boats and other recreational vessels anchoring, a practice which causes a great deal of damage (e.g. Jameson *et al.*, 1999).

Impacts from development

Tourism requires the development and operation of a large supporting infrastructure. The construction of, and conversion of land for, hotels, roads, esplanades, airports, ports and beaches can adversely impact coral reefs. In an assessment of Maldivian resort islands, Price and Firaq (1996) noted that reef health and quality were inversely correlated with resort age and proximity to the capital, Malé.

A major potential impact during the construction phase is from increased sedimentation, which can stress reefs through smothering, shading, abrasion and the inhibition of recruitment (Hubbard, 1997). Reef degradation caused by increased sedimentation arising from coastal modification, e.g. for ports and artificial beaches, has been reported from many areas, e.g. the Caribbean and Polynesia (Salvat, 2002; Burke and Maidens, 2004). In the Egyptian Red Sea area around Hurghada, coastal modification for touristic land reclamation has been the prime cause of reef degradation through increased quantities of fine sediment (Riegl and Velimirov, 1991; El-Gamily *et al.*, 2001). Reclamation of 3 million m^2 of reef flat for resort construction in the same area between 1994 and 1997 led to a sediment plume extending several kilometres offshore (Pilcher and Abou Zaid, 2000). Poorly managed resort construction can also affect reefs through deposition of cement dust and other construction wastes.

Resort operation results in increased environmental loads due to an artificially higher human population. This can create issues with the treatment and disposal of solid waste and wastewaters, and the supply of sufficient food, water and other consumables. The management of sewage and other nutrient-rich wastes is a critical issue, as corals are strongly oligotrophic. Nutrient pollution can lead to eutrophication, and coral mortality through increased competition from algae (Marszalek, 1981; Steneck, 1988). Reef stress attributed to sewage discharge from tourist areas has been reported from the Cayman Islands and Hawaii, amongst other destinations (Linton *et al.*, 2002; Brainard *et al.*, 2002). Where potable water is scarce, the dumping of desalination wastewaters has potential impacts not just due to localized heating of waters and possible coral bleaching, but also from chemical additives in the desalination process such as chlorine, copper and anti-scalants (Hoepner and Lattemann, 2002). Tourism in coastal areas inevitably results in increased demand for seafood, which can place reefs under greater fishing stress, and, although illegal in many destinations, the marine curio trade is also a traditional accompaniment of coastal tourism and can increase pressure on target species.

Other pressures include the discharge of anti-fouling paints, fuels and oily wastewaters from vessels associated with marine tourism, all of which are known to have adverse effects on marine biota (e.g. MacFarlane and Benville, 1986; Sorokin, 1995; Batley *et al.*, 1994; see Jaap *et al.*, this volume). This chapter mainly considers tourism in the context of shore-based development, but it is worth noting the potential impact of the global cruise industry, 58% of which is based in the Caribbean. A typical large cruise ship generates 8 tonnes of bilge water and 1 tonne of solid waste day^{-1}, requiring the provision of adequate handling facilities at ports of call (Sweeting and Swayne (2003) and The Ocean Conservancy (2002) quoted in Burke and Maidens, 2004). Apart from the large anchor systems associated with such vessels, groundings can be severe; the *Royal Viking Sun* cleared 2000 m^2 of coral in the Egyptian Straits of Tiran in 1996, breaking the reef superstructure (Ras Mohamed National Park, pers. comm.).

By comparison to many other commercial uses of coral reefs, such as fisheries and mining, the direct impacts of recreation and tourism are low. Mitigation measures for many of these impacts are well understood, and well-planned tourism is likely to offer the most sustainable and profitable use of reef resources. Tourism can provide incentives as well as financing for reef conservation through user fees in marine protected areas and other environmental tariffs (e.g. Driml, 1994; Lindsay and Holmes, 2002). However, there is frequently insufficient capacity for adequate planning and regulation in those countries endowed with coral reef resources, and the rapid growth associated with tourism development can outstrip attempts to generate sufficient management capacity.

One particular feature of tourism is the industry's centrifugal tendency to develop 'virgin' areas to meet demand for isolated beach resorts with high environmental quality as older resorts age. This tendency, combined with the rapid development associated with tourism, results in a pattern of urbanization which makes tourism impacts of particular concern to coral reef managers.

THE SOUTH SINAI AS A CASE STUDY

Growth of South Sinai as a tourist destination

The South Sinai has witnessed rapid development since 1982, when Egypt regained control of the Sinai Peninsula from Israel. This growth has been largely driven by the government's policy to reclaim desert areas and create settlements away from the crowded Nile Valley, set against a projected rise in national population from 72 million in 2003 to 103 million by 2025 (United Nations Population Division, 2002). Driven by domestic migration, South Sinai's population has risen from 29 000 (40% urban) in 1986 to an estimated 110 000 (75% urban) in 2003. Seven of South Sinai's eight cities are coastal, and urban population growth has been particularly strong in the Gulf of Aqaba, an increase from 3300 to 56 300 between 1986 and 2003 (Support for Environmental Assessment and Management, 2004). What were essentially frontier towns and villages in 1982 are now bustling urban centres well connected to the Nile heartland by transport links.

The development of the Gulf of Aqaba coastline, the 240-km stretch between Sharm el Sheikh and Taba, has been driven by tourism (Fig. 7.1). This demonstrates the potential power of this sector for economic development. The government of Egypt strongly supports the tourism sector, which accounts for over 11% of GDP and provides an import source of foreign exchange. In the fiscal year 2000/01, the most recent for which information is available, South Sinai accounted for 16% of all hotel accommodation in Egypt, 17% of employment in tourism establishments, and 19% of total revenues from tourism (Central Agency for Public Mobilization and Statistics, 2003).

To illustrate the speed of tourism development, the number of South Sinai tourist establishments rose from 5 in 1987 to 274 by September 2003 (Ormond *et al.*, 1997; Support for Environmental Assessment and Management, 2004). As the number of establishments rose, so did the average capacity per establishment, from 80 to 162 rooms per hotel between 1996 and 2003 (Support for Environmental Assessment and Management, 2004). This growth in hotel capacity has been particularly noticeable in four- and five-star classification accommodation (Fig. 7.2), reflecting the increasingly upmarket nature of South Sinai tourism. Similarly, tourist arrivals to South Sinai have grown from under 40 000 in 1988 to 2 million

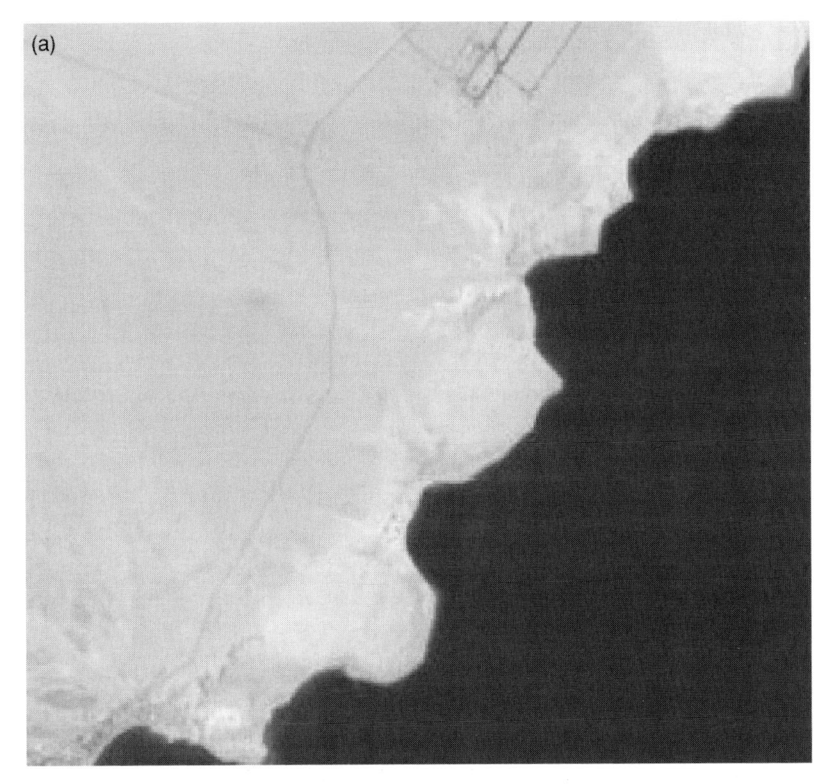

Figure 7.1 Area between Na'ama Bay and Sharm el Sheikh Airport in (a) the late 1980s and (b) 2004. (Sources: (a) Ras Mohamed National Park; (b) Support for Environmental Assessment and Management 2004.) (See also Plate 7.1 in the colour plate section.)

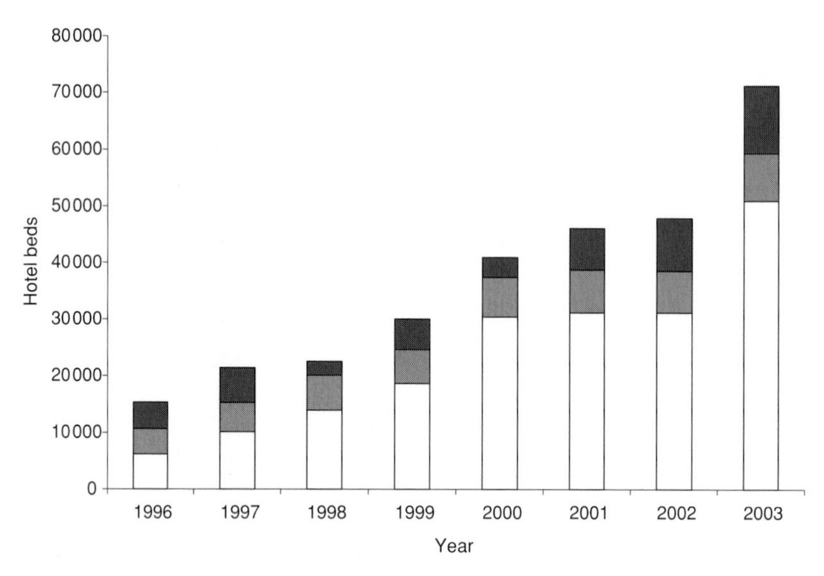

Figure 7.2 Growth of hotel accommodation in South Sinai, Egypt, 1996–2003, by classification: □ four- and five-star accommodation; ■ one-, two- and three-star accommodation; ■ unclassified accommodation. (Source: South Sinai Governorate Information Centre.) Data for 2003 accurate to end of September 2003.

in 2003 (South Sinai Governorate Information Centre, unpublished data). To the 2003 numbers must be added those visitors staying in private villas and holiday rental apartments for which no figures are kept.

In terms of geographic distribution, Sharm el Sheikh dominates. It accounts for 73% of all accommodation, and 88% of all five-star accommodation (Support for Environmental Assessment and Management, 2004). Its historical dominance of coastal tourism is set to continue under current development plans and predictions (Fig. 7.3), with a doubling in accommodation capacity by 2017. In Dahab, which was until recently a destination catering mainly for budget and backpacking travellers, a 350% increase in the number of four- and five-star hotels is planned by 2017. The 65-km stretch between Nuweiba and Taba is currently dominated by small beach camps catering for backpacking Israeli tourists, but four new five-star hotel resorts at Taba since 2000 have created a new market, particularly catering for British package tourists. With the improvement of Taba airport, and assuming an eventual recovery in the Israeli market, this area is also expected to grow significantly (910%) by 2017 (Support for Environmental Assessment and Management, 2004).

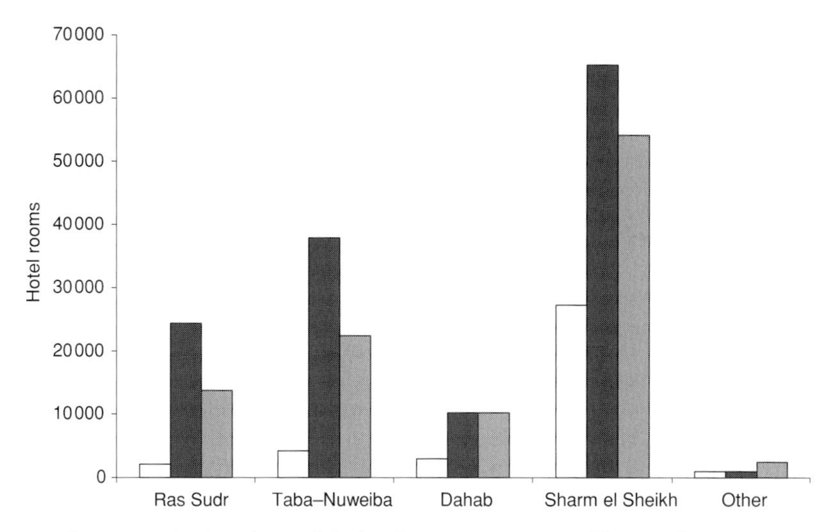

Figure 7.3 Projected growth in hotel rooms 2003–2017: □ currently operating rooms; ■ planned rooms; ▒ best estimates of actual completion. (Source: Support for Environmental Assessment and Management, 2004.)

The huge environmental load posed by these increases in tourist numbers, and the implied increase in residential population, certainly raise questions about the management of environmental impacts. However, the scale of development also raises concerns about long-term economic sustainability, particularly in the context of the globalized tourism market. The following two sections address these issues.

Managing the direct environmental impacts of tourism

Legislative framework

In South Sinai, the rapid growth of tourism-led development has placed an unprecedented level of pressure on central and local governmental regulators and enforcement agencies to upgrade institutional capacities for environmental management. Two major achievements have been the introduction and implementation of two legislative frameworks: Law 102 of 1983 and Law 4 of 1994.

Law 102/1983 provides the legal basis for the declaration of protected areas. It stipulates that without permission from the Egyptian Environmental Affairs Agency (EEAA), any activity within the protected areas leading to the destruction of the natural environment, biota or aesthetic quality of the area is prohibited. It also grants the EEAA authority to regulate recreational use within the protectorates, and to monitor all activities and enforce regulatory measures. Law 102/1983 also determines penalties for violations of regulations. The law is simple, comprehensive, and – at least on paper – authoritative.

The implementation of Law 102/1983 has relied, at least initially, on external funding. Between 1989 and 2002 the EC allocated € 23 million to implement the South Sinai Protectorate network and build institutional capacity and local and national levels. Between 1996 and 1998 the South Sinai Protectorate network expanded, adding four protected areas to Ras Mohamed National Park (established in 1983) to cover a total of 10 000 km^2 (Fig. 7.4). Within these protected areas, anchoring on corals, fishing (with the exception of Bedouin traditional fisheries in certain areas), fish feeding, and damage or collection of marine biota, including the collection or sale of marine curios, are prohibited. In addition, a mooring network for recreational vessels was supplied as an alternative to anchoring at major dive sites.

Since 2002, budgets for the protected areas have been provided by the Egyptian government. Modest fees are currently charged to all visitors to Ras Mohamed National Park and Nabq Managed Resource Protected Area. However, these fees and other revenues, e.g. fines imposed on violators, are not retained locally, but are directed to the national Environmental Protection Fund. Unfortunately, budget allocations back to the protected areas are not sufficient to develop programmes embarked on during the phase of support by foreign donors. For example, the number of vehicles and vessels available for patrolling and enforcement has declined due to the high cost of maintenance, and currently the mooring network is only approximately 50% operational. Resource limitations affect the protectorates' ability to monitor effectively the area's reefs. There are also problems with the control of snorkel and dive boats, solid waste management, and with fishing in various parts of the network.

The Nature Conservation Sector – the branch of the EEAA overseeing protected areas – has proposed mechanisms for retaining a fixed percentage of user fees and other revenues to upgrade service provisions, thereby ensuring financial sustainability. However, since the South Sinai is the largest contributor to the Environmental Protection Fund, which supports environmental management through Egypt and thereby distributes tourism's economic benefits across the country, this issue is likely to take some time to resolve. In the interim, the Nature Conservation Sector has developed partnerships with non-governmental organizations (NGOs) to extend management capacity at little or no cost to itself. A protocol for marine monitoring in the Dahab area has been agreed with a local NGO,

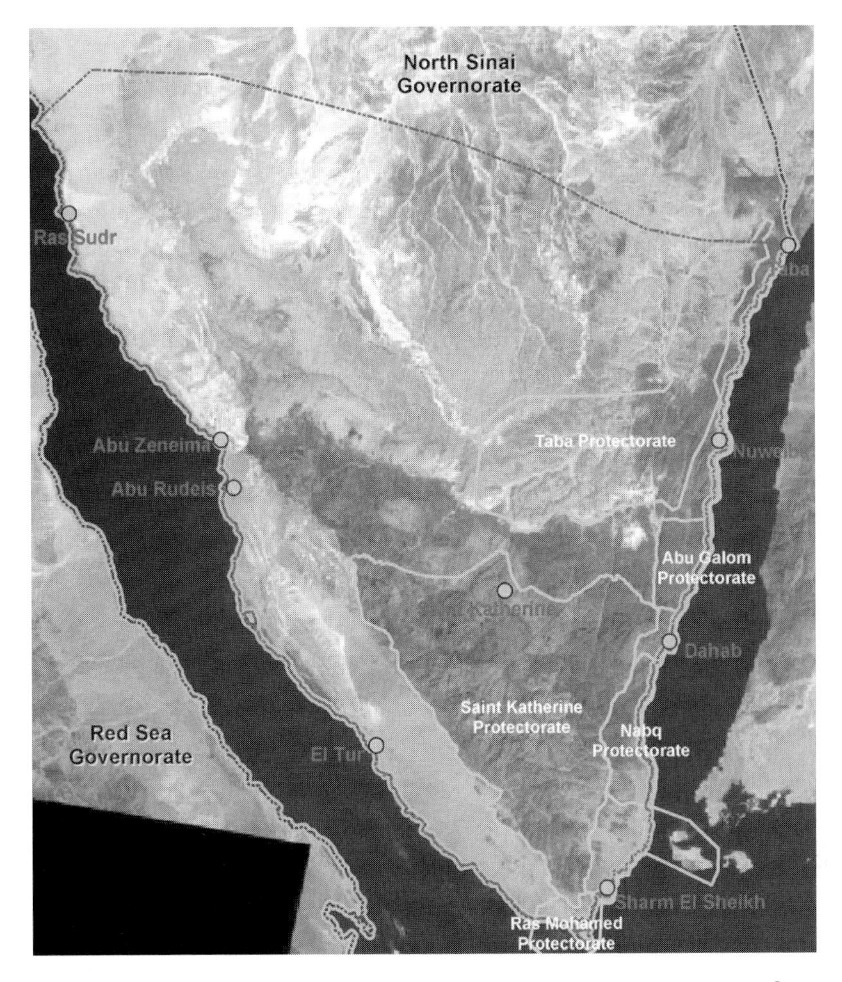

Figure 7.4 Protectorates and major cities of South Sinai. (Source: Support for Environmental Assessment and Management, 2004.) (See also Plate 7.4 in the colour plate section.)

whilst a partnership with a Nuweiba-based NGO has recently been approved to undertake solid waste management in Abu Galum Managed Resource Protected Area, with the NGO to self-finance through the sale of recycled materials and the charge of a user fee to tourists. A new EC-funded initiative, due to begin in 2005, should provide further institutional support through the upgrading of equipment, particularly enforcement and monitoring vessels. However, mechanisms are needed to guarantee long-term financial sustainability of the protected areas, and reduce dependency on external donors.

The second legislative framework, Law 4/1994, also known as the Law for the Environment, applies more generally across the environmental sector. It requires environmental impact assessments (EIAs) for all construction projects to be submitted to the EEAA (see Turner *et al.*, this volume), regulates and sets strict controls on construction within 200 m of the shoreline as well as any activity modifying the coastline. It also controls the transportation and disposal of construction wastes, prohibits all discharges of land-based sources of pollution within 500 m of the coast, requires ports to have facilities for managing solid waste, wastewaters and waste oils, and bans the discharge of polluting substances from ships or oil platforms. The law also details penalties for violation, including fines and jail terms.

Although the 200 m setback is often reduced to 50 m in most resort areas, and to 30 m in others, subject to agreements with the various agencies implementing Law 4/1994, resources have been devoted to the building of tourist facilities such as floating jetties and swim platforms, the establishment of underwater walkways, and awareness programmes, all intended to minimize impacts on reefs. The use of EIAs has also improved significantly since their first introduction in 1994. Numbers of submitted EIAs have steadily increased, and the process has benefited from assessment and refinement of the EIA procedure.

However, the effectiveness of implementation of Law 4/1994 has been hampered by insufficient resources. For example, until recently the South Sinai Governorate Environmental Management Unit responsible for the EIA process for construction projects, monitoring water quality, raising environmental awareness, coordinating with other environmental management bodies, and overseeing solid waste management, as well as playing a significant role in enforcement, had only four members of staff (who were poorly trained) and inadequate computing and monitoring equipment. However, a change in the designation of the unit in 2004 means when fully operational it will have a total of 50 staff. Training has been scheduled, and adequate equipment is being procured.

Problems with the EIA process also lie principally in the limited resources available to the appropriate administrative bodies, which have had to cope with a large workload based on comparatively little experience. The lack of quality and experience of private sector consultants employed to draft the EIAs has been a serious limitation in the system. Combined with the requirement to respond to EIAs within 60 days, and delays in transferring documents between South Sinai and Cairo, these limitations have meant that some projects have been approved despite the submission of substandard EIAs. Controlling the environmental impact of tourism development relies on the EIA process to identify mitigating and preventative measures, followed by enforcement and monitoring (Turner *et al.*, this volume). However, there is little outside inspection or monitoring of project compliance with EIA and operational standards. Although there have been notable successes, for example the mustering and prosecution of 170 legal cases against hotels between 1997 and 2002, consolidating the EIA framework remains an important challenge (de Grissac, 2002).

Given the expected growth of tourism development over the next 13 years, it will be crucially important to strengthen the EIA process and enforce compliance with regulations. Four measures should help to achieve this objective: increasing the number and qualifications of staff, raising the awareness of all stakeholders including investors and NGOs about the EIA process, implementation of inspection, monitoring and enforcement activities by the Environmental Management Unit, and developing the capacity of individual municipalities along the coast (Support for Environmental Assessment and Management, 2004).

Similar issues are identifiable when evaluating the effectiveness of anti-pollution measures. Principal sources of land-based pollution potentially affecting reefs are uncollected domestic wastes, sanitary wastes and poorly treated wastewaters, and the dumping at sea of construction waste. In terms of marine pollution, the principal concern is the potential for pollutant spills arising from shipping and oil and gas exploration in the Gulf of Suez. However, discharges of waste oils, wastewaters and solid waste from diving boats and other recreational vessels are considered a serious problem, particularly in the Sharm el Sheikh area. Capacities for planning, monitoring, pollution combating and environmental remediation, and – crucially – enforcement, are generally insufficient, and there is a need for greater budgetary allocation by the state to upgrade the resources available.

In summary, the passing of environmental laws has not alone been sufficient to guarantee high-quality environmental management. Sufficient technical and management capacity and human and financial resources need to be dedicated to the implementation of legal codes. In South Sinai, the allocation of resources and capacities for environmental management has lagged behind the rates of development and population growth, and behind the requirements of the legal code.

Current marine environment condition in South Sinai

The lack of a well-resourced, long-term integrated monitoring management programme for the South Sinai's coral reefs is a serious impediment to assessing the impacts of recent human development along the coasts. A

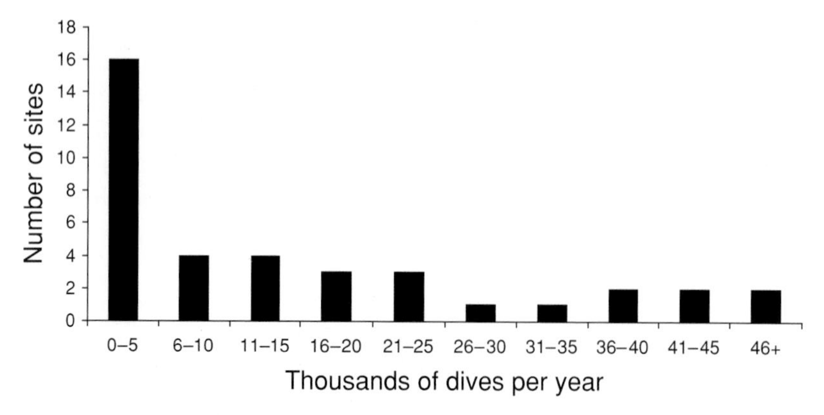

Figure 7.5 Distribution of diving intensity at sites around Sharm el Sheikh. (Source: Ras Mohamed National Park.)

number of projects have developed coral reef monitoring programmes, most notably in cooperation with British universities between 1994 and 1996, but these ended when their funding expired. It is frustrating that each successive monitoring project has used different methodologies and/or surveyed different sites, largely negating options for conventional comparison (but see Côté *et al.*, this volume).

There is evidence that coral cover has declined on Sinai reefs in the last decade. A 2001/02 video monitoring study by foreign and Egyptian scientists found hard coral cover values ranging from 5% to 30% in 2001 at seven reef sites within Ras Mohamed National Park compared to 15–60% in 1996 (Tilot, 2002). Annual Reef Check surveys similarly show that hard coral cover had fallen from a range of 8–62% in 1997 to 2–47% in 2002 (Reef Check, unpublished data). Although sample sizes are generally small and different sites have been monitored in different years, these figures suggest reef degradation but it is impossible at the moment to ascribe specific causal factors to these changes.

As in other seas, reef impacts from scuba diving and snorkelling have been observed in the Red Sea (Hawkins and Roberts, 1992, 1993), and diver numbers at some sites in the Sharm el Sheikh area may exceed greatly the proposed carrying capacity of these reefs (Hawkins and Roberts, 1992). A 2003 study by Ras Mohamed National Park showed that, out of 40 dive sites surveyed, a quarter received more than 25 000 dives yr^{-1} (Fig. 7.5). The most heavily visited sites were Ras Om Sid and Jackson Reef, with 60 000 dives yr^{-1}. As the National Park study surveyed only diving vessels (over 90% of diving in the area is conducted by boat), one must also take into account snorkellers from the shore and those on boat trips. The South Sinai Association for Diving and Marine Activities (pers. comm.) has estimated that divers represented just 25% of boat-based recreational visitors, the rest comprising snorkellers. The numbers of shore-based snorkellers and swimmers using the sea from front-row hotels is unknown, although the number was estimated to be 103 000 yr^{-1} at one station on the reef flat at Temple (W. Leujak and R. F. G. Ormond, unpublished data).

Whilst damage by recreational users is apparently unsustainable in some areas, particularly the heavily used sites between Ras Om Sid, Temple and Ras Katy, other sites reveal a mixed picture. Some heavily used offshore sites, such as Woodhouse and Jackson Reefs in the Straits of Tiran, and some sites within the protectorates, such as Ras Ghozlani and Marsa Bareika, show signs of only low levels of physical impacts (Mohamed Salem, pers. comm.). Most of the reefs that have been seriously degraded over the last 15 years appear to be those fringing reefs affected by impacts associated with the construction phase of hotel development. Whilst large-scale coastal modification and creation of artificial beaches was prevented in the area, the operational practices of developers during the construction phase were not always successfully monitored. In many areas, particularly between Ras Om Sid and Ras Nasrani, sedimentation arising from spills of aggregates and cement dust on site appears to have affected reefs. Frequently construction workers also used reef animals as sources of food, and used the reef itself for solid waste disposal. At sites such as Tower, Sodfa and Paradise along the heavily developed coast between Ras Om Sid and Na'ama Bay, hard coral cover is now below 8% (Ras Mohamed National Park, unpublished data; Reef Check, unpublished data).

In addition to the impacts from recreational users and urbanization, several other sites were affected by crown-of-thorns starfish infestations between 1994 and 2001. Sites such as Shark's Bay and Gordon Reef were severely impacted, and the protectorates organized the collection of over 60 000 individual starfish between 1998 and 1999. Outbreaks of these corallivorous starfishes have been linked to human disturbance, especially terrestrial runoff (e.g. Brodie, 1992), among other causes.

Despite the negative impression of the above review, there may be grounds for cautious optimism. The construction of first-row hotels along the Sharm el Sheikh coast has now largely halted, if only because there are no more available sites. The containment of nutrient pollution has been largely successful, as has protection of the coast's natural topography, which prevents shore access to many parts of the reef. Relieved from pressures of construction waste dumping and trampling, some areas may yet recover to an extent. There are initial signs of such a recovery, with coral recruitment running high at several sites with low coral cover, including Near Garden, Tower, Fiasco and Ras Bob. Gordon Reef is also showing strong signs of recovery, with over 70 colonies m^{-2} (Ras Mohamed National Park, unpublished data.).

Further north in Dahab, and between Nuweiba and Taba, a similar scale of construction has not yet taken place. Reef impacts regarded as most significant in those areas are the loss of reef fish due to over-harvesting, and wind-blown solid wastes, particularly plastics. However, there are ambitious plans for hotel development and urbanization in these areas until 2017. If sufficient lessons can be learned from the construction phase in Sharm el Sheikh, as Sharm learned from Hurghada (see below), and capacity for planning, monitoring and enforcement improved, then it is possible that the impacts of development in the Gulf of Aqaba and elsewhere in Egypt will be less severe.

Whilst no one would suggest that tourism development has not affected the reefs of South Sinai, it is instructive to compare their condition to those of Hurghada, on the mainland Egyptian Red Sea coastline. By the early 1990s the reefs around Hurghada had suffered from coastal modification and increased sedimentation, boat anchoring on corals, tourism-driven over-fishing and curio collection, and discharges of wastewaters (e.g. Riegl and Velimirov, 1991; Hawkins and Roberts, 1994; El Gamily *et al.*, 2001). By contrast the majority of near-shore reefs around Sharm el Sheikh are currently in better condition than those of Hurghada, even though Sharm el Sheikh has long exceeded Hurghada's 1990 level of visitation. Unlike Sharm el Sheikh, Hurghada suffers from a lower market value, is seen by consumers as a less fashionable, less attractive destination, and attracts tourists with less money to spend. This is reflected in the differential recreational value-added of coral reefs in the two areas, estimated for 2000 as US$15.2 million for Hurghada and US$36.2 million for Sharm el Sheikh, despite similar numbers of visitors (Cesar, 2003b). It is a repeat of that set of economic and consumer patterns that tour operators in Sharm el Sheikh wish to avoid.

The management of tourism quality

Sustaining coral reef protection is strongly linked to maintaining the quality of tourism. Tourism quality, broadly speaking, is both the quality that the resort offers, and the financial returns and type of tourist that the destination receives. Tourism quality, therefore, embraces standards in

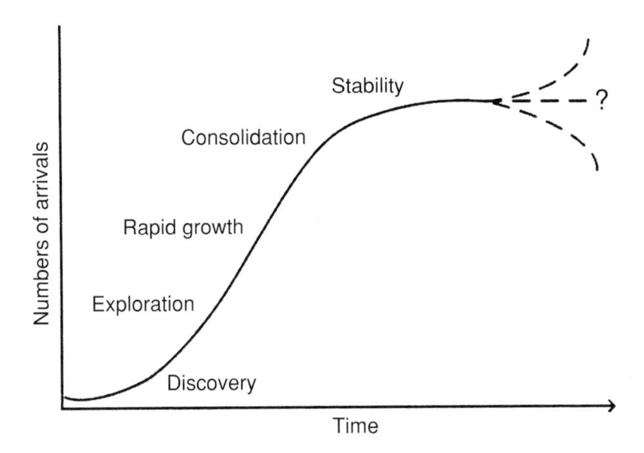

Figure 7.6 The tourism life cycle, showing the resort's evolution from initial discovery to a mass-market destination with an uncertain future. (Adapted from Butler, 1980.)

accommodation, food, services and infrastructure, the type and range of tourist activities and products, and the environmental awareness, cultural sensitivity and experiences desired by the tourists. Managing tourism quality is a task perhaps more challenging than enacting immediate environmental protection, as changes beyond the destination's control, for example upheaval in the global tourism market or downturns in the economies of source markets, can have great impacts. There are also known problems with sustaining tourism quality associated with product life cycles.

Tourism life cycles

Butler (1980) described how popular tourist resorts move through a life cycle in which continuing development and increasing tourist numbers lead to a degradation of natural resources, and a resulting tendency to stagnation and a decline of visitor numbers (Fig. 7.6). With increasing popularity the resort passes though a typical pattern of discovery, exploration, rapid growth, consolidation, stability and then either decline or renewal. The possibility of entering a stage of destination decline due to overdevelopment is a serious threat to resort sustainability, and the south coast of Spain and Malta are two examples of destinations attempting to deal with this problem. Overdevelopment is not only an issue of direct impacts on environmental quality. If growth in the quantity of accommodation is not controlled, supply will exceed demand, leading to cut-throat competition between hotels and tour operators. As hotels generally run on a low-profit basis and owe money to investors, cuts in prices quickly turn into cuts in maintenance and external spending, e.g. on maintaining environmental quality and reef conservation. The destination then edges towards the bottom end of the market, usually associated with cheap packages in all-inclusive resorts which provide less income to the local economy. As hotels and operators are receiving less money per bed sold, they therefore try to increase occupancy by further lowering prices. Customer perception of the resort changes, and it begins to repel old guests and attract new guests with lower expectations of quality. Tourism, being a consumer product, is essentially a fashion accessory, and destinations behave similarly to other types of brands. Once a resort loses the market-place perception of being a leading brand, it is very difficult to recapture that position.

Sharm el Sheikh is most likely in the consolidation stage of this life-cycle model, after discovery in the 1970s and 1980s, and rapid growth during the 1990s (Fig. 7.7). Earlier exploration-driven tourists have been replaced by mass-market 'sun-seekers', with lower demands for quality. Tourists, particularly high-paying guests, perceive tourism quality as not just about the quality of the environment and services, but also about the quality of other guests. There is no doubt that in that sense there has been a loss of tourism quality in Sharm el Sheikh. Some wealthy divers and other earlier clientele now go elsewhere, to more exclusive resorts. There is concern that if this trend continues, the economic incentive to invest in environmental management could become negligible. Ultimately there is a risk that, should prices fall too low, the incentive and ability to invest in resort infrastructure will also decrease, leading to dilapidation and total decline. This is the worst-case scenario that tourism managers plan to avoid.

A similar simple model is of recreational succession, which examines more specifically the loss of environmental quality with increased development (Clark and Stankey, 1979 and Stankey (1985) quoted in Orams, 1999). In this model, the initial discovery and use of a site for recreation result in some deterioration in environmental quality. The original visitors, who searched for pristine areas, move on and are replaced by greater numbers of visitors with lower expectations of environmental quality, and the supply of infrastructure to cope with the greater number of visitors results in further environmental degradation. Meanwhile the original pioneers have discovered a new area, which will then undergo the same successional sequence.

Again, the experience of Sinai corresponds to this model, particularly with respect to the scuba diving market. The scuba market was particularly important to the growth of Sharm el Sheikh, as it was pioneering divers who created the initial demand for accommodation. At the same time as Sharm el Sheikh was undergoing this initial development, recreational scuba was

(a)

(b)

Figure 7.7 White Knights area of Sharm el Sheikh in (a) 1997 and (b) 2002. (Photos: Philip Jago.)

becoming cheaper, more available and more fashionable. Sharm el Sheikh capitalized, and continues to capitalize, on the fashionability of scuba and the exoticism of coral reefs to attract guests. As the numbers of divers and snorkellers in the water increased, with subsequent crowding and environmental damage, the diving pioneers were replaced by a new breed of less-experienced mass-market scuba divers with lower expectations of reef health – a recreational form of the shifting-baseline syndrome (Sheppard, 1995). Those pioneering divers have since moved onto Marsa Alam and other sites in the southern Egyptian Red Sea, as well as diving in Eritrea and Sudan. One consequence of this tendency is known as the centrifugal nature of tourism, implying the constant search for untouched locations and their subsequent development, and the gradual creep of human infrastructure and loss of wilderness areas. Another consequence has been that Sharm el Sheikh and other resorts in Sinai are facing increasing competition from other scuba destinations both inside and outside Egypt.

Exogenous threats

Reef conservation in tourist destinations such as the South Sinai is also at the mercy of exogenous threats, because of the economic impacts of downturns in visitor arrivals due to regional or global political instability, war, acts of terrorism or natural disasters. Tourism in Egypt has been vulnerable to such threats, with wars in the Arabian Gulf in 1991, 2003 and 2005, domestic terrorist attacks against tourists, particularly in 1997, 2004 and 2005, and of course the events of 9/11 which created market-place apprehension about the Middle East in general. In Sinai the consequences of these events have been, historically, a sharp fall in visitor arrivals followed by a lowering of prices, a subsequent recovery of demand and then a gradual recovery of prices. (Following the attacks of summer 2005 bargains were available through travel agents and arrival numbers appeared to recover quickly, although remaining below the usual for the time of year.) The real risk to tourism quality, and concomitant risk to incentives for reef protection, is that in the phase during which low prices are used to attract guests the destination loses fashionability and experiences a downshift in market perception, aggravating or even precipitating longer-term economic and environmental problems.

How tourists perceive South Sinai

It is clear that South Sinai's resorts are no longer catering to guests who are predominantly attracted by the area's coral reefs. Results from the Support for Environmental Assessment and Management (2004) tourism survey showed that the top five motivations for foreigners travelling to South Sinai were climate (82%), beaches (44%), snorkelling and water sports (33%), good value for money (27%) and short travel time (23%). Diving was a mere sixth, and cultural and religious tourism, and desert safaris all came further down the list. Of those surveyed, 92% stayed for less than two weeks. The small sample size ($n = 453$) and short time-frame (two months) of the survey limit the generality of the results, but they do correspond to what is anecdotally reported. The majority of tourists in South Sinai are on short-term breaks, and are most likely to be choosing their holiday destination based on a combination of guaranteed sun, access to the sea, value for money and proximity to Europe.

Interestingly, when asked about the most enjoyed aspects of their holiday, tourists ranked coral reefs/Red Sea (73%) first, followed by weather/climate (58%), beauty of landscape (35%), beaches (31%), and accommodation, service and food (26%). In addition, a very large number of respondents (78%) undertook one or more excursions whilst on holiday, with the most popular being boat trips (30%), cultural visits such as trips to St Katherine monastery and Mount Sinai (27%), desert safaris (23%), snorkelling trips (22%) and diving (22%), despite the relative unimportance of these activities as reasons for choosing the South Sinai as a destination. The top five dislikes, other than the Sharm el Sheikh airport which ranked first for one-third of respondents, were accommodation and food (18%), waste and rubbish (15%), quality of service (14%), noise (9%) and sea and beach pollution (8%). Poor value for money (6%) and overcrowding of dive sites (4%) were also mentioned (Support for Environmental Assessment and Management, 2004).

South Sinai's natural resources, and its reefs in particular, therefore still have a powerful role in supporting tourism, even if they may not be the principal motivating factor behind destination choice, particularly for first-time visitors. In a way, this is worrisome for coral reef conservation because it may indicate that the consumer surplus of a holiday in South Sinai is higher than the destination can afford in the long term. In other words, if tourists are purchasing their holidays based on a combination of climate, price and travel time attributes, this implies that the unique qualities of South Sinai, such as its coral reefs, may be undervalued in the market place. With cheap package holidays available to sunny destination close to Europe, for example Mediterranean destinations such as Tunisia, or the Canary Islands, South Sinai may be competing too heavily in terms of price, rather than developing a marketing strategy based on its strengths and aimed at a higher end of the market. In addition, the higher importance placed by tourists on high standards in tourism facilities than environmental quality suggests that poor accommodation, food and services will obstruct attempts to situate the destination in the top end of the tourism market, with its concomitant environmental benefits, even if the implementation of coral reef conservation and management is first rate.

Sustaining reef-based tourism in South Sinai

It is important to stress that the tourism situation in this region is evolving quickly. Indeed, the rapid pace of development has been one of the principal problems in the management of both environment and tourism in South Sinai, as the usual cycles of policy systems (the identification of problems, and the creation and implementation of solutions) often work on longer timescales than the dynamics of the systems they attempt to govern (Jobbins, 2003). Nonetheless, it is possible to develop a general strategy for improving the tourism product in South Sinai, and, by extension, coral reef management. The challenge for South Sinai, and for other resort areas whose economies rely on reef-based tourism, is to maintain, or even improve, the quality and sustainability of the tourism product during the rapid growth and consolidation phases of the destination life cycle, and avoid dependence on mass-market, low-price tourism in which reef resources are undervalued. The loss of tourism quality is a chronic threat that can lead to long-term underinvestment in environmental management.

Recognizing that coral reefs provide significant net benefits to tourism in the region, a coherent management plan for their sustainable recreational use must be developed. This plan will need to balance the medium- and long-term survival of a limited amount of reef space, and its medium- and long-term benefits, against the pressure for maximizing revenues in the short term. Similar approaches need to be developed for the management of sensitive areas visited by desert safaris, and for cultural heritage sites. There needs to be implementation of programmes for tackling marine and noise pollution and solid waste management, and procedures for environmental impact assessments need to be reviewed and upgraded. Institutional development and capacity-building are needed to support all of these actions, particularly in terms of monitoring, enforcement, public awareness, community participation in management and coordination between administrative organizations, and sustainable financing must be secured to ensure their long-term success. The publication of South Sinai's Governorate Environmental Action Plan, summarizing objectives, policies, targets and actions developed through extensive community consultation, is an important milestone to achieving these aims (Support for Environment Assessment and Management, 2004).

Because of the link between environmental quality and tourism life cycles, it is imperative that the South Sinai maintains itself at the top end of the market, offering excellent facilities and a pristine environment. To draw recreational pressure away from reefs, alternative activities should be offered to tourists. These touristic opportunities can range from health tourism, desert safaris, trekking, rock-climbing, sailing, windsurfing, horse-riding and educational tourism, all of which are currently underexploited. These are niche markets with strengths of their own, adding resilience to the basic 'sun, sea and sand' product in the market place in addition to offering respite to coral reef ecosystems.

CONCLUSIONS

The World Tourism Organization predicts three major industry trends over the next twenty years: an increase in long-haul travel, an increase in speciality market segments, and combinant holidays such as beach and special interest combinations (World Tourism Organization, 2001). The latter two are the strongest hope for reef-based destinations to avoid sliding towards the mass market all-inclusive resort, which is usually associated with poor environmental protection. Tourism is by no means a necessarily 'green' industry with minimal impacts on coral reefs. Encouraging dive tourism in an island, perhaps in order to develop alternative livelihoods and undercut over-fishing, may well backfire should the environmental pressures of tourism be poorly managed. Limiting these impacts requires considerable investment in development control, mitigation of direct construction impacts, waste and sewage management, reef management, public awareness, and enforcement. However, if properly managed, tourism development need not spell disaster for coral reefs. Environmental management, combined with serious attention to the cultivation of tourism quality, may generate tourism of a net benefit to reef conservation, particularly if sustainable revenues can be sourced from a tourism industry that puts high values on local natural resources.

ACKNOWLEDGEMENTS

The author would like to acknowledge the input, comments and work of his colleagues at the EEAA/UK DfID Support for Environmental Assessment and Management Programme (SEAM) and South Sinai Governorate, particularly Phil Jago, Atwa Hussein, Rafik Riad, Magda Banasiak and David Sims. Harold Goodwin also provided useful insights, and Isabelle Côté and John Reynolds made many helpful comments on the initial draft. The author would like to thank the SEAM Programme, the EEAA, and South Sinai Governorate for allowing use of the Governorate Environmental Action Plan data. The contents of this paper are the author's own, and do not necessarily reflect the position or policy of the SEAM Programme, EEAA or South Sinai Governorate.

REFERENCES

Barker, N. H. L. and Roberts, C. M. (2004). Scuba diver behaviour and the management of diving impacts on coral reefs. *Biological Conservation*, **120**, 481–9.

Batley, G. E., Chapman, J. C. and Wilson, S. P. (1994). Environmental impacts of antifouling technology. In *Biofouling: Problems and Solutions*, eds. S.Kjelleberg and P.Steinberg, pp. 49–53. Sydney, NSW: University of New South Wales.

Brodie, J. E. (1992). Enhancement of larval and juvenile survival and recruitment in *Acanthaster planci* from the effects of terrestrial runoff: a review. *Australian Journal of Marine and Freshwater Research*, **43**, 539–54.

Brainard, R., Friedlander, A., Gulko, D. *et al.* (2002). Status of coral reefs in the Hawaiian archipelago. In *Status of Coral Reefs of the World: 2002*, ed. C. R. Wilkinson, pp. 238–50. Townsville, QLD: Australian Institute of Marine Science.

Burke, L. and Maidens, J. (eds.) (2004). *Reefs at Risk in the Caribbean*. Washington, DC: World Resources Institute.

Butler, R. W. (1980). The concept of a tourist area cycle of evolution: implications for management of resources. *Canadian Geographer*, **1**, 5–12.

Central Agency for Public Mobilization and Statistics (2003). *Economic Census of 2000/2001: Statistics on the Elements of Activities of Hotels, Tourist Villages, and Pensions in the Public and Private Sectors*. Cairo: CAPMAS.

Cesar, H. (1996). *Economic Analysis of Indonesian Coral Reefs*. Washington, DC: World Bank.

Cesar, H., Burke, L. and Pet-Soede, L. (2003a). *The Economics of Worldwide Coral Reef Degradation*. Amsterdam: Cesar Environmental Economics Consulting. Available online at http://www.icran.org/pdf/cesardegradationreport.pdf

(2003b). *Economic Valuation of Egyptian Coral Reefs*, USAID contract LAG I–00-99-00014-00. Amsterdam: Cesar Environmental Economics Consulting.

Clark, R. N. and Stankey, G. H. (1979). *The Recreation Opportunity Spectrum: A Framework for Planning, Management, and Research*, General Technical Report No. PNW-98. US Department of Agriculture Forest Service, Pacific Northwest Forest and Range Experiment Station.

Davis, D and Tisdell, C. (1995). Recreational scuba-diving and carrying capacity in marine protected areas. *Ocean and Coastal Management*, **26**, 19–40.

de Grissac, A. J. D. (2002). *Gulf of Aqaba Protectorates Development Programme: Final Report*, unpublished report. Nature Conservation Sector, Egyptian Environmental Affairs Agency / Carl Bro International.

Dixon, J. A., Scura, L. F. and van't Hoff, T. (1993). Meeting ecological and economic goals: marine parks in the Caribbean. *Ambio*, **22**, 117–25.

Driml, S. (1994). *Protection for Profit. Economic and Financial Values of the Great Barrier Reef World Heritage Area and Other Protected Areas*, Research publication no. 35. Townsville, QLD: Great Barrier Reef Marine Park Authority.
Fernandes, L. (1995). *Integrating Economic, Environmental, and Social Issues in an Evaluation of Saba Marine Park, N. A., Caribbean Sea*. Honolulu, HI: Honblue. Also available online at http://www.mina.vomiban/Pubs/
El-Gamily, H. I., Nasr, S. and El-Raey, M. (2001). An assessment of natural and human-induced changes along Hurghada and Ras Abu Soma coastal area, Red Sea, Egypt. *International Journal of Remote Sensing*, **22**, 2999–3014.
Harriott, V. J., Davis, D. and Banks, S. A. (1997). Recreational diving and its impact in marine protected areas in Eastern Australia. *Ambio*, **26**, 173–9.
Hawkins, J. P. and Roberts, C. M. (1992). Effects of recreational SCUBA diving on fore-reef slope communities. *Biological Conservation*, **62**, 171–8.
(1993). Effects of recreational diving on coral reefs: trampling of reef flat communities. *Journal of Applied Ecology*, **30**, 25–30.
(1994). The growth of coastal tourism in the Red Sea: present and future effects on coral reefs. *Ambio*, **23**, 503–8.
Hawkins, J. P., Roberts, C. M., Van't Hof, T. *et al.* (1999). Effects of recreational SCUBA diving on Caribbean coral and fish communities. *Conservation Biology*, **13**, 888–97.
Hoepner, T. and Lattemann, S. (2002). Chemical impacts from seawater desalination plants: a case study of the northern Red Sea. *Desalination*, **152**, 133–40.
Hubbard, D. K. (1997). Dynamic processes of coral-reef development. In *Life and Death of Coral Reefs*, ed. C. Birkeland, pp. 43–67. New York: Chapman and Hall.
Jameson, S. C., Ammar, M. S. A., Saddalla, E., Mostafa, H. M. and Riegl, B. (1999). A coral damage index and its application to diving sites in the Egyptian Red Sea. *Coral Reefs*, **18**, 333–9.
Jobbins, G. (2003). The effects of stakeholder interactions on capacity for integrated coastal governance in Morocco and Tunisia. *Aquatic Ecosystem Health and Management*, **6**, 455–64.
Kay, A. M. and Liddle, M. J. (1989). Impact of human trampling in different zones of a coral reef flat. *Environmental Management*, **13**, 509–20.
Lindsay, G. and Holmes, A. (2002). Tourist support for marine protection in Nha Trang, Viet Nam. *Journal of Environmental Planning and Management*, **45**, 461–80.
Linton, D., Smith, R., Alcolado, P. *et al.* (2002). Status of coral reefs in the Northern Caribbean and Atlantic Node of the GCRMN. In *Status of coral reefs of the world: 2002*, ed. C. R. Wilkinson, pp. 277–302. Townsville, QLD: Australian Institute of Marine Science.
MacFarlane, R. and Benville, P. (1986). Primary and secondary stress response of striped bass exposed to benzene. *Marine Biology*, **92**, 245–54.
Marszalek, D. S. (1981). Effects of sewage effluents on reef corals. *Proceedings 4th International Coral Reef Symposium*, **1**, 15–20.
Medio, D., R. F. G. Ormond and M. Pearson (1997). Effects of briefing on rates of damage to corals by scuba divers. *Biological Conservation*, **79**, 91–5.

Muthiga, N. A. and McClanahan, T. R. (1997). The effect of visitor use on the hard coral communities of the Kisite Marine Park, Kenya. *Proceedings 8th International Coral Reef Symposium*, **2**, 1879–82.

Neil, D. (1990). Potential for coral stress due to sediment resuspension and deposition by reef walkers. *Biological Conservation*, **52**, 221–7.

Orams, M. (1999). *Marine Tourism: Development, Impacts and Management.* London: Routledge.

Ormond, R., Hassan, O., Medio, D., Pearson, M. and Salem, M. (1997). Effectiveness of coral protection programmes in Ras Mohamed National Park, Egyptian Red Sea. *Proceedings 8th International Coral Reef Symposium*, **2**, 1931–6.

Pilcher, N. and Abou Zaid, M. (2000). *The Status of Coral Reefs in Egypt.* Townsville, QLD: Global Coral Reef Monitoring Network. Available online at http://www.reefbase.org.

Price, A. R. G. and Firaq, I. (1996). The environmental status of reefs on Maldivian resort islands: a preliminary assessment for tourism planning. *Aquatic Conservation: Marine and Freshwater Systems*, **6**, 93–106.

Reboton, C. and Calumpong, H. P. (2000). How much damage do divers and snorkelers do to corals? *Proceedings 9th International Coral Reef Symposium*, **1**, 783–6.

Riegl, B. and Velimirov, B. (1991). How many damaged corals in the Red Sea? A quantitative survey. *Hydrobiologia*, **216/217**, 249–56.

Roberts, L. and Harriott, V. J. (1994). Recreational scuba diving and its potential for environmental impact in a marine reserve. In *Recent Advances in Marine Science and Technology 1994*, eds. O. Bellwood, H. Choat and N. Saxena, pp. 695–704. Townsville, QLD: James Cook University.

Rodgers, K. S. and Cox, E. F. (2003). The effect of trampling on Hawaiian corals along a gradient of human use. *Biological Conservation*, **112**, 383–9.

Rouphael, A. P. and Inglis, G. J. (1997). Impacts of recreational scuba diving at sites with different reef topographies. *Biological Conservation*, **82**, 329–36.

(2001). Take only photographs and leave only footprints? An experimental study of the impact of underwater photographers on coral reef dive sites. *Biological Conservation*, **100**, 281–7.

Salvat, B. (2002). Status of Southeast and Central Pacific coral reefs in the Polynesia Mana Node': Cook Islands, French Polynesia, Kiribati, Niue, Tokelau, Tonga, Wallis and Futuna. In *Status of Coral Reefs of the World: 2002*, ed. C. R. Wilkinson, pp. 203–15. Townsville, QLD: Australian Institute of Marine Science.

Support for Environmental Assessment and Management (2004). *South Sinai Governorate Environmental Action Plan.* Cairo: SEAM, Egyptian Environmental Affairs Agency.

Sheppard, C. (1995). The shifting baseline syndrome. *Marine Pollution Bulletin*, **30**, 766–7.

Sorokin, Y. I. (1995). *Coral Reef Ecology.* Berlin: Springer-Verlag.

Steneck, R. S. (1988). Herbivory on reefs: a synthesis. *Proceedings 6th International Coral Reef Symposium*, **1**, 37–49.

Talge, H. (1992). Impact of recreational divers on scleractinian corals at Looe Key, Florida. *Proceedings 7th International Coral Reef Symposium*, **2**, 1077–82.

Tilot, V. (ed). (2002). *Video Coral Reef Monitoring: The Gulf of Aqaba Monitoring Programme*, Gulf of Aqaba Protectorates Development Programme SEM 04/220/027-A Egypt, unpublished report. Cairo: Egyptian Environmental Affairs Agency.

Tratalos, J. A. and Austin, T. J. (2001). Impacts of recreational SCUBA diving on coral communities of the Caribbean island of Grand Cayman. *Biological Conservation*, **102**, 67–75.

United Nations Population Division (2002). World Population Prospects: the 2002 Revision. Department of Economic and Social Affairs of the United Nations Secretariat, New York.

Woodland, D. J. and Hooper, J. N. A. (1977). The effect of human trampling on coral reefs. *Biological Conservation*, **11**, 1–4.

World Tourism Organization (2001). *Tourism 2020 Vision*, vol. 7, *Global Forecast and Profiles of Market Segments*. Madrid: WTO.

(2004). International tourism receipts. *World Tourism Barometer*, **2**(2), 2–3.

8

Longer-term impacts of climate change on coral reefs

CHARLES SHEPPARD
University of Warwick

INTRODUCTION

Most accounts of coral bleaching rarely take the story further than an initial report of the event, yet it has become clear that longer-term effects may occur at several scales: those of the corals themselves, of the wider ecological community which is based upon the corals and the three-dimensional reef structure they create, and of the human communities which depend on the coral ecosystem for food, wave protection or tourism-related revenues. Several factors change profoundly in areas where mass mortality follows coral bleaching, as was particularly evident following the severe warming event of 1998. During this period, substantial proportions of corals were killed on reefs throughout the tropics, but most particularly in the Indian Ocean where mortality was commonly 50–100% in shallow water. This chapter describes and predicts some of the consequences of changes induced by coral mortality.

First, I clarify two definitions. The distinction is emphasized between coral bleaching and coral mortality. These two terms are commonly conflated, perhaps because they have a clear relationship (McClanahan, 2004). In this chapter, bleaching (perhaps obviously) refers to the blanched appearance of corals following zooxanthellae expulsion. This state may last from days to several months, and a bleached coral may recover, or it may die. Where recovery occurs, the bleaching story usually ends simply – indeed it may never really have started other than at the coral's own physiological

Coral Reef Conservation, ed. Isabelle M. Côté and John D. Reynolds.

level. When bleached corals die in large numbers, however, as seen in 1998, changes become considerable at all scales.

The term 'warming' is used here as a shorthand way of describing the impact that afflicted reefs, especially in 1998, and at other times before and since. Other factors contributing to bleaching are numerous. Increased photosynthetically active radiation (PAR) may overload the symbiotic zooxanthellae's photosystem II and, in the Indian Ocean, came about not because of any increase in the Sun's radiation as some popular accounts have suggested, but because changes in the Indian monsoon led to prolonged periods of glassy calm seas, and the latter led to less surface reflection of light and greater penetration of incident light into the water. To illustrate the significance of calm seas, an underwater photographer can detect a difference of at least one *f*-stop at the same site between rough and calm conditions at the same time of day, and the difference can be further amplified by turbidity or mild loads of suspended particulates in rougher conditions. This effect was detectable statistically by an increased variance of annual mean wind speed, as happened in Chagos for example (Sheppard, 1999a). Again in 2004, corals in the same area were affected by windless and glassy conditions for several weeks during the period of warmest sea surface temperature (SST), which again led to widespread bleaching. In the Seychelles, mortality of most juvenile corals resulted, while in Chagos they recovered. The UV component of this increased light has been suggested as being especially important but, whether this is the case or not, examples of partially killed corals where the irradiated part died and the shaded part survived were common (Fig. 8.1). While acknowledging the wide range of contributory factors, 'warming' is used here for simplicity.

DIFFERENTIAL MORTALITY OF SPECIES

The differential susceptibility of different genera and species to warming was quickly evident during the 1998 bleaching event. *Acropora*, the most diverse genus and commonly the most abundant, was particularly affected, to the degree that it became a rare genus in some areas, such as the Arabian Gulf. Areas such as the zones 5–15 m deep on seaward reef slopes of atolls, previously dominated by *Acropora* tables, were denuded and vast fields of branching corals typical of lagoonal areas died (Fig. 8.2). At first, such areas were conspicuous by their expanses of dead, standing skeletons of *Acropora* or branching *Porites*, but as these became weakened by bioerosion over the following two to three years, reefs decayed into coral rubble. By 2002, in shallow parts of the Arabian Gulf, the removal of the fields of

Figure 8.1 *Goniastrea* coral, with top surface killed during the severe bleaching event of 1998, showing living shaded surfaces. Photograph taken in Salomon atoll, Chagos Archipelago, 1999.

Figure 8.2 Dead *Acropora* stand on a Seychelles reef flat, at high tide. The dead colonies are now (2004) increasingly fragile, and the height of the dead stand is reducing.

Figure 8.3 Remnant of *Acropora palifera*, Chagos 2001. The colony standing is over 1.5 m tall. Previously, live *A. palifera* densely covered the substratum to the height of the dead remnant (Sheppard *et al.*, 2002).

'stagshorn' and tabular forms was near-total (Riegl, 1999, 2002; Sheppard and Loughland, 2002) and included areas where, ironically, long ago, Kinsman (1964) had noted that corals were more tolerant to warm temperatures than first had been suggested. No *Acropora* appeared to survive across vast areas, and the term 'reef' probably should no longer be applied to them. Indeed off Dubai, nearly 99% of the framework building has gone (Riegl, 2002).

Similar reports on the demise of *Acropora* have come from numerous localities, some of which lost large quantities of striking forms, such as the fields of table corals in places like the Maldives (Loch *et al.*, 2002). Another marked reduction of this previously dominant genus was seen in Chagos where *A. palifera* formerly provided a dense thicket between the surface to about 4 m depth; its near total elimination and subsequent disintegration meant that the shallow reef surface immediately seaward of the surf zone dropped by approximately the height of the colonies – over 1.5 m (Fig. 8.3).

There it had been noted after surveys in 1996 (i.e. before the mass mortality), that several species of *Acropora*, including *A. palifera*, had decreased in cover from values recorded in 1979, and no reason was evident for the modest but significant decline (Sheppard, 1999b). We can speculate that there had been one or more earlier mortality events which went unnoticed; new datasets of SST (see later) suggest these may have occurred. The demise of *Acropora* on these reefs has meant the loss of the main architectural species, which provided both wave resistance and a three-dimensional habitat structure on the reefs.

The other abundant member of the same family, *Montipora*, was not affected to the same degree. Being mostly small and encrusting species, monitoring of their abundance may have been neglected, but later surveys focussing on these species indicated that they survived better than did *Acropora*.

Massive *Porites* species were the main survivors of the 1998 bleaching event. Two notable members of this group are *P. lutea* and *P. solida*, along with *P. nodifera* which was the main survivor (from any genus) in the extremely heated Arabian Gulf where *Porites* species suffered 'only' a 50% mortality. The main failing of many surveys has been their inability to discriminate between species of this important genus. Faviids were good survivors, and in relative terms they became perhaps the most common family. In many reefs this diverse family had already dominated, but this dominance became much more conspicuous in the absence of the acroporids. In the Arabian Gulf, numerous faviid juveniles now occupy many of the vast expanses of denuded limestone on reefs previously covered by stagshorn. Given the known and presumed growth rates of these species, it is estimated that most colonies in the Gulf are younger than five years.

In the worst-affected areas such as the Indian Ocean, coral mortality from the 1998 event was commonly >90%, and in many areas it was nearly total in the region commonly termed the surface zone. The vertical extent of the deeper zone below this, where corals survived, has thus become very important in terms of directing population shifts on the whole reef. This topic is returned to later.

REPEAT MORTALITIES

The key issue must be addressed of whether mortality such as that of 1998 will recur, because if it does, the question is changed from one of recovery patterns and succession following a severe impact, to one of investigating the response of an ecosystem to a possibly permanent alternative stable state. Probably the first to substantially document SST curves in relation to reefs was Hoegh-Guldberg (1999) who used forecast data from model predictions, and the review by Hughes *et al.* (2003) reiterated the main points. Although the latter showed only a schematic graph for this relationship, with neither temperature units nor dates, both of these papers made the point clearly that rising SST was likely to cross 'lethal temperatures' for corals in the coming very few decades.

The dates when this threshold might be exceeded are close enough to demand attention, but one problem is that SST forecast from climate models suffers from two potential inaccuracies: plots of mean forecast SST (or warmest month SST) do not usually continue seamlessly onwards from historical data, and the disagreement between the two datasets may be greater than a degree, which is more than the difference between a 'normal' warm season and warm events which can cause widespread mortality. Secondly, the annual oscillation in forecast SST may be very different (greater or smaller) from that actually recorded, and the jump in warmest month values especially may be large. Since it is the warmest periods that cause the problem, an accurately forecast annual cycle is as vital as the forecast mean trend, as without it any estimate of when SSTs are predicted to reach a particular value may be inaccurate by several decades. Thus a method of adjusting and scaling forecast data was developed (Sheppard, 2003). This used HadISST1 data for the period 1871–2000 as the historical data for any one site, combined with skin data (equivalent to SST in marine areas) from the HadCM3 coupled climate model for forecast data (using the climate scenario IS92A), from 1950 to 2100. Both these datasets and the scenario are well researched and are arguably the most suitable and up to date for such treatment (Cubasch *et al.*, 2001; McAvaney *et al.*, 2001; Rayner *et al.*, 2003). They give global coverage, and an SST curve for any marine area can be produced. Figure 8.4a shows the Bahamas as an example.

The statistical method for obtaining a curve for a site is complicated (Sheppard, 2003); briefly, a first transformation 'locks' the historical data and simply adjusts each forecast data series by the mean difference in values in the overlapping data between 1950 and 1999 ($n = 600$ months). Then the seasonal amplitude of the forecast data series is scaled to match that of each site's historical data, using a method based on a substitution of standard deviations of residuals.

For any site, a curve may then be produced not only of SST from 1871 to 2100 but of the probability, in any year, of a specified temperature being reached. In the Bahamas example (Fig. 8.4b), the specified or target

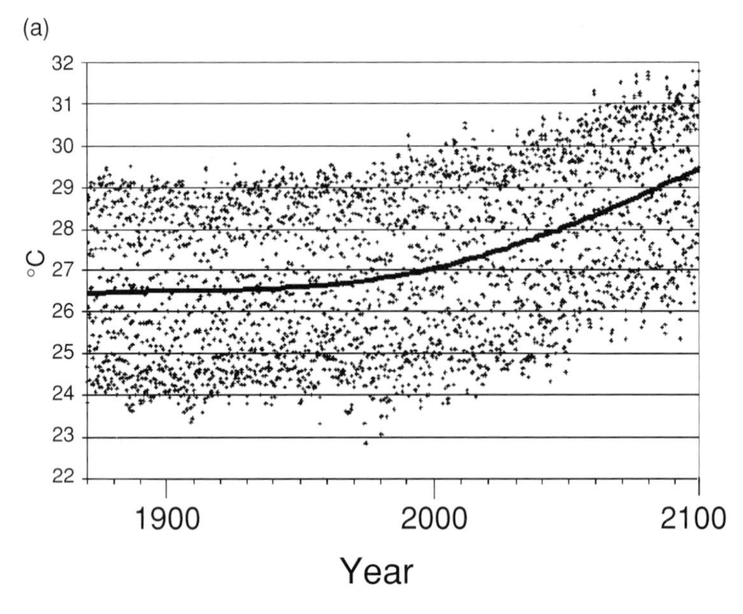

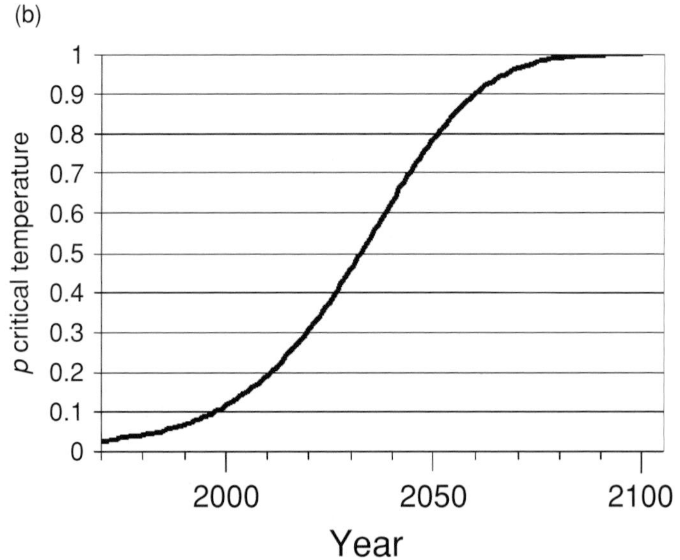

Figure 8.4 (a) Sea surface temperature (SST in °C) curve for eastern Bahamas, 1870–2100. Each dot is a monthly average, thick line is the fourth-order polynomial line of best fit. (b) Probability curve (based on warmest month temperatures) of temperature reaching a critical value, in this case the bleaching-inducing warm temperature of 1998. Thus, by approximately 2020, each year will have a probability of 0.3 of exceeding the 1998 threshold. For explanation of the statistical methods, see Sheppard (2003).

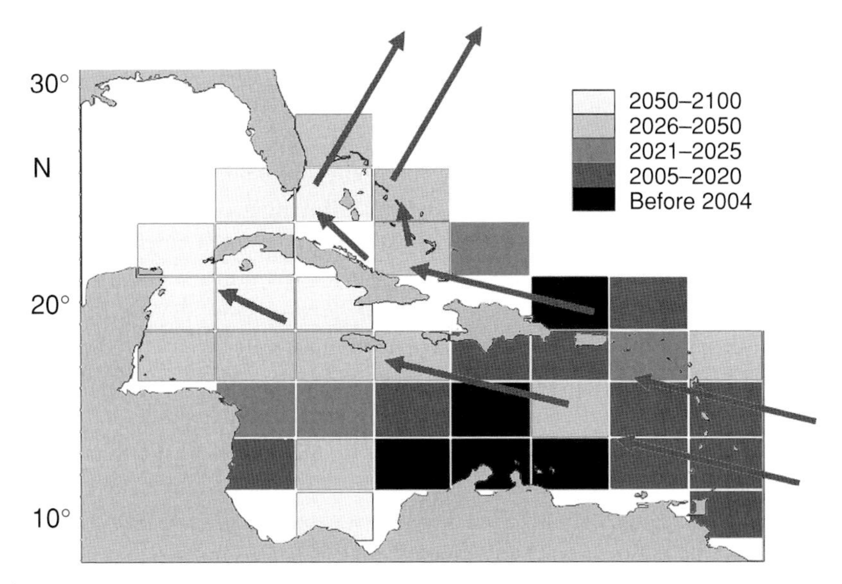

Figure 8.5 Dates, in the Caribbean, when temperatures are expected to reach the peak 1998 values with a probability of 0.5. Thick arrows show the broadscale currents.

temperature used is the warmest monthly value obtained from 1998, this being the value which affected corals in that year. Different temperatures killed corals from different geographical locations, and the method encompasses this differential, perhaps regional, coral acclimation (Gates and Edmunds, 1999; Pittock, 1999; Douglas, 2003), as well as encompassing the different absolute SSTs at each site and different rates of SST rise, all of which affect estimates of when rising temperatures will reach levels which proved to be lethal before.

The geographical resolution is coarse, being a function of the resolution of the climate models, but it is useful for examining regional patterns. With this dataset, the wide geographical spread and long time period offer opportunities for examining regional patterns in a way that cannot easily be accomplished using, for example, the very fine satellite SST data. The Caribbean basin offers an example (Fig. 8.5). This is examined in more detail in Sheppard and Rioja-Nieto (2005) where several unsurprising patterns are shown, such as the locations of warmer and cooler regions, areas of greater and smaller annual temperature ranges, and so on. Figure 8.5 also shows how the forecast dates of possible reef 'extinction' (as defined in Sheppard, 2003) travel in a wave from southeast to northwest. The overlying thick arrows illustrate the broad current pattern, so it is seen that, generally, the up-current and larvae source areas are likely to become 'extinct' first. This has serious implications for reef connectivity issues, as well as for issues of reef and fisheries management, as some Caribbean management plans appear to rely on the possibility of recruitment from up-current locations. This SST dataset is available from the author (Sheppard, 2005). Other locations for which data are available include the Indian Ocean (Sheppard, 2003), the Arabian region, the United Kingdom (Sheppard, 2004) and the Mediterranean (in preparation).

From all of these, it is clear that not only is the rise in SST nearly universal, but in some areas the time to reach temperatures which are known to have been lethal to corals in the past is very close. Almost everywhere, SST rise generally started around 1970 or so. It is also clear that any acclimation or heat tolerance of a modest 1 °C or so will postpone the extinction date of most coral reefs by many decades. The main point is, however, that whether recurrences of lethal SST values happen sooner or later, recurrence means that investigations should certainly focus on consequences of repeatedly and then terminally impacted reef systems rather than situations of recovery from a one-off impact. Many recent papers seem erroneously to view the situation as being the latter, happier condition. In fact, the SST of 2003, which was the second warmest year recorded, seems to confirm that repeat mortality is already taking place; in the Seychelles most of the new coral recruits that appeared a couple of years after the 1998 warming were seen in mid 2004 to have themselves been killed.

DEPTH OF THE AFFECTED ZONE

Coral mortality happens mainly in the 'surface' zone. The depth to which mortality extends is critical. Characteristic of the widespread mortality that followed the 1998 warming was the sight on reefs of a largely killed area from the surface to a certain depth, followed by a remarkably sharp transition zone, below which corals largely survived. The transition zone commonly ranged over a depth span of just 2 m. On the famous atoll Aldabra and its adjacent atoll Cosmoledo, for example, this sharp change occurred at about 10 m depth (Sheppard and Obura, 2005) (Fig. 8.6). Note that there were still some very low cover values at some sites below 10 m. In several reefs this transition depth was uniform over a long extent of reef even where the reef showed varied topography along its length. In other words, its location was not determined by the position of a morphological feature such as a 'drop-off' (though it coincided with one in some places).

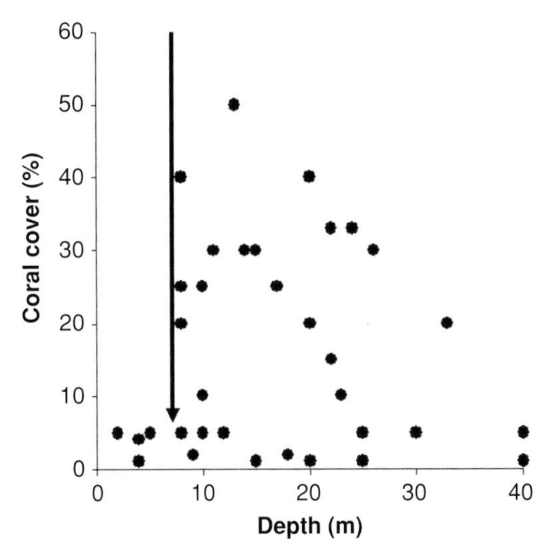

Figure 8.6 Coral cover in relation to depth (m) at Cosmoledo and Aldabra atolls. The vertical arrow shows the depth to which coral cover greatly declined following the 1998 bleaching event. These data were collected in 2002, hence some of the cover seen above 10 m was due to coral recruitment since the mortality. (Modified from Sheppard and Obura, 2005.)

The depths of these transition zones may be determined by post-hoc observations, but they show no obvious geographical pattern across the Indian Ocean (Table 8.1). Many reefs, especially on atolls, showed very high mortality to 10–12 m depth, while others, even in the same archipelago, showed near total mortality to over 40 m depth. All reefs may show patchiness, which illustrates the disadvantages of very brief surveys of perhaps just one site in a large region.

Insufficient data exist on real water temperature measurements at different depths to be certain, but it seems likely that the transition zone between where coral was largely killed and where it largely survived corresponded to a local thermocline that was established at the time of the peak or critical warming period. In the last few years several research groups have attached countless recording thermistors throughout the tropical seas, and it is hoped that enough will be recovered, unflooded, to provide useful information after the next large warming event.

Transition zones were not recorded for many of the sites from which heavy coral mortality has been reported. Many surveys simply reported mortality with no useful depth data. Many others reported coral cover from

Table 8.1. Depths in Indian Ocean atolls to which severely reduced coral cover was observed as a result of the mass bleaching event of 1998

Atoll	'Transition depth' (m)	Reference
Aldabra, Seychelles	8–12	Sheppard and Obura (2005)
Cosmoledo, Seychelles	8–12	Sheppard and Obura (2005)
Alphonse, Seychelles[a]	10–15	Spencer *et al.* (2000)
St Pierre, Seychelles[a]	10–15?	Spencer *et al.* (2000)
Seychelles, granitic islands	15	Turner *et al.* (2000)
Southern islands, Seychelles	10–20	Teleki *et al.* (2000); Teleki and Spencer (2000)
Mayotte	>30	Quod and Bigot (2000)
Masoala, Madagascar	10	D. Obura, pers. comm.
Felidu, Maldives	>30	McClanahan (2000)
Mulaku, Maldives	>30	McClanahan (2000)
North Malé, Maldives	>30	C. Anderson, pers. comm.
South Malé, Maldives	>30	C. Anderson, pers. comm. McClanahan (2000)
Ari, Maldives	>30	C. Anderson, pers. comm.
Vaavu, Maldives	>30	C. Anderson, pers. comm.
Addu, Maldives	6–10	C. Anderson, pers. comm.
Salomon, Chagos	8–15	Sheppard *et al.* (2002)
Peros Banhos, Chagos	8–15	Sheppard *et al.* (2002)
Great Chagos Bank (west)	>30	Sheppard *et al.* (2002)
Egmont, Chagos	>30	Sheppard *et al.* (2002)
Diego Garcia, Chagos	>30	Sheppard *et al.* (2002)
Northern Kenya, East Africa	10–15	Obura (2002)
Southern Kenya, East Africa	>20	Obura *et al.* (2000a)
East Africa mainland	15–20	Obura *et al.* (2000b)
Rodriguez	2.5	Turner, pers. comm.
Socotra	12–15	Turner, pers. comm.
Abu Dhabi, UAE[b]	3–5	Sheppard and Loughland (2002)

[a]Measurements were only taken at 10 and 15 m, so the 'transition depth' lies between these two values.
[b]In Arabian Gulf, the maximum depth in inshore sites is 12 m.
Source: Sheppard and Obura (2005).

a few depths only, such as from horizontal transects at 5 m and 20 m, and unfortunately, even where the shallower site exhibited very low cover and the deeper one high or normal cover, there may be no extractable information on where the amount of coral cover suddenly changed – or indeed whether the change was sudden. Given that many locations were surveyed only rarely, sometimes just once, this omission represents a loss of potentially important information – important because of issues of coral reservoirs and sources of larvae (see below).

Numerous researchers now make use of excellent SST data, updated regularly, which provide surface temperature over the entire ocean. The criticism may be made that these do not reflect the temperature of the water that actually surrounds most of the corals, below the surface skin of the sea. The fact that most SST values literally may only record the temperature of a thin surface film may be conveniently overlooked. This limitation may not matter on reef flats which, although sometimes the most extensive part from a planar perspective, are really only extreme and distorted peripheral 'outposts' of coral reefs, but it probably does matter greatly for the reef slopes where cover is high and diversity is greatest. The extent to which this misuse of the term 'surface' is important is debatable. Given the various depths of the transition zones observed post hoc (Table 8.1), it may be supposed that the SST could be taken as being a surrogate of, or may reflect in some close way, the temperature of a depth span of water which extends over the zone of killed corals. But this, as we have seen, is variable, extending to 10 m depth in some areas and to >40 m in others. Only post-hoc observation of how deep the transition zone actually extended can tell us how deep the 'surface' layer was at the important time. And here too, the actual value will not be the same as that at the surface itself where cooling rain, evaporation and surface warming have greatest and immediate effects. This difference may be important where attempts are made to transfer exactly measured 'surface' temperature values to laboratory aquaria for experimentation purposes.

Given the obvious point that different species are preferentially found at different depths on a reef, the consequences of different transition depths to overall coral composition are marked. Obligate shallow corals, of which there are many species, clearly were greatly reduced no matter how shallow the transition zone was (unless the reef escaped the warming impact entirely, which occurred in a few places). Obligate deep species, such as several leafy forms, may have escaped intact whatever the transition depth. But the majority of species thrive in intermediate depths, where illumination is sufficient and where sediment and wave action are not too great. These depths range between 5 to 20 m, depending on the area, and support the greatest coral diversity. This range encompasses the boundary between killed and not-killed, in the examples collated in Table 8.1. The effect of the mortality may therefore differ greatly between areas, and these differences may be one reason why it has not proved easy to deduce any sort of standard or consistent set of consequences to the 1998 severe mortality.

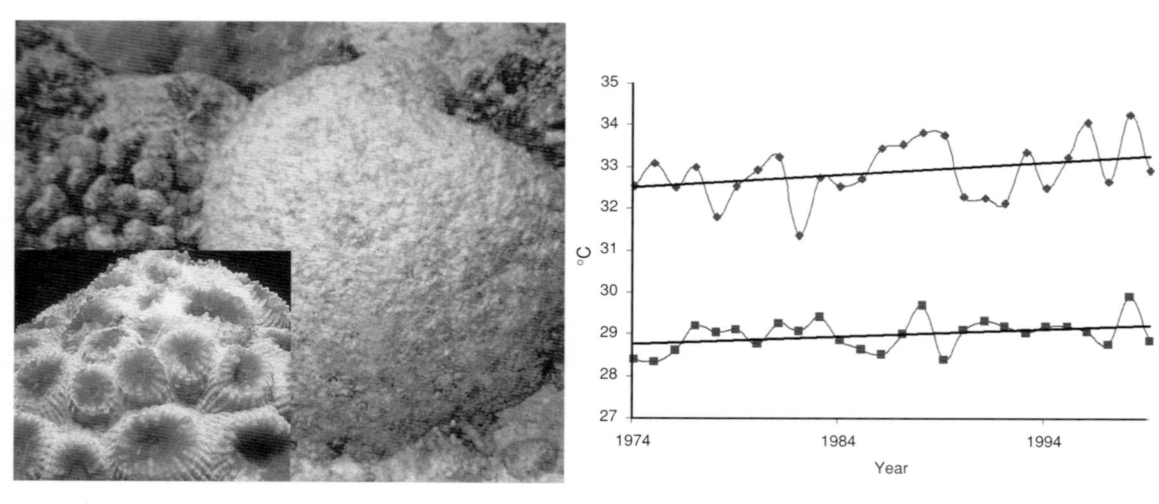

Figure 8.7 Sea surface temperatures for the warmest month of each year in the Arabian Gulf (Bahrain site; top trace) and Indian Ocean (Chagos site; bottom trace) from 1974 to 2000. Note that every year the Gulf values are at least 2.5°C warmer than the values that were lethal in the central Indian Ocean (about 30°C), yet about 50 Indian Ocean coral species thrived in the former for most of this period. Photos: the dead colony is an eroded *Favia pallida* in Chagos (1999); inset is a live coral of same species in Arabian waters. (See also Plate 8.7 in the colour plate section.)

THE SURVIVING SPECIES POOL AND CHANGES TO CORAL ASSEMBLAGES

The combination of differential sensitivity amongst species and different vertical extents of the 'killed zone' on different reefs produces a complex array of factors distorting the reef's surviving coral assemblage and future pool of planulae. Previous discussions of generalized effects of marine pollution on corals have tended to consider 'corals' or 'coral reefs' as a whole, without needing to differentiate between species at different depths. With temperature, this need is greater.

To this should be added another layer of complexity arising from different susceptibilities of different clades of zooxanthellae. It appears that the so-called clade D is more resistant to heat than others, and there are signs that this clade is increasing in frequency in reefs affected by bleaching at the expense of less tolerant but perhaps faster growing clades (Baker *et al.*, 2004). This fact probably lies behind many observations of acclimation in which it is observed that, for example, a common coral species such as *Favia pallida* can survive temperatures of 33 °C annually in the Arabian Gulf, but is killed at temperatures of below 30 °C in oceanic parts of the Indian Ocean (Fig. 8.7). Even within one atoll where a species' mortality on seaward slopes may have been nearly total, survival of the same species in the lagoon may have been 50%. The suggestion that survival in the lagoon presumably arose because of acclimation to warmer water was never more than a tautology; clade differences of the zooxanthellae may provide the explanation.

The important point is that the balance between species may change. Previously abundant species may become rare, as has happened in the Arabian Gulf. Even surviving adults appeared not to reproduce for a couple of years after 1998. Thus a hypothesis that arises from the interplay of differential susceptibility and depth is that there will be a shift in type of coral assemblage, given continued warming events. If numerical aspects of a population are a consequence of every species' life-history characters (reproduction rate, growth rate, aggressiveness, ability to crowd out or shade others, etc.), then reduction of major characteristics such as reproductive rates and mean size of live colonies would be expected to lead to a change in the equilibrium of the assemblage.

Evidence that such a shift in coral species composition is occurring comes from the Arabian Gulf, the sea which already is considerably warmer than most other places. Arabian Gulf reefs are relatively simple. Most are patch reefs, rising from depths of only about 12 m (Basson *et al.*, 1977).

Table 8.2. All coral species identified in 15 hrs of diving surveys in the Arabian Gulf in 2002. Species are categorized into three groups according to abundance. Prior to 1998, 50–70 species would have been expected in this region

Status 2–4 years after mortality	Species
Most abundant	*Porites nodifera* Klunz.
	Porites compressa Dana
	Porites lutea Ed. and Haime
Most new recruits	*Acropora cytherea* (Dana)
	Acropora pharaonis (Ed. and Haime)
	Favia speciosa (Dana)
	Favia pallida (Dana)
	Turbinaria mesenterina (Lam.)
Uncommon	*Acanthastrea echinata* (Dana)
	Anomastrea irregularis Marenz.
	Coscinarea monile (Forsk.)
	Cyphastrea serailia (Forsk.)
	Favia favus (Forsk.)
	Favites abdita (Ellis and Sol.)
	Platygyra daedalea (Ellis and Sol.)
	Plesiastrea versipora (Lam.)
	Siderastrea savignyana Ed. and Haime
	Acropora valenciennesi (Ed. and Haime)

Corals on reefs in the south (Qatar and Abu Dhabi) are organized into two main zones: a shallow zone to about 3 m dominated by *Acropora*, and a deeper zone dominated by *Porites*. Faviids are abundant throughout and a few species are endemic (Sheppard and Sheppard, 1991). These simple reefs have poor diversity compared to those of the Indian Ocean, showing a little more than 50 species. Warming in 1998 in Saudi Arabia, Bahrain, Qatar and the United Arab Emirates caused heavy or total mortality of corals on reefs to about 3 m depth, followed by lower mortality in deeper parts, the survivors being mainly large *Porites*. Most other genera were heavily affected. Following 1998, the shallow zone became vast plains of mobile stagshorn rubble, and corals are still absent from many such areas. *Acropora* also disappeared from the deeper zone, along with about half the other corals too. Table 8.2 shows all species seen in 15 hours of searching in Abu Dhabi's reefs four years later.

This Arabian transect produces information on changes in time and space (Fig. 8.8). The map (a) is overlaid with $1^\circ \times 1^\circ$ cells from which historical SST is available. The two right-hand panels of Fig. 8.8 (b and d) show

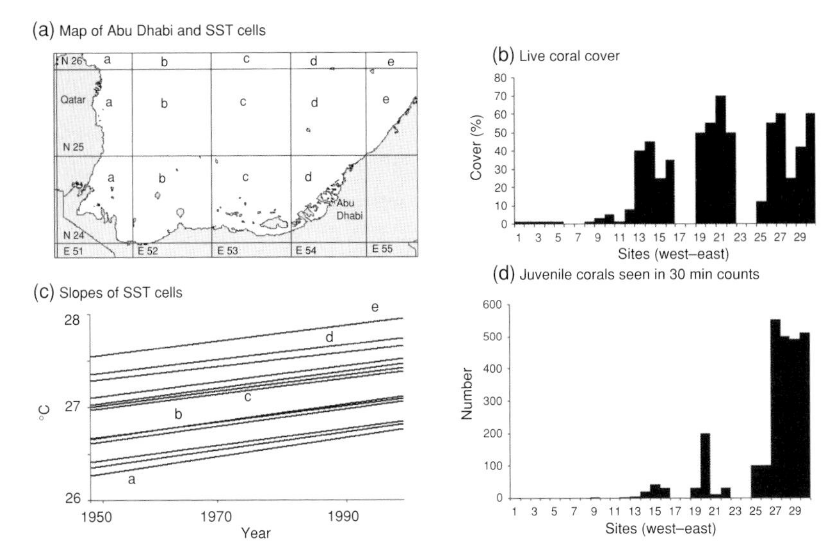

Figure 8.8 (a) Location of 500-km-long transect sampled across the Arabian Gulf in 1999. The grid marks cells of 1 degree of latitude and longitude, for each of which monthly SST data were taken. (b) Percentage live coral cover and (d) numbers of juvenile corals seen per 30-min survey, along the transect. A total of 30 sites were sampled. Sites in the histograms are arranged along a west-to-east axis. (c) Simple regression lines of SST vs. time from 1951 to 1999 for each of the 14 cells in the map. Lines in (c) marked a–e correspond to cells on the map with the same letter. Note that there are two lines 'e' directly superimposed on each other.

that coral survival, expressed as live coral cover, and numbers of juvenile corals (age <4 yr) were markedly higher towards the east along this coast (Sheppard and Loughland, 2002). This pattern of recovery can be related to the SST pattern. The SST in 14 1° × 1° cells was plotted over a 50-yr period for this area (Fig. 8.8c). For clarity, only lines of best fit are shown for each of the temperature curves; it should be noted that the summer–winter SST range here is in the order of 15 °C (air temperature range is nearly 25 °C). The pattern shows rising temperatures through the 50-yr series of about 0.2 °C per decade, but the rate of temperature increase has accelerated to about 0.45 °C per decade in the last 20 years.

In any one year, temperature increases towards the east. It can be seen that, broadly, the mean temperature field at any location is similar to that which is seen in the 1° × 1° cell immediately to its east approximately 30 years earlier. A basic anticlockwise water circulation pattern is presumed for the Gulf, and though this idea is not based on much measurement, the thermal pattern shown here supports it. The bay is large and shallow, and water has a known easterly drift along the coast of the United Arab Emirates, during which time it presumably warms slightly in summer. A further data point for this transect can be extracted from Riegl (1999) who surveyed in Dubai, about 50 km further east. The pattern and trend remain consistent.

Clearly, despite the overall warmer temperatures towards the east, conditions favoured corals there in terms of both survival and recruitment. Nowhere was there much *Acropora*, and in the west there was virtually no coral of any species. Neither was *Porites* well represented amongst new juveniles. By far the majority of new recruits were of *Favia speciosa* and the morphologically similar *F. pallida*, both widespread but previously scarce members of the Gulf community (Sheppard and Sheppard, 1991), which are now very abundant towards the east. During this survey, however, juveniles of these two species accounted for over 90% of the total numbers of new recruits. Many were located on dead *Acropora* tables, whose imminent collapse (many already had collapsed) suggests rather insecure prospects for the juveniles, but many had commenced growth on dead *Porites* and other massive species, or on other bare substrata, providing sometimes very high cover. The important point is that the warmer end of the transect (by about 1.5 °C and 30 years equivalent) has a richer coral assemblage, and one which has changed in composition.

Much has been made of the high survival of some genera, notably *Porites*. But although *Porites* was the best survivor in this Arabian Gulf transect, as it was throughout the Indo-Pacific, it was the dominant dead species in the Gulf below 4 m too; in terms of cover an average 33.2% ($\pm$ 14.9% SD, $n = 16$ locations) died in these waters. It was by no means unaffected.

In the Caribbean, coral mortality may lead to a phase shift, where algae replace corals as the dominant group resulting in an alternative community (Precht and Aronson, this volume). In the Arabian Gulf this shift has not happened. Even though the Arabian Gulf supports substantial areas of *Sargassum* and its relatives in locations where conditions preclude corals (Sheppard *et al.*, 1992), at the times of these surveys, these algae had not occupied the large expanses of dead corals. The replacement organisms here were different corals. Based on current colony densities, if even a small proportion of the new faviids continue to grow they will in due course rival *Porites* for dominance. The reasons remain unknown, but may be found in different levels of fecundity, competition or rates of change to more warm tolerant clades of zooxanthellae.

This change in species dominance may be extrapolated speculatively. Given a general warming SST trend throughout the Indo-Pacific, with recruitment skewed towards groups of survivor species which did not dominate previously, especially towards species found below any local thermocline or transition depth, the Arabian Gulf pattern may forecast the future nature of coral reefs over a wider area. Of course, acclimation may happen, but observations from the Seychelles in 2004 showed heavy mortality of new recruits, and in Chagos atolls the same year over 65% of newly recruited *Acropora* were strongly bleached, indicating both that the bleaching threshold had again been exceeded and that there has not been a conspicuous build-up of resistance to it yet.

The temperature pattern from most of these SST traces shows a rise starting in about 1970, and the ecological change arose from the 1998 event. Thus the last 30 years have been insufficient time to permit much acclimation, and if there has been any (see Baker *et al.*, 2004) it appears to have arisen from a massive mortality event, not from the preceding gradual rise in temperature.

CORAL MORTALITY AND WAVE ENERGY ACROSS REEF FLATS

The demise of the shallowest corals of all, on reef flats, may have marked physical consequences too. Reef flats and the reef crest provide the main break to the energy of oncoming waves. Its corals include species that are the least likely to recover. Following Gourlay's (1996a, 1996b, 1997) work on waves on reefs, Sheppard *et al.* (2005) have constructed a spreadsheet to compute wave energy striking a shore behind a reef flat, for a wide range of different situations, including those following coral mortality.

Propagation of wave energy onto shore is not straightforward: waves breaking at the edge of the reef create a water set-up, which in turn drives secondary wavelets, sometimes called solitons, towards the shore. One offshore wave may create a set-up which generates one, two or three wavelets. Apart from offshore wave height and periodicity, several variables affect wave energy transmission: width of the reef flat, depth of water over it, the angle of the reef slope where waves break and the roughness of the reef flat. Sheppard *et al.* (2005) hypothesized that the reduction of dead coral skeletons to rubble over the years following a mass mortality would drop the upper surface of the reef flat, thus effectively increasing still water depth. Furthermore, when previously rich and topographically complex corals were reduced to a planar expanse of rubble, then to sand and even to bare, underlying flat limestone, the roughness would also decline, leading to less friction. This scenario was examined on 14 reef flats in the

Figure 8.9 Typical reef flats in the Seychelles, 2004. (a) Beau Vallon, Mahé Island, reef flat 135 m wide on a low tide. (b) Praslin Island, reef flat 205 m wide. (c) La Digue reef flat 225 m wide. (d) The narrow reef flat at Fisherman's Cove, Mahé, 65 m wide. All photos taken on calm days to show waves breaking at the edge of the reef flat. The darker patches under water are seagrasses near shore, and dead coral further out. (Photographs by the author.) (See also Plate 8.9 in the colour plate section.)

Seychelles. Complications to this work were that each reef flat was composed of several zones between shore and reef crest, the outer ones usually supporting corals (or dead coral skeletons) and the inner ones supporting seagrass beds, sand or rubble. This complication was only one of detail, however, requiring numerous subunits to be measured and averaged, the average values then being input into the reef flat model.

Within the variable water depth, we added sea-level rise. True sea-level rise is a minor component compared with the 'pseudo-sea-level rise' caused by the drop in the reef flat in zones where coral skeletons were being eliminated, but is still an appreciable addition with clear effects (Woodworth *et al.*, 2004). Seagrasses were assumed to keep up with real sea-level rise. For areas of sand and rubble we assumed (in the absence of usable data) a 'default' value in which these zones stayed the same throughout. Any variable can be changed according to preference, and the model is available on the 'Research' tab in Sheppard (2005). The variables and results that

Figure 8.10 Dead reefs of the Seychelles, 2004. (a) Edge of expanse of dead branching *Porites* coral on a Seychelles reef flat. Some tips are living, mainly new recruits but possibly with some older survivors; most of the top is now covered with the alga *Turbinaria*. The packed branches extend about 0.6 m above the sand-covered platform. (b) Edge of expanse of dead branching *Acropora* staghorn coral on a Seychelles reef flat. These packed branches extend about 0.5 m above the platform. (c) Seagrass bed on reef flat. Seagrass is assumed in this model to be able to keep up with sea-level rise and appears to be doing so. (d) Fringing reef crest, showing lack of live coral and eroding surface with a rounded reef crest. Prior to the coral mortality of 1998, reef crests supported live coral which grew to approximately the low-tide level where they formed a steep slope and sharp angle. (See also Plate 8.10 in the colour plate section.)

we calculated, assumed or otherwise selected are also available, as are all parameter test results (Sheppard *et al.*, 2005).

The Seychelles reefs are an important and economically valuable national resource (Fig. 8.9). Many reef flats were, before 1998, covered with 0.5-m-high thickets of staghorn corals which reached low tide level, but which now are largely dead (Fig. 8.10a, b). For each reef, two time periods in addition to the present were estimated or measured: a time approximately a decade ago when reef flat corals were healthy and still reached low-water level, and a time about a decade in the future when skeleton disintegration has progressed to its endpoint. The progression assumed is shown in Fig. 8.11 and the term 'decade' is not intended to be precise. Offshore

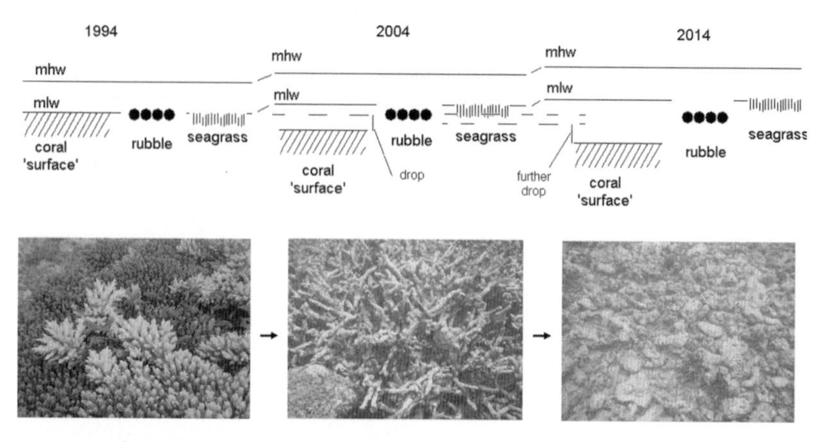

Figure 8.11 Top: Schematic of progression of change on reef flats as a result of bleaching-induced coral mortality (mhw, mean high water; mlw, mean low water). Bottom: examples of conditions seen (corals only) at each step of the degradation process. (See also Plate 8.11 in the colour plate section.)

wave height was kept standard at 1.25 m, and periodicity was 5.2 s throughout, both being mean annual values for the Seychelles (Voluntary Observing Ship programme and South African Data Centre for Oceanography). Figure 8.12a shows the percentage of offshore energy reaching shore, averaged for all 14 reefs, for a decade ago, for the present time and for a decade in future. Although the main variable controlling energy is width of reef flat, which remains the same throughout, changes in water depth and reef roughness due to coral mortality nevertheless result in marked increases in transmitted energy over time. This may also be expressed as percentage change compared to the present (Fig. 8.12c). On any one reef, transmitted energy has approximately doubled over the past decade, but is expected to increase by twice that amount over the next decade (assuming new coral growth continues to be suppressed on the reef flats). Following the energy changes to date, effects on shores have become of considerable concern (Fig. 8.12b, d); the further doubling in energy in the next decade may be increasingly damaging.

Several interesting and sometimes counter-intuitive results arise from the model. One comes from the change in slope in the wave-breaking area; with crest coral mortality, a slight rounding-off of the wave breaking zone reduces the rise in energy transmission, i.e. it had an opposite or moderating effect. Another point is that the greater wave energy generated may increase the quantity of sand pushed towards islands, countering erosion for as long as there is a supply of increased sand production from

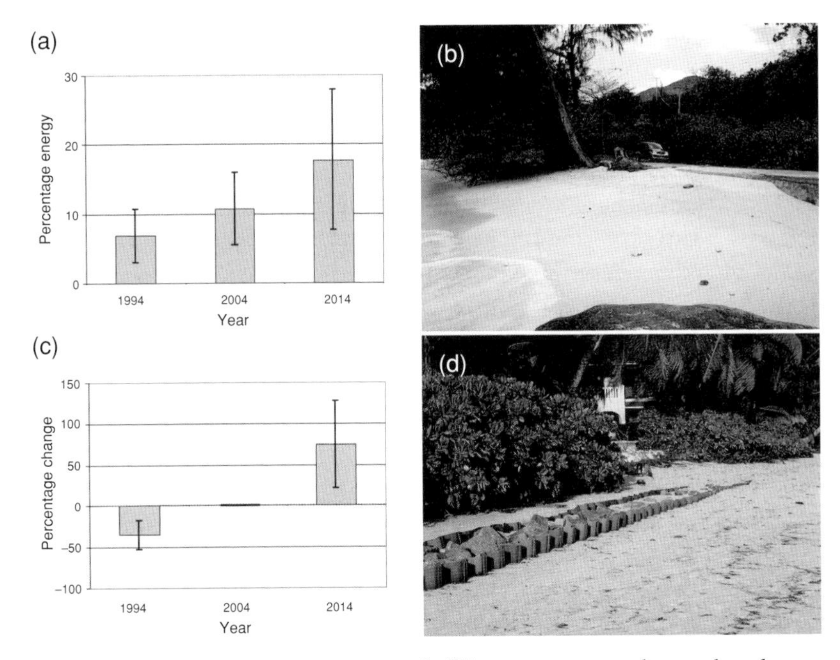

Figure 8.12 (a) Average percentage of offshore wave energy that reaches shores in three different decades. Average values of 14 reefs; bars are standard deviations. (b) Increased energy changes pumping increased sand production onto a road. (c) Percentage changes in wave energy reaching shores compared to the present. The zero on the y axis represents 2004. Average of all 14 reefs; bars are standard deviations. The shores behind these reefs are now receiving, on average, 35% more wave energy than 10 years ago. Wave energy is projected to increase by 75% in the next decade, owing to coral mortality and reef degradation. (d) Emergency steel pilings inserted on beach by a hotel to resist erosion. Note elevation of the hotel. (See also Plate 8.12 in the colour plate section.)

dead coral colonies (D. Hopley, pers. comm.). This effect, however, may not last beyond the final disintegration of the dead colonies, as erosion of the underlying platform will be slower than that of the friable coral colonies.

Stormy conditions drive major changes to shores, of course, but persistent increases in wave energy of a lesser amount are likely to both maintain any storm-induced changes and to promote them further. What happens to any shore which is struck by a doubling of wave energy depends of course on what the shore is made of; the granitic shores of the Seychelles may not suffer noticeably, but limestone, and especially sandy shores, can change markedly. Stories of undermined roads and property along limestone shores from the Caribbean to the Pacific are numerous and increasing, while sandy beaches of a 'classical' sort are subjected to something approximating the Brunn rule (Brunn, 1962, 1988; Brunn and Schwartz, 1985; Leatherman *et al.*, 2000). This rule states, and demonstrates, that horizontal loss can be approximately two orders of magnitude greater than vertical sea-level rise, common multiples being of the order of $\times 150$. This extent of loss is more than enough to remove all sand from a tourist beach, exposing the jagged karst rock beneath. Since waves are so important in determining the very existence and survival of a coral cay, partly from sand pumping (Gourlay, 1988), the increase in energy resulting from sea-level rise and from coral mortality may prove to be critical.

CONCLUSIONS

In conclusion, the potential for medium- to long-term change to coral communities and to reefs is clear, given continuing temperature-induced coral mortality. However, reef growth and coral colony growth are not the same thing. Vertical reef accretion may be about 4 mm yr^{-1} (Buddemeier and Smith, 1988) which, if sustained, is generally sufficient to cope with sea level rise. Brown (1997) noted that values of reef accretion range from 1 to 10 mm yr^{-1} and that a sea-level rise of more than this upper value may result in reef 'drowning'. She pointed out, however, that annual and inter-annual variations in sea level may be up to 30 cm, so that several years of background sea-level rise would be needed before much effect would be noticed. The values of reef drop (causing pseudo-sea-level rise) following just one episode of lethal warming noted here are considerably greater in extent.

Heavy mortality of the shallow corals changes this balance between reef growth and reduction. Perhaps the earliest example of what this change can mean comes from Panama (Eakin, 1992) where a reef which had been depositing about 10 t $CaCO_3$ ha^{-1} yr^{-1} is now eroding at about 2.5 t $CaCO_3$ ha^{-1} yr^{-1}, which equates to a vertical loss of about 6 mm yr^{-1}. This reversal followed a 50% coral mortality after the 1982 El Niño. Removal of substantial amounts of material from the top of a reef can have the same effect as a sea-level rise of an equivalent amount. In many countries, notably the Maldives' capital city of Malé and southwest Sri Lanka, mining of reef material for limestone can remove as much as 0.5 m over extensive parts of the reef flat. The pseudo-sea-level rise that this extraction has created has led to erosion of the shoreline and property upon it. Mortality of corals as a result of warming is creating drops of nearly equal depth but over very much greater areas.

The changes we may expect over the next few years, therefore, may be substantial. These include ecological and productivity distortions which may come about from community and biodiversity changes, as well as consequences to shorelines formerly protected by thriving reefs. The present paper has focused upon benthic changes acting on corals and on consequences from mortality of the latter, but several other related and undoubtedly important issues have been less well studied. Less work has been done, but is badly needed, for example, on soft corals which are another major occupier of reef space. The mortality of these related cnidarians was as extensive as it was for stony corals, in the Indian Ocean at least, and personal observations in the latter area suggest that recovery of soft corals has been less successful than it has for stony corals, leaving areas still largely devoid of either forms. Regarding fishes, while initial observations in the badly affected Chagos Archipelago suggested that changes to that group in the first few years were not very dramatic (Sheppard *et al.*, 2002), more recent observations there suggest that where reefs have now been reduced to planar, two-dimensional surfaces instead of rugose, three-dimensional structures, fish *quantity* has recently become considerably reduced (unpublished observations). This reduction in associated groups, many not researched in detail at all, should not be a surprise to anyone, including decision-makers and politicians. To use a terrestrial analogy helpful to the latter group, if a rainforest is felled, the birds and monkeys eventually disappear too; this is becoming clear on many reefs worldwide and we expect a number of quantitative studies documenting this in the near future. One of the clearest conclusions that can be made from these results is that current responses by decision-makers to the changes that are occurring lag woefully behind the rates of change themselves, yet considerable management activity is now needed to counter, where possible, some of the deleterious consequences that are resulting from changes on coral reefs.

REFERENCES

Baker, A. C., Starger, C. J., McClanahan, T. T. and Glynn, P. W. (2004). Coral's adaptive response to climate change. *Nature*, **430**, 741.

Basson, P. W., Burchard, J. E., Hardy, J. T. and Price, A. R. G. (1977). *Biotopes of the Western Arabian Gulf.* Dhahran: Aramco.

Brown, B. E. (1997). Disturbances to reefs in recent times. In *Life and Death of Coral Reefs*, ed. C. Birkeland, pp. 354–78. New York: Chapman and Hall.

Brunn, P. (1962). Sea level rise as a cause of shore erosion. *American Society of Civil Engineers Proceedings, Journal of Waterways and Harbors Division*, **88**, 117–30.

1988. The Brunn Rule of erosion by sea-level rise: a discussion on large-scale two and three-dimensional usages. *Journal of Coastal Research*, **4**, 627–48.

Brunn, P. and Schwartz, M. L. (1985). Analytical predictions of beach profile change in response to a sea level rise. *Zeitschrift für Geomorphologie N.F. Supplement*, **57**, 33–50.
Buddemeier, R. W. and Smith, S. V. (1988). Coral reef growth in an era of rapidly rising sea level: predictions and suggestions for long term research. *Coral Reefs*, **7**, 51–6.
Cubasch, U., Meehl, G. A. and Boer, G. L. (2001). Projections of future climate change. In *Climate Change 2001: The Scientific Basis*, ed. Intergovernmental Panel on Climate Change, pp. 525–82. Cambridge: Cambridge University Press.
Douglas, A. W. (2003). Coral bleaching: how and why? *Marine Pollution Bulletin*, **46**, 385–92.
Eakin, C. M. (1996). Where have all the carbonates gone? A model comparison of calcium carbonate budgets before and after the 1982–1983 El Niño at Uva Island in the Eastern Pacific. *Coral Reefs*, **15**, 109–19.
Gates, R. D. and Edmunds, P. J. (1999). The physiological mechanisms of acclimatisation in tropical reef corals. *American Zoologist*, **39**, 30–43.
Gourlay, M. R. (1988). Coral cays: products of wave action and geological processes in a biogenic environment. *Proceedings 6th International Coral Reef Symposium*, **2**, 491–6.
(1996a). Wave set-up on coral reefs. I. Set-up and wave generated flow on an idealized two dimensional horizontal reef. *Coastal Engineering*, **27**, 161–93.
(1996b). Wave set-up on coral reefs. II. Set-up on reefs with various profiles. *Coastal Engineering*, **28**, 17–55.
(1997). Wave set-up on coral reefs: some practical applications. In *Proceedings 13th Australian Coastal and Ocean Engineering Conference*, pp. 959–64.
Hoegh-Guldberg, O. (1999). Climate change, coral bleaching and the future of the world's coral reefs. *Marine and Freshwater Research*, **50**, 839–66.
Hughes, T. P., Baird, A. H., Bellwood, D. R. *et al.* (2003). Climate change, human impacts, and the resilience of coral reefs. *Science*, **301**, 929–33.
Kinsman, D. J. J. (1964). Reef coral tolerance of high temperatures and salinities. *Nature*, **202**, 1280–2.
Leatherman S. P., Zhang, K. and Douglas, B. (2000). Sea level rise shown to drive coastal erosion. *Eos*, **81**, 55–7.
Loch, K., Loch, W., Schumacher, H. and See, W. (2002). Coral recruitment and regeneration on a Maldivian reef 21 months after the coral bleaching event of 1998. *Marine Ecology*, **23**, 219–36.
McAvaney, B. J., Covery, C. and Joussaume, S. (2001). Model evaluation. In *Climate Change 2001: The Scientific Basis*, ed. Intergovernmental Panel on Climate Change, pp. 471–523. Cambridge: Cambridge University Press.
McClanahan, T. R. (2000). Bleaching damage and recovery potential of Maldivian coral reefs. *Marine Pollution Bulletin*, **40**, 587–97.
(2004). The relationship between bleaching and mortality of common corals. *Marine Biology*, **144**, 1239–45.
Obura, D. (2002). Status of coral reefs in Kiunga Marine Reserve, Kenya. In *Coral Reef Degradation in the Indian Ocean: Status Report 2002*, eds. O. Linden, D. Souter, D. Wilhelmsson and D. Obura, pp. 47–54. Kalmar, Sweden: CORDIO.

Obura, D., Suleiman, M., Motta, H. and Schleyer, M. (2000a). East Africa. In *Status of Coral Reefs of the World: 2000*, ed. C. Wilkinson, pp. 65–76. Townsville, QLD: Australian Institute of Marine Science.
Obura, D., Uku, J. N., Wawiye, O. P., Mwachireya, S. and Mdodo, R. (2000b). Kenya: reef status and ecology. In *Coral Reef Degradation in the Indian Ocean*, eds. D. Souter, D. Obura and O. Linden, pp. 25–34. Stockholm: CORDIO.
Pittock, A. B. (1999). Coral reefs and environmental change: adaptation to what? *American Zoologist*, **39**, 10–29.
Quod, J.-P. and Bigot, L. (2000). Coral bleaching in the Indian Ocean islands: ecological consequences and recovery in Madagascar, Comoros, Mayotte and Reunion. In *Coral Reef Degradation in the Indian Ocean*, eds. D. Souter, D. Obura and O. Linden, pp. 108–13. Stockholm: CORDIO.
Rayner, N. A., Parker, D. E., Horton, E. B. *et al.* (2003). Global analyses of SST, sea ice and night marine air temperature since the late nineteenth century. *Journal of Geophysical Research, Atmospheres*, **108**, 440–7.
Riegl, B. (1999). Corals in a non-reef setting in the southern Arabian Gulf (Dubai, UAE): fauna and community structure in response to mass mortality. *Coral Reefs*, **18**, 63–73.
(2002). Effects of the 1996 and 1998 positive sea-surface temperature anomalies on corals, coral diseases and fish in the Arabian Gulf (Dubai, UAE). *Marine Biology*, **140**, 29–40.
Sheppard, C. R. C. (1999a). Changes in some weather patterns in Chagos over 25 years. In *Ecology of the Chagos Archipelago*, vol. 2, eds. C. R. C. Sheppard and M. R. D. Seaward, pp. 45–52. London: Linnean Society.
(1999b). Changes in coral cover on reefs of Chagos over 18 years. In *Ecology of the Chagos Archipelago*, vol. 2, eds. C. R. C. Sheppard and M. R. D. Seaward, pp. 91–100. London: Linnean Society.
(2003). Predicted recurrences of mass coral mortality in the Indian Ocean. *Nature*, **425**, 294–7.
(2004). Sea surface temperature 1871–2099 in 14 cells around the United Kingdom. *Marine Pollution Bulletin*, **49**, 12–16.
(2005). SST dataset and energy models. Available online at http://www.bio.warwick.ac.uk/res/frame.asp?ID=42.
Sheppard, C. R. C. and Loughland, R. (2002). Coral mortality and recovery in response to increasing temperature in the southern Arabian Gulf. *Aquatic Ecosystem Health Management*, **5**, 395–402.
Sheppard, C. R. C. and Obura, D. (2005). Corals and reefs of Cosmoledo and Aldabra atolls: extent of damage, assemblage shifts and recovery following the severe mortality of 1998. *Journal of Natural History*, **39**, 103–21.
Sheppard, C. R. C. and Rioja-Nieto, R. (2005). Sea surface temperature 1871–2099 in 38 cells in the Caribbean region. *Marine Environments Research*, **60**, 389–96.
Sheppard C. R. C. and Sheppard, A. L S. (1991). Corals and coral communities of Arabia, *Fauna of Saudi Arabia*, **12**, 7–192.
Sheppard, C. R. C., Price, A. R. G. and Roberts, C. J. (1992). *Marine Ecology of the Arabian Area: Patterns and Processes in Extreme Tropical Environments*. London: Academic Press.

Sheppard, C. R. C., Spalding, M., Bradshaw, C. and Wilson, S. (2002). Erosion vs. recovery of coral reefs after 1998 El Niño: Chagos reefs, Indian Ocean. *Ambio*, **31**, 40–8.
Sheppard, C. R. C., Dixon, D. J., Gourlay, M., Sheppard, A. L. S. and Payet, R. (2005). Coral mortality increases wave energy reaching shores behind reef flats: examples from the Seychelles. *Estuarine, Coastal and Shelf Science* in press.
Spencer, T., Teleki, K. A., Bradshaw, C. and Spalding, M. D. (2000). Coral bleaching in the southern Seychelles during the 1997–1998 Indian Ocean warming event. *Marine Pollution Bulletin*, **40**, 569–86.
Teleki, K. A. and Spencer T. (2000). Reef systems of the islands of the southern Seychelles. In *Coral Reef Degradation in the Indian Ocean*, eds. D. Souter, D. Obura and O. Linden, pp. 87–93. Stockholm: CORDIO.
Teleki, K. A., Downing N., Stobart R. and Buckley R. (2000). The status of the Aldabra atoll coral reefs and fishes following the 1998 coral bleaching event. In *Coral Reef Degradation in the Indian Ocean: Status Report 2000*, eds. D. Souter, D. Obura and O. Linden, pp. 114–23. Stockholm: CORDIO.
Turner, J., Klaus, R. and Englehardt, U. (2000). The reefs of the granitic islands of the Seychelles. In *Coral Reef Degradation in the Indian Ocean*, eds. D. Souter, D. Obura and O. Linden, pp. 77–86. Stockholm: CORDIO.
Woodworth, P. L., Gregory, J. M. and Nicholls, R. J. (2004). Long term sea level changes and their impacts. In *The Sea*, vol. 13, eds. A. R. Robinson, J. McCarthy and B. J. Rothschild, pp. 717–52. Cambridge, MA: Harvard University Press.

Plate 2.4 Underwater photograph taken at the Long-Term Study (LTS) reef at 6 m depth on the West Fore Reef at Discovery Bay, Jamaica, in March 2004. Recovery of the herbivorous sea urchin *Diadema antillarum* has reduced macroalgal cover from $>60\%$ to $<5\%$, while increasing the cover of crustose coralline algae and the abundance of coral recruits on a substratum of *Acropora* rubble. In the last few years there has been a conspicuous increase in recruits of *A. palmata*, one of which appears in the centre of the photograph.

Plate 2.5 Underwater photograph of *Acropora cervicornis* thickets filling in the voids between large, century-old colonies of *Montastraea annularis* at ~6 m depth at Dairy Bull Reef, Jamaica, in July 2003. The view in this photograph is reminiscent of the coral assemblage of the north coast of Jamaica in the 1960s and 1970s. This reef has shown dramatic increases in coral cover and reductions in macroalgae in the past few years, coincident with the recovery of *Diadema antillarum* and in the near-absence of herbivorous fish.

Plate 3.1 Ikonos satellite image of Andros (Bahamas) showing a mangrove-lined coastal creek (left inset), a lagoon with seagrass beds (right inset) and patch reefs, and an outer reef crest with *Montastraea* reef to the seaward edge of the image (middle inset).

Plate 4.1 Model of a cold-water reef, composed of various underwater photos taken on Norwegian *Lophelia* reefs. (Courtesy of Fosså *et al.*, 2000.)

Plate 4.2 Living *Lophelia pertusa* colonies on top of a Norwegian reef. (Courtesy of André Freiwald, IPAL-Erlangen.)

Plate 4.4 (a) Intact reef. (Courtesy of the JAGO-Team.) (b) Reef after a trawl has passed. (Courtesy of Fosså *et al.*, 2002.) (c) Coral caught in trawl gear. (Courtesy of Jim Reid, DFO-Canada.) (d) Lost net on reef. (Courtesy of IFREMER, ARK-19/3a, 2003.)

Plate 4.4 (*cont.*)

Plate 4.4 (*cont.*)

Plate 4.4 (*cont.*)

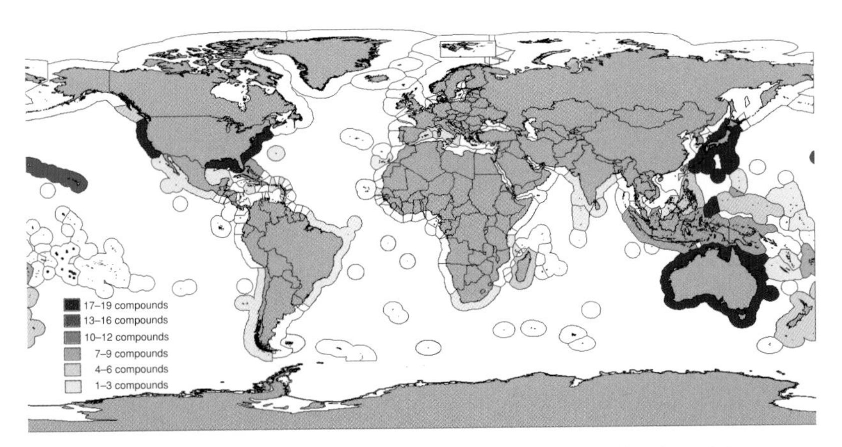

Plate 6.15 Distribution and number of novel marine compounds. The origin (recorded as national exclusive economic zones (EEZs)), and number of novel marine compounds sampled from the literature (American Chemical Society Database) are used as surrogates for location and relative intensity of bioprospecting activity. The data suggest that collection is focused on countries with coral reefs and the national waters of countries that conduct research into marine natural products. (Source: Hunt and Vincent, in press.)

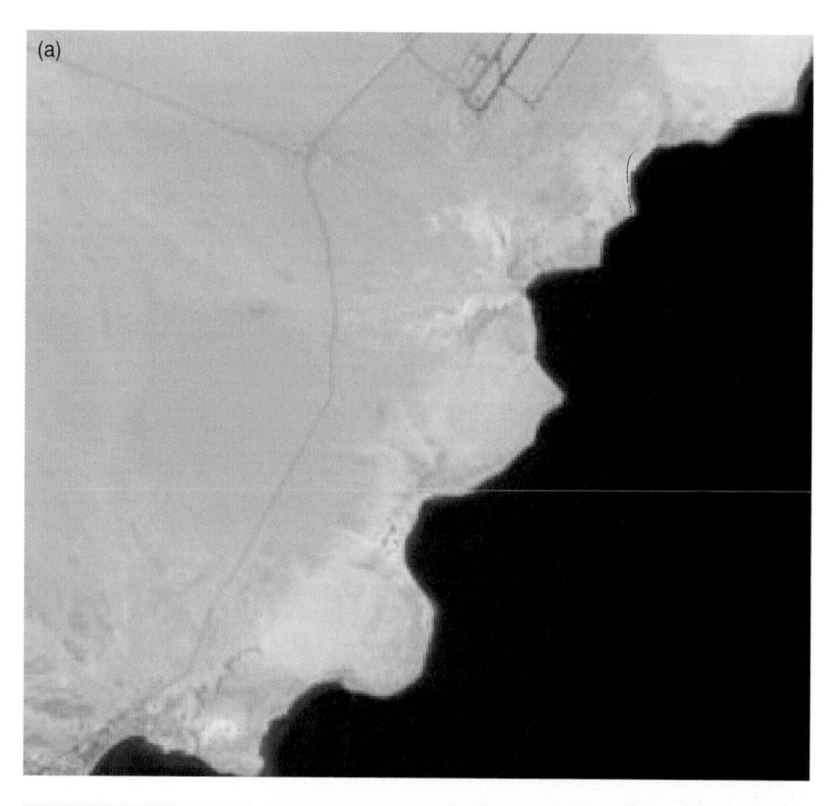

Plate 7.1 Area between Na'ama Bay and Sharm el Sheikh Airport in (a) the late 1980s and (b) 2004. (Sources: (a) Ras Mohamed National Park; (b) Support for Environmental Assessment and Management 2004.)

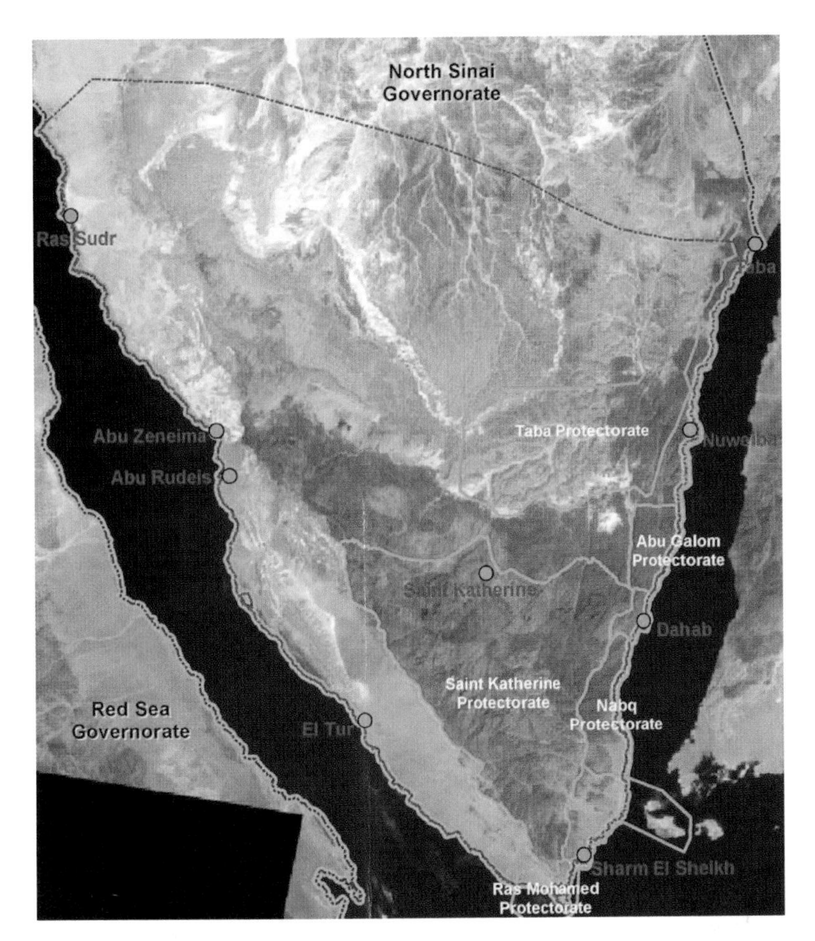

Plate 7.4 Protectorates and major cities of South Sinai. (Source: Support for Environmental Assessment and Management, 2004.)

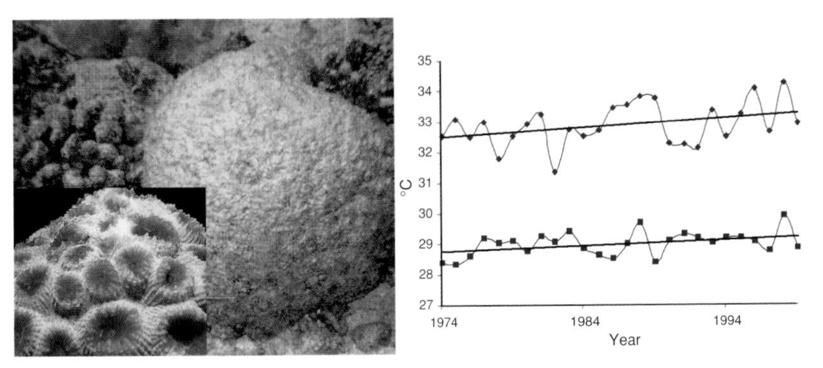

Plate 8.7 Sea surface temperatures for the warmest month of each year in the Arabian Gulf (Bahrain site; top trace) and Indian Ocean (Chagos site; bottom trace) from 1974 to 2000. Note that every year the Gulf values are at least 2.5°C warmer than the values that were lethal in the central Indian Ocean (about 30°C), yet about 50 Indian Ocean coral species thrived in the former for most of this period. Photos: the dead colony is an eroded *Favia pallida* in Chagos (1999); inset is a live coral of same species in Arabian waters.

Plate 8.9 Typical reef flats in the Seychelles, 2004. (a) Beau Vallon, Mahé Island, reef flat 135 m wide on a low tide. (b) Praslin Island, reef flat 205 m wide. (c) La Digue reef flat 225 m wide. (d) The narrow reef flat at Fisherman's Cove, Mahé, 65 m wide. All photos taken on calm days to show waves breaking at the edge of the reef flat. The darker patches under water are seagrasses near shore, and dead coral further out. (Photographs by the author.)

Plate 8.10 Dead reefs of the Seychelles, 2004. (a) Edge of expanse of dead branching *Porites* coral on a Seychelles reef flat. Some tips are living, mainly new recruits but possibly with some older survivors; most of the top is now covered with the alga *Turbinaria*. The packed branches extend about 0.6 m above the sand-covered platform. (b) Edge of expanse of dead branching *Acropora* staghorn coral on a Seychelles reef flat. These packed branches extend about 0.5 m above the platform. (c) Seagrass bed on reef flat. Seagrass is assumed in this model to be able to keep up with sea-level rise and appears to be doing so. (d) Fringing reef crest, showing lack of live coral and eroding surface with a rounded reef crest. Prior to the coral mortality of 1998, reef crests supported live coral which grew to approximately the low-tide level where they formed a steep slope and sharp angle.

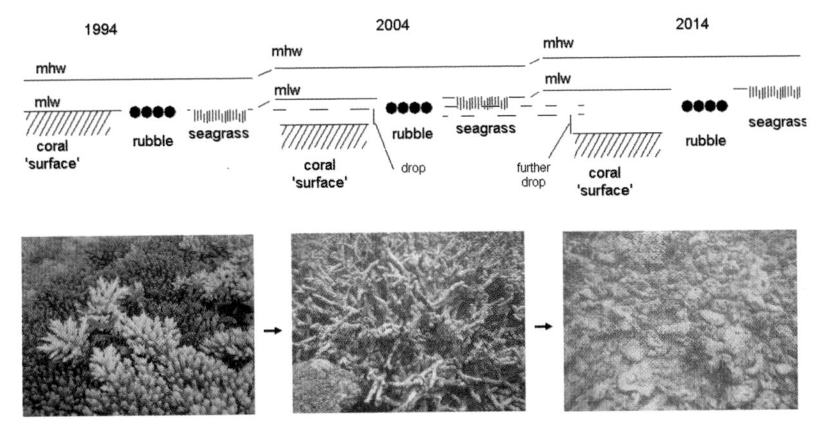

Plate 8.11 Top: Schematic of progression of change on reef flats as a result of bleaching-induced coral mortality (mhw, mean high water; mlw, mean low water). Bottom: examples of conditions seen (corals only) at each step of the degradation process.

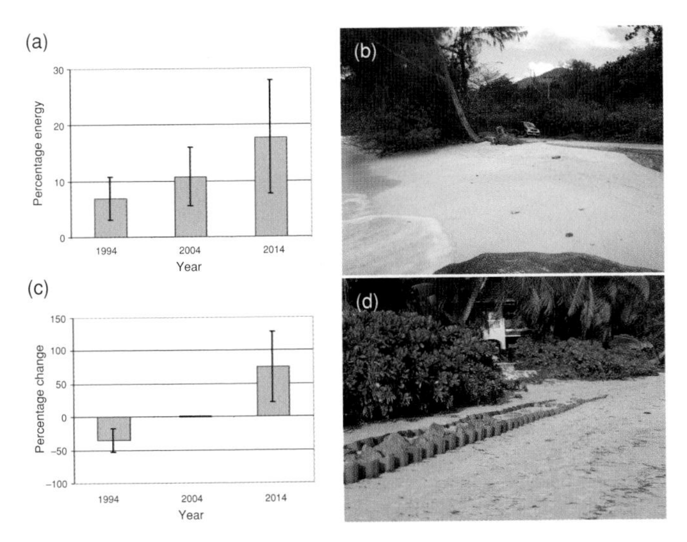

Plate 8.12 (a) Average percentage of offshore wave energy that reaches shores in three different decades. Average values of 14 reefs; bars are standard deviations. (b) Increased energy changes pumping increased sand production onto a road. (c) Percentage changes in wave energy reaching shores compared to the present. The zero on the y axis represents 2004. Average of all 14 reefs; bars are standard deviations. The shores behind these reefs are now receiving, on average, 35% more wave energy than 10 years ago. Wave energy is projected to increase by 75% in the next decade, owing to coral mortality and reef degradation. (d) Emergency steel pilings inserted on beach by a hotel to resist erosion. Note elevation of the hotel.

Plate 10.3 Implementation team for assessment of management effectiveness of Malindi Marine Park, Kenya. (Photograph by Sue Wells.)

Plate 10.4 Meeting with fishers at Kisite Marine Park, Kenya to review preliminary results of assessment of MPA management effectiveness. (Photograph by Sue Wells.)

Plate 10.5 Local communities such as this women's group in the village adjacent to Kisite Marine Park, Kenya, were very positive about the assessment of MPA management effectiveness. (Photograph by Sue Wells.)

Plate 10.7 Coral mining at Mnazi Bay-Ruvuma Estuary Marine Park, Tanzania. (Photograph by Sue Wells.)

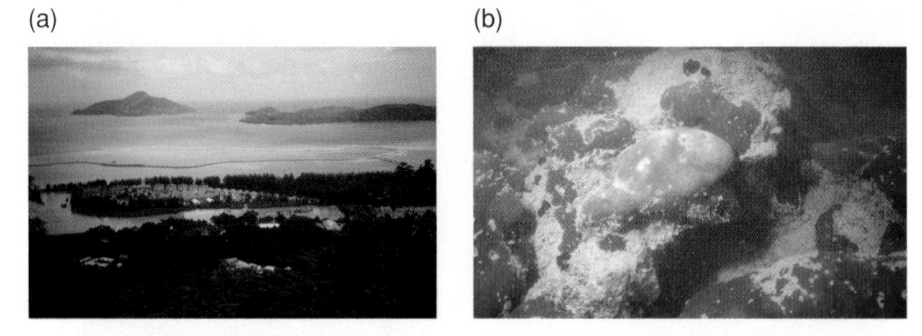

Plate 11.2 (a) Land reclamation on inshore coral reefs between the main island of Mahé and Ste Anne's Marine Park, Seychelles in 1999. (b) Coral covered in sediment in the Marine Park. Mitigation measures should have been proposed in the EIA and put in place to prevent sediment from drifting into the Marine Park because of its high tourism value.

Plate 11.3 The 'environmental attributes' assessed by EIA include (a) coral reef fauna and flora and (b) cultural heritage, such as this temple and arch constructed out of coral. The 'environmental elements' assessed within each attribute include penetration of light and movement of water, essential to reef processes in (a).

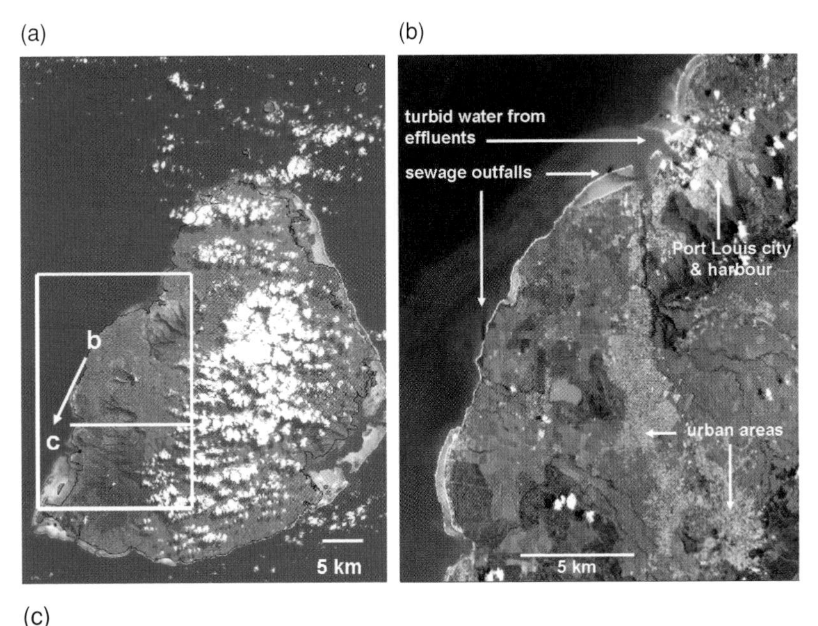

(c)

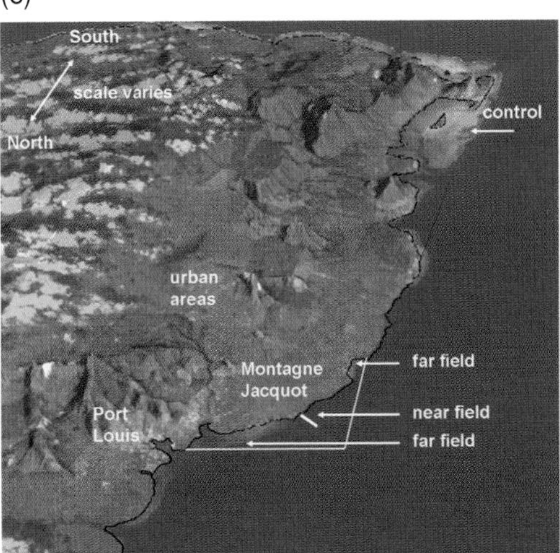

Plate 11.5 (a) Landsat satellite imagery of Mauritius showing coral reefs and lagoon areas. Boxes (b) and (c) (with arrow showing angle of view) are enlarged in the corresponding images. (b) Turbid water extending south along the coastline from Port Louis and existing sewage discharges serving urban areas. (c) Three-dimentional view from north looking south along west coast to show position of the new outfall, predicted mixing zone and near field, far field and control site locations used in the monitoring.

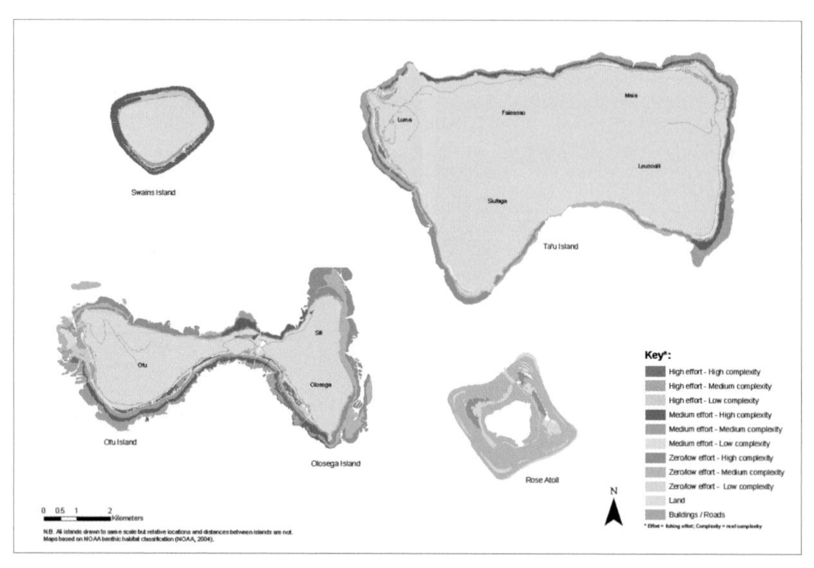

Plate 12.4 Map showing spatial variation in direct use fishery (subsistence and artisanal) values for four islands in American Samoa. (From Spurgeon *et al.*, 2004.)

Plate 16.4 (a) Divers removing rubble debris from a reef and (b) loading debris into metal baskets for transport away from the reef, Broward County, Florida, 2004. (Photographs by Richard Shaul.)

Plate 16.4 (*cont.*)

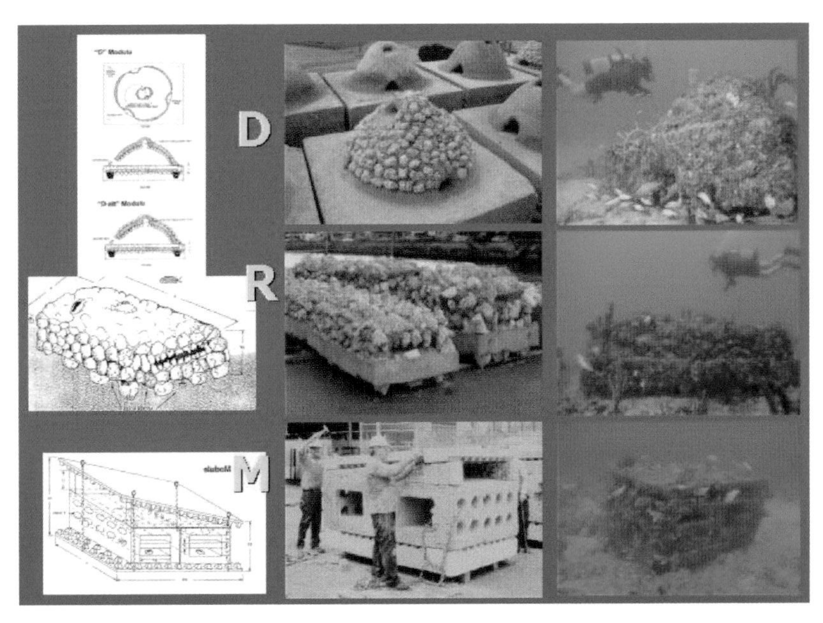

Plate 16.6 Reef restoration modules used to restore an area off Miami Beach, 1991. D, Dome; R, Reef module; M, Motel. D and R designed by Harold Hudson, US Patent #5215406. (Images courtesy of Miami-Dade County, Florida.)

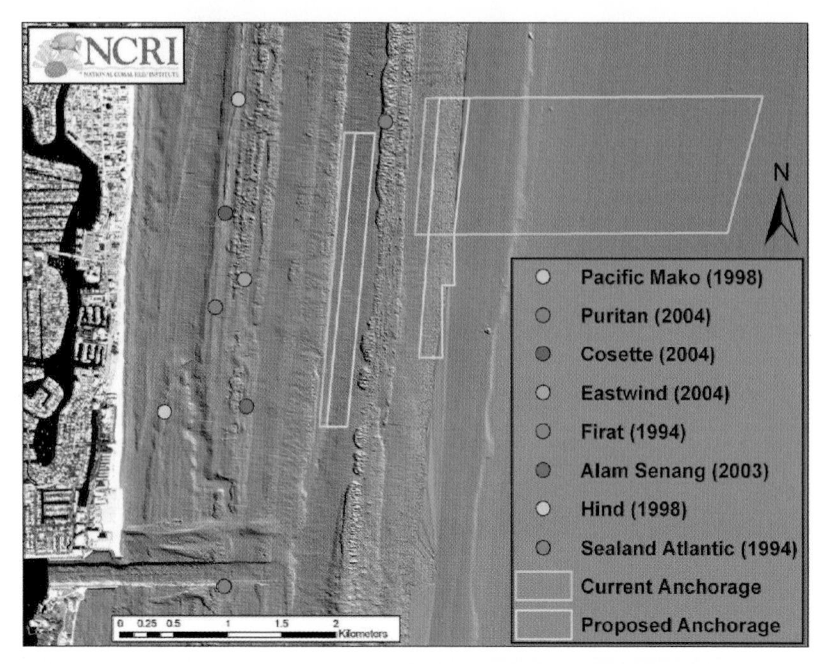

Plate 16.7 Map of coast of Broward County, Florida, identifying multiple ship mishaps, 1994–2004. The symbols indicate the positions of the ships. The anchorage and recommended changes are displayed in yellow and blue lines, respectively.

PART III

The way forward: tools and approaches

9

New approaches to estimating recent ecological changes on coral reefs

ISABELLE M. CÔTÉ
Simon Fraser University

TOBY A. GARDNER
University of East Anglia

JENNIFER A. GILL
University of East Anglia

DAVID J. HUTCHINSON
University of Liverpool

ANDREW R. WATKINSON
University of East Anglia

INTRODUCTION

Things are getting worse. Few conservation biologists would dispute this statement, but one of the major obstacles to understanding exactly how poorly nature is faring is the paucity of data on trends in the state of natural habitats, particularly at the global scale (Balmford *et al.*, 2003). Jenkins *et al.* (2003), for example, were able to derive annual rates of change in aerial extent for only four of the nine natural habitats they considered. Of these, tropical forests, mangroves and seagrass beds have declined globally in area in the past decades, although the data for the latter two are not robust. Measuring the rate of change, either in the extent or state of habitats and ecosystems, is important for several reasons. First, rate of change is an indicator of ecosystem health that is easily understood by the public and decision-makers, and hard figures that are statistically robust can be used

Coral Reef Conservation, ed. Isabelle M. Côté and John D. Reynolds.
Published by Cambridge University Press.

in conservation lobbying and advocacy. Second, measuring rates of change in natural habitats permits a quantitative assessment of the effectiveness of conservation interventions and environmental policies. Third, establishing trends in rates of change allows us to put current rates of change into context. This can be important, for example, when assessing whether we are likely to reach goals such as the target set by the Convention on Biological Diversity to reduce the rate of biodiversity loss by 2010 (UNEP, 2003; Balmford *et al.*, 2005).

There is a clear need for more information to be collected on both the area and state of natural habitats. Remote-sensing techniques can often provide rapid assessment data on the area of ecosystems across large spatial scales. However, whenever ecological degradation precedes reductions in areal extent, ground surveys may be necessary to detect the warning signs of community shifts. For example, while the area of coral reefs can be readily measured remotely, it is not yet possible to derive broad-scale information on coral and algal cover – two major indicators of coral reef health – from remote sensors (Mumby *et al.*, 2004). Unfortunately, global *in situ* monitoring programmes are expensive and can be difficult to implement and support on a long-term basis. New programmes will also take some years to yield visible trends. Alternatively, better use can be made of information already collected at the local or regional level (Buddemeier, 2001). For example, many small-scale ecological studies have been carried out for practical or academic purposes in the past decades in a variety of habitats. These studies often provide data on extent or composition of the study habitat, and can potentially be assembled to provide a picture of ecological change over a longer period than the duration of individual studies.

Gardner *et al.* (2003) recently demonstrated the usefulness of amalgamating existing datasets for assessing ecological changes occurring on Caribbean coral reefs. Coral reefs are an important ecosystem in terms of biodiversity and for the invaluable goods and services they provide to millions of coastal dwellers at tropical latitudes (Moberg and Folke, 1999). Qualitative global assessments of the state of coral reefs exist (e.g. Bryant *et al.*, 1998; Wilkinson, 2000), but there is no reliable global estimate of the rate at which coral reefs are being lost (Jenkins *et al.*, 2003). Gardner *et al.* (2003) assembled data on live hard coral cover from a large number of published and unpublished studies carried out across the Caribbean basin. Although the average duration of each study was only eight years, the collated data allowed Gardner and co-workers to recreate the pattern of change over the past 25 years, providing the first quantitative regional estimate of coral loss and giving a clear context for the changes occurring today.

The aim of this chapter is to evaluate methods used to integrate existing small-scale datasets to assess long-term and large-scale patterns of ecological change. We focus on coral reefs of the Caribbean region, because of data availability, but we believe that our conclusions are generally applicable to other regions. We first compare three amalgamation methods: simple averaging, vote-counting and meta-analysis, and review briefly the advantages of the latter. We then examine the performance of different meta-analytical metrics in measuring the rate of change in coral and macroalgal cover, and consider the effect of combining studies which have used different field methodologies. The accuracy of estimates of change generated using meta-analyses is then verified in comparisons with estimates generated from coordinated survey programmes using standardized methodologies. Finally, using meta-analysis we confirm the accuracy of large-scale survey programmes based on volunteer effort and, for the first time, generate estimates of change in coral cover for regions other than the Caribbean.

ASSEMBLING A DATABASE ON CARIBBEAN CORAL REEFS

Coral reefs have been extensively monitored in the Caribbean, particularly over the past three decades. Much of this monitoring has been carried out during the course of postgraduate or postdoctoral studies at single locations. Thus, time series of information on the composition of benthic cover are typically short and spatially focused.

We obtained data on hard coral and macroalgal cover for reefs within the wider Caribbean basin through electronic and manual literature searches, as well as personal communication with reef scientists, site managers and institutional librarians. Electronic literature searches were conducted using the Scientific Citation Index (SCI) and Aquatic Sciences and Fisheries Abstracts (ASFA) from 1981 to 2001 and 1988 to 2001, respectively. All relevant references cited in these publications were also checked. Studies were selected if (1) they reported percentage of cover of live hard coral or macroalgae (including fleshy and calcareous species), (2) they used replicated measurements, and (3) they reported from two or more years from a site within the region. Each sampling area treated as a site by researchers was considered as a separate site in our database. However, when a single site crossed a steep depth contour, transects were separated into groups of similar depth (e.g. Dustan and Hallas, 1987). All values were converted to percentage of total area, if not originally reported in this way. Cover values of $<1\%$ were rounded up to 1% in each case.

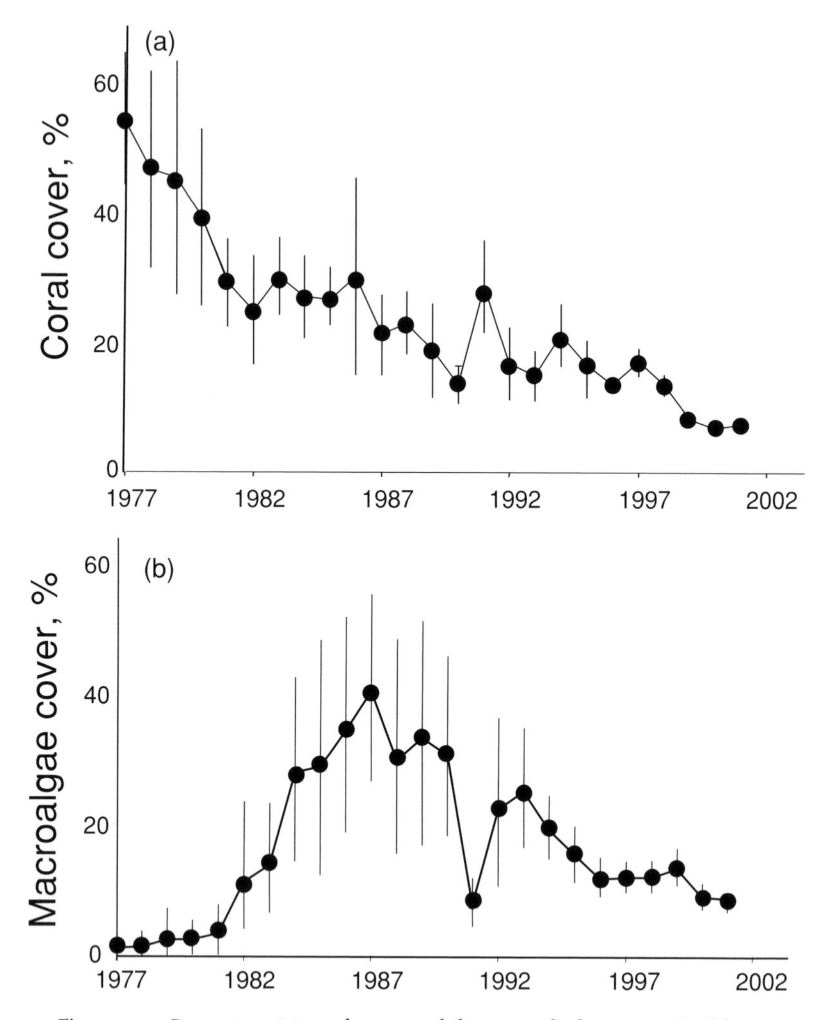

Figure 9.1 Percentage (a) coral cover and (b) macroalgal cover on Caribbean reefs from 1977 to 2002. Means are shown ± 95% (bootstrapped) confidence intervals. (a) is modified from Gardner *et al.* (2003).

For the purpose of this chapter, as in Côté *et al.* (2005), we omitted the data provided by the Caribbean Coastal Marine Productivity (CARICOMP) monitoring programme, which were included in the overall rate of change in coral cover reported by Gardner *et al.* (2003). This was done to allow an explicit comparison of the rates of change generated by this programme to those of the meta-analysis of small-scale studies. Other differences with the dataset of Gardner *et al.* (2003) are the addition of two studies from St Lucia and Saba, which together contribute 61 new sites.

The database used in this chapter consisted of 294 sites for which estimates of hard coral cover were available. Macroalgal cover was reported for 170 of these sites. The durations of individual time series ranged from 2 to 27 years, with the years of study onset ranging from 1970 to 1999. The years prior to 1977 did not yield enough data to permit the calculation of annual mean cover (Fig. 9.1), but these early data were included in meta-analyses.

AMALGAMATING STUDIES BY SIMPLE AVERAGING

The simplest way to amalgamate short-term small-scale studies is to generate yearly measures of the target habitat components which are obtained from averaging all values available each year. Figure 9.1 shows the patterns of change in coral (Fig. 9.1a) and macroalgal cover (Fig. 9.1b) obtained in this way for the Caribbean region from 1977 to 2001 (see also Gardner *et al.*, 2003).

Hard coral cover has declined steadily, from an average of 55% in 1977 to ~10% in 2001 (Fig. 9.1a), although there is some indication of a reduction in the absolute amount of coral lost in the most recent years. This represents an 82% decline in coral cover in 24 years. These statistics reflect fairly well the changes in coral cover experienced at most sites. Of the 294 sites reporting coral cover in the study, 243 (83%) lost coral cover during their period of study.

The pattern of change in macroalgal cover is markedly different from that of coral cover. Macroalgal cover appears to have increased quickly in 1982 from previously very low levels, peaked in 1987 at ~40% cover, and decreased rapidly to reach a stable level of ~15% which has been maintained since 1996 (Fig. 9.1b). The endpoints of this time series yield a 650% increase in 24 years.

Examination of the changes in macroalgal cover at individual sites reveals that this inferred regional pattern is an artefact. The majority of sites (114/170 sites, or 67%) reported increases in macroalgal cover over their study period, but the magnitude of these increases was greater earlier than later in the time series (Fig. 9.2). Thus sites which were monitored prior to 1987 (e.g. Jamaica: Hughes, 1994) show an extremely rapid rise in macroalgal cover around 1982/83, followed by stabilization at high levels of cover. By contrast, most of the sites monitored in the 1990s exhibit much more modest increases in macroalgal cover (Fig. 9.2). The gradual addition

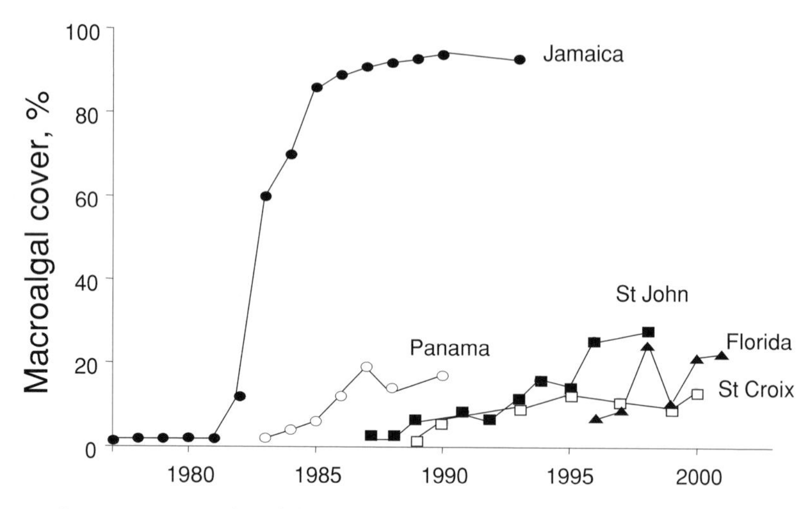

Figure 9.2 Examples of change in percent macroalgal cover at individual Caribbean reefs from 1977 to 2001. ● Rio Bueno reef, Jamaica (data from Hughes, 1994); ○ Point 23 site, San Blas, Panama (Shulman and Robertson, 1996); ■ Yawzi Point reef, St John, US Virgin Islands (Edmunds, 2002); □ Conch reef, Florida (Porter *et al.*, 2002); ▲ BI5 site, Buck Island National Park, St Croix, US Virgin Islands (Bythell et al., 2000).

of new sites to the dataset, which showed slower increases in macroalgal cover, thus resulted in an apparent but false decline in mean macroalgal cover at the regional level.

Such artefacts in data amalgamation by averaging can be avoided if one considers only studies with similar times of onset. However, this will often unduly restrict sample sizes. Alternatively, one could use a method which specifically considers the patterns of change at individual sites in the amalgamation process. Two methods allow this: vote-counting and meta-analysis.

AMALGAMATING STUDIES BY VOTE-COUNTING

In vote-counting, studies are divided into categories according to whether they are statistically significant and whether they support the hypothesis under test. The proportions of studies 'voting' for or against the hypothesis are then counted, and the hypothesis is supported if a significant proportion of studies find in its favour.

Vote-counting has been used previously to examine patterns of change in coral reef communities. Connell (1997), for example, considered the results of 23 long-term quantitative studies of coral abundance to assess coral recovery following various disturbances (e.g. storms, coral bleaching, pollution). In the first instance, statistical testing of coral cover before and after each disturbance was carried out and, depending on the outcome, studies were deemed to support or counter hypotheses about recovery.

We subjected our Caribbean dataset to a vote-counting analysis. The information needed to carry out a *t*-test comparing coral cover at the start and end of a time series was given for 195 sites. Although 144 of these sites had lower coral cover at the end than at the start of their study period, this difference was significant only for 61 of the sites. The other sites showed either no statistically detectable change in coral cover (122 sites) or a significant increase in coral cover (12 sites). Overall, therefore, significantly more sites showed no change or an increase in coral cover than a decrease in coral cover ($X_1^2 = 27.3$, $p < 0.001$).

Similar results were found for macroalgal cover. The information necessary for statistical testing was provided for 120 sites. Of these, 64 had more macroalgae at the end of their study period. However, this difference was significant for only 35 sites. Again, significantly more sites showed no change (68 sites) or a decrease in macroalgae (17 sites) than an increase ($X_1^2 = 20.8$, $p < 0.001$).

From this analysis, we should conclude that there have not been significant changes in either coral or macroalgal cover across the Caribbean since 1977. This would be a mistake. Because it considers only significant results, vote-counting can be overly conservative (Hedges and Olkins, 1985), particularly in ecological studies where sample sizes, and hence statistical power, are often low. This fact is well illustrated by the increasing proportions of Caribbean sites showing significant changes in coral and macroalgal cover with increasing numbers of replicates used to measure change (Fig. 9.3). Connell (1997) made a similar argument when adding a threshold change criterion (i.e. declines of more than 33% are significant) to his statistical significance criterion. In this way, some studies with large, but non-significant effect sizes, because of small sample sizes, were deemed to support various hypotheses under test. The following method, meta-analysis, formalizes this approach to amalgamating results.

AMALGAMATING STUDIES: AN INTRODUCTION TO META-ANALYSIS

Meta-analysis is a set of methods designed to summarize quantitatively research findings across studies (Hedges and Olkins, 1985). A detailed

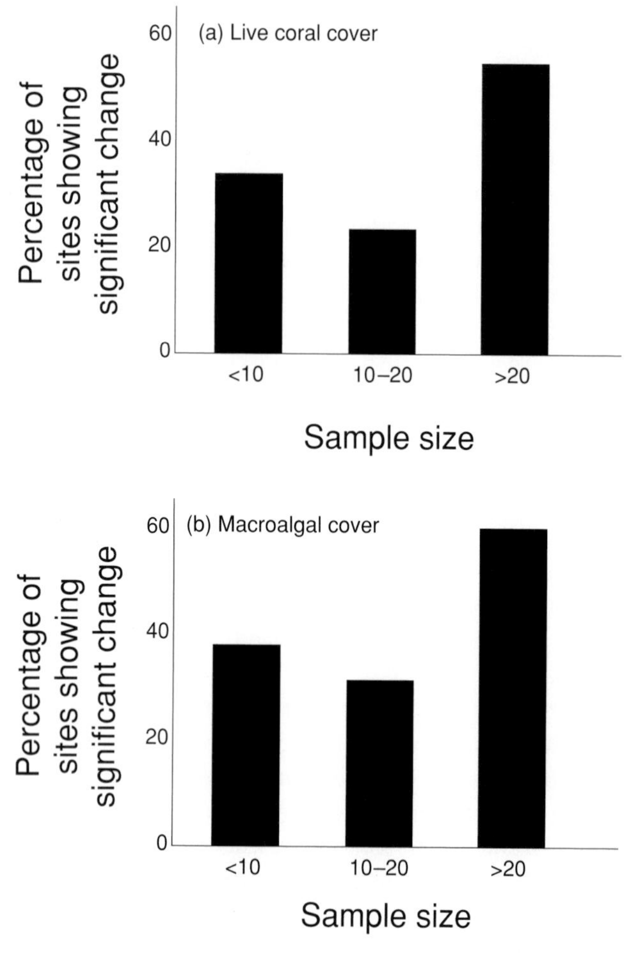

Figure 9.3 Percentage of sites showing a significant change in (a) live coral cover ($n = 73$ sites) and (b) macroalgal cover ($n = 52$ sites) in relation to sample size used to generate estimates of change. Sample sizes represent the total number of replicates used in the start and end years of monitoring of each site.

discussion of the statistics of meta-analysis is beyond the scope of this paper but is provided in Hedges and Olkin (1985) and Cooper and Hedges (1994). Only the main steps of a generic meta-analysis are described here.

In meta-analysis, the outcomes of different studies are expressed in terms of a common currency called 'effect size'. Common measures of effect size are the standardized difference between means of experimental and control groups (*d*) or the Pearson product moment correlation coefficient (*r*). However, a wide range of other effect size metrics can be used which may be more appropriate to the question posed than *d* or *r* (Osenberg *et al.*, 1999; see below).

The effect sizes derived from individual studies are weighted, in the case of coral cover, by the area of the survey generating the estimates of cover (Côté *et al.*, 2005). They are then combined to yield a common estimate of the magnitude of the effect, bounded by confidence intervals generated by bootstrapping (Rosenberg *et al.*, 2000). Mean effect sizes are considered significant when the confidence intervals do not include zero. The homogeneity of effect sizes among studies is examined to determine whether all studies share a common effect size. If there is evidence of heterogeneity, studies can be divided into biologically meaningful subgroups and the overall effect sizes for each subgroup recalculated and compared with the statistic Q_M (referred to as Q_B in Hedges and Olkins, 1985) in a manner analogous to an analysis of variance. The significance of Q_M is then tested against a distribution generated from 5000 iterations of a randomization test (Adams *et al.*, 1997; Rosenberg *et al.*, 2000). Effect sizes can also be related to continuous variables in a regression-like manner (Rosenberg *et al.*, 2000). These tests allow the identification of factors that explain significant amounts of variance in effect size (Cooper and Hedges, 1994). All meta-analyses presented in this chapter were conducted using the software MetaWin (v.2) (Rosenberg *et al.*, 2000).

Meta-analysis offers three important advantages over other methods of research synthesis. First, meta-analysis considers the results obtained by individual studies (unlike averaging), regardless of their statistical significance (unlike vote-counting). Meta-analysis overcomes the problem of low statistical power caused by small sample sizes by weighting the outcome of each study by a correlate of sample size. Larger, more robust studies are therefore given more weight in the analysis. A second, related advantage of meta-analysis is that the likelihood of Type-II errors (i.e. failing to reject the null hypothesis when it is false), which is high for individual studies with low sample sizes or weak treatment effects, is reduced through the amalgamation of all studies into a single analysis. This can be a great advantage for conservation research where committing such an error can be more harmful than committing a Type-I error (i.e. rejecting the null hypothesis when it is true). In the case of estimating rates of change in a particular habitat, a Type-II error would lead one to believe wrongly that rates of change are not significantly different from zero, which would have serious consequences for declining habitats or species. Finally, meta-analysis provides a quantitative estimate of the overall magnitude of the effect under study as well as its statistical significance. In conventional vote-counting, the number of significant findings may bear no relationship to the magnitude of an effect, and vote-counting does not provide information on the latter. This makes meta-analysis a more objective method of synthesis than narrative reviews.

A number of criticisms have, however, been levelled at meta-analysis. These include: (1) the lack of uniformity in studies pooled in meta-analytical reviews, both in terms of methods used and in terms of robustness, (2) the possibility that the studies included in meta-analyses are not representative of all the studies that have been carried out, and (3) potential non-independence of data if, for example, a single study yields multiple effect sizes included in a single meta-analysis. The first issue can be addressed by having clear selection criteria for studies to be included in a meta-analysis (Englund *et al.*, 1999) and testing specifically for effects of method on effect sizes. There is evidence in ecological studies for the second issue, i.e. a greater likelihood of publishing significant than non-significant results (Jennions and Møller, 2002). However, meta-analytical methods allow the assessment of the extent of this problem through the examination of distribution of effect sizes and the calculation of the number of unpublished, non-significant studies necessary to overturn a significant overall effect size (Rosenberg *et al.*, 2000). Finally, the issue of non-independence of data can be examined by focused or hierarchical tests of homogeneity.

THE IMPORTANCE OF CHOOSING THE RIGHT EFFECT-SIZE METRIC

The effect-size metric chosen must be matched to the question posed (Osenberg *et al.*, 1999). A number of effect-size metrics could be used to examine ecological change over time. In this section, we examine the behaviour of three candidate metrics to assess rates of change on coral reefs.

The first, C_{Rp}, is simply defined as:

$$C_{\mathrm{Rp}} = (C_{\mathrm{end}} - C_{\mathrm{start}}) / d \qquad (9.1)$$

where C_{start} and C_{end} are the percentage cover of a given benthic component at the start and end of the monitoring period of a site, and d is the monitoring interval. The main advantage of a measure such as C_{Rp} is its simplicity; however, the magnitude of the numerator may be greatly influenced by initial cover, i.e. sites with high cover in the first survey have greater scope to show decreases in cover, and vice versa, making comparisons among sites unfair.

A second metric has been proposed which takes into account variation in initial cover. C_{Ri} is calculated as:

$$C_{Ri} = 100 \cdot [(C_{end} - C_{start})/C_{start}]/d \tag{9.2}$$

This metric, which is similar to C_R in Gardner *et al.* (2003) (although their d was the number of monitoring years rather than monitoring interval) still has intuitive appeal. However, it is only valid if the change in cover is linear over time.

A third metric, C_{Rg} (the geometric rate of change: Côté *et al.*, 2005), may be better suited to non-linear time series:

$$C_{Rg} = 100 \cdot [1 - (C_{end}/C_{start})^{1/d}] \tag{9.3}$$

The annual rates of change in Caribbean coral cover obtained with each of these three metrics applied to our dataset are shown in Fig. 9.4a. The effect sizes are presented both weighted by survey area, to give studies which surveyed larger portions of reef more weight, and unweighted. In this case, the usual weighting used in meta-analyses, i.e. the inverse of the sample variance (Hedges and Olkin, 1985) has been omitted because of statistical problems related to temporal auto-correlations in time series. The estimates are similar qualitatively: all three metrics indicate that coral cover has declined significantly (i.e. the confidence intervals do not encompass zero and all means are negative). However, the magnitudes of the decline differ, ranging from ~2% per annum (C_{Rp}) to 12% per annum (C_{Rg}).

For macroalgal cover, the estimated annual rates of change differ both qualitatively and quantitatively (Fig. 9.4b). Macroalgal cover appears to have remained essentially unchanged in the past 25 years when measured with C_{Rp}. By contrast, C_{Ri} reveals a massive rate of increase, of the order of ~70% per annum, while C_{Rg} also gives a significant, but much more modest, rate of macroalgal increase. What are the true annual rates of change?

The three metrics behave very differently when applied to the same hypothetical scenarios of change (Table 9.1). A good metric should preserve both the proportionality of both cases of decline (i.e. a 50% to 5% loss is proportionately similar to a 10% to 1% loss) and both cases of increase in cover, as well at the symmetry between declines and matching increases. Table 9.1 shows that C_{Rp} does not preserve the proportionality of the declines or increases but is symmetric, yielding similar rates with opposite signs for equal declines and increases. The metric C_{Ri} does preserve

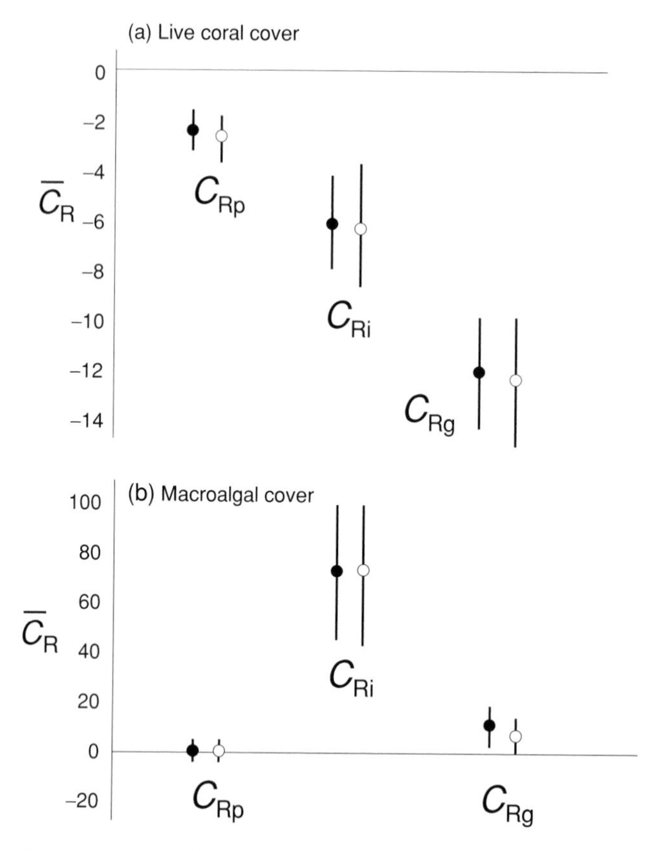

Figure 9.4 Annual rates of change in (a) live coral cover and (b) macroalgal cover, estimated by three effect size metrics (see text). Means are shown ± 95% bootstrapped confidence intervals; ● unweighted estimates ($n = 294$); ○ estimates weighted by survey area ($n = 249$).

the proportionality of the changes, but is not symmetric – it either underestimates losses, or overestimates increases, or both; C_{Rg} both preserves proportionality and is largely symmetric with respect to declines and increases.

Superficially each metric appears to provide a measure of annual change but they are potentially the source of considerable confusion. Consider the meaning of a 10% loss. The implication of C_{Rp} is that the loss of coral will always be an absolute loss of 10%, no matter what the initial cover value is: 50% will decline to 40% in the first year and to 30% the next, while 10% cover will decline to 0%. In contrast, C_{Ri} indicates that there will always be a 10% loss relative to the initial value. So, if the initial value is 50%, cover will decline to 45% in the first year and then to 40%, whereas if the initial

Table 9.1. Annual rates of change in cover obtained using three effect size metrics for simulated declines and increases in cover

	Decline in 10 years		Increase in 10 years	
Metric	50% to 5%	10% to 1%	5% to 50%	1% to 10%
C_{Rp}	−5%	−1%	+5%	+1%
C_{Ri}	−10%	−10%	+100%	+100%
C_{Rg}	−22.6%	−22.6%	+29.2%	+29.2%

value is 10%, the cover value will decline first to 9% and then to 8% (i.e. 10% of the initial cover value is lost each year). However, C_{Rg}, is based on the geometric mean and provides a measure of relative decline. A 10% loss per year from an initial cover of 50% would result in a cover value of 45% in the first year and 40.5% in the second year, whereas a 10% loss from 10% initial cover would result in 9% in the first year, to 8.1% in the second year. The differences between C_{Ri} and C_{Rg} may not appear very large but they accumulate over time.

Clearly which metric is appropriate depends on the pattern of decline or increase. In most cases we are concerned with relative change and C_{Rg} is thus likely to be the most suitable metric for the purposes of measuring the rate of change in benthic cover on coral reefs. This may not always be the case, and our example illustrates that a thorough investigation of the mathematical behaviour of different effect size metrics is recommended.

EFFECT OF SURVEY METHODS

One of the strengths of meta-analysis is its ability to combine results from different studies addressing a similar question using a variety of experimental methods. While this amalgamation is sometimes viewed as being akin to mixing apples and oranges, Rosenthal (1991) argued that generalizing over studies is essentially similar to generalizing over subjects within studies. Nevertheless, meta-analysis allows the direct examination of the effect of using different survey methods on effect sizes.

Four different methods were used in assessing the sessile benthic community on coral reefs in our dataset: line-intercept transects, video transects (followed by point count analysis), photoquadrats (followed by point count or photogrammetric analysis) and quadrats assessed visually *in situ*. The biases involved in using some of these methods have been relatively well

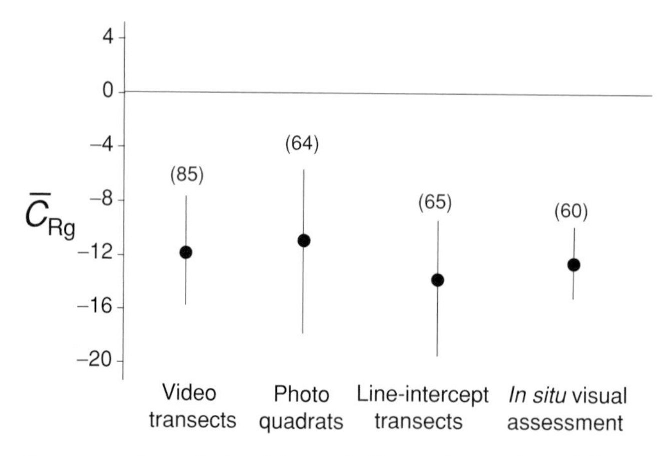

Figure 9.5 Annual rate of change in live coral cover derived from studies using different sampling methods. Means are shown ± 95% bootstrapped confidence intervals. Sample sizes are shown in parentheses.

studied (Done, 1977), and the methods are often remarkably consistent, at least in terms of estimating change in coral cover (e.g. video transects vs. chain transects: Rogers and Miller, 2001; quadrats vs. line-intercept transects: Chiappone and Sullivan, 1991; quadrats vs. video transects: Garrison *et al.*, 2000).

The four commonly used methods in our database yielded mean rates of decline in coral cover that range narrowly between 11.4% (photoquadrats) and 14.6% (line-intercept transects) ($Q_{M3} = 0.01$, $p = 0.81$) (Fig. 9.5). It therefore seems that differences in methodology among studies do not introduce significant biases, at least for analyses of live coral cover. However, sampling method does appear to be important when measuring other benthic components of coral reefs. Côté *et al.* (2005), for example, found significant differences among methods in estimates of rates of change in macroalgal cover, using a similar meta-analytical framework as that presented here.

The effect of amalgamating studies that vary in sampling methods and various other ways can also be assessed by comparing our meta-analysed estimates of change in coral cover to rates obtained from coordinated monitoring programmes using standardized methodologies. Two such programmes of reef monitoring are on-going in the Caribbean region: the CARICOMP and Reef Check programmes (UNESCO, 1998; Hodgson and Liebeler, 2002).

CARICOMP, the Caribbean Coastal Marine Productivity programme, is an international monitoring network which began in 1990 with funding from UNESCO. The network comprises 27 institutions in 17 countries across the wider Caribbean, which are involved to varying degrees in the monitoring activities. Fully participating institutions undertake yearly ecosystem measurements using standardized methodology on relatively undisturbed coral reefs (one to four reefs per country) and in other coastal habitats, along with oceanographic and meteorological measurements. Transect sites are permanently marked to allow repeated surveys of the same locations. The 'best' reef zones are specifically chosen as transect sites (i.e. areas with the most *Montastrea annularis* coral, or if this species is rare, areas with high coral diversity: CARICOMP, 2001). Most CARICOMP data currently available cover the period from 1993 to 2001.

The second ongoing programme, Reef Check, was developed in 1996 as a volunteer, community-based monitoring protocol designed to measure the health of coral reefs on a global scale. Reef Check is active in 60 countries worldwide, including 15 Caribbean nations. Reef Check scientists train teams of volunteers to identify and record, in a standardized manner, global and regional indicators of reef health, such as live coral cover and easily recognizable fish and invertebrate species. Keen amateurs can also contribute since the methodology and data sheets are available on the internet. Because the programme is based on volunteer effort, transect locations are not marked and the same sites are usually not surveyed repeatedly. This therefore precludes calculation of rates of change at each site. Instead, annual rates of change in coral cover were derived from the mean coral covers of both the earliest year and the latest year of data for each country. Reef Check data for live coral cover were available for the period from 1997 to 2004.

The rates of decline in coral cover obtained from the 'grab-bag' of studies compares well, for matching years, with the rates obtained with CARICOMP ($Q_{MI} = 0.007$, $p = 0.58$) (Fig. 9.6) and Reef Check data ($Q_{MI} = 0.02$, $p = 0.27$) (Fig. 9.6). This suggests again that the variation in methods that characterizes meta-analyses of disparate studies is not important, at least as far as coral cover is concerned. Moreover, it may not be necessary to monitor the very same sites repeatedly to measure large-scale changes in gross habitat categories.

TOWARDS A GLOBAL ESTIMATE OF RATE OF CORAL DECLINE

The close match between the annual rates of live coral cover loss obtained with CARICOMP, Reef Check and the amalgamation of small-scale data (Fig. 9.6) highlights the potential for community-driven programmes to

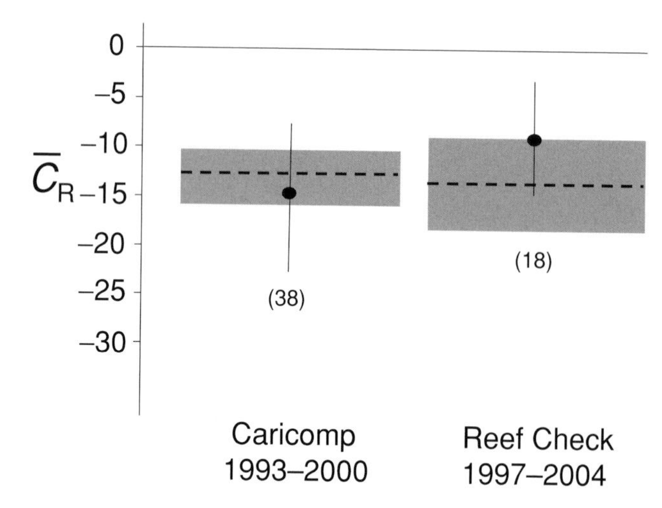

Figure 9.6 Annual rates of change in live coral cover derived from the CARICOMP and Reef Check monitoring programmes. Means are shown ± 95% bootstrapped confidence intervals. Sample sizes are given in parentheses. The mean annual rates of change in live coral cover derived from meta-analyses of small-scale studies and carried out for the same time spans as the two monitoring programmes are shown with dashed lines. The confidence intervals for these rates are indicated by the grey areas.

contribute significant amounts of good data to the goal of measuring ecological change. Data holdings for Reef Check, for example, increased from 350 reefs in 11 countries in the first five years of programme to more than 3500 reef locations in 56 countries three years later, reflecting the increasing interest and willingness of the general public to participate in coral reef monitoring and conservation (G. Hodgson, Reef Check Foundation, pers. comm.). Such programmes may therefore be an important source of data in the future, as well as fulfilling a crucial role in public awareness and education.

The global coverage of Reef Check offers an opportunity to estimate recent rates of change in coral cover not only for the Caribbean but for other regions of the world, as well as a first global estimate of decline (Fig. 9.7). Sample sizes are necessarily limited because data are analysed at the country level, rather than by reef. This constraint affects the Red Sea region in particular, but the results are nevertheless revealing. The Caribbean region boasts a highly significant rate of loss of coral cover, but both the Indian and the Pacific regions show non-significant rates of coral decline (i.e. the confidence intervals overlap zero). This is perhaps not surprising given that data series for most countries in these two regions began after 1998, the most severe mass coral bleaching year on record (Wilkinson, 1998, 2000).

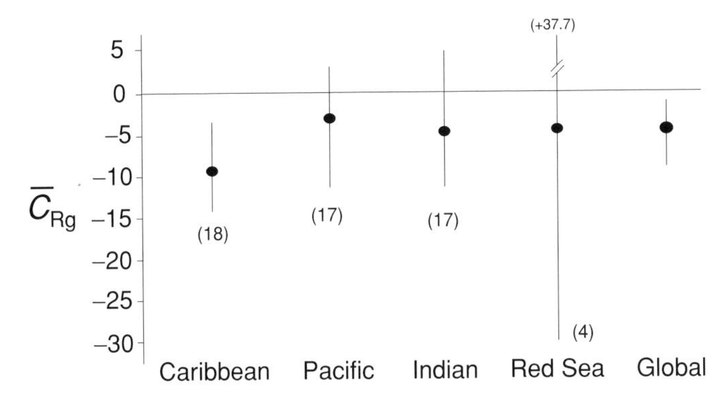

Figure 9.7 Annual rates of change in live coral cover for different regions of the world derived from the Reef Check monitoring programme. Means are shown ± 95% bootstrapped confidence intervals. Sample sizes are given in parentheses.

This bleaching event killed approximately 16% of reefs globally (Wilkinson, 2000), but many of the reefs that were not killed have shown some recovery since 1998 (Wilkinson, 2004), which was captured in the Reef Check surveys. At a global scale, coral cover has declined by ~5% yr^{-1} since 1997 (Fig. 9.7).

A PLEA FOR A GLOBAL REPOSITORY OF CORAL REEF DATA

Meta-analyses will produce reliable results if a large amount of representative data is considered. The task of assembling as complete a dataset as possible of coral and other benthic cover is made difficult by the fragmented distribution of coral reef data. Many partial repositories of data exist, which cater to specific monitoring programmes (e.g. for Reef Check, CARICOMP, Reef Keepers, the Atlantic and Gulf Rapid Reef Assessment (AGRRA), etc.), most of which have only regional mandates. Few repositories have a truly global remit, which entails pulling together information from disparate sources. The closest is ReefBase, the global database on coral reefs developed by the World Fish Centre (2005). It consolidates information on the location, extent, status, threats and management of coral reefs around the world and is a major source for Reefs at Risk analyses. This is the central repository for the Global Coral Reef Monitoring Network (GCRMN), which publishes biannual summaries on the status of the world's coral reefs (National Oceanic and Atmospheric Administration, 2005). However, its holdings of coral status information are often narrative rather than numerical, and they include a fraction of what is truly available.

Our own data-mining exercise revealed that many data are not published – more than one-third (about 38%) of the data used in our Caribbean analyses was obtained from grey literature (e.g. unpublished reports or dissertations) or from personal communications. A wealth of information clearly exists, which has been collected by individuals as part of independent study, often of topics unrelated to coral reef health or conservation, rather than as part of organized monitoring schemes. However, these valuable data are not readily available without determination by those assembling datasets and openness by those owning data.

We feel strongly that a global data archive should be created to hold such information, as well as to bring together the disparate databases that currently exist. Researchers should be encouraged to contribute routinely to the holdings of this global archive and its access for analysis should be made easy. Data territoriality may prevent the success of such an endeavour. Although we encountered virtually universal cooperation in our efforts to assemble Caribbean data, we know that for some it may be difficult to share their data. Clearly, for a global archive to succeed, contributors must benefit. There has to be a careful and transparent assessment of intellectual property rights of the contributed data. For example, data contributors should be able to cite work done using their unpublished data when compiling internal reports, submitting funding applications, etc. This would encourage researchers to view the submission of data to such a central repository as one of their 'project deliverables'. Hopefully, in time, applicants for funding who demonstrate this willingness to share useful data will be more successful. In addition, data contributors should be allowed to state what they are prepared to allow their data to be used for, as well as what their own research needs are. Thus, rather like an online car-pool system, people should be able to post vacancies as well as requests. In this way contributors should soon become beneficiaries of the archive.

Ultimately, the greatest benefit of a global information repository will be not to researchers but to coral reefs. Pooling all available data will allow scientists to assess more quickly the rates of ecological change on reefs in all regions of the world, their biological and human correlates and responses to conservation interventions, which may point the way to solutions.

CONCLUSIONS

Meta-analysis offers a powerful tool to estimate quantitatively current rates of ecological change in a variety of habitats and to reconstruct recent patterns of change. It offers two particularly significant advantages for conservation. First, by using existing data collected for a variety of purposes, meta-analysis removes the need to wait for coordinated monitoring programmes to generate evidence of ecosystem stress. The task of collecting this information is arduous, however, because of the lack of a global repository of coral reef data. Second, monitoring and evaluation are not usually specifically linked to the identification of stressors, which creates an obstacle to transposing scientific information into policy and legislative frameworks (Risk, 1999). Meta-analysis allows an examination of the causes of change (e.g. Gardner *et al.* (2005) on the effects of hurricanes on rates of coral decline), producing results which can feed directly into management and mitigation programmes. Creating a direct link between science and action is the only way to protect coral reefs for the future.

ACKNOWLEDGEMENTS

We are grateful to Richard Aronson, Rolf Bak, John Bythell, Don Catanzaro, Leandra Cho, Peter Edmunds, Ginger Garrison, Francisco Geraldes, Catriona Glendinning, Keith Hackett, Alastair Harborne, Edwin Hernandez-Delgado, Zandy Hillis-Starr, Walt Jaap, Lisa Kellogg, Tim McClanahan, Melanie McField, Jeff Miller, Thad Murdoch, Richard Nemeth, William Precht, Caroline Rogers and Gene Shinn for contributing unpublished data or manuscripts in press. Thank you also to Gregor Hodgson and the Reef Check Foundation for making their data easily accessible.

REFERENCES

Adams, D.C., Gurevitch, J. and Rosenberg, M. S. (1997). Resampling tests for meta-analysis of ecological data. *Ecology*, **78**, 1277–83.

Balmford, A., Green, R. E. and Jenkins, M. (2003). Measuring the changing state of nature. *Trends in Ecology and Evolution*, **17**, 326–30.

Balmford, A., Bennun, L., ten Brink, B. *et al.* (2005). The convention on biological diversity's 2010 target. *Science*, **307**, 212–13.

Bryant, D. L., Burke, L., McManus, J. and Spalding, M. (1998). *Reefs at Risk*. New York: World Resources Institute.

Buddemeier, R. W. (2001). Is it time to give up? *Bulletin of Marine Science*, **69**, 317–26.

Bythell, J. C., Hillis-Starr, Z. M. and Rogers, C. S. (2000). Local variability but landscape stability in coral reef communities following repeated hurricane impacts. *Marine Ecology Progress Series*, **204**, 93–100.

CARICOMP (2001). *Manual of Methods for Mapping and Monitoring of Physical and Biological Parameters in the Coastal Zone of the Caribbean, Levels 1 and 2*. St Petersburg, FL: CARICOMP Data Management Center and Florida Institute of Oceanography.

Chiappone, M. and Sullivan, K. M. (1991). A comparison of line quadrat transect versus linear percentage sampling for evaluating stony coral (Scleractinia and Milleporina) community similarity and area coverage on reefs of the Central Bahamas. *Coral Reefs*, **10**, 139–54.

Connell, J. H. (1997). Disturbance and recovery of coral assemblages. *Coral Reefs*, **16** (Suppl.), S101–S113.
Cooper, H. M. and Hedges, L. V. (1994). *Handbook of Research Synthesis*. New York: Russell Sage Foundation.
Côté, I. M., Gill, J. A., Gardner, T. A. and Watkinson, A. R. (2005). Measuring coral reef decline through meta-analyses. *Philosophical Transactions of the Royal Society*, **360**, 385–95.
Done, T. J. (1977). A comparison of units of cover in ecological classification of coral communities. *Proceedings 3rd International Coral Reef Symposium*, **1**, 9–14.
Dustan, P. and Hallas, J. C. (1987). Changes in reef coral community of Carysfort reef, Key Largo, Florida – 1974 to 1982. *Coral Reefs*, **6**, 91–106.
Edmunds, P. J. (2002). Long-term dynamics of coral reefs in St. John, US Virgin Islands. *Coral Reefs*, **21**, 357–67.
Englund, G., Sarnelle, O. and Cooper, S. D. (1999). The importance of data-selection criteria: meta-analyses of stream predation experiments. *Ecology*, **80**, 1132–41.
Gardner, T. A., Côté, I. M., Gill, J. A., Grant, A. and Watkinson, A. R. (2003). Long-term region-wide declines in Caribbean corals. *Science*, **301**, 958–60.
(2005). Hurricanes and Caribbean coral reefs: immediate impacts, recovery trajectories, and contribution to long-term coral decline. *Ecology*, **86**, 174–84.
Garrison, V., Shinn, E. A., Miller, J. *et al.* (2000). *Isla de Culebra, Puerto Rico: Changes in Benthic Cover on Three Reefs (1991–1998)*, Technical Report for the Water Resources Division. St Petersburg, FL: US Geological Survey.
Hedges, L. V. and Olkin, I. (1985). *Statistical Methods for Meta-Analysis*. New York: Academic Press.
Hodgson, G. and Liebeler, J. (2002). *The Global Coral Reef Crisis: Trends and Solutions*. Los Angeles, CA: Reef Check Foundation.
Hughes, T. P. (1994). Catastrophes, phase-shifts, and large-scale degradation of a Caribbean coral reef. *Science*, **265**, 1547–51.
Jenkins, M., Green, R. E. and Madden, J. (2003). The challenge of measuring global change in wild nature: are things getting better or worse? *Conservation Biology*, **17**, 20–3.
Jennions, M. D. and Møller, A. P. (2002). Publication bias in ecology and evolution: an empirical assessment using the 'trim and fill' method. *Biological, Reviews*, **77**, 211–22.
Moberg, F. and Folke, C. (1999). Ecological goods and services of coral reef ecosystems. *Ecological Economics*, **29**, 215–33.
Mumby, P. J., Skirving, W., Strong, A. E. *et al.*, (2004). Remote sensing of coral reefs and their physical environment. *Marine Pollution Bulletin*, **48**, 219–28.
National Oceanic and Atmospheric Administration (2005). *Global Coral Reef Monitoring Network*. Available online at http://coral.aoml.noaa/gov/gcrmn
Osenberg, C. W., Sarnelle, O., Cooper, S. D. and Holt, R. D. (1999). Resolving ecological questions through meta-analysis: goals, metrics and models. *Ecology*, **80**, 1105–17.
Porter, J. W., Kosmynin, V. and Patterson, K. L. (2002). Detection of coral reef change by the Florida Keys Coral Reef Monitoring Project. In *The Everglades, Florida Bay, and Coral Reefs of the Florida Keys: An Ecosystem Sourcebook*, eds. J. W. Porter and K. G. Porter, pp. 749–69. Boca Raton, FL: CRC Press.

Risk, M. J. (1999). Paradise lost: how marine science failed the world's coral reefs. *Marine and Freshwater Research*, **50**, 831–7.
Rogers, C. S. and Miller, J. (2001). Coral bleaching, hurricane damage, and benthic cover on coral reefs in St John, US Virgin Islands: a comparison of surveys with the chain transect method and videography. *Bulletin of Marine Science*, **69**, 459–70.
Rosenberg, M. S., Adams, D.C. and Gurevitch, J. (2000). *MetaWin v.2: Statistical Software for Meta-Analysis*. Boston, MA: Sinauer.
Rosenthal, R. (1991). *Meta-Analytic Procedures for Social Research*. New York: Sage Publications.
Shulman, M. J. and Robertson, D. R. (1996). Changes in the coral reefs of San Blas, Panama: 1983 to 1990. *Coral Reefs*, **15**, 231–6.
UNEP 2003. United Nations Environment Programme. Available online at http//www.biodiv.org/meetings/gbc~2010
UNESCO (1998). *CARICOMP: Caribbean Coral Reef, Seagrass and Mangrove Sites*, Coastal Region and Small Island Papers No. 3. Paris: UNESCO.
Wilkinson, C. (1998). *Status of Coral Reefs of the World: 1998*. Townsville, QLD: Australian Institute of Marine Science.
(2000). *Status of Coral Reefs of the World: 2000*. Townsville, QLD: Australian Institute of Marine Science.
(2004). *Status of Coral Reefs of the World: 2004*. Townsville, QLD: Australian Institute of Marine Science.
World Fish Centre (2005). *ReefBase*. Available online at http://www.reefbase.org

10

Assessing the effectiveness of marine protected areas as a tool for improving coral reef management

SUE WELLS

INTRODUCTION

Marine protected areas (MPAs) are considered an essential tool for protection of coral reefs (Roberts *et al.*, this volume). Indeed, protected areas are now seen as a key mechanism for achieving the Convention on Biodiversity (CBD)'s overall goal of a significant reduction in the rate of biodiversity loss by 2010. A global target has therefore been set requiring 'at least 10% of the world's ecological regions effectively conserved', with representative protected area systems established by 2010. Recognizing that MPAs are lagging behind terrestrial protected areas, the deadline for the establishment of representative protected area systems in the marine environment has been extended to 2012.

While there has been a great deal of enthusiasm for the establishment of MPAs with coral reefs around the world, it has often proven easier to set them up than to manage them successfully. As emphasized in many chapters in this book, monitoring and assessment of conservation actions are essential and can lead to greatly improved management. Effectiveness of performance, and accountability, are increasingly demanded across all sectors of society and conservation is no exception (Margoluis and Salafsky, 1998). Indeed, the CBD recommends that appropriate methods, standards, criteria and indicators for evaluating the effectiveness of protected area management and governance should be developed and

Coral Reef Conservation, ed. Isabelle M. Côté and John D. Reynolds.

adopted by 2008, and 30% of protected areas 'assessed' in each country by 2010. Monitoring the effectiveness of protected areas has therefore acquired some urgency and many methods are being developed and tested at present.

Despite a steady growth in the number of MPAs in recent decades, many of which include coral reef habitat, there has also been a well-documented decline in the health of reefs worldwide, including those found within MPAs (Gardner *et al.*, 2003; Wilkinson, 2004). This indicates that MPAs are in fact perhaps not yet having their intended impact as far as improvements in coral reef health are concerned. This chapter thus looks at how such assessments might contribute to improved management of coral reefs. First, I will briefly describe the range of methods that are available for monitoring management effectiveness. Then, I will illustrate the key issues with a review of recent case studies from East Africa. I will conclude with a summary of important lessons that are being learned.

METHODS FOR ASSESSING MANAGEMENT EFFECTIVENESS

The need for tools and guidelines to evaluate the ecological and managerial quality of protected areas was first recognised at the 1992 World Parks Congress in Venezuela, with the result that in 1996 the IUCN set up a Management Effectiveness Task Force under the World Commission on Protected Areas (WCPA) to look at this issue (Hockings, 1998; Hockings and Philips, 1999). A framework methodology was published by the Task Force (Hockings *et al.*, 2000) to provide general guidance in the development of assessment systems for protected areas and to encourage basic standards for assessment and reporting. This is being used as a basis for many of the specific assessments methods now being developed, including those for use by protected areas supported through the Global Environment Facility (GEF) (Mulongoy and Chape, 2004).

As with programme evaluation in other sectors, it is now recognized that it is necessary not only to review the resources dedicated to an activity, and how well they are used, but also to answer the more fundamental question of whether objectives are being achieved. The framework methodology therefore comprises six components relating to the three key elements of protected area establishment and management (Fig. 10.1):

(1) Design: What is the *context* in which the MPA exists, and what is its vision? How appropriate is the *planning*?

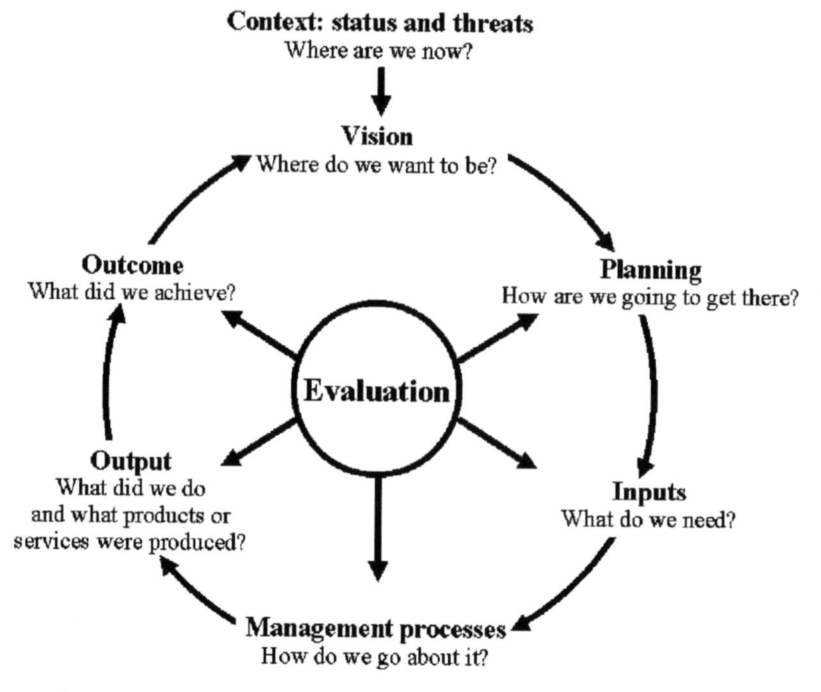

Figure 10.1 Project management cycle for protected areas.

(2) Management systems and processes: what *inputs* are needed? What is the management *process*?
(3) Delivery of objectives: What are the *outputs*/products? What are the *outcomes*/impacts?

The six main principles of an assessment, as identified in the framework methodology, are that:

- the aim must be to improve management and generate positive change, not to compete with other protected areas;
- the guidelines should be adapted to the site – there is no single correct method;
- assessments must be participatory and involve the stakeholders;
- the type of assessment should be chosen according to available resources and capacity;
- if possible, biophysical, socio-economic, cultural and management issues should all be included;
- results and recommendations from the assessment must be followed up.

Common steps in all the methods are:

- analysing the biophysical and socio-economic characteristics of the site (if not already available) to define clearly the values (i.e. why the protected area was established) and management objectives;
- identifying indicators for measuring effectiveness (indicators for existing monitoring activities can be reviewed for their suitability);
- analysing status and trends in biodiversity, socio-economic issues, threats and governance, using qualitative and numerical rating systems if appropriate;
- reviewing and revising the preliminary assessment results with stakeholders, usually through workshops and discussions;
- preparing a report with recommendations to improve management.

Assessments should be repeated (e.g. every two to three years) and preferably mainstreamed into the MPA's monitoring and reporting system, perhaps in association with the periodic review of the management plan, in order to ensure adaptive management. The following are examples of methods currently being used or tested.

Detailed assessments

IUCN/WCPA-Marine, the Worldwide Fund for Nature (WWF) and the National Oceanic and Atmospheric Administration (NOAA) have developed a method aimed at helping MPAs select and use appropriate indicators for assessing management effectiveness that focus on the outputs and outcomes (or impact) of an MPA (Pomeroy *et al.*, 2004). This method has been piloted at 17 sites worldwide. For this method, the MPA ideally needs clear, formally stated objectives, a management plan and baseline data from when it was established, and should have been in operation for at least two years. This method helps to provide new information and emphasizes the importance of quantitative monitoring programmes, but is time-consuming. The Nature Conservancy has also developed a method that provides a detailed assessment of impact and outcomes (Parrish *et al.*, 2003; The Nature Conservancy, 2000). Two measures are used: the extent to which threats are being reduced as a result of conservation actions, which may be relatively easy to measure; and the ecological integrity of the area, which is more difficult to assess, particularly if the focus of a protected area is biodiversity in general, rather than specific species. For this reason, a limited number of conservation 'targets' are determined, based on the objectives of the protected area. Key ecological attributes for each target are identified as well as the acceptable range of variation for each attribute. A rating for the status of each target can then be determined; if any of the key ecological attributes exceeds its acceptable range of variation, the target cannot be considered to have been successfully 'conserved'. This method thus requires detailed information on the targets, as well as monitoring data indicating trends.

Broad assessments

Methods for assessing the full management cycle (Fig. 10.1) include one developed through the UN Foundation/UNESCO/IUCN-WCPA project *Enhancing our Heritage*, designed specifically for World Heritage Sites (Hockings *et al.*, 2004). It uses worksheets for each of the six components (*context, planning, inputs, processes, outputs, outcomes*) that can be adapted to individual protected areas. The tables are filled in, preferably by a team of people familiar with the site and using all available data, and are then reviewed by other stakeholders. The worksheets involve assigning qualitative (in some cases semi-qualitative) ratings to a number of predetermined criteria. It has been used at a number of World Heritage sites and is adaptable to both well-developed and established protected areas, and to those with less capacity and fewer skills in management and research. This approach has the advantage of low cost, direct involvement of the manager, and a greater likelihood of feedback into management and sustainability, although a potential obstacle is that it depends on the management agency's objectivity. It has been used with some success for at least two MPAs: Aldabra Special Reserve in the Seychelles and Greater St Lucia Wetland Parks in South Africa, and in both cases aspects of the management are being adapted in line with the results of the assessments.

A similar, but slightly simpler, method has been developed for MPAs in the western Indian Ocean (Wells and Manghubai, 2005). The assessment can be carried out in about two to three months. A small 'implementation team', comprising MPA personnel, key stakeholders, and sometimes consultants, leads the assessment and ensures that data are collected and worksheets compiled. These are reviewed by staff and stakeholders in consultative workshops, and a report and recommendations are produced. Questionnaires are used for obtaining feedback from some stakeholder groups. The method and results of some pilot tests in East Africa are described below.

Scorecards

A scorecard, developed by the World Bank for use in GEF projects related to MPAs, provides an even simpler method (Staub and Hatziolos, 2003). It

Table 10.1. Percentage cover by MPAs and no-take areas of the continental shelf (to 200 m depth) in Kenya, Tanzania and Mozambique

	Kenya	Tanzania	Mozambique
Area of continental shelf (km²)	8 460	17 903	73 300
Area of MPAs (km²)	735	1 378	2 920
Percentage of continental shelf protected	8.7	7.7	4.0
Area of no-take (km²)	54	66	est. 40
Percentage of continental shelf no-take	0.6	0.4	0.1
Total area of coral reef (km²)[a]	630	3 580	1 890
Percentage of coral reef no-take	8.6	1.9	2.1

[a] From Spalding *et al.* (2001).

focuses on the *process* component of the management cycle. If repeated at intervals, it will help to track progress. The scorecard is filled out by MPA staff, and makes use of immediately available information and the knowledge of the personnel, and should take a maximum of half a day to complete. The disadvantage of this is that it does not assess the impact of the MPA as this requires analysis of data from monitoring programmes.

MPAS AND CORAL REEF MANAGEMENT IN EASTERN AFRICA

Over the last decade, countries of the western Indian Ocean have greatly increased their investment in MPAs and there are now over 50 MPAs (see examples in McClanahan, this volume). As part of its programme to promote the establishment of MPAs in Eastern Africa, WWF has recently carried out an analysis of the current status of MPAs in three countries: Kenya, Tanzania and Mozambique (WWF Eastern African Marine Ecoregion, 2004). Considering both fully protected sites and those managed for multiple uses, the number and area covered by MPAs has increased significantly in recent years (Table 10.1, Fig. 10.2). Kenya has the shortest coastline and smallest continental shelf and current MPA coverage is 8.7%, much of which was gazetted in the 1970s. Tanzania, with a much longer coastline and larger continental shelf, has 7.7% contained within MPAs, mostly declared in the 1990s and 2000s. Mozambique has the longest coastline and the largest continental shelf, and has only 4% within MPAs.

The question of what is meant by the term 'effectively conserved' is also a particular issue in the marine environment and has led to extensive debate about whether MPAs can be effective if they are not closed to fishing (Côté

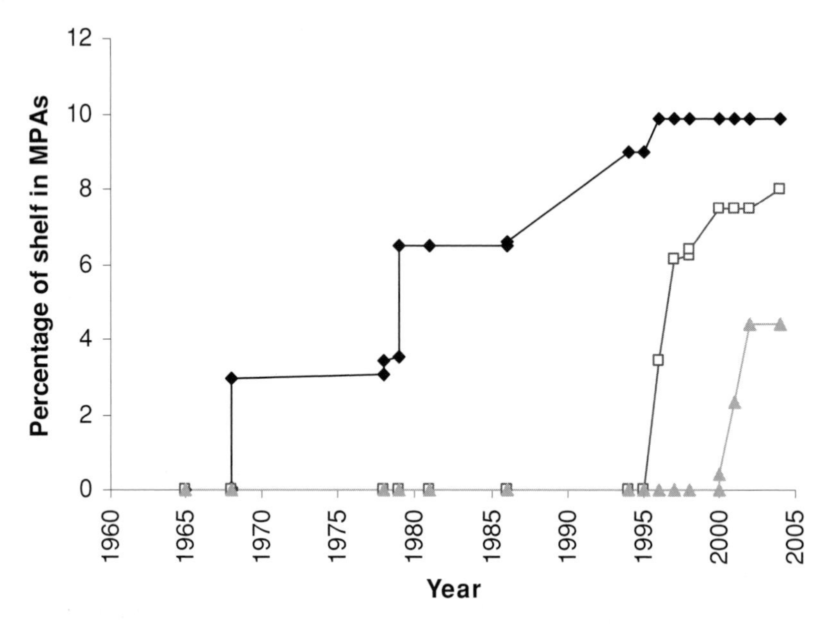

Figure 10.2 Percentage of continental shelf located within MPA from 1960 to end 2004 for three East African countries (◆Kenya; □ Tanzania; ▲Mozambique).

et al., 2001; Agardy *et al.*, 2003; Halpern, 2003). At the 5th World Parks Congress in Durban, South Africa in September 2003 it was recommended that 20–30% of each marine habitat should be closed to exploitation, a target based on recent research findings (Roberts *et al.*, 2003) and now being considered for incorporation in some form into the CBD's programme of work.

However, in the three countries analysed, a very much smaller proportion of marine habitat is no-take (Table 10.1). In Kenya, all MPAs termed 'marine parks' are fully protected (unlike 'marine reserves' which allow non-destructive forms of fishing) and cover about 0.6% of the continental shelf. It should be noted that countries use different terminology for MPAs under their protected area legislation, with 'marine park', 'marine reserve', 'sanctuary' etc. being used to describe different management regimes. In Tanzania only about 0.4% of the continental shelf is closed to fishing, through a variety of mechanisms. In mainland Tanzania, no-take areas include: MPAs designated as marine reserves; no-take zones within the multiple-use marine parks; and reefs that have been closed to fishing within the collaborative management areas of northern Tanzania (which are not currently considered part of the MPA network as their primary objective is fishery management rather than biodiversity conservation). On Zanzibar, three of the MPAs have very small closed areas. In Mozambique, no-take zones are being established within the National Parks but information on area coverage is not available; however, they are estimated to cover no more than 40 km^2, or 0.05% of the continental shelf.

However, if coral reefs alone are considered, the figures for no-take areas are rather better (Table 10.1). Our knowledge about the MPAs allows us to extrapolate that all the no-take areas are essentially on coral reefs, as these are considered to be the key areas within MPAs needing full protection. We also know the extent of coral reef in each country from the work of Spalding *et al.* (2001). On that basis, 8.6% of reefs in Kenya, 1.8% of reefs in Tanzania and 2.1% of reefs in Mozambique are fully protected. Although still a long way from the recommended 20–30% fully protected, this shows some progress, given the importance of reefs in these countries for artisanal fishing.

In addition to simple percentage area targets, the CBD also requires that national MPA networks are 'representative' of the full suite of biodiversity in the area. Despite considerable research and survey work over the last two decades, it is still only possible to assess representation within the current MPA network on a presence/absence basis, as was the case in the 1980s. The majority of MPAs within these three countries indeed have reefs. However, we still do not have information at the more detailed level to show how much is included within each MPA (and in multiple use MPAs it is considerably more than just the no-take areas); equally we have no information on the extent to which different types of coral reef lie within MPAs. This is despite the fact that coral reefs are probably the most studied ecosystem and, as mentioned above, global mapping programmes have provided estimates of the area of this habitat in each country (Spalding *et al.*, 2001).

Assessing management effectiveness of Eastern African MPAs

Assessments of the management effectiveness of eight MPAs in Eastern Africa in 2003 provided useful insight into some of the problems currently being encountered in MPA management (Wells, 2004). An early version of the workbook by Wells and Manghubai (2005) was used. The MPAs were selected to represent a range of types of management and situations:

- five in Kenya: Malindi Marine Park and Reserve, Watamu Marine Park and Reserve, Kiunga Reserve, Mombasa Marine Park and Reserve, and Kisite Marine Park/Mpunguti Marine Reserve;

- two in Tanzania: Mnazi Bay-Ruvuma Estuary Marine Park and Mafia Island Marine Park;
- one in Seychelles: Cousin Island Special Reserve.

Method

Each site was provided with a small sum (US$2000–3000) to cover some of the costs, such as meetings or hiring additional assistance. It was expected that the MPAs themselves would provide in-kind support (e.g. staff time, use of vehicles), and some financial input where possible, particularly since the aim is to make such initiatives a regular part of the management cycle.

The assessment started with an introductory workshop for the eight sites. Each site formed an implementation team and drew up a work plan. Implementation teams varied in composition. For Watamu Marine Park and Reserve, the implementation team included representatives from non-governmental and community-based organizations, as well as a Japanese International Cooperation Agency (JICA) volunteer; for Kisite the team included one of the key village elders. The other sites in Kenya, and those in Tanzania and Seychelles, had teams comprising primarily MPA staff (Fig. 10.3). In Kenya, a national coordinating team was set up with staff from the Kenya Wildlife Service Coast office in Mombasa, which provided technical and logistical assistance, and has overseen production of an annotated bibliography of references and research reports relevant to all sites.

The worksheets were compiled by the implementation teams, with assistance from the national coordinators and technical support from IUCN's Eastern Africa Regional Office. All sites followed the same general approach, but made minor modifications to the worksheets according to their needs. For input from some of the stakeholder groups, a questionnaire was developed to collect information and opinions in a workshop setting, as the worksheets were found to be too complex for some of the community stakeholders (e.g. fishermen and boat operators). The completed sheets were reviewed by stakeholders at workshops (Fig. 10.4), informal meetings or through correspondence. The process took three to four months, depending on the capacity and other work schedules of the MPA.

Results in relation to management process

All the MPAs involved found a benefit in the assessments. This was so even though the concept of self-assessment is not yet well understood in the three countries surveyed. This is particularly the case where government institutions are involved, so that some MPA staff found it difficult to

Figure 10.3 Implementation team for assessment of management effectiveness of Malindi Marine Park, Kenya. (Photograph by Sue Wells.) (See also Plate 10.3 in the colour plate section.)

acknowledge areas where improvement was needed, for fear that this might result in some form of retribution.

It helped MPA staff to think about the reasons behind the establishment of the site, how their management activities can have an impact on both biodiversity and stakeholders, and how even small, insignificant management issues can affect the overall success of an MPA. All the assessments showed that better communication is needed with stakeholders. In several instances, the assessment was the first time that the MPA staff had approached a stakeholder group for information and opinions. In all cases, the stakeholders expressed great appreciation of the exercise (Fig. 10.5). The assessments, particularly through the questionnaires, also revealed that stakeholders are often very ignorant of the aims of the MPA, the legislation relating to it, and how it operates. This indicates a need for provision of more targeted information.

The assessments showed that the longer-established MPAs had developed the basic capacity for effective management, although all lacked adequate staff and assured funding. Basic enforcement arrangements had been set up in all cases, with boundaries and zones demarcated but most had

Figure 10.4 Meeting with fishers at Kisite Marine Park, Kenya to review preliminary results of assessment of MPA management effectiveness. (Photograph by Sue Wells.) (See also Plate 10.4 in the colour plate section.)

flaws in the design of these. Few MPA staff could explain on what basis the location of boundaries or zoning schemes had been determined.

All the MPAs had, or were preparing, management plans, but no MPAs had standards for best practices in management. It was felt the assessments had provided very useful information for the revision of their respective management plans. In Kenya, the management plans should be reviewed after five years, and the plans for each MPA are due for revision. Recommendations included, for example, the suggestion that Malindi and Watamu MPAs should have separate management plans. The two MPAs currently have a joint plan, as the sites are adjacent to each other. However, the detailed information gathered during the assessment indicated that there are sufficient differences between the sites that separate plans would be useful, with some form of coordinating mechanism to ensure joint management of common issues, such as the Marine Reserve (which encompasses the two Marine Parks). Mnazi Bay MPA used the assessment as a capacity-building exercise to help identify the issues to be taken into consideration in the preparation of their management plan.

Figure 10.5 Local communities such as this women's group in the village adjacent to Kisite Marine Park, Kenya, were very positive about the assessment of MPA management effectiveness. (Photograph by Sue Wells.) (See also Plate 10.5 in the colour plate section.)

The assessments should ideally have included an analysis of the financial status of the MPAs, but most sites lacked the resources or capacity to do this. However, a simple analysis of funding requirements in relation to available sources for Mafia Island Marine Park in Tanzania revealed the very large size of donor contributions compared to government or other support. The situation was probably similar at other MPAs, demonstrating the progress that will be required if MPAs in this region are to become financially sustainable. Indeed, although there has been a major increase in both MPA establishment and management in East Africa over recent years, this has been paralleled by increased donor investment, through WWF, IUCN, the World Bank and several bilateral agreements. Funding through WWF alone to these three countries increased from US$18 000 in 1992 to the current investment of over US$1 460 000 yr^{-1} (Fig. 10.6).

Results in relation to coral reef health

As mentioned earlier, improved management systems are only one component of 'effective' management. The ultimate determinants of success are whether the objectives are being met, and a conservation impact

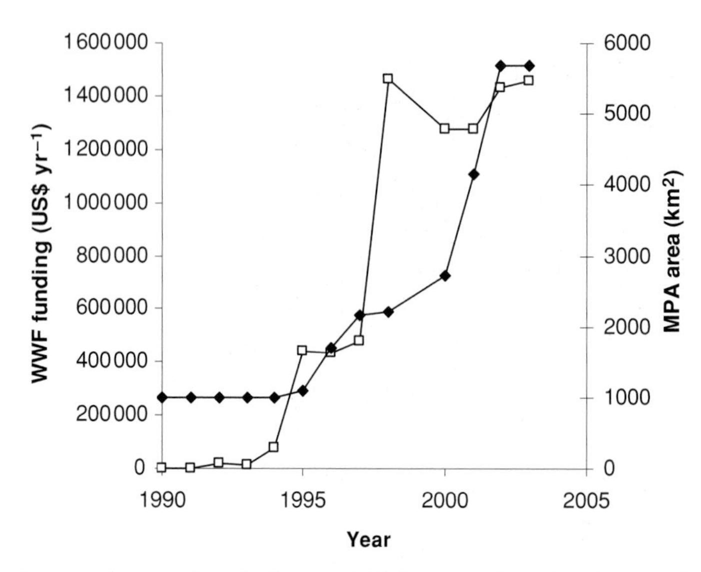

Figure 10.6 Growth in funding available by WWF (□) and in the area of MPAs in Eastern Africa (◆) from 1990 to 2005. Note different scales on the two axes.

achieved. Most of the MPAs had objectives that relate both to biodiversity conservation and improved livelihoods, but in many cases these were insufficiently defined for measuring progress towards their achievement. This was reflected in the fact that the management plans tended to be issue-driven (i.e. based on an analysis of the threats to the area at the time the plan was prepared) rather than objective-oriented, and thus did not lay out a strategy for reaching the overall aim of the MPA. This was the case, for example, for the management plan of Mnazi Bay–Ruvuma Estuary Marine Park, where coral mining for lime is a major threat to reefs (Fig. 10.7). The assessments were thus extremely useful in helping staff and stakeholders to think carefully about the site and to identify what the most important elements of 'biodiversity' are (the management targets) and how the MPA should be managed to protect these. Coral reefs were key features of all the MPAs but often little thought had been given to particular management approaches required.

However, even once the objectives were more clearly designed, in most cases data were not available to show the progress made towards achieving the objectives. Although some MPAs in Eastern Africa have been in place for 20–30 years, few have good baseline surveys from before protection started. This is a common situation in other parts of the world as well (Mosqueira *et al.*, 2000).

Figure 10.7 Coral mining at Mnazi Bay-Ruvuma Estuary Marine Park, Tanzania. (Photograph by Sue Wells.) (See also Plate 10.7 in the colour plate section.)

Equally importantly, although all MPAs undertook some monitoring, this was often inappropriately designed, or inadequately maintained to provide sufficiently long datasets to show trends. It was found that the results of monitoring and research activities were often not easily available to MPA managers and staff, particularly if carried out by external research organizations. This highlighted the need for more structured and sustainable monitoring programmes, using methods that MPA staff can participate in, and mechanisms to ensure that copies of data and results are kept at each MPA site, and are understood and available to all MPA staff. Monitoring needs to be designed not only to measure trends in biophysical and socio-economic parameters, but also to assess the effectiveness of management. Monitoring manuals address this issue (e.g. Bunce *et al.*, 2003; English *et al.*, 1997; Wilkinson *et al.*, 2003), but the programmes themselves often focus more on designing sampling protocols and collecting data than on analysing results in relation to management, reporting the conclusions back to managers and advising on how they should be adapting their management.

The main monitoring programmes in the MPAs assessed were for coral reef health (mainly fish and corals), and in some cases mangroves and turtle nesting. Cousin Island was exceptional in having a model seabird monitoring programme, the results of which were used extensively in the management of the reserve. Socio-economic monitoring was limited at all sites, although there had been considerable investment in staff training; data on fish catch and tourism were available at some sites, but often not in a form that could readily be used for the assessment.

In Kenya, two research organizations (Wildlife Conservation Society's Coral Reef Conservation Project and CORDIO – Coral Reef Degradation in the Indian Ocean) carry out research on and monitoring of the reefs in the Kenyan MPAs in association with the Kenya Wildlife Service. Much of this work points towards MPAs being effective at enhancing fish populations. McClanahan *et al.* (1999) found that the no-take MPAs of Chumbe (Zanzibar) and Kisite (Kenya) have larger fish biomass (sometimes 3.5 times greater) and a higher diversity of fish species than reefs that were being fished off Dar es Salaam and in the Tanga region (see McClanahan, this volume). The abundance of three groups of economically important species (triggerfish, surgeonfish and parrotfish) is higher in no-take sites than in fished areas (McClanahan and Arthur, 2001). McClanahan (2000) also showed that the no-take areas at Malindi, Watamu, Mombasa, Kisite and Chumbe have led to the recovery of the heavily overfished triggerfish *Balistapus undulatus* in those MPAs within 5–10 years (although 30 years may be necessary for full recovery). Some of these effects may be due to the fact that MPAs have been established in particularly diverse areas, but nevertheless it seems that well-enforced no-take sites can have a positive impact on reef fish.

Impacts that MPA management might have had on corals themselves, however, may have been largely obscured by the El Niño-associated coral bleaching event of 1998, which caused widespread coral mortality reaching 50–90% in some areas. Reefs inside and outside MPAs were affected (Obura *et al.*, 2002). In Kenya, reefs within MPAs suffered greatest damage because these had more vulnerable coral communities, with species that are less tolerant to stress (McClanahan *et al.*, 2001). There are some indications that reefs within MPAs recovered faster than those outside, although this was very variable (Obura *et al.*, 2002). In addition, the widespread use of destructive fishing methods (beach seines and dynamite), which is progressively being brought under control, has had significant impact on corals in the region. Efforts to regulate these methods have been country-wide rather than specifically linked to MPAs. Important factors determining reef health may thus be related to coral bleaching and the use of destructive fishing gears, rather than the existence of MPAs per se.

CONCLUSIONS

Scientific studies have demonstrated the importance of MPAs for the protection of coral reefs but management is often ineffective, with the result that reef health continues to decline. Simple methods to assess management effectiveness will help to improve management but for useful assessments, we need much better monitoring programmes than those which are currently in place at most MPAs, with data analysed on regular basis. This will require skilled, committed people, and thus greater investment in resources for training and education (see also Browning *et al.*, this volume).

Monitoring programmes must be fully linked into management and the results made available to the people who can adapt management plans and actions appropriately. This will require more active collaboration between scientists and managers, to ensure that the best methods are used, and that where skills and capacity for advanced methods are lacking, simple techniques are used. The introduction of regular assessments of management effectiveness will help to move this process forward, by revealing gaps in data, monitoring systems and capacity. The first assessment of an MPA tends to be incomplete whatever method is used, but is invaluable for discovering where monitoring, other data gathering exercises, and information management systems need improvement. Monitoring of reefs is well advanced compared to many other marine ecosystems. The challenge now is to make this monitoring management-oriented. While this is not a new idea (e.g. Wells, 1995), the gap between researchers and managers still needs to be closed.

ACKNOWLEDGEMENTS

This chapter resulted from a number of studies and discussions with numerous colleagues involved in marine conservation in East Africa. In particular, I would like to thank the IUCN Eastern Africa Regional Programme and the WWF Eastern Africa Marine Ecoregion programme for their support. I would also like to acknowledge the following individuals for their contributions and roles in the various initiatives discussed in the paper: Sangeeta Mangubhai, Neil Burgess, Nyawira Muthiga, Melita Samoilys and Amani Ngusaru. Thanks are due also to Isabelle Côté and John Reynolds for encouraging the publication of the chapter and for editiorial assistance.

REFERENCES

Agardy, T., Bridgewater, B., Crosby, M. P. *et al.* (2003). Dangerous targets: differing perspectives, unresolved issues, and ideological clashes regarding marine protected areas. *Aquatic Conservation: Marine and Freshwater Ecosystems*, **13**, 1–15.

Bunce, L., Townsley, P., Pomeroy, R. and Pollnac, R. (2000). *Socio-Economic Manual for Coral Reef Management.* Townsville, QLD: Australian Institute of Marine Science.

Côté, I. M., Mosqueira, I. and Reynolds, J. D. (2001). Effects of marine reserve characteristics on the protection of fish populations: a meta-analysis. *Journal of Fish Biology*, **59** (Suppl. A), 178–89.

English, S., Wilkinson, C. and Baker, V. (1997). *Survey Manual for Tropical Marine Resources*, 2nd edn. Townsville, QLD: Australian Institute of Marine Science.

Gardner, T. A., Côté, I. M., Gill, J. A., Grant, A. and Watkinson, A. R. (2003). Long-term region-wide declines in Caribbean corals. *Science*, **301**, 958–60.

Halpern, B. (2003). The impact of marine reserves: do reserves work and does reserve size matter? *Ecological Applications*, **13**, S117–S137.

Hockings, M. (1998). Evaluating management of protected areas: integrating planning and evaluation. *Environmental Management*, **22**, 337–46.

Hockings, M. and Phillips, A. (1999). How well are we doing? Some thoughts on the effectiveness of protected areas. *Parks*, **9**(2), 5–14.

Hockings, M., Stolton, S. and Dudley, N. (2000). *Evaluating Effectiveness: A Framework for Assessing the Management of Protected Areas.* Gland, Switzerland: IUCN. Available online at http://www.enhancingheritage.net

Hockings, M., Stolton, S., Dudley, N. and Parrish, J. (2004). *The World Heritage Management Effectiveness Workbook: How to Build Monitoring, Assessment and Reporting Systems to Improve the Management Effectiveness of Natural World Heritage Sites.* Brisbane, QLD: University of Queensland. Available online at http://www.enhancingheritage.net

Margoluis, R. and Salafsky, N. (1998). *Measures of Success: Designing, Managing and Monitoring Conservation and Development Projects.* Washington, DC: Island Press.

McClanahan, T. R. (2000). Recovery of a coral reef keystone, *Balistapus undulates* in East African marine parks. *Biological Conservation*, **94**, 191–8.

McClanahan, T. R. and Arthur, R. (2001). The effect of marine reserves and habitat on populations of East African coral reef fishes. *Ecological Applications*, **11**, 559–69.

McClanahan, T. R., Muthiga, N. A., Kamukuru, A. T. Machano, H. and Kiambo, R. W. (1999). The effects of marine parks and fishing on coral reefs of northern Tanzania. *Biological Conservation*, **89**, 161–82.

McClanahan, T. R., Muthiga, N. A. and Mangi, S. (2001). Coral and algal changes after the 1998 coral bleaching: interaction with reef management and herbivores on Kenyan reefs. *Coral Reefs*, **19**, 380–91.

Mosqueira, I., Côté, I. M., Jennings, S. and Reynolds, J. D. (2000). Conservation benefits of marine reserves for fish populations. *Animal Conservation*, **4**, 321–32.

Mulongoy, K. J. and Chape, S. (eds.) (2004). *Protected Areas and Biodiversity: An Overview of Key Issues*, UNEP-WCMC Biodiversity Series No. 21. Montreal: Convention on Biodiversity Secretariat.

Obura, D., Celliers, L., Machano, H. *et al.* (2002). Status of coral reefs in Eastern Africa: Kenya, Tanzania, Mozambique and South Africa. In *Status of the Coral Reefs of the World: 2002*, ed. C. Wilkinson, pp. 63–77. Townsville, QLD: Australian Institute of Marine Science.
Parrish, J. D., Braun, D. P. and Unnasch, R. S. (2003). Are we conserving what we say we are? Measuring ecological integrity within protected areas. *BioScience*, **53**, 851–60.
Pomeroy, R. S., Parks, J. E. and Watson, L. M. (2004). *How is Your MPA Doing? A Guidebook of Natural and Social Indicators for Evaluating Marine Protected Areas Management Effectiveness*. Gland, Switzerland: IUCN.
Roberts, C. M., Andelman, S., Branch, G. (2003). Ecological criteria for evaluating candidate sites for marine reserves. *Ecological Applications*, **13** (Suppl.), S199–S214.
Spalding, M. D., Ravilious, C. and Green, E. P. (2001). *World Atlas of Coral Reefs*. Berkeley, CA: University of California Press.
Staub, F. and Hatziolos, M. E. (2003). *Score Card to Assess Progress in Achieving Management Effectiveness Goals for Marine Protected Areas*. Washington, DC: World Bank. Available online at http://www.MPAscorecard.net
The Nature Conservancy (2000). *The Five-S Framework for Site Conservation: A Practitioner's Handbook for Site Conservation, Planning and Measuring Conservation Success*. Arlington, VA: TNC, Available online at http://nature.org/summit/files/five_s_eng.pdf
Wells, S. M. (1995). Science and management of coral reefs: problems and prospects. *Coral Reefs*, **14**, 177–81.
(2004). *Assessment of Management Effectiveness in Selected Marine Protected Areas in the Western Indian Ocean*. Nairobi: IUCN Eastern Africa Regional Programme.
Wells, S. M. and Mangubhai, S. (2005). *Assessing Management Effectiveness of Marine Protected Areas: A Workbook for the Western Indian Ocean*. Nairobi: IUCN Eastern African Regional Programme.
Wilkinson, C. (2004). *Status of Coral Reefs of the World: 2004*, vols. 1 and 2. Townsville, QLD: Australian Institute of Marine Science.
Wilkinson, C., Green, A., Almany, J. and Dionne, S. (2003). *Monitoring Coral Reef Marine Protected Areas: A Practical Guide on How Monitoring Can Support Effective Management of MPAs*. Gland, Switzerland: IUCN.
WWF Eastern African Marine Ecosystem (2004). *Towards the Establishment of an Ecologically Representative Network of Marine Protected Areas in Kenya, Tanzania and Mozambique*. Dar es Salaam, Tanzania: WWF.

11

Environmental impact assessment for coral reefs: advocating direct protective approaches

JOHN R. TURNER
University of Wales at Bangor

RICHARD BOAK
Water Management Consultants Ltd

REBECCA KLAUS
University of Wales at Bangor

DEOLALL DABY
University of Mauritius

EMILY HARDMAN
University of Wales at Bangor

INTRODUCTION

Arguably, there is little that coastal zone managers can do to minimize the impact of natural disturbances to coral reefs, such as cyclones and hurricanes, boom and bust in echinoderm populations, coral bleaching, disease and climate change (Bellwood *et al.*, 2004). However, protection can be afforded to reefs from degradation arising from the construction and operation of coastal developments such as marinas, prawn farms, desalination plants, sewage treatment works, hotels and other large-scale developments, thereby maximizing the resilience of reefs to natural perturbations. Coral reefs occur adjacent to many rapidly developing regions, and it is important not to allow concerns over large-scale natural impacts to diminish the need for continued protection of reefs at the national, regional and local levels (Wilkinson, 2004; Jaap, this volume).

Coral Reef Conservation, ed. Isabelle M. Côté and John D. Reynolds.
Published by Cambridge University Press.

Environmental impact assessment (EIA) is a tool that can be used to identify the likely impacts from human activities before they arise (Clark, 1996), and to put into place measures to minimize damage from those impacts that are unavoidable. Monitoring during both construction and operation is essential to determine whether mitigation measures work (Lincoln-Smith, 1991). EIA is a powerful environmental protection device if the assessment is undertaken thoroughly, and all recommendations are followed by the developer and operator, and enforced by the regulating authority. Unfortunately, EIA is often inadequate (Fairweather, 1989, 1993) or worse, not carried out, and coral reefs are needlessly degraded by developments, devaluing their role in coastal protection (Sheppard, this volume), fisheries (McClanahan, this volume), tourism (Jobbins, this volume) and as repositories of biodiversity.

Monitoring of the condition of an environment before a development begins, and then again after the resulting damage (e.g. Underwood, 1994), might help in gaining compensation after the event by proving impact, but this in itself does not actually protect environments, such as a coral reef which may change state rather than recover (Knowlton, 1992). Instead, a method of monitoring and detecting impacts as they arise is required, such that the causes of damage can be identified and removed or modified immediately (Gray *et al.*, 1991). This approach embodies the concept of feedback monitoring (Gray and Jenson, 1993) and is a form of adaptive management (Constable, 1991).

In this chapter, the process of EIA as a tool in coastal zone management for coral reef protection is outlined, and key problems identified. While a failed EIA/development may receive media interest, there are rarely transparent reports or publications to document the facts (Sheppard, 2003), and hence we draw largely on examples from personal observation. The integration of feedback monitoring to provide reactive management is strongly recommended and demonstrated here by describing a case study of construction of a sewage outfall in a coral reef environment in Mauritius, in which we are currently involved.

ENVIRONMENTAL IMPACT ASSESSMENT IN THE COASTAL ZONE

Environmental impact assessment is used to provide coastal zone managers with indications of the likely consequences of their actions to allow a development (e.g. construction of a shrimp farm), or a programme (e.g. fisheries aid project) to proceed, or to enact new legislation (e.g. establishment of

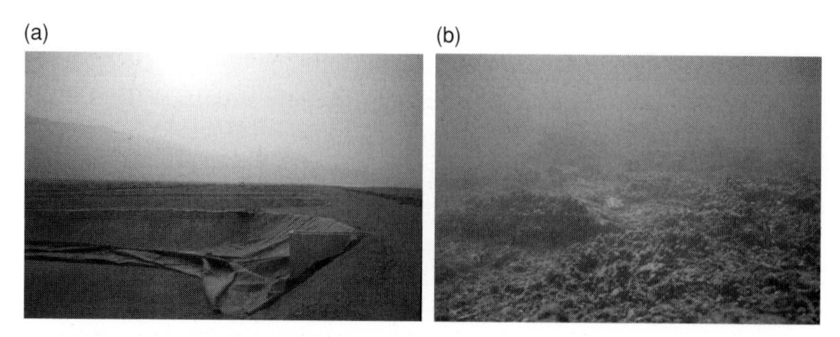

Figure 11.1 (a) A failed shrimp farm in Oman lays landward of (b) a degraded coral reef. An EIA should have identified the water quality problems which caused farm to fail and reef to die.

a statutory marine reserve). Used properly, EIA does not necessarily stop development, for most governments have policies for both development and environmental protection. Instead, it reduces conflict in the coastal zone by making the development take place at an appropriate location and in an environmentally acceptable manner. EIA should therefore lead to better use of coastal resources by ensuring that planned new activities complement the physical and biological interactions in an area of coast, and the human uses of that area. EIAs for coastal zone developments are complex to undertake because of the many stakeholders using a sea area (e.g. Brown, this volume), the relatively uncontained nature of many marine processes, and the difficulty in establishing background impacts that may have synergistic effects. For example, in northern Oman, a failed shrimp farm now lies unused, just landward of a section of reef reduced to rubble (Fig. 11.1). Although the reason for failure of the farm and the sequence of events that killed the reef is unreported, an EIA would have identified that water quality would be difficult to maintain in the ponds due to high evaporation, and that saline effluent would be released into adjacent coastal waters. Whether the effluent caused death of the reef is unclear in this instance, for close by was a desalination plant, which already released hypersaline water near the reef. The shallow waters also experienced regular stratification in summer, potentially causing a synergistic impact on the reef.

A further example of the need for effective EIA is evident on the steep, granitic island of Mahé in the Seychelles, where a lack of flat lands for infrastructure, industry and housing has resulted in the construction of islands on inshore shallow patch reefs (Fig. 11.2). An effective EIA would have ensured that the nearby coral reefs of Ste Anne's Marine Park, the recreational value of which was more than US$18 million in 2003, would be protected from

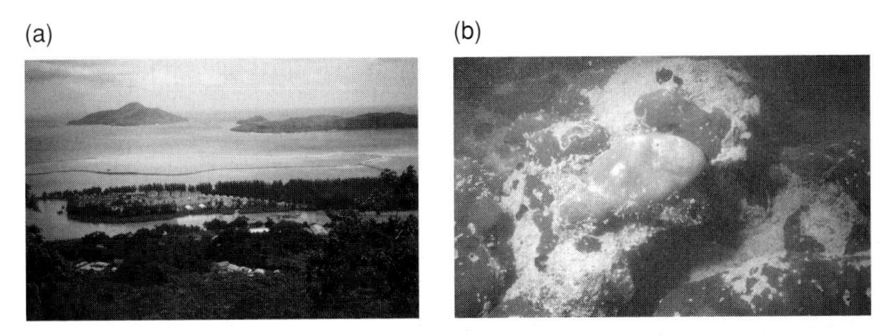

Figure 11.2 (a) Land reclamation on inshore coral reefs between the main island of Mahé and Ste Anne's Marine Park, Seychelles in 1999. (b) Coral covered in sediment in the Marine Park. Mitigation measures should have been proposed in the EIA and put in place to prevent sediment from drifting into the Marine Park because of its high tourism value. (See also Plate 11.2 in the colour plate section.)

sediment drift arising from the construction. If mitigation measures were attempted, they proved inadequate because much sediment was observed on these reefs during the construction period in 1999. High coral mortality did occur at Ste Anne's, but also on most shallow reefs around Mahé, due to the 1998 coral bleaching event (Turner *et al.*, 2000a). It is therefore not clear how much of the coral mortality was due to sedimentation from the construction project.

ENVIRONMENTAL IMPACT

An environmental impact is a change in an environmental parameter over a specified period of time and within a defined area, resulting from a particular activity when compared with the situation that would have occurred had the activity not been initiated. An impact may therefore be positive or negative. An impact must be identifiable from other causes of long-term trends in that environmental parameter over time.

For coral reefs, many long-term trends of environmental decline have been documented. For example, coastal water quality has deteriorated over recent decades around most reefs near human settlements (Bryant *et al.*, 1998; Spalding *et al.*, 2001). Long-term declines in coral cover and in numbers of large herbivores and predatory fish have been recorded (e.g. Jackson, 1997; Gardner *et al.*, 2003; Côté *et al.*, this volume). Recent events such as the mass mortality of *Diadema* urchins and acroporid corals on Caribbean reefs, and coral bleaching worldwide (Hughes, 1994; Hughes *et al.*, 2003; Precht and Aronson, this volume) are shaping these trends in change.

It is important for an EIA to consider all impacts. Moreover, an EIA should differentiate impacts arising from causes unrelated to the development (such as steady reduction in water quality in the area due to other effluents) and natural events (such as seasonal changes and storms) from those arising either directly (e.g. sediment smothering of corals due to dredging) or indirectly (e.g. deforestation of a watershed causing soil erosion and release of fine sediments, which are carried by rivers onto reefs where they smother coral) from a development project.

Social impact assessment (SIA) examines the consequences of impacts and environmental changes on people and organizations (Clark, 1996), and usually involves a cost–benefit analysis (Spurgeon, this volume). SIA is either conducted separately or as part of an EIA, depending on the likely impact of a development project on employment, relocation, price changes, accessibility, changing roles and health risks. For example, Socotran fishers used to fish only for their own communities off the undeveloped island of Socotra. The construction of roads, a refrigeration plant and port, and regular visits by factory ships to the island in recent years have resulted in fishers intensifying their fishing activities because they now have access to a wider market, but the impacts of these developments have not been adequately assessed in social terms. The resulting increased wealth might soon be expected to bring about social change because of new demand for consumer goods, and increased travel between what were relatively isolated communities on the island. Further, the increased fishing effort has increased the need for managed fisheries within the Marine Zoning Plan for Socotra (Klaus *et al.*, 2003).

THE PROCESS OF ENVIRONMENTAL IMPACT ASSESSMENT

Origin and application

Environmental impact assessment originated in the USA under the National Environment Policy Act (NEPA) of 1969, before being adopted by the United Nations in 1972. It has since become embodied in many national laws (e.g. Australia in 1975, the European Union in 1985). Many funding agencies, including the World Bank, now require EIAs for funded projects (World Bank, 1994) and EIA is mandatory for large-scale projects throughout the world (e.g. Bamber, 1990). Projects that are likely to have significant effects on the environment (e.g. ports, power stations, nuclear waste treatment) must be assessed in all cases, while EIAs for projects that may have significant effects (e.g. marinas, reclamation, resort hotels) may become mandatory depending on scale (e.g. only those hotels with 80 or more rooms may be subject to EIA).

Project action and alternatives

It is important that all phases of a development are assessed by the EIA, such that impacts arising from both the construction phase and operation phase are considered. A baseline environmental survey is often required, to allow the impacts of specific project actions over known locations to be detected. Consultants are usually contracted by the developer to conduct the EIA and to report their results in a consultation document, the Environmental Impact Statement. Alternatives to the proposed project are also examined, both in relation to location (e.g. resort hotel on mainland beach or offshore island) and method (e.g. primary treatment and long sea outfall or tertiary treatment and short sea outfall). The alternative of 'no project action' should always be examined, for other options may be foreclosed by the development (e.g. a marina in an area proposed as a marine reserve). It may be worse to do nothing (e.g. when the proposal is for a new primary sewage treatment outfall beyond the reef to replace old outfalls depositing untreated sewage within lagoons). The choice of the preferred project must be justified in the Environmental Impact Statement. Legislation requires the developer to: (a) describe the site, design and scale of the project; (b) describe measures to avoid, reduce or remedy any significant adverse impacts (so-called 'mitigation measures'); (c) provide data to support the identification and assessment of the main environmental effects of the development; and (d) provide a non-technical summary which indicates any issues to be resolved, such as unknown effects (e.g. oceanographic currents might be unrecorded for the area, hence extent of effect cannot be calculated).

Analysis and assessment

Technical knowledge is required to specify in the Environmental Impact Statement all production processes, quantities of materials used and expected residues and emissions. A thorough description of the environment to be affected must also be provided. Scientific and socio-economic knowledge is required to identify the likely impact of each major action on the environment by considering eight key 'environmental attributes': (1) human population and cultural heritage, (2) fauna and flora, (3) noise, (4) soil, (5) water, (6) air, (7) climate and (8) landscape (Fig. 11.3). Specialist analysis is then necessary to assess within each environmental attribute, the effects on appropriate 'environmental elements', such as: light penetration,

(a)

(b)

Figure 11.3 The 'environmental attributes' assessed by EIA include (a) coral reef fauna and flora and (b) cultural heritage, such as this temple and arch constructed out of coral. The 'environmental elements' assessed within each attribute include penetration of light and movement of water, essential to reef processes in (a). (See also Plate 11.3 in the colour plate section.)

water movement, dissolved oxygen, suspended solids, thermal pollution, faecal coliforms, threatened species and so forth, and any interactions that may occur between these.

Analyses in complex environments such as coral reefs require a thorough understanding of the processes and functional values of reef habitats and communities (Bellwood *et al.*, 2003; Mumby and Harborne, this volume). Wherever possible, all effects on environmental elements must be quantified. This is best done by measuring mean and variance values, and applying a weighting to distinguish impacts of different importance, and within different alternative development schemes. Forecasting is usually required, and models must use either accepted procedures or be rigorously described.

Magnitude and risk

The geographical extent, magnitude at that spatial scale, and duration of any impact must be considered, and then the risk associated with that impact assessed. An impact may be highly site-specific (such as a 10-°C thermal rise over a 100-m plume), localized (e.g. faecal coliforms in sewage), regional (e.g. mangrove removal for prawn farms), national (e.g. implementation of water-quality legislation) or international (e.g. radioactive pollution). An impact of low magnitude causes negligible alteration to environmental elements, while a medium impact will notably cause alteration, and one of high magnitude will severely alter natural processes or social functions. Impacts of short duration may last 0–5 years, while medium-term impacts might have an effect for 5–15 years and long-term impacts continue for over 15 years. Risks are high when there is uncertainty, statistically low confidence levels, and where an impact is severe and irreversible, and cannot be mitigated, or has long-term cumulative or synergistic effects. For example, using chlorine as a secondary sewage treatment might be considered a high risk if industrial wastewaters of variable content and unknown origin are treated along with diurnal pulses of domestic sewage, and the effluent discharges onto a coral reef. Although the effects of chlorine on temperate fresh and brackish water species are relatively well researched (Abarnous, 1982; Hall *et al.*, 1982; Hose *et al.*, 1989), the toxicity, persistence and bioaccumulation effects of chlorine on tropical marine organisms are not known. Sewage outfalls often provide rich fishing grounds; hence, a high risk to human health may result.

Consultation and public awareness

Public consultation is essential throughout the EIA process (Clark, 1996). The intention and consent to develop must be made public. Local people and all authorities concerned must be given an early opportunity to express their opinions (see also Brown, this volume). Issues of concern are identified by the EIA consultant, and the scope of the Environmental Impact Statement is determined by consulting widely with all stakeholders. Consultation is sought during the initial planning stages, again while identifying impacts of concern, and in response to the draft Environmental Impact Statement.

Failure to consult adequately can lead to public aggression towards a project, delay, compromised developments, increased costs and compensation. For example, in 2000 a developer began preparation for construction of a hotel on a small island within a lagoon in a marine park in Mauritius. Planning permission for the development had been granted many years before, when there were no EIA requirements. Without an EIA, potential impacts were not identified or mitigated, and initial shore-side excavations to prepare access to the island caused runoff onto some of the best shallow-water coral reefs in Mauritius. An EIA was later prepared but arguments over the progression of the works then arose between all involved, including the developer and regulating authorities, national non-governmental organizations outraged at the ecological damage, and divided local people who saw the development either providing employment or ruining their livelihoods and environment. A well-prepared EIA with extensive public consultation might have ensured an appropriate development without significant impact.

Environmental Impact Statement review

The final Environmental Impact Statement is reviewed by the regulating authorities (e.g. a national environment protection agency) and categorized as either Category 1 – when the Environmental Impact Statement adequately describes the environmental impact of the proposed project and alternatives; Category 2 – when there is insufficient information to assess fully the environmental impact of the proposed project, but a preliminary determination can be made and further information is requested; or Category 3 – when the Environmental Impact Statement inadequately analyses the environmental impacts of the proposed project and/or alternatives, and substantial revision is required concerning potential hazards before the development can be considered.

Review packages are available to assist coastal zone managers in undertaking quick, accurate and reproducible reviews (e.g. Colley and Lee, 1990). Reviews generally alert people to areas of weakness (e.g. the rationale for justification of conclusions is not given or unsuitable methods used), concealment (e.g. biased or inaccurate supporting data) or omission, rather than refute findings.

PROBLEMS IN ENVIRONMENTAL IMPACT ASSESSMENT

The traditional process of EIA is well documented and prescribed (e.g. Wathern, 1988; Carpenter and Maragos, 1989; Bamber, 1990; UNEP, 1990; Sorenson and West, 1992; World Bank, 1999). EIA should identify the likely consequences of implementing particular activities for the biogeophysical environment and for human health and welfare, and should convey this information at a stage when it can affect the decision to sanction the proposal.

Unfortunately, it is apparent that EIA often fails (Buckley, 1989; Fairweather, 1989, 1994; Underwood, 1990; Sheppard, 2003), and environments such as coral reefs are often damaged as a result. EIA may fail because the Environmental Impact Statement is inadequately prepared or reviewed, or more usually a combination of both. Common problems are a lack of rigorous exploration of project alternatives, sources of error due to a poor scientific approach, inadequate quantification of potential impacts, and overlooked environmental issues. For example, sand-dune extraction for building material and subsequent urban development has occurred on many islands, such as Mauritius, causing coastal areas to flood. In many cases, no account was taken of the effects of coral reef bleaching in 1998, which subsequently caused reef tops to degrade and the mined shores became exposed to increased overwash during storm surges (see also Sheppard, this volume).

Lack of will, priority and capacity may also result in an Environmental Impact Statement being ignored, or EIA not being conducted in the first place. It is not uncommon for an Environmental Impact Statement to be shelved on the pretence that the developer and regulating authorities have met their legal requirements, where the parties have failed to appreciate the need to commit resources to implement the recommendations made. The Environmental Impact Statement may be ignored because it is simply too large and unfocused and the generality of the data contained may fail to provide workable mitigation measures. Although the development may be of the type mandatory for EIA, the EIA may not be undertaken because of other priorities, such as emergency measures or national security. In Kuwait, for example, a military marina base is currently being constructed for border security on the offshore island of Al Maradam, which is surrounded by nearly one-third of the nation's coral reefs, yet no mitigation measures to protect the reefs are evident (Fig. 11.4a). EIA fails when, presumably to save costs, the Environmental Impact Statement for a particular project at a particular location is used for another project or another location, without a further EIA being conducted. EIA may also fail because impacts from construction may have been adequately assessed, but the impacts under operating conditions or expansion of the project have not. Finally, perhaps the commonest cause of failure of EIA is linked to the failure to ensure that the mitigation measures suggested are actually implemented (Fig. 11.4b), and that impacts predicted actually occur within the estimated range. Baseline monitoring of the environment is therefore required before development begins, and should be repeated during the construction and operational phases.

More recent developments in EIA (e.g. Morrisey, 1993) involve a rigorous hypothesis-based approach to determine whether a significant impact will occur and did occur. This approach requires examination of the causes

Figure 11.4 Some causes of failure of EIA. (a) In Kuwait, for reasons of national security, no EIA was conducted for this military base, even though construction affected a large proportion of the nation's few coral reefs. (b) Silt curtains, proposed as a measure to contain the sediment generated by this hotel development project adjacent to a marine park in Mauritius, were poorly installed and maintained.

of past disturbances to identify which variables should be measured, and monitoring before and after the development to detect change inconsistent with background change. To this end, the World Bank (1999) recommends the preparation of an Environmental Management Plan, in which the findings of the Environmental Impact Statement are linked to the implementation and operation of the project. The Environmental Management Plan summarizes: key impacts and their significance; realistic and cost-effective mitigation measures; a monitoring programme to ensure that mitigation measures are implemented and have their intended result, and that remedial measures are undertaken; the legal and institutional framework behind the mitigation; an implementation schedule; and the cost of implementing the mitigation measures and monitoring programme.

MONITORING

Monitoring programmes to detect environmental impacts should follow the Before–After/Control–Impact (BACI) approach, first recommended by Green (1979), and later developed into so-called 'Repeated Measures' or 'Beyond-BACI' designs by Green (1993) and Underwood (1991, 1992, 1993, 1994, 1996). In the original designs, rigorous monitoring of areas likely to be disturbed by a development is compared to control areas before and after the development project, and the data are subjected to analysis of variance to detect significant impacts. The improved and asymmetrical designs of Underwood (1991, 1992, 1993, 1994) similarly seek to detect impacts caused by the development, but when compared with many control areas, and against a background of natural variation over time. Implicit in these designs is the ability to detect the magnitude of the difference in measured variables between numerous control sites and a disturbed site over time. This ability increases with sample size and can be measured quantitatively with a power analysis (Green, 1989; Fairweather, 1991, Peterman, 1990; Peterson, 1993; Sheppard, 1999). Statistical power calculates the probability of an impact being detected when there is no change in the measured variable in response to the disturbance (a Type-I error), and conversely, when an impact is not detected when there is a change in the measured variable in response to the disturbance (a Type-II error). A Type-I error might lead to costly mitigation measures that were not required, but clearly the environmental consequences of committing a Type-II error are more serious in EIA, since such impacts will not be mitigated and could prove catastrophic or expensive to address in the long run. EIA should adopt monitoring designs which are more likely to make a Type-I error, and thereby follow the precautionary principle.

Rigorous monitoring designs are not without their problems. Such designs are expensive to implement, because to achieve adequate statistical power, sampling must be conducted at the site which is expected to be disturbed and at a wide range of control sites, sometimes over a wide geographical area, and replicated at irregular times throughout the seasons to detect natural change. Another common problem arises because major developments, especially industrial ones, often occur together and degrade a wide area, and it is not possible to find sufficient comparable control sites outside this area.

In the context of coral reefs, monitoring surveys are particularly expensive because it is usually necessary to measure a wide range of variables to assess benthic cover, macroinvertebrate and fish abundance and water quality. Costs can be reduced by selecting only those parameters in which change can be detected, but this requires knowledge of the magnitude of the potential impact on specific variables, and hence a baseline survey, pilot project, or past experience of effects are required. Such surveys necessarily require underwater and boat-based work, and are time-consuming to complete, and have significant logistical and safety constraints requiring more personnel and hence cost, than comparable surveys on land.

In developing countries, it can be particularly difficult to secure the funding for a comprehensive monitoring programme within an EIA. To ensure that sufficient funds are available, it is essential that EIA requirements are specified when developments are proposed and hence the developer is responsible for the costs of the EIA, which should be identified at the tendering stage. Unfortunately, scientists often join EIA consultancy teams late in the process after the programme has been set, and there is often an insufficient window of opportunity to undertake surveys at an appropriate number of control sites over time to give the survey sufficient power to detect impact adequately.

At present, the Environmental Impact Statement review process addresses the adequacy of the content of the statement, rather than refuting its findings. Insufficient responsibility rests with the developer to prove that their project actions are not harming the environment. Instead, it is the regulating authorities who must prove that a development will degrade the environment – this usually takes place only during prosecution and for compensation, after damage has occurred – and it is often difficult for them to pass on the cost to the developer of the rigorous monitoring required. Although the costs of monitoring surveys with replication at numerous control sites (and at different times of year) appear high, they are usually a minor proportion of the overall cost of a large-scale development which needs mandatory EIA (e.g. less than 1.5% in the case study below), and are likely to be exceeded by the costs of remedial measures, compensation claims, and social costs if reef damage occurs.

Underwood (1996) critically analysed the BACI monitoring designs and favoured the complex Beyond BACI designs which are most likely to reliably detect an impact, but these require sampling over wide geographic regions and over long periods of time. Kaly and Jones (1997) proposed a modified 'minimum' BACI design for monitoring impacts on coral reefs, on the basis that neither funding nor time will support full Beyond-BACI designs in many developing countries. Their design focused sampling effort to measure the extent of impact away from the primary impact site to provide an assessment of both magnitude and spatial scale of impact. With limited resources, additional sampling through space rather than through time is more affordable because of the high costs of mobilizing numerous surveys. They tested their minimum design on a dredging project in Funafuti lagoon, Fiji, and showed that the power to detect changes in fish abundance and cover of coral and algae was high (mean $\pm$ 1 SE: 90.9% $\pm$ 2.8%). Importantly, they incorporated 'during' sampling between 'before' and 'after' sampling, such that monitoring was conducted when maximum short-term effect could be documented, allowing adaptive management of the development. Perhaps the most important problem of BACI-like monitoring designs in EIA is that monitoring to record damage resulting from the construction or operation of a development does not actually protect a coral reef, because the damage has been done by the time an impact has been detected.

What is therefore required for effective environmental protection is a form of monitoring which can detect impacts as they occur, and provide feedback such that the project action can be changed immediately to stop further damage.

FEEDBACK MONITORING

A new surveillance framework for marine environmental hazard assessment was developed by Gray *et al.* (1991), in which changes in variables were compared at affected and control sites, and feedback loops were used to control discharges. Gray and Jensen (1993) further developed the approach into one of 'feedback monitoring' where continuous testing of the effect of an ongoing project is undertaken near and far from the development site. It is expected a priori that any impact should be confined to the 'near field' and that no effects due to the development should occur in the 'far field'. Through consultation with stakeholders, including the developer, regulating authority, representatives of major user groups and EIA consultants, impact thresholds for the near field are agreed. Monitoring of key environmental variables is then carried out in the near field during construction, using adequate replication to allow statistical testing, and if the agreed thresholds are exceeded, feedback loops are enacted to monitor the same variables in the far field to determine whether the impact is solely due to the development. If the project action is identified as causing the impact, then a feedback loop requires construction activity to stop immediately.

Feedback monitoring thus detects impacts as they occur, and provides a mechanism to stop the harmful action until conditions improve, or to modify the action to prevent further damage. Such reactive or adaptive management of developments is considered a potentially cost-effective approach for coral reef protection during projects in developing regions, because effort can be focused on monitoring only specific variables, for the most part only in the near field, and damaging activities can be curtailed immediately, thereby preventing excessive unrecoverable damage to a reef. The following section presents a case study in which feedback monitoring was implemented into an EIA for a large wastewater treatment plant and sea outfall in Mauritius, Western Indian Ocean.

A CASE STUDY OF FEEDBACK MONITORING: CONSTRUCTION OF A WASTEWATER OUTFALL ON A CORAL REEF IN MAURITIUS

There are many studies of the impacts of sewage discharges on coral reefs (e.g. Pastorok and Bilyard, 1985; Bell, 1991; Gast *et al.*, 1999; Edinger *et al.*, 2000). Most show that discharging sewage effluent into lagoon embayments can cause significant coral reef degradation. At Kaneohe Bay, Hawaii, for example, the introduction of secondary treatment failed to improve water quality, which declined severely when a sewage outfall was placed in the lagoon. Eventually, relocation of the outfall to an offshore, deep-water site with maximum dispersion and mixing was required to prevent further damage to the reef (Maragos *et al.*, 1985; case study by Maragos in Clark, 1996; Grigg, 1995). The problem of where to locate wastewater outfalls arises more and more frequently, as developing countries begin to control the effluents which they currently discharge untreated into the sea. Mauritius can be seen as a case in point.

Mauritius (20° S, 58° E) is the largest island (1869 km^2) of the Mascarenes Archipelago, located some 875 km from the east coast of Madagascar. The island has a volcanic mountainous topography (maximum altitude 828 m). The 258-km-long coastline is surrounded by 240 km^2 of lagoons and coral reefs (Turner and Klaus, 2005). Fringing reefs are only absent from two short stretches of coast (15.5 km in the south and 10.5 km in the west) (Fig. 11.5a), although coral colonies do grow on the younger volcanic flows of these steep slopes. Lagoons are generally shallow (less than 3 m deep), range from 0 to 8 km in width from beach to reef, and contain a variety of habitats including beaches, mangroves, lagoon channels, sand and seagrass beds, sparse coral heads and patch reefs. The reef flat is narrow (<25 m wide) and the shallow reef front is normally dominated by an algal ridge or robust *Acropora* corals to 5 m depth. Below this, spurs and grooves of the outer slopes descend, composed of a diverse range of hard (161 species) and soft corals. At greater depths (20–50 m), basalt rock is colonized by corals, soft corals, sponges and algae.

The coral reefs of Mauritius, like many in the Indian Ocean, are threatened by anthropogenic impacts (reviewed by Turner *et al.*, 2000b; Wilkinson, this volume), many of which have indirect effects on reefs, and the lagoons and their patch reefs are most vulnerable. Wastewater effluents from light industry and urbanized centres around the capital city of Port Louis are discharged untreated on the west coast, mostly within 500 m of the shore (Figs. 11.5b, 11.6a). Lagoons are contaminated by pathogens from

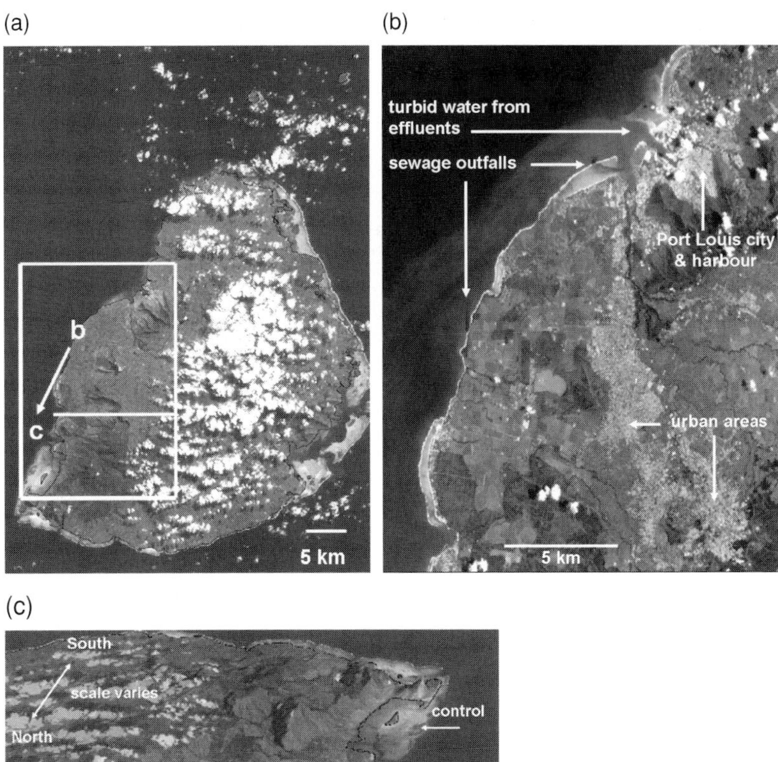

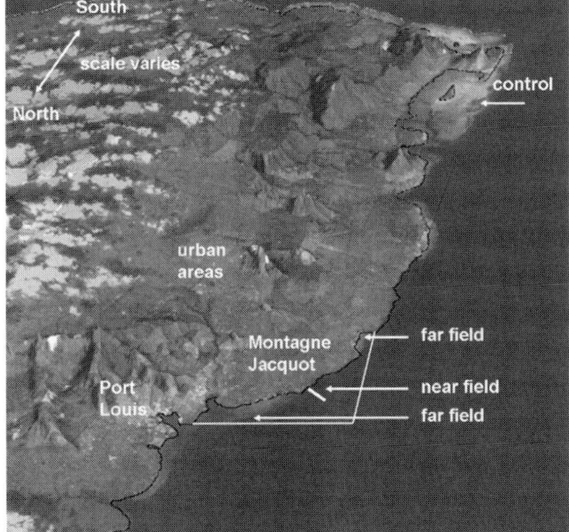

Figure 11.5 (a) Landsat satellite imagery of Mauritius showing coral reefs and lagoon areas. Boxes (b) and (c) (with arrow showing angle of view) are enlarged in the corresponding images. (b) Turbid water extending south along the coastline from Port Louis and existing sewage discharges serving urban areas. (c) Three-dimentional view from north looking south along west coast to show position of the new outfall, predicted mixing zone and near field, far field and control site locations used in the monitoring. (See also Plate 11.5 in the colour plate section.)

Figure 11.6 Effects of untreated effluent discharges on the west coast of Mauritius. (a) Poor inshore water quality is a concern and swimming within some of the lagoons is considered unsafe on health grounds. (b) Coral reefs close to outfalls are degraded, with high cover of filamentous and macroalgae and heavy sedimentation.

sewage and nutrient levels are several orders of magnitude greater within lagoons than outside reef waters (Daby, 2001; Daby *et al.*, 2002). Along the central west coast, discharges have increased water turbidity and the frequency of algal blooms, and have resulted in a proliferation of filamentous algae and corals smothered in sediment (Thomassin *et al.*, 1998) (Fig. 11.6b).

Since the early 1990s, Mauritius has been implementing a sewerage master plan, where old works, which lack treatment, are abandoned in favour of new wastewater plant with primary treatment and chlorination and offshore deep-water outfalls. One of the new sewage treatment stations was located at Montagne Jacquot, 6 km south of Port Louis on marginal lands and opposite a 10.5-km break in the fringing reef, where the rocky seabed slopes steeply to depths of over 1000 m (Fig. 11.5b, c). An exciting and novel plan to inject the wastewaters into a volcanic lava tube which extends from under the site of the plant, and emerges as cracks and fissures in the seabed, was abandoned by the World Bank, following consideration of an Environmental Impact Statement (Water Management Consultants Ltd, 2000), which highlighted possible risks of lava tunnel blockage, unknown underground strata causing discharges offsite and potential loss of unknown biodiversity from within tunnels. A conventional sea outfall was the preferred alternative (Black and Veatch International, 1997), designed to discharge at a depth of more than 30 m, 645 m out to sea onto the volcanic slope. Public concern about the development was high, because an outfall constructed earlier, north of Port Louis, had caused substantial damage to a reef and lagoon, resulting in claims for compensation from fishers. Therefore an Environmental Management Plan was prepared to link the EIA to implementation and operation of the project (Water Management Consultants Ltd, 2004a). The Environmental Management Plan provided the opportunity to introduce feedback monitoring into this development. The plan addressed four areas:

(1) how the predicted adverse impacts of construction of the outfall would be mitigated;
(2) how baseline information about the existing state of the environment would be employed to assess the positive and negative effects of the construction and operation;
(3) how threshold impacts would be identified and tested during the construction and operational phases of the development by feedback monitoring; and
(4) how the long-term positive and negative impacts of operation should continue to be assessed.

These four aspects are addressed below.

Impacts and mitigation

A number of impacts were predicted. On operation, the outfall and new wastewater treatment plant were predicted to improve marine environmental conditions overall, because two existing outfalls discharging untreated effluent would close. However, it was thought unlikely that there would be significant improvement in conditions at the discharge point in the near field, because only primary treatment with chlorination for disinfection was to be employed. Secondary treatment, involving chemical treatment or UV radiation and no chlorination was an alternative action recommended in the Environmental Impact Statement (Water Management Consultants Ltd, 2000), but this alternative was not adopted as the preferred action. Significant impacts on the coral reef were predicted during outfall construction and these could have been avoided if the alternative action of injection into the lava tunnel had been adopted. The need to cut and suction dredge, lay foundation material and armour the pipeline would displace mobile species and destroy benthic communities in the vicinity of the pipeline. Furthermore, heavy civil-engineering equipment would need to travel to and anchor at the site, and spoil would need to be dumped, and hence the spread of impacts beyond the work site had to be constrained.

Mitigation measures were proposed (Water Management Consultants Ltd, 2004a) to control movements of excavation machinery on shore;

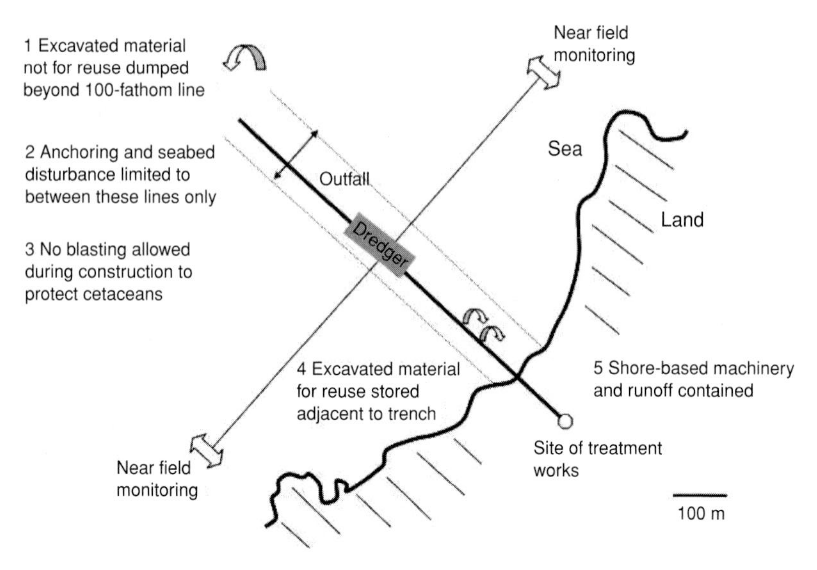

Figure 11.7 Five mitigation measures proposed during the construction of a wastewater outfall at Montagne Jacquot, Mauritius in 2004. Monitoring in the near field will take place opposite the path of the dredger as it works along the route of the planned outfall.

prevent runoff from land-based works; restrict anchoring of vessels to designated areas alongside the pipe; deploy silt curtains to reduce horizontal dispersion of fine sediments; dump excavated materials in designated areas; use clean rock and gravel for pipeline armouring; and maintain a strict ban on using explosives underwater to prevent damage to fish and cetaceans over the wider area (Fig. 11.7).

Baseline environmental survey

A baseline environmental survey was commissioned (Water Management Consultants Ltd, 2002, 2004b). Survey sites were established within the areas predicted to be affected by the construction and operation of the outfall, and control sites were selected away from the area of influence, following a minimum BACI design. Using data on effluent composition, a north–south tidal flow of 0.2 m s^{-1}, and offshore winds for 97% of the year, a dilution and tidal dispersion model was used to define the mixing zone of the effluent plume. The predicted mixing zone extended 6.5 km north and 4.5 km south of the outfall (Fig. 11.5c) and encompassed Port Louis harbour and new port-side tourist and commercial developments, two lagoon and coral reef areas, and the Albion Fisheries Research Centre aquaculture facility. The plume was not predicted to reach the reefs of the northwest and southwest which are important residential and tourism resort areas.

A benthic survey was conducted at a near field site, 100 m south of the proposed pipeline route, with stations at 6–8 m, 17–18 m and 27–30 m depth. Little was to be gained by surveying the actual footprint of pipe construction since major disturbance was expected here. Two far field control sites at the limits of the mixing zone were identified, and stations were established in comparable reef habitats at 1–3 m within the lagoons, and 6–8 m on fore-reef slopes. Further comparable habitats were surveyed at additional control sites, located off the southwest tourism zone in a rural area bound by inland mountain forest reserve and lacking industrial or domestic wastewater discharges. At each station, replicate permanent monitoring transects and water-quality monitoring stations were established. Baseline surveys were conducted under worst-case-scenario conditions with winds blowing plumes from the existing discharges onshore and across the near and far field sites.

Unexpectedly, a low-profile spur-and-groove coral reef without reef crest was found on the steep rock slope at the development site, with 34% coral cover at 18 m depth and extending from 4 m depth to more than 33 m. Coral species composition was typical of other reefs on the west coast of Mauritius, but the reef was degraded due to sediment from existing sewage plumes, especially on the shallower and less steep reef slopes at 6–8 m and 27–30 m. On the steeper slope at mid-depths, however, coral colonies were exceptionally healthy.

Coral and fish biodiversity was lower at the near field sites (48 coral species; 44 fish species) when compared to control sites (71 coral species; 62 fish species). Sedimentation rates were higher at the near fields (mean $\pm$ 1 SD: 4.98 ± 0.66 mg $cm^{-2}d^{-1}$) than at the control sites (2.66 ± 0.55 mg $cm^{-2}d^{-1}$) and measurements of photosynthetically active radiation (PAR) were more typical of coastal waters at near field sites (K_d PAR $= 0.168 \pm 0.030$) compared with oceanic waters at the control sites (K_d PAR $= 0.074 \pm 0.013$).

Development of impact thresholds and feedback loop

It was agreed from the onset that the thresholds criteria should meet five conditions. First, they must include parameters that are simple to measure on site, providing instant feedback without laboratory or computational analysis. Second, changes in these parameters must be detectable and indicative of changing conditions predicted to have the greatest impact on coral reef organisms. Third, the monitoring system must distinguish

Table 11.1. Agreed thresholds for the monitored parameters of dissolved oxygen and light penetration during construction were developed using guidelines from literature, National Environment Protection Regulations (2003) Guidelines for Coastal Water Quality, and results of a baseline environmental survey

Monitored parameter	Dissolved oxygen (DO)	Attenuation of light (coefficient of attenuation of photosynthetically active radiation, K_d PAR)
Guidelines from literature	7.8 mg l^{-1} in 30 °C seawater >4 mg l^{-1} for healthy marine communities median of 7 mg l^{-1} over 24 hrs (ie. >80% saturation) (Clark, 1996; Desa *et al.*, 2005)	0.03–0.11 for clear oceanic waters 0.15–0.71 coastal waters (Kirk, 1994)
National Environment Protection Regulations (Government of Mauritius, 2003) Guidelines for Coastal Water Quality	2 mg l^{-1} for industrial waters 5 mg l^{-1} for conservation, recreation and fishing waters	Light penetration in discharging waters to be within 10% of other non-discharging waters
Baseline survey indications during worst-case conditions (onshore wind)	9.9 mg l^{-1} offshore 6.8 mg l^{-1} at proposed site 6.0 mg l^{-1} in the inner harbour 5.8 mg l^{-1}at existing discharge	0.08 at proposed site (clear oceanic type water) 0.19–0.24 at existing discharging outfall
Agreed thresholds for near field	<2 mg l^{-1} unacceptable 2–4 mg l^{-1} of concern >4 mg l^{-1} acceptable	>0.15 unacceptable 0.1–0.15 of concern <0.1 acceptable (and should be within 10% of the comparable control site values at the time of measurement)

changes caused by the construction from other anthropogenic and natural variation. Fourth, the process of daily measurements must be safe given that large construction machinery will be operating, and sea conditions may not be calm. Finally, thresholds must be precautionary but realistic, because the cost of bringing construction to a stop is expensive in terms of standby rates for machinery such as cutter-dredgers and side-dumping stone-hopper vessels.

To set impact thresholds and devise feedback loops, the EIA used both national water-quality regulations and results of the baseline environmental survey. In Mauritius, the former takes the form of the Environment Protection (Standards for effluent discharge into the ocean) Regulations 2003 (Government of Mauritius, 2003) which provides quantified guidelines for coastal water quality based on the resources present and activities undertaken. For example, waters around coral reefs, mangroves, and seagrasses must meet the most stringent requirements for pH, dissolved oxygen, nutrients, faecal coliforms and heavy metals, while the standards to be met by waters receiving industrial and agricultural discharges can be lower. These national guidelines, together with the results obtained from the baseline environmental survey, and knowledge from experience and the literature, informed stakeholder debate, and a consensus was reached.

It was agreed that dissolved oxygen and light penetration would prove the most informative and practical measures upon which to base feedback monitoring during construction. Activities such as cut and suction dredging, rock dumping for armouring and infill, cement laying and onshore land modifications were predicted to increase fine suspended sediments causing turbidity and smothering marine life. High turbidity would be expected to change the quantity and quality of underwater irradiance, thereby reducing photosynthetic production and impeding vision in mobile fauna. Smothering of marine organisms would disrupt photosynthetic, feeding and respiratory processes. These effects would cause stress immediately, reduce productivity and increase mortality if sustained. On this basis, and in light of existing literature and national regulations (Table 11.1), threshold criteria and feedback loops were defined as shown in Fig. 11.8

The site engineer, who is employed independently of the construction company, will ensure that the contractor monitors dissolved oxygen and light attenuation daily, especially during construction activities such as dredging, cutting and armouring of the pipeline. While either parameter remains acceptable, no reaction is required. If, however, one or both near field thresholds are exceeded, then measurements must be made at the far field sites. If they are still exceeded here, then measurements must be made

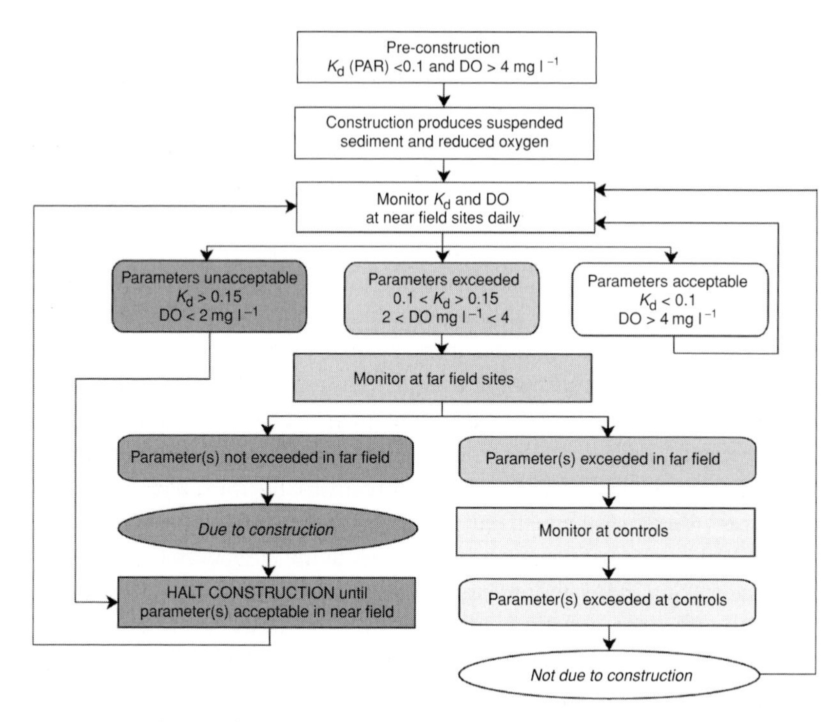

Figure 11.8 The feedback monitoring loop for reactive management designed for the construction of the wastewater outfall at Montagne Jacquot, Mauritius. The loop is based on agreed thresholds for levels of dissolved oxygen (DO) and the coefficient of attenuation of downwelling light (K_d PAR). These environmental parameters are measured in the near field (see Fig. 11.7), and compared with the agreed criteria. Additional monitoring at far field and control sites is conducted when necessary, to determine whether the development is causing an impact. Construction is halted and modified if found to be the cause of the impact.

at the control sites. If the parameters are also exceeded there, then the deteriorated conditions are deemed to be due to other phenomena and not to the construction. However, if the parameters were not exceeded at the far field site, then construction activities must cease until conditions improve, activities must be changed or additional mitigation measures must be put into place. As an additional source of independent monitoring, an environmental technician from the University of Mauritius will make random weekly measurements to verify contractor data and maintain quality control.

Long-term monitoring during plant operation

The third objective of the Environmental Management Plan was to assess the long-term impacts of the operation of the sea outfall. Positive impacts were predicted (except for the area immediately around the outfall) because of the closing down of existing outfalls, better quality of effluent and greater dispersion. It is expected to take longer for the marine environment to recover than it did to deteriorate, and hence long-term monitoring is required. In designing the long-term monitoring programme, three main principles were followed. First, long-term monitoring must be directly related to the baseline environmental survey using the same survey sites, so that changes in the condition of the marine environment can be assessed. Second, survey methods, sampling techniques and analysis methods must be the same as for the baseline survey to ensure data comparability. Third, sampling frequency should be random, to prevent synchronising with natural biological cycles. Feedback loop monitoring will be based on new threshold criteria for environmental parameters relevant to operation, rather than construction, for compliance with the Mauritius Environment Protection Act (2003) Standards for effluent discharge into the ocean. Long-term monitoring was specified for the first three years of operation, with recommendations for continuation to monitor the performance of treatment plant and outfall.

Construction of the outfall began in late 2004. This is the first time that feedback monitoring will be employed in an environmental impact assessment in Mauritius, and represents an important management initiative to prevent further impact on already stressed reef environments. Similar monitoring loops for the reactive management of construction activities are being introduced on the Great Barrier Reef (e.g. Chinn and Marshall, 2003). It is encouraging to see a small island state, such as Mauritius, at the environmental forefront in terms of efforts to adopt adaptive management practices.

LESSONS LEARNED

Environmental impact assessment is an important and powerful tool, which should allow coastal zone managers to minimize harmful environmental impacts from new developments. However, if EIA were truly effective, then coastal development activities should not be having the negative impact that they do have on coral reefs at global scales. EIA is ineffective where there is a lack of will-power, lack of public consultation, poor capacity in technical, scientific, legal and institutional areas, and a lack of financial resources. For EIA to work, a scientific approach is essential to ensure that all significant impacts are predicted and that their effects can be measured with accuracy and precision. Only with this knowledge can mitigation measures be implemented and their effectiveness continually tested. Short-term and long-term monitoring is required during pre-development, construction, operation and in many cases decommissioning phases. Failure to detect an impact which occurs and causes a change in a coral reef ecosystem can have serious implications for reef recovery and human livelihoods. Falsely detecting an impact when one does not occur may result in the ineffective deployment of resources. Although scientifically robust monitoring is expensive (due to asymmetrical designs with many control sites and repeated measures), the costs (usually up to several hundred thousand dollars) are usually a very minor proportion of the cost of a major development (tens of millions of dollars), and of the remedial actions and compensation that might result.

The challenge is for monitoring programmes in EIA to become an established procedure, which is built into every development project from its inception. In order to do this, urgent changes are needed in the way developments are managed. Responsibility is currently held by regulating authorities to show that impacts from developments occur. This responsibility needs to be transferred onto the developer, who should prove that their development will have no impact before approval is granted, and should demonstrate this during construction and operation. Feedback monitoring is a form of adaptive management which commits the developer to an automatic cessation or modification of activities should an unacceptable change in a parameter occur. The main advantage of feedback monitoring is that the developer has to pay for the monitoring to be carried out by an independent observer (with institutional support to provide quality control and specialist advice) and this is, in itself, an incentive to use less damaging methods in the construction. Only key parameters need to be measured, and normally only in the near field, and hence resources can be focused where they matter most. The procedure is simple in concept and execution, scientifically rigorous and cost-effective, and hence can be implemented in developing countries provided that there is a will.

CONCLUSIONS

Feedback monitoring is strongly advocated here, using simply measured and agreed indicating thresholds to forewarn of negative impacts and allowing for immediate reactive management during construction, as an additional mitigation measure in environmental impact to protect coral reefs. At the beginning of this chapter, we suggested that there was little coastal managers could do to minimize directly the impact of natural disturbances on coral reefs, but that they should be able to protect them from the harmful effects of development activities. If the direct protective measures discussed here are deployed against anthropogenic impacts, then coral reef resilience will be better served and reefs may be more able to respond to natural perturbations (Bellwood *et al.*, 2004). Improved EIA, embodying adaptive management, is a practical, transferable technique, which should help to conserve coral reefs.

ACKNOWLEDGEMENTS

We thank the following parties involved in the case study in Mauritius: the Waste Water Management Authority of the Republic of Mauritius; K. Seetiah (water-quality technician, University of Mauritius); Daniel Pelicier, Vassen Kauppaymuthoo and Xavier Pigeot (baseline survey and logistics, Delphinium Ltd Mauritius); Olivier Tyack (Mauritius Marine Conservation Society); Richard Wilson (sanitation engineer); Toby Sherwin (ocean modeller, CAMS Bangor); Ken Edworthy (hydrologist, Water Management Consultants Ltd); Richard Speece (anaerobic treatment specialist, Vanderbilt University, Nashville, TN). We also thank Isabelle Côté and John Reynolds, the Zoological Society of London and the Fisheries Conservation Foundation for the opportunity to present this work.

REFERENCES

Abarnous, A. (1982). The chlorine effluents in the sea: chemical aspects of water chlorination and evaluation of the toxicity for the environment. *Science et Pêche*, **321**, 1–11.

Bamber, R. N. (1990). Environmental Impact Assessment: the example of Marine Biology and the UK power industry. *Marine Pollution Bulletin*, **21**, 270–4.

Bell, P. R. F. (1991). Status of eutrophication in the Great Barrier Reef Lagoon. *Marine Pollution Bulletin*, **23**, 89–93.

Bellwood, D. R., Hoey, A. S. and Choat, J. H. (2003). Limited functional redundancy in high diversity systems: resilience and ecosystem function on coral reefs. *Ecological Letters*, **6**, 281–5.

Bellwood, D. R., Hughes, T. P., Folke, C. and Nystrom, M. (2004). Confronting the coral reef crisis. *Nature*, **429**, 827–33.

Black and Veatch International (1997). *Montagne Jacquot Environmental Sewerage and Sanitation Project: Environmental Impact Assessment Report*. BVI with Servansingh Jadav and Partners, July 1997.

Bryant, D., Burke, L., McManus, J. and Spalding, M. (1998). *Reefs at Risk: A Map-Based Indicator of Threats to the World's Coral Reefs*. Washington, DC: World Resources Institute

Buckley, R. (1989). What's wrong with EIA? *Search*, **20**, 146–7.

Carpenter, R. A. and Maragos, J. (1989). *How to Assess Environmental Impacts on Tropical Islands and Coastal Areas*. Honolulu, HI: East–West Center.

Chin, A. and Marshall, P. (2003). Reactive monitoring at Nelly bay harbour using environmental monitoring to manage marine construction activities. In *Monitoring Coral Reef Marine Protected Areas*, eds. C. Wilkinson, A. Green,

J. Almany and D. Shannon, pp. 34–5. Townsville, QLD: Australian Institute of Marine Science.

Clark, J. R. (1996). *Coastal Zone Management Handbook*. Boca Raton, FL: CRC Press.

Colley, R. and Lee, N. (1990). Reviewing the quality of environmental statements. *The Planner*, **76**, 12–14.

Constable, A. J. (1991). The role of science in environmental protection. *Australian Journal of Marine and Freshwater Research*, **42**, 527–38.

Daby, D. (2001). A review and critical assessment of coastal water quality in Mauritius. *Science and Technology, Research Journal, University of Mauritius*, **8**, 59–83.

Daby, D., Turner, J. R. and Jago, C. (2002). Microbial and nutrient pollution of coastal bathing waters in Mauritius. *Environment International*, **27**, 555–66.

Desa, E., Zingde, M. D., Vethamony, P. *et al.* (2005). Dissolved oxygen: a target indicator in determining use of the Gulf of Kachchh waters. *Marine Pollution Bulletin*, **50**, 73–9.

Edinger, E., Limmon, G. V., Jompa, J. *et al.* (2000). Normal coral growth rates on dying reefs: are coral growth rates good indicators of reef health? *Marine Pollution Bulletin*, **40**, 404–25.

Fairweather, P. G. (1989). Environmental Impact Assessment: where is the science in EIA? *Search*, **20**, 141–4.

(1991). Statistical power and design requirements for environmental monitoring. *Australian Journal of Marine and Freshwater Research*, **42**, 55–67.

(1993). Links between ecology and ecophilosophy, ethics and the requirements of environmental management. *Australian Journal of Ecology*, **18**, 3–19.

(1994). Improving the use of science in environmental assessments. *Australian Zoologist*, **29**, 217–23.

Gast, G. J., Jonkers, P. J., van Duyl, F. C. and Bak, R. P. M. (1999). Bacteria, flagellates and nutrients in island fringing coral reef waters: influence of the ocean, the reef and eutrophication. *Bulletin of Marine Science*, **65**, 523–38.

Gardner, T. A., Côté, I., Gill, J. A., Grant, A. and Watkinson, A. R. (2003). Long-term region-wide declines in Caribbean corals. *Science*, **301**, 958–60.

Government of Mauritius (2003). *Environment Protection (Standards for Effluent Discharge into the Ocean) Regulations 2003*. Port Louis: Government of Mauritius.

Gray, J. S. and Jensen, K. (1993). Feedback monitoring: a new way of protecting the environment. *Trends in Ecology and Evolution*, **8**, 267–8.

Gray, J. S., Calamari, D., Duce, R. *et al.* (1991). Scientifically based strategies for marine environmental protection and management. *Marine Pollution Bulletin*, **22**, 432–40.

Green, R. H. (1979). *Sampling Design and Statistical Methods for Environmental Biologists*. New York: John Wiley.

(1989). Power analysis and practical strategies for environmental monitoring. *Environmental Research*, **50**, 195–205.

(1993). Applications of repeated measures designs in environmental impact and monitoring studies. *Australian Journal of Ecology*, **18**, 81–98.

Grigg, R. W. (1995). Coral reefs in an urban embayment in Hawaii: a complex case history controlled by natural and anthropogenic stress. *Coral Reefs*, **14**, 253–66.

Hall, L. W., Burton, D. T. and Liden, L. H. (1982). Power plant chlorination effects on estuarine and marine organisms. *Critical Reviews in Toxicology*, **10**, 27–48.
Hose, J. E., Di Fiore, D., Parker, H. S. and Sciarrotta, T. (1989). Toxicity of chlorine dioxide to early life stages of marine organisms. *Bulletin of Environmental Contamination and Toxicology*, **42**, 315–19.
Hughes, T. P. (1994). Catastrophes, phase shifts, and large-scale degradation of a Caribbean coral reef. *Science*, **265**, 1547–51.
Hughes, T. P., Baird, A. H., Bellwood, D. R. *et al.* (2003). Climate change, human impacts, and the resilience of coral reefs. *Science*, **301**, 929–33.
Jackson, J. B. C. (1997). Reefs since Columbus. *Coral Reefs*, **16**, S23–S32.
Kaly, U. L. and Jones, G. P. (1997). Minimum sampling design for assessing the magnitude and scale of ecological impacts on coral reefs. *Proceedings 8th International Coral Reef Symposium*, **2**, 1479–84.
Kirk, J. T. O. (1994) *Light and Photosynthesis in Aquatic Ecosystems.* Cambridge: Cambridge University Press.
Klaus, R., Jones, D. A., Turner, J. R., Simoes, N. and Vousden, D. (2003). Integrated marine and coastal management: a strategy for conservation and sustainable use of marine biological resources in the Socotra Archipelago. *Journal of Arid Environments*, **54**, 71–80.
Knowlton, N. (1992). Thresholds and multiple stable states in coral reef community dynamics. *American Zoologist*, **32**, 674–82.
Lincoln-Smith, M. P. (1991). Environmental Impact Assessment: the roles of predicting and monitoring the extent of impacts. *Australian Journal of Marine and Freshwater Research*, **42**, 603–14.
Maragos, J. E., Evans, C. and Holtus, P. (1985). Reef corals in Kaneohe Bay six years before and after termination of sewage discharges (Oahu, Hawaiian Archipelago). *Proceedings 5th International Coral Reef Symposium*, **4**, 189–94.
Morrisey, D. J. (1993). Environmental Impact Assessment: a review of its aims and recent developments. *Marine Pollution Bulletin*, **26**, 540–5.
Pastorok, R. A. and Bilyard, G. R. (1985). Effects of sewage pollution on coral reef communities. *Marine Ecology Progress Series*, **21**, 75–189.
Peterman, R. M. (1990). Statistical power analysis can improve fisheries research and management. *Canadian Journal of Fisheries and Aquatic Science*, **47**, 2–15.
Peterson, C. (1993). Improvement of environmental impact analysis by application of principles derived from manipulative ecology: lessons from coastal marine case histories. *Australian Journal of Ecology*, **18**, 21–52.
Sheppard, C. R. C. (1995). Editorial: The shifting baseline syndrome. *Marine Pollution Bulletin*, **30**, 766–7.
(1999). How large should my sample be? Some quick guides to sample size and the power of tests. *Marine Pollution Bulletin*, **38**, 439–47.
(2003). Editorial: Environmental carpetbaggers. *Marine Pollution Bulletin*, **46**, 1–2.
Sorensen, J. and West, N. (1992). *A Guide to Impact Assessment in Coastal Environments.* Nawagansett, RI: University of Rhode Island: Coastal Resources Center.
Spalding, M. D., Ravilious, C. and Green, E. P. (2001). *World Atlas of Coral Reefs.* Berkeley, CA: University of California Press.

Thomassin, B. A., Gourbesville, P., Gout, B. and Arnoux, A. (1998). Impact of an industrial and urban sewage off a coral fringing reef at Mauritius (Indian Ocean): modelling plumes, distribution of trace metals in sediments and effects of the eutrophication on coral reef communities. In *Engineering for Sustainable Use of the Oceans: Conference Proceedings*, pp. 301–5.

Turner, J. R. and Klaus, R. (2005). Coral reefs of the Mascarenes, Western Indian Ocean. *Philosophical Transactions of the Royal Society A*, **363**, 229–50.

Turner, J. R., Jago, C., Daby, D. and Klaus, R. (2000a). The Mascarene Region. In *Seas at the Millennium: An Environmental Assessment*, vol. 2, *The Indian Ocean to the Pacific*, ed. C. R. C. Sheppard, p. 253–68. Amsterdam: Pergamon.

Turner, J. R., Klaus, R. and Engelhardt, U. (2000b). The reefs of the granitic islands of the Seychelles. In *Coral Reef Degradation in the Indian Ocean*, eds. D. Souter, D. Obura and O. Linden, p. 77–86. Stockholm: CORDIO/Swedish Agency for Research Cooperation.

Underwood, A. J. (1990). Experiments in ecology and management: their logics, functions and interpretations. *Australian Journal of Ecology*, **15**, 365–89.

(1991). Beyond BACI: experimental designs for detecting human environmental impacts on temporal variations in natural populations. *Australian Journal of Marine and Freshwater Research*, **42**, 569–87.

(1992). Beyond BACI: the detection of environmental impacts on populations in the real, but variable world. *Journal of Experimental Marine Biology and Ecology*, **161**, 145–78.

(1993). The mechanics of spatially replicated sampling programmes to detect environmental impacts in a variable world. *Australian Journal of Ecology*, **18**, 99–116.

(1994). On beyond BACI: sampling designs that might reliably detect environmental disturbance. *Ecological Applications*, **4**, 3–15.

(1996). *Environmental Design and Analysis in Marine Environmental Sampling*, Intergovernmental Oceanographic Commission Manuals and Guides No. 34. Paris: UNESCO.

UNEP (1990). *An Approach to Environmental Impact Assessment for Projects affecting the Coastal and Marine Environment*. UNEP Regional Seas Reports and Studies No. 122. Nairobi: UNEP.

Water Management Consultants Ltd (2000). *Environmental Sewerage and Sanitation Project, Environmental Impact Assessment of Treated Wastewater Disposal via Borehole Injection, Mauritius*, Final Report No. 1539/R1, ed. R. Wilson, K. Edworthy, J. R. Turner *et al.* Shrewsbury: Water Management Consultants Ltd.

(2002). *Montagne Jacquot Environmental Monitoring*, Interim Report No. 1725/R1, eds. R. Boak, J. R. Turner and D. Daby. Shrewsbury: Water Management Consultants Ltd.

(2004a). *Montagne Jacquot Environmental Sewerage and Sanitation Project, Updated Environmental Management Plan*, Final Report No. 1884/R1, ed. R. Boak. Shrewsbury: Water Management Consultants Ltd.

(2004b). *Montagne Jacquot Environmental Sewerage and Sanitation Project, Report on Baseline Survey of Marine Environment*. Wastewater Management Authority, eds. R. Boak, J. R. Turner, R. Klaus, E. Hardman and D. Daby. Shrewsbury: Water Management Consultants Ltd.

Wathern, P. (1988). *Environmental Impact Assessment: Theory and Practice*. London: Unwin Hyman.
Wilkinson, C. (ed.) (2004). *Status of the Worlds Coral Reefs: 2004*. Townsville, QLD: Australian Institute of Marine Science.
World Bank (1994). *Environmental Assessment Sourcebook*, Vol. 3, *Guidelines for Environmental Assessment of Energy and Industry Projects*, World Bank Technical Paper No. 154. New York: Environment Department, World Bank.
(1999). *Environmental Management Plans: Environmental Assessment Sourcebook Update No. 25*. New York: Environment Department, World Bank.

12

Time for a third-generation economics-based approach to coral management

JAMES SPURGEON
Jacobs Babtie, UK

INTRODUCTION

This chapter conveys a simple but critical message. Coral reefs provide an immense yet still underestimated value to society. Benefits include, amongst other things: food, recreation, education, health, coastal protection, support of other ecosystems and species, and enjoyment from social, cultural and spiritual aspects, as well as income generation and livelihood support (see Spurgeon, 1992; Moberg and Folke, 1999; Cesar, 2002; Whittingham *et al.*, 2003; Ahmed *et al.*, 2004). Regrettably though, corals are in serious decline and efforts to manage and protect them are generally inadequate and significantly under-resourced in terms of money and management skills.

In recent years economic approaches have been recognized as potentially providing powerful underpinning support for effective coral reef protection. However, given the continuous decline in status of corals (Wilkinson, 2004; Wilkinson, this volume) and the current unprecedented dynamic nature of the global economy, it is time for an updated economics-based approach. The approach needs to be more effective in demonstrating the benefits from enhancing coral management and protection, and should facilitate the maximization of potential long-term benefits derived from healthy coral reefs. To achieve this we need to broaden the issues explored, go well beyond just 'knowing' the 'numbers', and embrace a far more integrated and radical 'third-generation' economics-based approach.

Coral Reef Conservation, ed. Isabelle M. Côté and John D. Reynolds.

Aim and contents

An introduction to coral reef economics and a fairly comprehensive set of different coral reef values can be found elsewhere (e.g. Spurgeon, 1992; Cesar, 2002; Ahmed *et al.*, 2004). Consequently, to avoid replication, this chapter mainly focuses on highlighting how approaches to coral reef economics have developed and broadened, and how they need to further evolve in the future to aid coral conservation measures. A principal aim is thus to provoke thought and much needed change.

The introduction sets the scene by stressing some of the problems faced both in terms of our proficiency in estimating economic values for coral reefs, and with respect to the ever-growing threats to coral reefs in the turbulent and dynamic global market that now exists. The chapter then outlines the 'first-generation' approach based on a welfare economics perspective and the concept of total economic value. A more integrated 'second-generation' approach is then detailed, highlighting additional perspectives to be considered for a more holistic appreciation of coral values that includes: economic impacts; financial aspects; socio-economics and other indicators. The concept of a new 'third-generation' approach is then proposed. Finally, the chapter concludes by recommending steps to facilitate application of second- and third-generation economic approaches, thereby leading to improved coral reef management.

An immense yet underestimated value

The most authoritative and credible estimate of the global value of coral reefs to date is that by Cesar *et al.* (2003), who estimated net benefits of 'nearly US$ 30 billion year^{-1}' to the global economy. Using a 3% discount rate and a 50-year timeframe, the corresponding global asset value of coral reefs is thus nearly US$800 billion. The relative composition of this value in terms of key goods and services is provided in Fig. 12.1. It is based on an extrapolation of economic values from various studies and assumes a world area of 284 000 km^2 of coral reefs, representing an average value of US$0.10 m^{-2} yr^{-1} of coral.

However, this estimate significantly underestimates the true value of corals. This is partly because many other benefits such as social, cultural, pharmaceutical and sand generation are omitted, but also because the biodiversity/non-use value (18% of the total) is probably vastly underestimated. For example, the American Samoa case study outlined later in this chapter reveals that non-use values, which represent the enjoyment gained by individuals without necessarily making personal use of the corals, could

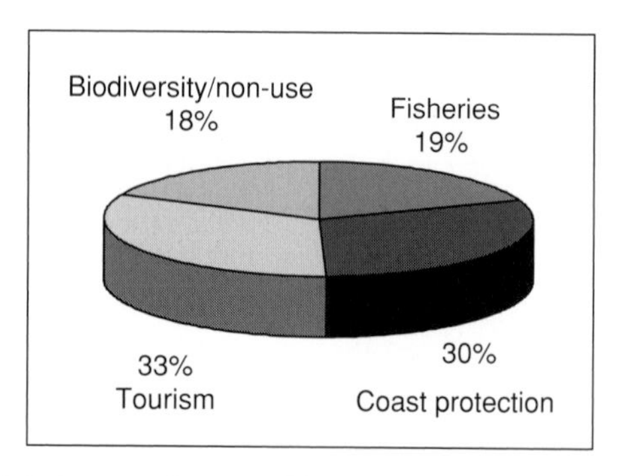

Figure 12.1 Relative contribution of various goods and services to the global value of coral reefs. (Modified from Cesar *et al.*, 2003.)

account for over 88% of the total annual value of their coral reefs. However, use values, particularly recreational use values, are admittedly relatively low in American Samoa.

It is worth noting that the widely publicized paper by Costanza *et al.* (1997), which estimated the value of the world's ecosystem services and natural capital, implied a global value of corals of US\$377 billion yr^{-1}. This estimate was based on an assumed value of US\$6075 ha^{-1} yr^{-1} for 620 000 km^2 of coral reefs, or an equivalent of US\$0.60 m^{-2} yr^{-1}. The benefits evaluated for coral reefs comprised recreation (50%), coast protection (45%), food production (4%) and waste treatment (1%). However, the overall estimates for all habitats valued, including corals, is acknowledged to be uncertain due to well-recognized limitations in the valuation approach (e.g. Costanza *et al.*, 1997, 1998). Certainly for coral reefs, it appears to have extrapolated values from relatively high-value sites and applied them to all other coral reefs. For the specific services it represents, the value is thus probably an overestimate. However, other coral values with fewer estimates of value in the literature were omitted (e.g. non-use values, indirect services, medical and pharmaceutical uses, etc.) so the overall estimated coral value may actually be an underestimate.

To add reality to these large numbers, and to highlight their potential underestimation, it is interesting to note the outcome of a recent ship-grounding incident in Yemen. In August 2004, the *Iran Ardebil* ran aground on Mayyoun Island, damaging 2350 m^2 of coral reef. Despite the fact that corals there support minimal tourism and fishing activities, and provide no coast protection function, the shipping insurance company paid damage compensation of US\$1.9 million to the Yemen government. This represents

US\$809 m^{-2} or US\$30 m^{-2} yr^{-1} assuming a 3% annuity discount rate. The claim and settlement were based on restoration and monitoring costs (see also Jaap *et al.*, this volume), backed by strong arguments relating to their non-use value (i.e. the relative uniqueness and quality of corals in the vicinity of the incident). Although strictly speaking a 'legal' rather than an 'economic' value, the value of US\$30 m^{-2} yr^{-1} is real in that it was actually paid and could be drawn upon in the future to inform other coral damage incidents.

Decline in coral status, inadequate management and increasing pressures

The fact that global coral reef status is under serious threat, with some locations facing particularly drastic degradation, is well documented. According to Wilkinson (2004), at a global level, 20% of the world's corals have been effectively destroyed, 24% are at imminent risk of collapse through human pressure, and a further 26% are under longer-term threat of collapse. The slow growth of corals and their strict requirement for certain conditions further compound the severity of this problem.

Meanwhile, in the Caribbean, Burke and Maidens (2004) report that 64% of corals are currently threatened by human activities (10% very high, 33% high and 21% medium threat). Around 60% of Caribbean corals are threatened by over-fishing, 35% are threatened by inland sediment and pollution, and 33% by coastal development. Coral cover in this region has declined from 55% to *c.* 10% in the past three decades (Gardner *et al.*, 2003; Côté *et al.*, this volume). Disease and rising sea temperatures serve to intensify those impacts which stem from anthropogenic activities, thereby causing additional loss of corals and keystone organisms (Harvell *et al.*, 1999; McWilliams *et al.*, 2005; Precht and Aronson, this volume).

The inadequate and under-resourced management and protection of coral reefs is also widely acknowledged (e.g. Wilkinson, 2004), but less often quantified. Burke and Maidens (2004) report that in the Caribbean, only 20% of corals are within marine protected areas (MPAs), and only 6% of the 285 MPAs are effectively managed.

Unfortunately, given today's unprecedented dynamic business climate and the key trends affecting the global economy, the status of the world's coral reefs is likely to decline further. Figure 12.2 highlights some key trends and associated consequences likely to have adverse effects on coral reefs. Whilst some trends are well recognized, others are perhaps more subtle. Examples include technological advances that will lead to more efficient

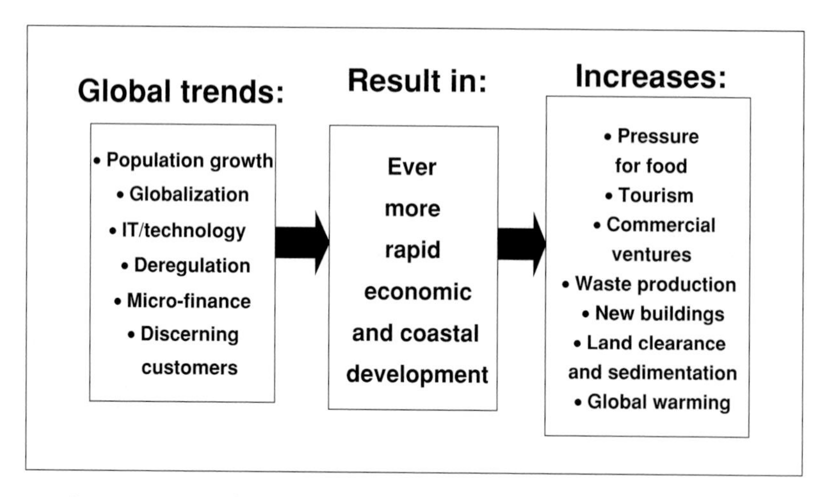

Figure 12.2 Key global trends likely to have adverse effects on coral reefs.

fishing techniques, increased micro-finance initiatives that will result in better-off local communities demanding more resources, and increasingly discerning global consumers who will desire a greater variety of products and activities to satisfy their more sophisticated demands.

The potential solution

So what is the solution to all this gloom and doom? There is of course no single solution. The answer lies in tackling the issues in a multitude of creative ways at all levels. In order to slow down and reverse current trends, whatever approaches are adopted certain features are required (see Box 12.1.). Costanza (2003) also stresses the need for a dramatic shift in the way we approach science if we are to end up with a sustainable and desirable world to live in. Amongst other things, he advocates a consilient transdisciplinary approach that draws upon: envisioning; a pragmatic philosophy built on complex systems theory and modelling; a multiscale approach; and a consistent theory of cultural and biological co-evolution.

FIRST-GENERATION ECONOMIC VALUATION APPROACHES

Welfare economics

The *Concise Oxford Dictionary* describes economics as the 'practical science of the production and distribution of wealth'. A strand of economics most

Box 12.1 Necessary features of future solutions to protect coral reefs

(1) Address the root causes of problems.
(2) Radical and innovative yet simple to implement.
(3) Collaborative, involving a blend of organizations such as governments, businesses, academic institutions, NGOs and local groups.
(4) Supported by appropriate politicians, businesses, 'personalities' and local people.
(5) Supported by appropriately targeted awareness campaigns at all levels.
(6) Holistic, integrated and multidisciplinary in approach.
(7) A mix of global, regional and local regulations and market-based instruments.
(8) 'Third-generation' economics-based approaches.

relevant to the use and management of coral reefs is neoclassical 'welfare economics', which can be defined as the 'science guiding the optimum allocation of scarce resources between competing uses for the maximization of human welfare'. Few could argue that this is not what humans should be striving for with respect to managing and protecting coral reefs for the long term.

At the heart of neoclassical welfare economics is the concept of measuring welfare (i.e. utility or individual preferences). This is generally achieved by measuring people's 'willingness to pay' for additional (marginal) units of a good or service, and aggregating it to determine total net benefits (i.e. less costs) for a national economy.

A few decades ago it became apparent that conventional economic and welfare economic approaches that relied on market prices failed to account for the true value of environmental goods and services. This is because some environmental goods (e.g. certain fish and recreational use) and most services (e.g. coastal protection) are not traded and thus have no recognizable market value. As a result, government decision-makers would make inappropriate decisions resulting in serious degradation of natural resources. This led to the introduction of 'environmental economics' as a means of helping to correct such 'market failures' (e.g. see Pearce *et al.*, 1989).

Box 12.2 Potential applications of welfare economics to coral reef management

(1) To prioritise where expenditure is best targeted.
(2) To enhance decision-making for optimising welfare.
(3) To highlight the winners and losers and facilitate equitable distribution.
(4) To help justify additional management costs and expenditure.
(5) To inform damage assessments and determine appropriate compensation.
(6) To help control people's behaviour and utilization of resources.
(7) To enhance revenue generation.
(8) To maximize benefits.
(9) To minimize costs.

Environmental economics predominantly focuses on the development and application of environmental valuation and economic instruments, although it does address other issues such as international trade and sustainability. Environmental valuation involves estimating monetary values for environmental goods and services. Economic instruments are market-based means of incorporating non-market-based environmental values (i.e. externalities) within the decision-making process (i.e. internalized).

When its inadequacies are appropriately corrected for, approaches based on welfare economics give rise to various potentially valuable applications that can assist coral reef management. These uses are briefly outlined in Box 12.2.

Total economic values

The first generation of economic-based approaches applied to coral reefs was predominantly that of welfare economics, focusing on different components of the concept of total economic value (TEV). Examples include Hodgson and Dixon (1989), Spurgeon (1992), Cesar (1996), and numerous others cited by Cesar (2002), and Ahmed *et al.* (2004). The key elements of the TEV concept are highlighted in Fig. 12.3 and are described in more detail in Spurgeon (1992) and Cesar (2002). The main point of TEV is that ecosystems such as coral reefs provide benefits and value to individuals and society, not only from direct uses, for example from tourism and

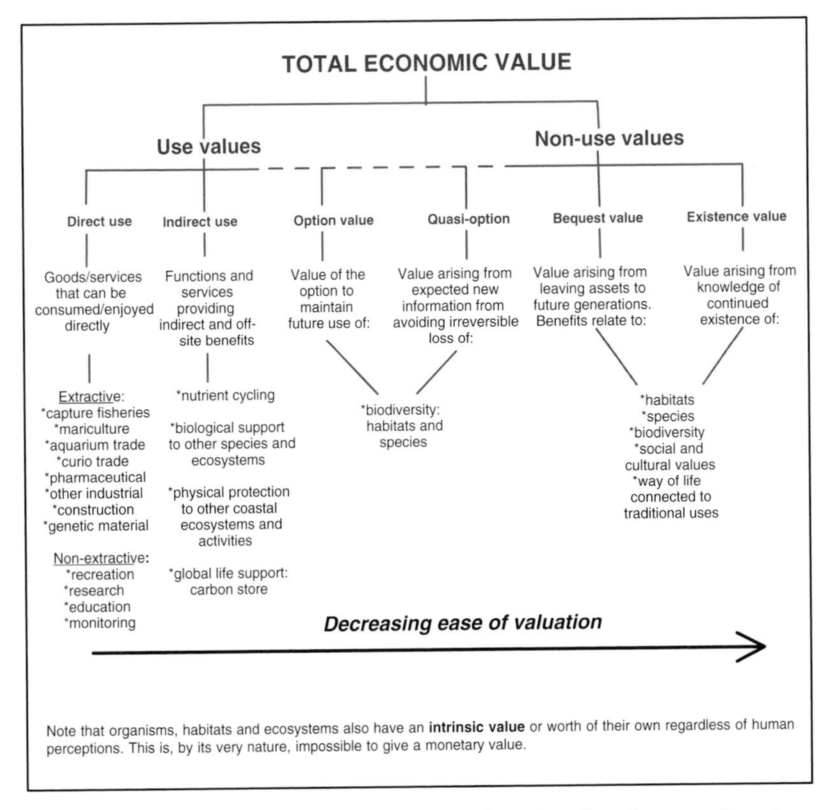

Figure 12.3 The concept of total economic value. (Based on Spurgeon (1992) and Barton (1994).)

fisheries, but also from indirect uses and without necessarily any actual use (i.e. non-use value).

Indirect-use values relate to the fact that benefits can accrue indirectly (i.e. off-site), away from coral reefs, for example through providing a coastal protection function whereby wave energy is absorbed hence protecting nearby resources on land (e.g. Sheppard, this volume). Non-use values relate to the fact that people may derive benefit simply from knowing that corals continue to exist, with motives relating to their own personal satisfaction (existence value), for the benefit of future generations (bequest value), for their own possible future use (option value) or for other people's current use (altruistic value). Organisms, habitats and ecosystems also have an 'intrinsic value' or worth regardless of human perceptions. It is impossible to place a monetary value on intrinsic value, but it should not be ignored.

Economic welfare valuation techniques

Many techniques are available to estimate the economic welfare value of environmental goods and services, as summarized in Table 12.1. Further details and guidance on how they can be applied can be found in Hufschmidt *et al.* (1983), Grigulas and Congar (1995), Dixon *et al.* (1997) and Bennett and Blamey (2001).

Examples of applications

The number of neoclassical welfare valuation studies conducted to date is expanding, but is still limited. Applications tend to focus either on specific types of value at a specific location, or on partial/complete valuations assessing impacts of different management or development options on a range of key values for a location or country. A comprehensive range of such examples is reported in Cesar (2002) and Ahmed *et al.* (2004).

More sophisticated examinations of specific values include studies by Rudd and Tupper (2002) and Weilgus *et al.* (2003). They have explored recreational and non-use values associated with specific coral reef attributes using choice experiments (e.g. effects of water quality, and abundance and size of fish and corals). Rudd and Tupper (2002) found that divers in the Turks and Caicos were willing to pay at least US$10 more per dive to observe larger or more abundant Nassau groupers (*Epinephelus striatus*). Weilgus *et al.* (2003) found that divers in Israel were willing to pay US$2.60 and US$1.20 per increased unit of fish diversity and water visibility, respectively, per dive.

There are also applications at a global and regional level, albeit using many crude assumptions. Examples include Cesar *et al.*'s (2002) global estimate of coral reef value, Burke *et al.*'s (2002) estimate for Southeast Asia and Burke and Maidens' (2004) estimate for the Caribbean. Average net benefit values applied for these studies range from US$700 to US$270 000 km^{-2} for tourism; US$14 500 to US$41 000 km^{-2} for fisheries; US$2000 to US$1 000 000 km^{-2} for coast protection; and US$2400 to US$75 000 km^{-2} for aesthetic/biodiversity value.

An example of a recent state-of-the-art first-generation economic welfare study attempting a more complete valuation of coral reef values is one undertaken in American Samoa (Spurgeon *et al.*, 2004; Spurgeon and Roxburgh, in press). As outlined in Box 12.3, it incorporates monetized social and non-use values as well as key ecosystem service values. The study estimated an annual value of coral reefs of US$1.3 million without non-use,

Table 12.1. Environmental valuation techniques

Category of technique	Name of technique	Description of approach
Market-price based	Market values	This approach is based on the assumption that the value of a good is based on its price in the market place. The value of the good is taken as the market price, less the cost of production and any transfer payments made, such as taxes and subsidies.
	Change in productivity	Changes in environmental quality can lead to changes in productivity and production costs, which in turn lead to changes in the volume and price of goods. For example, a decline in coral reef quality will lead to a decline in artisanal fishery catch and hence loss of market value.
	Damage costs avoided	Under this approach, the value of an environmental asset, such as coastal or flood protection, is taken to be represented by the saving made by avoiding damage to assets it protects. For example, the value of coastal defence provided by a beach or coral reef would be considered to be equal to the cost of repairing or replacing infrastructure and buildings damaged by erosion and flooding.
	Substitute/ surrogate prices	The substitute or alternative cost approach values a particular environmental service or good according to the market value of available substitutes. If an alternative good or service that provides a similar benefit has a market value, then the market price for this can be used as a proxy for the non-marketed good or service. For example, fish consumed at a subsistence use level can be assumed to have the same value as similar fish sold in a nearby market.
	Defensive or preventative expenditure	Defensive expenditures, such as the provision of extra-filtration for purifying water, are considered as minimum estimates of the benefits of environmental improvements. Such an increase in quality must provide a benefit to the individual at least as great as the cost of the defensive equipment, because otherwise the individual would settle for lower quality and avoid spending the money.
	Expected values	Value is based on potential revenues (less potential production costs) multiplied by probability of occurrence.
Cost-based	Replacement cost	The value of an environmental asset (or the function it performs) can be given a proxy value based on the cost of replacing the function with an alternative. For example, the value of a coral reef's shoreline protection function can be estimated based on the cost of providing an equivalent man-made shoreline protection scheme.

(*cont.*)

Table 12.1. (*cont.*)

Category of technique	Name of technique	Description of approach
Revealed preference/surrogate market (uses market-based information to infer a non-marketed value)	Travel cost method	This technique centres on the expenditure incurred by households or individuals in order to reach recreational sites, such as diving destinations, and uses these expenditures as a mean of measuring willingness to pay for the recreational activity. The sum of the cost of travelling, including the opportunity cost of time and any entrance fee, gives a proxy for market prices in estimating demand for the recreational opportunity provided by the site under investigation. By observing these costs and the number of trips that take place at each of the range of prices, it is possible to derive a demand curve and hence overall value for the particular site.
	Hedonic price	This approach seeks to isolate the contribution that environmental attributes make to the total market value of an asset. For example, the proportion of the price differential between two otherwise identical houses accounted for by being within a protected area or overlooking a healthy coral reef reveals an individual purchaser's valuation of the importance of that attribute.
Stated preference/construed market approach (questionnaire surveys to ask people's direct willingness to pay)	Contingent valuation	This is a carefully constructed and analysed questionnaire survey technique asking a representative sample of respondents how much they are willing to pay (WTP) for an environmental benefit or what they are willing to accept (WTA) in compensation for a loss. The questionnaire format thus stimulates a hypothetical (contingent) market for a particular good.
	Choice experiments	As above, however, respondents are presented with several short descriptions of a composite good (e.g. a good, such as a diving destination, described in terms of a number of valuable characteristics, such as fish diversity, fish abundance, coral health, and price to pay). Each description is treated as a complete package and differs from the other packages in respect to one or more of the good's characteristics. Respondents then select their preferred package (pairwise comparison) based on their personal preferences. It is then possible to isolate the effects that variation in individual characteristics has on the price.
Transfer of values	Benefit (value) transfer	This methodology uses the transfer of economic values estimated in one context and location in order to estimate values in a similar or different context and location. The values should ideally be adjusted based on key criteria and variations that apply in the different contexts and locations. This technique is increasingly being used when it is not feasible to carry out primary data collection.

Source: Spurgeon *et al.* (2004).

Box 12.3 Total economic valuation case study: American Samoa

Aim The study aimed to determine the total economic value of coral reefs and mangroves for all five main islands of American Samoa (Pacific Ocean). By estimating different current and potential values it was hoped that this would assist with the design and implementation of an Integrated Coastal Zone Management strategy.

Approach The study comprised four main data gathering processes: a review of literature; interviews with technical experts on the islands; focus groups with representatives of selected villages; and a willingness-to-pay questionnaire survey targeted at local residents on the main islands of Tutuila and Ofu.

The willingness-to-pay survey attempted to elicit the value that local residents place on maintaining the islands' coral (and mangroves) in terms of both enjoyment from subsistence fishing and non-use value (evaluated based on willingness to contribute money or time subsequently converted to money, based on a standard wage rate). Non-use value for visitors and the US public were based on assumed benefit transfer values (see Table 12.1). Fishery values were based on market and substitute prices, and coastal protection benefits were calculated based on cost savings from delaying the installation and repair of coastal protection structures.

Based on the identification of potential threats and opportunities, total potential benefits (over 25 years) were also evaluated and compared under a business-as-usual (BAU) scenario and an optimum sustainable management (OSM) scenario.

Results The estimated annual coral value was around US$10 million, comprising: subsistence fishery US$650 000; artisanal fishery US$45 000; recreation US$75 000; indirect fishery US$70 000; coast protection US$450 000; resident non-use US$3.6 million; visitor non-use US$215 000; and US public non-use possibly in the order of US$5 million. The breakdown of TEV below shows that non-use value (which includes a strong element of social and cultural value) represents potentially around 88% of overall benefits. The value equates to an average US$0.05 m^{-2} yr^{-1}, but site-specific values were considerably higher (up to US$2.5 m^{-2} yr^{-1}), particularly where the corals are important for fisheries, coastal protection, recreation and their protected area status.

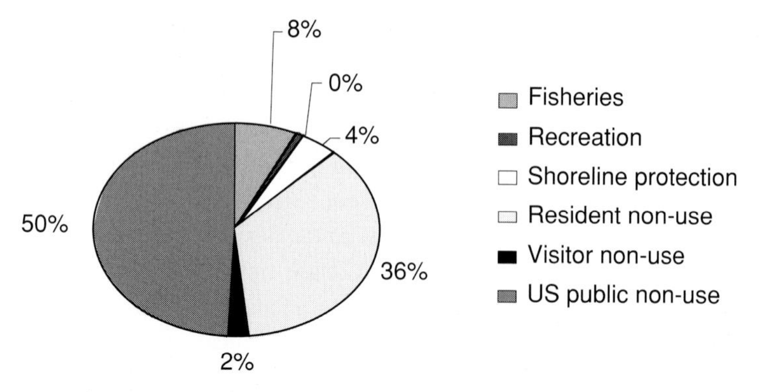

Other key findings were that:

- Ongoing beach mining has resulted in a cost of US\$0.5–2.3 million yr^{-1} (i.e. US\$90–450 m^{-3} bag of sand/coral rubble) due to the resulting need for man-made coastal protection installations. This excludes the considerable potential lost recreational value.
- There is much scope to enhance and increase capture of fishery, tourism and non-use values.
- An OSM scenario could result in benefits that are five times greater than those of the BAU scenario in 25 years time.

Contributors The project was undertaken by James Spurgeon, Toby Roxburgh and Stefanie O'Gorman of Jacobs, Dr Nick Polunin of the University of Newcastle upon Tyne, Robert Lindley of the Marine Resource Assessment Group (MRAG) and Doug Ramsey of the National Institute of Water and Environmental Management (NIWA). It was conducted for the American Samoa Department of Commerce and Coral Reef Advisory Group (CRAG), and was funded by the US National Oceanic and Atmospheric Administration.

US\$5 million including resident and visitor non-use values, and possibly an additional US\$5 million (between US\$0.5 million and US\$100 million or more) for potential US citizen non-use value. The case study reveals that non-use values in this instance could represent at least 88% of the overall value. As such, this suggests that the non-use value of Fig. 12.1 is perhaps a considerable underestimate. An interesting innovation of the American Samoa study was that the different values were mapped out and determined on a spatial basis around the islands using remote sensing and geographical information system (GIS) technology (see Fig. 12.4).

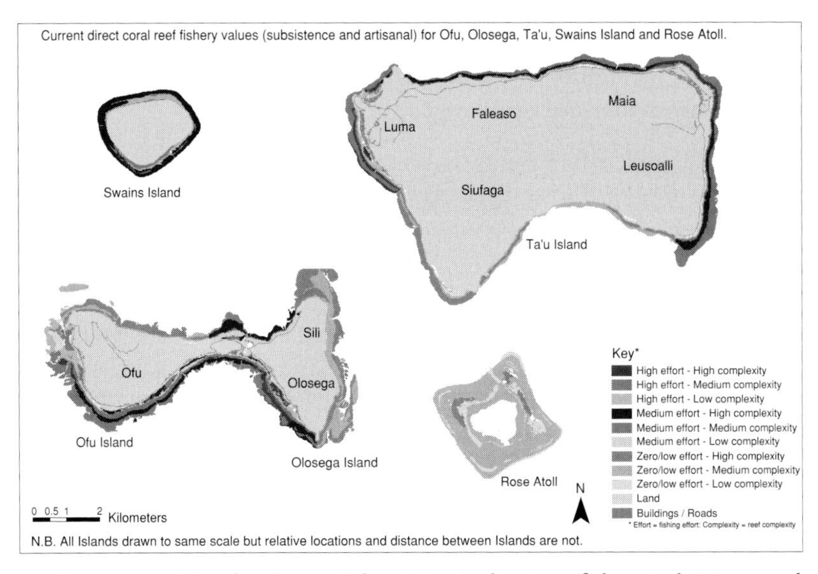

Figure 12.4 Map showing spatial variation in direct use fishery (subsistence and artisanal) values for four islands in American Samoa. (From Spurgeon *et al.*, 2004.) (See also Plate 12.4 in the colour plate section.)

SECOND-GENERATION APPROACHES TO CORAL REEF VALUATION

Comprehensive first-generation neoclassical welfare-based economics approaches encompassing the concept of TEV are still only just becoming relatively mainstream and accepted by decision-makers. However, over the past decade or so, growing concern from a number of academics and think-tanks has arisen, highlighting the fact that neoclassical welfare economics is failing us when it comes to more sustainable and equitable decisions regarding use of the planet's valuable resources. Box 12.4 provides a brief summary of thinking behind the need to evolve from a purely neoclassical approach to resource allocation decision-making, in particular highlighting the advent of ecological economics.

Consequently, a potential second-generation economics-based approach to valuing coral reefs has arisen, although it does not yet appear to have been fully applied. It can best be described as an approach that draws upon and fully integrates a far wider mix of indicators of 'value', as advocated to an extent by ecological economists. Five main categories of such 'values' are outlined and briefly compared in Table 12.2. Note that most existing coral reef valuation studies tend to focus on one category of value, rarely addressing the full range of other value types.

Box 12.4 A summary of thoughts on the need to embrace alternatives to neo-classical welfare economics

In an attempt to move away from neo-classical economics, Costanza (1989) presented what he proclaimed to be a new discipline of 'ecological economics'. It was introduced as a new field that addresses 'the relationships between ecosystems and economic systems in the broadest sense'. He went on to say: 'It will include neoclassical environmental economics and ecological impact studies as subsets, but will also encourage new ways of thinking about linkages between ecological and economic systems.' Later, Costanza *et al.* (1991) suggested an additional interpretation of ecological economics. They stressed the transdisciplinary nature of ecological economics and the fact that it focused more directly on the problems rather than the particular intellectual tools and models used to solve them, thereby ignoring arbitrary intellectual turf boundaries.

Interestingly, Pearce and Barbier (2000) argue that ecological economics is not a new discipline as such, rather a new category of analysis, or synthesis of approaches, where a single discipline approach will not suffice. However, Pearce (2006) does acknowledge five features of ecological economics that distinguish it from environmental economics. These are that ecological economics tend to (1) place greater emphasis on the Earth's 'limits' and regard environmental problems as more serious, (2) reject the substitutability assumption implicit in neoclassical production functions, (3) reject the 'smoothness' of various production functions in neoclassical economics suggesting a preference for quantity-based regulations rather than economic instruments, (4) be more suspicious of discounting future costs and benefits and monetizing environmental damage, and (5) stress the well-known fact in welfare economics that what is economically efficient is not necessarily optimum from the standpoint of a social welfare function.

Far more radical arguments have been put forward by Ekins *et al.* (1993) and Robertson (1999) who state the urgent need for a 'new economics'. Ekins *et al.* (1992) suggest that 'economic progress should be directed to the well-being of people and the earth, and quality of life rather than quantity of consumption and accumulation'. Robertson (1999) promotes the subordination of money-based calculations and values to real-life considerations and ethical and political values.

More recently, Gowdy (2004) claims that welfare economics is undergoing a revolution, as revealed by relatively modern 'experiment-based' economics approaches. He points out that the need for interpersonal comparisons of utility, the requirement to consider the social context of decision-making, and the complexity of human behaviour necessitate a shift from mainstream economic theories and policies towards an empirical science-based approach to environmental policy and sustainability. Getzner *et al.* (2005) also question the appropriateness of a purely monetary orientated welfare-based approach to inform decision-making, and suggest that alternatives such as multi-criteria analysis and 'citizens' juries' should be considered alongside, and in some instances instead of, environmental valuation methods.

More attempts at resource valuation should ideally be second-generation studies that capture the essence of all the categories of value identified in Table 12.2. Unfortunately, this is rarely the case for any natural resource, let alone corals. In part this is due to the complexities involved and the budgetary constraints of adequately quantifying such a broad mix of values; a problem regularly manifested in narrowly scoped terms of reference for such studies. Where different categories of value are considered together, it is essential that they are not all simply added together, because of issues of double-counting and incompatibility. An appropriate format for presenting the results is thus required where different values (e.g. financial, economic and non-monetary) can be displayed together.

Spurgeon *et al.* (2005) provide an example of a study that combines welfare values (recreational consumer surplus and non-use values) with socio-economic impacts (visitor and management expenditures, both direct and knock-on, and associated jobs), as well as integrating other environmental indicators (e.g. extent of ecosystem services, social, cultural, educational, health and research values). The study assessed the economic costs and benefits of protecting 300 areas of conservation value (Natura 2000 sites) in Scotland under the EU Habitats and Birds Directives.

The comparison was made at both a national (for all 300 sites) and local level (12 case study sites). An integrated 'appraisal summary table' reporting format was developed to reveal a broad range of associated costs and benefits and to highlight which stakeholder groups gained the benefits and incurred the costs. It is worth noting that annual non-use values from protecting all 300 sites was US$58 million (51%) for Scottish residents (2.3 million households) and US$54 million (48%) for visitors to Scotland who did not

Table 12.2. Alternative approaches to assessing 'economic-related' values

Approach	Objective	Methods used	Example
Welfare economics (encompassing total economic value)	To guide the optimum allocation of scarce resources between competing uses for the maximization of human welfare	• Environmental valuation techniques • Benefit (value) transfers • Total economic value • Cost–benefit analysis	Spurgeon *et al.* (2004) calculated an annual TEV of around US$10 million for America Samoa based on fishery, recreation, coastal protection and non-use values and compared future TEV under different management scenarios (see Box 12.3).
Economic impact analysis	To assess the contribution to, and/or the effect on, local, regional and national economies (e.g. in terms of expenditures and jobs)	• Input–output models • Expenditure surveys • Value transfers • Multiplier effect	Hazen and Sawyer (2001) estimated that the coral reefs of southeast Florida generate US$4.4 billion worth of local sales and US$2 billion of income, and support 71 300 jobs.
Socio-economic analysis	To understand and quantify the social, cultural, economic and political aspects of individuals, organizations and communities	Qualitative and quantitative: • Focus groups • Surveys • Interviews • Visualization techniques • Stakeholder analysis	Hoon (2003) identified 24 different types of socio-economic benefits from coral reefs on Agatti Island (west of India). She also found that 12% of poor households on the island depended on coral reefs for 100% of their incomes, and 59% of poor households relied on reefs for 70% of their incomes.

Financial analysis	To determine the financial viability and sustainability of enterprises and organizations, by focusing on transaction/market-based costs and benefits	• Budget forecasts • Profit and loss accounts • Cash flow analysis • Balance sheets • Business plans	The Coastal Zone Management Authority and Institute of Belize (2003) undertook a financial analysis to assess financing options for planned marine park and coastal management in Belize. They estimated potential revenues from Belizeans and non-Belizeans of over BZ$5 million and identified a financing gap of BZ$322 000.
Other non-monetary 'value'-based approaches	To highlight the relative importance of biodiversity and other natural and man-made assets and features	Environmental and Social Impact Assessments • Sustainability indicators • Index of captured ecosystem value • Multi-criteria analysis scoring and weighting techniques • Energy-based approaches	Fernandes *et al.* (1999) used multi-criteria analysis to determine the relative importance of various ecological, economic, social and global objectives and indicators amongst different stakeholders for Saba Marine Park. The approach also highlighted the fact that enhanced education and enforcement were commonly agreed by the stakeholders to be the best means of improving upon all four objectives.

visit the sites (17 million), compared to an estimated US$0.85 million (1%) consumer surplus user value for site visitors (2.7 million adult visits per year). These values (at exchange rate UK£1 = US$1.89) were based on fairly rigorous and comprehensive contingent valuation surveys.

First- and second-generation economic instruments

Economic instruments are a means of internalizing environmental values which are otherwise excluded from market prices. Box 12.5 gives a few examples relevant to coral reef management. Synergy (2001), Morris (2002) and Spergel and Moye (2004) provide useful additional information, options and examples. The instruments are considered together here as 'first- and second-generation' because although they are generally based on welfare economics theory, an integrated approach to developing them is likely to enhance their implementation success. Such instruments have a number of potentially important functions, including the control of human behaviour and resource overuse (e.g. through taxes and fees to restrict consumption and use) and raising revenues for management and conservation. However, economic instruments are not without their problems (Panayotou, 1994) and only work effectively under certain conditions and when strategically planned and implemented.

THIRD-GENERATION APPROACHES TO CORAL REEF VALUATION

In order to improve the chances of protecting coral reefs for future generations, we should not only strive to implement a second-generation economics-based approach, but also explore a new 'third-generation' (3G) approach. This approach could be considered as just an extension to the 'ecological economics' approach, whereby certain disciplines, characteristics and objectives are given slightly more emphasis. Key features of a 3G approach would involve focusing on the following:

(1) Incorporating modern and appropriate 'business management' principles and approaches.
(2) Gaining a better understanding of what the values mean and knowing how to make the most of them.
(3) Involving appropriate use of innovation, technology and collaboration.
(4) Accounting more fully for the concepts of quality of life, spirituality, and inter-generational equality.

Box 12.5 Examples of economic instruments relevant to coral reef management

- **User and entrance fees** (e.g. Bonaire and Bunaken Marine Parks)
- **Fines** (e.g. Egypt, USA and Mexico, for coral damage)
- **Licences** (e.g. fishing in USA)
- **Tradable quotas** (e.g. fishing in New Zealand)
- **Concessions** (e.g. tourism in Togean Islands and Komodo Island, Indonesia)
- **Hotel taxes** (e.g. Turks and Caicos Islands)
- **Environmental taxes** (e.g. discharge and carbon taxes)
- **Deposits** (e.g. returning bottles in USA)
- **Socially responsible investment funds** (e.g. Asian Conservation Company, Philippines)

Incorporating business management principles

The proliferation of business schools and the volume of research undertaken around the world to understand and improve how businesses work are staggering. The future management of coral reefs, both within and outside protected areas, cannot afford to ignore this valuable knowledge base. However, the significance of adopting the latest and most appropriate business management techniques is not yet apparent to many within the coral reef management community. Notable exceptions include Jameson *et al.* (2002) and Merckl (2003).

Virtually all management decisions within a business can be explained by this basic strategy formula:

$$profit = quantity \times margin$$

where margin is calculated as selling price minus cost. Businesses generally exist to make a profit, which can primarily be achieved by increasing the quantity of products (units) they sell, increasing the selling price of each unit, or reducing the cost of producing each unit.

With minor modifications this formula can equally be applied to enhancing the management of coral reefs. The formula instead becomes:

$$benefit = quantity \times net\ surplus$$

where net surplus is the sum of producer surplus, consumer surplus and other benefits.

In this case, one seeks to maximize 'welfare benefit' or overall 'surplus' rather than profit. There are two main types of surplus. 'Producer surplus' is the margin or profit made by individuals, businesses and organizations providing products and services (i.e. the selling price less production costs). Consumer surplus is the amount of additional satisfaction (welfare), in terms of enjoyment and quality of life, that people gain over and above what they have to pay (i.e. money) in order to derive pleasure from that good or service (i.e. an individual's maximum willingness to pay less selling price). 'Other benefits' encompass additional benefits that remain elusive to monetary valuation, not least intrinsic value.

Those people and organizations with responsibilities and influence over coral reef health should ideally be seeking to maximize this total welfare benefit accruing to society. This can be achieved by using business-related concepts that seek to 'optimise'(1) the quantity or goods used (e.g. fish caught) or people using a reef (e.g. tourists visiting); (2) the selling price; and (3) the costs of production and management. The overall optimizing approach should generally tend towards an increase in quantity and selling price and a reduction in costs, but to an optimal level that takes into account issues such as sustainable yields, carrying capacity, congestion costs, and the availability of substitute sites, goods and services, etc. As any business would do with such valuable assets, a precautionary approach should also be taken, particularly when setting optimum limits for extractive uses. For example, with respect to coastal tourism development, understanding and managing tourism life cycles and recreational succession (Jobbins, this volume) is essential for optimum and sustainable economic gain.

Interest in business management approaches has begun in the context of marine protected areas (MPAs), a key tool in coral reef conservation and management. However, few MPAs are managed as effectively as they could be, often due to inappropriately trained and inexperienced managers, inadequate funding and severe political and administrative constraints (Wells, this volume). Indeed, Merckl (2003) believes that the lack of an effective network of MPAs is not due to a shortage of funding but due to a lack of capacity in terms of adequate professional and business management skills. The goal of financial self-sufficiency has been much discussed but is generally far from fully realized. However, a business approach forces managers to consider financial viability from the outset and to optimize their approach in the face of intense and growing competition between MPAs for funds and visitors (e.g. Jameson *et al.*, 2002). Merckl (2003) quite rightly proposes the need for a professionally managed, conservation-focused, protected area management company. It will only be through maximizing benefits, capturing a broad range of values and minimizing costs, that MPAs will ultimately be financially sustainable. The challenge is to devise ways to capture the disperse benefits that are so often remote from those who pay the costs.

Numerous approaches and tools from several distinct disciplines within the sphere of business management could be used to significantly enhance coral reef benefits to society, reduce management costs and help reach conservation objectives. Some such approaches are highlighted in Table 12.3. A further explanation of these and many other methods and tools can be found in the following texts: Rosenfield and Wilson (1999), de Wit and Meyer (1999), Drury (2001), Slack *et al.* (2001), Johnson and Scholes (2002) and Kotler *et al.* (2002).

Better understanding of values and making the most of them

A second requirement of the 3G approach is that we need to have a far better and more detailed understanding of different coral reef values. Current coral reef valuation studies merely scratch the surface when it comes to calculating and understanding coral reef values. In particular, we need to grasp fully the potential implications of gaining a more in-depth understanding of people's consumer surplus and non-use values. Much can also be gained from better understanding of the value of other ecosystem functions, as well as pharmaceutical, social, cultural, spiritual, health, educational, and research benefits, to name but a few.

This knowledge will allow us to carry out more accurate and complete valuations of coral reefs and help improve decision-making that affects these ecosystems. In addition, it will enable more appropriate economic instruments and regulatory mechanisms to be developed that help protect corals and raise the vital revenues needed to contribute to their protection.

A better understanding of consumer surplus is particularly needed for benefits gained by fishers and recreational users. We could learn a great deal more about different market segments and the associated differences in levels of willingness to pay for different features. Then, using various methods such as price discrimination, product differentiation, capacity management techniques, business plans and competitor analysis (e.g. of other nearby dive sites and marine parks), actions could be taken to increase overall consumer surplus as well as the amount of money appropriated in ways such as visitor fees or fishing licences, to support site management.

For example, price discrimination can be achieved by providing a range of different prices for visitor entry. Such options include simply setting different rates for foreign and local visitors. However, options could go far beyond this, with a variety of different priced entry packages being offered. For example, alternatively priced packages could allow access to different

Table 12.3. Examples of potential business approaches to help enhance MPA and coral reef benefits and revenues, and reduce associated management costs

Discipline	Methods and tools that could be used
Marketing	• Market segmentation, targeting and positioning • Modifying the marketing mix for services (i.e. product, price, promotion, place/distribution, process, physical evidence and people) • Product differentiation and branding • Competitor analysis
Operations management	• Capacity management • Performance objectives • Total quality management
Organizational behaviour	• Motivational theory • Group dynamics • Change management techniques
Strategy	• PESTLE analysis (i.e. understanding the political, economic, societal, technical, legal and environmental context) • Porter's generic strategies model (i.e. selecting a business strategy based on either cost leadership, differentiation or market focus) • Porter's five forces model (i.e. understanding the competitive forces of supplier and buyer powers, barriers to entry, threat of substitutes, and degree of rivalry) • Porter's value chain (i.e. identifying cost and differentiation opportunities associated with the main business activities of inbound and outbound logistics, operations, marketing and sales, service, procurement, technology development, human resources management and firm infrastructure) • Ansoff's diversification matrix (i.e. identifying options for diversification based on new or existing customers and related or unrelated technologies) • Ashridge mission model (i.e. development of a reinforcing strategy based on defining an ethos and purpose and developing appropriate associated values and actions) • Scenario planning (i.e. developing strategies based on understanding the potential implications of alternative future scenarios)
Financial and management accounting	• Activity-based costing • Cash flow management • Business plans • Budgets/profit and loss

locations (of differing quality and features), or provide different level of information (leaflet, pamphlet, maps and membership options, etc.). Different quality guides, transport and meals could also be offered by parks for groups of different sizes at varying prices. The options are numerous. Much can be learned from terrestrial parks and well-run commercial visitor attractions. Furthermore, advantages available to a fully coordinated international or national network of MPAs could be significant, both in terms of economies of scale and potential marketing and pricing strategies.

Considerable scope also exists for enhancing and appropriating (capturing) non-use values. Unfortunately, non-use value has received much bad press because many people think it is simply too hypothetical and nebulous, and therefore not particularly relevant. However, non-use value becomes increasingly important the more we understand it. It reflects the importance people attach to maintaining coral reefs so that other people can benefit from them, either now or in the future. As such, it can encompass many of the wider social and cultural values humans associate with corals, and can be of significant value.

Non-use values are measured in terms of how much people are willing to contribute (e.g. through money, labour or other means) to ensure that the resource continues to remain in the same (or better) quality and quantity. In a sense, non-use value can be considered in exactly the same way as consumer surplus. However, there is rarely a market to capture this benefit, so virtually all the value usually remains uncaptured outside the market-place. The most common ways of capturing this benefit are through charity collections and subscriptions; user fees, donation boxes and 'friends of. . .' schemes where visitors are informed of the site's ongoing maintenance requirements; and through government tax.

The amounts stated by respondents in willingness-to-pay (or contribute) surveys are likely to represent values that they would pay without complaining if forced to pay, if they felt others were paying and if they thought the contribution was being spent wisely. If users do not have to pay, they generally will not (like consumer surplus). The easier it is for them to pay and the more they are encouraged in an appropriate way, the more likely it is that they would contribute that money (or their time).

Non-use values can be enhanced and appropriated using exactly the same principles and business approaches as for consumer surplus. Some charities have recognized this and are becoming increasingly business-like in their strategy to raise funds. The war to capture non-use values has been raging for a while, and will continue with increasingly sophisticated and daring tactics.

Involving innovation, technology and collaboration

In the same way that businesses are transforming and adjusting to today's rapidly changing global economy, 3G economics-based approaches need to involve appropriately modern solutions. Decision-makers, NGOs, academics and consultants with an interest in managing and protecting coral reefs should be constantly looking towards cost-effective innovative approaches, appropriate technology and broadly but well-targeted collaborations in both undertaking of valuation studies and development of suitable economic and regulatory instruments.

Accounting for spirituality, quality of life and inter-generational equity

A shift has been taking place globally over the past decade or so stressing the significance and resurgence of a more spiritual approach to life, human values and connectivity with the Earth (e.g. Covey, 2004). The 3G economics-based approaches will need increasingly to acknowledge and reflect this reality.

Governments and businesses are already beginning to do this too. For example, the UK government is focusing its policies on how it can build a better 'quality of life' for its citizens (DETR, 1999). Some large companies are now looking at 'ethos'-based strategies to determine how they should best develop, grow and compete in the future (Cummings and Wilson, 2003). Given the high level of spiritual and quality of life connections that many fishing communities have with coral reefs (for example in the Pacific), it is clearly an area that needs careful consideration. Determining how best to deliver inter-generational equality is something that will also become increasingly important. Results from the Millenium Ecosystem Assessment (Reid *et al.*, 2005) showing that two-thirds of the world's ecosystem services are in decline hammer this point home. Building in the concepts of 'sustainability', fully accounting for all environmental values in policy and economic decision-making, and changing individual behaviour patterns are critical steps that must be taken. Dealing appropriately with the problems of using economic 'discount rates' (see Pearce *et al.*, 1989) in decision-making to reflect people's preference for money now also needs resolving.

THIRD-GENERATION ECONOMIC INSTRUMENTS

There is scope for a wide range of novel 3G economic instruments. However, many will simply be variations of current ideas and applications. Hallmarks of 3G economic instruments will include an appropriate blend of sophistication, simplicity, practicality, imagination and boldness.

Possible examples, amongst many others, include:

- A more ambitious and well-thought-out approach to using price discrimination for user fees, for divers, snorkellers, and general park visitors that is cost-effective to administer (e.g. Bonaire Marine Park).
- Applications of carbon tax credits and offsets to corals. Forests and tree-planting schemes are benefiting significantly from the current focus on these carbon-based instruments, and considerable work has been undertaken in looking at seagrasses for sequestering carbon (K. Teleki, pers. comm.). However, not only do corals have a value in helping to store carbon (Emerton, 1998), but also they are one of the most adversely impacted habitats from increased carbon dioxide emissions and global warming (Hughes *et al.*, 2003). They surely deserve some of the increasingly available carbon funds.
- New and innovative ways of ensuring equitable distribution of coral-reef-related revenues amongst local communities, particularly from high-value extractive uses such as bioprospecting, the marine aquarium trade and the live fish trade (see Vincent, this volume).
- Development of approaches to consider and internalize impacts on coral reefs from land-based sources through river basin management initiatives and land-use-based economic instruments.
- Exploring ways in which coral coastal protection services can be internalized, for example through contributions from protected settlements, tourist facilities and other benefiting commercial operations.

CONCLUSION: THE NEXT STEPS

Some important steps associated with economics-based approaches to improve the fate of coral reefs are as follows.

(1) Raise the profile of the importance, value and status of corals and their continuing degradation to all stakeholders, in particular those in influential positions, and highlight what can be done. Carefully and strategically planned educational and awareness campaigns need to be targeted at all levels, including children, local communities, the general public, tourists, reef managers, local government officials and politicians (e.g. see Browning *et al.*, this volume). A far more powerful 'values'-based message needs to be put across. In addition, influential politicians, organizations, corporations and appropriate personalities around the world should be specifically targeted to either add their voice to the plight of coral reefs or to impose changes that will help

protect corals. Key individuals to target would be those known to dive and holiday in coral reef locations, those keeping marine aquaria, and those who could most readily make a difference (e.g. politicians in America and Australia where the Kyoto Agreement has yet to be signed).

(2) Undertake further well-targeted studies to fill gaps in our understanding of coral values, and to explore current and potential applications of economic instruments. Greater levels of funding should be allocated to studies and pilot activities that attempt to demonstrate in the field how economics-based approaches can be used to increase our understanding of the societal values of corals, raise additional revenues for coral management and reduce coral management costs.

(3) Develop and provide appropriate guidance and training in integrated economic-based approaches and relevant business management techniques to coastal managers and relevant decision-makers. There is a need to provide simple, fully integrated and readily available guidance materials and training for coastal managers and relevant decision-makers on the potential for economic and business approaches to be adopted to enhance coral reef protection and management. The guidance and training should complement other international initiatives (e.g. the Global Coral Reef Monitoring Network's *Socio-Economic Manual for Coral Reef Management* (Bunce *et al.*, 2000) and the Conservation Finance Alliance's (2004), *Conservation Finance Guide* and should highlight both current and potential best practice and strategies for implementing effective change.

(4) Seek to better understand and address the root causes of coral degradation, in particular through modification of incentive structures and institutional arrangements. A more coordinated and strategic approach to identifying the most critical root causes of degradation and putting in place an optimum achievable portfolio of local, regional and international measures to address them is required. A key focus should be to analyse current incentive structures (from behavioural and market perspectives associated with both consumers and producers) and determine the necessary behavioural, market and institutional changes required to rectify the problems.

ACKNOWLEDGEMENTS

The author would like to thank Robert Costanza, Isabelle Côté, John Dixon, Robert Henderson, John Reynolds, Toby Roxburgh and Kristian Teleki for their comments on an earlier draft.

REFERENCES

Ahmed, M., Chong, C. K. and Cesar, H. (2004). *Economic Valuation and Policy Priorities for Sustainable Management of Coral Reefs*. Penang, Malaysia: World Fish Center.

Barton, D. N. (1994). *Economic Factors and Valuation of Tropical Coastal Resources*, SMR Report No. 14/94. Bergen, Norway: University of Bergen.

Bennett, J. and Blamey, R. (eds.) (2001). *The Choice Modelling Approach to Environmental Evaluation*. London: Edward Elgar.

Bunce, L., Townsley, P., Pomeroy, R. and Pollnac, R. (2002). *Socio-Economic Manual for Coral Reef Management*. Townsville, QLD: Australian Institute of Marine Science.

Burke, L. and Maidens J. (2004). *Reefs at Risk in the Caribbean*. Washington, DC: World Resources Institute.

Burke, L., Selig, L. and Spalding, M. (2002). *Reefs at Risk in Southeast Asia*. Washington, DC: World Resources Institute.

Cesar, H. J. S. (ed.) (2002). *Collected Essays on the Economics of Coral Reefs*. Coral Reef Degradation in the Indian Ocean (CORDIO), Kalmar, Sweden: Kalmar University.

Cesar, H. J. S. (1996). *Economic Analysis of Indonesian Coral Reefs*. Washington, DC: World Bank.

Cesar, H. J. S., Burke, L. and Pet-Soede, L. (2003). *The Economics of Worldwide Coral Reef Degradation*. Arnhem, Netherlands: Cesar Environmental Economics Consulting (CEEC).

Coastal Zone Management Authority and Institute of Belize (2003). *Operationalizing a Financing System for Coastal and Marine Resource Management in Belize*, Strategy paper. Belize City, Belize.

Conservation Finance Alliance (2004). *Conservation Finance Guide*. Conservation Finance Alliance.

Costanza, R. (1989). What is ecological economics? *Ecological Economics*, **1**, 1–7.

(2003). A vision of the future of science: reintegrating the study of humans and the rest of nature. *Futures*, **35**, 651–71.

Costanza, R., Daly, H. E. and Bartholemew, J. A. (1991). Goals, agenda and policy recommendations for ecological economics. In *Ecological Economics: The Science and Management of Sustainability*, ed. R. Costanza. New York: Columbia University Press.

Costanza, R. d'Arge, R., de Groot, R., *et al.* (1997). The value of the world's ecosystem services and natural capital. *Nature*, **387**, 253–60.

(1998). The value of ecosystem services: putting the issues in perspective. *Ecological Economics*, **25**, 67–72.

Covey, S. R. (2004). *The 8th Habit: From Effectiveness to Greatness*. London: Simon and Schuster.

Cummings, S. and Wilson, D. (2003). *Images of Strategy*. Oxford: Blackwell.

DETR (1999). *A Better Quality of Life: A Strategy for Sustainable Development in the UK*. London: HMSO.

de Wit, R. and Meyer, R. (1999). *Strategy Synthesis: Resolving Strategy Paradoxes to Create Competitive Advantage*. London: Thomson.

Dixon, J. A., Scura, L. F., Carpenter, R. A. and Sherman, P. B. (1997). *Economic Analysis of Environmental Impacts*. London: Earthscan Publications.

Drury, C. (2001). *Management Accounting for Business Decisions*. London: Thomson.

Ekins, P., Hillman, M. and Hutchison, R. (1992). *Wealth beyond Measure: An Atlas of New Economics*. London: Gaia Books.
Emerton, L. (1998). *Djibouti Biodiversity: Economic Assessment*. Nairobi: IUCN Eastern Africa Regional Office.
Fernandes, L., Ridgley, M. A. and van't Hof, T. (1999). Multiple criteria analysis integrates economic, ecological and social objectives for coral managers. *Coral Reefs*, **18**, 393–402.
Gardner, T. A., Côté, I. M., Gill, J. A., Grant, A. and Watkinson, A. R. (2003). Long-term region-wide declines in Caribbean corals. *Science*, **301**, 958–60.
Getzner, M., Spash, C. L. and Stagl, S. (eds.) (2005). *Alternatives for Environmental Valuation*. London: Routledge.
Gowdy, J. M. (2004). The Revolution in welfare economics and its implications for environmental valuation and policy. *Land Economics*, **80**, 239–57.
Grigulas, T. A. and Congar, R. (eds.) (1995). *Environmental Economics for Integrated Coastal Area Management: Valuation Methods and Policy Instruments*. Nairobi: UNEP Regional Sea Reports and Studies No. 164.
Harvell, C. D., Kim, K., Burkholder, J. M. *et al.* (1999). Emerging marine diseases: climate links and anthropogenic factors. *Science*, **285**, 1505–10.
Hodgson, G. and Dixon, J. A. (1989). *Logging versus Fisheries and Tourism in Palawan: An Environmental and Economic Analysis*, Occasional Paper No. 7. Honolulu, HI: Environmental and Policy Institute.
Hoon, V. (2003). A case study from Lakshadweep. In *Poverty and Reefs*, vol. 2, eds. E. Whittingham, J. Campbell and P. Townsley, pp. 188–226. Paris: UNESCO.
Hufschmidt, M. M., James, D. E., Meister, A. D., Bower, B. T. and Dixon, J. A. (1983). *Environment, Natural Systems, and Development: An Economic Valuation Guide*. Baltimore, MD: Johns Hopkins University Press.
Hughes, T. P., Baird, A. H., Bellwood, D. R. *et al.* (2003). Climate change, human impacts, and the resilience of coral reefs. *Science*, **301**, 929–33.
Jameson, S. C., Tupper, M. H. and Ridley, J. M. (2002). The three screen doors: can marine protected areas be effective? *Marine Pollution Bulletin*, **44**, 1177–83.
Johns, G. M., Leeworthy, V. R., Bell, F. W. and Bonn, M. A. (2001). *Socio-Economic Study of Reefs in South-East Florida*. Report to NOAA. Hollywood, FL: Hazen and Sawyer.
Johnson, G. and Scholes, K. (2002). *Exploring Corporate Strategy*. Upper Saddle River, NJ: Prentice Hall.
Kotler, P., Armstrong, G., Saunders, J. and Wong, V. (2002). *Principles of Marketing*. Upper Saddle River, NJ: Prentice Hall.
McWilliams, J. P., Côté, I. M., Gill, J. A., Sutherland, W. J. and Watkinson, A. R. (2005). Accelerating impacts of temperature-induced coral bleaching in the Caribbean. *Ecology*, **86**, 2055–60.
Merckl, A. (2003). Problem is shortage of capacity, not revenue sources: proposing a new approach to financing protected areas. *MPA News*, **5**, 5.
Millennium Ecosystem Assessment (2005). *Ecosystems and Human Well-being: Synthesis*, Washington, DC: Island Press.
Moberg, F. and Folke, C. (1999). Ecological goods and services of coral reef ecosystems. *Ecological Economics*, **29**, 215–33.
Morris, B. (2002). *Transforming Coral Reef Conservation in the 21st Century: Achieving Financially Sustainable Networks of Marine Protected Areas* Washington, DC: The Nature Conservancy.

Panayotou, T. (1994). *Financing Mechanisms for Environmental Investments and Sustainable Development*. Environmental Economics Series. Nairobi: UNEP Paper No 15.

Pearce, D. W. (2006). An intellectual history of environmental economics. *Annual Review of Energy and the Environment*, **27**, 57–81.

Pearce, D. W. and Barbier, E. (2000). *Blueprint for a Sustainable Economy*. London: Earthscan Publications.

Pearce, D. W., Markandya, A. and Barbier, E. (1989). *Blueprint for a Green Economy*. London: Earthscan Publications.

Robertson, J. (1999). *The New Economics of Sustainable Development: A Briefing for Policy Makers*. London: European Commission.

Rosenfield, R. H. and Wilson, D.C. (1999). *Managing Organizations: Text, Readings, and Cases*. New York: McGraw Hill.

Rudd, M. A. and Tupper, M. H. (2002). The impact of Nassau grouper size and abundance on Scuba diver site selection and MPA economics. *Coastal Management*, **30**, 133–51.

Slack, N., Chambers, S. and Johnston, R. (2001). *Operations Management*. Upper Saddle River, NJ: Prentice Hall.

Spergel, B. and Moye, M. (2004). *Financing Marine Conservation: A Menu of Options*. Washington, DC: WWF Center for Conservation Finance.

Spurgeon, J. P. G. (1992). The economic valuation of coral reefs. *Marine Pollution Bulletin*, **24**, 529–36.

Spurgeon, J. P. G. (2004). Valuation of coral reefs: the next ten years. In *Economic Valuation and Policy Priorities for Sustainable Management of Coral Reefs*, eds. M. Ahmed, C. K. Chong and H. Cesar, pp. 50–8. Malaysia: World Fish Center.

Spurgeon, J. P. G. and Roxburgh, T. (in press). A blueprint for maximizing sustainable coastal benefits: the American Samoa case study. *Proceedings 10th International Coral Reef Symposium*.

Spurgeon, J. P. G. Roxburgh, T., O'Gorman, S. *et al.* (2004). *Economic Valuation of Coral Reefs and Associated Habitats in American Samoa*, Jacobs Report prepared for the American Samoa Government Department of Commerce (DOC).

Spurgeon, J. P. G., Roxburgh, T., O'Gorman, S. *et al.* (2005). *An Economic Assessment of the Costs and Benefits of Natura 2000 Sites in Scotland: Full Report*. Edinburgh: Scottish Executive Environment and Rural Affairs Department and Scottish Natural Heritage.

Synergy (2001). *Sustainable Financing of Coastal Management Activities in Eastern Africa: Final Report*. Oxford: SEACAM.

Weilgus, J., Chadwick-Furman, N. E., Zeitouni, N. and Schechter, M. (2003). Effects of coral reef attribute damage on recreational welfare. *Marine Resource Economics*, **18**, 225–37.

Whittingham E., Campbell, J. and Townsley, P. (eds.) (2003). *Poverty and Reefs*, vols. 1 and 2. Paris: UNESCO.

Wilkinson, C. (ed.) (2004). *Status of Coral Reefs of the World: 2004*, vol. 1. Townsville, QLD: Australian Institute of Marine Science.

13

Collaborative and community-based conservation of coral reefs, with reference to marine reserves in the Philippines

ANGEL C. ALCALA
Silliman University Marine Laboratory

GARRY R. RUSS
James Cook University

PORTIA NILLOS
Silliman University Marine Laboratory

INTRODUCTION

Coral reefs have served as a source of many useful products for humankind for ages. The most important product is fish. Exploitation of reef resources during the early twentieth century did not have much discernible negative effects on coral reef ecosystems in some parts of Southeast Asia (e.g. some areas in central Philippines), probably because of the small numbers of people exploiting the resources. This situation has changed dramatically. Human-induced stresses exacerbated by occasional natural perturbations such as coral bleaching and infestations of crown-of-thorns starfish threaten the survival of coral reef ecosystems. It is estimated that 30% of coral reefs has already been severely damaged and close to 60% may be lost by 2030 (Wilkinson, 2004). The 20 000 km^2 of Philippine coral reefs are no exception. Destructive fishing and sedimentation have taken a heavy toll of this fragile ecosystem. Only about 30% of coral reef stations surveyed remain in good to excellent condition (Gomez *et al.*, 1994).

Coral Reef Conservation, ed. Isabelle M. Côté and John D. Reynolds.
Published by Cambridge University Press.

Protection of coral reefs in the country began in the mid-1970s with the establishment of the first working marine reserve at Sumilon Island, central Philippines in 1974 (Alcala, 1981, 1988; Alcala and Russ, 1990). In the period 1976–80, the University of the Philippines Marine Science Center (now Marine Science Institute), Silliman University, and the Bureau of Fisheries conducted the first nation-wide survey of Philippine coral reefs (Gomez *et al.*, 1981). However, the need to protect and manage coral reefs was not officially recognized by the Philippine government until 1993, the year when the Coastal Environment Program of the Department of Environment and Natural Resources was established (DENR DAO 19, series of 1993). The International Coral Reef Initiative (ICRI) launched in Dumaguete City, Philippines, in May 1995, highlighted at that time the urgent need for protective management of coral reefs, and this need was reiterated in the Manila ICRI Symposium in 2003 (see Department of Environment and Natural Resources, 2004). Underwater surveys of coral reef fish since the early 1980s have revealed a much reduced fish density and fish biomass on many reefs. Only 5–10% of the original reef fish standing stock biomass remains today on many fringing reefs in the country (Silliman University – Angelo King Center for Research and Environmental Management (SUAKCREM), unpublished data). Likewise, the fish catch, as measured by catch per unit effort (CPUE) of small-scale fishers, has been drastically reduced over the years due to habitat destruction and over-fishing (Alcala and Russ, 2002; Green *et al.*, 2003).

The predominant activity in coral reef conservation in many areas of the world is the establishment of marine parks, marine protected areas (MPAs) and no-take marine reserves. In the Philippines there has been a steady rise in the number of marine parks and no-take marine reserves (mostly coral reefs) since the early 1980s to more than 400 official and unofficial MPAs at the present time (Pajaro *et al.*, 1999). They appear to be the most viable management tools (Russ and Alcala, 2003) for coastal and marine resource management (CRM) projects favouring collaboration among various stakeholders of marine resources (Ferrer *et al.*, 1996) as long as external economic pressures remain low or negligible (Chua, 2004). Therefore, for purposes of the present chapter, coral reef conservation will be discussed in relation to MPAs and no-take marine reserves.

Collaborative and community-based resource management approaches are relatively new initiatives. Although they were used for the management of agricultural resources in the early 1970s (Alcala, 1998), they were not applied to the conservation of marine and coastal ecosystems in most parts of the world until the early 1980s (White, 1988; Pomeroy, 1994; Alcala,

1998). The exceptions are the island states in the South Pacific with a tradition of local community involvement in short-term marine resource protection (Ruddle and Johannes, 1985). These approaches developed because of the failure of top-to-bottom government management characterized by control, monitoring and surveillance by central government agencies. Such failures forced people to seek other solutions to the worsening problems of fishery and resource depletion and environmental degradation (Williams, 1994).

Collaboration for coral reef conservation with varying degrees of participation of the collaborating partners can now be found in many parts of the world (Chua, 2004). Partnerships among government agencies, international or local non-government organizations (NGOs), financing institutions, the private sector and academic institutions are common in the Philippines. Collaboration may be viewed as occurring at various stages of the preparation of conservation and management projects, namely, conceptualization, planning and implementation (White *et al.*, 2002). The extent of the participative effort of the partners varies, but usually it is the government agencies that manage the projects. This chapter will review collaborative and non-community-based conservation initiatives reported from various countries of the world and those that are community-based (co-managed by local communities and local government units) in the Philippines, where this mode of management of CRM projects incorporating MPAs and no-take marine reserves has been actively pursued since the 1970s (Ferrer *et al.*, 1996).

The objectives of this chapter are (1) to investigate whether collaborative and community-based conservation projects, as defined above, have been effective in (a) improving fisheries through increased fish catch rates, (b) conserving biodiversity, (c) improving livelihoods, and (d) successfully managing stakeholder conflicts; and (2) to show the importance of human social and political structures in determining the outcomes of community-based effort.

SELECTING AND SCORING MARINE PROTECTED AREAS AND RESERVES

Published papers in internationally and locally refereed scientific journals, conference proceedings, books and unpublished reports were searched for information on MPAs established worldwide. A few MPAs not reported in the literature but known to the authors have also been considered. Only

MPAs and no-take marine reserves protected for at least five years (assumed capable of exporting fish biomass to surrounding fished areas) and with some documentation were included. Fisheries co-management or collaborative schemes not involving MPAs, for example those described by Khan *et al.* (2004) in Africa and those managed mainly by government agencies with little community involvement discussed in Department of Environment and Natural Resources (2004, pp. 41–5) are not dealt with here. Short-term community-managed reef areas in Pacific Island states such as the Solomon Islands (Smith *et al.*, 2000; Aswani and Hamilton, 2004), and the Cook Islands, Samoa and Fiji (King and Faasili, 1998, Mackay, unpublished data) were excluded from the analysis. About 12 MPAs in Cambodia, Indonesia and Vietnam established in the early 1990s with no monitoring data were also excluded (UP-MSI, ABC, ARCBC, DENR, ASEAN 2002).

A total of 54 MPAs established in 16 countries met the above criteria. These MPAs fall into two categories. The first group are MPAs (n = 28, each generally in thousands of ha in area, and mostly on coral reefs) established and managed primarily by government agencies (collaborative but not community-based because of the low level of participation or non-participation of local communities) (Table 13.1). The second group is composed of 26 MPAs in the Philippines which have either two national laws, the Local Government Code of 1991 and the Fishery Code of 1998, or one law, the National Integrated Protected Areas Act of 1992, as their legal framework (Table 13.2). Although the implementers of these projects are the local government units and the people's organizations working together, other collaborators (e.g. NGOs and academe) may participate at the policy level of management. No coral reef MPAs were known or found to have been implemented by local communities in other countries.

The MPAs and no-take marine reserves were scored positively (Yes) for (1) fisheries, if fish density and/or fish biomass were higher inside than outside the no-take zone, (2) biodiversity, if there was an increase in live coral cover and/or in number of reef macroinvertebrates such as sea cucumbers, (3) livelihoods, if either (1) or (2) occurred even though spillover has not been demonstrated (in these cases, spillover was assumed to have occurred based on other studies (e.g. Russ and Alcala, 2003; Halpern, 2003)) and if fish yield had increased and income-generating activities such as those associated with ecotourism were occurring, and (4) conflict management, if cooperation among stakeholders was evident and if violations of the

Table 13.1. Assessment of government-managed, private sector-managed or non-community-based MPAs (mostly coral reef) at least five–10 ha in area and protected for at least five years in various parts of the world

Name of reserve/country	Improved fisheries?	Improved marine biodiversity?	Provided human livelihoods?	Stakeholder conflicts managed?	Factors promoting sustainability (e.g. institutionalized)	Area (ha); year established; source
1. Alegre Resort Marine Reserve, Philippines	Yes	Yes	Yes	Yes	Alegre Resort	20; 1990; Stockwell, pers. comm.
2. Apo Reef Seascape, Philippines	Yes (some parts)	Yes	No	No	Government – Dept. of Environment and Natural Resources	*c.* 20 000+; KKP and DENR Rept., unpublished 2003
3. Arnavon Island Marine Conservation Area, Solomon Island	Yes	Yes	Yes	No data	Government initiated? Co-management by communities; Nature Conservancy Support	No area reported; 1995; Smith *et al.* (2002)
4. Balicasag Marine Reserve, Philippines	Yes	Yes	Yes	No	Government (PTA)	20; 1986; Stockwell (2004), Philreefs (2003)
5. Bunaken Marine Park, Manado, Indonesia	Yes	Yes	Yes	No	Government; tourism receipts support the park	90 000 (whole MPA); early 1990s; Devantier *et al.* (2004)
6. De Hoop Marine reserve, S. Africa	Yes	No data	Yes, fishery	Yes, no conflicts	Full government support	36 000; 1985; Roberts and Hawkins (2000); Gell and Roberts (2002)
7. Discovery Bay, Jamaica[a]	Yes	Yes	No	No	Fishers' organization	108;1995; Woodley and Sary (2000)
8. Duka Bay Marine Reserve, Misamis Oriental, Philippines	No data	Yes	Yes	No	Private resort maintains reserve	*c.* 10; >5; B. Stockwell (pers. comm.)
9. Edmonds Underwater Park, USA	Yes	No data	No, but recreational benefits	Yes	Full government support	10.1; 1970; Robert and Hawkins (2000)

10. Galapagos Marine Reserve, Ecuador	Yes	No data	Yes, fishing, tourism	Yes	Government ?	Not given; 1986; Roberts and Hawkins (2000)
11. Hol Chan Marine Reserve, Belize	Yes	No data	Yes, tourism, some fishing	Yes	Tourism income	260; 1987; Roberts and Hawkins (2000)
12. Hundred Islands National Park, Philippines	No	No	No, clam pouching	No	Government (tourism)	*c.* 1000?; 1940; UP-MSI *et al.* (2002)
13. Initao Marine Park, Philippines	No	No	No	No	Government (Department of Environment and Natural Resources)	*c.* 100?; 1994; Aliño *et al.* (2002)
14. Jewelmer, Bugsuk Island, Palawan, Philippines	No data	Yes	Yes	No	Private sector	10 000; 1979; A. Alcala (pers. obs.)
15. Kisite Marine National Park, Kenya	Yes	Yes	Yes, tourism	Yes, but fishing inside reserve	Government management	23 000 (whole MPA); 1978; Gell and Roberts (2002)
16. Leigh Marine Reserve, New Zealand	Yes	Probably yes	Yes	No, consultation necessary	Strong government support	518; 1977; Walls (1998)
17. Long Island, Kokomohua, New Zealand	Yes	No data	No, but recreational benefits	Yes; no conflicts	Full government support	Not given; 1993; Gell and Roberts (2002)
18. Mombasa Marine National, Park, Kenya	Yes	No data	Yes probably	No, negative effects	Government support	620; 1987; Gell and Roberts (2002)
19. Nabq Protected Area, Egypt	Yes	Probably yes	Yes, CPUE increased	Yes, through community meetings	Locals as paid community rangers; government funded	12 200 (whole MPA); (1992); Gell and Roberts (2002)
20. Saba Marine Park, Netherlands Antilles	Yes	Yes	Yes, tourism, fishing	Yes, no problems	Tourism income for park management	Not given; 1984; Roberts and Hawkins (2000)

(cont.)

Table 13.1. (*cont.*)

Name of reserve/country	Improved fisheries?	Improved marine biodiversity?	Provided human livelihoods?	Stakeholder conflicts managed?	Factors promoting sustainability (e.g. institutionalized)	Area (ha); year established; source
21. Sagay Marine Reserve, Philippines	Yes	Yes	Yes	No	LGU w/PAMB, institutionalized	32 000; 1985; Marañon (pers. comm.); Webb *et al.* (2004)
22. Sambos Ecological Reserve, Florida, USA	Yes	No data	Yes	No, commercial fishers object	Government funded, NOAA implementer	3087; 1997; Gell and Roberts (2002)
23. Soufriere Marine Management Area, West Indies	Yes	No data	Yes	No, illegal fishing	Tourism income support	Not given; 1995; Gell and Roberts (2002)
24. Tabarca Marine Reserve, Spain	Yes	Yes	Yes	Yes, no conflicts	Government ? Also local support	100; 1986; Gell and Roberts (2002)
25. Tsitsikamma National Park, S. Africa	Yes (probably)	No data	Yes, fishery (probably)	Yes, no conflicts	Full government support	Not given; 1964; Gell and Roberts (2002)
26. Tubbataha National Marine Park, Palawan, Philippines	Yes	Yes	Yes	Yes	PCSD-WWF support	32 000; 1988; Mejia *et al.* (2002)
27. Uluikoro Marine Reserve, Fiji	Yes	Yes	Yes	Probably no, poaching occurring	Income generation incentive planned; community support	100; 1996; Mackay (unpubl. data)
28. Virgin Island National Park, US Virgin Is.	Yes but only briefly	No data	No	No, fishing inside park	None, protection failed	2.287; 1962; Gell and Roberts (2002)

[a] Intended to be a community–based marine protected area.

Table 13.2. Assessment of coral reef collaborative and community-based marine reserves in the Philippines at least 5 ha in area and protected by local communities and/or local government units for at least four to five years.

Name of reserve/country	Improved fisheries?	Improved marine biodiversity?	Provided human livelihoods?	Stakeholder conflicts managed?	Factors promoting sustainability (e.g. institutions[a])	Area (ha); year established; source
1. Acha Reef Fish Sanctuary, San Andres, Quezon	No	No	No data	No	Co-managed by LGUs, NGOs, community	20; 1996; Aliño *et al.* (2002)
2. Alibijaban Fish Sanctuary, San Andres, Quezon	Yes	No data	No data	No	Co-managed by NGO and LGU	225; 1996; Aliño *et al.* (2002)
3. Apo Island Marine Sanctuary, Dauin, Negros Oriental	Yes	Yes	Yes	Yes	Strong community effort	11; 1982–86; Russ and Alcala (1996); Philreefs (2003)
4. Bagongbanua Island Marine Reserve, Guiuan, Samar	Yes	Yes	Yes	No	NGO support	50; 1991; ?
5. Baliangao Wetland Park, Misamis Occidental	Yes	No	Yes	Yes	Baliangao, Plaridel communities	74;1991; De Guzman (2004); Ferrer (1996)
6. Balingasay Marine Reserve, Bolinao, Pangasinan	Yes	No data	Yes	No	NGO–PO–LGU–academe partnership	Not given; 1999; Campos *et al.* (2002)
7. Bongalonan Marine Reserve, Negros Or.	Yes	No	Yes	Yes	LGU–PO collaboration	*c.* 15; 1987; Aliño *et al.* (2002)
8. Cabacongan Fish Sanctuary, Cabilao, Bohol	Yes	Yes	Yes	Yes	Assurance of support from fees	11.8; 1997; Philreefs (2003)
9. Danjugan Island, Marine Reserve, Negros Occidental	Yes	No	Yes	Yes	PO–NGO cooperation	102; 1999–2000; Philreefs (2003)
10. FISHER Sanctuaries, Palawan	Yes	No data	Yes	Yes	PO–NGO–LGU; needs planning after Foundation for Philippine Environment support runs out	*c.* 50?; 1991; Foundation for the Philippine Environment (2004)
11. Gilutongan Marine Sanctuary, Cebu	Yes	Yes	Yes	Yes	Tourism as source of income; Government	10; 1991; Ross *et al.* (2000), Philreefs (2003)
12. Loculan Shoal Marine Sanctuary, Misamis Occidental	No	No	No	No	Management not sustained; poor management	Not known; not known; Philreefs (2003)
13. Lomboy Fish Sanctuary, Bohol	Yes	Yes	No data	Yes	LGU–Local community support strong	8.6; 1995; Philreefs (2003)

(*cont.*)

Table 13.2. (*cont.*)

Name of reserve/country	Improved fisheries?	Improved marine biodiversity?	Provided human livelihoods?	Stakeholder conflicts managed?	Factors promoting sustainability (e.g. institutions)	Area (ha); year established; source
14. Magsaysay Network of Marine Sanctuaries, Misamis Oriental	Yes	No	Yes	Yes	Academe–community partnership	87.7;1994–2000; Adan (2004)
15. Malalison Island Sanctuary, Antique	Yes	No	Yes	Yes	Community–SEAFDEC cooperation	28; 1991; Primavera (2002)
16. Pamilacan Island Fish Sanctuary, Bohol	Yes	No data	Yes (but not as result of sanctuary)	Yes	LGU–academe–PO cooperation	*c.* 15; 1986; Philreefs (2003)
17. Port Barton Marine Park, Palawan	No	Yes	No	No data	No data	74 483 (whole reserve); 1998; Philreefs (2002)
18. San Salvador Island Marine Sanctuary, Zambales	Yes	Yes	No	Yes	NGO–PO	127; 1989; Christie (2000, 2004)
19. Sibulan Marine Reserve, Negros Oriental	No	Yes	No	No	LGU–PO	6; 1997; Philreefs (2003)
20. Sogod Bay Marine Sanctuaries (network)	Yes	Yes	No	No	LGU–PO–NGO	*c.* 50; 1993–94; Estacion and Calumpong (2002)
21. Sumilon Marine Reserve, Cebu	Yes	No	Yes	Yes	NGO–PO–LGU	50; 1974; Alcala (1981); Russ and Alcala (1990)
22. Taklong Island National Marine Reserve, Guimaras	Yes	No data	No	Yes	Lacks support from community	1100; 1990; Philreefs (2003)
23. Tuka Marine Sanctuary, Saranggani	Yes	Yes	No data	Yes	Mostly managed by LGU	10; 1998; Philreefs (2003)
24. Tulapos Marine Sanctuary, Siquijor	No	Yes	No data	Yes	Philippine Department of Environment and Natural Resources, LGU. PO managed	14; 1994; Aliño *et al.* (2002)
25. Triton Island Fish Sanctuary, Zamboanga Sur	No data	No data	No	No	LGU supported	50; ?;Dollar (2002)
26. Twin Rocks, Cathedral Rock, Arthur's Rock Sanctuary, Batangas	No	Yes	Yes	Yes	Co-managed by private sector, POs and LGU	>10; 1991; Philreefs (1993)

[a] PO, people's organization; LGU, local government unit.

no-take zones were non-existent or occurred rarely. If the above conditions were not met, the MPAs were given negative (No) scores. 'No data' was given as a score when no information was available. We then compared the effects of the two groups of MPAs on fisheries, biodiversity, livelihoods and conflict management using these simple Yes or No scores against the criteria mentioned above.

EFFECTS OF COMMUNITY-BASED CONSERVATION PROJECTS WITH MPAS AND MARINE RESERVES: AN EMPIRICAL ANALYSIS

The majority of the 28 coral reef and non-reef MPAs of various sizes and protected for varying numbers of years in 16 countries worldwide (Table 13.1) were managed primarily by central governments and their agencies. Many of them received financial support from international NGOs and international funding agencies and had minimal, if any, involvement by local communities and local governments. Reports on these MPAs indicate that most of them probably caused an improvement of fisheries, marine biodiversity, and livelihoods of stakeholders (Fig. 13.1). However, these MPAs were not very effective in resolving resource user conflicts. Serious conflicts were reported at 15 of 27 MPAs (one MPA had no data) (Fig. 13.1). Strong enforcement mechanisms made possible by large budgets available to the managers were probably the main reason for the success of these MPAs. With few exceptions, not much detailed information on positive effects (other than those mentioned) of these 28 MPAs is available.

The second group of MPAs, all found in the Philippines and established, co-managed and maintained jointly by organized communities and local government units, is not much different from the first group (Fig. 13.1, Table 13.2). Fisheries, biodiversity and livelihoods were all probably improved, as in the non-community-based MPAs. The difference is that in this latter group of coral reef MPAs managed by community organizations and local government units, not only were fisheries, biodiversity and incomes reported to have been improved but also stakeholder conflicts were successfully managed in 18 of the 26 MPAs, resulting in only occasional problems (Fig. 13.1). The community-based and community-managed MPAs and no-take marine reserves tended to be more successful in managing user conflicts than the centrally managed ones (Fig. 13.1). The relative success of this group of MPAs lies in the participative nature of the processes used in their planning, establishment and management.

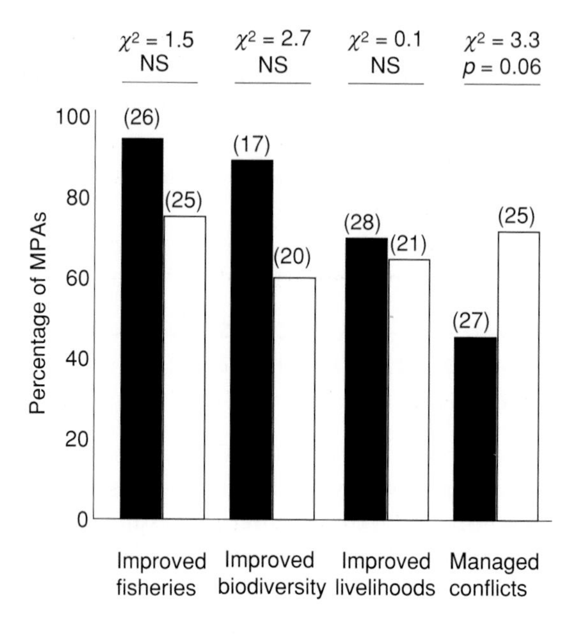

Figure 13.1 Percentage of community-managed (open bars) and non-community-managed (black bars) MPAs and reserves showing success at improving fisheries, biodiversity and livelihoods, and at managing stakeholder conflicts. A total of 26 community managed or collaboratively managed and 28 non-community-managed MPAs were considered. Sample sizes (indicated in parentheses) differ from these totals when no information was available for some MPAs.

CAUSES OF CONFLICT IN MPA MANAGEMENT

The reasons for the conflicts in 12 of the first group of MPAs (those managed by central governments and their agencies) were as follows: (a) the local fishers were excluded from decision-making in the establishment of MPAs (5 MPAs), (b) the fishers and local community felt that they did not benefit from MPAs, or if they did, there was no equitable distribution of benefits (5 MPAs), (c) there were unresolved disagreements between recreational fishers and government (1 MPA), and (d) there was lack of enforcement (1 MPA).

In four of the second group of MPAs, there are three reasons: (a) ineffective enforcement (2 MPAs), (b) ineffective community organizing effort (1 MPA), and (c) lack of management plan (1 MPA). Apparently, despite the use of social processes in the establishment and management of these MPAs, certain inadequacies have remained unresolved, indicating the importance of a continuing social component in coral reef conservation.

For both groups of MPAs, it is important that the rules and regulations contained in the management plans are enforced. This is the only way that an MPA can function well to deliver the benefits of protection. The strength of community-based conservation programmes lies mainly in community organizing and information, education and communication activities, as these tend to prevent or manage interpersonal and user conflicts in the enforcement of MPAs.

TWO CASE STUDIES IN CENTRAL PHILIPPINES: APO AND SELINOG MARINE RESERVES

The results of our research on marine reserves and community work on two islands (Apo and Selinog) in the Bohol (Mindanao) Sea, central Philippines, will now be described (Alcala and Russ, 2001; A. T. White *et al.*, unpublished data). On both islands, the empowered people's organizations and local government units have effectively managed the coral reef resources as evidenced by the positive effects on the fish standing stock and livelihoods. It should also be noted that the local communities on both islands, through their vigilance, have effectively excluded fishers from other areas, thereby avoiding user conflicts.

Apo Island (Fig. 13.2) is a 70-ha island with a population of 700 people, situated about 9 km from the nearest point of southeastern Negros Island. It is surrounded by 1.06 km^2 of coral reef to 60-m depth. A 22.5-ha marine sanctuary (no-take reserve) was established on the southeastern side in 1982. The combined community and local government units have protected the no-take reserve continuously since 1982. Its legal framework was originally a municipal ordinance and later the Local Government Code of 1991. However, since 1994, it has become a national protected area under the NIPAS Act of 1992. The fished area outside of the no-take zone was protected from all forms of destructive fishing. Largely volunteer work by the Bantay Dagat (sea wardens) is responsible for protection. In the no-take marine reserve, coral cover has remained high despite the bleaching event in 1998 (Fig. 13.3). Five species of sea cucumbers occur in fairly high densities of 1–2 individuals per square metre and two species of giant clams (*Tridacna*) have reappeared (Calumpong *et al.*, 1997). The biomass of target fish (four families) increased inside the reserve 4.6 times over 18 years of protection (Fig. 13.4) (Alcala *et al.*, 2005). The biomass of predatory fish increased 17.3 times over the same period (Russ and Alcala, 2003). Large

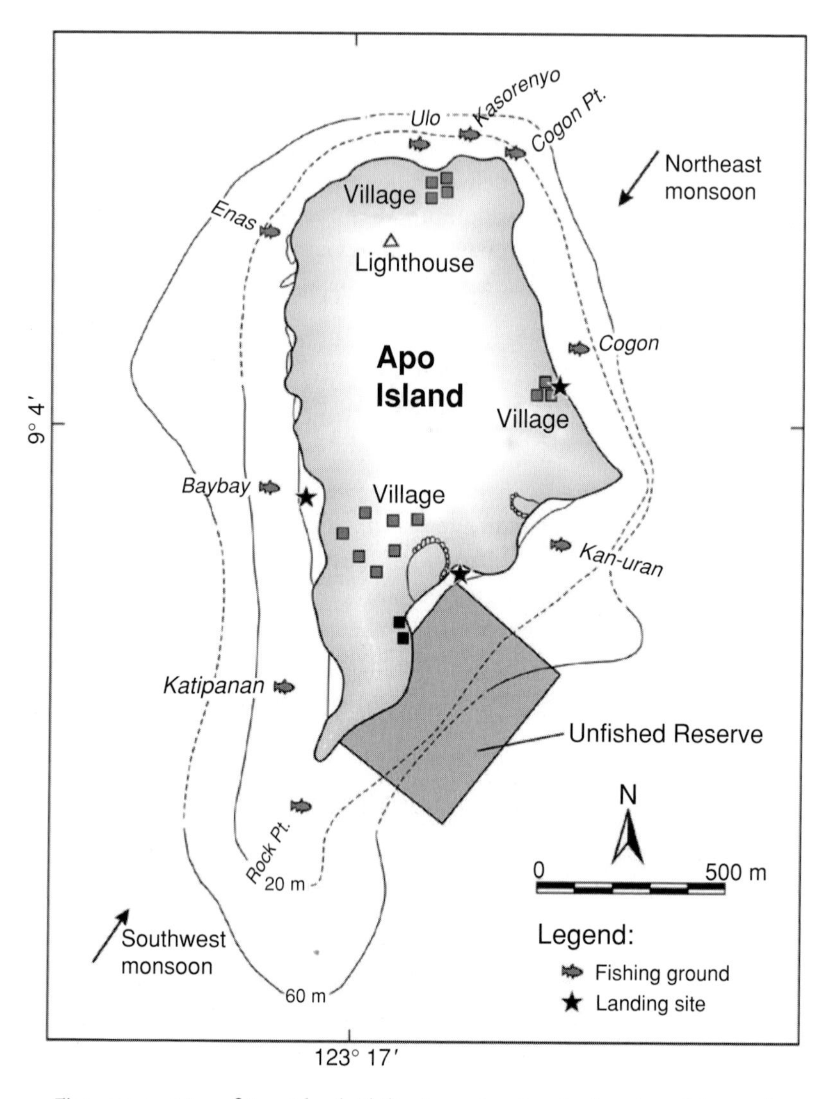

Figure 13.2 Map of Apo Island, Philippines, showing the location of the marine reserve.

predatory fish and surgeons (40–75% of yield) increased by factors of 17 and 3, respectively over 18 years of protection (Fig. 13.5). Outside the reserve, biomass of these fish increased significantly closer to than farther from the reserve boundary. Catch rates by hook and line of surgeonfish were significantly higher closer to than farther away from the no-take reserve (Fig. 13.6) (Russ *et al.*, 2004; Alcala *et al.*, 2005). About 63% of hook and line catch

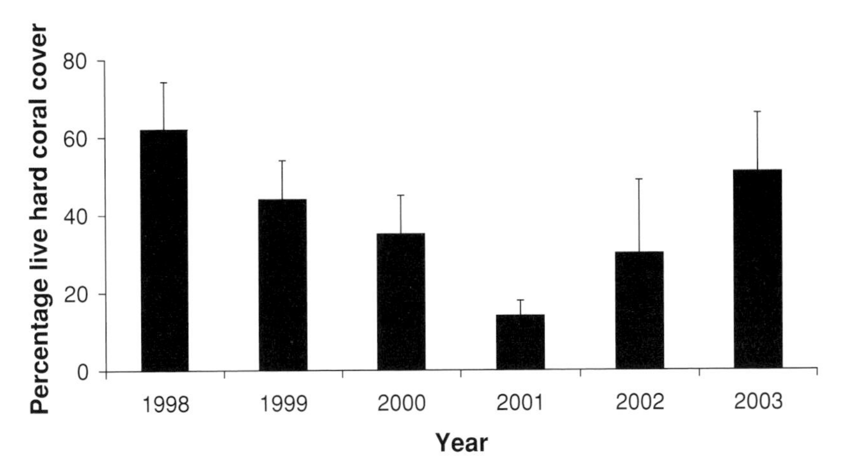

Figure 13.3 Mean percentage of live hard coral cover of Apo no-take marine reserve; decreasing percentage is due to coral bleaching. Error bars are SE of means. (Data from Raymundo (2004) and L. J. H. Raymundo and A. Maypa, Reef Check Report.)

records for one species of surgeonfish were within 200 m of the two ends of the reserve (Russ *et al.*, 2003). Combined, the data provide evidence for spillover.

There was a strong positive correlation between years of protection and targeted fish biomass in the reserve but not between years of protection and total yield (Alcala *et al.*, 2005) (Fig. 13.4). Total yield was about 15 to 20 t yr^{-1} yet fishing effort was reduced (Russ *et al.*, 2004). These results, and the evidence for spillover, suggest that marine reserves help maintain or even enhance local fishery yields in the long term (Alcala *et al.*, 2005). Both stable fisheries and a thriving ecotourism on the island worth about US$200 000 a year (of which US$35 000 come from divers' fees) (Cadiz and Calumpong, 2000; Alcala and Russ, 2002) have enhanced the living standard of the community on the island. In 2003, a project on women's health and family planning was started on the island to complement the coral reef protection programme.

The other island with a no-take marine reserve managed by local government units and people's organizations is Selinog Island (Fig. 13.7), also situated in the Bohol (Mindanao) Sea. The island is about 22 km away from Dapitan City, Zamboanga del Norte province, on Mindanao Island. Its land area is 78 ha, surrounded by 70 ha of coral reef and sandy areas. The island population is about 832 persons. The 7-ha no-take coral reef reserve on the northeastern side of the island was established in 2000. It started as

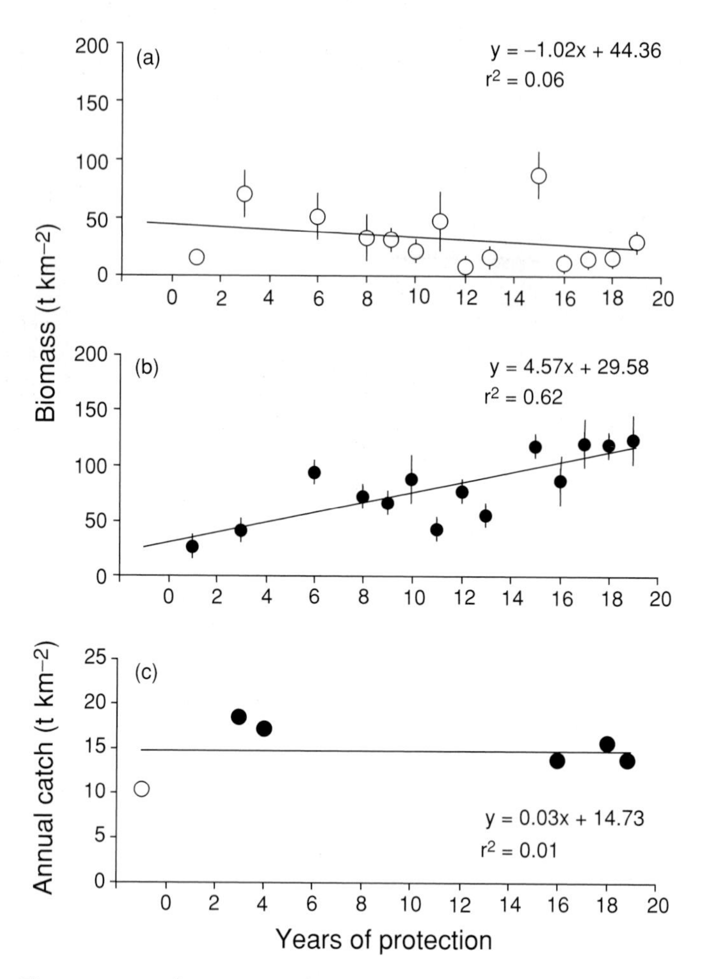

Figure 13.4 Underwater visual census estimates of bromass and annual catch of reef (food) fish of families Acanthuridae, Carangidae, Lutjanidae and Lethrinidae at Apo; (a) non-reserve biomass (1983–2001), (b) reserve biomass (1983–2001), and (c) total annual catch (1979–2001) (Alcala *et al.*, 2005).

a local initiative (Fig. 13.8) under the Local Government Code but has been recommended as a national MPA. Coral cover is high and large invertebrates have been protected. Target (food) fish biomass was 17.21 ± 3.91 (SE) kg per 500 m^2 (reserve) and 6.88 ± 3.5 kg per 500 m^2 (non-reserve) in 2002. The CPUE for hook and line fishers fishing outside the no-take marine reserve ranged from 1.5–2.1 kg $fisher^{-1}$ hr^{-1} for 10 months in 2001–2002. The mean number of fish species per 500 m^2 inside the reserve was 50.0 ± 3.3 while outside, it was 35.8 ± 2.6 (SUAKCREM, unpublished

Figure 13.5 A 15-kg jack (*Caranx ignobilis*) caught by hook and line in Apo Island non-reserve in 2004. There is evidence that this fish was nursed in the Apo marine sanctuary. (Photograph by Aileen Maypa.)

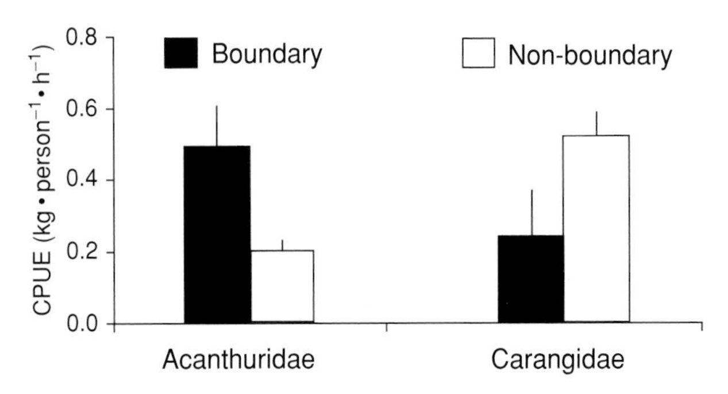

Figure 13.6 Hook and line catch per unit effort (CPUE) close to (within 200 m of boundary) and far from Apo no-take reserve in 2000/1 (Russ *et al.*, 2004). Error bars are standard errors.

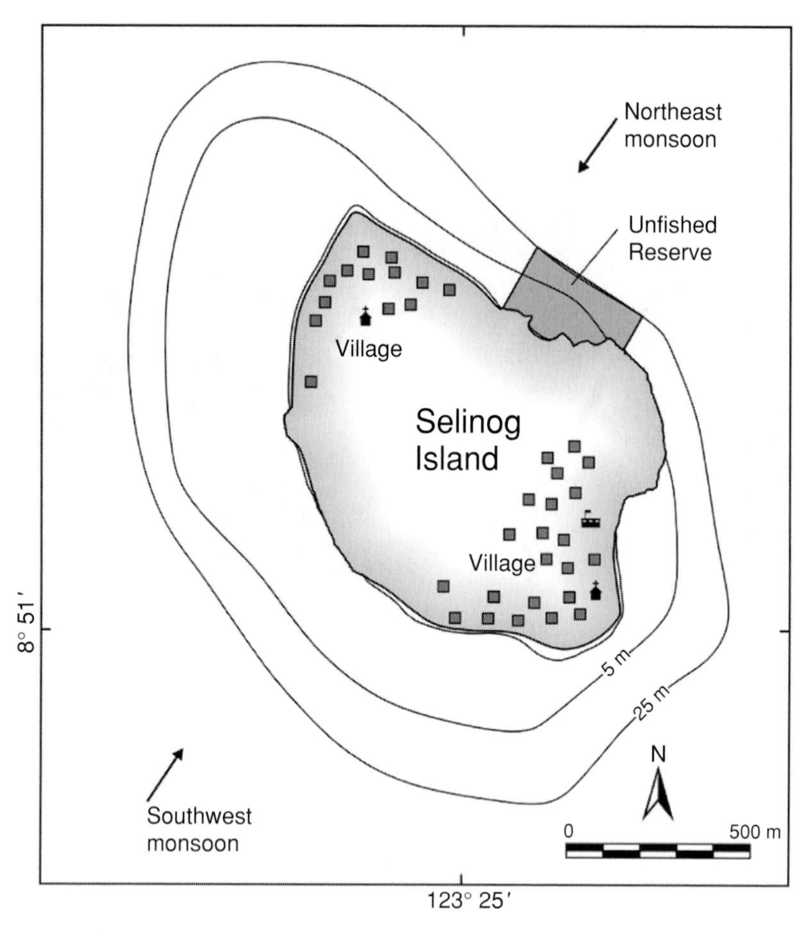

Figure 13.7 Map of Selinog Island, Philippines, showing the location of the marine reserve.

data, 2004). These quantitative monitoring data suggest positive effects of protection. The number of fish species observed outside the Selinog reserve is similar to the number of fish species observed in newly established marine reserves in nearby areas (Napo: 34.2 ± 2.3; Canlucani: 31.5 ± 2.3) (SUAKCREM, unpublished data). Fish yield data from the fished areas gathered over a period of two years are currently being analysed, and a study to determine fishery spillover effects will soon be conducted. Selinog Island is beginning to attract tourists but is not yet earning much from tourism. Livelihood activities are the concern of two people's organizations. One produces high-quality salt in addition to managing the marine reserve, and the

Figure 13.8 Community members and social scientists discussing the establishment of Selinog Island marine reserve in 2000. (Photograph by Jasper Maypa.)

other is involved in catering to visitors on the island, particularly producing attractive mats woven from local materials (Fig. 13.9). The salt has provided an income of about US$500 over a period of four months in the summer of 2004. Although not much, this income plus other earnings from mats and from catering to island visitors helps in reducing fishing pressure on the stressed fisheries. As on Apo Island, income from environment-friendly activities has served as incentive for sustainable management of coral reef resources.

ROLE OF HUMAN SOCIAL AND POLITICAL STRUCTURES IN CORAL REEF CONSERVATION

It has become clear over the years that coral reef conservation has a major social or human dimension (see also Brown, this volume). This is a more difficult part of conservation compared to the scientific aspects, which are more straightforward (Alcala, 1998; Bunce *et al.*, 1999; Alcala and Russ, 2000). The root causes of coral reef degradation in developing countries are poverty and high population growth rates. These two factors in turn combine to cause high exploitation rates on coral reef resources, resulting in physical damage and depletion of these resources.

Figure 13.9 Women of Selinog Island, Philippines, displaying the mats made of *Pandanus* leaves for sale in 2001. (Photograph by Juvie Chavez.)

In the majority of cases involving coral reef and reef resource conservation, the issues of fisheries and marine biodiversity are predominant. In developing countries, such issues are often of local concern, involving fewer stakeholders, compared to more complex trans-boundary issues requiring international and regional approaches in the context of integrated coastal resource management. These issues are in general adequately addressed by local partnerships. A partnership involving people's organizations in a local community (village), local government units and a non-government academic research organization (Fig. 13.10) has been shown to be an effective approach to coral reef conservation in central Philippines (Alcala, 1998; Alcala and Russ, 2000, 2001). Each partner has a specific role to play. The people's organizations in the local communities formulate management plans for the protected areas and development plans for their communities. The local government units provide the ordinances serving as part of the legal framework for MPAs and no-take marine reserves under the mandate of two national laws (Local Government Code of 1991 and Fishery Code of 1998). These two national laws mandate that local government

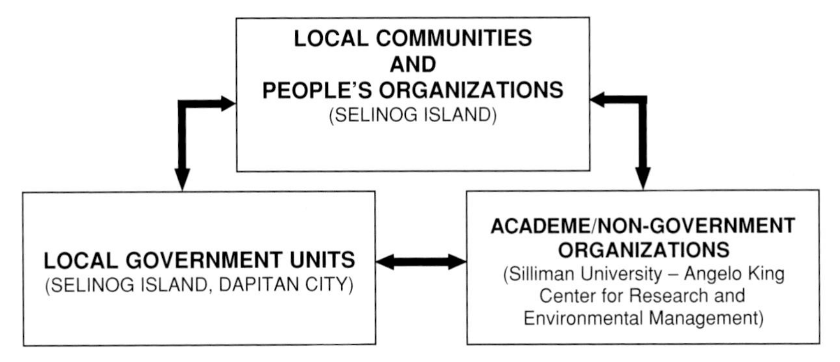

Figure 13.10 Schematic depiction of the tripartite partnership among the local community, the local government units, the non-government organizations and the academe, which supports the management of Selinog Island marine reserve in the Philippines.

units, NGOs and people's organizations collaborate in managing marine and coastal resources found in areas 15 km from the shoreline. Local government units also serve to institutionalize these projects by including them in municipal development plans and support non-reef-related livelihood activities to reduce exploitation pressure on coastal resources. Academic institutions or NGOs access funding to start conservation projects and often serve as initiators of projects. They improve the scientific knowledge of the communities and provide training in community organization, in networking with similar conservation initiatives and in developing leadership and management skills. This training results in improved capacity and empowerment of local governmental units and local communities to protect and manage their coral reef resources. Under the tripartite scheme they are the implementers of conservation projects. The academe or NGO partners are facilitators but may participate at the policy level of management by membership on management boards.

The basic social structure for community-based coral reef conservation is in the local communities. This consists mainly of organized people's organizations. A people's organization may be a group of fishers, fish vendors, community leaders, influential persons and other members of coastal communities. An organized local community has a set of officers and committees for various purposes, such as marine protection, livelihood, etc. Enforcement is effected by volunteers receiving minimum allowances, not salaries. They are educated in conservation biology, empowered to exert their rights to facilitate a productive environment, trained to conceptualize environment-friendly income-generation projects, implement rules and regulations of MPAs, formulate management plans, network with other MPAs and monitor their MPAs over time. The village chairperson or captain plays an important role in all of these activities.

In the Philippines, the socio-political process needed for the legal framework of community-managed MPAs begins at the *barangay* (i.e. village) level, with the passing of a resolution for coral reef protection by the village head and the barangay council. The next step is the passing of a Municipal Ordinance (the sanctuary's legal basis) by the Municipal Council as recommended by the Council's chair of environment. The third step is the approval of the Municipal Ordinance by the Municipal Mayor. The fourth and last step is approval for implementation by the Provincial Council and Provincial Governor. This approval is ministerial as the Municipal Ordinance is automatically approved a month after enactment at the municipal level, whether or not signed by the provincial officials.

To ensure sustainable coral reef conservation, four kinds of activities, usually initiated and conducted by the academe or NGO partners, have been found necessary. The first of these are information, education and communication activities, which are part of community organising processes resulting in the formal organization of communities; establishment of protected areas; setting up of income-generating projects; and stabilizing population through women's health projects (see also Brown, this volume). Through these activities, changes in human behaviour from purely exploitative to conservation are effected and an inter-generational commitment to conservation is maintained. The second major activity, the establishment of MPAs and no-take marine reserves, is necessary to allow degraded coral reefs and their resources to recover and yield fishery products. MPAs must be monitored regularly to provide feedback on the results of protection to the communities. The third major activity, the provision of environment-friendly income-generation projects to the communities, allows poor fishers to realize some income, reduces the level of fishery activities and serves as source of funds for the maintenance of the MPAs. The fourth activity serves to stabilize the population dependent on coral reef resources through family planning and women's health interventions.

COMMUNITY-BASED VERSUS NON-COMMUNITY-BASED REEF CONSERVATION

Collaborative management of coral reefs, with or without the participation of local communities, is more effective than top-to-bottom, centralized modes of management. This has been shown by examples in the

Philippines (Alcala, 1998; White *et al.*, 2002). However, among collaborative MPAs, those that are managed primarily by organized communities and local government units appear to be more successful (that is, more sustainable) than those without local stakeholder participation (Oracion, 2003; Pollnac *et al.*, 2003). The advantage of the former management mode is the presence of committed local community organizations and cooperative local government units working together as project implementers under the two enabling national laws (Local Government Code and Fishery Code) with community (not personal) agenda.

But even among the community-managed MPAs, there are bound to be a certain percentage of failures in management because social factors are in general difficult to control (Alcala, 1998). This must be borne in mind in order to avoid making hasty and misleading assessments, such as that of Christie (2004), who labelled MPAs with personal conflicts in management as social failures. Such conflicts should be viewed as challenges to, not as failures in, management.

The similarity of the two groups of MPAs in the present study (one group managed mainly by government agencies and the other mainly by local communities) in improving fisheries and biodiversity is not surprising, as many studies have shown that protection increases species richness, fish abundance and fish biomass at specific sites over time (e.g., Mosqueira *et al.*, 2000; Roberts and Hawkins, 2000; Russ *et al.*, 2003) and at different sites in a region at any point in time (Russ *et al.*, 2005). Thus it does not matter who implements conservation projects, or what strategies are employed, to achieve positive results. What does matter is effective enforcement, with the use of political and financial support for the managers of MPAs (Department of Environment and Natural Resources, 2004, pp. 108–18).

However, in terms of managing conflicts in resource use, co-management by local communities and local governments offers a more effective way of working with the various stakeholders to avoid resource use conflicts. The main reason for this is that such schemes are well placed to readily address complaints by local fishers that they are ignored in decision-making in the establishment of MPAs, or that they do not benefit from MPAs. The small sizes (usually less than hundreds rather than thousands of hectares) of community-managed reserves cannot account for the ease in settling conflicts in these reserves because this factor is amply counterbalanced by the large budgets and the large numbers of personnel in large non-community-managed MPAs. The lack of understanding or misunderstanding on the part of local fisher communities results mainly from a lack of conversations between them and the MPA managers.

There is, however, one difficulty inherent in community-based schemes. This is the length of time required to establish MPAs to be managed by local communities. For example, Apo marine sanctuary took almost four years to establish and Selinog a little more than a year (Alcala, 2001). Selinog took less time because of the local awareness of the success of Apo, showing that learning from actual successful examples plays an important role in the establishment of community-managed MPAs.

In developing countries, the most important expectation of local communities regarding MPAs and marine reserves is that these protected areas will export adult fish biomass to fished areas to improve catches. However, it is only in a few areas of the world that spillover or export of adult fish biomass has been documented (e.g. Alcala and Russ, 1990; Russ and Alcala, 1996; Johnson *et al.*, 1999; McClanahan and Mangi, 2000; Roberts *et al.*, 2001; Russ *et al.*, 2003, 2004; Alcala *et al.*, 2005). Many of the MPAs reviewed in this chapter are assumed to export fish biomass outside of no-take zones because of the high fish biomass inside these zones. Data on spillover effects and income from economic activities related to protection when reported to local communities are very important as they serve as incentives for maintaining the commitment to conservation (Alcala and Russ, 2000). MPAs have also been considered as the best options for marine resource management in developing countries for other reasons, such as the ease in setting them up, ease in managing them, incomes from tourism, insurance against fisheries collapse, etc. (Russ *et al.*, 2004). But much remains to be done on MPAs, in both the biological and the social science aspects (White and Green, 2004).

ACKNOWLEDGEMENTS

We are indebted to the Zoological Society of London through Dr Isabelle Côté and Dr John Reynolds for inviting one of us (A.C.A.) to participate in the Symposium on Coral Reef Conservation in London on 16–17 December 2004. The study was supported by a Fellowship on Marine Conservation from the Pew Trusts to A.C.A. and G.R.R. Jasper Leif Maypa of SUAKCREM prepared the illustrations.

REFERENCES

Adan, W. R. (2004). Multiple small-scale marine sanctuaries in municipal waters: the Magsaysay example. In *Turbulent Seas: The Status of Philippine Marine Fisheries*, pp. 232–6. Cebu City, Philippines: Coastal Resource Management Project of the Department of Agriculture–Bureau of Fisheries and Aquatic Resources.

Alcala, A. C. (1981). Fish yields of coral reefs of Sumilon Island, central Philippines. *National Research Council of the Philippines Research Bulletin*, **36**, 1–7.

(1988). Effects of protective management of marine reserves on fish abundances and fish yields in the Philippines. *Ambio*, **17**, 194–9.
(1998). Community-based coastal resource management in the Philippines: a case study. *Ocean and Coastal Management*, **38**, 179–86.
Alcala, A. C. and Russ., G. R. (1990). A direct test of the effects of protective management on abundance and yield of tropical marine resources. *Journal du Conseil International pour l'Exploration de la Mer*, **49**, 40–7.
(2000). Role of socio-economic factors in coral reef protection and management. *Proceedings 9th International Coral Reef Symposium*, **1**, 29–32.
(2001). Local partnership for coastal and marine resource management: the case of Selinog Island. *Tropical Coasts*, **8**(2), 4–9.
(2002). Status of Philippine coral reef fisheries. *Asian Fisheries Science*, **15**, 177–92.
Alcala, A. C., Russ, G. R., Maypa, A. P. and Calumpong., H. P. (2005). A long-term, spatially replicated, experimental test of the effect of marine reserves on local fish yields. *Canadian Journal of Fisheries and Aquatic Sciences*, **62**, 98–108.
Aliño, P. M., Miclat, E. F. B., Nañola Jr, C. L., Roa-Quiaoit, H. A. and Campos, R. T. (eds.) (2002). *Atlas of Philippine Coral Reefs*. Quezon City, Philippines: Goodwill Trading Co.
Aswani, S. and Hamilton, R. (2004). The value of many small vs. few large marine protected areas in the Western Solomon Islands. *SPC Traditional Marine Resource Management and Knowledge Information Bulletin*, **16**, 3–14.
Bunce, L., Gustavson K., Williams, J. and Miller, M. (1999). The human side of reef management: a case study analysis of the socioeconomic framework of Montego Bay Marine Park. *Coral Reefs*, **18**, 369–80.
Cadiz, P. L. and Calumpong, H. P. (2000). Analysis of revenues from ecotourism in Apo Island, Negros Oriental, Philippines. *Proceedings 9th International Coral Reef Symposium*, **2**, 771–4.
Calumpong, H. P., Estacion, J. S., Lepiten, M. V. and Acedo, C. E. (1997). *Status of the Coastal Resources of the Negros Learning Site*. Manila, Philippines: Silliman University Marine Laboratory and the Center of Excellence in Coastal Resources Management.
Campos, W. L., Beldia II, P. D. and Aliño, P. M. (eds.) (2002). *Workshop Proceedings of the AFMA Marine Fishery Reserves Program: Foundation of a National Fish Sanctuary Strategy*. Miag-ao, Iloilo: UP in the Visayas.
Christie, P. (2000). Learning from the case of the San Salvador Island (Philippines) Marine Protected Area. *Proceedings 9th International Coral Reef Symposium*, **2**, 801–5.
(2004). Marine protected areas as biological successes and social failures in Southeast Asia. In *Aquatic Protected Areas as Management Tools*, ed. J. B. Shipley, pp. 155–64. Bethesda, MD: American Fisheries Society.
Chua, T. E. (2004). Integrated coastal management as framework for management of coral reefs and other coastal ecosystems. *Proceedings 2nd International Tropical Marine Ecosystems Management Symposium*, 24–7 March 2003. Philippines DENR, Manila.
De Guzman, A. B. (2004). Exporting economic benefits from marine reserves: a case study of the coastal fishery of Danao Bay, northern Mindanao,

Philippines. *Proceedings 2nd International Tropical Marine Ecosystems Management Symposium*, 24–7 March 2003, pp. 475–82.

Deguit, E. T. and Marales, M. B. (2002). The Gilutungan Marine Sanctuary: benefits gained from proper management, p. 45–52. In Campos, W. L. and P. D. Beldia II (eds). Workshop Proceedings of the AFMA Marine Fishery Reserves Program on the formulation of a National Fish Sanctuary Strategy. Miag-ao, Iloilo: UP in the Visayas.

Department of Environment and Natural Resources (2004). *Proceedings 2nd International Tropical Marine Ecosystems Management Symposium*, 24–7 March 2003, Manila, 578 pp.

Devantier, L., Alcala, A. C. and Wilkinson, C. (2004). The Sulu-Sulawesi Sea: environmental and socioeconomic status, future prognosis and ameliorative policy options. *Ambio*, **33**, 693–702.

Dollar, N. (2002). Triton Island fish sanctuary. In *Workshop Proceedings of the AFMA Marine Fishery Reserves Program on the formulation of a National Fish Sanctuary Strategy*, eds. W. L. Campos and P. D. Beldia II, pp. 140–45. Miag-ao, Iloilo: UP in the Visayas.

Estacion, J. S. and Calumpong, H. P. (eds.) (2002). *Sogod Bay Post-Resource and Social Assessment Monitoring*, FRMP Information Paper. Quezon City, Philippines: Bureau of Fisheries and Aquatic Resources, Department of Agriculture.

Ferrer, E. M., Polotan-de la Cruz, L. and Agoncillo-Domingo, M. (eds.) (1996). *Seeds of Hope: A Collection of Case Studies on Community-Based Coastal Resources Management in the Philippines.* Quezon City, Philippines: College of Social Work and Community Development.

Foundation for the Philippine Environment (2004). *Sustaining Biodiversity Conservation Initiatives*, Site-Focused Projects 2003 Report. Quezon City, Philippines: FPE.

Gell, F. R. and Roberts, C. M. (2002). *The Fishery Effects of Marine Reserves and Fishery Closures.* Washington, DC: Worldwide Fund for Nature.

Gomez, E. D., Alcala, A. C. and San Diego, A. C. (1981). Status of Philippine coral reefs, 1981. *Proceedings 4th International Coral Reef Symposium*, **1**, 275–82.

Gomez, E. D., Alino, P. M., Yap, H. T. and Licuanan, W. R. I. (1994). A review of the status of Philippine reefs. *Marine Pollution Bulletin*, **29**, 62–8.

Green, S. J., White, A. T., Flores, J. O., Carreon III, M. F. and Sia, A. E. (2003). *Philippine Fisheries in Crisis: A Framework for Management.* Cebu City, Philippines: Coastal Resource Management Project of the Department of Environment and Natural Resources.

Halpern, B. S. (2003). The impact of marine reserves: do reserves work and does reserve size matter? *Ecological Applications*, **13**, S117–S137.

Johnson, D. E., Funicelli, N. A. and Bohnsack, J. A. (1999). Effectiveness of an existing estuarine no-take fish sanctuary within the Kennedy Space Center, Florida. *North American Journal of Fisheries Management*, **19**, 436–51.

Khan, A. S., Mikkola, H. and Brummett, R. (2004). Feasibility of fisheries co-management in Africa. *World Fish Center Quarterly*, **27**, 60–4.

King, M. and Faasili, U. (1998). Village fisheries management and community-owned marine protected areas in Samoa. *World Fish Center Quarterly*, April–June, 34–8.

McClanahan, T. R. and Mangi, S. (2000). Spillover of exploitable fishes from a marine park and its effect on the adjacent fishery. *Ecological Applications*, **10**, 1792–805.

Mejia, M. N., Ledesma, M. and Dygico, M. (2002). An update on conservation efforts in Tubbataha National Marine Park and World Heritage Site in Palawan, Philippines. In *Workshop Proceedings of the AFMA Marine Fishery Reserves Program on the Formulation of a National Fish Sanctuary Strategy*, eds. W. L. Campos and P. D. Beldia II, pp. 77–84. Miag-ao, Iloilo: UP in the Visayas.

Mosqueira, I., Côté, I. M., Jennings, S. and Reynolds, J. D. (2000). Conservation benefits of marine reserves for fish populations. *Animal Conservation*, **3**, 321–32.

Oracion, E. G. (2003). The dynamics of stakeholder participation in marine protected area development: a case study in Batangas, Philippines. *Silliman Journal*, **44**, 95–137.

Pajaro, M., Olano, F., San Juan, B. and Nozawa, C. M. (1999). Inventory of marine protected areas in the Philippines. In *Proceedings of the Workshop on Marine Protected Areas in the Philippines*, eds. A. J. Uychiaoco, S. Schoppe, P. Aliño and R. Hermes,. Quezon City, Philippines: Coral Reef Information Network of the Philippines.

Philreefs (Coral Reef Information Network of the Philippines) (2003). *Philippine Coral Reefs through Time: Workshop Proceedings*. Quezon City, Philippines: Coral Reef Information Network of the Philippines (Philreefs), University of the Philippines Marine Science Institute.

Pollnac, R. B., Thiele, M. T., Eisma, R. V. *et al.* (2003). Factors influencing the sustainability of integrated coastal management projects in the Philippines. *Silliman Journal*, **44**, 37–74.

Pomeroy, R. S. (ed.) (1994). *Community Management and Common Property of Coastal Fisheries in Asia and the Pacific: Concepts, Methods and Experiences*. ICLARM Conf. Proc. 45.

Primavera, Y. H. (2002). The coral reef fisheries of Malalison Island, west central Philippines two years after fish sanctuary protection. *UPV Journal of Natural Sciences*, **1/2**, 120–32.

Raymundo, L. J. H. (2004). Reef check in Apo Island Marine Reserve: a six-year report. Unpublished report submitted to Reef Check International.

Roberts, C. M. and Hawkins, J. P. (2000). *Fully Protected Marine Reserves: A Guide*. Washington, DC: Worldwide Fund for Nature.

Roberts, C. M., Bohnsack, J. A., Gell, F., Hawkins, J. P. and Goodridge, R. (2001). Effects of marine reserves on adjacent fisheries. *Science*, **294**, 1920–3.

Ross, M. A., White, A. T., Sitoy, A. C. and Menguito, T. (2000). Experience from improving management of an 'urban' marine protected area: Gilutongan Marine Sanctuary, Philippines. *Proceedings 9th International Coral Reef Symposium*, **2**, 641–6.

Ruddle, K. and Johannes, R. E. (1985). *The Traditional Knowledge and Management of Coastal Systems in Asia and the Pacific*. Paris: UNESCO.

Russ, G. R. and Alcala, A. C. (1996). Do marine reserves export adult fish biomass? Evidence from Apo Island, central Philippines. *Marine Ecology Progress Series*, **132**, 1–9.

(2003). Marine reserves: rates and patterns of recovery and decline of predatory fish, 1983–2000. *Ecological Applications*, **13**, 1553–65.

Russ, G. R., Alcala, A. C. and Maypa, A. P. (2003). Spillover from marine reserves: the case of *Naso vlamingii* at Apo Island, Philippines. *Marine Ecology Progress Series*, **264**, 15–20.

Russ, G. R., Alcala, A. C., Maypa, A. P., Calumpong, H. P. and White, A. T. (2004). Marine reserve benefits local fisheries. *Ecological Applications*, **14**, 597–606.

Russ, G. R., Stockwell, B. and Alcala, A. C. (2005). Inferring versus measuring rates of recovery in no-take marine reserves. *Marine Ecology Progress Series*, **292**, 1–12.

Smith, M. P. L., Bell, J. D., Pitt, K. A., Thomas, P. and Ramohia. P. (2000). The Anarvon Islands Marine Conservation Area: lessons in monitoring and management. *Proceedings 9th International Coral Reef Symposium*, **2**, 621–5.

Stockwell, B. (2004). Section 3: Fish Standing Stock. In *Bohol Marine Triangle Project (BMTP): Biodiversity Inventory, Assessment and Monitoring*, ed. H. P. Calumpong. Quezon City, Philippines: Foundation for the Philippine Environment.

UP-MSI, ABC, ARCBC, DENR, ASEAN. (2002). *Marine Protected Areas in Southeast Asia*. Los Baños, Philippines: ASEAN Regional Centre for Biodiversity Conservation, Department of Environment and National Resources.

Walls, K. (1998). Leigh Marine Reserve, New Zealand. Parks. *World Commission on Protected Area of the IUCN*, **8** (2), 5–10.

Webb, E. L., Maliao, R. J. and Siar, S. V. (2004). Using local user perceptions to evaluate outcomes of protected area management in the Sagay Marine Reserve, Philippines. *Environmental Conservation*, **31**, 138–48.

White, A. T. and Green, S. (2004). Successful marine protected areas require broad support: the Philippine case. In *Proceedings 2nd International Tropical Marine Ecosystems Management Symposium*, 24–27 March 2003, pp. 267–77.

White, A. T., Salamanca, A. and Courtney, C. A. (2002). Experience with Marine Protected Area planning and management in the Philippines. *Coastal Management*, **30**, 1–26.

Wilkinson, C. (ed.). (2004). *Status of the Coral Reefs of the World*: 2004. Townsville, QLD:. Australian Institute of Marine Science.

Williams, M. J. (1994). Foreword. In *Community Management and Common Property of Coastal Fisheries in Asia and the Pacific: Concepts, Methods and Experiences*, ed. R. S. Pomeroy. ICLARM Conf. Proc. 45.

Woodley, J. D. and Sary, Z. (2000). Development of a locally managed fisheries reserve at Discovery Bay, Jamaica. *Proceedings of the 9th International Coral Reef Symposium*, **2**, 627–33.

14

Education as a tool for coral reef conservation: lessons from marine protected areas

LISA J. BROWNING
Reefology

R. ANDREW O. FINLAY
Atkins Water

LORNA R. E. FOX
Reefology

INTRODUCTION

Education is pivotal to the success of coral reef conservation. From local to global and from policy to practice, public understanding of human interactions with the natural world plays a vital role in the development of sustainable solutions to environmental challenges. Without it, how can we possibly expect individuals – be they politicians, fishers or tourists – to compromise short-term interests for long-term gain? In the context of the modern shift towards participatory decision-making, stakeholder education has the potential to become the most powerful and fundamental force in the sustainable management of the marine environment. Many conservation programmes have long recognized this potential and have sought to realize it in diverse ways.

This chapter – published during the first year of the UN Decade of Education for Sustainable Development – considers the role of education in coral reef conservation, including drivers for education, tools and techniques and evaluation. We focus in particular on marine protected areas (MPAs) because these are the coral reef conservation tool that has made greatest use of educational initiatives. There is a host of MPA programmes,

Coral Reef Conservation, ed. Isabelle M. Côté and John D. Reynolds.
Published by Cambridge University Press.

centres, services and materials designed to engage the interest of the general public or specific groups in the coral reef environment and associated issues. But do these programmes really work? And how do they interact with other conservation tools? Although most of the examples we have included relate to education in MPAs, we believe that the points arising from them also have a wider significance.

EDUCATION FOR SUSTAINABILITY

Definitions

These days, no profession is without its own sector-specific jargon, often ambiguous or impenetrable to the unacquainted. Education is no different, and there is a plethora of terms in use, sometimes applied interchangeably or inconsistently. For the purposes of this chapter, the range of terminology will be kept to a minimum (primarily the terms in italics below). *Education* will be defined in the widest sense, to include any action that seeks to increase awareness and understanding. This includes *formal education* (aimed at students at schools, colleges, universities and other academic institutions) and *non-formal education* (aimed at specific non-academic groups or the general public).

Environmental education (EE) is a long-established term, usually referring to formal and non-formal education contributing to understanding of the environment and our human interrelationship with it. EE may focus largely on the natural environment, or include the man-made, cultural and technological environment (Thomson and Hoffman, 2003). *Education for sustainable development* (*ESD*; sometimes called education for sustainability or sustainability education) is a more recent addition to the vocabulary, bringing a wider dimension and purpose than is typical of EE. ESD 'enables people to develop the knowledge, values and skills to participate in decisions about the way we do things individually and collectively, both locally and globally, that will improve the quality of life now without damaging the planet for the future' (Education for Sustainable Development and Global Citizenship, 2005). Closely related to ESD are education for global citizenship and education for participatory democracy, both of which focus on the role of individuals in the local and global society. Education for global citizenship 'enables people to understand the global forces which shape their lives and to acquire the knowledge, skills and values that will equip them to participate in decision making, both locally and globally, which promotes a more equitable and sustainable world' (Education for Sustainable Development and Global Citizenship, 2005).

Aims and objectives

Environmental education (here viewed as an integral aspect of ESD) has been defined as comprising three critical components: awareness, leading to understanding, which in turn creates the potential and capacity for appropriate actions (Thomson and Hoffman, 2003). The objectives of EE, as outlined by the 1977 Tbilisi Intergovernmental Conference on Environmental Education (UNESCO–UNEP, 1978; UNESCO, 1980), are as follows:

(1) Awareness – to help social groups and individuals acquire an awareness and sensitivity to the total environment and its allied problems (and/or issues).
(2) Sensitivity – to help social groups and individuals gain a variety of experiences in, and acquire a basic understanding of, the environment and its associated problems (and/or issues).
(3) Attitudes – to help social groups and individuals acquire a set of values and feelings of concern for the environment and motivation for actively participating in environmental improvement and protection.
(4) Skills – to help social groups and individuals acquire skills for identifying and solving environmental problems (and/or issues).
(5) Participation – to provide social groups and individuals with an opportunity to be actively involved at all levels in working toward resolution of environmental problems (and/or issues).

It is plain that these general principles lend themselves readily to the context of coral reef conservation, from the global to the local scale, providing an overarching set of objectives for all educational activity.

International drivers for EE and ESD

The need for EE was formally recognized by the international community at the UN Conference on the Human Environment in Stockholm, in June 1972 (UNESCO, 1980). The UN's *Agenda 21* (UN, 2005) went further, placing education at the heart of sustainable development. *Agenda 21* is among the most important guidelines for education for sustainable development and was formulated during the historic UN Conference on Environment and Development (UNCED), also known as the Earth Summit, held in Rio de Janeiro in June 1992.

Chapter 36 of *Agenda 21* states that 'education, including formal education, public awareness and training should be recognised as a process by which human beings and societies can reach their fullest potential', whereby 'education is critical for promoting sustainable development and improving the capacity of the people to address environment and development issues'. In addition, it indicates that formal and non-formal education are indispensable in changing people's attitudes so that they have the motivation to assess and address their sustainable development concerns. *Agenda 21* sets the objective of promoting broad public awareness as an essential part of the global education effort to strengthen attitudes, values and actions that are compatible with sustainable development (Connect, 1992).

The pivotal role of education was reaffirmed at the World Summit on Sustainable Development in Johannesburg in August/September 2002 (UNESCO, 2005). Later in the same year, the UN General Assembly adopted a resolution to launch the UN Decade of Education for Sustainable Development (DESD) 2005–2014, identifying UNESCO as the lead agency. The vision of the DESD is 'a world where everyone has the opportunity to benefit from quality education and learn the values, behaviour and lifestyles required for a sustainable future and for positive societal transformation'. Education is seen as 'the primary agent of transformation towards sustainable development, increasing people's capacities to transform their visions for society into reality' (UNESCO, 2005). The proposed objectives of the Decade are to:

(1) Give an enhanced profile to the central role of education and learning in the common pursuit of sustainable development.
(2) Facilitate links and networking, exchange and interaction among stakeholders in ESD.
(3) Provide a space and opportunity for refining and promoting the vision of, and transition to sustainable development – through all forms of learning and public awareness.
(4) Foster increased quality of teaching and learning in education for sustainable development.
(5) Develop strategies at every level to strengthen capacity in ESD.

Another driver for education is the global promotion of participatory decision-making. Stakeholder dialogue and participation in decision-making serve to incorporate public values, knowledge and experience into decisions (see Brown, this volume). This has the potential to improve the quality, sustainability and enforceability of decisions, by resolving conflict, building trust and creating 'buy-in' (Acland, 1990, 2002). This approach is being driven forward by initiatives such as the UN Economic Commission for Europe (UNECE) Aarhus Convention: Access to Information, Public Participation in Decision-Making and Access to Justice in Environmental Matters. According to the UNECE (2005):

> (t)he Aarhus Convention is a new kind of environmental agreement. It links environmental rights and human rights. It acknowledges that we owe an obligation to future generations. It establishes that sustainable development can be achieved only through the involvement of all stakeholders. It links government accountability and environmental protection. It focuses on interactions between the public and public authorities in a democratic context and it is forging a new process for public participation in the negotiation and implementation of international agreements.

In the context of this Convention, education is a vital tool for engaging and informing stakeholders in decision-making processes.

ESD as an emerging profession

Linked to the growing status of ESD in international policy is the development of ESD as a profession in its own right. One of the key factors in the emergence of the profession is the provision of academic training and recognized qualifications. For example, in 1994, a pioneering course was established in the UK: the Masters/Postgraduate Diploma in Environmental and Development Education at South Bank University, London. The first course of its kind in the UK, the M.Sc./Pg.Dip. offered the chance to gain professional training in the field of EE/ESD. The course came about as a partnership between the university and WWF–UK, with funding from WWF–UK, the European Community, Oxfam, CAFOD and Christian Aid (S. Sterling, pers. comm.). It was set up during a time that saw the convergence of environmental and development education and the arrival of the concept of ESD (Huckle and Sterling, 1996). The course sought to recognize the multidisciplinary nature of ESD and to cover a range of aspects including environmental and development education within the formal education system, issues in participation, critical analysis of media coverage of environmental and development issues, how local and global factors interact north/south, and education for sustainability.

Similar courses are now offered at universities in Australia (La Trobe), South Africa (Rhodes) and the USA (University of New Hampshire). Over the coming years, graduates of courses such as these will help to raise standards and increase consistency in the profession, firmly grounded in an understanding of the principles of education for sustainable development.

EDUCATION AND MARINE CONSERVATION

The overarching aims of ESD are presented above, but what are the desired outcomes specifically relating to the marine environment? Two informal

Table 14.1. Delegate responses from the Coral Reef Conservation Conference, London, December 2004, to the question: 'What would be the benefits of greater public understanding of the marine environment?'

People would take greater personal responsibility for the health of the marine environment, for example by doing more recycling and choosing sustainable seafood and tourism.
You'd get more informed participation in stakeholder dialogue processes that form part of decision-making, leading to more sustainable decisions.
More pressure on politicians and policy makers.
There would be more public support and understanding when difficult decisions have to be made . . . for example, if coastal re-alignment is necessary because of sea level rise, or if a fishery has to be closed or MPA regulations enforced.
Making our jobs [in conservation] easier – less of an uphill struggle.
More funding for research and conservation.
More people – and a greater diversity of people – would be attracted to careers in conservation, bringing in skills from business, media, psychology, social sciences and so on.
Increased membership of environmental organizations.
More appreciation of less 'charismatic' species.
Better co-operation with the media.
Greater appreciation of the value of the marine environment.
More enjoyment of the marine environment.

surveys have identified the variety of potential benefits from increased public understanding of the marine environment, as perceived by a portion of the coral reef conservation and UK marine conservation communities. At the Coral Reef Conservation Conference hosted by the Zoological Society of London in December 2004, delegates were asked by one of the authors to answer the question: 'What would be the benefits of greater public understanding of the marine environment?' Some of the responses are shown in Table 14.1.

Written responses to the same question, provided by delegates at The Wildlife Trusts' UK Conference on Public Understanding of the Marine Environment in London in January 2005 showed political pressure and acceptance of personal responsibility for the state of the marine environment as the two most widely recognized benefits, though a further 19 categories of benefit were also cited (The Wildlife Trusts, unpublished data) (see Table 14.2). Note that some of the categories overlap and are subject to interpretation. For example, acceptance of 'Personal responsibility' for the marine environment is closely related to 'Sense of ownership' and both of these might entail 'Public participation' in conservation projects, 'Stakeholder participation' in decision-making and exertion of 'Consumer choice'.

Table 14.2. Delegate responses from the Conference on Public Understanding of the Marine Environment, London, January 2005

Issue	Number of mentions[a]
Taking personal responsibility for the marine environment	26
Exerting political pressure	24
Exerting consumer choice/power	10
More effective protected areas	10
Better management of the sea	9
More public participation in marine conservation	9
Greater appreciation of the marine environment	8
Wider understanding of human impacts on the sea	8
Wider understanding of the value of marine resources	7
More funding for conservation	6
Sense of ownership of the sea	5
Better integration of local/traditional knowledge	4
Socio-economic gains	3
Difficult decisions made easier	3
Higher baseline for education	2
Increased public profile of the marine environment	2
Greater awareness of safety issues at sea	2
Greater stakeholder participation	2
Higher media profile for the sea and marine issues	1

[a] Number of delegates' responses ($n = 55$) in which this issue was mentioned.

A lack of awareness and understanding of coral reefs has been identified as one of the main threats to the survival of these ecosystems (Nicholson and Schreiner, 1973), and the survey responses suggest a range of underlying factors, from insufficient public understanding of human impacts on the marine environment to a lack of stakeholder engagement in decision-making. These factors apply at a range of spatial scales and suggest the need to target a variety of stakeholder sectors, including local and international leaders, local communities, tourists and consumers of marine products. However, many of the factors are most relevant – making education potentially most effective – at the local level. For this reason, much of the next section focuses on local education, specifically relating to marine protected areas.

EDUCATION AND MARINE PROTECTED AREAS

Designation, implementation and management of marine protected areas (MPAs) is widely regarded as an important approach to the management of fisheries, biodiversity and other marine resources (White, 1988; Kenchington, 1990; Kelleher and Kenchington, 1991; Gubbay, 1993, 1995; McNealy, 1994; Russ and Alcala, 1999; Dayton *et al.*, 2000; White and Vogt, 2000). An MPA is an area or zone within the marine or coastal environment where resource extraction and/or human access are regulated or prohibited. It can be an effective way to protect breeding and juvenile fish, guard against overfishing and ensure a sustainable breeding population that can help to enhance fish stocks outside of the MPA (Pauly, 2000). There is a wealth of evidence that suggests that areas without MPAs will suffer continuous decline of fisheries while those areas with active MPAs experience an increase in fish catches (White, 1986a; Roberts and Polunin, 1991; Russ and Alcala, 1999). A coral reef unaffected by natural and human disturbances produces 25 t km^{-2} yr^{-1} of fish while a destroyed reef yields less than 5 t km^{-2} yr^{-1} (Bolido and White, 1997; see also McClanahan, this volume).

Alongside sustaining fish stocks for future generations, MPAs are often designated for the conservation of biodiversity and as multiple-use management tools. Integrated protection of a number of biological coastal resources, such as coral reefs, mangroves or seagrass beds, and sometimes non-biological resources such as historic wrecks, can provide productive areas for tourism and heritage and biodiversity conservation, as well as 'no-take zones' for fisheries management.

The relationship between MPAs, education and participation

Experience in MPA management shows that the success of conservation management programs depends critically on the support of local people (Kaza, 1988; Lemay and Hale, 1989; Christie *et al.*, 1990; Alcock, 1991; Kelleher and Kenchington, 1991; Kriwoken, 1991; Kenchington and Bleakley, 1994; White *et al.*, 1994; Wells and White, 1995; Alder, 1996a; Attwood, 1997; Balgos, 1999; Bunce *et al.*, 1999; Mascia, 1999; Russ and Alcala, 1999; White and Vogt, 2000). In an international study of the governance of MPAs in the Caribbean, Mascia (1999) found that participation in the development and management of MPAs varied extensively between stakeholder groups and that low involvement was a main factor in the failure of MPA management.

However, engaging the participation and support of local communities is rarely straightforward. The marine environment – being 'out of sight and out of mind' – is typically less well understood, less valued and less appreciated than the terrestrial environment. Communities may be quite unaware of the concept and cost implications of unmanaged or mismanaged marine resources (Kenchington, 1990). As a result, public support for the designation and management of MPAs may be low.

An example of this can be seen in research conducted by Bunce *et al.* (1999), which discussed the socio-economics of coral reef management with particular reference to the Montego Bay Marine Park, Jamaica. Relations among user groups of the MPA were found to be generally poor. This was because there were limited interactions between fishers and hoteliers, in large part due to their different socio-economic backgrounds. Furthermore, antagonistic relations had developed between the fishers and the water-sports operators because each group felt that the other was threatening their livelihood. Serious conflict existed between the Marine Park managers and fishers, as the fishers believed that they had been unfairly targeted in measures to protect marine resources. Most hotel resorts and water-sports operators generally recognized, and were concerned about, the impacts of their own activities and their guests' activities. In contrast, most fishers did not perceive fishing to be having a major impact on the reefs. Perhaps of greater importance were the misunderstandings of the fishers and some hoteliers regarding the Marine Park regulations, particularly boundary locations. Furthermore, there was a general lack of awareness of management activities, which contributed to a lack of confidence in the ability of the Park staff to manage the Park's resources (Bunce *et al.*, 1999). All of these factors, coupled with a low awareness of the marine environment, contributed to the lack of public support and community involvement in the management of MPA.

Education is a critical component in addressing the lack of community support and involvement (White, 1986b; Alcock, 1991; Kelly, 1992; Christie *et al.*, 1994; Kaza, 1995; Dikstehius, 1996; Attwood, 1997; Selendy, 1998; Balgos, 1999; Bunce *et al.*, 1999; Collins and Dickinson, 1999; White and Vogt, 2000), not only conveying the potential future benefits of the MPA, but also the interests, sensitivities and constraints of other resource-users (Brown, this volume). Indeed, Alcock (1991) claims that the most important method for managing natural resource areas is the implementation of a well-designed education programme, one which informs and educates users about the values of the area and about nature conservation, not by direct teaching but by experience. Conversely, inadequate or inappropriate education has been highlighted as one of the many causes of unsuccessful MPAs (Cabanban and White, 1981; Kaza, 1988; Sivalingham, 1991; Kelly, 1992; Christie *et al.*, 1994; Kenchington and Bleakley, 1994; Wells and

White, 1995; Alder, 1996a; Dikstehius, 1996; Selendy, 1998; Bunce *et al.*, 1999; Spruill, 1999).

Kelly (1992) studied a total of 15 marine agencies and MPAs from the UK, USA, Canada, Ecuador and Australia, to review the effectiveness of public communication techniques in the resolution of marine resource management problems. In this study, managers consistently identified education as a critical tool in MPA management. The objectives of their MPA education programmes were as follows, in order of priority (Kelly, 1992):

(1) Enhance the experience of MPA users.
(2) Inform users of regulations controlling use.
(3) Provide information to ensure the safety of users.
(4) Encourage environmentally responsible behaviour.
(5) Seek information exchange for incorporation into management planning – traditional knowledge.

Environmental education stimulates participation at a local level, as it not only provides knowledge and information about the environment but also seeks to promote a change in attitude and behaviour (Kelly, 1992; Dikstehius, 1996). Among local communities, this can result in a determination to search for solutions to problems arising from their interactions with their environment (Renhack *et al.*, 1992; Rodriguez-Martinez and Ortiz, 1999).

A well-designed education and public involvement programme can also generate political and public enthusiasm for the MPA and its goal and objectives. Establishment of a sense of ownership will generate pride and commitment (Kelleher and Kenchington, 1991). It may also attract the support of the government, so increasing the chances of obtaining logistical support and funding for the future maintenance of the MPA. Community support for successful MPAs may also contribute to the establishment of new MPAs, as seen throughout the Philippines (Alcala *et al.*, this volume).

It is interesting to note that in literature on the subject of MPAs, there has been a shift in emphasis on the importance of public participation and education. In the *Coral Reef Management Handbook* (Kelleher and Lausche, 1984), a four-line paragraph on public participation is incorporated into an extensive outline of the issues that need to be considered when establishing an MPA. However, in the IUCN report *Guidelines for Establishing MPAs* (Kelleher and Kenchington, 1991), which is based on the previous report by the same authors, the section on public participation has been elaborated. Not only does it highlight the importance of public participation, but also provides details of procedures that can be used to ensure effective and appropriate public participation. What is of particular interest is that the use of education to catalyse involvement of the public is not mentioned in the 1984 guidelines but is recognized in its own section in the review in 1991, as one of the most important components of MPA management.

Education providers

Hayashi (1991) outlined the responsibility that administrative bodies, schools and non-governmental organizations (NGOs) have in delivering environmental education. NGOs are a major driving force behind environmental education in MPA management throughout the world, providing the staff resources, time and technical expertise to carry out effective educational programmes (White, 1997; Selendy, 1998; Walters *et al.*,1998; Spruill, 1999). NGOs have the flexibility to target a range of stakeholders including local communities, school children and tourists. For example, Shoals Rodrigues, a Mauritian NGO, works with local fishers, the local community, schools and visitors to the island to raise awareness of the importance of the marine environment (Shoals Rodrigues, 2004). In the Philippines, the Coastal Resource Management Project (CRMP) has been very successful in establishing community-based MPAs with a strong emphasis on education (Green *et al.*, 2000; Sotto *et al.*, 2001).

Where MPAs have a legal underpinning, the authority responsible for managing them frequently has a remit for environmental education, whether through visitor centres, museums or other media. For example in Australia, the Great Barrier Reef Marine Park Authority (2004) provides a range of educational services and materials.

Universities are often active in carrying out marine education, whether education and technical training of students or raising awareness amongst local communities. Student groups and environmental departments can often obtain funding to carry out educational and monitoring initiatives. In the Philippines, Silliman University has supported many projects by providing technical assistance and funding in preparation, planning, implementation and monitoring of MPAs (White, 1986b, 1989; Walters *et al.*, 1998; Russ and Alcala, 1999). Furthermore, many universities have marine laboratories that provide technical courses for students or professionals on a whole host of marine-related subjects. Participants spend weeks or whole semesters staying on location studying the marine environment first hand. Links between NGOs and universities are also common, and these links frequently have an international dimension. For example, Coral Cay Conservation's programme in Belize, which culminated in the designation of a number of MPAs, was delivered in partnership with University College Belize (Coral Cay Conservation, 2004).

Schools also play an important role in environmental education. However, delivery is strongly limited by the content of the teaching curricula, course books and teacher training programmes. The extent to which EE and ESD have been incorporated into formal education varies greatly from country to country. At primary and secondary level at the current time, elements of ESD/EE are often addressed through the geography or science parts of the curriculum rather than being integrated across all subject areas.

It is important to understand that even if the EE content of the student curriculum is lacking, opportunities – or 'hooks' on which EE themes can be hung – can almost invariably be found. For example, the theme of 'Animals and their environment' in the Mauritian curriculum can be used to introduce coral reef conservation. However, delivery is then reliant on the willingness and confidence of individual teachers to identify and exploit the opportunities. The accessibility of teaching materials (for example, those produced by MPA education programmes), outreach services and visitor centres to support study is also a significant factor. The cost and health and safety implications of outdoor teaching are further considerations that affect the ability of teachers to develop EE/ESD within their teaching (see for example Department for Education and Employment, 1998; Professional Association of Teachers, 1997).

One of the major challenges presented by *Agenda 21* is the reorientation of primary, secondary and tertiary education to address sustainability (McKeown *et al.*, 2005). A reoriented approach would provide the principles, skills, perspectives and values necessary to promote sustainable lifestyles and development. This might be achieved through changes to academic curricula and teacher training programmes.

One example of a 'reoriented' curriculum is the International Baccalaureate Primary Years Program (International Baccalaureate Organization, 2005), which is offered at IBO accredited international schools around the world. It has a holistic approach to the individual and the whole school, advocating the development of the individual's whole being – physical, emotional and mental. The curriculum covers six trans-disciplinary themes (including 'Who we are', 'How the world works', 'How we organize ourselves' and 'Sharing the planet'). Within these broad themes, the teacher chooses a specific topic (for example, 'Reduce, reuse, recycle') for investigation over a fixed timescale and, after a period of teacher input, the pupils are responsible for taking investigation of the subject in their chosen direction or directions. The written curriculum incorporates five essential elements – concepts, skills, attitudes, action and knowledge – and the core attitudes and principles are a crucial part of each school day. There is less top–down control of learning and more ownership by the learner of his/her own learning experience.

Identifying audiences

Identifying target audiences is the key to maximizing the effectiveness of initiatives, staff and resources (Kaza, 1995). Schoolchildren, as the marine environmental custodians of the future, are a popular focus (Hooper, 1992; Russel, 1992; Gough and Robottom, 1995; Rowe and Probst, 1995; Rodriguez-Martinez and Ortiz, 1999; Finlay, 2000) and, notwithstanding the limitations of formal teaching curricula described above, are a relatively straightforward audience. Political sensitivities and vested interests may be less acute when dealing with children than with adults, and an educator has the luxury of an audience that is likely to be interested in their environment and eager to learn. In a sense, educating children is the easy option. However, if MPAs are to have a rapid impact on the health of the marine environment, it is likely that educational effort will also need to be directed at other stakeholder groups. For example, an MPA may need to orientate its programmes towards tourists, local leaders, government officials or influential community members (Smith, 2001).

At the outset of a programme in Honduras, local community leaders, schoolteachers and senior staff within the local dive industry were identified as the most influential stakeholders in the short term, and were the focus of a number of training and capacity-building initiatives (Browning, 2000). In South Africa, many of the community-based MPAs and participative management systems have recognized a specific and urgent need for fisheries education (Mann-Lang, 1998) to provide local communities with as much information as possible about new initiatives, and to develop measures in partnership rather than imposing changes (Badalamenti *et al.*, 2000).

Learning approaches

There is no single formula for successful ESD/EE. Education must be sensitive and adapted to the local circumstances, objectives and target stakeholders. However, as our understanding of how people learn increases, broad approaches to EE/ESD are gradually evolving. One of the mantras of education comes from Albert Einstein, who said that 'Learning is experience.

Figure 14.1 Students at Utila Public School, Honduras, create clay models of coral polyps. (Photograph by Lisa J. Browning.)

Everything else is just information.' Direct, often hands-on, experience is thus at the heart of many EE/ESD programmes, for both the formal and non-formal sectors. Figure 14.1 shows an example of hands-on learning.

Good environmental education 'is learner centred, providing students with opportunities to construct their own understandings through hands-on, minds-on investigation; involves engaging learners in direct experience and challenges them to use higher-order thinking skills; is supportive of the development of an active learning community where learners share ideas and expertise and prompt continued inquiry; provides real-world contexts and issues from which concepts and skills can be used' (North American Association for Environmental Education, 1996).

An understanding of the importance of play as a vehicle for learning has also emerged (Bennett *et al.*, 1997) and games now feature strongly in many programmes, particularly those aimed at children (see for example Cornell, 1989, 1998; Horsfall, 1997; Browning, 2002). Figure 14.2 shows an example of environmental games in action.

Various learning models have helped provide a conceptual framework for the development of environmental education. One particular model presents three alternative learning styles – visual, kinaesthetic and auditory (Sumner, 2004). It is acknowledged that any individual will learn through a mixture of these styles, but will show a preference for one of the three. Visual learners learn through seeing things. They like to have activities

Figure 14.2 Children dressed up as customs officers search baggage for smuggled 'coral'. An activity devised by Reefology for London Aquarium's Reef Week. (Photograph by Lisa J. Browning.)

demonstrated to them, to be shown things, look at things, or see pictures or diagrams. These people benefit from using images and objects in activities. They will remember what they learn by how things look. Kinaesthetic learners like to be hands-on, learning through physical activities, movement and touch. They learn most effectively through physically enacting something, walking through the movements or by touching and feeling. They benefit from using real objects and movement in learning. Auditory learners learn through hearing things. They respond well to verbal instructions, and enjoy listening to stories. These people may look away when listening, and may seem to be focused on something else. However, they are listening and may be taking in the story or event in immense detail. They may benefit from music or sounds accompanying their learning. Most stakeholder groups will be expected to comprise a mixture of visual, kinaesthetic and auditory learners (typically a 40/30/30 split). By incorporating all three learning styles in the learning and teaching approach, be it through hands-on activities, drama or rich sensory experiences, the efficiency and effectiveness of teaching is increased (Sumner, 2004).

Tools

The basic educational resources available to MPA programmes are staff and educational materials. Personal contact with the public in the form of tours, walks or visits to schools and community groups is a common

Figure 14.3 Students at Utila Methodist Community College, Honduras, graduate from Reefology's Utila Sea School programme. (Photograph by Lisa J. Browning.)

educational tool used in developed and developing countries (Kaza, 1988, 1995; Rodriguez-Martinez and Ortiz, 1999). Working with schools, whether through student visits to the MPA or outreach visits of MPA staff into schools, provides access to the heart of the community, and serves as an avenue for contact with teachers, parents and other adults (Fig. 14.3). For example in Fiji, after a five-week coral reef education programme, the pupils of Yadua Island school delivered a coral reef concert for the rest of the community, in which pupils acted out various coral reef issues such as the value of coral reefs in terms of providing fish for food and the threat to coral reefs such as litter (Finlay, 2002). During the school project, the children made *sulus* with coral reef themes and messages so that they would have a lasting reminder of the coral reef project which they proudly displayed during the community concert (Fig. 14.4). Similarly in Honduras, an outreach programme with local schools on the island of Utila included the creation of sea life costumes for a marine-themed group in the Utila Carnival procession.

Community outreach programmes and liaison with local leaders may have the most direct influence in addressing local practices that harm the marine environment (Hudson, 1984; Kaza, 1988, 1995; Green *et al.*, 2000; White and Vogt, 2000). Many education providers have adopted educational strategies that communicate information to the stakeholders of MPAs through workshops and seminars. The hope is that this will create ownership and, fundamentally, empowerment so that the community begins to

Figure 14.4 Pupils making *sulus* with coral reef protection themes at the school project on Yadua Island, Fiji. (Photograph by R. A. O. Finlay.)

take responsibility for protecting marine resources (Christie *et al.*, 1994; White *et al.*, 1994; White, 1997; Balgos, 1999). Community outreach programmes require diplomacy, but it is often the most important arena for interpretive efforts (Kaza, 1988, 1995). For example, the Coastal Resource Management Project in the Philippines delivers annual MPA fisherfolk ceremonies in which the local community is empowered to restore natural resources by planting mangrove propagules in areas that have been cut down (Finlay, 2001) (Fig. 14.5).

The person-to-person approach is known to be very effective in conveying conservation values and promoting participation. However, most MPAs do not have funds to support full-time educational staff. Even in the USA, the largest MPAs have only a small team of staff to cover resource protection, enforcement, administration, planning and education. In some programmes (for example Browning, 2000), volunteers may be recruited to support or substitute for paid staff, but the investment in time and resources can still be very high. Another way of increasing the efficiency of staff-led education is to employ the 'cascade effect', training trainers and teachers who will then pass on the learning to a much wider audience than would be achievable through a single educator or small team. In Mauritius, Shoals Rodrigues (2004) runs workshops for local teachers, in order to enable them to undertake environmental education themselves (Figs. 14.6 and 14.7). In Fiji, the Institute of Marine Resources at the University of the South

Figure 14.5 Members of the local community planting mangroves as part of the annual MPA fisherfolk ceremony in the Philippines. (Photograph by R. A. O. Finlay.)

Pacific conducted a 12-day 'Train the trainers' Coral Reef Monitoring Workshop. Government fisheries officers from all of the countries in the South West Pacific underwent intensive awareness-raising on the threats to and importance of coral reefs (Finlay and Taylor, 2002). The participants also learnt coral reef monitoring methodology, data analysis and report-writing skills in order to train their own local teams in-country (Fig. 14.8). The aim of the workshop was to raise awareness and enable each country to prepare reports on the status of their country's coral reefs for submission to the Global Coral Reef Monitoring Network.

Facilities such as visitor centres, displays, interpretative signage and self-guided nature trails are another means of reaching an audience, as well as helping to develop the identity of a site. In the Philippines, signboards positioned on the main road have been used to show the way to marine reserves and also to promote the educational and awareness values of the reserves (White and Vogt, 2000). Outdoor interpretive aids work well for the self-guided visitor as a reminder of the boundaries of the protected area, but they are subject to vandalism and weathering. However, if members of the community are involved in the plans, design and construction of facilities, this may encourage protection.

Much larger audiences may be reached through educational materials, whether these are in print, on film or in digital formats. Printed materials

Figure 14.6 Participants in a teachers' workshop run by Shoals Rodrigues try out a pollution-themed activity for children. (Photograph by Lisa J. Browning.)

such as brochures, posters, pamphlets and books help to establish an image for a MPA, as well as communicating important conservation messages. Even inexpensively produced posters can promote community support for the marine environment by presenting beautiful and inspiring images of local fish, birds or underwater scenes.

In addition to materials aimed at the general public, marine education programmes often produce materials specifically for schools. For example, in 2004, the Office of the Advisor for Conservation of the Environment in Oman commissioned the production of an interactive CD-Rom for use in all schools across the country (Kennedy, 2003). The CD introduces students to the marine ecology of Oman, using colourful visual media to explore the key wildlife habitats and marine processes that support them. The pupil is able to navigate through different habitats and is introduced to natural processes by talking marine creatures and video footage of wildlife. For each habitat, a multiple-choice quiz tests the student's knowledge and awards points and audio applause for correct answers. It is a fun way to educate children using visual and audio aids that stimulate the child's participation through interacting with the marine creatures within the programme.

More widely, the role of digital media, particularly the internet, is revolutionizing environmental education. For example, the Organization for

Figure 14.7 Shoals Rodrigues staff and volunteers demonstrate model fish created during a teachers' workshop. (Photograph by Lisa J. Browning.)

Education and Science Integration (2005) is using the internet to link schools in New York State with scientists working with local communities on ecologically sustainable projects such as MPAs in the South West Pacific (S. Birch, pers. comm.) The scientists and project participants act as educators and role models during classes via video documentaries, web-based discussion forums, web-conferencing presentations and live video and audio link-ups. This interactive 'real-time' connection enables students to experience a tropical coral reef environment from their classroom and communicate directly with scientists in the field. This undoubtedly is far more stimulating and exciting for a child than reading or looking at pictures in a textbook, and aims to contribute to two-way learning and a building of understanding between distant communities.

Increasingly, there are efforts to gather and share materials between education providers in order to prevent providers from having to 'reinvent the wheel', thus saving time and resources. To mark the International Year of the Reef in 1997, a partnership comprising the Institute of Marine Sciences at the University of Southern Mississippi, the National Sea Grant College Programme and the Sea Grant College Programme of Puerto Rico compiled and published a book of coral reef activities from around the world, as an aid for middle-school teachers (Walker *et al.*, 1997). The book

Figure 14.8 Government fisheries officers learning coral reef surveying methodology at a training workshop in Fiji. (Photograph by R. A. O. Finlay.)

was published in both English and Spanish. The International Coral Reef Information Network (2005) has developed a Coral Reef Education Library, a web-based tool to signpost educators to educational materials from around the world. There are currently over 100 materials in the virtual library. Educational web-based portals and pathfinders also offer a useful signposting service for educators (for example, Eduscapes, 2005; 42eXplore, 2005)

The mass media, such as movies, television and newspapers, have played an important part in building public awareness of environmental problems as they have the advantage of reaching very large numbers of people (Kaza, 1995). Reef Check had enormous media success when film star Leonardo di Caprio attended a launch event (www.reefcheck.org) and Pixar/Disney's film *Finding Nemo* turned a cartoon coral reef fish into a global celebrity, recognized by millions of adults and children worldwide. This type of education has its limitations, however, as the message is rarely in the control of conservationists and often places emphasis on superficial or sensational aspects of the question. What is more, there is a disparity in the availability of these media between developed and developing countries, due to the high cost of equipment and production (Kaza, 1988, 1995).

EVALUATION OF THE EFFECTIVENESS OF ENVIRONMENTAL EDUCATION

Evaluation should be an integral part of all environmental education. Indeed, education programmes should be built around a continuous cycle of design, delivery, evaluation and redesign (Thomson and Hoffman, 2003).

The Council for Environmental Education (2004) describes the aims of evaluation of ESD as:

- To measure learning – to find out who has learned what
- To assess progress – to find out whether objectives have been met
- To improve the quality of the programme – to reflect on what is happening and plan further developments
- To enhance accountability – to demonstrate results to funders, managers and colleagues within the organization
- To communicate results – to those directly involved, to colleagues within the organization and to wider audiences
- To build up a body of evidence of effectiveness in ESD – to help understand what works (and in what ways) in a variety of contexts.

In practice, evaluation is rarely built into the development of ESD programmes (Jacobson, 1991) due to a number of factors including the difficulty (perceived and real) of measuring the results of programmes, especially in the long term. Reflecting on the aims of EE/ESD (see p. 421), it is understandable that educators and programme managers would be daunted by the task of evaluating how successful they have been in addressing the five key elements: awareness, sensitivity, attitudes, skills and participation.

While awareness, sensitivity, participation and skill levels are relatively simple to measure in the short term (unless the audience is large, widely dispersed or hard to access), it is much more difficult to measure longer-term learning and even harder to assess the impact of learning on attitudes and values. Furthermore, it is very difficult to separate changes in behaviour, attitude and values arising from a specific education programme from changes brought about by other complementary educational activities, media coverage, peer pressure and other factors. Other obstacles to evaluation include a lack of time, resources and expertise, and conflicting expectations and requirements from funders and managers (Council for Environmental Education, 2004). To address this lack of evaluation, several authors and organizations have published guidance, case studies and advice on a common-sense approach (McNamara, 1999; Stokking *et al.*, 1999; Robson,

2000; Walford, 2001; Thomson and Hoffman, 2003; Council for Environmental Education, 2004). Two of the key messages from McNamara's guide are that it is better to attempt some form of evaluation than nothing at all, and that the main concern when evaluating a programme is to collect and understand information that will be relevant to decisions.

The most straightforward parameter in which to measure change is 'awareness' (that is, understanding of the environment and sensitivity to issues and concerns). As such, this is the focus of the majority of evaluation efforts. For example, an evaluation was carried out to assess the effectiveness of the 'Train the trainers' workshop described in the previous section, in which government fisheries officers from countries in the South West Pacific attended a 12-day workshop on coral reef monitoring. The evaluation test was devised by the coordinators (Finlay and Taylor, 2002) to allow the initial knowledge levels of the participants to be determined, so guiding the structure of the training and allowing the workshop to be assessed. The test included sections on coral reef ecology, the importance of coral reefs and threats to the coral reef environment. The participants were also tested on their newly acquired knowledge of the Australian Institute of Marine Science (AIMS) coral reef monitoring methods for assessing the state of coral reef resources. Figure 14.9 shows that the participants' general knowledge of coral reefs improved, with the average score increasing from 53.6% (before the workshop) to 78.8% (after the workshop). The participants' average performance in the coral reef monitoring test increased from 51.7% to 83.5%. No further studies were undertaken to assess longer-term retention of the information.

Another straightforward evaluation of awareness (Finlay, 2002) highlighted the importance of sustained educational programmes. At a school on Yadua Island in Fiji, twelve 9–12-year-old pupils spent five weeks learning about the importance of coral reefs to their local community and the current threats to the reefs and hence to their families' income and livelihoods. Before the education programme started, the pupils were given a test to establish a baseline of their knowledge level with regard to coral reefs. After the project finished, the same test was administered and the study concluded that the class' overall knowledge of coral reefs had increased by 21%. Before the education programme, children of all ages had a very similar knowledge level, but there was a higher increase in knowledge level amongst younger pupils, suggesting that the project catered better for the more junior pupils. No further education work was undertaken, but six months later the test was repeated with the same pupils. The children's knowledge levels had fallen back to within 2% of their original level,

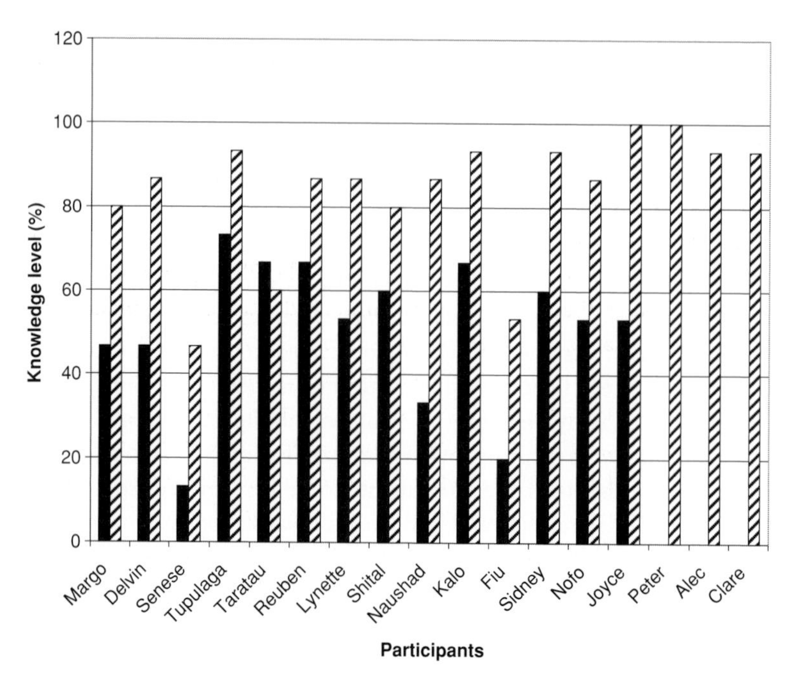

Figure 14.9 Mean knowledge levels of participants before (black bars) and after (hatched bars) a 'Train the trainers' marine education programme in Fiji.

highlighting the principal weakness of short-term initiatives and the importance of sustained input (Finlay, 2002).

Going beyond the measurement of 'awareness' to an assessment of 'skills' and 'participation' has also been attempted in a number of situations. In 1990, a training and education programme on alternatives to the use of cyanide for collecting aquarium fishes commenced on Luzon Island in the Philippines (Pajaro, 1994). The programme trained the local fishers in sustainable fishing techniques using nets. Objectives included organizing the trainees into core groups or associations to empower them to become self-reliant and to ensure sustainability of aquarium fishes and invertebrates as a resource. From 1990, 475 trainees participated in 15 training workshops at 11 sites. Of the 176 trainees monitored, 29% changed to using nets; the remainder persisted in using cyanide but most (50–90%) used it at a lower intensity.

There is evidence that even very short educational interventions can be effective. Medio *et al.* (1997) conducted educational briefings to recreational divers before entry into the water, which also proved beneficial in reducing their impact on marine resources. A single environmental awareness briefing reduced the rate of diver contact with the reef from 1.4 to 0.4 contacts diver^{-1} per 7-min observation period. The authors concluded that diver behaviour could be influenced by the use of educational tools, and divers' physical impact on corals could in this way be considerably reduced.

Far fewer studies have attempted to evaluate a change in attitudes and values. However, the following study took a comprehensive approach, considering levels of awareness, attitudes, skills and participation after 25 years of community-based coral reef management in the Philippines. White and Vogt (2000) found that the local governments developed an understanding of the importance of protecting their coral reefs. In addition, many had introduced active community-based enforcement of local fisheries laws through locally formed organizations with support from deputized fish wardens (see Alcala *et al.*, this volume). Furthermore, the accomplishment included increased awareness among the resort community of how to limit negative reef impacts. This was evidenced by the use of anchor buoys and trained personnel, by the careful disposal of wastewater from beach hotels, by the setting of proper channels for solid waste disposal from boats and resorts, and by attempts to work with the larger community to facilitate sustainable use of the area (White and Vogt, 2000).

One of the difficulties often encountered in evaluation of awareness, attitudes and other parameters is that a baseline level is seldom recorded at the outset of the initiative. This is especially true of long-running programmes. Alder (1992) is one of few authors to quantify community awareness and attitudes before and after an education programme, in this case six years of education in the Cairns Area of the Great Barrier Reef (GBR) Marine Park. From 1985, marine park awareness surveys of public education programmes targeted non-specific users as well as specific users within the Cairns Area and Park-wide. The aim of these programmes included increasing public awareness of the Marine Park's existence and its multiple uses, and changing the behaviour patterns of users. In 1991, respondents to surveys placed greater importance on management of the GBR than in 1985. In 1991, 84% of respondents felt that management of the GBR was very important. In 1985, only 45% agreed strongly that the GBR should be managed and 47% disagreed. Some of these changes in user attitude can be partially attributed to education programmes conducted by managers, various conservation organizations, industry associations and government agencies. Hence, education has been successful in increasing public awareness and improving attitudes towards the MPA. It remains to be shown, in this case, that these positive changes in user knowledge and perceptions have led to improved MPA performance.

Table 14.3. Examples of evaluation studies

Location	Type of programme evaluated	Audience	Key changes recorded	Conclusions of evaluation	Reference
South West Pacific	Coral reef monitoring training workshop	Government fisheries officers	• Participants' knowledge levels increased due to training	• Training workshop increased participants' awareness and skills in short term.	Finlay and Taylor (2002)
Yadua Island, Fiji	School coral reef education programme	Local schoolchildren	• Knowledge levels increased during five week education programme • Awareness levels of younger children increased more than older children from initial baseline • Six months after programme ended, knowledge levels of all children had reduced to initial baseline level prior to education	• Programme was effective in raising awareness of coral reefs • Programmes are only beneficial in long term if educational input is sustained • This particular programme catered better for younger children	Finlay (2002)
Luzon Island, Philippines	Training programme on sustainable fishing techniques for aquarium trade	Local fishers	• 29% of fishers monitored changed fishing techniques • 50–90% of fishers that retained unsustainable methods reduced intensity of fishing	• Training was effective in changing attitude of fishermen • Training was effective in changing fishing technique of a large percentage of fishermen	Pajaro (1994)

Red Sea	Pre-dive briefings on environmental impacts	Recreational scuba divers	• Amount of damage to corals caused by direct diver contact was reduced by pre-dive briefing	• Even short, simple educational activities can be effective	Medio *et al.* (1997)
Philippines (country-wide)	Community-based coral reef management	Local community, i.e. fish wardens, tourism sector, local and national government	• Increased level of support from tourist resorts • Increased enforcement of reef protection with use of locally empowered fish wardens	• Education of key stakeholders was crucial to success of coral reef management plan	White and Vogt (2000)
Great Barrier Reef, Australia	Various education programmes	Local community	• Between 1985 and 1991, percentage of community that felt that effective management of GBR was important increased from 45% to 84%	• Education programmes were effective at changing attitude of local community • Not clear if change in attitude had any direct impact on MPA	Alder (1992)
Cebu, Philippines	MPA education programmes	Local fishers	• Direct relationship between success of MPA management and level of knowledge of fishers responsible for MPA management • Level of knowledge related to amount of education undertaken and age of MPA, with older MPAs being more successful	• Education of local community responsible for MPA management is an important component in success of MPA. • Education programmes must be sustained to be effective	Finlay (2001)

The link between increased awareness and MPA success is evident in a study conducted in the Philippines, which investigated knowledge levels of fishermen responsible for the management of their local MPAs (Finlay, 2001). Each MPA had been established by the local community, with support and environmental education from the Coastal Resource Management Project. In comparison with the newer MPAs, the older MPAs that had undergone a greater number of environmental awareness and technical fisheries management workshops were being managed by fishermen with much greater knowledge of coral reef ecology, human impacts and sustainable management techniques. As a result, the older MPAs were being managed more successfully than the younger MPAs: they had higher abundances of coral and fish and there was less conflict among stakeholders.

To summarize, evaluation of coral reef education programmes from around the world has shown them to be effective in improving awareness, sensitivity, attitudes, skills and participation amongst stakeholders (Cabanban and White, 1981; Alder, 1992; Russ and Alcala, 1999; Finlay, 2002). In turn, these changes have contributed to improved management of MPAs. However, there are relatively few published examples of these effects (see Table 14.3 for a summary).

INTERACTION OF EDUCATION WITH OTHER TOOLS

In their summary of 25 years of community and cooperative-based reef conservation in the Philippines, White and Vogt (2000) concluded that effective coastal resource management is more than a problem of simple environmental education or law enforcement. Approaches that mobilize those people who use the resources daily are necessary to ensure wide participation and potentially long-lasting effects.

Environmental education does not possess the factual and scientific certainty that coastal managers, funding bodies and other decision-makers like to work towards. Changing attitudes and behaviour is a long-term process and investment in education only occasionally yields immediate visible benefits (Dikstehius, 1996). People must see some immediate results of their management efforts if they are to remain committed to a management programme intended to improve their environment. Education can provide the initial understanding of why a management programme is needed, but only observable results can sustain management efforts (White *et al.*, 1994; White and Vogt, 2000).

Effective conservation management of coral reefs usually requires legally enforceable rules for the conduct of people within the area and of those whose actions affect the area (Hudson, 1984). However, most countries with coral reefs lack the financial resources (or willingness to commit resources) effectively to enforce coral reef protection. In addition, management based solely upon strict enforcement has been shown to be less effective than incentive-based systems linked to compliance with the rules of the MPA (Mascia, 1999).

Amongst the best forms of enforcement are education and peer pressure, which can be extremely effective and relatively cheap compared to other enforcement measures (Hudson, 1984). Few countries can afford the cost of top–down enforcement in the presence of a generally hostile public. Conversely, costs of enforcement can be very low where public support exists (Kelleher and Kenchington, 1991).

The cost of a well-designed education programme may be offset by the reduction in enforcement effort in the medium to long term (Alcock, 1991). Recreational and commercial users that are aware of coral reef management plans and supportive of management decisions require less effort in surveillance, patrols or policing. In most cases, positive community education programmes cost less than repair to damaged coral reefs and legal prosecutions for infringements (Alcock, 1991). In this context, prosecution may be viewed as the final option of management when education, peer group pressure and participation have failed.

Unfortunately, the benefits of education programmes are often slow to manifest themselves. Resource managers are often reluctant to assign adequate funding for education programmes since it is difficult to demonstrate the benefits of such programmes in the short term (Alder, 1996b).

Education programmes are generally costly. In the management of the Cairns Area of the GBR Marine Park from 1985 to 1991, the cost and effectiveness of education and enforcement programmes were evaluated using an awareness survey (Alder, 1996b). Both programmes were effective in meeting programme objectives. However, while education costs per person were approximately one-tenth of the cost of enforcement, the total cost for education programmes was twice that of the enforcement programmes.

For this reason it is important to combine evaluation with cost–benefit analysis. Very few studies of this nature have been published. An exception is that by White *et al.* (2000), which involved a simple cost–benefit analysis for the Gilutongan MPA off Olango Island in the Philippines. The analysis estimated the total cost of supporting coastal resource management and the total benefits that would be derived from increases in tourism, fisheries, coastal protection, seaweed farming and aesthetic or biodiversity assets. Education, training and community liaison accounted for one-third of the total costs of coastal resource management. Other costs included reef surveys, monitoring, buoy maintenance, law enforcement, staffing and other costs. The total cost of management was US$21 000 km^{-2} yr^{-1}; however, if properly managed, the total potential benefits amounted to US$200 000 km^{-2} yr^{-1}.

Education and enforcement programmes clearly interact with other management activities, and neither programme can totally replace the other. Some users will willingly comply with management measures, others will comply in response to education, but there will be another group that will only respond to enforcement activities. There will also be users that persistently disregard park rules and regulations and will continue to present a problem to managers. For these individuals, education in association with enforcement actions is necessary.

Overall it seems that combining community participation, environmental education, economic incentives and legal mandates in a manner appropriate for a particular MPA, together with long-term institutional support from government, NGOs, and academic and other institutions, offers the greatest possibility of success (White and Vogt, 2000).

CONCLUSIONS: RECOMMENDATIONS FOR THE FUTURE

Education is now widely accepted as a fundamental tool in the sustainable management of coral reefs. MPA managers and other leaders increasingly understand the need to allocate resources for the provision of education, in order to raise awareness, change behaviour and promote public participation in decision-making. However, there is still an enormous potential for increasing the scope, range and effectiveness of coral reef education. We suggest four priorities for the next 10 years.

First, there needs to be greater integration of education into mainstream conservation. In order for education to deliver coral reef conservation, it must take its place at the heart of conservation initiatives. Education should be viewed as a long-term commitment rather than a 'quick fix', and resources allocated accordingly. Professional educationalists must increasingly be included at senior management level in conservation institutions to facilitate this process. Objectives for education programmes should be tightly associated with overall conservation objectives, identifying the critical stakeholders (as opposed to the most accessible or least challenging ones) with which to engage in order to achieve these objectives.

Second, good practice must be disseminated and resources shared. Signposting and virtual library schemes such as the International Coral

Reef Information Network (2005) Coral Reef Education Library must be properly funded and widely promoted to facilitate this. Transferable (i.e. not site- or country-specific) educational materials about coral reefs and conservation issues should be made available in a comprehensive range of languages and formats. Opportunities for education providers to share ideas and resources face to face (for example conferences and workshops) should be developed at a local, regional and global level. This recommendation is very much in keeping with the objectives of the Decade of Education for Sustainable Development 2005–2014. The coral reef conservation community should exploit links with the DESD to secure the necessary funds and other resources.

Third, EE should be integrated into formal curricula. The coral reef conservation sector should promote and support the 'reorientation' of school curricula as guided by *Agenda 21*, as this will make a profound difference to the ability of teachers to address reef conservation and sustainability issues.

Finally, evaluation should be embraced by education providers as a means of verifying and demonstrating the effectiveness of their programmes. Evaluation should be integrated into all education programmes and the findings disseminated. Complementary to programme-specific evaluation, data should be gathered at appropriate spatial scales to gauge public awareness of, attitudes towards, and participation in coral reef conservation. These data will provide a baseline for future studies to investigate the changing 'climate' of public awareness. Cost–benefit analysis should also be applied more widely, to inform management decisions and resource allocation.

REFERENCES

Acland, A. F. (1990). *A Sudden Outbreak of Common Sense: Managing Conflict through Mediation*. London: Hutchinson.

(2002). *Consensus-Building*. London: Environment Council.

Alcock, D. (1991). Education and extension: management's best strategy. *Australian Parks and Recreation*, **27**, 15–17.

Alder, J. (1992). Have six years of marine park education changed community attitudes and awareness? *Proceedings 7th International Coral Reef Symposium*, **2**, 1043–51.

(1996a). Have tropical marine protected areas worked? An initial analysis of their success. *Coastal Management*, **24**, 97–114.

(1996b). Costs and effectiveness of education and enforcement, Cairns Section of the Great Barrier Reef Marine Park. *Environmental Management*, **20**, 541–51.

Attwood, C. G. (1997). Review of the state of marine protected areas in South Africa. *South African Journal of Marine Science/Suid-Afrikaanse Tydskrif vir Seewetenskap*, **18**, 341–67.

Badalamenti, F., Ramos, A. A., Voultsiadou, E. *et al.* (2000). Cultural and socio-economic impacts of Mediterranean marine protected areas. *Environmental Conservation*, **27**, 110–25.

Balgos, M. C. (1999). *Assessing the Impacts of Public Education: Evaluation of Education Programmes in Marine Protected Areas in the Philippines.*

Bennett, N., Wood, E. and Rogers, S. (1997). *Teaching through Play: Teachers' Thinking and Classroom Practice.* Buckingham: Open University Press.

Bolido, L. and White, A. (1997). Reclaiming the island's reefs. *People and the Planet*, **6**(2), 22–23.

Browning, L. J. (2000). *Reefology's Education Initiatives in Utila, Honduras 1999–2000*, unpublished report. Eastleigh, UK: Reefology.

(2002). *Coast and Ocean: Wildlife Watch Leaders' Activity Guide.* Newark, UK: The Wildlife Trusts.

Bunce, L., Gustavson, K., Williams, J. and Miller, M. (1999). The human side of reef management: a case study analysis of the socioeconomic framework of Montego Bay marine park. *Coral Reefs*, **18**, 369–80.

Cabanban, A. S. and White, A. T. (1981). Marine conservation programme using non-formal education at Apo Island, Negros Oriental, Philippines. *Proceedings 4th International Coral Reef Symposium*, **1**, 317–21.

Christie, P., White, A. T. and Buhat, D. (1990). San Salvador Island marine conservation project: some lessons for community-based resource management. *Tropical Coastal Area Management*, **5**, 7–11.

(1994). Community-based coral reef management on San Salvador Island, the Philippines. *Society and Natural Resources*, **7**, 103–17.

Collins, M. A. J. and Dickinson, A. (1999). *Enhancing Environmental Awareness through Marine Education.* Zanzibar: Ims.

Connect, E. (1992). UNCED the Earth Summit (The Rio Declaration on Environment and Development and Agenda 21). *UNESCO–UNEP Environmental Education Newsletter*, **27**, (2).

Coral Cay Conservation (2004). *Case Study: Belize.* Available online at http://www.coralcay.org/science/belize.php

Cornell, J. (1989). *Sharing Nature with Children II: A Sequel to the Classic Parents' and Teachers' Nature Awareness Guidebook.* Nevada City, CA: Dawn Publications.

(1998). *Sharing Nature with Children: The Classic Parents' and Teachers' Nature Awareness Guidebook*, 20th Anniversary edn. Nevada City, CA: Dawn Publications.

Council for Environmental Education (2004). *Measuring Effectiveness: Evaluation in Education for Sustainable Development.* Reading, UK: CEE.

Dayton, P. K., Sala, E., Tegner, M. J. and Thrush, S. (2000). Marine reserves: parks, baselines, and fishery enhancement. *Bulletin of Marine Science*, **66**, 617–34.

Department for Education and Employment (1998). *Health and Safety of Pupils on Educational Visits.* London: DfEE.

Dikstehius, O. W. (1996). Environmental education: a tool for coastal management? *Coastal Management*, **24**, 339–353.

Eduscapes (2005). *Eduscapes: A Site for Life-Long Learners of All Ages.* Available online at http://www.eduscapes.com

Education for Sustainable Development and Global Citizenship (2005). Home page. Available online at http://www.esd-wales.org.uk

Finlay, R. A. O. (2000). Litter lessons in Utila. *Reef Encounter*, **29**, 14–15.
(2001). Increasing environmental knowledge of fisherfolk through education: its role in the success of Marine Protected Areas in the Philippines. M.Sc. thesis, University of Newcastle upon Tyne.
(2002). *Yadua School Coral Reef Environmental Project*. Unpublished report for the National Trust of Fiji.
Finlay, R. A. O. and Taylor, O. J. S. (2002). *The IMR–GCRMN South West Pacific Coral Reef Monitoring Workshop*, Final Report. Suva, Fiji: Global Coral Reef Monitoring Network and Institute of Marine Resources.
42eXplore (2005). *Thematic Pathfinders for All Ages: Coral Reefs*. Available online at http://www.42explore.com/reef:htm
Gough, A. G. and Robottom, I. (1995). Towards a socially critical environmental education: water quality studies in a coastal school. *Journal of Curriculum Studies*, **25**, 301–16.
Great Barrier Reef Marine Park Authority (2004). Home page. Available online at http://www.gbrmpa.gov.au
Green, S. J., Monreal, R. P., White, A. T. and Bayer, T. G. (2000). *Coastal Environmental Profile of Northwestern Bohol, Philippines*. Cebu City, Philippines: Coastal Resource Management Project.
Gubbay, S. (1993). Management of marine protected areas in the UK: lessons from statutory and voluntary approaches. *Aquatic Conservation – Marine and Freshwater Ecosystems*, **3**, 269–280.
(ed.) (1995). *Marine Protected Areas: Principles and Techniques for Management*. London: Chapman and Hall.
Hayashi, S. (1991). Enclosed seas and coastal areas as models of the global environment: three conditions of realising Sustainable Development and Environmental Education. *Marine Pollution Bulletin*, **23**, 513–17.
Hooper, C. N. (1992). Building coral reef conservation awareness through education and interpretation programmes at the Waikiki Aquarium. *Proceedings 7th International Coral Reef Symposium*, **1**, 1057–64.
Horsfall, J. (1997). *Play Lightly on the Earth: Nature Activities for Children 3–9 Years Old*. Nevada City, CA: Dawn Publications.
Huckle, J. and Sterling, S. (1996). *Education for Sustainability*. London: Earthscan Publications Ltd.
Hudson, B. (1984). User and public education and enforcement. In *Coral Reef Management Handbook*, eds. R. A. Kenchington and B. Hudson, pp. 147–60. Jakarta, Indonesia: UNESCO.
International Baccalaureate Organization (2005). *Primary Years Program*. Available online at http://online.ibo.org
International Coral Reef Information Network (2005). *Coral Reef Education Library*. Available online at http://www.coralreef.org
Jacobson, S. K. (1991). Evaluation model for developing, implementing, and assessing conservation education programmes: examples from Belize and Costa Rica. *Environmental Management*, **15**, 143–50.
Kaza, S. (1988). Community involvement in marine protected areas. *Oceanus*, **31**, 75–86.
(1995). Marine education and interpretation. In *Marine Protected Areas: Principles and Techniques for Management*, ed. S. Gubbay, pp. 174–98. London: Chapman and Hall.

Kelleher, G. and Kenchington, R. (1991). *Guidelines for Establishing Marine Protected Areas*. Gland, Switzerland: IUCN.
Kelleher, G. and Lausche, B. (1984). Review of legislation. In *Coral Reef Management Handbook*, eds. R. A. Kenchington and B. E. T. Hudson. Jakarta, Indonesia: UNESCO.
Kelly, G. C. (1992). Public participation and perceived relevance as critical factors in marine park management. *Proceedings 7th International Coral Reef Symposium*, **1**, 1033–7.
Kenchington, R. A. (1990). *Managing Marine Environments*. New York: Taylor and Francis.
Kenchington, R. A. and Bleakley, C. (1994). Identifying priorities for marine protected areas in the Insular Pacific. *Marine Pollution Bulletin*, **29**, 3–9.
Kennedy, F. (2003). *Wild Oman Interactive CD-Rom: Marine Environment of Oman*. Oman: Five Oceans, LLC.
Kriwoken, L. K. (1991). The Great Barrier Reef Marine Park: an assessment of zoning methodology for Australian marine and estuarine protected areas. *Maritime Studies*, **36**, 12–21.
Lemay, M. and Hale, L. (1989). *Coastal Resources Management: A Guide to Public Education Programmes and Materials*. West Hartford, CT: Kumbrian Press.
Mann-Lang, J. B. (1998). The role of education in fisheries management in South Africa. In *African Fishes and Fisheries Diversity*, eds. L. Coetzee, J. Gon and C. Kulongowski. Grahamstown, South Africa: Fisa/Paradi.
Mascia, M. B. (1999). Governance of marine protected areas in the Wider Caribbean: preliminary results of an international mail survey. *Coastal Management* **27**, 391–402.
MeKeown, R., Hopkins, C., Rizzi, R. and Chrystalbridge, M. (2005). *Education for Sustainable Development Toolkit*, Available online at http://www.esdtoolkit.org
McNamara, C. (1999). *Basic Guide to Outcomes-Based Evaluation in Non-Profit Organizations with Very Limited Resources*. Available online at http://www.managementhelp.org/evaluatn/outcomes.htm
McNealy, J. A. (1994). Marine protected areas for the 21st century: working to provide benefits to society. *Biodiversity and Conservation*, **3**, 340–405.
Medio, D., Ormond, R. F. G and Pearson, M. (1997). Effect of briefings on rates of damage to corals by SCUBA divers. *Biological Conservation*, **79**, 91–5.
Nicholson, S. and Schreiner, B. K. (1973). *Community Participation in City Decision Making*. Milton Keynes, UK: The Open University.
North American Association for Environmental Education (1996). *Environmental Education Materials: Guidelines for Excellence*. Washington, DC: NAAEE.
Organization for Education and Science Integration (2005). Home page. Available online at http://www.oedsi.org
Pajaro, M. G. (1994). Using education to stop destructive fishing practices: a partial success in several communities. In *Collaborative and Community-Based Management of Coral Reefs*, eds. A. T. White, L. Z. Hale, Y. Renard and L. Cortesi. West Hartford, CT: Kumbrian Press.
Pauly, D. (2000). Fisheries in the Philippines and in the world: an overview. *Tambuli: A Publication for Coastal Management Practitioners*, **6**, 23–5.
Professional Association of Teachers (1997). *Safety on School Trips: A Teachers and the Law Booklet*. Derby, UK: PAT.

Renhack, A. M. O., Zee, D. M. W., Cunha, E. S. and Portilho, M. F. (1992). Topics of environmental education programmemes in coastal areas. *Water Science and Technology*, **25**, 253–9.
Roberts, C. M. and Polunin, N. V. C. (1991). Are marine reserves effective in management of reef fisheries? *Reviews in Fish Biology and Fisheries*, **1**, 65–91.
Robson, C. (2000). *Small Scale Evaluation: Principles and Practice*. London: Sage Publications.
Rodriguez-Martinez, R. and Ortiz, L. M. (1999). Coral reef education in schools of Quintana Roo, Mexico. *Ocean and Coastal Management*, **42**, 1061–68.
Rowe, R. and Probst, C. (1995). Connecting with local culture. *Educational Leadership*, **53**, 62–4.
Russ, G. R. and Alcala, A. C. (1999). Management histories of Sumilon and Apo marine reserves, Philippines, and their influence on national marine resource policy. *Coral Reefs*, **18**, 307–19.
Russel, S. H. (1992). Promoting coral reef conservation monitoring and research through experimental education programmes. *Proceedings 7th International Coral Reef Symposium*, **1**, 1071–7.
Selendy, J. M. H. (1998). Marine information management and environmental education. In *Coral Reefs: Challenges and Opportunities for Sustainable Management*, eds. M. E. Hatziolos, A. J. Hooten and M. Fodor, pp. 147–50. Washington, DC: World Bank.
Shoals Rodrigues (2004). *Marine Research, Training and Education*. Available online at http://www.shoals-rodrigues.org
Sivalingham, P. M. (1991). Environmental education and nongovernmental activities in protecting the enclosed coastal sea of the Malacca Straits. *Marine Pollution Bulletin*, **23**, 807–9.
Smith, R. (2001). *Information, Education and Communication Advisor for Cebu Province*. Cebu City, Philippines: Coastal Resource Management Project.
Sotto, F. B., Gatus, J. L. I., Ross, M. A., Portigo, M. F. L. and Freire, F. M. (2001). *Coastal Environmental Profile of Olango Island, Cebu, Philippines*. Cebu City, Philippines: Coastal Resource Management Project.
Spruill, V. (1999). *Public Education of Ocean Issues: An Invitation for Participation from the Marine Science Community*. Washington, DC: SeaWeb.
Stokking, H., Van Aert, L., Meilberg, W. and Kaskens, A. (1999). *Evaluating Environmental Education*. Gland, Suitzerland: IUCN.
Sumner, I. (2004). *Finding Your Own Way to Learn*. London: City and Guilds.
Thomson, G. and Hoffman, J. (2003). *Measuring the Success of Environmental Education Programmes*. Calgary: Canadian Parks and Wilderness Society/Network for Environmental Education.
UN (2005). *Agenda 21*. Available online at http://www.un.org/esa/sustdev/agenda21.htm
UNECE (2005). Access to Information, Public Participation in Decision-Making and Access to Justice in Environmental Matters. Available online at http://www.unece.org/env/pp
UNESCO (1980). *Environmental education in the light of the Tbilisi Conference*. Paris, France: UNESCO.
(2005). *World Summit on Sustainable Development*. Available online at http://portal.unesco.org/education

UNESCO–UNEP (1978). *Intergovernmental Conference on Environmental Education*, Final Report. Paris: UNESCO.

Walford, G. (2001). *Doing Qualitative Educational Research: A Personal Guide to the Research Process*. London: Continuum.

Walters, J. S., Marargos, J., Siar, S. and White, A. T. (1998). *Participatory Coastal Resource Assessment: A Handbook for Community Workers and Coastal Resource Managers*. Cebu City, Philippines: Coastal Resource Management Project and Silliman University Centre of Excellence in Coastal Resource Management.

Walker, S. H., Newton, R. A. and Ortiz, A. (eds.) (1997). *Coral Reefs: An English Compilation of Activities for Middle School Students*. Ocean Springs, MS: University of Southern Mississippi. Available online at http://www.aquarium.usm.edu/coralreef/index.html.

Wells, S. and White, A. T. (1995). Involving the community. In *Marine Protected Areas: Principles and Techniques for Management*, ed. S. Gubbay, pp. 61–84. London: Chapman and Hall.

White, A. (1986a). Marine reserves: how effective as management strategies for Philippine, Indonesian and Malaysian coral reef environments? *Ocean Management*, **10**, 137–59.

(1986b). The marine conservation and development programme of Silliman University, Philippines. *Tropical Coastal Area Management*, **1**, 1–4.

(1988). *Marine Parks and Reserves: Management for Coastal Environments in Southeast Asia*. Manila, Philippines: International Centre for Living Aquatic Resources Management.

(1989). The marine conservation and development programme of Silliman University as an example for Lingayen Gulf. In *Towards Sustainable Development of the Coastal Resources of Lingayen Gulf, Philippines*, eds. G. Silvestre, E. Miclat and T. E. Chua, pp. 119–23. Manila, Philippines: ICLARM.

(1997). Collaborative and community-based management of coral reef resources: lessons from Sri Lanka and the Philippines. In *Workshop on Integrated Reef Resources Management in the Maldives*, eds. D. J. Nickerson and M. H. Maniku. Madras, India: BOBP.

White, A. T. and Vogt, P. H. (2000). Philippine coral reefs under threat: lessons learnt after 25 years of community-based reef conservation. *Marine Pollution Bulletin*, **40**, 537–50.

White, A. T., Hale, L. Z., Renard, Y. and Cortesi, L. (1994). *Collaborative and Community-Based Management of Coral Reefs: Lessons from Experience*. West Hartford, CT: Kumbrian Press.

White, A. T., Ross, M. and Flores, M. (2000). Benefits and costs of coral reef and wetland management, Olango Island, Philippines. In *Collected Essays on the Economics of Coral Reefs*, ed. H. S. J. Cesar, pp. 215–27. Stockholm: CORDIO.

15

Adaptive institutions for coral reef conservation

KATRINA BROWN
University of East Anglia

INTRODUCTION

Institutions are the formal and informal rules that govern the way natural resources such as coral reefs are managed. They range from policy and legislative frameworks to local informal collective action, property rights, and norms and rules. Protected areas and other conservation and management designations, regulations, laws and local management networks are therefore all institutions relevant to conservation.

There is a substantial theoretical and empirical literature that discusses the characteristics of apparently 'successful' institutions for terrestrial protected area management (Agrawal, 2001; Pretty, 2002; McShane and Wells, 2004). However, relatively little social science analysis has been devoted to marine protected areas or coral reefs. What work has been done has focused on coastal management and, to a lesser extent, fisheries (e.g. Alcala *et al.*, this volume).

This chapter examines institutional dimensions of marine protected areas (MPAs) and whether the design principles identified for terrestrial protected areas are applicable to marine resources. It argues that successful institutions for managing resources such as coral reefs should be efficient and effective in meeting their goals, be equitable in their outcomes and enjoy legitimacy among the relevant actors and institutions. To do this they need to be adaptive. Adaptive institutions are those that are able to deal with dynamic and fluctuating ecological conditions and resources; that recognize and manage a range of users and uses, and the trade-offs between them; and which can learn from and adapt to experience.

Coral Reef Conservation, ed. Isabelle M. Côté and John D. Reynolds.

Drawing on empirical research in MPAs in the eastern Caribbean (Brown *et al.*, 2001, 2002), the analysis identifies and discusses the features of management institutions which enable them to become adaptive. These include the inclusion of key stakeholders in management processes, the recognition and integration of plural forms of knowledge, and the development of open, transparent and legitimate forms of decision-making. These features mean that rules which govern MPAs are upheld and enforced by users themselves, reducing costs and conflicts, and enhancing the likelihood of successful conservation which yields equitable and sustainable benefits from these diverse and important resources. However, the analysis also recognizes the importance of supra-local processes and influences, and that cross-scale and multiple-scale linkages need explicit recognition and development.

WHY INSTITUTIONS MATTER FOR CORAL REEF CONSERVATION

Institutions are socially constructed constraints that structure human interaction through definition of formal rules, laws and constitutions, and informal norms of behaviour, conventions, self-imposed codes of conduct, and their enforcement characteristics. Enforcement characteristics have ethical and cognitive dimensions, as well as regulatory dimensions. Institutions have been called the 'rules in use'. The term institution is often used synonymously with, and confused with, organization. However, an institution is a system of rules that can exist without organizations or can encompass many different organizations within its structure.

The study of institutions relevant for environmental management has emerged as a mainstream field in social sciences within the last two decades (McCay and Acheson, 1987; Berkes, 1989; Ostrom, 1990; Bromley *et al.*, 1992; Baland and Plateau, 1996; National Research Council, 2002). It brings together a range of perspectives and methods from, for example, political science, economics, sociology, anthropology and management sciences. Interdisciplinary synthesis between these diverse insights has, since the late 1980s, led to the development of an integrative set of propositions and analytical frameworks. Agrawal (2002) observes that there has been remarkable progress in this period and convergence on understanding of what kind of institutional arrangements account for sustainable resource use. These insights have occurred partly as a result of development in the field of non-cooperative game theory but more directly as a result of an explosion of empirical research on common property resource management and common-pool resources (e.g. in forestry: Gibson *et al.*, 2000; water and irrigation: Ostrom, 1990; fisheries: Acheson, 1988; drylands: Jodha, 1986; international agreements: Young, 1996; and collections such as Berkes, 1989; Bromley *et al.*, 1992; Hanna *et al.*, 1996; and the *Digital Library of the Commons*, 2005). Common property resources share two important characteristics. First, users or managers of common property resources are able to control access of other users, or exclude outsiders from using the resource. Second, in using the resource each user is able to subtract from the welfare of all others. These two universal characteristics of the commons are referred to as the *exclusion problem* and the *subtractability problem*. Ostrom *et al.* (1999) define common pool or common property resources as those 'in which (i) exclusion of beneficiaries through physical and institutional means is especially costly, and (ii) exploitation by one user reduces resource availability for others'. Typical common pool resources are forests and woodlands, rangelands and common grazing, and fisheries.

The most widely cited work in institutional analysis for natural resource management by Ostrom (1990) identifies eight design principles for successful institutions in terms of their sustainability and persistence. Agrawal (2002) has expanded on these design principles to produce a comprehensive set of enabling conditions for successful management based on three decades of common property research. This synthesis recognizes factors intrinsic to the institutions themselves as well as characteristics of the resources they seek to manage, the user groups and the external context within which they work. These elements of resource use among multiple actors and diverse environments, along with the connections between them, are summarized in Fig. 15.1.

There are, of course, limits to the explanatory powers of the hybrid theories of common property resource management. Much of the analysis of successful institutions is derived from studies of local-level natural resource management, and success is assumed to equate to those institutions that endure over time. Successful institutions are therefore those which are continuous and relatively stable. This conclusion overlooks specific aspects which may be especially important when examining the sustainability of resource use beyond one locality, and for complex and fluctuating systems. This approach to understanding 'success' does not necessarily take account of changing resource or environmental conditions; an enduring institution that depletes natural resources over time could well be seen as successful. The dynamics of changing conditions, not only in ecological terms, but also socially and economically, need also to be considered. Thus institutions researchers such as Steins and Edwards (1999) have called for a greater

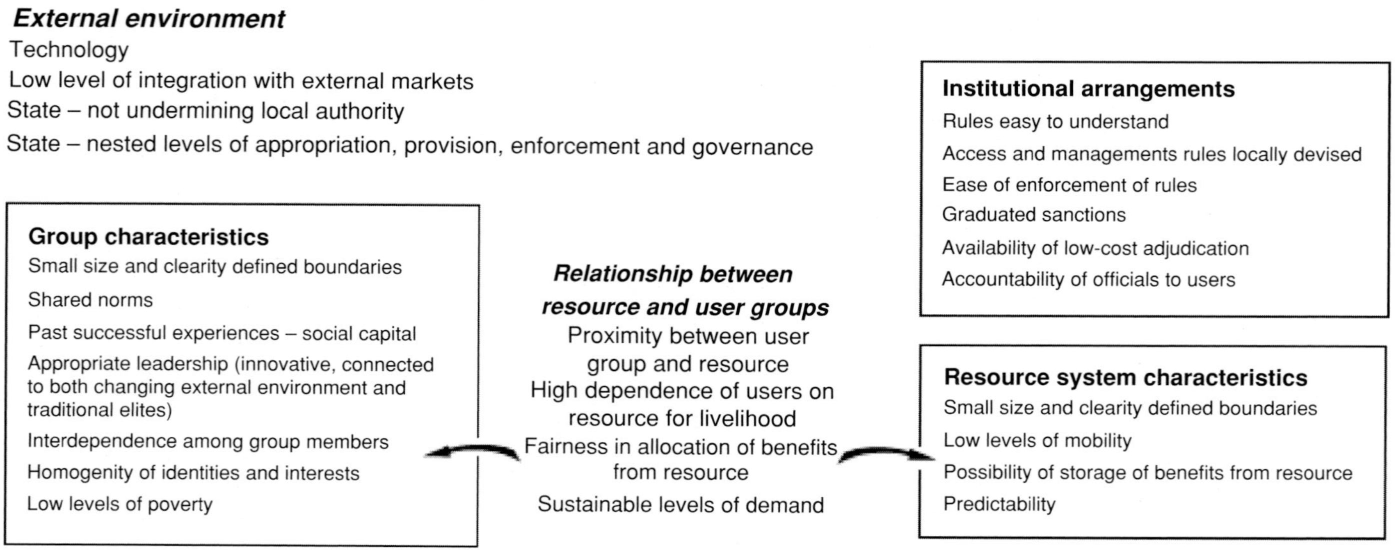

External environment

Technology

Low level of integration with external markets

State – not undermining local authority

State – nested levels of appropriation, provision, enforcement and governance

Group characteristics

Small size and clearity defined boundaries

Shared norms

Past successful experiences – social capital

Appropriate leadership (innovative, connected to both changing external environment and traditional elites)

Interdependence among group members

Homogenity of identities and interests

Low levels of poverty

Relationship between resource and user groups

Proximity between user group and resource

High dependence of users on resource for livelihood

Fairness in allocation of benefits from resource

Sustainable levels of demand

Institutional arrangements

Rules easy to understand

Access and managements rules locally devised

Ease of enforcement of rules

Graduated sanctions

Availability of low-cost adjudication

Accountability of officials to users

Resource system characteristics

Small size and clearity defined boundaries

Low levels of mobility

Possibility of storage of benefits from resource

Predictability

Figure 15.1 Enabling conditions for sustainable collective management of coastal resources. (From Brown *et al.* (2002), adapted from Agrawal (2001).)

consideration of contextual factors in examining common property institutions. In the case of coral reefs, these contextual factors are central to the evolution of institutional arrangements and the effectiveness of how institutions work. These contextual factors are pronounced in the 'resource system characteristics' identified by Agrawal (2002) and listed in Fig. 15.1.

A first significant contextual factor affecting the evolution of institutions for coral reefs and MPAs is the highly dynamic nature of coastal and marine ecosystems. Five particular characteristics pose problems for successful coral reef and coastal resource management. First, ecological boundaries are often poorly defined and highly dynamic, e.g. boundary between salt and fresh water changes on daily, seasonal and annual basis. Second, complex and large-scale ecological linkages, e.g. of nutrients and fish and invertebrate larvae which disperse over large distances in the plankton, are characteristic of coral reef habitats. Third, highly migratory species are prevalent in oceans, e.g. cetaceans, large pelagic fish, turtles. Migration is often linked to breeding and feeding behaviour, and to ocean currents. Fourth, with changing technologies, many users are located physically distant from the resources themselves. Finally, property rights to different resources are often very poorly defined, and are often overlapping and competing, for example to species, fishing areas and resources at the land–water interface.

These factors clearly exacerbate the exclusion and subtractability problems outlined above. But the list of factors also indicates that institutions are at once a cause and a solution to coral reef degradation. The competing and overlapping nature of property rights and users lead inevitably to diverse and competing governmental responsibility for coastal regions and resources. Indeed, the inability of different agencies and levels of government involved in coastal management to work together is often cited as a major reason for the failure of conservation initiatives (Cicin-Sain, 1993; Alder, 1996; Tompkins *et al.*, 2002). Thus it is widely held that the problems faced by coastal zones are exacerbated by conventional institutional frameworks. For example, conventional management processes have tended to segment concerns and deal with problems on an isolated and uncoordinated basis. Regulatory and political structures can also encourage damaging behaviour, and poor planning regulations allow developments at the coast which put both ecosystems and people at risk.

The solution often proposed to address these institutional problems is to integrate different agencies and elements of coastal management. There has been widespread adoption of the language and objectives of so-called 'integrated coastal management' (ICM), with competing and apparently ever-widening definitions and claims to its benefits (Clark, 1996;

Cicin-Sain and Knecht, 1998; Kay and Alder, 1999; Beatley *et al.*, 2002; Harvey and Caton, 2003). The 'integrate"' approach seeks to deal with the drivers or factors that lead to the degradation of coastal resources in at least three major ways. First, integration should ideally address conflicts between different uses and users of coastal resources. Second, it should improve processes of coastal planning and management in order to regulate increasing demands on resources. Third, by promoting institutional change, particularly the processes through which decisions are made about coastal zones and their resources, integration seeks to yield benefits in both the effectiveness and efficiency of what coastal management organizations actually deliver. The latter issue, of actual institutional change, increasingly implies more inclusive decision-making, building capacity, and promoting inter-sectoral and inter-agency coordination.

No one could doubt the benefits of greater integration in planning and decision-making. Yet the core of ICM focuses on integration of *government* planning and agencies. This focus, I argue, fails to account for the polycentric nature of coastal governance. Governments are but one actor in the governance of coastal resources. The others include self-governing resource management and social norms of resource use governing socially acceptable settlement, extractive and recreational uses of resources. Therefore the single most important set of integrating processes in coastal resource management is not those between agencies and formal organizations with bounded jurisdictions and responsibilities. Rather the important linkages are those 'vertical' connections and networks between different governance elements, i.e. those that comprise knowledge systems, social norms of resource use and decision-making fora. These connections are fostered by deliberative democratic structures of debate and inclusion. Such connections and structures enable inclusive management through building legitimacy and equity (see Young, 2000), and have been demonstrated in the context of coastal resources and marine protected areas and in co-management of fisheries, to yield positive results in terms of objective ecological goals (Berkes *et al.*, 2001; Brown *et al.*, 2002; Alcala *et al.*, this volume). Rather than being integrated therefore, I argue, that institutions need to be *adaptive* in order to successfully manage coastal and marine resources such as coral reefs.

WHAT ARE ADAPTIVE INSTITUTIONS?

The concept of an adaptive institution for resource management brings together ideas from ecology on adaptive management (Berkes and Folke,

1998) and from social sciences on adaptive co-management and collaborative or social learning (Lee, 1993; Parson and Clark, 1995; Ruitenbeek and Cartier, 2001). Adaptive institutions for resource management are those that able to deal with ecological dynamics but also with shifting economic, political and social landscapes. The measurement and conceptualization of adaptability has been discussed widely within the context of resilience of social–ecological systems. Walker *et al.* (2004), for example, identify adaptability as the capacity of actors within a social–ecological system to manage or influence resilience. They relate adaptability to the ability to change resource management practices and to manage processes of change within the governance landscape. It is the latter of these elements, that of being able to cope with changing societal demands, preferences and power structures, that I emphasize as central to the success or otherwise of institutions that deal with critical sustainability issues for coral reef and MPA management.

Can adaptability be observed, measured and promoted? The most important empirical base and insight into adaptive institutions in this context has been the emerging literature and experience on adaptive ecosystem management. Put simply, institutions need to be adaptive to undertake adaptive management (e.g. Ruitenbeek and Cartier, 2001; Olsson *et al.*, 2004). Adaptive institutions therefore require mechanisms by which the rights and responsibilities of stakeholders can be defined and shared, mechanisms for learning over time, and capacity and mechanisms to deal with the inter-temporal dimensions of ecosystem dynamics. These characteristics may require dramatic change and upheaval of the ways things are generally undertaken: adaptive co-management often means not only allowing change, but also surrendering power to other stakeholders. These challenging elements of adaptive management further require a number of additional elements, synthesized by Olsson *et al.* (2004) and Tompkins *et al.* (2002) to include: enabling legislation that creates social space for ecosystem management; the ability to monitor and respond to environmental feedbacks; and leaders and individuals to translate and make sense of diverse languages and lexicons of governments, lay people and science. Indeed, at its core adaptive management means recognizing, embracing and treating multiple values and different forms of knowledge as valid (Berkes, 1999). This element of adaptive management is often shown to be the most difficult and counter-intuitive to managers with traditional scientific training. Embracing knowledge diversity is opposed because it flies in the face of a need to control nature and challenges underlying discourse, often engrained from Western colonial interpretations of environmental problems (Ruitenbeek and Cartier, 2001; Adams and Mulligan, 2003).

Adaptive institutions are crucial to securing resilient MPAs. These characteristics of inclusion of diverse interests and actors, the ability to change structures, and the ability to work across scales are important in this context because of the nature of MPAs, as outlined in the previous section. First, the nature of the polycentric governance of marine protected areas, allied to the complexity and diffuse nature of the ecosystems and resources, means that adaptation is the only feasible means of management. Second, adaptive institutions can potentially be successful in meeting the aims of sustainable extractive and non-consumptive use of marine protected areas because they are likely to be more legitimate than protected areas based on regulation or simple exclusion of uses. Inclusion is good for the instrumental reason that it is effective. More users abide by the rules if they helped to create them and they also help to enforce the rules. While some of the characteristics of adaptive institutions are increasingly recognized by advocates of 'integrated' coastal zone management in its more progressive formulations (Francis and Torell, 2004), it is the key elements of adaptation that remain crucial to success.

BUILDING ADAPTIVE INSTITUTIONS

We are far from adaptive institutions in most of the MPAs around the world. In order to move towards this adaptability for sustainable coral reef management, I argue in this section that there are three key pressure points. These elements put people at the centre of the conservation paradigm (Brown, 2003a) and include: (1) inclusion of all relevant stakeholders and mechanisms for giving them voice in decision-making, (2) acknowledgement of the diverse sets of values and knowledge of different stakeholders, and (3) working across spatial, social and administrative scales. This section discusses each of these aspects of adaptive institutions in turn and, using the example of a MPA in the eastern Caribbean, the Buccoo Reef Marine Park in Tobago, examines how they can be implemented for coral reef conservation.

Inclusionary mechanisms

Calls for the greater participation of various stakeholders in management of coastal and reef resources are widespread and have almost become the new received wisdom of natural resource management in both terrestrial and marine systems (Cooke and Kothari, 2001). The motivation for these calls stems partly from the perception that resource management works better when the relevant (local) actors are more involved in various aspects of management, and partly because greater participation is seen as more fair and democratic. These discussions are entering mainstream science literature; for example, Francis and Torell (2004) present three arguments for increasing participation in coastal management. First, that this enhances the interchange between local ecological knowledge and scientific knowledge which will have positive synergies. Second, that it is in the interests of more democratic decision-making and management. Third, that increased participation is likely to add to legitimacy – the perception of fairness of decisions made. Thus they identify both instrumental and intrinsic reasons for greater participation by particularly local stakeholders. For example, instrumentally, recent quantitative analyses also demonstrate that community-led coral reef protected areas are as effective in improving fisheries, biodiversity and livelihoods, and more effective in resolving conflicts among stakeholders, than MPAs with traditional top–down management (Alcala *et al.*, this volume).

A range of models of increasing participation can be observed, including participatory, collaborative and co-management approaches (Pretty and Pimbert, 1994). These have been variously described and categorized, for example as 'ladders', 'steps' or 'wheels' of participation (Treby and Clark, 2004). These models recognize not only that participation comes in many forms, from passive consultation exercises to positive empowerment of stakeholders, but also that they often involve many stages and different processes. Participation happens at many points in the management process, from problem identification, to implementation, monitoring and evaluation. Hughey *et al.* (2000), for example, present a continuum of classification of stakeholders involvement in fisheries management. This ranges from *advisory management* which represents a government-led approach with limited consultation with stakeholders, through *co-management* with a more equal sharing of power and decision-making responsibility between government and stakeholders, to *self-management*, where fishers decide their own operating regime within a framework established by government.

Despite various experiments with co-management, most stakeholder participation in coral reef management represents more passive forms of involvement. Within co-management and collaborative arrangements, government agencies still commonly have the greater power in decision-making and defining the rules, and local stakeholders are included to enforce and monitor rules. Exceptions do exist (see Alcala *et al.*, this volume) but these often require radical changes in legislative framework to support the shift in power and finances (for example the case of Soufrière

Marine Management Area in St Lucia; see Sandersen and Koester, 2000). Building adaptive institutions requires a shift towards the self-management or self-organizing type of participation, and I argue that this entails a more systematic consideration of *who* is included and *how* they are included.

The identification and analysis of stakeholders have been established areas of study in social and management sciences since the 1980s (Mitroff, 1983). Stakeholders are not just a set of undifferentiated people who live close to or who use resources from a coral reef or MPA. Stakeholders are a diverse group that exist at many scales, not just the local level. Brown *et al.* (2002, p. 53), for example, present a typology of coastal actors and interests on a broad continuum of scales, identifying global and international wider society, national, regional, local off-site and local on-site as levels of this continuum.

The analysis of stakeholders at Buccoo Reef Marine Park in Tobago revealed 20 different sets of stakeholders with interests in and influences over the marine park (Fig. 15.2). The *importance* of these stakeholder groups was assessed according to how their livelihoods were impacted upon by changes in management of the marine park, and their *influence* by how much power they had in decisions and over the outcome of decisions. Importance refers to the degree to which the stakeholder is considered a focus of the decision to be made, and those who will be directly affected by decisions. Important stakeholders might therefore include subsistence fisherfolk whose livelihoods depend on access to a reef. But importance varies according to the objectives of management; thus in exclusive zones, important stakeholders may be conservation groups or even scientists. Influence is dictated by the stakeholder's control of, or access to, power and resources. Influential stakeholders might include well-established lobbying groups, wealthy land-owners or respected religious leaders who are already engaged in decision-making processes. In the case of Buccoo Reef, influential stakeholders who were not immediately visible in local discussions about the reef management included land developers, responsible for development of tourist and other infrastructure, and hoteliers, as well as the government agencies responsible for national and local enforcement of development and MPA regulations (the Town and Country Planning Department and the Marine Park Manager).

Using this approach the relative levels of influence and importance determine whether a stakeholder is classified as primary, secondary or external. *Primary stakeholders* have little influence over the outcome of management decisions, but their welfare is important to decision-makers. Often primary stakeholders are those who stand to lose most from decisions,

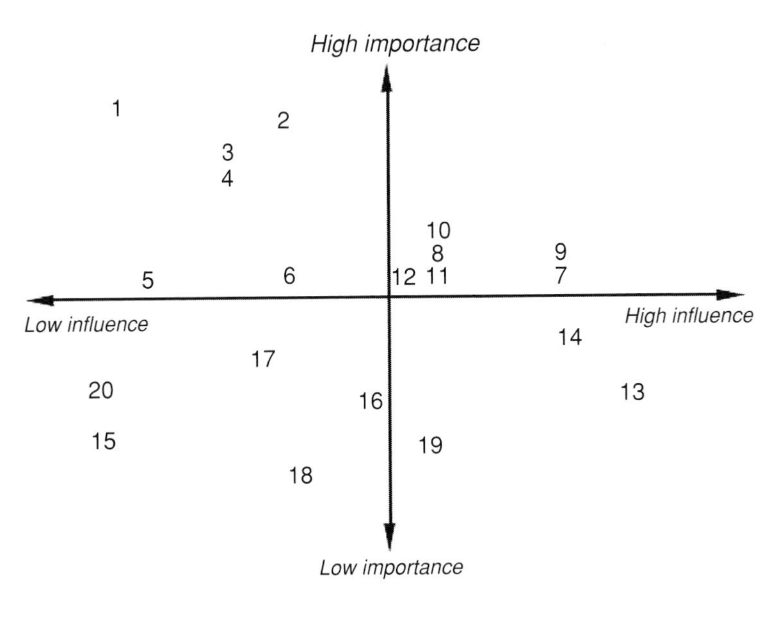

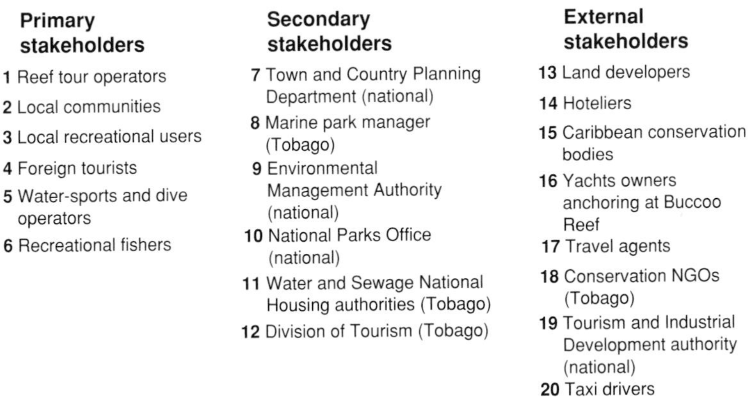

Figure 15.2 Stakeholders in Buccoo Reef Marine Park, Tobago, ranked along axes of influence and importance. From Brown *et al.* (2002).

although this is not always the case. In the case of Buccoo Reef, primary stakeholders included foreign tourists and those directly connected to tourism activities as well as local communities (Fig. 15.2). *Secondary stakeholders* can influence decisions because they are predominantly decision-makers and those engaged in implementing decisions. They are relatively unimportant because their welfare is not a priority but it is crucial to recognize them as stakeholders not as neutral in the management process.

In Tobago, secondary stakeholders were mainly department and authorities at various governmental levels (Fig. 15.2). Finally, *external stakeholders* are those individuals or groups who can exert significant influence over the outcome of a process but their interests are not important. With respect to Buccoo Reef Marine Park, these include a wide range of stakeholders, from land developers and hoteliers (both high influence) to conservation NGOs and taxi drivers (both low influence) (Fig. 15.2).

Other ways have been suggested of analysing the characteristics and dimensions of stakeholders. Mikalsen and Jentoft (2001), for example, assessed stakeholders in Norwegian fisheries according to their power, legitimacy and urgency. From this they identified three groups: *definitive* stakeholders, who possess all three qualities and thus have an unequivocal claim on management; *expectant* stakeholders who possess two out of the three attributes; and *latent stakeholders* who possess only one.

Analysing stakeholders using importance and influence identifies who should be included in what aspects of management. However, there is no a priori or natural set of stakeholders to be included. Depending on the objective, it may be more important to engage with either influential or important stakeholders, or with on-site or off-site ones.

How then are stakeholders included in decision-making and other management processes? Under the definition of adaptive institutions outlined above, an active form of participation which involves self-organisation and collaborative learning is necessary. The term 'deliberative inclusionary processes' (DIPs) covers a range of participatory policy processes, management practices and community empowering actions. A useful review of DIPs is provided by Holmes and Scoones (2000). Deliberation means careful consideration or discussion; it implies that decisions require social interaction and debate. Participants are expected to reflect on, evaluate and re-evaluate their own and others' positions, and the process of deliberation itself aims to bring about some kind of transformation of values, and foster negotiation between participants. Inclusion is the action of including different participants in the process. A wide range of procedural techniques, mechanisms and methods have developed under the broad umbrella of DIPs (see Holmes and Scoones, 2000; Brown *et al.*, 2002). Typical principles adopted in DIPs include working with small groups of people; focusing on the future and on common ground; urging full attendance and participation; incorporating the widest range of interest; and seeking public commitments to action. The kinds of mechanisms and methods include citizens juries, focus groups, issue forums, participatory rural appraisal, visioning exercises and various types of workshops and working groups.

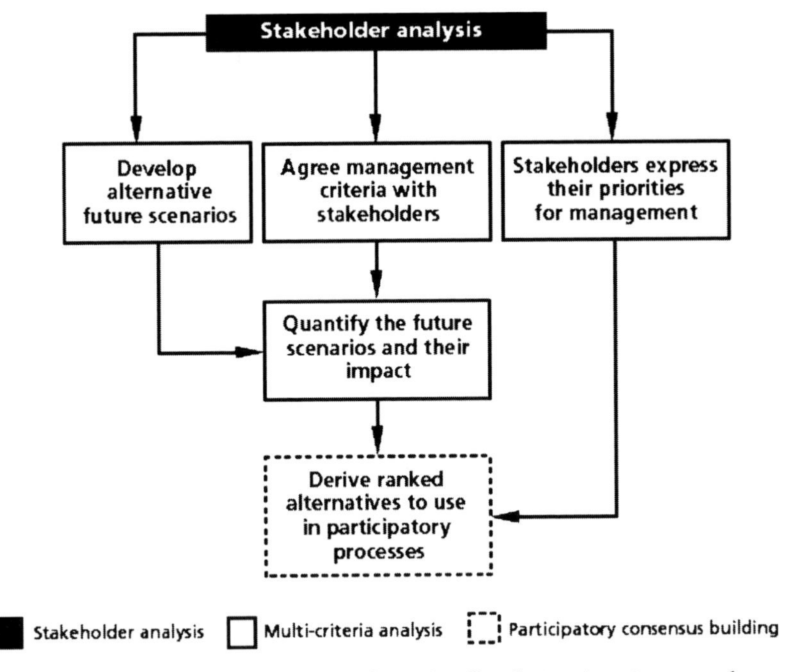

Figure 15.3 Conceptual framework for trade-off analysis. (From Brown *et al.*, 2002.)

At Buccoo Reef a set of these techniques were combined to develop a novel approach to decision-making and management which included the diverse users of the reef (Brown *et al.*, 2002). This approach has been labelled 'trade-off analysis' and focuses on including the values and interests of all those concerned with coastal resources into decision-making processes, as shown in Fig. 15.3. Using a framework of multi-criteria analysis, the approach engages stakeholders in the research process in order to evaluate the trade-offs between users and uses of coastal resources, and to negotiate and design effective, efficient, legitimate and equitable governance structures (Adger *et al.*, 2003).

Trade-off analysis is particularly focused on the problems and dilemmas of those parts of the developing world where the natural resources of the coast form significant and necessary resources for livelihood resilience. Here the dilemmas and trade-offs for sustaining the coast are especially acute and immediate, given the high biodiversity and ecosystem values and the acute dependence on coastal and marine resources for livelihoods. In addition to trade-off analysis, other methodologies have been proposed to facilitate the development of ICM which use consensus, flexible institutional arrangements based on issues and not sectors, and more equal power in decision-making (see Kay *et al.*, 2003).

The key lessons from trade-off analysis are that the initial identification and analysis of stakeholders are critically important. This determines who is included in participatory processes. Excluding important stakeholders is often a problem in participatory approaches to natural resource management; it results in stakeholders losing trust in the process. Second, working with small groups builds confidence, especially for stakeholders who feel intimidated by expressing their views in public fora. It is necessary to employ different techniques to engage with different stakeholders and to be persistent. DIPs take time, energy and resources; they will not happen overnight. However, they provide a critical opportunity and necessary framework within which to explore and understand different stakeholders' perspectives, preferences, values and knowledge, a necessary aspect of the co-learning process in adaptive institutions.

Fostering co-learning: integrating different knowledge and values

In addition to inclusion of all relevant stakeholder and transparent, open decision-making, adaptive institutions also involve the flow of information and knowledge between stakeholders, and the integration of knowledge and experience into management. Knowledge concerns the way people interpret, understand and apply meaning to the world and to their experiences. Conventional scientific knowledge is contrasted with local or traditional knowledge. Local or traditional knowledge is seen both as an obstacle and as an opportunity for coral reef conservation. But knowledge – whether local, traditional or scientific – cannot be viewed as a static resource. Within the notion of adaptive institutions developed here, different forms of knowledge are seen to bring valuable perspectives and they are integrated and utilized, and combined in a co-learning process. Ecological knowledge is a key link between social and ecological systems and can be used to interpret and respond to signals of ecosystem change (Olsson and Folke, 2001).

Berkes' (1999) definition of 'traditional ecological knowledge' shows knowledge as both cumulative and dynamic, building on experience and adapting to change and how it relates to institutions. It requires that we take account of how knowledge is embedded within the management strategies, social institutions and ultimately the world-views of different actors. It also views knowledge, practice and institutions as evolving and adapting to changes in contexts and circumstances (Berkes *et al.*, 2001). Berkes identifies four interrelated levels of ecological knowledge. The first, which is based on empirical observations, consists of local knowledge of animals, plants, soils and landscapes. According to Berkes, local knowledge in itself is not enough to ensure sustainable use of resources, although it might be sufficient to fulfil short-term survival objectives. At the second level, local knowledge is associated with a set of practices, tools and techniques, which requires an understanding of ecological processes. A third level develops social institutions, social organization, cooperation between resource users to enforce systems of management. Fourthly, a world-view, or paradigmatic knowledge, gives meaning to individual perceptions of the environment, and in turn shapes observations and social institutions. Local or traditional ecological knowledge is an integral part of social learning processes necessary for adaptive institutions. Social learning is how people learn to behave and use knowledge in social environments through interaction and deliberation. It thus helps to build the trust necessary for successful collaboration. The interplay between different forms of knowledge has been termed hybrid knowledge or knowledge-in-action by Blaikie *et al.* (1997), or fusion knowledge by Brown (2003a).

Scientific and local knowledge may sometimes appear in conflict, but a recent study by Wilson (2003) demonstrates that the cause of disagreements may in fact be the institutional context in which knowledge is used and negotiated. His study shows the importance of institutional frameworks for building agreement and collaborative management between fishers and scientists. In examining seven areas of dispute between fishers and scientists in a case study of bluefish management in the USA, he found that for five areas of dispute – the usefulness of survey data, usefulness of fishers' observations, environmental factors, fishing pressure and offshore displacement – scientists and fishers shared understanding of the issue, but the dispute was rooted in institutional sources. For example, fishers and scientists displayed nearly completely mutual understanding of the displacement hypothesis – that the observed decline in bluefish is an illusion created by a substantial and sustained movement of bluefish offshore. This was taken to be common sense by fishers, built up from consistent observation. However, although the hypothesis was supported by many scientists, it did not fit into the main model used to assess fish stocks. Only in case of two disputes – on ageing of bluefish and effort measurement – was there a clear cultural difference at the root of the disagreement. This relates to how people perceive and value the factors themselves. Although cultural and institutional factors contributed to each dispute, the importance of institutions in

On ecology
'When we lose the coral we lose the beach due to wave action' (*fisherman*)

'Everything that happens on this island makes its way to the water eventually' (*reef tour operator*)

On the tourism and economy
'We're headin' towards Barbados' (*reef tour operator*)

'Economic benefits may be good now, but what will happen in the future?' (*Bon Accord villager*)

Figure 15.4 Local views of ecological and economic changes occurring at Buccoo Reef, Tobago.

distorting and widening the gap between different forms of knowledge was clear. Shared understandings are institutional products, and Wilson argues that fisheries social scientists have overdrawn the idea that fishers and scientists see the world differently and have therefore underplayed the degree to which the rules governing management and stakeholder interactions create these apparent gaps in how the world is seen.

The development of trade-off analysis demonstrates how local knowledge can be at once validated and integrated into a decision-making process. Figure 15.4 shows some of the quotes from different Buccoo Reef stakeholders recorded in focus group discussions. These comments reveal different perspectives on the Buccoo Reef ecosystem. The comments were discussed by the focus groups, and they were used in presentations and also in scientific publications arising from research at Buccoo. For example, the quotes on ecology reveal how people observe and explain the linkages between different ecosystem components, and how they recognize the importance of land-based activities in affecting the reef. When discussing the development of tourism and its effects on the local economy, many expressed a preference for small, locally based tourism rather than large-scale, high-volume tourism they had heard about on other islands. These were concepts and ideas that other stakeholders could relate to and that were expressed in their own terms. When we discussed these views with them, we validated stakeholder knowledge and values and at the same time built their confidence and trust in being able to express and deliberate on them.

Different forms of knowledge and different values were integrated into decision-making process throughout trade-off analysis. Table 15.1 shows some of the techniques used at different stages of the process. This

Table 15.1. Stages in trade-off analysis, sources of knowledge and values, and techniques employed to draw out and integrate opinions and perceptions

Stage in trade-off analysis	Whose knowledge and values?	Techniques employed
Identifying drivers of change	Local residents and resource users; local planners, government agencies and NGOs; university scientists and researchers	Series of interviews; expert brainstorming group; review of scientific and policy literature, local plans and planning applications
Developing scenarios of future management	Local resource managers and planners; primary and secondary stakeholders including local users, tourist operators and NGO representatives, local parish councils; scientists and researchers; external stakeholders (tourism authority)	One-to-one interviews and series of small focus groups – feedback using quotes from stakeholders; envisioning exercises with stakeholder groups – 'How will Tobago look in 10 years time?'; expert brainstorming group; review of scientific and policy literature, local plans and planning applications
Defining criteria	Research team and resource managers	Brainstorming, expert consultation
Assessing impacts of management options on criteria	Research team and resource managers	Ecological and social surveys; secondary data from scientific and economic literature
Evaluating options	Weightings by stakeholder groups – articulation of values	Focus groups; contingent valuation survey of recreational users; survey of informal business people; one-to-one interviews; consensus-building workshop

demonstrates how what people understood about changes in the Buccoo Reef ecosystem, and what caused those changes, their preferences for different development options, and their values, in terms of the criteria by which options should be assessed and the weightings they gave to those criteria, were brought together. Deliberation and co-learning were part of the dynamics of the trade-off analysis process. There was continual feedback to participants about new knowledge and findings, about what other stakeholders thought. It was only in the final stages that large meetings were held and the priorities for action – at local, national and regional level – and personal commitments and responsibilities were decided upon.

The scale issue

Many examples of apparently successful participatory and inclusionary processes of coral reef management exist throughout the world. However these processes often encounter constraints at supra-local scales. For example, Walker *et al.* (2004) note that adaptive management has frequently failed because existing governance structures have not allowed it to function effectively. Torell *et al.* (2004) show the importance of recognizing the nested nature of coastal governance in order to achieve even the first of their four orders of coastal governance outcomes. The enabling conditions must be in place at local, regional and national scales. Their study of implementing ICM in Tanzania highlights the importance of national frameworks to support ICM. This is confirmed by our empirical analysis of the constraints to co-management of marine protected areas in Trinidad and Tobago (see Tompkins *et al.*, 2002). Some of these constraints can be related to the misfit of institutions to the ecosystems they seek to manage or between the different institutions involved in managing multiple coastal and marine resources associated with coral reef systems (Pritchard *et al.*, 1998). The concept of institutional fit has been discussed primarily in the context of terrestrial resource management (for example, Brown, 2003b) and rarely applied to marine systems, a recent exception being Hutchinson (2003).

In the ideal situation, co-management of resources, shared responsibility between institutions of the state and of local resource users, leads to reduced enforcement costs, the sharing of knowledge and information on the resource, and systematic learning between all parties. This situation is portrayed in Fig. 15.5 with the two main protagonists being institutions of the state (top) and the community (bottom). All communities exhibit heterogeneity in their internal and external networks (depicted as arrows within and external to the locality). A meta-analysis awaits to be undertaken among the successful examples of co-management (reviews: Berkes *et al.*, 2001; Brown *et al.*, 2002) on the patterns of interaction and other factors that explain their persistence and sustainability. At present Olsson *et al.* (2004) and Tompkins *et al.* (2002) have hypothesized prerequisites for sustained

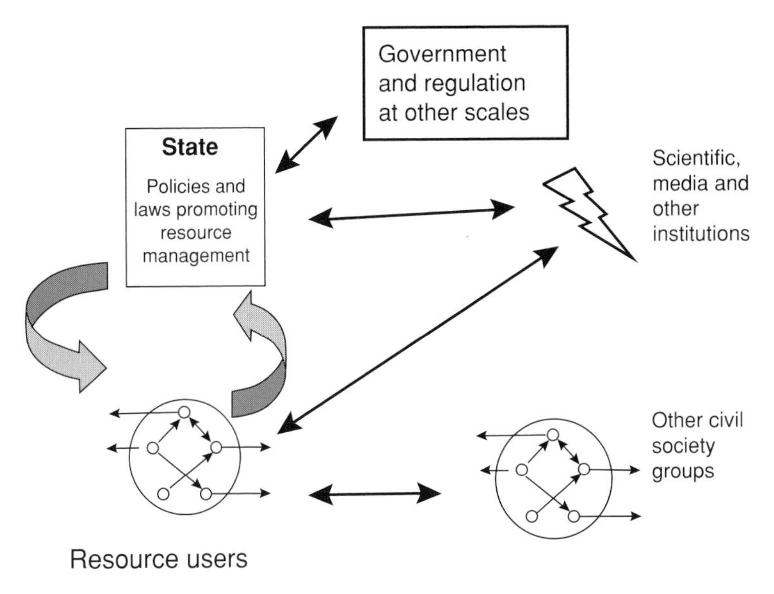

Figure 15.5 Interactions between institutions and stakeholders across scales.

interaction that include: (a) enabling constitutional order and legislation; (b) the ability for organizations to monitor and adapt their co-management experiments; and (c) the presence of leaders and agents for change.

Clearly although we can observe successful local-scale institutions for co-management of MPAs, these initiatives are not sufficient to address the scale of degradation and rapid rates of decline of coral reef systems worldwide (e.g. Gardner *et al.*, 2003). As Bellwood *et al.* (2004) point out, most MPAs or restricted-take areas are instigated too late, and management of tropical fisheries is invariably initiated after exploitation has peaked, and when dwindling stocks are likely to decline in a 'shifting baseline' scenario. Adaptive institutions should work across scales and make linkages between networks of MPAs and other conservation areas in order to scale up the adaptive management of individual locations to larger spatial and temporal scales (see also Roberts *et al.*, this volume).

CONCLUSIONS

Institutions provide an umbrella term and an analytical perspective for understanding the management and use of resources associated with coral reefs, ranging from the traditional uses and rights of local fishers, to the rules and enforcement of MPAs and exclusion zones, to the national and international legislative frameworks. Most research on institutions for natural resource management and conservation has been carried out in terrestrial systems. Marine systems such as coral reefs provide some special challenges for institutions, and this chapter has argued that in order to foster resilience of coral reefs adaptive institutions are necessary. These are characterized as being inclusionary, self-organizing, learning and working across scales. This chapter has used examples from the literature and from empirical research and development of trade-off analysis at Buccoo Reef Marine Park in Tobago to illustrate how adaptive institutions can be fostered for coral reef conservation and some of the enabling conditions necessary for them.

An understanding of institutional dynamics and the governance system is a prerequisite to designing and implementing successful conservation measures to halt or slow coral reef degradation. Just as scientific or technical solutions instigated without an understanding of the processes by which ecosystems work are 'flying in the dark', making rules without understanding governance and institutions is likely to be ineffective.

ACKNOWLEDGEMENTS

I am indebted to many of my colleagues and collaborators who have helped in my research in this broad area and especially to Neil Adger and Emma Tompkins who have been instrumental in developing ideas and insights. Research in Trinidad and Tobago was originally funded by Department for International Development through its Natural Resources Systems Programme.

REFERENCES

Acheson, J. M. (1988). *The Lobster Gangs of Maine*. Hanover, NH: University Press of New England.

Adams, W. M. and Mulligan, M. (2003). *Decolonising Nature: Strategies for Conservation in a Post-Colonial Era*. London: Earthscan Publications.

Adger, W. N., Brown, K., Fairbrass, J. *et al.* (2003). Governance for sustainability: towards a 'thick' analysis of environmental decision-making. *Environment and Planning A*, **35**, 1095–110.

Agrawal, A. (2001). Common property institutions and sustainable governance of resources. *World Development*, **29**, 1649–72.

(2002). Common resources and institutional sustainability. In *The Drama of the Commons*, National Research Council, pp. 41–85. Washington, DC: National Academy Press.

Alder, J. (1996). Have tropical marine protected areas worked? An initial analysis of their success. *Coastal Management*, **24**, 96–114.

Baland, J. and Platteau, J. (1996). *Halting Degradation of Natural Resources: Is There a Role for Rural Communities?* Oxford: Clarendon Press.

Beatley, T., Brower, D. J., Schwab, A. K. *et al.* (2002). *An Introduction to Coastal Zone Management*. Washington, DC: Island Press.

Bellwood, D. R., Hughes, T. P., Folke, C. and Nystrom M. (2004). Confronting the coral reef crisis. *Nature,* **429**, 827–33.
Berkes, F. (ed.) (1989). *Common Property Resources: Ecology and Community-Based Sustainable Development.* London: Belhaven Press.
(1999). *Sacred Ecology: Traditional Ecological Knowledge and Resource Management.* Philadelphia, PA: Taylor and Francis.
Berkes, F. and Folke, C. (1998). Linking social and ecological systems for resilience and sustainability. In *Linking Social and Ecological Systems,* eds. F. Berkes and C. Folke, pp. 1–25. Cambridge: Cambridge University Press.
Berkes, F., Mahon, R., McConney, P., Pollnac, R. C. and Pomeroy, R. S. (2001). *Managing Small-Scale Fisheries: Alternative Directions and Methods.* Ottawa: International Development Research Centre.
Blaikie, P., Brown, K., Dixon, P. *et al.* (1997). Knowledge in action: local knowledge as a development resource and barriers to its incorporation in natural resource research and development. *Agricultural Systems,* **55**, 217–37.
Bromley, D. W., Feeney, M., Mckean, M. A. *et al.* (eds.) (1992). *Making the Commons Work: Theory, Practice and Policy.* San Francisco, CA: Institute for Contemporary Studies Press.
Brown, K. (2003a). Three challenges for a real people-centred conservation. *Global Ecology and Biogeography,* **12**, 89–92.
(2003b). Integrating conservation and development: a case of institutional misfit. *Frontiers in Ecology and the Environment,* **1**, 479–87.
Brown, K., Adger, W. N., Tompkins, E. *et al.* (2001). Trade-off analysis for marine protected area management. *Ecological Economics,* **37**, 417–34.
Brown, K., Tompkins, E. L. and Adger, W. N. (2002). *Making Waves: Integrating Coastal Conservation and Development.* London: Earthscan Publications.
Cicin-Sain, B. (1993). Sustainable development and integrated coastal management. *Ocean and Coastal Management,* **21**, 11–43.
Cicin-Sain, B. and Knecht, W. (1998). *Integrated Coastal and Ocean Management: Concepts and Practices.* Washington, DC: Island Press.
Clark, J. R. (1996). *Coastal Management Handbook.* Boca Raton, FL: CRC Press.
Cooke, B. and Kothari, U. (eds.) (2001). *Participation: The New Tyranny?* London: Zed Books.
Digital Library of the Commons (2005). Database. Available online at http://dlc.dlib.indiana.edu/
Francis, J. and Torell, E. (2004). Human dimensions of coastal management in the Western Indian Ocean region. *Ocean and Coastal Management,* **47**, 299–307.
Gardner, T. A., Côté, I. M., Gill, J. A., Grant, A. and Watkinson, A. R. (2003). Long-term region-wide declines in Caribbean corals. *Science,* **301**, 958–60.
Gibson, C. C., McKean, M. A. and Ostrom, E. (eds.) (2000). *People and Forests: Communities, Institutions and Governance.* Cambridge, MA: MIT Press.
Hanna, S. S., Folke, C. and Maler, K.-G. (eds.) (1996). *Rights to Nature: Ecological, Economic, Cultural and Political Principles of Institutions for the Environment.* Washington, DC: Island Press.
Harvey, N. and Caton, B. (2003). *Coastal Management in Australia.* Oxford: Oxford University Press.

Holmes, T. and Scoones, I. (2000). *Participatory Environmental Policy Processes: Experiences from North and South,* IDS Working Paper No. 113. Brighton, UK: Institute of Development Studies, University of Sussex.
Hughey, K. F. D., Cullen, R. and Kerr, G. N. (2000). Stakeholder groups in fisheries management. *Marine Policy,* **24**, 119–27.
Hutchinson, D. J. (2003). Institutional misfit in tropical ecosystems: a test using marine protected areas. Ph.D. thesis, School of Development Studies, University of East Anglia, UK.
Jodha, N. S. (1986). Common property resources and rural poor in dry regions of India. *Economic and Political Weekly,* **21**, 27.
Kay, R. and Alder, J. (1999). *Coastal Planning and Management.* London: E. and F.N. Spon.
Kay, R., Alder, J., Brown, D. and Houghton, P. (2003). Management cybernetics: a new institutional framework for coastal management. *Coastal Management,* **31**, 213–27.
Lee, K. (1993). *Compass and Gyroscope: Integrating Science and Politics for the Environment.* Corvelo, CA: Island Press.
McCay, B. J. and Acheson, J. M. (eds.) (1987). *The Question of the Commons: The Culture and Ecology of Communal Resources.* Tucson, AZ: University of Arizona Press.
McShane, T. O. and Wells, M. P. (eds.) (2004). *Getting Biodiversity Projects to Work: Towards More Effective Conservation and Development.* New York: Columbia University Press.
Mikalsen, N. H. and Jentoft, S. (2001). From user groups to stakeholders? The public interest in fisheries management. *Marine Policy,* **25**, 281–92.
Mitroff, I. I. (1983). *Stakeholders of the Organizational Mind.* San Francisco, CA: Jossey-Bass.
National Research Council (2002). *The Drama of the Commons.* Washington, DC: National Academy Press.
Olsson, P. and Folke, C. (2001). Local ecological knowledge and institutional dynamics for ecosystem management: a study of Lake Racken Watershed, Sweden. *Ecosystems,* **4**, 85–104.
Olsson, P., Folke, C. and Berkes, F. (2004). Adaptive co-management for building resilience in social–ecological systems. *Environmental Management,* **34**, 75–90.
Ostrom, E. (1990). *Governing the Commons.* Cambridge: Cambridge University Press.
Ostrom, E., Burger, J., Field, C. B., Norgaard, R. B. and Policansky, D. (1999). Revisiting the commons: local lessons, global challenges. *Science,* **284**, 278–82.
Parson, A. E. and Clark, W. C. (1995). Sustainable development as social learning: theoretical processes and practical challenges for the design of a research programme. In *Barriers and Bridges to the Renewal of Ecosystems and Institutions,* eds. L. Gundersen, C. S. Holling, and S. S. Light, pp. 428–60. New York: Columbia University Press.
Pretty, J. (2002). People, livelihoods and collective action in biodiversity management. In *Biodiversity, Sustainability and Human Communities,* eds. T. O'Riordan and S. Stoll-Kleemann, pp. 61–86. Cambridge: Cambridge University Press.

Pretty, J. and Pimbert, M. (1994). *Participation, People and the Management of National Parks and Protected Areas: Past Failures and Future Promise.* Geneva, Switzerland: United Nations Research Institute for Social Development.
Pritchard, L., Colding, J., Berkes, F., Suedin, U. and Folke, C. (1998). *The Problem of Fit between Ecosystems and Institutions.* Bonn: IHDP.
Ruitenbeek, J. and Cartier, C. (2001). *The Invisible Wand: Adaptive Co-Management as an Emergent Strategy in Complex Bio-Economic Systems,* CIFOR Occassional Paper No. 34. Bogor, Indonesia: Centre for International Forestry Research.
Sandersen, H. T. and Koester, S. (2000). Co-management of tropical coastal zones: the case of the Soufriere Marine Management Area, St Lucia, WI. *Coastal Management,* **28**, 87–97.
Steins, N. and Edwards, V. (1999). A framework for analysing contextual factors in common pool resource research. *Journal of Environmental Policy and Planning,* **1**, 205–21.
Tompkins, E., Adger, W. N. and Brown, K. (2002). Institutional networks for inclusive coastal zone management in Trinidad and Tobago. *Environment and Planning A,* **34**, 1095–111.
Torell, E. C., Amaral, M., Bayer, T. G. *et al.* (2004). Building enabling conditions for integrated coastal management at the national scale in Tanzania. *Ocean and Coastal Management,* **47**, 339–59.
Treby, E. J. and Clark, M. J. (2004). Refining a practical approach to participatory decision-making: an example from coastal zone management. *Coastal Management,* **32**, 353–72.
Walker, B., Holling C. S., Carpenter, S. R. and Kinzig, A. (2004). Resilience, adaptability and transformability in social–ecological systems. *Ecology and Society,* **9**, 5. Available online at http://www.ecologyandsociety.org/vol9/iss2/art5
Wilson, D. C. (2003). Examining the two cultures theory of fisheries knowledge: the case of bluefish management. *Society and Natural Resources,* **16**, 491–508.
Young, I. M. (2000). *Inclusion and Democracy.* Oxford: Oxford University Press.
Young, O. (1996). Rights rules and resources in international society. In *Rights to Nature: Ecological, Economic, Cultural and Political Principles of Institutions for the Environment,* eds. S. S. Hanna, C. Folke and K.-G. Maler, pp. 245–63 Washington, DC: Island Press.

16

Coral reef restoration with case studies from Florida

WALTER C. JAAP
Florida Fish and Wildlife Research Institute and Lithophyte Research, Florida

J. HAROLD HUDSON
Florida Keys National Marine Sanctuary

RICHARD E. DODGE
Nova Southeastern University

DAVID GILLIAM
Nova Southeastern University

RICHARD SHAUL
Sea Byte, Inc., Florida

INTRODUCTION

While a coral reef may appear to be a formidable mass, its structure is easily damaged by disturbances. This is because reefs are layer cakes of coral skeletons, remains of other calcifying organisms, and sediment infill (in some cases even sedimentary strata). Typically 30–40% of the reef mass is void space which may be either filled with loose sediments or remain open. Fungi, algae, sponges, snails and fish work like miners to rasp, dissolve or bore through the coral skeletons, creating a labyrinth of tunnels and spaces.

The structural fragility of coral reefs leads to susceptibility to a number of disturbances. Natural events that have immediate impacts on their structure include meteorological phenomena (hurricanes, typhoons, frontal events, severe doldrums), earthquakes and tsunamis, and lava flows.

Coral Reef Conservation, ed. Isabelle M. Côté and John D. Reynolds.
Published by Cambridge University Press.

A class-five hurricane may totally destroy a high-profile coral reef, as occurred with Hurricane Hattie in Belize and Hurricane Allen in Jamaica (Stoddart, 1962; Woodley *et al.*, 1981). On the other hand, smaller storms and fast-moving large storms are less destructive. Hurricanes Donna and Betsy (1960 and 1964) and Andrew (1992) damaged coral reefs off the Florida Keys, but reefs appeared to recover within ten years after Donna (Springer and McErlean, 1962; Shinn, 1976). Some of these natural stress agents have a spatial context of entire ocean basins, e.g. the 1998–99 mass bleaching event (Goldberg and Wilkinson, 2004). Others are more moderate in space and time such as a hurricane that influences hundreds of hectares of reef. Glynn (1984) documented severe coral mortality after an El Niño warming in the Galápagos Islands and on reefs off the Pacific coast of Panama.

Many anthropogenic activities also cause acute physical damage to reefs. These often have smaller spatial signatures than major natural disturbances. Impacts include ship groundings, dredging operations, coastal development, fibre-optic cable and gas pipeline installations, and anchoring incidents.

In this chapter, we review options for restoration of coral reefs following acute structural damage caused by a variety of anthropogenic activities. We begin with a brief review of the kinds of impacts that are amenable to restoration, followed by a survey of techniques. These are illustrated by case studies in Florida, in which many of the methods in use today were pioneered. We conclude with some general guidelines and recommendations, including criteria for evaluating success.

PHYSICAL INJURIES AMENABLE TO RESTORATION

Anthropogenic and physically destructive activities that impact coral reefs include dredging channels and harbours, dredge-mining sand for beach renourishment, vessel groundings, anchoring on coral reefs, and coastal development. Any of these incidents may degrade or destroy a coral reef.

Dredging impacts typically involve a dredge cutter head colliding with the reef (by design or accidentally), ground tackle from the dredge damaging the reef, dumping dredge materials on the reef, and sediment- or silt-related insults from the dredging process or beach runoff. Additionally, dredging creates chronically high levels of turbidity which destroy corals from lack of light and sediment smothering (Courtenay *et al.*, 1974; Dodge and Vaisnys, 1977; Marszalek, 1981; Salvat, 1987; Blair *et al.*, 1990; Brown *et al.*, 1990; Rogers, 1990). Mining operations that employ dredges have resulted in coral reef degradation in Thailand (Brown *et al.*, 1990; Clarke

Figure 16.1 Forms of damage to coral reef structure. (a) Fractured coral: *Montastraea cavernosa, Alam Senang* grounding, 2003, Broward County, Florida. (Photograph by D. Gilliam.) (b) Rubble berm, *Eastwind* grounding, Broward County, Florida. (Photograph by W. Jaap.) (c) Scarified reef substratun and embedded hull paint, *Eastwind* grounding. (Photograph by W. Jaap.)

Table 16.1. Abundance of Cnidaria on the spur formation at Looe Key Reef, Florida, before and after the *Columbus Iselin* grounding in 1994

Attribute	Before (Wheaton and Jaap, 1988)	After Jaap (unpublished injury survey, 1994)
n = number of quadrats (1 m^2)	54	50
Number of cnidarian species	36: 22 stony coral, 14 octocoral	1 stony coral
Density of stony coral species (m^2)	3.59 ± 2.05	0.02
Density of octocoral species (m^2)	2.89 ± 2.08	0
Density of stony coral colonies (m^2)	8.76 ± 5.39	0.06
Density of octocoral colonies (m^2)	5.65 ± 4.91	0
Total number of colonies	900	3
Shannon–Weiner Diversity Index (H' log base e)	2.87	0.01
Pielou's Evenness Index (J'_n)	0.80	0.1

et al., 1993). Mining coral for construction is also reported to result in reef injuries (Brown and Dunne, 1988; Clark and Edwards, 1994).

Ship groundings on coral reefs have occurred ever since humans first built boats and began going to sea. Modern steel ships pose a much greater threat to a coral reef than a wooden sailing ship. Their impacts can dislodge and fracture corals (Fig. 16.1a), pulverize coral skeletons into small debris-rubble, displace sediment deposits (Fig. 16.1b), flatten the topography (Fig. 16.1c) and destroy or fracture the reef platform. Salvage operations often result in collateral injuries due to inappropriate methods and poor control of operations. In some cases, the ship's hull is ruptured and cargo and fuel are spilled on the reef (Hawkins *et al.*, 1991).

Large ship groundings cause fundamental changes in reef topography and biological communities. For example, when the *Columbus Iselin* foundered in the spur and groove habitat at Looe Key Reef, Florida in 1994, it was possible to compare impacts with quantitative studies of the cnidarian community that had been made prior to the incident (Wheaton and Jaap, 1988). The wreck devastated organisms (Table 16.1). The ship remained hard aground on the reef for several days, causing structural injuries to the reef foundation from the pounding of the hull. Large ship groundings have been occurring with regular frequency throughout the area off the southeast Florida coast (Table 16.2) and have degraded significant reef habitat.

Small boat groundings (vessels less than 30 m long) also occur chronically in many shallow reef areas. For example, in the Florida Keys,

Table 16.2. Summary of large ship groundings off southeast Florida, 1973–2004

Region	Number of groundings	Habitat area injured (m^2)
Palm Beach, Broward	9	21 008
Monroe County	14	14 597
Dry Tortugas	5	17 836
Total	28	53 441

approximately 60–90 small vessel groundings on coral reefs are reported annually (Florida Fish and Wildlife Law Enforcement records); however, it is likely that two to three times that number go unreported.

Cruise ships have run into reefs in Egypt and the Cayman Islands (Jaap and Moorelock, 1997). Examples of places where abandoned ships are found atop reefs include Greater Corn Island, Nicaragua, Aves Island, Venezuela, and Rose Atoll, American Samoa. Recent groundings include the US Research Vessel *Maurice Ewing*, which ran into a reef off the Yucatan Peninsula, Mexico (February 2005), and a freighter, *Cape Flattery*, which ran into a reef off Oahu, Hawaii, on 5 February 2005, resulting in severe coral injuries.

Anchor and chain damages occur in many areas (Davis, 1977). The size of the anchor, frequency of anchoring and local weather conditions have a direct impact on the magnitude of the damages. In many tourist areas, chronic small-boat anchor damage to coral reefs has been mitigated by installing moorings buoys, which eliminate the need to anchor on the reef (Halas, 1985, 1997). Smith (1988) documented the chronic anchoring problem off George Town, Grand Cayman, British West Indies: cruise ships anchoring off the port devastated acres of reef. A typical large ship anchor weighs several tons and is attached to the ship by a heavy chain. As the ship responds to any change in the wind, tides and current, the anchor chain is dragged across the reef, which can dislodge and fracture corals for hundreds of metres (Smith, 1988). Often these damages go unnoticed because they occur in deep water or remote areas. For example, the container vessel *Diego* anchored on the Tortugas Banks on 2 October 2002, remained anchored for several days (until discovered), and dislodged hundreds of corals. The *Diego's* anchor and chain were estimated to weigh 15 tonnes. A team of divers turned approximately 200 large coral colonies right side up. Restoration was challenging because of logistics, depth (25 m) and winter weather. All of the larger corals were eventually secured back onto the reef with hydraulic cement.

Figure 16.2 *Xestospongia muta* (giant barrel sponge) severed by fibre-optic cable installation, Broward County, Florida, 2001. (Photograph by Steve Addis.)

Trawlers and other types of fishing gear can harm coral reefs. Trawls can dislodge and abrade corals. Trawling devastated coral communities off Alaska (Krieger, 2001), Ireland (Wheeler *et al.*, 2003) and Norway (Fosså *et al.*, 2001; Hovland *et al.*, 2001). In Alaska the principal corals affected are octocorals, while in the North and Irish Seas extensive injuries have been sustained by colonies of *Lophelia pertusa* (see Corcoran and Hain, this volume). The latter eventually led to legislation protecting these deep reefs from trawling activity.

Coastal engineering projects, such as fibre-optic cable and gas pipeline installation, occur worldwide and have resulted in reef injures from physical impacts (Fig. 16.2) and deterioration of water quality.

A SURVEY OF RESTORATION TECHNIQUES

The technology and science of coral reef restoration have made strides in recent decades but we are still at a pioneer level in our understanding and development of solutions. At this juncture, we have incomplete information as to what does or does not work, the cost-efficacy of various techniques and the types of resources best suited to specific problems. An assortment of basic scientific information is available and is beginning to be applied towards restoration activity. For example, understanding of reproduction

Figure 16.3 Triage station for corals after grounding of the *Federales Pescadores*, Broward County, Florida, 2004. Corals were salvaged and set upright until they were reattached. (Photograph by W. Jaap.)

and larval settlement attributes of coral species can be applied towards strategies such as manipulation of reproduction (and generation of large volumes of larvae) as well as stimulation of settlement at a specific location. An ultimate application of such strategies might be to reseed large areas that have suffered coral loss from predators, bleaching or minor tropical cyclone damage. However, the challenges of achieving this are formidable; somehow multiple species must be inspired to produce larvae simultaneously and settle in the target area. Below, we review techniques that have been applied to small-scale restoration around the world.

Primary restoration: salvage and triage

Dislodged organisms (e.g. sponges, octocorals and stony corals) from any injury event can be used to repopulate any area in need of restoration (see below). The organisms are collected by divers and set aside in areas where they will be out of harm's way (Fig. 16.3). This is a typical procedure prior to dredging or other construction projects (Birkland *et al.*, 1979; Bouchon *et al.*, 1981; Fukunishi *et al.*, 1998; Dodge *et al.*, 1999). Corals have been transported above water using plastic holding crates and wet burlap with a transport time of approximately 1 hour (Jaap and Morelock, 1997). The organisms survived following the actual restoration. Recently, a consultant for the US Navy salvaged corals that would have been destroyed in a harbour engineering project in Key West. These corals (approximately 2000) were on seawalls and pilings. They were removed with hammer and chisel and transplanted to reefs, nursery areas and public aquaria, and a few were donated to research projects. In Japan, a patent was filed for suspending *Acropora* fragments on a rope and allowing them to grow (Omori and Okubo, 2004). The researchers reported difficulties in obtaining fragments and a high cost of labour and transport. A study of coral fragments in Okinawa (July 1992 to November 1994) reported that *Cyphastrea serailia* fared the best (approximately 75% survival) and *Montipora digitata* fared poorly (no survival); higher survival was found in shallow water with strong tidal currents for *Acropora formosa* and *A. nobilis* (Japan Marine Science and Technology Center, 1991). Survival rates for transplanted Scleractinia are highly variable; branching species, such as *Acropora* spp., often have good survival rates (Table 16.3).

Rubble and framework restoration

In cases with severe physical impact, dealing with the attendant rubble and framework stability may be significant tasks requiring a substantial labour effort. Stabilizing large masses of rubble on the reef using cement or other materials is not recommended; the rubble is vulnerable to destabilization by large swells and storms. Instead, we recommend moving rubble off the reef using divers and containers. R. Shaul (unpublished data) used cage-like containers and pillow-type lift bags to move large volumes of rubble from a ship-grounding site in Mexico and off Fort Lauderdale, Florida (Fig. 16.4).

Once the framework is exposed, the task is to inspect for fractures and instability. If the inspection reveals that the framework is satisfactory, reconstruction options can be addressed. For example, organisms can be reattached directly, or artificial reef structures can be created.

Transplantation and reattachment

A central issue in deciding whether transplantation is appropriate as a restoration option is the degree to which natural recovery is limited by larval supply or post-settlement mortality. Edwards and Clark (1998) showed that in some cases natural processes might be preferable over transplantation for medium to long time-frames. Exceptions include cases where larval supply

Table 16.3. Survival rates of transplanted scleractinian and hydrozoan corals

Species	Survival rate: Time (months)	Survival rate: Percent	Reference
Acropora microphalama	17	100	Okinawa General Bureau, Development Agency (1997)
Acropora prominens	12	51.8	Auberson (1982)
Acropora humilis	24	79.9	Clark and Edwards (1995)
Acropora tenuis	12 and 24	25 to 100	Clark and Edwards (1995)
Acropora hyacinthus	12 and 17	24 after 12 months; 17 after 17 months	Plucer-Rosario and Randall (1987)
Acropora hyacinthus	24	49	Clark (1997)
Acropora divaricata	24	80.6	Clark and Edwards (1995)
Acropora cytherea	24	50	Clark and Edwards (1995)
Montipora foliosa	15	100	Okinawa General Bureau Development Agency (1997)
Montipora stellata	15	100	Okinawa General Bureau Development Agency (1997)
Montipora digitata	12	10 to 80	Marine Parks Center (1995)
Echinopora lammellosa	3	80	Kaly (1995)
Leptastrea purpurea	28	0	Clark and Edwards (1995)
Pocillopora damicornis	7	100	Harriott and Fisk (1988)
Pocillopora damicornis	17	100	Okinawa General Bureau Development Agency (1997)
Seritopora hystrix	43	13	Okinawa General Bureau Development Agency (1997)
Stylopora pistillata	18	39	Japan Marine Science and Technology Center (1991)
Porites lichen	28	100	Clark and Edwards (1995)
Porites lobata	28	97	Clark and Edwards (1995)
Porites nigrescens	28	84	Clark and Edwards (1995)
Porites lutea	28	92	Clark and Edwards (1995)
Heliopora corulea	12	100	Auberson (1982)
Millepora dichtoma	12	68	Auberson (1982)
Millepora platyphylla	12	58	Auberson (1982)
Montastraea cavernosa	50	76.5	Continental Shelf Associates (2004)
Meandrina meandrites	50	100	Continental Shelf Associates (2004)
Dichocoenia stokesii	50	90.9	Continental Shelf Associates (2004)
Diploria clivosa	50	86.5	Continental Shelf Associates (2004)
Solenastrea bournoni	50	100	Continental Shelf Associates (2004)

Figure 16.4 (a) Divers removing rubble debris from a reef and (b) loading debris into metal baskets for transport away from the reef, Broward County, Florida, 2004. (Photographs by Richard Shaul.) (See also Plate 16.4 in the colour plate section.)

Figure 16.5 *Solenastrea bournoni* (smooth star coral) reattached to reef off Broward County, Florida, using hydraulic cement. *Alam Senang* grounding, 2003. (Photograph by Bruce Graham.)

is limited, recruitment mortality is high and a large number of detached corals and fragments are available for transplanting. Often, the resource trustee advocates transplantation of dislodged corals as their standard policy.

Many restoration projects have succeeded in reattaching corals (Fig. 16.5). People typically use hydraulic cement (Neely, 1988) or Portland cement supplemented with moulding plaster and sand. Cement will enter solution and generate a plume; caution should therefore be exercised to minimize deposition of cement residue around the work site. Epoxy is an alternative to cement (Jaap and Morelock, 1997), which is expensive but works well for reattaching smaller, fragile corals.

Other methods include stainless steel wire and plastic cable ties to reattach branching corals (Kaly, 1995; Iliff *et al.*, 1999; Bruckner and Bruckner, 2001). Octocorals (plumes and sea fans) require a rod or other structure for support. Kaly (1995) reported the results of experiments at Lizard Island, Great Barrier Reef, with nails, cable ties and epoxy to transplant and reattach corals. This study included impacts of exposure to air. Measurements included growth, partial and total mortality, attachment, bleaching,

Table 16.4. Survivorship of transplanted organisms at Lizard Island, Great Barrier Reef

Species	Mortality and growth	Attached to substratum	Best method of attachment	Tolerance to exposure
Stylophora pistallata	Partial with nails	No	Epoxy	Yes
Acropora gemmifera	Same as controls	Most did	Epoxy	Minor problems
Echinopora lamellosa	Partial mortality at site B	A few did	Epoxy	Unclear
Favia stelligera	Time was insufficient to tell	No	Epoxy or nails	Yes
Rumphella spp.	Site B fragments fared better	A few did	Epoxy	Most specimens tolerated exposure

Source: Kaly (1995).

and formation of new branch tips in branching species. About 5% of the corals could not be found during the second data collection effort after 3.5 months. The overall results were positive for non-exposed treatments that used epoxy for attachment (Table 16.4). Kaly (1995) reported that it would cost A\$580 000 to transplant coral at a density of 245 000 fragments ha^{-1} (24.5 fragments m^{-2}, A\$58.00 m^{-2}). Cost is based on a four-person dive team, transplanting 500 corals day^{-1} and does not include logistics, which may cost as much as the labour and materials depending on the distance of the work site from the staging area.

Transplantation efforts are mostly focused on the Scleractinia. Success is high when the corals are healthy and water quality is satisfactory. For example, in the Dominican Republic a resort was confronted with the loss of a large thicket of *Acropora palmata* from harbour dredging. The entire thicket was moved out of harm's way and relocated. The corals were then moved and cemented into a new location.

Conversely, sponges such as the barrel sponge, *Xestospongia muta*, and the loggerhead sponge, *Sphiospongia vesparia*, are very difficult to reattach. They do not reattach if severed from the bottom. However, injured colonies will generate new tissues if sponge material remains firmly attached to the sea floor. Smaller demosponges will survive and prosper. They can be secured by pushing them into holes and crevices in the rock.

Artificial reef structures

The nature, quality and three-dimensionality of artificial reef substrata have been examined to better understand whether these fulfil the habitat requirements of corals (Clark and Edwards, 1994; Gilliam *et al.*, 1995; Jaap, 2000). Nevertheless, there remains a moderate knowledge gap. Additional research would be useful on artificial substratum type and function, together with the attendant ecology that it may influence (Spieler *et al.*, 2001).

In cases where a ship, dredge or tropical cyclone has scarified the reef surface, replacement of topographic structure is recommended. The local materials and technological skills often dictate methods. The material texture and complexity are important; Dahl (1973) identified rugosity as a very important consideration in marine benthic diversity. For example, there are cases where limestone boulder modules were installed in close proximity to cement structures with a smooth surface. After ten years, the limestone boulder structure was totally covered with algae, sponges, octocorals and stony corals, whereas the smooth cement structure had only a thin film of algae.

A central goal is to mimic nature as closely as possible. Limestone structures can be fabricated with concrete as a base and adhesive to hold the boulders in place. The concrete can be pH-adjusted to near 7 to reduce alkalinity. Typical installation includes precision placement on the sea floor using a crane and divers. In other situations, a metal frame is placed as a template on the sea floor; the frame is filled with rock from a barge and a crane, and then moved with the crane. Rock pyramids with a 6 m × 6 m footprint were constructed using a temporary metal frame to contain the rock in Tampa Bay; these pyramids were about 1.5 m high. Rocks of 0.5 to 1 m in diameter created topography and refuge habitat. Multi-layers of boulders in a polygon tens of metres long and wide were created in deeper areas by positioning a barge over the designated area and pushing the rock into the sea with a tractor. Inspections reported no collateral damage (Sea Byte, 2001).

Pre-constructed structures (modular reef units) include designs that resemble an elongated pyramid with a horizontal concrete pipe imbedded on the long axis and covered with a layer of limestone boulders (0.25 to 0.50 m in diameter) immersed in concrete (Fig. 16.6). Another method that has been used successfully is Hudson's 'reef crown' structure, used for restoration of a small structural flaw in shallow reefs. This method is described in detail under the *Connected* case study (p. 500).

Where possible, modules should be placed downstream of known recruitment sources. Hydrodynamic microgyres retain water (and larvae) for prolonged periods (Carlton *et al.*, 2001), thus resulting in superior recruitment in the area of the gyre. Placement and structural design of

Figure 16.6 Reef restoration modules used to restore an area off Miami Beach, 1991. D, Dome; R, Reef module; M, Motel. D and R designed by Harold Hudson, US Patent #5215406. (Images courtesy of Miami-Dade County, Florida.) (See also Plate 16.6 in the colour plate section.)

the modules should work toward generating microgyres, for example by creating a small cul-de-sac in the side of a structure or placing modules together to create a cul-de-sac.

The reconstructed elements should be stable enough to withstand nominal waves and currents. The adjacent areas should not change because of reconstruction, for example through build-up of sediments which can bury organisms such as sponges, octocorals and stony corals. Restoration should blend in with the natural habitat; ships, aeroplanes and other waste materials should not be used as replacement structures for restoring a shallow-water coral reef. During the 1960s, there was an aggressive artificial reef programme off Fort Lauderdale, Florida, using motor-vehicle tyres. Subsequently, the tyres dispersed and have become a nuisance, impacting natural reefs. The local government is trying to find creative ways to remove them.

Mineral accretion technology

Electrical currents have been applied in iron fixtures to enhance coral growth (Kudo and Yabiku, 1988; Shumacher and Shillak, 1994; Van Treck and Schumacher, 1997, 1999; Schumacher, *et al.*, 2000). Creating mineral accumulations from electrical current is often referred to as 'Biorock' (Hilbritz *et al.*, 1977; Hilbertz, 1992). An iron grid is placed in the restoration area, power cables are run from the metal grid to an electrical power source (windmill generator or batteries) and coral fragments are attached to the grid system. An electrical current is supplied to the grid from a power source, enhancing coral calcification and growth. Goreau *et al.* (2004) reported that zooxanthellae densities and the mitotic index were higher in corals that were grown on a Biorock system in Indonesia. The technical complexity of grids, electricity and cables makes this method challenging to operate in remote coral reef locations. Additionally, grids are not a natural feature of coral reefs and present a risk of collateral injury from storms. Although this methodology has shown promise in experiments, it has not been tested at the scale of thousands of square metres, typical in coral reef restoration. It may prove useful in coral nurseries to expedite the growth of corals in non-reef areas.

Seeding corals and coral larvae

Seeding of coral fragments involves removal of corals from healthy colonies from a donor site, to be transplanted to target sites. This is one way to reintroduce corals quickly to large areas with intact reef substrata. Fragments can either be transplanted to the target site directly or held in coral nurseries (see case studies below) and allowed to grow to a suitable size (Auberson, 1982; Nishihira, 1994; Chen and Xiaog, 1995; Clark and Edwards, 1995; Gil-Navia, 1999; Lindahl, 2000; Bowden-Kirby, 2001a). After attaining this size, the corals can be further fragmented to propagate additional stock.

Seeding coral fragments has been successful in a number of restoration projects. For example, following an *Acanthaster planci* predation event at Green Island on the Great Barrier Reef of Australia (Harriott and Fisk, 1988), *Acropora* and *Pocillopora* species fragments were seeded throughout the area where the *Acanthaster* predation had extirpated virtually all the corals. Many of the fragments survived and grew into bush-like colonies upwards of 0.5 m in four to five years.

The success of seeding depends very much on the species used. *Acropora* species, for example, are well known for their ability to generate new colonies from fragments (Tunnicliffe, 1981; Highsmith, 1982; Kobayashi, 1984; Wallace, 1985; Harriott and Fisk, 1988). Fragments of *A. cervicornis, A. palmata* and *A. prolifera* will grow and generate new colonies under conditions of good water quality, low predator pressure and favourable fragment position (i.e. not in silty sediments) (Tunnicliffe, 1981; Garcia *et al.*, 1996; Bowden-Kerby, 2001, 2002). In fact, growth in all transplanted *Acropora* species is faster than in almost all other scleractinian species.

Coral larvae rather than fragments can also be seeded into an injured area; larvae for seeding are typically obtained by collecting gravid corals from the wild and allowing them to spawn in the laboratory (Richmond, 1995). Larvae are then nurtured until mature and ready for settling, and taken to the restoration site. Coral larval production rates in these experiments are moderate.

Heyward *et al.* (2002) carried out an elaborate field experiment in western Australia, which included floating larval culture ponds, a water circulation system, reef-retaining enclosures and a larval delivery system. Following a mass coral-spawning event, the surface slick of eggs, sperm and larvae was collected and placed in floating larval culture ponds. An estimated 4 million coral embryos of 18 *Acropora* species were captured. After a seven-day maturation period, larvae were delivered by gravity through a hose to settlement tents covering terracotta tiles. On control sites, beyond the tents, natural coral settlement was less than one recruit per tile over a three-week period. In contrast, the number of recruits per tile within the tents ranged from 0.17 to 68 with a 20-minute input of larvae and 80 to 384 in tents with a 12-hr larval input. The experiment documented that mass larval seeding can enhance settlement significantly; however, this specific method is limited to areas with predictable mass spawning followed by large slicks of gametes and larvae.

Another method that can potentially enhance the rate of coral larval settlement is the use of settlement attractors such as glycosaminoglycan (a sulphated polysaccharide). This is produced by coralline algae (*Hydrolithon boergesenii*) and induces *Agaricia agaricites humilis* larvae to settle (Morse *et al.*, 1994, 1996; Morse and Morse, 1996). Products such as this – the equivalent of 'coral flypaper' – could presumably be developed for other species and synthesized for use in restoration projects. However, we are unaware of any restoration projects that have applied this method.

Diadema antillarum relocation

The 1983–84 mass mortality of *Diadema antillarum* contributed to a proliferation of algae and a reduction in suitable substrata for coral larval settlement on western Atlantic coral reefs (Lessios *et al.*, 1984; Precht and Aronson, this

Table 16.5. Coral reef habitat estimates, Florida, east coast

Region (county)	Habitat area (ha)	Capitalized value (billons of 2001 US$)	Annual usage (person days, millions)
Palm Beach	12 000	1.4	2.83
Broward	8 300	2.8	5.46
Miami-Dade	7 200	1.6	6.22
Monroe	115 290	1.8	3.64
Total	142 790	7.6	18.15

Source: Johns *et al.* (2001).

volume). Experimental work documented the importance of *D. antillarum* urchins in grazing control of the benthic algae and enhancing coral larval settlement (Sammarco, 1980). To this day, urchin populations remain low on most western Atlantic reefs; however, in some areas (e.g. Setson Bank, Florida Middle Grounds) there are sizeable urchin populations and benthic algae are well grazed.

Attempts to introduce *D. antillarum* to reefs with abundant algae have met with limited success. Rearing *D. antillarum* in the laboratory and releasing them in the wild also has a poor record. Laboratory-reared *D. antillarum* have high mortality due mainly to predation. By contrast, capturing wild *D. antillarum* and sequestering them onto a reef to create artificially increased densities has been moderately successful: algae cover on manipulated reefs was reduced and there were more smaller corals (The Nature Conservancy, 2004).

FLORIDA REEF RESTORATION CASE STUDIES

Historical overview

The subtropical coral reef ecosystem off the Florida peninsula parallels the coast from Palm Beach to the western-most Florida Keys, Dry Tortugas. It includes an estimated 142 790 ha of coral reef habitat (Table 16.5). The Straits of Florida have always been an important shipping thoroughfare; ships transit the Straits of Florida as they navigate to and from Europe, the east coast of the USA, Canada, eastern Caribbean, Gulf of Mexico, Panama Canal and Central America. Vessel traffic includes tankers, bulk carriers, cargo containers, research vessels, cruise ships, fishing vessels and warships. Ship groundings have occurred in the Florida region for centuries.

Many British, Spanish, French and American sailing ships ended up on the reefs; numerous reefs are named for ships that foundered there. For example, Looe Key Reef is named for the HMS *Looe*, wrecked on the reef in 1744 (Peterson, 1955). The Straits of Florida are challenging to navigate; in the northern areas, the course to follow is north or south, but this changes to east or west in the southern portion of the Straits. If the ship's pilot veers too far east, the vessel is at risk of grounding on reefs off Cuba and Cay Sal Bank; if the pilot strays too far west, the vessel may go up on Florida coral reefs. A major boundary current, the Gulf Stream, is situated in the Straits of Florida. This also complicates navigation and was very difficult to master during the age of sail.

In 1850s, the US Coast Survey sent Louis Agassiz to survey the reefs and develop a plan to reduce the shipping losses (Agassiz, 1852). The plan was to build lighthouses on the most treacherous reefs, e.g. Carysfort, Fowey, American Shoal. The string of lighthouses provides visual warning of the reefs. In spite of radar, global positioning systems (GPS), electronic charting, depth recorders and satellite navigation systems, ship pilots still manage to run aground on coral reefs. Most of the recent groundings are the result of human errors (Table 16.2; Fig. 16.7).

The history of reef restoration can be traced to incidental work carried out in conjunction with marine aquaria. As aquaria designed displays that used reef organisms as an attraction, aquarists became more knowledgeable and skilled in sustaining the reef organisms and they developed unique ways to cement corals onto rock structures. Scientific researchers also became competent in manipulating corals in experiments. For example, in the early part of the twentieth century, Vaughan (1916) cemented corals on cement plates in Dry Tortugas and Goulding Cay, Bahamas, for growth rate experiments.

When the freighter *Wellwood* went aground at Molasses Reef, in the Key Largo National Marine Sanctuary in 1984, the ship and salvage operations heavily impacted 1282 m^2 of coral reef habitat (Hudson and Diaz, 1988). Injuries included fracturing the reef foundation, dislodging coral formations and individual coral colonies, and multiple injuries from towing cables scraping across the reef. The *Wellwood* was moved from the reef after lightering cargo and bunker fuel. Portland cement was used in an initial attempt to stabilize the loose reef rubble (J. H. Hudson, unpublished data). A small number of corals (casualties from the grounding) were transplanted back onto the reef. Half of the transplants were dislodged the following year by Hurricane Kate, but a survey by Hudson in 1994 revealed that remaining transplants were still attached and healthy. The reef framework was

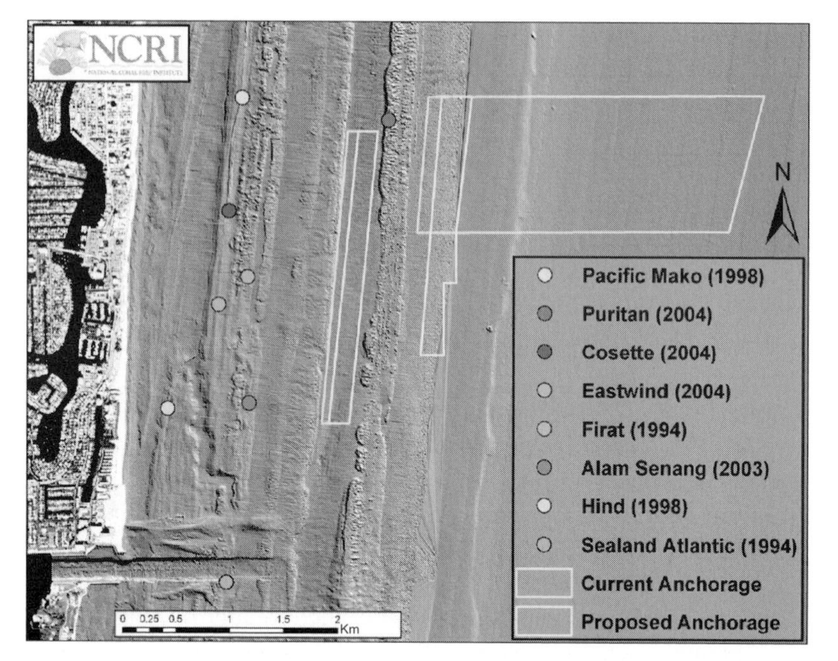

Figure 16.7 Map of coast of Broward County, Florida, identifying multiple ship mishaps, 1994–2004. The symbols indicate the positions of the ships. The anchorage and recommended changes are displayed in yellow and blue lines, respectively (See also Plate 16.7 in the colour plate section.)

stabilized in 2001, when 25 concrete and limestone modules and 2 tonnes of limestone boulders were set atop the loose rubble in the injured area (Hudson and Franklin, in press).

In 1989, three major groundings occurred in the Florida Keys within a few months: the *Alec Owen Maitland* (Carysfort Reef, 880 m^2), *Elpsis* (Elbow Reef, 2605 m^2) and *Mavro Vetranic* (Pulaski Shoal, 15 800 m^2). After the three groundings, the Florida Keys National Marine Sanctuary was created by the state of Florida and the federal government for greater resource protection. The *Elpsis* and the *Alec Owen Maitland* sites were restored using various materials to sequester the loose fragments. Restoration did not occur at the *Mavro Vetranic* site.

In the 1990s, restoration lessons learned in the previous decade began to be implemented. In 1994, for example, a grounding occurred at Looe Key Reef when a research vessel, the *Columbus Iselin*, ran onto the reef and sat atop the shallow spurs for several days, crushing and pulverizing structure over 345 m^2. This time, a detailed restoration plan was developed and executed. The restoration included clearing debris and replacing the missing structure using historical information (aerial photography). Limestone boulders and fibreglass reinforcement rods were used to form the perimeter area. The interior was backfilled with smaller limestone rocks and Portland cement. The replacement matched the area, shape and depth of the missing reef structure. No coral transplanting took place. The restored spurs are stable and some recruitment of juvenile corals has occurred. The final legal settlement for this grounding was the greatest for any incident to date (~US$10 000 m^{-2}). This project was unique because it restored the structure of the lost spur formations to near-original status. This technique can be used when the area is well mapped and there is a strong management incentive to restore structural features.

Not all restoration efforts during the 1990s were similarly successful, as shown by the container ship *Houston*, which ran aground south of Maryland Shoal in 1997, damaging 7107 m^2 of reef (Shaul *et al.*, 1999). Some of the injuries, including multiple sponge and coral damage and crushed reef structure, were the result of trying to free the ship by operating engines and propeller. Innovative methods, which were thought to be hurricane-resistant, were incorporated into the restoration. Articulated concrete mats were laid across rubble fields and large boulders were set atop the mats to secure loose rubble. Epoxy resin was poured over the rubble berms to secure them. Craters created from the vessel's propeller wash were backfilled with moderate-sized rock. However, upon the arrival of Hurricane George, some 18 months after the restoration was completed, the articulated mats broke apart and elements were scattered, several large boulders were moved, and one of the rubble berms was mobilized by the storm. Lessons learned were important in designing better subsequent restoration projects. Articulated mats do not withstand hurricane-force seas and rubble deposits are difficult to hold in place in a major storm event. In subsequent projects the rubble was moved off-site and use of articulated mats in shallow water was discontinued.

Experimental case studies

USS Memphis

In February 1993, the US nuclear submarine *Memphis* grounded on a coral reef off Dania Beach, southeast Florida. The grounding caused extensive physical and biological damage to the reef structure and to the coral community (about 1000 m^2 of injury). As part of a claim by the state of Florida against the USA, the impact of the grounding was assessed through field and photographic studies. The National Oceanic and Atmospheric Administration (NOAA) habitat equivalency analysis (HEA) was used to calculate the additional reef area that was required in order to compensate for the injury (see p. 504).

A hypothesis-driven multivariate experiment was carried out to test the efficacy of various coral reef restoration methods. The experimental design used a series of concrete structures to study benthic recruitment, growth and survival of corals. Substrata (tile material) were tested for recruitment based on exterior structural complexity (tiles containing calcium carbonate, calcium carbonate with iron added, and a tile that included commercial 'biofilm' material). Coral transplanting experiments included replicates of two species to measure survival and growth rates (Banks *et al.*, 1999). Cores were extracted from *Montastrea cavernosa* and *Meandrina meandrites* and cemented with epoxy on the reef structures. Core voids were backfilled with cement plugs. Quarterly data collection was initiated in October 2001, 12 months after the artificial reefs were deployed. Tiles were recovered at 1-, 3-, 7-, 14-, 21- and 60-day intervals and examined microscopically for settlement of organisms.

Tiles incorporating the calcium carbonate and biofilm did not differ in the settlement rate of bacteria or diatoms; however, discs with iron filings had a significantly slower settling rate (Dodge *et al.*, 2000; Quinn *et al.*, 2001, in press; Glynn *et al.*, 2002; Robinson and Rogerson, 2001; Fahy, 2003; Fahy *et al.*, in press). After 23 months, 100% of the *Montastrea cavernosa* and 27.5% of the *Meandrina meandrites* transplants retained their original tissue surface area or exhibited evidence of growth. The remaining 72.5% of the *Meandrina meandrites* transplants showed varying degrees of partial tissue mortality (Fig. 16.8). All donor colonies survived; tissue regenerated in core holes, but not over an entire concrete plug. There was minimal tissue mortality from coring. Species-specific differences in transplant growth and mortality, noted in this study, indicate that species selection is an important consideration in coral reef restoration efforts. Based on the experiments, coring for coral transplants and using biofilms or iron to expedite recruitment were discontinued.

Bal Harbor dredge mitigation

In 1999, during a beach renourishment project off Miami Beach, a reef was severely injured by dredge-induced sedimentation. To fulfil court-ordered mitigation, a restoration project was initiated using reef modules. Benthic community abundance data were collected on four occasions during the 35-month study at random stations on modules, and coral reef reference

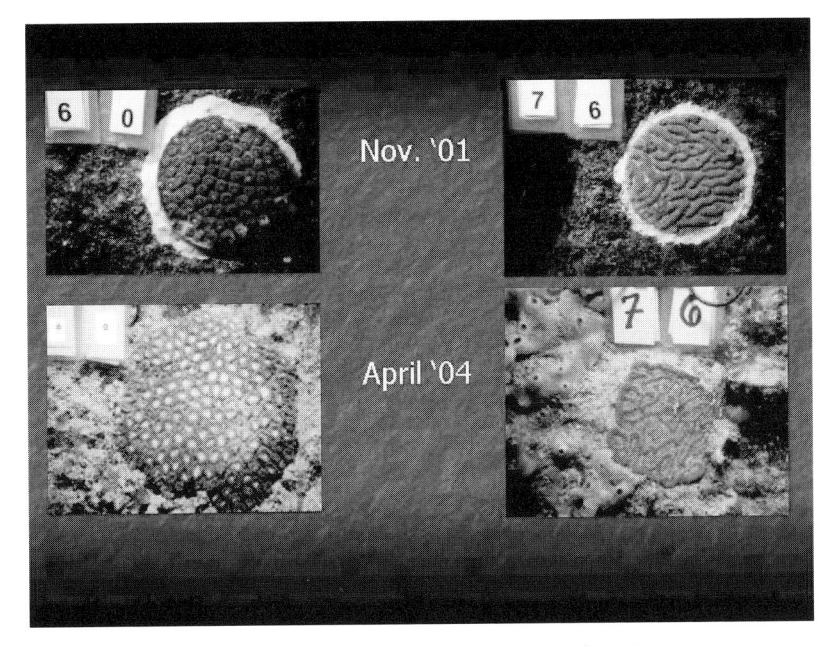

Figure 16.8 Comparison of results of transplantation of *Montastraea cavernosa* (giant star coral) and *Meandrina meandrites* (maze coral) in the *Memphis* Restoration Project, Broward County, Florida, November 2001 and April 2004. Photographs on left are *M. cavernosa*: top, coral plug recently attached to the structure; bottom, same 29 months later (note the growth around the edge of the plug). Right photos are *M. meandrites*: top, at time of attachment; bottom, 29 months later (note tissues have receded). (Photographs by David Gilliam.)

sites near the project. Quadrats and photography were used to collect data on the relative abundance of algae and sessile animals. In the first six months, the most abundant and diverse fauna found growing on restoration structures were sponges, *Holopsamma helwigi* and *Dictyonella ruetzleri*, which cumulatively comprised 45% of all sponge colonies (Table 16.6).

During the monitoring period, the number of species doubled and the number of individuals increased fourfold. The greatest increases in abundance were observed in algae, sponges and scleractinian corals (Table 16.6). The latter two groups exhibited maximum proliferation after two years. The greatest difference between the restoration and reference sites was the moderate abundance of octocorals on the latter and their total absence on the former. Species richness at the restoration sites exceeded that at the reference sites (Fig. 16.9). The benthic community analyses (Bray Curtis Similarity, classification and ordination) show that the reference and restored areas remain somewhat different because of the richer sponge and stony

Table 16.6. Number of species and individuals observed attached and growing on restoration structures, Bal Harbor Restoration Project

	December 1999		August 2000		April 2001		November 2001	
Taxon	Species	Number	Species	Number	Species	Number	Species	Number
Algae	5	36	8	64	7	50	10	80
Porifera	9	95	15	211	23	573	17	572
Hydrozoa	1	4	1	2	4	12	2	13
Octocorallia	0	0	0	0	0	0	0	0
Actinaria	0	0	0	0	1	1	0	0
Scleractinia	1	3	4	7	10	33	13	31
Zooanthidea	0	0	1	2	2	5	1	1
Bryozoa	2	21	1	18	2	38	4	14
Ascidians	0	0	1	2	2	5	1	1
Total	22	179	34	330	56	768	54	737

Source: Modified from Miami-Dade Department of Environmental Resource Management (2003).

coral components in the restored samples and the moderately abundant octocorals found in the reference sampling sites. The most likely explanation for this difference is that the restoration sites had greater topographic complexity than the reference locations, providing a multitude of microhabitats. By contrast, on the natural reefs, relief was not greater than 1 m. The project documents that limestone structures are stable and effectively recruit sponges and stony corals. Topographic complexity is an important aspect in the settlement of algae, sponges and stony corals. Lack of octocoral recruitment is puzzling as they are often the most abundant settling organisms shortly after physical disturbances.

M/V *Connected*

The grounding of the M/V *Connected*, an 18-m Viking sport cruiser, on Western Sambo Reef, off Key West, Florida in 2001, resulted in a challenging restoration effort. The vessel caused extensive injury to *Acropora palmata* habitat along the 157-m-long grounding track and a salvage removal path in depths ranging from 0.9 to 1.5 m. Injury to reef substratum was 202 m^2. This restoration required four elements in a single prefabricated structure: stabilizing substratum, three-dimensional relief, a means of reattaching viable coral fragments, and installation in turbulent shallow water.

To resolve this dilemma, the 'Reef Crown', a pre-cast concrete and limestone rock module (Fig. 16.10), was designed and fabricated by Harold Hudson of the Florida Keys National Marine Sanctuary. The 1.2-m high, 227-kg hollow cylinders were transported as close as feasible to the injury site; after winching the module over the side of the boat, lift bags and

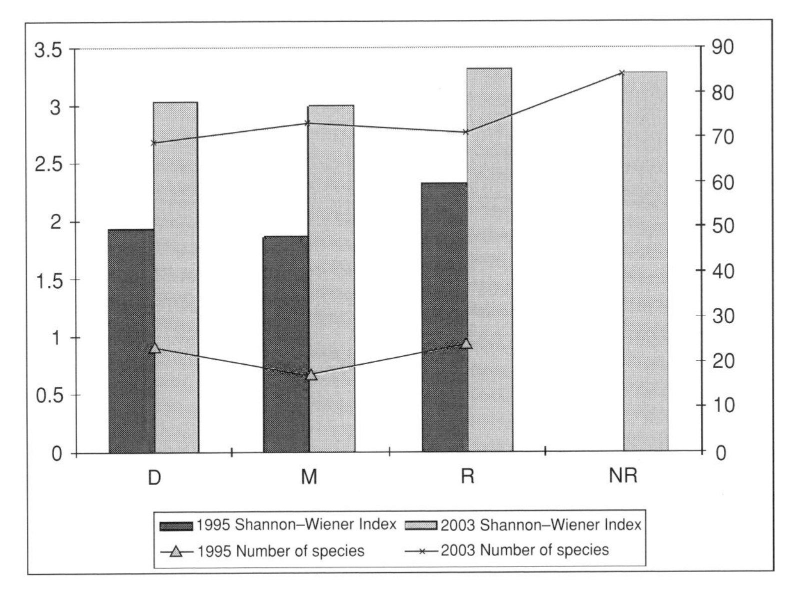

Figure 16.9 Changes in species diversity (Shannon–Weiner Species Diversity Index and numbers of species), Bal Harbor Project, Miami-Dade County, Florida. D, dome modules; M, motel module; R, reef replacement module; NR, natural reef reference sites.

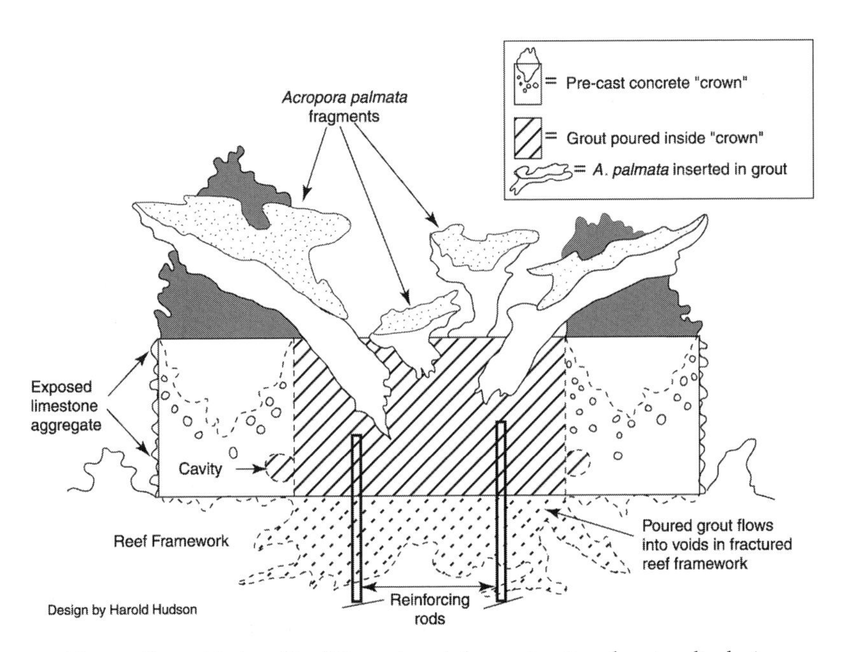

Figure 16.10 Hudson 'Reef Crown' module construction drawing displaying side perspective.

styrofoam flotation blocks kept the Reef Crowns afloat. Divers guided them to the precise area of deployment and slowly deflated the lift bags. Cement grout was poured into each module, penetrating crevices, holes and other irregularities in the reef and forming a permanent bond between the Reef Crown and the underlying reef. Live *Acropora palmata* fragments salvaged from the injury were installed in the fresh cement. Twenty Reef Crown units were used to repair the *Connected* grounding site during June and July 2001.

Two years after Reef Crown deployment, coralline algae had encrusted the exposed limestone rock surfaces. Coralline algae build-up retards boring and grazing organisms that can erode the limestone. In addition, corals and other encrusting biota that settle and grow on the modules will increase the biodiversity in the area. Reef Crowns were designed and fabricated to last indefinitely and were considered to be hurricane resistant. Hurricane Frances tested this with sustained winds of 43 knots (80 km h^{-1}) at Key West Airport Meteorological station in August 2004. The hurricane had no visible effect on any of the 20 Reef Crowns installed at the M/V *Connected* site. Reef Crown units were also used to restore two other sites in the Florida Keys National Marine Sanctuary and Biscayne National Park.

The benefits of the Reef Crowns are that they can be deployed in shallow, turbulent conditions. Fabrication does not require high technology; construction and deployment costs are not prohibitive to export to developing countries; and the training to build and deploy Reef Crowns is not challenging. The system can be modified (size, shape) to meet local conditions.

The Coral Nursery Project

In 2001, the Coral Nursery Project was developed by Nova Southeastern University, the Broward County Department of Planning and Environmental Protection and Ocean Watch Foundation to collect dislodged coral colonies and transplant them to a nursery site where they could continue to grow and be available as donor colonies for restoration activities. The project also aimed to provide reef managers with coral species-specific and colony-size specific transplantation success information, and to play a large role in public awareness and education by recruiting volunteers with interests in diving and the marine environment to assist with coral and data collection and to learn about coral identification and transplanting procedures.

Corals of opportunity (5–40-cm size class) are collected by hand from reefs in 12 m depth or less. Corals are immediately transported using the 'dry method', whereby they are brought aboard the boat and covered with a wet fabric, such as a towel (Becker and Mueller, 2001), and transported to the coral nursery. Colony size, species identity, percent mortality, presence of bleaching, and presence of encrusting organisms are recorded. Corals are generally out of the water for less than 2 hr.

Corals are transplanted to the nurseries using Portland Type II cement (Auberson, 1982; Harriott and Fisk, 1988; Hudson and Diaz, 1988; Jaap, 2000). All transplanted colonies are mapped, tagged and photographed, to monitor condition and growth.

More than 300 corals of opportunity, representing 17 species, have been transplanted into the nursery so far. Since June 2001, 250 of the colonies, representing 14 species, have been monitored quarterly. Of these, 240 (96.0%) were still securely attached to the nursery substrata and alive in January 2004. Survival was 98.5% for the 6 most abundant species, and 8 of the 14 species transplanted had 100% survival over this monitoring period.

The very high colony survival rates provide resource managers with information on the utility of using corals of opportunity as a source of transplant donor colonies for coral reef restoration. The management and administration require skilled and experienced people. The motivation is non-monetary; volunteers enjoy the experience and in many cases become spokespersons for coral reef conservation. The project shows evidence that government, academic and volunteer NGO organizations can execute projects that benefit society. Corals of opportunity and coral nurseries should become important tools in the future of coral reef restoration.

GENERAL GUIDELINES AND RECOMMENDATIONS

The following is a summary of what has been learned from a variety of reef injury and restoration experiences and literature sources. While some of the information is qualitative in nature, a recapitulation can provide a valuable starting point for continued research and actual on-site restoration activities. Regardless of the restoration method used, the human expectation of rapid recovery is unrealistic. Natural reef creation is a process of centuries; technologies and skills cannot build a functioning coral reef in a few months. Nevertheless, many useful lessons have been learned and provide a reasonable set of tools for restoration projects.

Preliminary assessment

Careful planning is important for any restoration (Causey, 1990; Jaap 2000). Plans should be based on understanding the problem and applying solutions that have a good track record, validated in the field on several occasions. Assessment is always an important aspect in anthropogenic disturbances because of the legal ramifications. Methods include aerial photography coupled with ground-truth surveys (Julius *et al.*, 1995; Hudson and Goodwin, 2001) and *in situ* techniques using nominal coral reef sampling methods: quadrats, transects, photography, and video. Integrated GPS and photography (film and digital) and/or video require a GPS receiver to georeference the injuries. Resultant data are processed to create maps of the injuries and to quantify the various types of injury. Assessment helps in defining the scale and nature of the restoration. Alternative high-tech assessment methods include a system of subsurface sound-emitting buoys that are deployed in a triangular configuration. A diver receiver-module processes the sound signals and triangulates the position. Injury categories are coded in the software. The buoy locations are georeferenced using a GPS receiver. Injury data are compiled, the injuries are quantified (planar area) and maps can be generated electronically. If there are databases (seismic–sonar profiles) that document topography, they can be used to contrast with post-incident seismic data. These data are helpful in depicting topographic losses and in planning the restoration.

Scaling

In Florida and US territorial jurisdiction, the injury data are used to compute interim loss of ecological services (Mazzotta *et al.*, 1994; Julius *et al.*, 1995; Fonseca *et al.*, 2000; Milon and Dodge, 2001). The method is referred to as habitat equivalence analysis (HEA). This provides a means to scale restoration activities relative to the injuries and the expected recovery time. The input includes the injury area (which may be divided into resource subunits and/or injury categories), recovery time, and the discount rate. The discount rate is the willingness of resource-users to pay a fee for speeding up the recovery of ecological services. The rate for discounting interim losses should reflect the social rate of time preference, the rate at which society is willing to substitute between present and future consumption of natural resources with certainty. A large body of economics literature exists concerning which rate(s) best measures the social rate of time preference. These data may be viewed at the NOAA website (NOAA, 2005). Among the rates recommended are the real rate of interest and the government borrowing rate. A rate of 3% is typically used, based on the average discount rates that the Federal Reserve banks charge the member banks to borrow.

As an example of HEA evaluation, suppose a reef injury of 1000 m^2 includes 750 m^2 of moderate injuries expected to require 15 years to return to pre-incident condition, and 250 m^2 that is severely injured and expected to require 100 years to recover. Two sets of inputs for HEA computations are 750 m^2, 15 years, 3% discount and 250 m^2, 100 years, and 3% discount. HEA reports that moderate injuries are compensated for with a 164.93 m^2 project and the severe injuries are compensated for with a project of 518.12 m^2. At this juncture, the resource managers and researchers would design a project(s) that would be equivalent of 683.05 m^2 in area. Historically, the types of compensatory projects have ranged from creating artificial reefs, educational programmes, installing anchor moorings and navigational warning markers, to adding radar transmitters (RACON beacons) to lighthouses.

The spatial area can be converted to the equivalent currency by a cost estimate to create an artificial reef that has a footprint of 683 m^2. In the period 2000–2005, Florida artificial reef projects typically used 16 000–19 750 ts ha^{-1} and the rock cost was US$75.00–91.00 t^{-1} (procurement and deployment). Thus the cost to build a 683-m^2 reef ranges from $81 960 to $122 760. This value could be used to scale the project (non-artificial reef) and requires the responsible party to compensate for the lost of ecological services.

Monitoring the results to assess success

Stability and biological attributes are fundamental to repairing a natural reef with foreign materials. A hurricane will move virtually everything if wind speed is over 161 km hr^{-1} and/or if it is moving very slowly (16 km hr^{-1} or less). Larger reef modules barely moved at all during Hurricane Andrew (1993); however, Hurricane George (1997) resulted in multiple movements at the *Houston* restoration site. Non-hurricane storms with few exceptions do not result in movement. Measurements are typically focused on stability: constructed materials should not move or have structural failures. Biological attributes include species richness, evenness, biological cover, disease, competition and recruitment of juveniles. The typical strategy is to compare the restored reef habitat with reference sites that are representative of the pre-injury status.

At the onset, unless there was a major transplanting effort, the structural restoration components will appear barren. Within a period of one month to a year the recovery is typified with algae colonizing the rocks. Sponges succeed algae. Off southeast Florida, after approximately three years, sponges are abundantly colonizing rocks. After two to five years, coral settlement progresses and colonies 2–10 cm in diameter are common. Performance of a restoration project is considered satisfactory if the biological attributes meet or exceed those of the reference sites. Multivariate community analysis, Bray Curtis Similarity coefficient and multi-dimensional scaling (MDS) are useful tools to compare reference and restored sites (Clarke and Warwick, 2001). If the restoration is progressing satisfactorily, the Bray Curtis Similarity coefficient values will converge to reach a high degree of similarity (>85%). The MDS plot will document spatial convergence of the restoration and reference sites. Vector of HEA points over time provides an indication of direction of change; the reference and restored plots will be moving in the same general direction toward convergence.

Site monitoring should have a timescale relevant to the potential for full recovery. For example, if the site is expected to recover within ten years, monitoring should be for that time span, with more intensive sampling at the onset and reduced effort toward the end. Monitoring is the only way to determine the success of the restoration, to document status and trends and to correct problems (Gomez and Yap, 1984; Likens, 1988; Rogers, 1988; Swanson and Sparks, 1990; Rogers *et al.*, 1994; Done, 1997; Connell *et al.*, 1997). Any project that is worthy of restoration is worthy of monitoring status and trends.

Transplanted organisms

The methods used include visual observations, photography and video. During transplanting, a map is compiled of transplanted organisms, including installed reference markers and GPS coordinates. Sample size for the transplanted organisms should be sufficiently large to support rigorous status and trend analysis. Typically, a few species are sufficiently abundant to test the efficacy of the effort: are the growth and health of species in the restoration and reference areas similar?

Attachment and adhesion are important. If most transplanted organisms remain attached, this component is considered a success; however, if 20% or more of the reattached organisms are dislodged without a major storm event, remedial action is called for. Equally important is the vitality of the transplanted organisms. Sampling should include colour, bleaching, competition with benthic algae, disease and percentage of cover by functional groups (stony coral, sponge, octocoral, benthic algae, rock). Sampling must include sites and corals (same taxa) from an adjacent non-impacted area to provide a reference sample for vitality.

Recruitment

Natural recruitment and colonization of space by organisms in the restoration project are monitored using visual observations, photographs, video and experiments. Evaluating reference sites and restored sites documents progress. The local setting will have a significant influence on recovery. Areas downstream from sizeable reef populations with a delivery source (currents and prevailing winds) will generally recruit well while isolated areas will not. Recruitment in the restored area should generally match the reference sites.

CONCLUSIONS

Coral reef restoration is not a substitute for good stewardship of a very important ecosystem that is susceptible to degradation and collapse from a multitude of anthropogenic impacts. Coral reef restoration has a limited and expensive toolbox that can in some circumstances correct problems at a scale of tens of hectares. During the past decades we have perfected methods to transplant corals and replace topographic structure. Transplanted coral survivability is equivalent to the corals in the reference community. Some headway has been made in the field of coral reproductive biology: generating and harvesting larvae, stimulating settlement and generating new colonies. Recognizing the pittance of funding that has supported coral reef restoration research, it is not surprising that progress is slow (National Research Council, 1992). Human expectations are often very unrealistic; the palaeontological record indicates that reef creation is a slow process with some reefs growing less than 1 m in 1000 years (Hoffmeister and Multer, 1964; Shinn *et al.*, 1977). There are no methods for instantaneously creating a functioning coral reef. As we continue the efforts to learn and understand what works and is possible, the technologies will improve; however, we cannot offer great hope with all of the multiple stressors that impede coral reef vitality, e.g., continuing climate heating, rising sea level, land-based pollution of the water, and degradation from anthropogenic insults (Wilkinson, 2004, this volume).

REFERENCES

Agassiz, L. (1852). Florida reefs, keys, and coast. *Annual Report of the Superintendent of the Coast Survey*, **1851**, 107–34.

Auberson, B. (1982). Coral transplantation: an approach to re-establishment of damaged reefs. *Kalikasan*, **11**, 158–72.

Banks, K., Dodge, R. E., Fisher, L. E., Stout, D. and Jaap, W. C. (1999). Grounding of the nuclear submarine USS *Memphis* on a southeast Florida coral reef: impact, assessment, and proposed restoration. In *International Conference on Scientific Aspects of Coral Reef Assessment, Monitoring, and Restoration*, Fort Lauderdale, FL, 14–16 April, abstract and poster.

Becker, L. C. and Mueller, E. (2001). The culture, transplantation, and storage of *Montastraea faveolata, Acropora cervicornis,* and *Acropora palmata*: what have we learned so far? *Bulletin of Marine Science*, **69**, 881–96.

Birkland, C., Randall, R. H. and Grimm, G. (1979). *Three Methods of Coral Transplantation for the Purpose of Re-establishing a Coral Community in the Thermal Effluent Area at the Tanguisson Power Plant.* Guam: University of Guam.

Blair, S. M., Flynn, B. S. and Markley, S. (1990). Characteristics and assessment of dredge-related mechanical impact to hard-bottom reef areas off northern Dade County, Florida. *Proceedings 10th American Academy of Underwater Science, Diving for Science Symposium*, 5–14.

Bouchon, C., Jaubert, J. and Bouchon-Navano, Y. (1981). Evolution of a semi-artificial reef built by transplanting coral heads. *Tethys*, **10**, 173–6.

Bowden-Kerby, A. (2001). Low-tech reef restoration methods modeled after natural fragmentation processes. *Bulletin of Marine Science*, **69**, 915–31.

(2002). Coral transplantation modeled after natural fragmentation processes: low tech tools for coral reef restoration and management. Ph.D. dissertation, University of Puerto Rico, Mayaguez.

Brown, B. E. and Dunne, R. P. (1988). The environmental impact of coral mining on coral reefs in the Maldives. *Environmental Conservation*, **15**, 159–65.

Brown, B. E., LeTissier, M. D. A., Scoffin, T. P. and Tudhope, A. W. (1990). Evaluation of the environmental impact of dredging on intertidal coral reefs at Ko Phuket, Thailand, using ecological and physiological parameters. *Marine Ecology Progress Series* **65**, 273–81.

Bruckner, A. W. and Bruckner, R. J. (2001). Condition of restored *Acropora palmata* fragments off Mona Island, Puerto Rico, two years after the *Fortuna Reefer* ship grounding. *Coral Reefs*, **20**, 235–43.

Carlton, J. H., Brinkman, R. and Doherty, P. J. (2001). The effects of water flow around coral reefs on the distribution of pre-settlement of fish (Great Barrier Reef, Australia). In *Oceanographic Processes of Coral Reefs*, ed. E. Wolanski, pp. 209–30. Orlando, FL: CRC Press.

Causey, B. D. (1990). Biological assessment of damage to coral reefs following physical impacts resulting from various sources, including boat and ship groundings. *Proceedings 10th American Academy of Underwater Science, Diving for Science Symposium*, 49–57.

Chen, G. and Xiaog, S. (1995). A study on the transplantation of reef-building corals in Sanya waters, Hainan Province. *Tropic Oceanology*, **14**, 51–7.

Clark, S. and Edwards, A. J. (1994). The use of artificial reef structures to rehabilitate reef flats degraded by coral mining in the Maldives. *Bulletin of Marine Science*, **55**, 26–46.

(1995). Coral transplantation as an aid to reef rehabilitation: evaluation of a case study in the Maldive Islands. *Coral Reefs*, **14**, 201–13.

Clark, T. (1997). Tissue regeneration rate of coral transplants in a wave-exposed environment, Cape D'Aguilar, Hong Kong. *Proceedings 8th International Coral Reef Symposium*, **2**, 2069–74.

Clarke, K. R. and Warwick, R. M. (2001). *Change in Marine Communities: An Approach To Statistical Analysis and Interpretation*, 2nd edn. Plymouth, UK: Primer-E.

Clarke, K. R., Warwick, R. M. and Brown, B. E. (1993). An index showing breakdown of seriation related to disturbance in a coral reef assemblage. *Marine Ecology Progress Series* **102**, 153–60.
Connell, J. H. (1997). Disturbance and recovery of coral assemblages. *Proceedings 7th International Coral Reef Symposium*, **1**, 9–22.
Continental Shelf Associates (2004). *Monitoring Reattached Stony Corals at the Firat Grounding Site*, final report, surveys 1–4, Technical Report to Polaris Applied Sciences and the Florida Marine Research Institute. Juno, FL: Continental Shelf Associates.
Courtenay, W. R., Herrema, J., Thompson, M. J., Azzinaro, W. P. and Van Montfrans, J. (1974). *Ecological Monitoring of Beach Erosion Control Projects, Broward County, Florida and Adjacent Areas*, Technical Memoir No. 41. Fort Belvior, VA: US Army Corps of Engineers, Coastal Engineering Research Center.
Dahl, A. (1973). Surface area in ecological analysis: quantification of benthic coral reef algae. *Marine Biology*, **23**, 239–49.
Davis, G. E. (1977). Anchor damage to a coral reef on the coast of Florida. *Biological Conservation*, **11**, 29–34.
Dodge, R. E. and Vaisnys, J. R. (1977). Coral populations and growth patterns responses to sedimentation and turbidity associated with dredging. *Journal of Marine Research*, **35**, 715–30.
Dodge, R. E., Anderegg, D., Fergen, R. and Cook, P. (1999). *Sewer Outfall Coral Transplantation Project*. Dania Beach, FL: National Coral Reef Institute.
Dodge, R. E., Spieler, R. E., Gilliam, D. S. *et al.* (2000). Restoration of a Southeast Florida coral reef injured by the grounding of the nuclear submarine USS *Memphis* Poster presented at *9th International Coral Reef Symposium.*
Done, T. (1997). Decadal changes in reef-building communities: implications for reef growth and monitoring programs. *Proceedings 7th International Coral Reef Symposium*, **1**, 411–15.
Edwards, A. J. and Clark, S. (1998). Coral transplantation: a useful management tool or misguided meddling? *Marine Pollution Bulletin*, **37**, 474–87.
Fahy, E. G. (2003). Growth and survivorship of *Meandrina meandrites* and *Montastrea cavernosa* transplants to an artificial reef environment, and the effectiveness of plugging core hole sites in transplant donor colonies. M.Sc. thesis, Nova Southeastern University.
Fahy, E. G., Dodge, R. E., Fahy, D. P., Quinn, T. P., Gillian, D. S., and Spieler, R. E. (in press). Growth and survivorship of scleractinian coral transplants and the effectiveness of plugging core holes in transplant donor colonies. *10th International Coral Reef Symposium.*
Fonseca, M., Julius, B. and Kenworthy, W. (2000). Integrating biology and economics into seagrass restoration: how much is enough and why? *Environmental Engineering*, **15**, 227–37.
Fosså, J. H., Mortensen, P. B. and Furevik, D. M. (2001). The deep-water coral *Lophelia pertusa* in Norwegian waters: distribution and fishery impacts. *Proceedings 1st International Symposium of Deep-Sea Corals*, 194–5.
Fukunishi, K., Yonaha, K., Morita, S., Yamamoto, H. and Takaashi, Y. (1998). A planning method on harbor construction harmonizing with coral reef. *Proceedings Techno-Ocean 98 International Symposium*, 181–4.

Garcia, R. U., Alvarado, E. M. and Acosta, A. (1996). Regeneration of colonies of and transplants of *Acropora palmata* in the National Park Corales del Rosario, Colombian Caribbean. *Proceedings 8th International Coral Reef Symposium*, 68.

Gill-Navia, M. F. (1999). *Transplantation of Reef-Building Corals on the Rosario Archipelago, Columbian Caribbean*. National Dania Beach, FL: Coral Reef Institute.

Gilliam, D. S., Banks, K. and Spieler, R. E. (1995). Evaluation of a novel material for artificial reef construction. *Proceedings 6th International Conservation and Aquatic Habitat Enhancement Symposium*, 345–50.

Glynn, E. A., Quinn, T. P., Fahy, D. P. *et al.* (2002). Growth and survivorship of stony coral *Meandrina meandrites* and *Montastrea cavernosa* transplants to an artificial reef environment: a work in progress, poster presented at the *International Society for Reef Studies 2002 European Meeting*, Cambridge, UK.

Glynn, P. W. (1984). Widespread coral mortality and the 1982/83 El Niño warming event. *Environmental Conservation*, **11**, 133–46.

Goldberg, J. and Wilkinson, C. (2004). Global threats to coral reefs: coral bleaching, global climate change, disease, predator plagues, and invasive species. In *Status of Coral Reefs of the World: 2004*, vol. 1, ed. C. Wilkinson, pp. 67–92. Townsville, QLD: Australian Institute of Marine Science.

Gomez, E. D. and Yap, H. T. (1984). Monitoring reef conditions. In *Coral reef Management Handbook*, eds. R. A. Kenchington and B. E. T. Hudson, pp. 171–8. Jakarta: UNESCO.

Goreau, T. F., Cervino, J. M. and Pollina, R. (2004). Increased zooxanthellae numbers and mitotic index in electrically stimulated corals. *Symbiosis*, **37**, 107–20.

Halas, J. C. (1985). A unique mooring system for reef management in the Key Largo National Marine Sanctuary. *Proceedings 5th International Coral Reef Symposium*, **4**, 237–42.

(1997). Advances in environmental mooring technology. *Proceedings 7th International Coral Reef Symposium*, **2**, 1995–2000.

Harriott, V. J. and Fisk, D. A. (1988). Coral transplantation as a reef management option. *Proceedings 6th International Coral Reef Symposium*, **2**, 375–9.

Hawkins, J. P., Roberts, C. M. and Adamson, T. (1991). Effects of a phosphate ship grounding on a Red Sea reef. *Marine Pollution Bulletin*, **22**, 538–42.

Heyward, A. J., Smith, L. D., Rees, M. and Field, S. N. (2002). Enhancement of coral recruitment by in situ mass culture of coral larvae. *Marine Ecology Progress Series*, **230**, 113–18.

Highsmith, R. C. (1982). Reproduction by fragmentation in corals. *Marine Ecology Progress Series*, **7**, 207–26.

Hilbertz, W. (1992). Solar-generated building material from seawater as sink for carbon. *Ambio*, **21**, 126–9.

Hilbritz, W., Fletcher, D. and Krausse, C. (1977). Mineral accretion technology: application for architecture and aquaculture. *Industrial Forum*, **8**, 75.

Hoffmeister, J. E. and Multer, H. G. (1964). Growth rate estimates of a Pleistocene coral reef of Florida. *Geological Society of America Bulletin*, **75**, 353–8.

Hovland, M., Vasshus, S., Indreeide, A., Austdal, L. and Nilden, Ø. (2001). Mapping and imaging deep-sea coral reefs off Norway, 1982–2000. *Proceedings 1st International Symposium of Deep-Sea Corals*, 197–8.

Hudson, J. H. and Diaz, R. (1988). Damage survey and restoration of M/V *Wellwood* grounding site, Molasses Reef, Key Largo National Marine Sanctuary, Florida. *Proceedings 6th International Coral Reef Symposium*, **1**, 231–6.
Hudson, J. H. and Goodwin, W. B. (2001). Assessment of vessel grounding injury to coral reef and seagrass habitats in the Florida Keys National Marine Sanctuary, Florida: protocols and methods. *Bulletin of Marine Science*, **69**, 509–16.
Hudson, H. J. and Franklin, E. C. (in press). Coral reef restoration of a storm-disturbed vessel grounding site in the Florida Keys National Marine Sanctuary, USA.
Iliff, J. W., Goodwin, W. B., Hudson, J. H., Miller, M. W. and Timber, J. (1999). Emergency stabilization of *Acropora palmata* with stainless steel wire and nails: impressions, lessons learned and recommendations from Mona Island, Puerto Rico. *National Coral Reef Institution*, Abstract, 110.
Jaap, W. C. (2000). Coral reef restoration. *Ecological Engineering*, **15**, 345–64.
Jaap, W. C. and Morelock, J. (1997). *Baseline Monitoring Report, Restoration Project, Soto's Reef, Georgetown, Grand Cayman Island, British West Indies*. Seattle, WA: Holland America-Westours and Cayman Islands Department of the Environment.
Japan Marine Science and Technology Center (1991). *Report of the Coral Reef Project*. Tokyo: Japan Marine Science and Technology Center.
Johns, G. M., Leeworthy, V. R., Bell, F. W. and Bonn, M. A. (2001). *Socioeconomic Study of Reefs in Southeast Florida*, a Final Report. Fort Lauderdale, FL: Hazen and Sawyer.
Julius, B., Iliff, J., Hudson, J., Jones, C. and Zobrist, E. (1995). Natural resource damage assessment M/V *Jacquelyn L* grounding site, Western Sambo Reef, FKNMS, 7 July, 1991. Silver Spring, MD: US Department of Commerce and National Oceanic and Atmospheric Administration.
Kaly, U. L. (1995). *Experimental Test of the Effect of Methods of Attachment and Handling on the Rapid Transplantation of Corals*. Townsville, QLD: CRC Reef Research Centre.
Kobayashi, A. (1984). Regeneration and regrowth of fragmented colonies of the hermatypic corals *Acropora formosa* and *Acropora nasuta*. *Galaxea*, **3**, 13–23.
Krieger, K. J. (2001). Coral (*Primnoa*) impacted by fishing gear in the Gulf of Alaska. *Proceedings 1st International Symposium on Deep-Sea Corals*, 106–16.
Kudo, H. and Yabiku, I. (1988). Aquamarine project in Okinawa. *Proceedings Techno-Ocean Symposium*, 338–47.
Lessios, H., Robertson, D. and Cubit, J. (1984). Spread of *Diadema* mass mortality through the Caribbean. *Science*, **226**, 335–7.
Lindahl, U. (2000). Reef rehabilitation through transplantation of staghorn corals: artificial stabilization and effects of breakage and abrasion. *Proceedings 9th International Coral Reef Symposium*, Abstract, 228.
Likens, E. (1988). *Long-Term Studies in Ecology: Approaches and Alternatives*. New York: Springer-Verlag.
Marine Parks Center of Japan (1995). *Study on the Recovery of Coral Reef Ecological Systems*. Tokyo: Marine Parks Center of Japan.

Marszalek, D. S. (1981). Impact of dredging on a subtropical reef community, southeast Florida, USA. *Proceedings 5th International Coral Reef Symposium*, **1**, 147–53.

Mazzotta, M. J., Opaluch, T. and Grigalunas, T. (1994). Natural resource damage assessment: the role of resource restoration. *Natural Resources Journal*, **34**, 153–78.

Miami-Dade County Department of Environmental Resource Management (2003). *Bal Harbor Mitigation Artificial Reef Monitoring Program*, Progress Report for Bal Harbor Consent Order OGC 94–2842. Miami, FL: Miami-Dade County Department of Environmental Resource Management.

Milon, J. W. and Dodge, R. E. (2001). Applying habitat equivalency analysis for coral reef damage assessment and restoration. *Bulletin of Marine Science*, **69**, 975–88.

Morse, A. N. C. and Morse, D. E. (1996). Flypapers for coral and other planktonic larvae. *BioScience*, **46**, 254–62.

Morse, D. E., Morse, A. N. C., Raimondi, P. T. and Hooker, N. (1994). Morphogen-based chemical flypaper for *Agaricia humilis* coral larvae. *Biological Bulletin (Woods Hole)*, **186**, 172–81.

Morse, A. N. C., Iwao, K., Baba, M. *et al.* (1996). An ancient chemosensory mechanism to bring new life to coral reefs. *Biological Bulletin*, **191**, 149–54.

National Research Council (1992). *Restoration of Aquatic Ecosystems: Science, Technology and Public Policy*. Washington, DC: National Academy Press.

Neely, B. D. (1988). *Evaluation of Concrete Mixtures for Use in Underwater Repairs*, Technical Report REMR-18. Vicksburg, MS: US Army Corps of Engineers.

Nishihira, M. (1994). Transplantation of hermatypic coral using fragments of colonies: brief method using bamboo stick. *Biological Magazine, Okinawa*, **32**, 49–56.

NOAA (2005). www. NOAA.gov/restoration

Okinawa General Bureau, Development Agency (1997). *Research of Coral Transplantation in the Isigaki Port*. Okinawa, Japan: Okinawa General Bureau, Development Agency.

Omori, M. and Okubo, N. (2004). Previous research and undertaking of coral reefs restoration. In *Manual for Restoration and Remediation of Coral Reefs*, eds. M. Omori, and S. Fujiwara, pp. 3–13. Nature Conservation Bureau, Ministry of the Environment.

Peterson, M. L. (1955). The last cruise of the H. M. S. *Looe*. *Smithsonian Miscellaneous Collections*, **231**, 1–54.

Plucer-Rosario, G. P. and Randall, R. H. (1987). Preservation of rare coral species by transplantation: an examination of their recruitment and growth. *Bulletin of Marine Science*, **41**, 585–93.

Quinn, T. P., Glynn, E. A., Dodge, R. E. *et al.* (2001). Hypothesis-based restoration study for mitigation of a damaged S. E. Florida coral reef: a work in progress, poster presented at the *2001 Florida Artificial Reef Summit Artificial Reefs: Into the New Millennium*, Fort Lauderdale, FL.

Quinn, T. P., Fahy, E. G., Robinson, J. L., Dodge, R. E. and Spieler, R. E. (in press). Hypotheses-based restoration study for mitigation of a S. E. Florida U.S. A. coral reef damaged by the grounding of a nuclear submarine. *10th International Coral Reef Symposium*.

Richmond, R. (1995). Coral reef health: concerns, approaches and needs. In *Proceedings Coral Reef Symposium on Practical, Reliable, Low Cost Monitoring Methods for Assessing the Biota and Habitat Conditions of Coral Reefs*, pp. 25–8. Silver Spring, MD: US Environmental Protection Agency and National Oceanic and Atmospheric Administration.

Robinson, J. L. and Rogerson, A. (2001). Preliminary analysis of initial microfouling of a nearshore artificial reef in Broward County, Florida. Poster presented at the Annual Meeting of American Society for Limnology and Oceanography, Albuquerque, NM.

Rogers, C. S. (1988). Recommendations for long-term assessment of coral reefs: US National Park Service initiates regional program. *Proceedings 6th International Coral Reef Symposium*, **2**, 399–403.

(1990). Responses of coral reefs and reef organisms to sedimentation. *Marine Ecology Progress Series*, **62**, 185–202.

Rogers, C. S., Garrison, G., Grobber, R., Hillis, Z. M. and Franke, M. A. (1994). *Coral Reef Monitoring Manual for the Caribbean and Western Atlantic*. St John, US Virgin Islands: Virgin Islands National Park, Nature Conservancy and World Wildlfe Fund.

Salvat, B. (1987). Dredging on coral reefs. In *Impacts des Activités Humaines sur les Récifs Coralliens: Connaissances et Recommendations*, ed. B. Salvat, pp. 165–84. Paris: UNESCO.

Sammarco, P. W. (1980). *Diadema* and its relationship to coral spat mortality: grazing and competition and biological disturbance. *Journal of Experimental Marine Biology*, **45**, 245–72.

Schumacher, H. P. and Shillak, L. (1994). Integrated electrochemical and biological deposition of hard material: a nature-like colonization substrate. *Bulletin of Marine Science*, **55**, 672–9.

Schumacher, H. P., Treek, P., Eisinger, M. and Paster, M. (2000). Transplantation of coral fragments from ship groundings on electrochemically formed structures. *Proceedings 9th International Coral Reef Symposium*, **2**, 989–90.

Sea Byte (2001). *Gulfstream Natural Gas Pipeline Benthic Habitat Survey*. Tequesta, FL: Sea Byte.

Shaul, R., Waxman, G., Schmahl, G. P. and Julius, B. (1999). Using GIS to to conduct injury assessment, restoration and monitoring during the Contship *Houston* grounding. *Proceedings International Conference on Scientific Aspects of Coral Reef Assessment, Monitoring and Restoration* (abstract).

Shinn, E. A. (1976). Coral reef recovery in Florida and the Persian Gulf. *Environmental Geology*, **1**, 241–54.

Shinn, E. A., Hudson, J. H., Halley, R. B. and Lidz, B. (1977). Topographic control and accumulation rate of some Holocene coral reefs: south Florida and Dry Tortugas. *Proceedings 3rd International Coral Reef Symposium*, **2**, 1–7.

Smith, S. H. (1988). Cruise ships: a serious threat to coral reefs and associated organisms. *Ocean Shoreline Management*, **11**, 231–48.

Spieler, R. E., Gilliam, D. S. and Sherman, R. L. (2001). Artificial substrate and coral reef restoration: what do we need to know to know what we need? *Bulletin of Marine Science*, **69**, 1013–30.

Springer, V. and McErlean, A. (1962). Seasonality of fishes on a south Florida shore. *Bulletin of Marine Science of the Gulf and Caribbean*, **12**, 39–60.

Stoddart, D. R. (1962). Catastrophic storm effects on the British Honduras reefs and cays. *Nature*, **196**, 512–14.
Swanson, F. J. and Sparks, R. E. (1990). Long-term ecological research and the invisible place. *BioScience*, **40**, 502–8.
The Nature Conservancy (2004). *The* Diadema *Workshop Report*. Miami, FL: Nature Conservancy.
Tunnicliffe, V. (1981). Breakage and propagation of the stony coral *Acropora cervicornis*. *Proceedings of the National Academy of Sciences, USA*, **78**, 2427–31.
Van Trek, P. and Shuhmacher, H. (1997). Initial survival of coral nubbins by new transplantation technology: options for reef rehabilitation. *Marine Ecology Progress Series*, **150**, 287–92.
(1999). Artificial reefs created by electrolysis and coral transplantation: an approach ensuring the compatibility of environmental protection and diving tourism. *East Coast Shelf Science*, **49**, 75–81.
Vaughan, T. W. (1916). Growth rate of the Florida and Bahamian shoal-water corals. *Carnegie Institute, Washington, Year Book*, **14**, 221–31.
Wallace, C. (1985). Reproduction, recruitment and fragmentation in nine sympatric species of the coral genus *Acropora*. *Marine Biology*, **88**, 217–33.
Wheaton, J. L. and Jaap, W. C. (1988). *Corals and Other Prominent Cnidaria of Looe Key National Marine Sanctuary, Florida*. St Petersburg, FL: Florida Marine Research Publications.
Wheeler, A. J., de Haas, H., Huvenne, V. A. I., Onteys, F. X. and Theiede, J. (2003). Hydrodynamic and anthropogenic influences on deep-water corals on the Porcupine Bank, Irish margin: recent ROV results from ARK-XIX/3a. *Proceedings 2nd International Symposium on Deep-Sea Corals* (abstract), 87.
Wilkinson, C. (ed.) (2004). *Status of Coral Reefs of the World: 2004*, vols. 1 and 2. Townsville, QLD: Australian Institute of Marine Science.
Woodley, J. D., Chornesky, E., Clifford, P. *et al.* (1981). Hurricane Allen's impact on Jamaican coral reefs. *Science*, **213**, 749–55.

17

Redesigning coral reef conservation

CALLUM M. ROBERTS
University of York

JOHN D. REYNOLDS
Simon Fraser University

ISABELLE M. CÔTÉ
Simon Fraser University

JULIE P. HAWKINS
University of York

INTRODUCTION

Coral reefs are the most diverse shallow water marine ecosystem but in many parts of the world they are becoming degraded rapidly by a combination of human stresses and climate change (Birkeland, 1997; Wilkinson, this volume). Recent analyses suggest that at least 58% of corals reefs worldwide are directly threatened by human activities (Bryant *et al.*, 1998). Major stressors impacting reef habitats include sediment and nutrient pollution from coastal development, land clearing and agriculture, over-fishing, pest and disease outbreaks, and global warming (Polunin and Roberts, 1996; Birkeland, 1997; Hoegh-Guldberg, 1999).

An estimated 20% of reefs have already been destroyed (Wilkinson, this volume), while less than a half of the 16% of reefs seriously damaged by global warming-induced increases in sea-surface temperatures in 1998 have recovered (Wilkinson, 2000). Where reefs are exposed to multiple stresses recovery could be slow or may not occur (Connell, 1997). In the Caribbean, Gardner *et al.* (2003) have shown a region-wide decline in coral cover from 50% to 10% between 1977 and 2001. Spalding and Grenfell (1997) estimated that there are 20 000 km^2 of reefs in the Caribbean,

Coral Reef Conservation, ed. Isabelle M. Côté and John D. Reynolds.
Published by Cambridge University Press.

implying a loss of 8000 km^2 of coral in 24 years, or 333 km^2 of coral per year. Analyses of fossil records from the Caribbean suggest that recent reef degradation has been unprecedented over the last 100 000 years (Jackson *et al.*, 2001; Wapnick *et al.*, 2004; Precht and Aronson, this volume).

Degraded coral reefs are characterized by reduction in hard coral cover, declining structural complexity, increasing filamentous and fleshy algal cover, failing calcification, declining biomass and diversity of macrofauna, and increasing microbial biomass. Such changes are of great concern, not least because they imply substantial economic losses. Healthy reefs are self-repairing breakwaters that provide vital coastal protection services (Sheppard, this volume). These services have been estimated to be worth at least US$30 billion worldwide annually (Cesar *et al.*, 2003). The very existence of countries such as the Maldives and Tuvalu depends on reefs being healthy enough to keep pace with rising sea levels.

Loss of structural complexity will reduce carrying capacity of the reef for fish and other commercially important organisms (Roberts, 1996; Almany, 2004). This loss of production could cause great hardship for the growing human populations in developing countries who depend on reef fisheries for protein and income. Income from reef tourism represents an important earner, especially for developing countries, and is also intimately connected with attributes associated with healthy reefs. Tourists consistently rate high coral cover, structural complexity, fish biomass and abundance of large fish as factors that attract them to reefs (Rudd and Tupper, 2002). By contrast, low relief, algae, rubble and sediment-dominated reefs with low fish biomass and poor underwater visibility are least attractive (Williams and Polunin, 2000; Barker and Roberts, 2004).

Loss of biodiversity also implies substantial loss of option values from reefs. For example, many reef species are currently under investigation for pharmaceutically active or other commercially valuable compounds (Vincent, this volume). Cone snails represent one of the most promising groups for their rich diversity of neurotoxins. Compounds from these snails are already showing promise as treatments for cancer and as painkillers (Chivian *et al.*, 2003). Rapid and widespread degradation and loss of coral reefs thus represent a crisis not only for today's generations but also for those to come. The challenge is to find ways to protect and recover reefs before their rich diversity and plethora of values are irrevocably lost.

OBJECTIVES OF A CORAL REEF CONSERVATION AGENDA

A conservation agenda for coral reefs has two interdependent goals: (1) to maintain or rebuild the biological and structural integrity of reefs, and (2) to secure the sustained delivery of ecosystem services important to people. The second goal cannot be achieved without attaining the first. If we want reefs to continue to be of value to humanity, then conservation is a necessity, not a luxury.

Given the global scale of impacts like climate change, there are now no reefs that can be considered unaffected by human activity. Some remote and uninhabited regions, like the northwest Hawaiian Islands, still retain many characteristics of pristine reefs such as significant hard coral cover and fish biomass dominated by large, predatory animals (Friedlander and DeMartini, 2002). But such reefs are a rarity today (Pandolfi *et al.*, 2003). In most cases, management must interrupt and reverse ongoing processes of degradation. This must be achieved against background stresses of human population growth and global warming that will continue to build until at least the middle to late twenty-first century, regardless of what efforts we make today to ameliorate these pressures (Hughes *et al.*, 2003; Hoegh-Guldberg, 2004). While reefs are struggling to cope now, they must survive worse to come. Any management strategies we devise have to deal with this reality.

SCALING UP FROM LOCAL TO REGIONAL MANAGEMENT

In view of escalating pressures, most scientists now accept that it is unrealistic to expect to sustain or recover reefs to their pristine state. But this does not mean that we should abandon goals of maintaining biological or structural integrity. Keeping reefs alive and in working order is critical to the livelihoods of millions of people. What we need are management measures that will (1) maintain reef growth and structural complexity of habitats, (2) maintain or rebuild fish stocks and sustain fishery yields, (3) prevent, reverse or minimize local losses of species and (4) ensure that no species are driven to extinction globally. To meet these objectives, we will need to maintain local and regional sources of replenishment for reef species and prevent loss of key groups of organisms on which the functional integrity of reefs depends (Bellwood *et al.*, 2003, 2004). Preventing global extinctions will also require the creation of secure refuges at least somewhere within the geographic ranges of all species. This may seem an unrealistic proposition given the enormous species diversity harboured by reefs; however, the majority of reef organisms are characterized by large distributional ranges (Hawkins *et al.*, 2000), and hence each refuge can protect a large number of species. Furthermore, restricted-range species are concentrated into centres of endemism (Roberts *et al.*, 2002).

Local-scale management tools have been tested extensively over the last few decades and we are beginning to find winning formulae for reef protection and restoration. For example, marine reserves that are off-limits to all extractive and destructive uses have proven highly successful in rebuilding stocks of overexploited species and initiating recovery from destructive fishing practices (Roberts, 1998b; Mosqueira *et al.*, 2000; Gell and Roberts, 2003; Russ and Alcala, 2003). Many methods of rehabilitating damaged reefs have been tried in different habitats and at different scales with varying degrees of success (e.g. Clark and Edwards, 1999; Fox, 2004; Fox *et al.*, 2005; Jaap *et al.*, this volume). The linkage between watershed condition and impacts on downstream reefs has been well established (e.g. Wolanski *et al.*, 2003). Although rarely straightforward to implement, measures to reduce nutrient and sediment loads in runoff will pay local dividends in reduced stress to reefs (McCulloch *et al.*, 2003; McLaughlin *et al.*, 2003; Wolanski *et al.*, 2004), and may also improve resistance to other impacts such as diseases (Bruno *et al.*, 2003).

On their own, local management initiatives are insufficient. Many impacts on reefs operate across far larger scales than those amenable to local management action. Recent sea-water warming and coral bleaching events have spanned oceans (Sheppard, 2003), invasive species and diseases can rapidly engulf entire regions such as the Caribbean (Harvell *et al.*, 2004), and pollution can spread hundreds or thousands of kilometres from sources. These large-scale impacts can overwhelm local efforts to protect reefs. One reason for the failure of many management initiatives to reverse or even arrest reef decline, particularly with respect to corals (Birkeland, 2004), is that they are too few in number, too small and too isolated to combat stresses that operate across large scales. There is a huge schism between need for management action and the scale at which it is occurring. To tackle these stresses, we need to greatly enlarge the spatial extent of management and scale up the magnitude of our present efforts. The remainder of this chapter will explore how we can develop the regional dimension of a reef conservation agenda.

DEVELOPING REGIONAL NETWORKS OF MARINE RESERVES

Intensive reef degradation over large regions, like that seen in the Caribbean (Gardner *et al.*, 2003), causes regional decline of sources of replenishment for reef organisms. Reduced production of eggs and larvae undermines resilience, impairing recovery from impacts that cause mass mortality, such as storms or disease epidemics. Patterns of reef decline seen in recent decades fit a ratchet model in which impacts cause a succession of coral losses without significant recovery in between (Birkeland, 2004). Sources of replenishment need to be secured or rebuilt as a priority, and the ecological processes that allow corals to successfully recruit and survive need to be restored. Sources of replenishment need to be connected throughout regions via the linking effects of ocean currents and larval dispersal. A regional conservation strategy for reefs cannot be considered a success unless it also prevents species loss. These objectives can be met, in part, by developing networks of marine reserves.

Intensive fishing on coral reefs can reduce population sizes of exploited animals by 90% or more, and some of the most vulnerable species have been extirpated from large areas of their ranges (Reynolds *et al.*, 2002; Dulvy *et al.*, 2003; Hawkins and Roberts, 2004a, 2004b). Bellwood *et al.* (2003) argue that the loss of certain key functional groups of reef animals can render reefs incapable of recovery from impacts. In particular, they argue that loss of scraping and excavating parrotfishes removes an agent of 'reef conditioning' necessary for successful coral recruitment. Fishing is not the only route by which such species are lost. Epidemic disease caused massive decline in reef-building *Acropora* corals throughout the Caribbean in the 1980s (Precht and Aronson, this volume), to the extent that these coral species are now candidates for the US Endangered Species List (Precht *et al.*, 2004), and new disease outbreaks affect remaining reef-builders in this region such as *Montastrea* species (Nugues, 2002). While controlling disease may be difficult, reversing most of the effects of over-fishing is relatively straightforward (Gell and Roberts, 2003a), and rebuilding populations of scraping and excavating parrotfish could pave the way for recovery of corals (Bellwood *et al.*, 2003).

Marine reserves have proven highly effective in rebuilding stocks of exploited organisms (Mosqueira *et al.*, 2000; Halpern and Warner, 2002; Gell and Roberts, 2003b). Experience throughout the tropics suggests that reserves can increase population sizes of many species by several times within a few years of protection. For example, Russ and Alcala (2003) have documented a 17-fold increase in biomass of large predatory fish over 18 years of protection in the Apo Island marine reserve in the Philippines (see Alcala *et al.*, this volume). A network of marine reserves in St Lucia increased biomass of parrotfish by five times over a seven-year period (Hawkins and Roberts, 2004b). A meta-analysis of a large number of studies of marine protected areas (MPAs) around the world found that the abundance of fish species inside reserves is on average 3.7 times higher than outside reserves (Mosqueira *et al.*, 2000). Reproductive output of protected populations grows by larger multiples than densities due to increase in body size and egg production by protected animals. Hence marine reserves can rebuild local sources of replenishment, promoting recovery of reefs within and potentially around them.

However, marine reserves are typically small and isolated, limiting their role in promoting local and regional regeneration. Large-scale impacts such as coral bleaching and disease epidemics seriously compromise the ability of local protection to offset degradation or foster recovery (Jones *et al.*, 2004; Munday, 2004). To build regional resilience will require us to embark on a programme of marine reserve creation that is unprecedented in its ambition. Theoretical work suggests that coverage of marine reserves should be expanded to around 30% of the sea in order to maximize benefits to fisheries, ensure adequate representation of the full spectrum of habitats and species, and attain sufficient replication of them across different reserves (Gell and Roberts, 2003b; World Parks Congress, 2003). At these scales, reserves will function more effectively as sources for replenishment and recovery, exporting much larger numbers of offspring of reef organisms. If reserves are distributed throughout a region, local sources will sum to furnish regional benefits.

Building regional connectivity and resilience in reserve networks

Connectivity is the linkage of populations in space through processes of dispersal of eggs, larvae or other propagules, and movement of juvenile and adult organisms. Water currents that move organisms from place to place facilitate these connections but do not necessarily determine them. Today's large-scale depletion and removal of populations is breaking these connections. The effects of habitat fragmentation are well known in terrestrial systems, leading to progressive loss of species from isolated habitat 'islands' (Turner, 1996; Lens *et al.*, 2002) and possible breakdown in food-web structure and loss of ecosystem functionality (Terborgh *et al.*, 2001). Long-distance dispersal of reef species may keep connections among reefs open for longer than would be the case with less mobile terrestrial species. However, as the magnitude of larval production falls these links become ever more tenuous, and the possibility of rescue of declining populations through immigration decreases. Rebuilding connectivity of reefs at regional scales is an urgent priority if we are to interrupt processes of local species loss that are already well under way (Sadovy *et al.*, 2003; Hawkins and Roberts, 2004a, 2004b).

Where should reserves be located to promote connectivity and provide reef resilience at a regional scale? Reserves need to secure connectivity of populations among protected areas and between protected areas and surrounding reefs. In some cases, for example scallops on Georges Bank off the New England coast, the dispersal of eggs appears to map closely onto ocean current patterns (Gell and Roberts, 2003b). This suggests that currents can be a primary force determining patterns and scales of connectivity in the sea. Hence, currents might seem an obvious way of identifying linkages among populations in order to guide the placement of marine reserves. Roberts (1997), for example, used surface current patterns to explore possible dispersal routes and connectivity patterns in the Caribbean. However, several lines of evidence indicate that current patterns alone are an unreliable guide to connectivity.

Animals do not always (perhaps rarely) drift passively. Late-stage larvae of many reef fish appear to have strong swimming abilities, allowing them to swim against currents if necessary (Stobutzki, 1998). They may use these abilities, in combination with behaviours that promote local retention, to remain near natal reefs and recruit back to them (Lunow, 1999; Swearer *et al.*, 1999). Fish larvae may use sound cues to orientate towards coral reefs for settlement (Tolimieri *et al.*, 2000). There are also perplexing genetic breaks among populations over relatively short distances that have no apparent link to surface currents (at least to modern current patterns) (e.g. Lourie and Vincent, 2004; Rivera *et al.*, 2004). They suggest that other forces affect connectivity.

When the vectors driving connectivity are unknown, and these drivers probably vary widely among organisms, it is not possible to map connectivity patterns and use them to guide marine reserve placement at regional scales (Roberts, 2000). In any case, climate change could alter present patterns of connectivity, rendering reserve networks designed for today's conditions ineffective in future. Faced with similar levels of uncertainty, investors use risk-spreading and bet-hedging to create portfolios that should perform well regardless of how individual investments perform. We need to adopt a similar approach in conservation planning (Roberts *et al.*, 2001).

Creating only a few marine reserves – i.e. the situation that prevails today – is highly risky because each carries a high level of responsibility for success or failure. Furthermore, few and widespread reserves are unlikely to have significant levels of connectivity. Recent evidence from genetics, oceanography, biogeography and modelling suggest that scales of connectivity will typically vary from a few up to a few hundred kilometres through dispersal of eggs and larvae (Lockwood *et al.*, 2002; Gaines *et al.*, 2003; Grantham *et al.*, 2003; Ayre and Hughes, 2004). For both reasons, effective reserve networks will need to contain many reserves spaced from a few to a few tens of kilometres apart and covering a substantial fraction of the habitat present. Based on a growing body of evidence (reviewed in Gell and Roberts, 2003a, 2003b), the World Parks Congress in 2003 recommended that at least 20–30% of every habitat in the sea should be strictly protected (i.e. should be protected from all extractive uses and harmful levels of other uses) (World Parks Congress, 2003). Scaling up protection in this way would have immediate benefits for connectivity.

If reserves are to be successful for fishery management they must link with exploited populations outside their boundaries. If they are to be effective as conservation tools, then populations of species that are sensitive to human impacts must interconnect among different reserves. Roberts (1998a) has argued that there are connectivity grounds for wanting a substantial proportion of any management area to consist of no-take reserves, stating that 'the likelihood of reserves interacting effectively will fall steeply as the percentage of sea area protected falls. Given our uncertainties about pathways of interaction we must adopt a precautionary approach and aim for a significant percentage of the sea designated as no-take'. Here, we explore the connectivity effects of increasing the proportion of the sea that is protected.

Imagine a square management area in which square reserves are established. The management area covers 1 million km^2, with an edge of 1000 km. Reserves are created evenly across the whole area, protecting 5% or more of the total management area, and five different reserve sizes: 100 km^2, 1000 km^2, 10 000 km^2, 50 000 km^2 and 100 000 km^2. Figure 17.1 shows connectivity expressed as the distance between adjacent reserves. For the sake of simplicity, we assumed a linear relationship between connectivity and inter-reserve distance. In reality, this relationship may be negatively exponential, which will amplify the results shown in Fig. 17.1. Connectivity increases, i.e. the distance between reserves falls, as the proportion of the management area protected rises. The loss of connectivity with falling proportion of the management area protected can be compensated for, to some extent, by reducing the size but increasing the number of reserve units. For any given percentage of the management area protected, the smaller reserves are, the shorter distances will be between them. The largest gains in connectivity are made over the lower part of the range of percentages of the management area protected. For example, when increasing the proportion of protected area from 5% to 10%, there is a decrease in inter-reserve distance of 38%. By contrast, when total area protected increases from 30% to 35%, inter-reserve distance declines by only 10%.

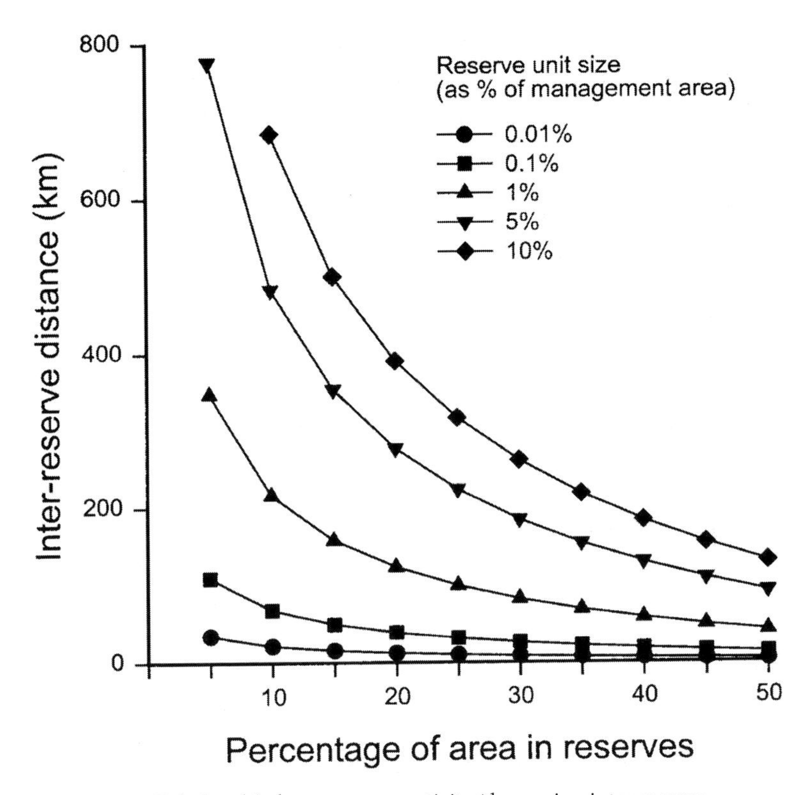

Figure 17.1 Relationship between connectivity (decreasing inter-reserve distance) and proportion of the management area protected for five different reserve sizes. In all cases, connectivity increases as a greater proportion of area is protected. In this simulation model square reserves were established evenly across a square management area covering 1 million km². Reserve unit sizes were 100 km² (0.01% of management area), 1000 km² (0.1%), 10 000 km² (1%), 50 000 km² (5%) and 100 000 km² (10%).

It should be remembered that small reserves make smaller targets for dispersing propagules. Figure 17.2 shows the 'target size' of reserves expressed as the number of angular degrees of horizon made up by reserves, for any given proportion of the management area protected. The fraction of the horizon made up of reserves, a proxy for connectivity, increases steeply as the proportion of the management area that is protected grows. The total target size of protected areas is four times greater when 30% of the area is protected compared to when only 5% is protected. However, expressed in this currency, gains in connectivity made by reducing reserve size, and so allowing closer spacing of reserves, are cancelled out by the reduced target

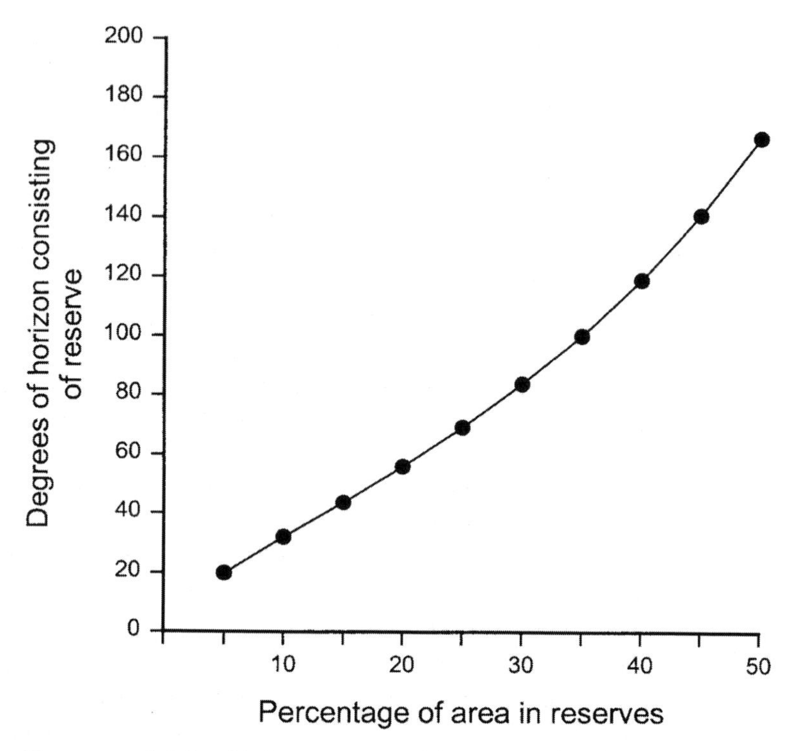

Figure 17.2 Relationship between connectivity, expressed as the number of angular degrees of horizon made up of marine reserves, a measure of 'target size' for dispersing propagules, and proportion of the management area protected. In this case, as more area is protected, reserves form increasingly large targets for dispersing larvae and propagules. In this simulation model, the target size of an individual reserve was taken as half of the sum of the length of the diagonal and length of a side of the square. The number of degrees of horizon covered by reserves does not differ with reserve unit size for any given proportion of the management area protected.

size of a small reserve. For any given proportion of the management area protected, there is no difference in target size presented by reserves of different sizes; that is, many small reserves together offer the same target to dispersing larvae as a single large reserve. Despite this invariance of target size with reserve unit size, many marine species disperse over short distances (Grantham *et al.*, 2003; Shanks *et al.*, 2003) and so the most appropriate measure of connectivity will be inter-reserve distance. Consequently we should not dismiss the idea of dividing up the total area protected into smaller reserve units to achieve connectivity gains. Quinn *et al.* (1993) examined the effects of reserve size and distribution on population densities of red sea urchin *Strongylocentrotus franciscanus*, a relatively short-distance disperser. They calculated that smaller, more closely spaced reserves would maintain higher population densities and catches than larger, more widely spaced reserves.

Our model is an oversimplification in that reserves are not spaced evenly in reality, nor are their shapes so regular. A random spacing of reserves would produce the same results on average, with some variance about the mean. However, reserves are not spaced randomly either, since in practice they depend on the distribution of habitat. Hence connectivity will be a function not only of the distribution of reserves and their sizes, but also the distribution of the habitat type protected. Nevertheless, the model helps to visualize some of the implications for connectivity of size, spacing and the fraction of the area protected.

Figure 17.3 shows for three reserve scenarios how connectivity builds as the number of reserves and their coverage rise. In this model, reserves are considered to be linked, i.e. animals or plants dispersing from them are able to reach an adjacent reserve, when they are within 25 km of each other. When there are very few reserves, the network is highly fragmented, and only local clusters of reserves are interconnected. As coverage grows, fragmentation decreases until, with a network of 30% reserve coverage, reserves are linked to many others either directly or through a series of stepping-stone recruitment events.

As we noted above, declining populations become fragmented in space partly because production of dispersive offspring falls. This problem can be offset by marine reserves. As populations of exploited species rebuild inside reserves so also will the absolute flows of propagules among reserves. If egg output from protected populations rises tenfold, a conservative estimate for many species given the scaling of body size and numbers (Gell and Roberts, 2003b), then the absolute flows of eggs and larvae should also increase tenfold. A reserve that received 100 recruits per year from another reserve should receive 1000 per year. The security of connections will increase with time since onset of protection, up to maxima that will be achieved after different periods for different species. For long-lived species like large groupers, connectivity benefits could continue to grow for decades.

Regional refugia

Marine reserve networks distributed throughout reef tracts should contain regional reef refugia. Regional refugia are areas that protect reefs capable

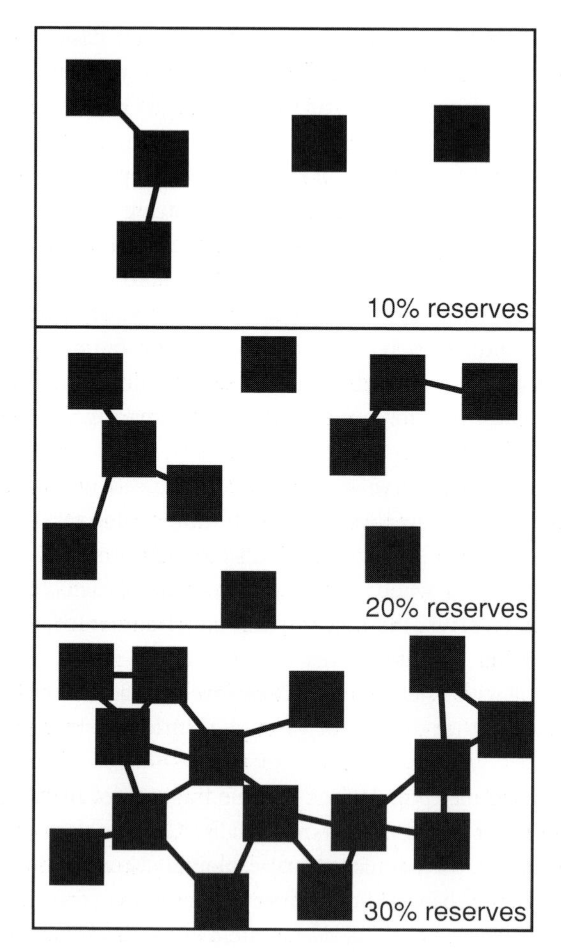

Figure 17.3 The effect of increasing marine reserve coverage on connectivity. Each reserve (black squares) covers 2% of the management area. Links show reserves that are ≤25 km apart, indicating connections among reserves for a species with a 25-km dispersal range. With 10% coverage (top panel) the network is highly fragmented. Connectivity increases rapidly with coverage until, in a network of reserves covering 30% of the management area (bottom panel), all reserves are linked.

of supplying regional benefits either now or in the future. Gardner *et al.* (2003), for example, argued for urgent protection of remaining regions of high coral cover in the Caribbean in the face of regional reef decline. Securing large coral populations in these areas would help maintain sources for replenishment to promote recovery.

There is a second reason to protect remaining areas that still have relatively intact populations of reef organisms. In the Pleistocene, regional refugia permitted the persistence of species unable to survive elsewhere in ice-bound temperate regions. In Europe, for example, many freshwater fish survived in the ice-free Danube Basin and were able to repopulate other regions during the milder Holocene (Hewitt, 1999). Reef degradation is causing the progressive loss of species that depend on corals and the structures they create (e.g. Jones *et al.*, 2004). If we are unable to arrest degradation quickly enough, then some species could become extinct and with them options for future recovery will disappear. Non-coral-dependent organisms are also affected by reef degradation and over-fishing. Protection in scattered and relatively small reserves may be insufficient to allow them to persist, even if the total coverage of such reserves is extensive. They include species that require several different habitats throughout life, such as the Caribbean rainbow parrotfish *Scarus guacamaia*. This species requires mangroves in its early life and reefs as adults (Mumby *et al.*, 2004). We also need to protect species that are highly vulnerable to removal by even relatively low levels of fishing effort, due to life histories that make these populations unable to replace lost individuals quickly enough (Reynolds *et al.*, 2001), and whose wide-ranging movements mean that only very large marine reserves can afford them secure refuge from fishing.

The same argument for creating regional refugia has been made in relation to coral bleaching. West and Salm (2003) argued that reefs in areas either resistant or resilient to coral bleaching mortality should be identified and protected. Features conferring some protection against bleaching include proximity to deep, cooler waters, strong currents, and shading by mountains. As the frequency and intensity of coral bleaching episodes rises, as models of global warming predict (e.g. Sheppard, 2003), many corals will find it increasingly difficult to survive. Protecting the few places where they can persist, or even thrive, could be critical to seeing species through the transition to a warmer world.

There is one important exception to the general difficulty of identifying source points for population replenishment at regional scales. Many species of grouper, snapper, wrasse, surgeonfish and other species gather at widely separated spawning aggregation sites (Sadovy, 1993). Historically, these have attracted thousands or tens of thousands of fish that travel tens or even a hundred or more kilometres to reach them. In recent years, many have been all but eliminated by targeted fishing on aggregations (Vincent and Sadovy, 1998). There is an urgent need to protect all spawning aggregations, including historic spawning sites, in the hope that they can eventually recover. Spawning aggregation sites represent a regional asset whose benefits often extend beyond national boundaries. They are an important component of any regional marine reserve network.

Regional refugia thus form an essential component of regional marine reserve networks and complement other protected areas and management distributed throughout regions. Although some protected areas could fulfil several of the regional roles described above, a region may need to protect several different areas to achieve all of these aims.

Different regions, different solutions

Every region presents different challenges for coral reef conservation. Cultural and political differences mean that what works in one region may not in another. For example, in some parts of the Pacific, there is still traditional tenure over marine resources and the authority of local village chiefs is respected. By contrast, in the Caribbean, village-level control over resources is unusual. But there are also important environmental differences among regions that set the context for and may constrain options for regional management.

Some regions are better endowed with reefs than others. Small and highly isolated reefs, such as Clipperton atoll in the eastern Pacific, or Rodrigues in the Indian Ocean, must depend almost entirely on self-replenishment to survive (Fig. 17.4). Such places represent regions unto themselves and local and regional conservation strategies amount to the same thing. By contrast, dense, archipelagic regions like the Philippines, Indonesia and the Great Barrier Reef support tens of thousands of square kilometres of reef habitat. Other things being equal, sources for replenishment in these regions will be much greater, especially taking into account the possibility of stepping-stone dispersal from reef to reef (Ayre and Hughes, 2004). Reefs should depend less on local sources of reproduction in such regions and so should be more resilient to local impacts.

Figure 17.4 suggests that resilience should increase with regional reef area and density. Intrinsic connectivity of reef regions will interact with extrinsic factors such as intensity of human use and success of management in controlling impacts. In combination they influence the scale of marine reserve areas needed to maintain adequate levels of recruitment. Reefs will need larger local sources of recruitment if they are isolated, so a larger fraction of marine reserve area is called for. Reefs will also need a larger area of reserves where intensity of use is high or management control outside reserves is limited. In such places, reefs will depend more on recruits derived from reserves for replenishment.

A similar effect of reef area and distribution also applies at the scale of individual reefs. Available external sources of recruitment to reefs within

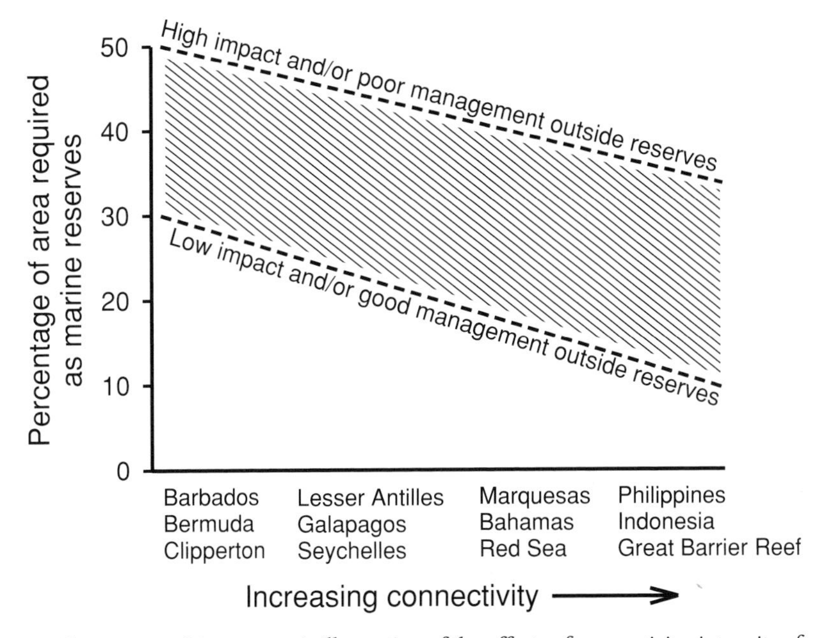

Figure 17.4 Diagrammatic illustration of the effects of connectivity, intensity of human use and management effectiveness on the proportion of reef area required as marine reserves. Areas with few and sparsely distributed reefs, such as Bermuda, are almost entirely reliant on self-replenishment to survive and will require relatively large areas of protected reefs. By contrast, reefs in dense archipelagic settings, like the Great Barrier Reef, may be supplied with recruits from many other reefs and will require a smaller proportion of reefs to be protected. Resilience should therefore increase with regional reef area and density. This intrinsic characteristic of reef regions interacts with intensity of human use and success of management in controlling impacts to influence the scale of marine reserve areas needed to maintain adequate levels of recruitment.

a region will vary depending on the proximity of that reef to others and to the area of those reefs. As noted earlier, current patterns do not necessarily determine connections among reefs. However, currents clearly do influence dispersal patterns (e.g. Limouzy Paris *et al.*, 1997; Domeier, 2004) and area of upstream reefs may be an indicator of likely sources and magnitude of external recruitment to a reef. Based on this simplifying assumption, Fig. 17.5 shows upstream reef area for 18 Caribbean sites (Roberts, 1997). Area was calculated based on maps of current strength and direction to identify the reefs from which a larva settling at a given site could have originated, assuming one and two months of passive dispersal. Upstream area differed by an order of magnitude, suggesting that connectivity is a property that varies considerably within regions. Designs for marine reserve networks

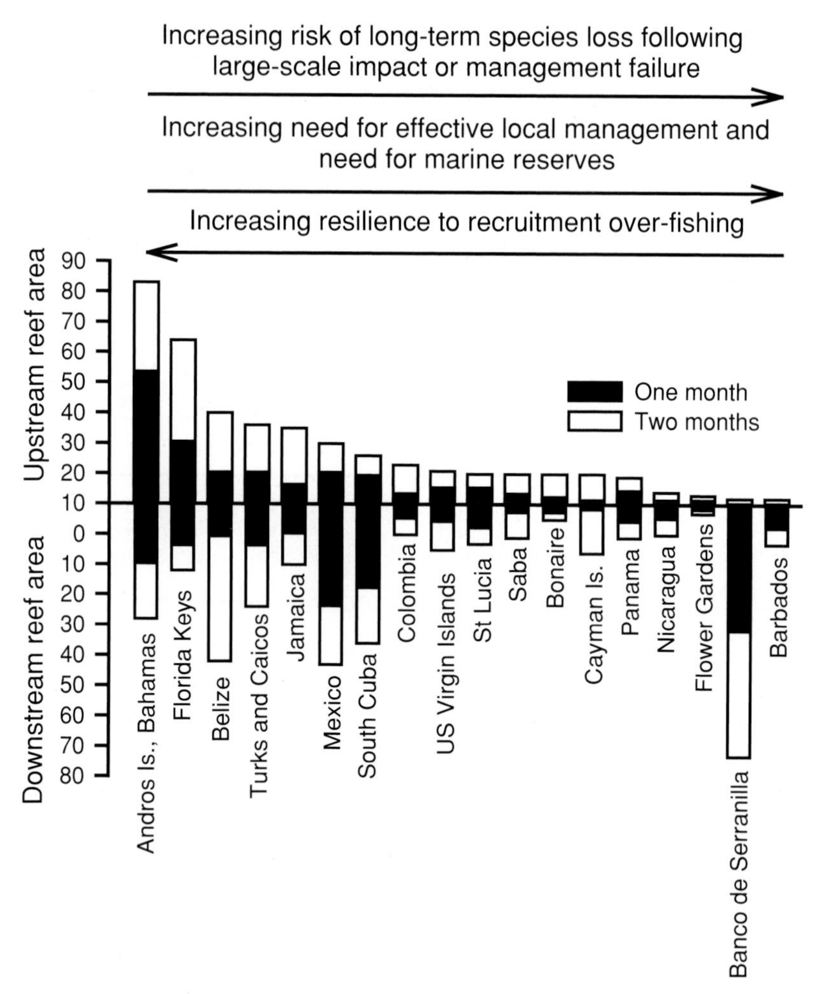

Figure 17.5 Area of reef (measured as the number of 0.5° × 0.5° cells with reefs) upstream and downstream of 18 reef sites in the Caribbean, based on direction and strength of current flows. The areas are greater for organisms with a two-month larval dispersal period than for shorter (one-month) periods. (Redrawn from Roberts, 1997.)

will need to accommodate this variation by increasing density and area of reserves in places with low connectivity.

Figure 17.5 also shows area of reef downstream of the 18 Caribbean sites. Like upstream area, this also varies by an order of magnitude, suggesting that some reefs could be much better sources of recruitment to distant reefs than others. Calculations such as this may help in identifying regional refugia that could act as sources for replenishment of large areas. Domeier (2004), for example, tracked the fate of buoyant drifter vials released over Riley's Hump, a protected spawning aggregation site for snappers that lies at the western end of the Florida reef tract. The distribution of recoveries suggests that currents from Riley's Hump could carry larvae to large areas of downstream reef in the Florida Keys.

In places that experience significant environmental fluctuations with resultant episodic mass mortalities of marine life, like the Galápagos Islands for example (Perry, 1984), exploitation or human-caused habitat degradation could make the difference between species disappearing or being able to persist despite the poor conditions. Under these circumstances more extensive marine reserves are warranted than in places with more stable conditions, i.e. 50% coverage for example rather than 30%. This will reduce the risk that species will be extirpated or will go extinct and should allow more rapid recovery of populations, including commercially important species, once conditions return to normal.

Developing regional conservation plans

With the recent exception of the Great Barrier Reef Marine Park, marine reserve creation has never been attempted on the large scale we advocate, nor has reserve placement been strategically guided across regions. The Great Barrier Reef Marine Park, covering 348 700 km^2 of sea, represents one end of the spectrum of regional management. It is a region unto itself, encompassing a complex archipelago of interconnected reefs that are a centre of endemism for reef species (Roberts *et al.*, 2002). Although large, management is tractable and simple since the reef falls within a single country. It is perhaps not surprising then that Australia is the first country to establish a representative, replicated network of marine reserves covering 33% of the area of marine habitats over such a large region. In most parts of the world, strategic planning for reef protection is less well developed, even at local scales.

Marine reserves have often been established in places where reefs have been regarded as exceptional in some way, or where local communities expressed a willingness to implement protection (Watson, 1999; Roberts, 2000). In the Philippines, for example, a national network of hundreds of marine reserves has been developing from a multitude of local village initiatives. Most Philippine reserves are extremely small, and the majority are not yet effectively managed (Wilkinson, 2004; but see Alcala *et al.*, this volume). Organic growth of reserve networks cannot be relied on to secure the future of reefs, either within nations or across regions. Strategic oversight is needed to coordinate and link local efforts, although we should emphasise that this is not the same thing as top–down imposition of management.

We suggest that planning regions be identified for every coral reef in the world, based on biogeographic, physical, oceanographic and ecological features. Regions would consist of areas where movement of water bodies and dispersal of organisms interconnect reefs. Between regions, such links would be much less well developed. As we explained above, scales of connectivity will also vary within regions and more isolated areas will be more dependent on local management. In places where reefs are very isolated, such as Easter Island, local and regional conservation plans will be the same. In other places, like the Hawaiian Islands, regional strategies can be pursued by a single nation. In most places though, the regional strategy will require collaboration among more than one nation, sometimes many (Roberts, 1997).

A key question remains: who should pay for coral reef protection? Protecting large-scale tracts of reef that still remain in a relatively intact condition may be beyond the means of the countries within whose waters they lie. The worldwide costs of maintaining a network of marine protected areas covering 20–30% of the sea has been estimated to be between US$5 billion and US$19 billion annually (Balmford *et al.*, 2004). These large sums are in fact less than the amount spent by world governments on harmful subsidies to industrial fishing (US$15–30 billion per year: Milazzo, 1998; Virdin and Schorr, 2001). The creation of a global reserves network would generate around 1 million full-time jobs directly linked to MPA protection (Balmford *et al.*, 2004) and substantial other economic benefits as a result of improved fisheries and ecosystem services (Costanza *et al.*, 1997). Since the MPA network is intended to provide regional and global benefits, it is appropriate for it to be financed largely by the international community. A similar approach is already being applied for terrestrial biomes through funds targeted at protecting biodiversity hotspots (e.g. the Critical Ecosystem Partnership Fund, 2005).

CONCLUSIONS

Our emphasis in this chapter has been on the development of regional-scale marine reserve networks that would protect nearly one-third of all coral reefs from extractive and destructive uses. A priority for regional planning is to identify regional refugia and spawning aggregation sites for inclusion in marine reserves. Clearly, this is only one element of a coral reef conservation agenda. We have concentrated on reserves because we believe that they are one of the most successful means we have of maintaining reef resilience in the face of global change and human population growth. But reserves need to be embedded within a framework of coastal management that includes comprehensive zoning of all marine activities, control of coastal development, and watershed management to limit input of pollutants. In essence, all of the sea needs to be planned like the largest marine parks, although even the best marine parks have to date had little success in controlling land-based activities.

ACKNOWLEDGEMENTS
Callum Roberts is grateful to The Pew Charitable Trusts for supporting this work.

REFERENCES

Almany, G. R. (2004). Differential effects of habitat complexity, predators and competitors on abundance of juvenile and adult coral reef fishes. *Oecologia*, **141**, 105–13.

Ayre, D. J. and Hughes, T. P. (2004). Climate change, genotypic diversity and gene flow in reef-building corals. *Ecology Letters*, **7**, 273–8.

Balmford, A., Gravestock, P., Hockley, N., McClean, C. J. and Roberts, C. M. (2004). The worldwide costs of marine protected areas. *Proceedings of the National Academy of Sciences USA*, **101**, 9694–7.

Barker, N. and Roberts, C. M. (2004). Scuba diver behaviour and the management of diving impacts on coral reefs. *Biological Conservation*, **120**, 481–9.

Bellwood, D. R., Hoey, A. S. and Choat, J. H. (2003). Limited functional redundancy in high diversity systems: resilience and ecosystem function on coral reefs. *Ecology Letters*, **6**, 281–5.

Bellwood, D. R., Hughes, T. P., Folke, C. and Nystrom, M. (2004). Confronting the coral reef crisis. *Nature*, **429**, 827–33.

Birkeland, C. (ed.) (1997). *Life and Death of Coral Reefs*. New York: Chapman and Hall.

(2004). Ratcheting down the coral reefs. *BioScience*, **54**, 1021–7.

Bruno, J. F., Petes, L. E., Harvell, C. D. and Hettinger, A. (2003). Nutrient enrichment can increase the severity of coral diseases. *Ecology Letters*, **6**, 1056–61.

Bryant, D., Burke, L., McManus, J. and Spalding, M. (1998). *Reefs at Risk: A Map-Based Indicator of Potential Threats to the World's Coral Reefs*. Washington, DC: World Resources Institute.

Cesar, H., Burke, L. and Pet-Soede, L. (2003). *The Economics of Worldwide Coral Reef Degradation*. Arnhem, Netherlands: Cesar Environmental Economics Consulting.

Chivian, E., Roberts, C. M. and Bernstein, A. (2003). The threat to cone snails. *Science*, **302**, 391.

Clark, S. and Edwards, A. J. (1999). An evaluation of artificial reef structures as tools for marine habitat rehabilitation in the Maldives. *Aquatic Conservation*, **9**, 5–21.

Connell, J. H. (1997). Disturbance and recovery of coral assemblages. *Coral Reefs*, **16** (suppl.), S101–S114.
Costanza, R., d'Arge, R., de Groot, R. *et al.* (1997). The value of the world's ecosystem services and natural capital. *Nature*, **387**, 253–60.
Critical Ecosystem Partnership Fund (2005). Home page. Available online at http://www.cepf.net/xp/cepf/
Domeier, M. L. (2004). A potential larval recruitment pathway originating from a Florida marine protected area. *Fisheries Oceanography*, **13**, 287–94.
Dulvy, N. K., Sadovy, Y. and Reynolds, J. D. (2003). Extinction vulnerability in marine populations. *Fish and Fisheries*, **4**, 25–64.
Fox, H. E. (2004). Coral recruitment in blasted and unblasted sites in Indonesia: assessing rehabilitation. *Marine Ecology Progress Series*, **269**, 131–9.
Fox, H. E., Mous, P. J., Pet, J. S., Muljadi, A. H. and Caldwell, R. I. (2005). Experimental assessment of coral reef rehabilitation following blast fishing. *Conservation Biology*, **19**, 98–107.
Friedlander, A. M. and DeMartini, E. E. (2002). Contrasts in density, size and biomass of reef fishes between the northwestern and the main Hawaiian islands: the effects of fishing down apex predators. *Marine Ecology Progress Series*, **230**, 253–64.
Gaines, S. D., Gaylord, B. and Largier, J. L. (2003). Avoiding current oversights in marine reserve design. *Ecological Applications*, **13**, S47–S46.
Gardner, T. A., Côté, I. M., Gill, J. A., Grant, A. and Watkinson, A. R. (2003). Long-term region-wide declines in Caribbean corals. *Science*, **301**, 958–60.
Gell, F. R. and Roberts, C. M. (2003a). Benefits beyond boundaries: the fishery effects of marine reserves. *Trends in Ecology and Evolution*, **18**, 448–55.
(2003b). *The Fishery Effects of Marine Reserves and Fishery Closures*. Washington, DC: WWF–US. Available online at http://www.worldwildlife.org/oceans/pdfs/fishery_effects.pdf
Grantham, B. A., Eckert, G. L. and Shanks, A. L. (2003). Dispersal potential of marine invertebrates in diverse habitats. *Ecological Applications*, **13**, S108–S116.
Halpern, B. S. and Warner, R. R. (2002). Marine reserves have rapid and lasting effects. *Ecology Letters*, **5**, 361–6.
Harvell, D., Aronson, R., Baron, N. *et al.* (2004). The rising tide of ocean diseases: unsolved problems and research priorities. *Frontiers in Ecology and the Environment*, **2**, 375–82.
Hawkins, J. P. and Roberts, C. M. (2004a). Effects of artisanal fishing on Caribbean coral reefs. *Conservation Biology*, **18**, 215–26.
(2004b). Effects of fishing on sex-changing Caribbean parrotfishes. *Biological Conservation*, **115**, 213–26.
Hawkins, J. P., Roberts, C. M. and Clark, V. (2000). The threatened status of restricted-range coral reef fish species. *Animal Conservation*, **3**, 81–8.
Hewitt, G. M. (1999). Post-glacial re-colonization of European biota. *Biological Journal of the Linnean Society*, **68**, 87–112.
Hoegh-Guldberg, O. (1999). Climate change, coral bleaching and the future of the world's coral reefs. *Marine and Freshwater Research*, **50**, 839–66.
(2004). Coral reefs in a century of rapid environmental change. *Symbiosis*, **37**, 1–31.

Hughes, T. P., Baird, A. H., Bellwood, D. R. *et al.* (2003). Climate change, human impacts and the resilience of coral reefs. *Science*, **301**, 929–33.

Jackson, J. B. C., Kirby, M. X., Berger, W. H. *et al.* (2001). Historical overfishing and the collapse of coastal ecosystems. *Science*, **293**, 629–38.

Jones, G. P., McCormick, M. I., Srinivasan, M. and Eagle, J. V. (2004). Coral decline threatens fish biodiversity in marine reserves. *Proceedings of the National Academy of Sciences, USA*, **101**, 8251–3.

Lens, L., VanDongen, S., Norris, K., Githiru, M. and Matthysen, E. (2002). Avian persistence in fragmented rainforest. *Science*, **298**, 1236–8.

Limouzy Paris, C. B., Graber, H. C., Jones, D. L., Ropke, A. W. and Richards, W. J. (1997). Translocation of larval coral reef fishes via sub-mesoscale spin-off eddies from the Florida current. *Bulletin of Marine Science*, **60**, 966–83.

Lockwood, D. R., Hastings, A. and Botsford, L. W. (2002). The effects of dispersal patterns on marine reserves: does the tail wag the dog? *Theoretical Population Biology*, **61**, 297–309.

Lourie, S. A. and Vincent, A. C. J. (2004). A marine fish follows Wallace's Line: the phylogeography of the three-spot seahorse (*Hippocampus trimaculatus*, Syngnathidae, Teleostei) in southeast Asia. *Journal of Biogeography*, **31**, 1975–85.

Lunow, C. (1999). Self-recruitment in a coral reef fish population. *Nature*, **402**, 802–4.

McCulloch, M., Fallon, S., Wyndham, T. *et al.* (2003). Coral record of increased sediment flux to the inner Great Barrier Reef since European settlement. *Nature*, **421**, 727–30.

McLaughlin, C. J., Smith, C. A., Buddemeier, R. W., Bartley, J. D. and Maxwell, B. A. (2003). Rivers, runoff, and reefs. *Global and Planetary Change*, **39**, 191–9.

Milazzo, M. (1998). *Subsidies in World Fisheries: A Re-Examination*. Washington, DC: World Bank.

Mosqueira, I., Côté, I. M., Jennings, S. and Reynolds, J. D. (2000). Conservation benefits of marine reserves for fish populations. *Animal Conservation*, **3**, 321–32.

Mumby, P. J., Edwards, A. J., Arias Gonzalez, J. E. *et al.* (2004). Mangroves enhance the biomass of coral reef fish communities in the Caribbean. *Nature*, **427**, 533–6.

Munday, P. L. (2004). Habitat loss, resource specialization, and extinction on coral reefs. *Global Change Biology*, **10**, 1642–7.

Nugues, M. M. (2002). Impact of a coral disease outbreak on coral communities in St Lucia: what and how much has been lost? *Marine Ecology Progress Series*, **299**, 61–71.

Pandolfi, J. M., Bradbury, R. H., Sala, E. *et al.* (2003). Global trajectories of the long-term decline of coral reef ecosystems. *Science*, **301**, 955–8.

Perry, R. (ed.) (1984). *Key Environments: Galápagos*. Oxford: Pergamon Press.

Polunin, N. V. C. and Roberts, C. M. (eds). (1996). *Reef Fisheries*. London: Chapman and Hall.

Precht, W. F., Robbart, M. L. and Aronson, R. B. (2004). The potential listing of *Acropora* species under the US Endangered Species Act. *Marine Pollution Bulletin*, **49**, 534–6.

Quinn, J. F., Wing, S. R. and Botsford, L. W. (1993). Harvest refugia in marine invertebrate fisheries: models and applications to the red sea urchin, *Strongylocentrotus franciscanus*. *American Zoologist*, **33**, 537–50.

Reynolds, J. D., Jennings, S. and Dulvy, N. K. (2001). Life histories of fishes and responses to exploitation. In *Conservation of Exploited Species*, eds. J. D. Reynolds, G. M. Mace, K. H. Redford and J. G. Robinson, pp. 148–68. Cambridge: Cambridge University Press.

Reynolds, J. D., Dulvy, N. K. and Roberts, C. M. (2002). Exploitation and other threats to fish conservation. In *Handbook of Fish Biology and Fisheries*, vol. 2, *Fisheries*, eds. P. J. B. Hart and J. D. Reynolds, pp. 319–40. Oxford, UK: Blackwell.

Rivera, M. A. J., Kelley, C. D. and Roderick, G. K. (2004). Subtle population genetic differences in the Hawaiian grouper, *Epinephelus quernus* (Serranidae) as revealed by mitochondrial DNA analyses. *Biological Journal of the Linnean Society*, **81**, 449–68.

Roberts, C. M. (1996). Settlement and beyond: population regulation and community structure. In *Reef Fisheries*, ed. N. V. C. Polunin and C. M. Roberts, pp. 85–112. London: Chapman and Hall.

(1997). Connectivity and management of Caribbean coral reefs. *Science*, **278**, 1454–7.

(1998a). Sources, sinks and the design of marine reserve networks. *Fisheries*, **23**, 16–19.

(1998b). Permanent no-take zones: a minimum standard for effective marine protected areas. In *Coral Reefs: Challenges and Opportunities for Sustainable Management*, pp. 96–100, eds. M. E. Hatziolos, A. J. Hooten and M. Fodor. Washington, DC: World Bank.

(2000). Selecting marine reserve locations: optimality vs. opportunism. *Bulletin of Marine Science*, **66**, 581–92.

Roberts, C. M., Halpern, B., Palumbi, S. R. and Warner, R. R. (2001). Designing networks of marine reserves: why small, isolated protected areas are not enough. *Conservation Biology in Practice*, **2**, 10–17.

Roberts, C. M., McClean, C. J., Veron, J. E. N. *et al.* (2002). Marine biodiversity hotspots and conservation priorities for tropical reefs. *Science*, **295**, 1280–4.

Rudd, M. A. and Tupper, M. H. (2002). The impact of Nassau grouper size and abundance on scuba diver site selection and MPA economics. *Coastal Management*, **30**, 133–51.

Russ, G. R. and Alcala, A. C. (2003). Marine reserves: rates and patterns of recovery and decline of predatory fish, 1983–2000. *Ecological Applications*, **13**, 1553–65.

Sadovy, Y. (1993). The Nassau grouper: endangered or just unlucky? *Reef Encounter*, **13**, 10–12.

Sadovy, Y., Kulbicki, M., Labrosse, P. *et al.* (2003). The humphead wrasse, *Cheilinus undulatus*: synopsis of a threatened and poorly known giant of the coral reef. *Reviews in Fish Biology and Fisheries*, **13**, 327–64.

Shanks, A. L., Grantham, B. A. and Carr, M. H. (2003). Propagule dispersal and the size and spacing of marine reserves. *Ecological Applications*, **13**, S159–S169.

Sheppard, C. R. C. (2003). Predicted recurrences of mass coral mortality in the Indian Ocean. *Nature*, **425**, 294–7.

Spalding, M. D. and Grenfell, A. M. (1997). New estimates of global and regional coral reef areas. *Coral Reefs*, **16**, 225–30.

Stobutzki, I. C. (1998). Interspecific variation in sustained swimming abilility of late pelagic stage reef fish from two families (Pomacentridae and Chaetodontidae). *Coral Reefs*, **17**, 111–19.
Swearer, S. E., Caselle, J. E., Lea, D. W. and Warner, R. R. (1999). Larval retention and recruitment in an island population of a coral-reef fish. *Nature*, **402**, 799–802.
Terborgh, J., Lopez, L., Nunez, P. *et al.* (2001). Ecological meltdown in predator-free forest fragments. *Science*, **294**, 1923–6.
Tolimieri, N., Jeffs, A. and Montgomery, J. C. (2000). Ambient sound as a cue for navigation by the pelagic larvae of reef fishes. *Marine Ecology Progress Series*, **207**, 219–24.
Turner, I. M. (1996). Species loss in fragments of tropical rain forest: a review of the evidence. *Journal of Applied Ecology*, **33**, 200–9.
Vincent, A. C. J. and Sadovy, Y. (1998). Reproductive ecology in the conservation management of fishes. In *Behavioural Ecology and Conservation Biology*, ed. T. Caro, pp. 209–45. New York: Oxford University Press.
Virdin, J. and Schorr, J. (2001). *Hard Facts, Hidden Problems: A Review of Current Data on Fishing Subsidies.* Washington, DC: World Wildlife Fund.
Watson, M. (1999). Paper parks: worse than useless or a valuable first step? *Reef Encounter*, **25**, 18–20.
Wapnick, C. M., Precht, W. F. and Aronson, R. B. (2004). Millennial-scale dynamics of staghorn coral in Discovery Bay, Jamaica. *Ecology Letters*, **7**, 354–61.
West, J. M. and Salm, R. V. (2003). Resistance and resilience to coral bleaching: implications for coral reef conservation and management. *Conservation Biology*, **17**, 956–67.
Wilkinson, C. R. (ed.) (2000). *The Status of Coral Reefs of the World: 2000.* Townsville, QLD: Australian Institute of Marine Sciences.
(ed.) (2004). *The Status of Coral Reefs of the World: 2004*, vols. 1 and 2. Townsville, QLD: Australian Institute of Marine Sciences.
Williams, I. D. and Polunin, N.V. C. (2000). Differences between protected and unprotected reefs of the western Caribbean in attributed preference by dive tourists. *Environmental Conservation*, **27**, 382–91.
Wolanski, E., Richmond, R., McCook, L. and Sweatman, H. (2003). Mud, marine snow and coral reefs: the survival of coral reefs requires integrated watershed-based management activities. *American Scientist*, **91**, 44–51.
Wolanski, E., Richmond, R. H. and McCook, L. (2004). A model of the effects of land-based, human activities on the health of coral reefs in the Great Barrier Reef and in Fouha Bay, Guam, Micronesia. *Journal of Marine Systems*, **46**, 133–44.
World Parks Congress (2003). *Recommendation 22.* Available online at http://www.iucn.org/themes/wcpa/wpc2003/pdfs/outputs/recommendations/approved/english/html/r22.htm.

18

Coral reef coda: what can we hope for?

NANCY KNOWLTON
Scripps Institution of Oceanography and Smithsonian Tropical Research Institute

THE RECENT PAST TO THE PRESENT: THREE PHASES OF CORAL REEF RESEARCH

Before heading into the future, a brief look at where we have come from and where we are now provides some perspective. Investigations of coral reefs began in earnest with the publication of Darwin's monograph *The Structure and Distribution of Coral Reefs* in 1842 (see Dobbs, 2005, for a history of the resulting controversy). However, their modern study, facilitated by the use of scuba, dates back only a little over half a century. Tom Goreau's pioneering work on Jamaican coral reefs (Goreau, 1959), the French research programme in Madagascar (reviewed by Thomassin, 1971), and the establishment by Joe Connell of the first permanent reef quadrats on the flats of Heron Island (summarized in Connell *et al.*, 1997) represent important early research efforts of this period. The first International Coral Reef Symposium (ICRS) was held in Mandapam, India, in 1969 and has been followed by nine since. The *Bulletin of Marine Science* started a coral reef section in 1978, and in 1982 the first issue of *Coral Reefs* was published.

Over this interval, the rate of production of coral reef studies has increased several fold; annual totals from BIOSIS searches of articles with the words 'coral' and 'reef' average under 75 for the 1970s, nearly 130 for the 1980s, nearly 220 for the 1990s, and over 320 since 2000, a rate of increase that exceeds that of articles retrieved with the search word 'marine' (Fig. 18.1). Unfortunately, this increase in interest has coincided (perhaps not coincidentally) with global declines in coral reef health (e.g. Gardner

Coral Reef Conservation, ed. Isabelle M. Côté and John D. Reynolds.
Published by Cambridge University Press.

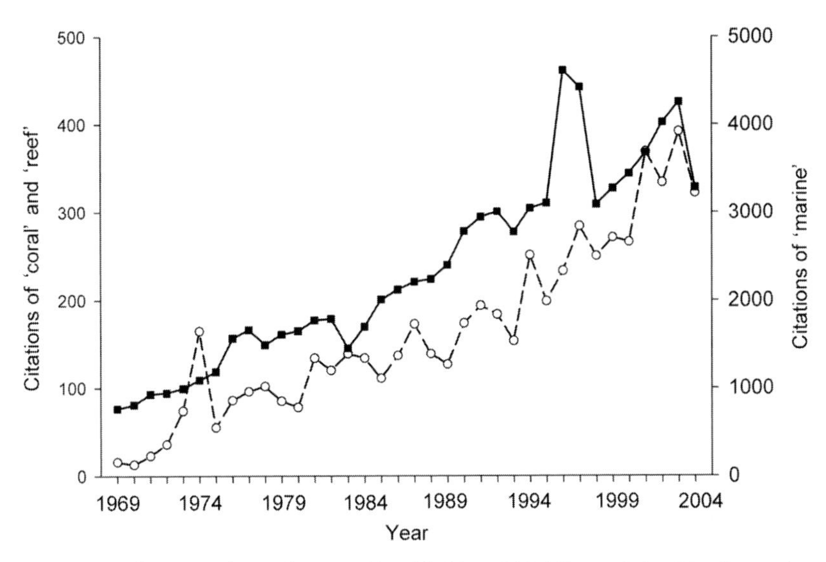

Figure 18.1 Numbers of papers identified in a BIOSIS search (23 March 2005) with keywords 'coral AND reef' (open circles) and 'marine' (solid sequence) from 1969 to 2004. The dip at 2004 reflects, at least in part, a time lag between publication date and entry into the database.

et al., 2003, Pandolfi *et al.*, 2003). 'The coming crisis' of Stoddart (1982) has clearly arrived (Bellwood *et al.*, 2004).

In examining this recent history of coral reef research, three overlapping phases, defined by the primary themes of study, emerge. In Phase I, most research concerned basic scientific questions such as the geology of reef formation, reef zonation, reef productivity, and the role of disturbance in shaping reef communities. There were concerns about the health of reefs, particularly the loss of coral cover in the context of *Acanthaster* outbreaks in the western Pacific, but even for this topic there was substantial disagreement as to whether people played any role in these outbreaks (e.g. Endean, 1977 vs. Frankel, 1977). In any case, research related to the interaction between people and reefs represented a small proportion of all coral reef research effort. None of the papers at the first ICRS in 1969 discussed any aspects of the reef–people interface, and in the second (1973) and third (1977) ICRSs, less than 10% did so, despite the fact that people have clearly had major impacts on reefs that go back centuries (Jackson, 1977; Pandolfi *et al.*, 2003).

The transition to Phase II, a focus on the decline of coral reefs and the nature of human impacts, is clearly seen in the fourth ICRS held in the Philippines in 1981, whose theme was *The Reef and Man*; over 25% of the 276 articles and abstracts addressed issues related to actual or potential human impacts. Since then, concern about human impacts has increasingly influenced the course of reef research, stimulated by the loss of much coral cover in the Caribbean due to coral disease and the die-off of the sea urchin *Diadema antillarum* in the 1980s, and the rising incidence of coral bleaching globally in the 1990s. In some cases the role of people has been accepted from the start, but in others the literature contains the record of debate over the role of people or the relative importance of their different impacts (thus paralleling the earlier *Acanthaster* controversies).

Phase III can be defined as research dedicated to determining how to conserve and restore coral reefs. Management was explicitly discussed as far back as the third ICRS in 1977, but its importance has increased dramatically since then. The organizers of both the seventh ICRS in Guam and the ninth ICRS in Bali specifically highlighted the role of management and the sustainable use of reef resources. The natural sciences originally dominated these discussions (e.g. calculations of yield, measurements of impacts and the optimal biological design of marine protected areas). The first session to focus explicitly on socio-economic issues took place in the fifth ICRS in 1985, and social science issues have increased in importance since then.

The contributions of this volume clearly reflect these research trends. In the category of Phase II research, we continue to monitor the status of reefs (Wilkinson, this volume) and increase our ability to detect change (Côté *et al.*, this volume). The debate over the role of people in reef decline is over, although the relative importance of factors, such as over-fishing versus other human impacts (Precht and Aronson, this volume), is not always clear. Overall, reefs probably continue to decline, and the amount of destruction in some regions, such as the Caribbean, rivals that seen for tropical forests (Côté *et al.*, this volume), the traditional poster child for human depredations on the planet. Moreover, some anthropogenic impacts, particularly those associated with climate change (Sheppard, this volume), will certainly worsen in the short term.

Most of the chapters in this volume are clearly a part of Phase III research, as they contain explicit recommendations for management. Some of these papers reflect uncertainty or debate within the natural-science community as to what should be done. For example, there is broad consensus as to the importance of marine protected areas (chapters in this volume by Wilkinson, McClanahan, Wells, Alcala *et al.*, and Roberts *et al.*), but the optimal locations are less clear. For example, does biodiversity hotspot analysis provide an effective method for prioritizing site selection (Roberts *et al.*, 2002), or will such a strategy miss many endemics located in more peripheral, lower-diversity locations ? Many possible criteria exist for prioritizing areas, but given limited resources, there is no clear agreement as to which are the most important. For example, what is the relative importance of current biodiversity versus likely future resilience? There is also much we don't know about the details of the processes that affect coral reefs. For example, within any location, what are the linkages that have the greatest impact on coral health and that offer the most potential for cost-effective interventions (Mumby and Harborne, this volume)? Finally, what should be done about damaged reefs – should they be ignored or restored (methods for which are improving), and if so how (Jaap *et al.*, this volume)?

This collection of chapters also clearly reflects the growing appreciation for socio-economic analyses. On the economic side, there is growing general appreciation for the value of reefs, although many aspects of reef value are still poorly measured, such as non-use value (Spurgeon, this volume) and ecosystems services that we take for granted (e.g. shoreline protection: Sheppard, this volume). Moreover, relying on economic values determined by the global marketplace (e.g. tourism) can leave reefs vulnerable when conditions change if other structures do not support their conservation (Jobbins, this volume). Globalization is widely recognized as a driver for some aspects of non-sustainable fishing (McClanahan, this volume), although some types of low-volume/high-value reef products may offer promise with respect to improving human welfare without having large negative impacts on reefs (Vincent, this volume). We also continue to learn, often through trial and error, what management strategies work best within the constraints of human social systems. Local participation (e.g. chapters by Wells, Alcala *et al.* and Brown, this volume) and quick feedback when things do go wrong (Turner *et al.*, this volume) are clearly beneficial. There is also much to be gained by making sure that people clearly understand the consequences of the choices they make (Brown, this volume; Browning *et al.*, this volume). Much of this acquired wisdom makes intuitive sense in retrospect, but other aspects of human behaviour are less obvious. There will be less error in the trials if social scientists are fully integrated in the process of decision-making. The fact that students of coral reefs are now increasingly interested and trained in both the natural and the social sciences bodes well for the future, to which I now turn.

THE FUTURE: WHAT CAN WE HOPE FOR?

One of the most discouraging things about coral reef science at present is the inverse correlation over the last several decades between the numbers of reef studies and numbers of living corals, or even worse, between the global numbers of marine protected areas (MPAs) on reefs and the amount of healthy coral on the planet. As Wells (this volume) points out, we are stronger on the output side than on the outcome side. Thus what we must hope for is Phase IV, the documentation of the reversal of regional trajectories of reef degradation, which remains largely on the horizon for now. What are the issues that will influence our success?

As a definition of success, a slight modification of that provided by Roberts *et al.* (this volume) serves well: (1) maintain reef growth and structural complexity, (2) maintain stocks and achieve sustainable yields for all resources harvested from reefs, (3) prevent, reverse or minimize local losses of species, and (4) minimize as much as possible the number of species driven to extinction. To this I would add (5) increase the well-being of people who live next to and depend upon coral reef habitats (because if this does not occur, the previous objectives are doomed to failure). Below I discuss five issues that I think will have the greatest impact on our chances to achieve these goals.

The role of human-dominated landscapes versus marine protected areas in preserving reef biodiversity

Although the limits of MPAs are well recognized in general (e.g. Allison *et al.*, 1998), this tool remains the central element in most strategies for coral reef conservation. In some situations, for example the spawning aggregations of tropical groupers, this is clearly an essential step (Sala *et al.*, 2001), and for reef fish in general, no-take areas can have measurable positive impacts (Mosqueira *et al.*, 2000; Gell and Roberts, 2003). Unfortunately, the efficacy of MPAs for restoring corals seems limited at best (Rogers and Beets, 2001). Moreover, a recent study showed that not only did corals decline inside and outside the reserves, but also that the decline in corals was tracked by a decline in the diversity of fishes (Jones *et al.*, 2004).

In this context it is interesting that among terrestrial biologists there is increasing interest in the importance of areas outside parks and reserves for preserving biodiversity (including in the tropics), in part because of the realization that dependence on parks alone will doom huge numbers of species to extinction (Parks and Harcourt, 2002). As a consequence, there have been serious efforts to study the role of human-dominated landscapes as havens for terrestrial biodiversity (e.g. Daily *et al.*, 2001, 2003) in order to develop strategies to maximize the opportunities for the coexistence of people and other organisms on shared lands. Because of the overwhelming focus on MPAs, no comparably serious effort has occurred for coral reef ecosystems in general (although the zoning schemes, such as that recently implemented on the Great Barrier Reef, implicitly depend on such a framework). We are woefully ignorant of the role that non-MPA areas should play in coral reef conservation, and whether there are steps that could be taken to make them more effective. The seascape-level perspective advocated by Mumby and Harbourne (this volume) points the way forward, for example by examining ontogenetic shifts by fish species between reef and non-reef habitats.

The potential for extinction in the sea

Although it is widely recognized that coral reefs are globally in dire straits in terms of declining percent cover of living corals, we are largely clueless when it comes to understanding the dynamics of actual extinction in the sea. It has been argued that extinction of marine organisms is less likely because of their broader distributions and large population sizes, but recent syntheses (Carlton *et al.*, 1999; Dulvy *et al.*, 2003) suggest that such logic is fallacious. Are we close to the brink of extinction for coral reef organisms?

Documented historical extinctions are rare in the sea (although abundant in the fossil record). In the tropics they are limited to the West Indian monk seal (Carlton *et al.*, 1999); the only coral reef invertebrate reported to go extinct was later rediscovered alive. However, there have been local extirpations of coral reef organisms (Dulvy *et al.*, 2003). This scarcity of examples is almost certainly in part an artefact of limited observations and poor taxonomy. Many small marine invertebrates, for example, have larvae with limited dispersal potential, much like that of terrestrial organisms. Although some brooding species apparently have surprisingly wide distributions (e.g. several coral species whose ranges span the breadth of the tropical Atlantic), it is almost certainly the case that some brooders are restricted to tiny areas and are thus highly vulnerable to localized habitat destruction. We simply do not know how many such species there are. Using species–area curve relationships (which admittedly make many assumptions), Carlton and colleagues (1999) estimated that between 10 000 and 50 000 species may have gone extinct assuming 5% loss of reefs, and that up to 400 000 may go extinct with the projected loss of 30% of reef area.

More worrying is the possibility that species currently with us are already doomed to extinction because they have reached a threshold of low density or because too much of their potential habitat has been destroyed. The former refers to the Allee effect, and seems particularly likely for free-spawning invertebrates where reproductive failure could occur due to large distances between potential mates (Gascoigne and Lipcius, 2004). For example, in the coral *Montastraea annularis*, fertilization success drops to near zero when the number of colonies spawning in an area is too low (Levitan *et al.*, 2004), so this is clearly a concern. On the other hand, *Diadema antillarum* has not continued to decline following what could have been a scenario of wholesale reproductive failure following mortality rates of at least 95% throughout its range, and indeed seems to be poised to recover (Edmunds and Carpenter, 2001; Miller *et al.*, 2003). In general, clear-cut cases of Allee effects in the sea remain elusive (Gascoigne and Lipcius, 2004), which is good news.

Even more difficult to predict are potential extinction debts on reefs. This evocative term (Tilman *et al.*, 1994) refers to the fact that once a certain percentage of the habitat has been destroyed, some species (often competitive dominants) might be doomed to extinction because they are out-competed by species with better dispersal potential. How such a scenario would play out on coral reefs remains to be seen; to date there have been just a handful of analyses and the models are highly simplistic (Stone, 1995; Stone *et al.*, 1996). Two points suggest this is something to worry about, however: (1) The diversity of corals and fishes is highly correlated with the amount of regionally available habitat (Bellwood and Hughes, 2001), and (2) the fossil record provides evidence that extinction can be associated with habitat reduction, for example, the loss of two once dominant branching corals (*Pocillopora* cf. *palmata* and 'organ-pipe' *Montastraea*) during a Pleistocene sea-level drop (Pandolfi, 1999, 2001).

Alternative stable or quasi-stable states

The possibility of alternative stable states is of concern to conservation biologists because they suggest that human activities could cause a major shift in community composition that would not be readily reversible. Despite their theoretical plausibility, few ecologically important examples have been documented in the sea (Knowlton, 2004). One possible example that has been discussed for several decades (Hatcher, 1984; Knowlton, 1992) is the transition from coral-dominated to macroalgal-dominated communities. Underlying this idea is the assumption that once unpalatable algae become established, it may be difficult for corals to recruit. The textbook case of such a transition has been the domination of Jamaican reefs by seaweeds following the loss of *Diadema* (Hughes, 1994). The potential for this to be an alternative stable state was made more likely by the apparent dependence of *Diadema* recruitment on well-grazed surfaces and potential Allee effects.

However, as noted above, *Diadema* appears to be slowly returning, suggesting that alternative stable state dynamics do not apply here (see also Precht and Aronson, this volume).

Barring catastrophic changes in the world's oceans (a not entirely impossible scenario, as discussed in the following section), quasi-stable alternative states probably pose more of a threat to coral reefs (Knowlton, 2004). Feedback loops in which some species have slow rates of recovery can have detrimental consequences for recovery of the system as a whole. In the Caribbean, for example, substantial coral mortality has occurred thanks to the prolonged nature of the *Diadema* recovery, which would not have occurred had recovery been relatively rapid.

The impact of future atmospheric change

Human activities are already having a global impact on the world's oceans, thanks to the emissions of greenhouse gases associated with industrialization. We are only just now seeing these changes, which will continue for some time even if we were to greatly reduce emissions tomorrow. This atmospheric change is detrimental to corals and thus reefs on several fronts, most importantly because of projected temperature increases and increasing ocean acidity; increasing intensity of tropical storms will also have localized impacts (Knowlton, 2001; Feely *et al.*, 2004; Gardner *et al.*, 2005; McWilliams *et al.*, 2005).

Coral bleaching is certainly a threat to the long-term persistence of extensive reef growth, particularly in the short term. What is unclear is the extent to which corals will be able to adapt to increasingly warm temperatures. Projections made based on past mortality rates and projections for future temperature increases (e.g. Hoegh-Guldberg, 1999) are probably too pessimistic. In particular, some types of zooxanthellae are known to be resistant to high temperatures (Rowan, 2004). At least some coral species can host these temperature-resistant symbionts, and they appear to be increasing in abundance, particularly in the aftermath of mass bleaching events (Baker *et al.*, 2004). The primary uncertainties revolve around the following questions: How many coral species can host temperature-resistant zooxanthellae? How quickly can temperature-resistant zooxanthellae spread (i.e. is bleaching, with its associated risks of mortality, required)? What are the costs to corals when they host stress-resistant zooxanthellae? Can range extension to now cooler waters lessen the impacts of mortality in warmer waters? Answers to these questions are not currently available.

We understand the likely consequences of increasing acidity even less well. What does seem to be the case is that increasing acidity will make calcification less easy, resulting in slower-growing or more fragile corals (Feely *et al.*, 2004). Both of these changes are problematic, since reef development is in essence a simple balance between growth and mortality, which must be net positive for reefs to continue. The slower growing or more fragile the corals, the more challenging are the conditions for net growth, particularly in combination with other factors, including the increased storm activity and disease prevalence (Harvell *et al.*, 2002) that are also projected to occur in a warmer world.

The human ability to respond

Herein lies the importance of the social sciences, both economics and the various fields that deal with how humans behave in a crisis situation. Economics will certainly play a major role, and for this reason accurate accounting of the value of coral reefs is an essential part of devising strategies to protect them. We are really just beginning to analyse the value of coral reefs, and some of the valuation analyses depend on aspects that are very difficult to quantify, such as existence values and ecological services. Moreover, people and governments do not always behave in an economically optimal fashion, and some kinds of approaches are more likely to achieve social change than others.

In the final analysis, the fate of reefs (and other forms of life on the planet) will hinge on how people perceive and respond to the crisis. In his recent book entitled *Collapse*, Diamond (2004) discusses how past societies have greatly differed in this respect, with some living in stable equilibrium with their environment and others simply vanishing. He highlights environmental degradation, climate, hostile neighbours, the collapse of friendly neighbours, and the ability of people to see and confront the problem. He is surprisingly optimistic with respect to the environmental challenges we face, but our ability to avoid societal collapse does not necessarily mean that reefs themselves will do well. The jury is still out as to when or even whether Phase IV of coral research will arrive.

CONCLUSIONS

There are many reasons to worry that need no repetition. There are, however, a few bright spots of hope, both social and biological. For me the most important of these are (1) the coming into effect of the Kyoto Protocol,

(2) the placement of 33% of the Great Barrier Reef in no-take zones, (3) the discovery of heat-resistant zooxanthellae and (4) the apparent beginning of the return of *Diadema* to Caribbean reefs. They are hardly grounds for complacency, but all is not yet lost.

REFERENCES

Allison, G. W., Lubchenco, J. and Carr, M. H. (1998). Marine reserves are necessary but not sufficient for marine conservation. *Ecological Applications*, **8** (suppl.), S79–S92.

Baker, A. C., Starger, C. J., McClanahan, T. R. and Glynn, P. W. (2004). Corals' adaptive response to climate change. *Nature*, **430**, 741.

Bellwood, D. R. and Hughes, T. P. (2001). Regional-scale assembly rules and biodiversity of coral reefs. *Science*, **292**, 1532–4.

Bellwood, D. R., Hughes, T. P., Folke, C. and Nystrom, M. (2004). Confronting the coral reef crisis. *Nature*, **429**, 827–33.

Carlton, J. T., Geller, J. B., Reaka-Kudla, M. L. and Norse, E. A. (1999). Historical extinctions in the sea. *Annual Review of Ecology and Systematics*, **30**, 515–38.

Connell, J. H., Hughes, T. P. and Wallace, C. C. (1997). A 30-year study of coral abundance, recruitment, and disturbance at several scales in space and time. *Ecological Monographs*, **67**, 461–88.

Daily, G. C., Ehrlich, P. R. and Sanchez-Azofeifa, G. A. (2001). Countryside biogeography: use of human-dominated landscapes by the avifauna of southern Costa Rica. *Ecological Applications*, **11**, 1–13.

Daily, G. C., Ceballos, G., Pacheco, J., Suzan, G. and Sanchez-Azofeifa, A. (2003). Countryside biogeography of neotropical mammals: conservation opportunities in agricultural landscapes of Costa Rica. *Conservation Biology*, **17**, 1814–26.

Darwin, C. (1842). *The Structure and Distribution of Coral Reefs*. London: John Murray.

Diamond, J. (2004). *Collapse: How Societies Choose to Fail or Succeed*. New York: Viking.

Dobbs, D. (2005). *Reef Madness: Charles Darwin, Alexander Agassiz, and the Meaning of Coral*. New York: Pantheon Books.

Dulvy, N. K., Sadovy, Y. and Reynolds, J. D. (2003). Extinction vulnerability in marine populations. *Fish and Fisheries*, **4**, 25–64.

Edmunds, P. J. and Carpenter, R. C. (2001). Recovery of *Diadema antillarum* reduces macroalgal cover and increases juvenile corals on a Caribbean reef. *Proceedings of the National Academy of Sciences, USA*, **98**, 5067–71.

Endean, R. (1977). *Acanthaster planci* infestations of reefs of the Great Barrier Reef. *Proceedings 3rd International Coral Reef Symposium*, **1**, 185–91.

Feely, R. A., Sabine, C. L., Lee, K. *et al.* (2004). Impact of anthropogenic CO_2 on the $CaCO_3$ system in the oceans. *Science*, **305**, 362–6.

Frankel, E. (1977). Previous *Acanthaster* aggregations in the Great Barrier Reef. *Proceedings 3rd International Coral Reef Symposium*, **1**, 201–15.

Gardner, T. A., Côté, I. M., Gill, J. A., Grant, A. and Watkinson, A. R. (2003). Long-term region-wide declines in Caribbean corals. *Science*, **301**, 958–60.

(2005). Hurricanes and Caribbean coral reefs: immediate impacts, recovery trajectories and contribution to long-term coral decline. *Ecology*, **86**, 174–84.

Gascoigne, J. and Lipcius, R. N. (2004). Allee effects in marine systems. *Marine Ecology Progress Series*, **269**, 49–59.
Gell, F. R. and Roberts, C. M. (2003). Benefits beyond boundaries: the fishery effects of marine reserves. *Trends in Ecology and Evolution*, **18**, 448–55.
Goreau, T. F. (1959). The ecology of Jamaican coral reefs. I. Species composition and zonation. *Ecology*, **40**, 67–90.
Harvell, C. D., Mitchell, C. E., Ward, J. R. *et al.* (2002). Climate warming and disease risks for terrestrial and marine biota. *Science*, **296**, 2158–62.
Hatcher, B. G. (1984). A maritime accident provides evidence for alternate stable states in benthic communities on coral reefs. *Coral Reefs*, **3**, 199–204.
Hoegh-Guldberg, O. (1999). Climate change, coral bleaching and the future of the world's coral reefs. *Marine and Freshwater Research*, **50**, 839–66.
Hughes, T. P. (1994). Catastrophes, phase shifts, and large-scale degradation of a Caribbean coral reef. *Science*, **265**, 1547–51.
Jackson, J. B. C. (1977). Reefs since Columbus. *Coral Reefs*, **16** (suppl.), S23–S32.
Jones, G. P., McCormick, M. I., Srinivasan, M. and Eagle, J. V. (2004). Coral decline threatens fish biodiversity in marine reserves. *Proceedings of the National Academy of Sciences, USA*, **101**, 8251–3.
Knowlton, N. (1992). Thresholds and multiple stable states in coral reef community dynamics. *American Zoologist*, **32**, 674–82.
(2001). The future of coral reefs. *Proceedings of the National Academy of Sciences, USA*, **98**, 5419–25.
(2004). Multiple 'stable' states and the conservation of marine ecosystsems. *Progress in Oceanography*, **60**, 387–96.
Levitan, D. R., Fukami, H., Jara, J. *et al.* (2004). Mechanisms of reproductive isolation among sympatric broadcast-spawning corals of the *Montastraea annularis* species complex. *Evolution*, **58**, 308–23.
McWilliams, J. P., Côté, I. M., Gill, J. A., Sutherland, W. J. and Watkinson, A. R. (2005). Accelerating impacts of temperature-induced coral bleaching in the Caribbean. *Ecology*, **86**, 2055–60.
Miller, R. J., Adams, A. J., Ogden, N. B., Ogden, J. C. and Ebersole, J. P. (2003). *Diadema antillarum* 17 years after mass mortality: is recovery beginning in St Croix? *Ecology*, **22**, 181–7.
Mosqueira, I., Côté, I. M., Jennings, S. and Reynolds, J. D. (2000). Conservation benefits of marine reserves for fish populations. *Animal Conservation* **4**, 321–32.
Pandolfi, J. M. (1999). Response of Pleistocene corals to environmental change over long temporal scales. *American Zoologist*, **39**, 113–30.
(2001). Geologically sudden extinction of two widespread late Pleistocene Caribbean reef corals. In *Evolutionary Patterns: Growth, Form, and Tempo in the Fossil Record*, eds. J. B. C. Jackson, S. Lidgard and R. K. McKinney, pp. 120–158, Chicago, IL: University of Chicago Press.
Pandolfi, J. M., Bradbury, R. H., Sala, E. *et al.* (2003). Global trajectories of the long-term decline of coral reef ecosystems. *Science*, **301**, 955–8.
Parks, S. A. and Harcourt, A. H. (2002). Reserve size, local human density, and mammalian extinctions in US protected areas. *Conservation Biology*, **16**, 800–8.
Roberts, C. M., McClean, C. J., Veron, J. E. N. *et al.* (2002). Marine biodiversity hotspots and conservation priorities for tropical reefs. *Science*, **295**, 1280–4.

Rogers, C. S. and Beets, J. (2001). Degradation of marine ecosystems and decline of fishery resources in marine protected areas in the US Virgin Islands. *Environmental Conservation*, **28**, 312–22.
Rowan, R. (2004). Thermal adaptation in reef coral symbionts. *Nature*, **430**, 742.
Sala, E., Ballesteros, E. and Starr, R. M. (2001). Rapid decline of Nassau grouper spawning aggregations in Belize: fishery management and conservation needs. *Fisheries*, **26**, 23–30.
Stoddart, D. R. (1982). Coral reefs: the coming crisis. *Proceedings 4th International Coral Reef Symposium*, **1**, 33–6.
Stone, L. (1995). Biodiversity and habitat destruction: a comparative study of model forest and coral reef ecosystems. *Proceedings of the Royal Society of London B* **261**, 381–8.
Stone, L., Eilam, E., Abelson, A. and Ilan, M. (1996). Modelling coral reef biodiversity and habitat destruction. *Marine Ecology Progress Series*, **134**, 299–302.
Thomassin, B. (1971). Revue bibliographique des travaux de la station marine de Tuléar (République Malgache) 1961–1970. *Tethys* (suppl.), **1**, 3–50.
Tilman, D., May, R. M., Lehman, C. L. and Nowak, M. A. (1994). Habitat destruction and the extinction debt. *Nature*, **371**, 65–6.

Index